il5 4/07

SUPERVISORY
MANAGEMENT

CHARLES R. GREER

W. RICHARD PLUNKETT

SUPERVISORY MANAGEMENT

ELEVENTH EDITION

CHARLES R. GREER
Neeley School of Business, Texas Christian University

W. RICHARD PLUNKETT
Formerly of Wright College, City Colleges of Chicago

PEARSON

Prentice
Hall

Upper Saddle River, New Jersey 07458

Library of Congress Cataloging-in-Publication Data

Greer, Charles R.
  Supervisory management / Charles R. Greer, W. Richard Plunkett.—11th ed.
    p. cm.
  Rev. ed. Of: Supervision : diversity and teams in the workplace 10th ed.
  Includes index.
  ISBN 0-13-229412-5
1. Supervision of employees. I. Greer, Charles R. Supervision. II. Plunkett, W. Richard (Warren Richard) III. Title.
  HF5549.P564 2007
  658.3'02—dc22

                                                                    2006010349

Editor-in-Chief: Vernon R. Anthony
Director of Production and Manufacturing: Bruce Johnson
Senior Acquisitions Editor: Gary Bauer
Assistant Editor: Jacqueline Knapke
Development Editor: Deborah Hoffman
Marketing Manager: Leigh Ann Sims
Marketing Coordinator: Alicia Dysert
Managing Editor-Production: Mary Carnis
Manufacturing Buyer: Ilene Sanford
Production Liaison: Denise Brown
Manager of Media Production: Amy Peltier
Media Production Project Manager: Lisa Rinaldi

Full-Service Production/Composition: Lindsey Hancock/Carlisle
  Publishing Services
Director, Image Resource Center: Melinda Reo
Manager, Rights and Permissions: Zina Arabia
Manager, Visual Research: Beth Brenzel
Manager, Cover Visual Research and Permissions: Karen Sanatar
Image Permission Coordinator: Nancy Seise
Senior Design Coordinator: Christopher Weigand
Cover Design: Vicki Kane
Cover Image: Mel Curtis/Photonica Amana America/Getty Images, Inc.
Printer/Binder: Von Hoffman Graphics, Inc./Owensville
Cover Printer: Phoenix Color

Photo Credits

Cover: Getty Images - Photonica Amana America, Inc., Mel Curtis; Page 6: Stock Boston, Bob Daemmrich; Page 13: Courtesy of Southwest Airlines Company; Page 22: Woodfin Camp & Associates, Michal Heron; Page 26: Getty Images Inc. - Stone Allstock, David Joel; Page 51: Getty Images Inc. - Stone Allstock, Don Bosler; Page 55: Getty Images, Inc.; Page 90: Peter Yates Photos, Peter Yates; Page 100: Getty Images, Inc.; Page 108: Getty Images Inc. - Stone Allstock, Walter Hodges; Page 112: Getty Images Inc. - Stone Allstock, Erik Dreyer; Page 143: Ore-Ida Foods, Inc.; Page 145: Getty Images Inc. - Stone Allstock, Bruce Ayres; Page 180: Photodisc/Getty Images; Page 182: Stock Boston, Billy E. Barnes; Page 184: Stock Boston, Bob Daemmrich; Page 194: Getty Images Inc. - Stone Allstock, Andy Sacks; Page 216: Xerox Corporation; Page 234: Woodfin Camp & Associates, William Hubbell; Page 244: The Image Works, Bob Daemmrich; Page 275: Spencer Rowell/Taxi/Getty Images; Page 277: Corbis/Stock Market, Maggie Steber; Page 278: Howard Grey/Stone/Getty Images; Page 280: Index Stock Imagery, Inc., Tom Tracy; Page 302: Getty Images Inc. - Stone Allstock, Walter Hodges; Page 307: Getty Images, Inc. - Taxi, Jurgen Reisch; Page 324: Fisher/Thatcher/Stone/Getty Images; Page 343: Photodisc/Getty Images; Page 358: Courtesy of the Saturn Corporation; Page 395: Getty Images Inc. - Stone Allstock, Donald Smetzer; Page 401: Photo Researchers, Inc., Blair Seitz; Page 428: Paul Thomas/Image Bank/Getty Images; Page 434: Getty Images Inc. - Stone Allstock, Michael Rosenfield; Page 464: Ghislain & Marie David de Lossy/Image Bank/Getty Images; Page 469: Getty Images/Digital Vision; Page 476: Ken Fisher/Stone/Getty Images; Page 479: Zigy Kaluzny/Stone/Getty Images; Page 504: Corbis/Stock Market, Chuck Savage; Page 516: The Image Works, Bob Daemmrich; Page 520: Richard Shock/Stone/Getty Images; Page 541: Stock Boston, Cary Wolinsky; Page 548: Woodfin Camp & Associates, Michael L. Abramson; Page 552: Larry Dale Gordon/Image Bank/Getty Images; Page 614: Patti McConville/Image Bank/Getty Images; Page 629: Contact Press Images Inc., Alon Reininger.

Pearson Prentice Hall™ is a trademark of Pearson Education, Inc.
Pearson® is a registered trademark of Pearson plc
Prentice Hall® is a registered trademark of Pearson Education, Inc.

Pearson Education Ltd.
Pearson Education Singapore, Pte. Ltd.
Pearson Education Canada, Ltd.
Pearson Education—Japan

Pearson Education Australia PTY, Limited
Pearson Education North Asia Ltd.
Pearson Educación de Mexico, S.A. de C.V.
Pearson Education Malaysia. Pte. Ltd.

10 9 8 7 6 5 4 3 2 1
ISBN: 0-13-229412-5

BRIEF CONTENTS

CONTENTS

Chapter 3

MANAGEMENT FUNCTIONS   88

Chapter 6
MOTIVATION   214

Chapter 7
LEADERSHIP AND MANAGEMENT STYLES   256

Chapter 8

LEADING CHANGE   298

Chapter 11

TRAINING   424

Chapter 12

MANAGING DIVERSITY   458

Chapter 14

DISCIPLINE 538

Chapter 15

COMPLAINTS, GRIEVANCES, AND UNIONS 574

PREFACE

TO THE STUDENT

INTENDED AUDIENCE

This text and supplementary resource package provide an excellent introduction to management functions and principles as they apply to supervisory management. This package can be used in 2- or 4-year colleges, proprietary schools, in-house corporate training or trade association courses, and supervisory management programs. Our primary goals are to engage students' interests, give clear explanations and examples that are suitable for beginners, and translate principles and theories into everyday supervisory management practice.

KEY CHAPTER-BY-CHAPTER UPDATES

- Chapter 1, "The Supervisor's Special Role," covers new material on ethics, diversity, information technology, and foreign ownership of companies.
- Chapter 2, "Management Concepts," includes an upgraded discussion of decision-making and delegation.
- Chapter 4, "Communication," discusses new material on e-mail etiquette, feedback, small group communications, and PowerPoint presentation skills.
- Chapter 5, "Building Relationships and Managing Conflict," covers new discussions of teams, building a better relationship with your boss, and managing conflict.
- Chapter 6, "Motivation," now has added coverage of ERG Theory, empowerment, and goal setting.
- Chapter 7, "Leadership and Management Styles," includes new leadership behaviors, principles of leadership, and new coverage on how women lead.
- Chapter 8, "Leading Change," incorporates new material based on Thomas Friedman's *The World Is Flat*, the myths and realities of change, and arranging the conditions for change, payoffs, and barriers to change.

- Chapter 9, "Teams and Groups," has new discussions of virtual teams, putting teams together, team development, desired teamwork behaviors, and effective team characteristics.
- Chapter 12, "Managing Diversity," is all new and covers increasing workforce diversity with views, practices, and skills for managing diversity.
- Chapter 14, "Discipline," contains new, expanded material on sexual harassment and employment at will.
- Chapter 16, "Security, Safety, and Health," includes an expanded discussion of risk factors and threats to computers and information systems security and a new exhibit on OSHA standards.

NEW TO THIS EDITION

REAL COMPANY "LECTURE LAUNCHER"

These features start each chapter and set the stage so that students can understand how upcoming chapter material relates to on-the-job practices. Each "Lecture Launcher" ends with questions that students should think about as they read through the chapter material. Companies covered include Southwest Airlines, Domino's Pizza, Starbucks, Hewlett-Packard, and Kodak.

NUMEROUS, UP-TO-DATE EXAMPLES FROM THE RECENT BUSINESS PRESS

These reinforce chapter concepts and are prevalent throughout all chapters. Material is drawn from sources such as the *New York Times, Investor's Business Daily, Quality Magazine,* and *Fortune.*

LEARNING OBJECTIVES AND KEY TERMS REFERENCED IN THE MARGINS

Key terms are defined in the margin when the term first appears, and learning objectives are noted in the margins when related material is first covered so that students can easily locate important text topics.

TWO NEW BUSINESS SKILLS EXERCISES

These exercises have been added to each chapter's assignment material. One of the exercises asks students to complete writing assignments, many of which simulate the kinds of correspondence required of supervisors on the job.

CORE FEATURES RETAINED IN THIS EDITION

ICONS RELATED TO IMPORTANT THEMES

These important themes run through the text and are highlighted with the following icons:

SUPERVISORS AND ETHICS, SUPERVISORS AND PERFORMANCE, AND SUPERVISING TEAMS BOXES

These boxes highlight recent discussions on the important themes of ethics, performance, and teamwork that run through this text.

ASSIGNMENT MATERIAL

This material has been upgraded and updated to reflect new chapter material. Each chapter includes the following:

- Instant Replays—provide a bulleted chapter summary that reviews key concepts
- Key Terms
- Questions for Class Discussion
- Assess This Situation
- Skill Building Exercises (New to this edition)
- Case Problems

SUPPLEMENTAL MATERIALS FOR STUDENTS AND INSTRUCTORS

COMPANION WEBSITE

Students can access a wealth of study aids at *www.prenhall.com/greer/greer*. The online Companion Website includes the following:

- Test-Prep Quizzes for each chapter, including true/false, multiple-choice, and short-essay questions.
- Objectives, key terms, and an overview for each chapter.

INSTRUCTOR'S MANUAL WITH TEST ITEM FILE

The Instructor's Manual with Test Item File for this text is available as a downloadable Word document at *www.prenhall.com/greer* at the Instructor's Resource Center and is also on the Instructor Resource CD. It contains a list of objectives, an outline, answers to text questions and cases, plus additional cases for each chapter. The test item file contains 75 to 100 multiple-choice, true/false, fill-in-the-blank, and essay questions for each chapter.

TEST GENERATOR

The test generator for this text is available for download at *www.prenhall.com/greer* at the Instructor's Resource Center and is also on the Instructor Resource CD. The program gives the instructor maximum flexibility in preparing tests and offers 75 to 100 multiple-choice, true/false, fill-in-the-blank, and essay questions for each chapter.

POWERPOINT LECTURE PRESENTATION PACKAGE

PowerPoint Lecture Presentation slides for each chapter are available for download at *www.prenhall.com/greer* at the Instructor's Resource Center and are also on the Instructor Resource CD.

INSTRUCTOR RESOURCE CD

The Instructor Resource CD (ISBN 013-243181-5)contains the Instructor's Manual with Test Item File, the Test Generator, and the PowerPoint Lecture Presentation. Instructors can request a copy through their local sales representative or by calling 1-800-526-0485.

ACKNOWLEDGEMENTS

This revision would not have been possible without the feedback and suggestions of the following reviewers:

Carolyn Ashe, University of Houston
Michael Drafke, College of DuPage
Samira Hussein, Johnson County Community College
Louise Kowalski, Erie Community College
Clay Lifko, Kirkwood Community College
Gregory Stephens, Kansas State University
Howard Williams, Elizabethtown Community and Technical College

We would like to express great appreciation to Liz Greer who performed much of the research for this revision. A big debt of gratitude is owed to Deborah Hoffman, Developmental Editor, who provided insightful guidance for improvement of the book, served as an excellent taskmaster, and was a wonderful source of support. Thanks to Gary Bauer, Senior Acquisitions Editor, who provided critical decisions for the project and support, and to Jackie Knapke, Assistant Editor, for her world-class efficiency and great attitude. In addition, special thanks to Peggy Conway, who worked tirelessly at night and on weekends to improve the supplemental materials. Special thanks also to John Greer and Elena Greer who developed the index and helped check the manuscript. Thanks also to Lindsey Hancock, Project Editor with Carlisle Publishing Services, for her encouraging oversight of the copyediting and production work. Thanks as well to Denise Brown, Senior Production Editor, for her help with permissions. Finally, thanks to Leigh Ann Sims, Senior Marketing Manager, for her enthusiastic support of the book.

Charles R. Greer
W. Richard Plunkett

We would also like to acknowledge the help of the following people on previous editions: Ray Ackerman, East Texas State University; Thomas Auer, Murray State University; Richard Baker, Mohave Community College; Raymond F. Balcerzak, Jr., Ferris State University; Gregory Barnes, Purdue University; James Baskfiled, North Hennepin Community College; Lorraine Bassette, Prince George's Community College; Charles Beavin, Miami-Dade Community College; James Bishop, Arkansas State University; Frederick Blake, Bee County College; Raymond Bobillo, Purdue University; Arthur Boisselle, Pikes Peak Community College; Jerry Boles, Western Kentucky University; Terry Bordan, Cuny-Hostos Community College; Joe Breeden, Kansas Technical Institute; Robin Butler, Lakeshore Technical Institute; Leonard Callahan, Daytona Beach Community College; Donald Caruth, East Texas State University; Donald S. Carver, National University; Joseph Castelli, College of San Mateo; Joseph Chandler, Indiana-Purdue University at Fort Wayne; Win Chesney, Sain Louis Community College-Meramac; Jackie Conway, Lenoir Community College; Gloria Couch, Texas State Technical Institute; John C. Cox, New Mexico State University; Roger Crowe, State Technical Institute at Knoxville; E. Jane Dews, San Jacinto College-South; Michael Dougherty, Milwaukee Area Technical College; M. J. Duffey, Lord Fairfax Community College; C. S. "Pere" Everett, Des Moines Area Community College; Lawrence Finley, Western Kentucky University; Ethel Fishman, Fashion Institute of Technology; Jack Fleming, Moorpark College; Randall Scott Frederick, Delgado Community College; Daphne Friday, Scared Heart College; Olene Fuller, San Jacinto College–North; Alfonso Garcia, Navajo Community College; John Guebtner, Tacoma Community College; Edwin A Giermak, College of Dupage; Tommy Gilbreath, University of Texas at Tyler; Cliff Goodwin, Indiana University-Purdue University; Edward Gott, Jr., Eastern Maine Vocational Technical Institute; Luther Guynes, Los Angles City College; Ed Hart, Elizabethtown Community College; Joann Hendricks, City College of San Francisco; Steven Herendeen, Indiana-Purdue University at Fort Wayne; Ron Herrick, Mesa Community College; Karen Heuer, Des Moines Area Community College; Larry Hill, San Jacinto College; Larry Holliday, Southwest Wisconsin Vocational Technical Institute; Eugene Holmen, Essex Community College; David Hunt, Blackhawk Technical Institute; Tonya Hynds, Purdue University–Kokomo; Jim Jackson, Johnson Technical College; William Jacobs, Lake City Community College; Joseph James, Jr., Lamar University–Port Arthur; Debbie Jansky, Milwaukee Area Tech; Carl F. Jenks, Purdue University; F. Mike Kaufman; George Kelley, Erie Community College–City Campus; Billy Kirkland,

Tarleton State University; Steve Kirman, Dyke College; Jay Knippen, University of South Florida; Thomas Leet, Purdue University; James Lewis, Gateway Technical Institute; Marvin Long, New River Community College; Dorix Lux, Central Community College–Platte; Cheryl Macon, Butler County Community College; Joseph Manno, Montgomery College; Manuel Mena, Suny College At Oswego; Michael Miller, Indiana University-Purdue University at Fort Wayne; Jerry Moller, Frank Philip's College; Sherry Montgomery, Sain Philip's College; Charles Moore, Neosho County Community College; Herff Moore, University of Central Arkansas; Jim Mulvihill, South Central Technical College; Jim Nestor, Daytona Beach Community College; Gerard Nistal, Our Lady of Holy Cross College; Smita Jain Oxford, Commonwealth College; Carolyn Patton, Stephen F. Austin State University; Jean Perry, Contra Costa College; Donald Pettit, Suffolk County Community College; Jerome Pilewski, University of Pittsburgh at Titusville; Sharon Pinebrook, University of Houston; Peter Randrup, Worwic Technical Community College; William Recker, Northern Kentucky University; Robert Redick, Lincoln Land Community College; James A. Reinemann, College of Lake County; Tom Reynolds, Southside Virginia Community College; Harriett Rice, Los Angeles City College; Ralph Rice, Maryland Technical College; Shirley Rickert, Indiana University-Purdue University at Fort Wayne; Charles Roegiers, University of South Dakota; Lloyd Roettger, Indiana Vocational Technical College; Pat Rothamel, Iowa Western Community College; Duane Schechter, Muskingum Community College; Robert Sedwick, Fairleigh Dickinson University; Sandra Seppamaki, Tanana Valley Community College; David Shepard, Virginia Western Community College; David Shufeldt, Clayton State College; David Smith, Dabney Lancaster Community College; Carl Sonntag, Pikes Peak Community College; Frank Sotrines, Washburn University; William Steiden, Jefferson Community College Southwest; Greg Stephens, Kansas Tech; John Stepp, Greenville Technical College; Lynn H. Suksdorf, Salt Lake Community College; Marge Sunderland, Fayetteville Technical Institute; George Sutcliffe, Central Piedmont Community College; H. Allan Tolbert, Central Texas Colleges; Daniel R. Tomal, Purdue University; Wes Van Loon, Matanuske-Sustain Community College; Peter Vander Haeghen, Coastline Community College; Mike Vijuk, William Rainey Harper College; W. J. Waters, Central Piedmont Community College; George White, Ohlone College; Ron Williams, Merced College; Willie Williams, Tidewater Community College; Bob Willis, Rogers State College; Ira Wilsker, Lamar University; Paul Wolff II, Dundalk Community College; Richard Wong, Olympic College; Robert Wood, Vance-Granville Community College; and Charles Yauger, Arkansas State University.

SUPERVISORY MANAGEMENT

CHARLES R. GREER

W. RICHARD PLUNKETT

CHAPTER 1

Objectives

After reading and discussing this chapter, you should be able to do the following:

1. List and define management skills every supervisor must possess and apply.
2. List the groups to whom the supervisor is responsible and the responsibilities that exist toward each group.
3. Explain the concepts of *effectiveness* and *efficiency* as they apply to a supervisor's performance.
4. Explain the supervisor's responsibilities in terms of ethics.
5. Discuss the possible effects on supervisors of current trends in U.S. business.
6. Describe the sources of supervisory personnel.

Reducing Turnover at Domino's Pizza

Many supervisors and managers have had the experience of working in the fast food industry. Companies in this industry provide entry-level job opportunities for young people who have limited jobs skills and little work experience. The supervisors and managers who run fast food restaurants face tremendous challenges as they commonly have a young and inexperienced workforce that must be able to provide quick service to customers who are typically in a hurry. Many of the part-time employees who work in such businesses are students who do not intend to stay on the job for a long time. In addition, working conditions are often problematic as the area in which employees work is often crowded and hot from the nearby stoves and ovens. The work is fast paced and in full view of customers who are waiting to be served or waiting on their orders.

The Supervisor's
Special Role

Unsurprisingly, such businesses have high employee turnover, which makes it difficult to provide high quality service when a large proportion of the employees have relatively little experience. Like most companies in this industry, Domino's Pizza was concerned about the high turnover in their stores. In one region, the annual turnover rate for the employees who made deliveries, cooked the pizzas, and took orders was topping out at 300 percent. While this is a very high turnover rate, the fast food industry often has turnover rates among hourly employees that approach 200 percent. By comparison, turnover in large- and medium-sized companies in other industries typically ranges between 10 to 15 percent per year. Not only was turnover for employees high, but there was high turnover among store managers as well—as they were staying for only three to six months. Turnover is costly in any business, even in the fast food industry, which is characterized by low hourly wages.[2]

Companies in the industry, such as Starbucks, have addressed turnover rates for its hourly employees with higher wages, and Starbuck's annual rate ranges between 80 to 90 percent. In contrast to such approaches, Domino's has approached the problem by upgrading the quality of its store managers. In addition to being more careful in hiring store managers, the company has been coaching its store managers in order to improve their supervisory skills. It has also provided more incentives for its store managers, such as expanded career opportunities and stock options. One of the key improvements has been that the store managers are establishing better relationships with employees. For example, they are becoming more skilled in helping employees learn from mistakes and are learning how to conduct discipline while preserving good relationships with employees. Domino's focus on its store managers is well placed as it has found that the performance of its stores is most affected by how good the store managers are, while location and marketing are of lesser importance. The changes made by Domino's have been impressive as it has been able to reduce turnover to 107 percent.[3]

Questions for Thought

1. What are some of the skills that good supervisors need to have?
2. What are some of the expectations that employees have of their supervisors?

Introduction

supervisor
a manager responsible for the welfare, behaviors, and performances of non-management employees (workers)

A **supervisor** is an employee (and member of the group called managers) who is responsible for the welfare, behaviors, and performances of non-management employees—called workers. (Throughout this text, the terms *worker, team member, subordinate*, and *associate* will be used interchangeably with the term *employee*.) The supervisor is a person in the middle, positioned between the workers and higher-level managers. Supervisors' managers and employees differ in attitudes, values, priorities, and in the demands they make on supervisors. Workers and managers often make conflicting demands. The supervisor must cope with conflicts while gaining a sense of job satisfaction and identity in the process.

Major changes throughout both the private and public sectors of our economy are reshaping the traditional behaviors of supervisors. Organizational efforts to become more cost-effective and to get closer to customers has tapped into the creativity of all employees by creating self-directed teams and pushing decision-making responsibilities into the hands of supervisors and their associates. As a result, supervisors are moving away from giving orders and commands, planning employees' work, making all decisions, and inspecting employees' output. Instead, they are leading by example, coaching, counseling, guiding, consulting with, and meeting employees' individual and collective needs.

As in the case of Domino's Pizza, empirical investigations are discovering that the quality of the supervisor and employee relationship is the most important determinant of morale, productivity, and reduction in turnover. In many work settings, there is more pressure than ever before, with greater pressures for speed, shorter deadlines, and risk. Organizations are also demanding higher quality performance from their workforces and are asking them to work harder. Conversely, many employees are becoming more concerned about the rewards for their efforts. Unsurprisingly, the supervisor's role is growing in importance.[4]

team leader
a supervisor working in a team who is responsible for its members

team facilitator
a supervisor in charge of teams but who is working outside them

In many organizations, supervisors are being rapidly transformed into team leaders and team facilitators. **Team leaders** serve on and lead a team, and **team facilitators** nurture one or more employee teams. Both are expected to determine the human, financial, material, and informational resources needed by their associates and to make certain that necessary support is provided. Supervision entails getting work done through the effective utilization of employees and other resources. Team leaders and team facilitators should support their associates by helping to create and nurture a committed, trained, competent, and enthusiastic workforce. As William Bridges, the author of *Job Shift*, puts it: The value of supervisors ". . . can be defined only by how they facilitate the work of teams or how they contribute to it as a member."[5]

Some companies have been disappointed with their application of teams. While we present examples of supervisors in team settings and stress that the use of teams is increasing, there are limitations to teams. The primary requirement for effective teams is that the team members share a compelling purpose. Without such a purpose teams can be ineffective.[6]

Governmental regulations, while not providing the most meaningful definition, also define the supervisor. The Taft-Hartley Act of 1947 says that any person who can hire, suspend, transfer, lay off, recall, promote, discharge, assign, reward, or discipline other employees or recommend such action while using independent judgment is a supervisor—a member of management. For the purposes of the Fair Labor Standards Act of 1938, commonly referred to as the minimum wage law, supervisors are distinguishable from regular employees only if (1) they spend no more than 20 percent of their time performing the same kind of work that their employees perform and (2) they are paid other than an hourly wage.

You may be familiar with the term **foreman**. While the term is used less frequently today, in some organizations it is used interchangeably with the word *supervisor* and usually refers to a supervisor of workers performing manufacturing activities.

Learning Objective Number One

foreman
a supervisor of workers in manufacturing

THREE TYPES OF MANAGEMENT SKILLS

No matter how supervisors are defined, they routinely must apply basic skills. The basic **management skills** required of all managers at every level in an organization can be grouped under three headings: interpersonal, technical, and conceptual.[7] Managers at different levels in an organization use one or another of these skills to a greater or lesser degree, depending on the manager's position in the organization and the particular demands of the circumstances at any given time. As Exhibit 1.1 illustrates, the supervisor's role requires less conceptual skill than does higher-level management. On the other hand, supervisors require more technical skill.

management skills
categories of capabilities needed by all managers at every level in an organization

INTERPERSONAL SKILLS

Interpersonal, human, or people skills determine the manager's ability to work effectively as a group or team member and to build cooperative effort within the group or team she leads. The manager also uses interpersonal skills to coordinate the interaction between that group and all the other groups with which it comes into contact.

Consider the lessons learned by team leaders in the Colorado-based XEL Company. This maker of communications equipment wanted to create a quality-obsessed environment "to become a model of workplace efficiency, dedicated to quality and teamwork."[8] The process began with a needs assessment in which team leaders asked associates what they wanted to learn and how. After trying ready-made courses and evaluating them, team leaders decided to design their own "XEL University [offering] 30 classes, on topics from soldering to problem solving."[9] Associates volunteered to participate, and spent, on average, nearly five hours each month in class. Major improvements and some dozen new patents were the result.

Proportions of Management Skills Needed at the Three Levels of Management.

EXHIBIT 1.1

Top management		
Middle management	INTERPERSONAL TECHNICAL CONCEPTUAL TIME	
Supervisory or first-line management		

Supervisors who have developed interpersonal skills know themselves well. They are tolerant and understanding of the viewpoints, attitudes, perceptions, and beliefs of others and are skillful communicators. People with interpersonal skills listen to others, are honest and open, and possess personalities that are pleasing to others. They create an atmosphere in which others feel free to express their ideas, and they make every effort to determine how intended actions will affect others in the organization. Supervisors who once held their employees' jobs have empathy for them—that is, supervisors have the ability to relate to what employees are experiencing and feeling. Managers at every level need interpersonal skills, but such skills are particularly important to supervisors. They must create and maintain an atmosphere of cooperation and harmony within and among the diverse individuals so often found in worker groups.

TECHNICAL SKILLS

Supervisors with technical skills understand and are proficient in specific kinds of activity. Their expertise may be in computer programming or repair, in utilizing precision equipment and tools, or in design. Technical skill involves specialized knowledge, analytical ability within that specialty, and facility in the use of the tools and techniques of the specific discipline.[10] Technical skills are the primary concern of training in industry, in public and private technical schools, and in community colleges. For example, Intel worked with community colleges in the design of two-year programs to train technicians to work in its microprocessor fabrication plants.[11]

Germany has a highly developed dual system that provides extensive technical training through apprenticeships with employers and classroom instruction. Its technical apprenticeship programs, which take from three to four years to complete, make it the world's leader in some areas of technology. The typical German supervisor has a highly technical background, often obtained through an apprenticeship, and views this expertise as the foundation for his or her authority.[12] It is no surprise that many other countries have studied Germany's technical training system.

As a supervisor, you will need good people skills to help your workers realize their full potential. Here, a supervisor at Glastron Boats takes time to assist an employee.

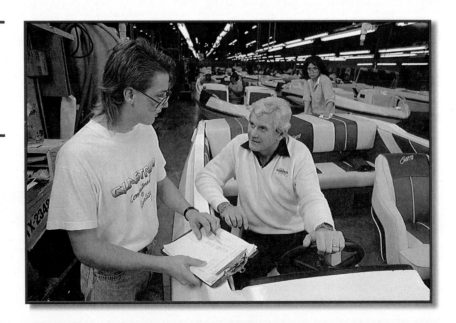

Technical skills are more important for supervisors than for mid-level and upper managers because the latter have responsibilities less closely related to the production, operations, service, and maintenance activities of the organization. Such skills are essential to supervisors for several reasons. Supervisors' influence over employees is a partial result of their technical competence. They must thoroughly understand the work they supervise, and they must be able to train others to do it. Without an understanding of their unit's machinery, equipment, procedures, and practices, they cannot adequately evaluate performance. As with human skills, technological skills can be learned and developed. Moreover, supervisors can be expected to supervise a growing number of technical workers. Projections of the fastest growing jobs through 2008 have included several technical jobs in the highest growth category, such as computer support specialists, systems analysts, desktop publishing specialists, data processing equipment repairers, and respiratory therapists.[13]

Practicing technical skills requires that you first possess them at a level sufficient both to apply them and to pass them along to others. Many supervisors are promoted from highly skilled jobs and then must turn around and supervise others who apply those same skills. If you are such a person, you have sound experience in skill applications. Such experience will prove quite useful to you when you are directing others who use those skills. But you will no longer have to execute your skills on the job as you had to when you were a worker. Your task is to help those you supervise to become as proficient as they can be in the execution of their skills.

CONCEPTUAL SKILLS

Managers with conceptual skills view their organizations as wholes with many parts, all of which are interrelated and interdependent. Supervisors must be able to perceive themselves and their employees, teams, and sections as part of and contributors to other sections and the entire organization. Every decision made by every manager can create a ripple effect that may influence others outside the particular decision-maker's control.

Consider the lessons learned by Randy Kirk, president of AC International in California. Kirk and his partner, Terry Brown, created a company specializing in bicycle accessories with only themselves as employees. They relied on outside suppliers for parts and felt that they had an ideal arrangement. Nonetheless, they soon began to receive customer complaints because their suppliers were unable to meet commitments. Quality and quantity of bike helmets became a problem even before the supplier had a fire and stopped production for several months. A second supplier of a key product went bankrupt. A third product was made in part by two different suppliers. This led to problems in shades of color and mating the different parts. The two entrepreneurs soon learned that if they made the parts themselves they would be less vulnerable to such shocks and in control of their products. With the help of several dozen employees, they began to make most of what they sold, used outside sources for a few services and raw materials, and reaped improvements to both quality and profits.[14] These entrepreneurs initially failed to anticipate and develop alternative plans for handling the shocks and ripple effects that they experienced. Their experience points out the need for conceptual thinking.

Acquiring a conceptual point of view becomes increasingly important as you climb higher on the management ladder. An employer must provide ways for you as a supervisor to know what is happening in other parts of the company and must inform you before changes are implemented. Internet sources, e-mail, official memos, reports, meetings, and workshops will also help keep you informed. Keeping in touch with fellow supervisors and reading the official correspondence that flows across your desk will make you a team player and help you and your people avoid unpleasant surprises.

THE SUPERVISOR'S RESPONSIBILITIES

Supervisors have responsibilities to three primary groups: their employees, their peers in management, and their superiors in management. They must work in harmony with all three groups if they are to be effective supervisors.

RELATIONS WITH EMPLOYEES

Supervisors have a responsibility to get to know their employees as individuals. Each employee, like his or her supervisor, has specific needs and wants. Each has certain expectations from work, certain goals to achieve through work, and fundamental attitudes and aptitudes that influence work performance. When supervisors get to know each employee as an individual, they are able to tailor their approach to each. Employees want to know that their supervisors care about them and are prepared to do something about their problems. As Lee Ledbetter, a team leader at the Fremont, California, GM/Toyota plant, puts it,

> Back when I worked in [another] GM [plant], I worked in the group for three months, and the foreman still didn't know my name. He'd come by and show me (my paycheck), and say "Hey, is that you?" Here, everybody knows everybody by their first name, right from the plant manager on down.[15]

A sure sign that supervisors care about their employees is common courtesy—using a person's name, a respectful tone of voice, personalized greetings, and sincere inquiries about the employee's health and well-being.

Getting to know employees well can be difficult. Some people are more open and outgoing than others. These obstacles, however, should not be used as excuses to avoid trying to know your employees. You will get to know your employees well only if you spend time with them and become familiar with their problems. If contacts with your people are informal, use the time for some casual conversation with them and find out what is going on in their lives. Your showing a sincere interest usually results in open responses from them. Only after you have a good understanding of your employees can you expect to be successful in your dealings with them.

Your major responsibilities to employees include the following:

- Getting to know them as individuals
- Giving them the respect and trust they deserve
- Valuing their uniqueness and individuality
- Assigning employees work that fits their abilities
- Listening to their concerns
- Treating them as they want to be treated

- Providing them with adequate instruction and training
- Enabling them to do and give their best
- Encouraging them to be lifelong learners
- Handling their complaints and problems in a fair and just way
- Safeguarding their health and welfare while they are on the job
- Praising and providing constructive criticism
- Providing examples of proper conduct at work

Among the most important of these is the last one. Team leaders and team facilitators must "walk the talk"—make their actions match their words. If these obligations are met, then employees will perceive their supervisors as leaders. Such supervisors gain the trust and respect of their employees—the keys to effective supervision and personal achievement. Your employees represent the most important group to whom and for whom you are responsible.

Supervisors fail when they exempt themselves from the rules, fail to make sacrifices asked of employees, or obtain extravagant perquisites. Such behavior can easily lead to an "us versus them" mentality that destroys teamwork and diminishes the role of employees. As an example of what *not* to do, on the same day that General Motors obtained concessions from its unionized workers, it announced a more lucrative bonus program for executives. The resentment aroused by this action was a factor that led to a strike several years later that virtually shut down the entire company's production facilities.[16]

RELATIONS WITH PEERS

Managers on the same level of management and possessing similar levels of authority and status are **peers**. Peers are the individuals with whom you must cooperate and coordinate if your department and theirs are to operate in harmony. Furthermore, Your peers normally constitute the bulk of your friends and associates at work. Your peers represent an enormous pool of talent and experience that will be yours to tap and contribute to if they view you in a favorable way. For this reason alone, it is to your advantage to cultivate their friendship. Your peers can teach you a great deal about the company, and they are often a fine source of advice on how to handle difficult situations that may arise. They can do more to keep you out of trouble than any other group in the company. In so many ways you need each other, and both you and they stand to benefit from a partnership or alliance based on mutual respect, trust, and the need to resolve common problems. If you share your expertise with them, you can expect them to share theirs with you.

s a supervisor, team leader, or team facilitator, you will be asked or assigned to serve on peer-group teams. In such cases, you will shape your reputation by the ways in which you foster a spirit of cooperation and teamwork. Your ability or inability to contribute and cooperate with peers can mean either success or failure in your career. Teams of peers are common at all organizational levels.

Linda Hill, a Harvard University professor, has noted the importance for supervisors to establish relationships with peers. She has found that supervisors need to develop peer relationships or peer networks for several reasons. These include obtaining information through peers, obtaining an additional means for getting things done, relying on peers for emotional support, and obtaining feedback. Interestingly, the supervisors she studied sometimes sought advice and feedback from peers in other parts of the organization who

peer
a person with the same level of authority and status as another

TEAMS

were on different career paths. These supervisors realized that it was better to receive criticism from peers than their bosses. Furthermore, any weaknesses revealed by their request for assistance were less likely to be used against them since these peers were in different career paths. In addition, in Hill's study, the importance of developing peer relationships was highlighted when some supervisors received instructions from their bosses to spend more time developing peer relationships.[17]

General Motors has recognized the value of teaming peers. The company uses vehicle launch center teams consisting of middle management specialists from engineering, design, and marketing to "evaluate car and truck proposals for cost, compatibility with other GM products, and marketability."[18] At the supervisory and worker levels, "GM is moving away from traditional assembly lines into smaller working units known as cells, where workers get more opportunity to design their own processes and thus improve output."[19] GM's Saturn operations are famous for self-managing teams and the inclusion of customers on its teams at every level.

Supervisors who are off in their own little worlds and unwilling to share their know-how are labeled uncooperative and antisocial, a reputation that jeopardizes their careers. Managers in higher positions in business have no need for withdrawn or isolated supervisors. In addition, most higher-level managers do not appreciate supervisors who are concerned about only their own units and who pursue their own units' objectives at the expense of the whole organization.

RELATIONS WITH SUPERIORS

middle manager
a manager of other managers or supervisors who reports to executives

If you are a supervisor, the person you report to is a **middle manager** who is accountable for your actions. Your boss is similar to you in being both a follower and a member of management. She executes all the functions of management and is evaluated on the basis of the performance of her employees. Like you, your boss must develop and maintain sound working relationships with her employees, peers, and superiors. Moreover, your boss has probably served an apprenticeship as a supervisor, so you can probably count on her understanding of your own situation.

Your responsibilities to your superiors, both line (having direct operational authority) and staff (having an advisory role to line managers and functional authority), can be summarized as follows:

- Valuing their uniqueness and individuality
- Giving them your best effort and the support they require
- Transmitting information about problems, along with recommendations for solving them
- Operating within company policies
- Promoting the company's goals
- Striving for constant improvement
- Seeking their counsel and using it
- Using the organization's resources effectively
- Keeping them informed about the unit's status

Learning Objective Number Three

To your boss, you owe allegiance and respect. You must be a loyal follower if you intend to be a successful leader. To the company's team of staff specialists, you are the person through whom their recommendations are implemented.

BEING EFFECTIVE AND EFFICIENT

Managers at every level are expected to perform their tasks with effectiveness and efficiency. *Managerial effectiveness* is defined as accomplishing stated goals.[20] Accomplishing stated goals means meeting deadlines. Effective managers think ahead and schedule work so that enough resources will be available to complete it on time. Those who accomplish stated goals carefully plan their work (set goals, priorities, timetables) and stick to their plans. An ineffective supervisor fails to meet deadlines, falls behind on projects, and receives poor performance ratings.

Efficiency is defined as doing things with a minimal expense of time, money, and other resources. The efficient supervisor avoids waste of all kinds. The inefficient supervisor spends too much of any resource while executing tasks. The inefficient supervisor also receives poor performance ratings and places future operations in jeopardy because the needed resources may not be available.

Clearly, a supervisor must be both effective and efficient. Effectiveness is probably the more important of the two because it means that, at a minimum, essential tasks will get done. Effectiveness with inefficiency can often be tolerated by organizations, at least in the short run. But efficiency without effectiveness is intolerable, even in the short run. Essentials remain undone and vital work is left incomplete.

SUPERVISORY ROLES

Like actors who have to learn their roles well, all supervisors are expected to learn and play specific roles in order to execute their duties successfully. The precise role of individual supervisors depends on their understanding of the job, as well as on the pressures, rewards, and guidelines brought to bear on them from inside and outside the organization. What follows is a brief but important discussion of the ways in which roles are assigned to, designed for, and perceived by each supervisor in a business enterprise. The authors are indebted to Robert L. Kahn and his associates and to Professor John B. Miner for much of this discussion.[21]

ROLE PRESCRIPTIONS

The employees, peers, friends, family, and superiors of supervisors help shape and define the kinds of roles the supervisors play and the way in which they play them. Demands made on the supervisors by these groups and their business organizations prescribe the roles (called **role prescriptions**) for them to follow. Through the expectations and demands placed on the supervisors, people help shape each supervisor's perception of his or her job. Organizational influences—such as policies, procedures, job descriptions, and union contracts—also exert influence on the roles of each supervisor. These multiple demands can and do create conflicts in the minds of supervisors: What should their roles be and how precisely should they play them?

Henry Mintzberg, a noted management researcher, developed a classic description of all management behavior with 10 roles (see Exhibit 1.2). Mintzberg developed the 10 roles through close observations of chief executives. He found that different

role prescription
the collection of expectations and demands from superiors, employees, and others that shapes a manager's job description and perception of his or her job

ExHIBIT 1.2	Mintzberg's management roles.

ROLE	DESCRIPTION	IDENTIFIABLE ACTIVITIES
INTERPERSONAL		
Figurehead	Symbolic head; obliged to perform a number of routine duties of a legal or social nature	Ceremony, status, requests, solicitations
Leader	Responsible for the motivation and activation of subordinates; responsible for staffing, training, and associated duties	Virtually all managerial activities involving subordinates
Liaison	Maintains self-developed network of outside contacts and informers who provide favors and information	Acknowledgments of correspondence, external board work; other activities involving outsiders
INFORMATIONAL		
Monitor	Seeks and receives a wide variety of special information to develop a thorough understanding of the organization and environment; emerges as a nerve center of internal and external information of the organization	Handling all correspondence and contacts concerned primarily with receiving information
Disseminator	Transmits information received from outsiders or from subordinates to members of the organization; some information factual, some involving interpretation and integration	Forwarding mail into the organization for informational purposes; verbal contacts involving information flow to subordinates
Spokesman	Transmits information to outsiders on organization's plans, policies, actions, results, and so forth; serves as expert on organization's industry	Board meetings; handling correspondence and contacts involving transmission of information to outsiders
DECISIONAL		
Entrepreneur	Searches organization and its environment for opportunities and initiates projects to bring about change	Strategy and review sessions involving initiation or design of improvement projects
Disturbance Handler	Responsible for corrective action when organization faces important, unexpected disturbances	Strategy and review involving disturbances and crises
Resource Allocator	Responsible for the allocation of organizational resources of all kinds—in effect the making or approving of all significant organizational decisions	Scheduling; requests for authorization; any activity involving budgeting and the programming of subordinates' work
Negotiator	Responsible for representing the organization at major negotiations	Negotiation

Source: Slight adaptation of Table 2 from *THE NATURE OF MANAGERIAL* WORK by Mintzberg, H. © 1973 Addison Wesley Longman. Adapted by permission of Person Education, Inc., Upper Saddle River, N.J.

managers emphasized different roles and spent varying amounts of time on each, depending on their personalities, the job at hand, and the situation. All supervisors play these roles on a day-to-day basis as they interact with higher-level managers, peers, associates, and people outside their organization.

ROLE CONFLICT

When conflicting and contradictory demands are made on supervisors, they may find themselves in awkward or difficult positions. How they react to such pressures and precisely what they do to cope with such conflicts depend on their own values and perceptions and on the circumstances of the **role conflicts**. Consider the following incident that happened in a suburb north of Chicago. Two paramedics discovered a conflict between the instructions in their medical manual and the provisions of Illinois law about the proper method of treatment for heart-attack victims. If the paramedics followed their manual, they believed they would be in violation of state law. If they followed the law, however, they believed they would be giving incorrect or outmoded treatment to their patients. Perplexed, they asked their hospital administrator for clarification of the treatment procedures. To their surprise, they received in reply a letter that called them incompetent and suspended them from their duties as paramedics! This example highlights a common job situation, in which an employee's training in organizational procedures contradicts the demands of the immediate boss. Role conflicts can and do occur, and when they do, they may create tensions and job dissatisfaction.

role conflict
a situation that occurs when contradictory or opposing demands are made on a manager

ROLE AMBIGUITY

Whenever a supervisor is not sure of the role he is expected to play in a given situation or how to play it, he is a victim of **role ambiguity**. Role conflict results from clearly contradictory demands. Role ambiguity results from unclear or nonexistent job descriptions,

role ambiguity
uncertainty about the role that one is expected to play

Employees love to work for Southwest Airlines. Here, a Southwest Airlines airport customer service agent dresses as a clown. Southwest Airlines has been chosen as *Fortune's* "Best Company to Work for in America." The company is known for its individuality and creativity.

orders, rules, policies, or procedures. When role ambiguity exists, supervisors may do things they should not do, may fail to do things they should do, and may find it hard to distinguish where one manager's job begins and another's ends.

General Electric (GE), a global company with 270,000 employees spanning several industries, provides a challenge for anyone attempting to eliminate role ambiguity. The company's former CEO, Jack Welch, who is widely recognized as one of the best business leaders in the world, emphasized the importance of communication. Welch's ability to communicate clearly and to gain enthusiasm for his ideas was legendary. He understood that effective communication requires repeated efforts to convey ideas to others. He also understood the importance of keeping things simple. One of the major differences between GE under Welch's leadership and many other companies was that its leaders and employees shared a common sense of direction. Welch was also legendary for his use of stretch targets as goals to eliminate ambiguity, set direction, provide clarity, and energize the company's workforce.[22]

ROLE PERFORMANCE

All organizations need their members to play their roles as prescribed. Exhibit 1.3 lists the "top 10 people strategies" at Southwest Airlines. Southwest Airlines, which is

EXHIBIT 1.3	**Southwest Airlines' top 10 people strategies.**

1. We encourage individuality and creativity—no clones.

2. We encourage and reward compassionate treatment of people.

3. We hire and fire based on attitude.

4. We have low tolerance for elitism.

5. We look for reasons to give awards and celebrate.

6. The customer is not always right.

7. We promote a family atmosphere.

8. We don't believe in a fancy compensation program.

9. We "do the right thing." There aren't many rules except for safety.

10. We have a high tolerance for mistakes, which is required for #9 above.

Source: Presentation by Libby Sartain, Vice President of People, Southwest Airlines to the Human Resource Management Roundtable, Texas Christian University, February 6, 1996.

unconventional and creative, has a reputation as being one of the best-managed companies in the United States. Southwest's superior management and unique culture led to its selection by *Fortune* magazine in 1998 as the best company to work for in the United States. Furthermore, after the September 11, 2001, attack on the World Trade Center, in contrast to many other airlines, Southwest did not lay off employees and was the only airline in the United States that had a profit for the quarter.[23] The strategies in Exhibit 1.3 provide a good set of guidelines for supervisors in many organizations. Point 3 indicates that having employees with good work attitudes is critical at Southwest; the company looks first for a good attitude. It feels that as long as an employee has a good work attitude, she can be trained for her job and role. Point 4 can be illustrated by several examples. Southwest's officers do not have big offices, and they give out their home phone numbers. They also perform the lowest-level jobs, such as handling baggage, one day every quarter. It is obvious that arrogant people do not fit in at Southwest. Point 6, which states that the customer is not always right, means that Southwest does not let its employees be abused by customers. This point is particularly relevant for supervisors in service industries. Keven Freiberg and Jackie Freiberg point out that Southwest Airlines feels that the manner in which employees are treated will be reflected in how employees treat customers.[24]

Learning Objective Number Four

GLOBAL

RESPONSIBILITIES FOR ETHICS

As with all other managers, supervisors are expected to take a leadership role in setting the standards for ethics, modeling ethical behavior, and enforcing standards necessary to maintain ethical conduct. Before delving further into this important responsibility, we first need a good understanding of the meaning of ethics. One definiftion of ethics is that it is a discipline focused on determining the rightness or wrongness of human conduct in a specific set of circumstances. Another useful definition of ethics, which is based on notions of honor and trust, states that ethics involves "obedience to the unenforceable."[25]

Supervisors will inevitably confront ethical dillemas, which will prove to provide difficult challenges for them. In order to handle such dilemmas, they need a decision framework, which will enable them to consider the dilemma from several ethical perspectives. One principle or persepctive, which is to provide the greatest good for the greatest number people, is called the **utilitarian principle**. While the value of this perspective is the cost-benefit approach upon which it rests, it does not protect the interests of the minority. Another perspective, the **rule-based principle**, maintains that one should act as a model for others or in a manner in which we would like to see all people behave in similar circumstances. This perspective is also defined by some as rule following, and there are obviously occassions when rigid adherence to a rule may not result in good decisions. Another aproach, the **golden rule principle**, which is also called the care-based approach, asks that we treat others as we would like to be treated.[26] The **justice-based principle** draws on notions of fairness in making decisions. Finally, the **rights-based principle** maintains that decisions should consider that all people have basic individual rights that should not be denied and that we should respect such rights.[27]

Having a working knowledge of such views or perspectives of ethics does not mean that it will now be easy to arrive at the right answers to ethical dilemmas by simply

utilitarian principle
an ethics perspective relying on cost-benefit analysis

rule-based principle
an ethics perspective that evaluates the desirability of a behavior in accordance to whether it could withstand scrutiny as a universal standard

golden rule principle
an ethics principle that specifies that people should treat others in a manner in which they would like to be treated

justice-based principle
an ethics perspective that emphasizes the criterion of fairness

rights-based principle
an ethics perspective that maintains that people have basic rights, which must be respected

applying these views. Despite some of the myths that ethical decisions are easy, ethical dilemmas, as opposed to moral decisions involving right and wrong, are complex and difficult. Nonetheless, after viewing the dilemma from all perspectives, there will likely be a clearer understanding of the action that should be taken. Furthermore, while these different perspectives can provide part of the answer, supervisors do not have to reach a decision entirely on their own. Help is available in most organizations, such as ethics officers who can help supervisors work through these issues.[28]

While deliberating on the issues involved in ethical dilemmas, supervisors must contemplate how various actions will affect others. They must think about the circumstances surrounding the intended action: his or her objectives, possible means available to achieve them, motives for taking the action, and possible consequences. Our moral and ethical thinking is affected by our personal values and by our experiences. Supervisors will occasionally need to decide whether to take actions that have negative consequences for some people and groups while they actually help others—an ethical dilemma. Ethical dilemmas have been defined as situations in which there are good reasons to select either one of two choices although only one choice is possible. In these situations, the decision involves conflicts in basic values, such as "truth versus loyalty, short-term versus long-term, individual versus community, and justice versus mercy."[29] Examples of such decisions include situations in which a government taxes one group to help another and some people are harmed to benefit others. In addition, when a business decides to stop manufacturing one item to produce a more profitable one, some employees and suppliers are hurt, whereas others benefit. The ethical person will do his best to refrain from taking actions that will be harmful to others, although this is not always possible in the most serious of ethical dilemmas. However, in those situations involving lesser challenges, supervisors should, at the very least, follow the centuries-old rule from the medical profession, which states "first, do no harm."[30]

Many professions and many corporations have stated codes of ethics, which their members are expected to live up to or incur some penalty. Such codes create boundaries around individuals' freedom to act. The decisions that supervisors must make each day have to be considered in terms of some kind of ethical test or code. If they are not, serious personal and legal problems can and will arise for both the supervisor and the employer. However, for most managerial positions, no clearly defined codes of conduct exist to provide exact guidance for behavior. In addition, pressures in business environments make for difficult ethical decisions, and employees sometimes use these pressures as excuses to justify unethical behavior. One type of excuse is to pass responsibility onto a supervisor who told the employee to do something unethical.[31] Since the pressures to comply with supervisors are high, taking individual responsibility is a challenge for many employees. Indeed, the Milgram studies at Yale University during the 1960s and 1970s, in which subjects made decisions to administer potentially lethal electrical shocks, indicate that people will do terrible things to others solely because someone with authority directed them to do so. This excuse could apply to all directed behaviors, regardless of how reprehensible, but the underlying truth is that in the final analysis, it is up to the employee to accept personal responsibility for her behavior.[32]

A second type of excuse is that everybody else is engaging in the same behavior, although such perceptions are seldom correct. While research has revealed that individuals are often strongly influenced by comparisons with others when looking for guidance in ambiguous situations, doing as the Romans do while in Rome does not excuse unethical behavior.[33] A third type of excuse involves situations in which individuals fail to fulfill ethical obligations to act by claiming that the problem is not their concern.[34] This excuse often fails to withstand close scrutiny when we apply the following guideline: "We cannot always count on others to do the right thing, and there will be times when we ought to be involved, even if it is inconvenient, time-consuming, or puts our jobs—or our lives—on the line."[35] A final type of excuse is that behaviors that would not be tolerated in our personal lives, such as deception and bluffing, are permissible in business. Again, this type of excuse fails when we apply the idea that morality in business cannot rest on different principles from those that apply in everyday morality.[36]

While business pressures sometimes cause people to make unethical decisions, there is evidence that profitability and good ethics go hand in hand. For example, Wetherill Associates, a small company of 480 employees, provides us with an illustration of the fact that high standards of conduct are not inconsistent with high profitability. The company has high standards of conduct, and its recent return on equity was 33 percent. As an indication of the firm's view of ethics, there are no sales targets at Wetherill because the company's leaders feel that such standards cause employees to lie when their performance is lagging.[37] Another example of the company's application of ethics is provided by the following: "Recently a new salesman proudly announced: 'Wow! I came up with a whopper to get that customer off my back.' His office mates were not amused. They made him call the customer back and tell the truth."[38] This last example indicates that supervisors are not alone in their desire for ethical conduct. When employees believe in the ethics of the organization, they also help their supervisors enforce standards of ethical conduct.

As a supervisor, you have not only ethical concerns but legal ones as well. You are charged to act both ethically and lawfully. Just refraining from doing things that are illegal is not enough. It may be legal to fire a person you do not like for that reason alone. But is it ethical to do so? What may be the consequences to you, to your associates, and to your company if you do so? Furthermore, your reputation is far too precious to waste on hasty, ill-thought-out decisions that fail to consider both the law and ethics. Times will come when you are asked to act in a way that you believe is immoral or unethical. What will you say to a boss who makes such a request of you? Are you prepared to cover up for a derelict employee? Once you are caught in a lie, your integrity is gone, and it is almost impossible to retrieve. Without personal codes of conduct and values we will struggle to defend our own actions, and the actions of others may compromise our integrity. It is better to leave an environment that is unethical than to remain and become so ourselves. As noted earlier, supervisors should remember that they do not have to resolve ethical dilemmas entirely by themselves. People are available in most organizations who can help supervisors and managers work through the issues. The important thing to remember is to get help from others. Exhibit 1.4 provides a set of guidelines that will help supervisors make decisions about ethical issues.

This chapter's section on supervising ethics deals with ethical lapses involving price fixing, which is an area where supervisors who deal with sales personnel must exercise caution.

EXHIBIT 1.4	Guidelines for ethical decision-making.

1. Do not end your search for the right answer with a solution that simply complies with the law.

2. Consult with respected and knowledgeable others in the organization who have experience dealing with ethical issues.

3. Apply the different ethics perspectives as a framework for analyzing the impact on everyone potentially affected by the decision.

4. Attempt to determine how you would feel about the issue from the perspectives of the parties affected by the decision.

5. Consider how you would feel about your decision if the facts were made public, such as by being reported on television on in the newspaper.

6. Examine potential decision alternatives for consistency with your basic values, such as concerns for honesty, fairness, and others.

7. Reflect upon your intentions and clarify what you want to accomplish with the decision.

8. Whenever possible, consult with everyone potentially affected by your decision prior to arriving at a final answer.

9. Examine the "rightness" of potential alternatives by comparing them with the long-term consequences.

10. Understand that there may be negative personal consequences in the short term for adhering to ethical principles, but there is no other alternative for the long term.

11. Be certain of the causes, people, principles, and organizations that are deserving of your loyalties.

Sources: Gary W. Davis. "Digging Into Ethics," *Association Management,* (October 2003): 26–33. Rushworth Kidder, Address to the Graduate Management Admissions Council, Dallas, Texas (June 18–21, 2003). Rushworth Kidder. *How Good People Make Tough Choices: Resolving the Dilemmas of Ethical Living,* New York: Simon & Schuster, 1996. Laura Nash. "Ethics Without the Sermon," *Harvard Business Review,* (November/December 1981): 78–90. Kathryn Tyler. "Do the Right Thing," *HR Magazine* (February 2005): 99–201.

WORKFORCE TRENDS AFFECTING SUPERVISORS

Learning Objective Number Five

As noted earlier, it is clear that supervisors are operating in more demanding work environments, and that the role they play is increasing in importance. The work environment, in which supervisors must operate, has changed in several important ways.

SUPERVISORS AND ETHICS

During a recent year, companies in the United Kingdom loaded pirated software, having an estimated value of $1 billion, onto their business computers.[39] Furthermore, a recent survey indicates that illegal software is used by approximately one-third to one-half of small to mid-sized firms in Singapore.[40] California software company Mitchell 1 is taking action against approximately 60 automotive businesses in Canada for using pirated copies of its shop management software.[41] Such examples of infringements on software copyright protection create serious ethical problems and legal issues, which can expose a company to significant financial liabilities. Software piracy might not initially seem like an issue of importance to supervisors, but because of the pervasiveness of the problem, it can pose serious problems. Most companies are very careful to insure that pirated software is not used in their operations and supervisors are often in the best position to be aware of such violations. Accordingly, supervisors are expected to prevent such abuses and to enforce the organization's policies prohibiting the installation of such software on company computers.

Despite the liabilities associated with copyright infringements of software and other intellectual property, such as music and patents, advances in technology have created new opportunities for abuse and violations of copyrights. Recently the U.S. Supreme Court ruled against Grokster, a company that created and distributed software that enables individuals to swap music and movies over the Internet. As a result of the ruling and damages assessed against the firm, which may approach $50 million, Grokster announced that it would no longer market the software. In addition to the ruling against Grokster, the Recording Industry Association of America, which represents the interests of movie and music companies, has filed lawsuits against 15,000 individuals involved in such activities. Estimates of the number of people using file-sharing networks, in violation of copyright laws, provide an indication of the enormity of the problem as one firm has estimated that there over nine million such individuals. Because of the breadth of such practices, supervisors will need to educate employees, who may fail to appreciate the ethical and legal issues involved with digital piracy, about the importance of respecting software copyrights. They may also have to resist pressure from others in their organizations to cut corners by using such software and other protected intellectual property.

Source: Jeff Leeds. "Grokster Calls It Quits on Sharing Music Files," *New York Times* (November 8, 2005): C1, C18.

Not only has the role of the supervisor become more demanding, time consuming, and more reliant on greater skills, but the demands on employees are also increasing. As organizations have become more decentralized and flatter, there has been a reduction in the hierarchical distance, both organizationally and interpersonally, between supervisors and employees as their relationships are on a more equal plane. After years of downsizing and outsourcing, it is clear that organizations no longer place emphasis on keeping employees for the duration of their careers. Correspondingly, employees are more focused on rewards that occur in the short term as opposed to the long term.[42] A brief look at some major trends, beginning with the changing workforce, will provide insights into a few of the problems and opportunities they represent for all of us.

EMERGENCE OF NEW GENERATIONS OF WORKERS

There is often speculation about the differences in work values of different generations and how today's younger employees are different. (It should be noted at this point that humorists have observed that there is a time-honored tradition of older generations viewing young generations with some suspicion.) Any differences are important to the subject of this chapter because they can provide insights into the effectiveness of various incentives or approaches for changing behavior. Generations of particular relevance to supervisors include: (1) Baby Boomers, who were born between 1946 and 1964, (2) Gen-Xers, who were born between 1965 and 1977, and (3) Millennials, who were born between 1978 and 1995.[43]

Survey research is consistent with some of the speculations that there are differences between generations. Some important differences between Baby Boomers and Gen-Xers are that members of the latter cohort have a greater desire for quick promotions, are less loyal to their employing organizations, and are more "me" oriented. They also feel less strongly about the centrality of work in their lives. On the other hand, there is no difference between the two cohorts on their pride in craftsmanship. The same research indicates, from a comparison of work values in the mid-1970s, that the differences are more a result of the general experiences associated with a generation in time rather than with aging. This finding is consistent with the Gen X-ers' lower company loyalty and work commitment as they have grown up with layoffs, downsizing, and the use of temporary workers.[44] Unfortunately, they have learned from their parents' experience or have seen employees treated by some employers as if they were disposable.[45] As noted earlier, Gen X-ers tend to view work less centrally, and some researchers have described them as having "an attitude of 'working to live' versus one of 'living to work'."[46] On the other hand, there are predictions that the next age cohort of employees will be increasingly productive, as indicated in the following description.

> They are well educated and comfortable with technology, and multiculturalism in their schools has made them the most tolerant and open-minded of all generations; they view the world as global and connected 24 hours a day. They are also said to be proactive, possessing positive expectations and a willingness to fight for social justice in the workplace.[47]

In addition, there is good news for supervisors leading change efforts in the future as younger workers in the Millennial generation are predicted to have a number of characteristics that are very positive for the work environment:

> As a group, Millennials are unlike any other youth generation in living memory. They are more numerous, more affluent, better educated, and more ethnically diverse. More important, they are beginning to manifest a wide array of positive social habits that older Americans no longer associated with youth, including a new focus on teamwork, achievement, modesty, and good conduct. Only a few years from now, this can-do youth revolution will overwhelm the cynics and pessimists.[48]

GREATER DIVERSITY IN THE WORKFORCE

Nearly every nation today is a mix of peoples with different origins, values, and traditions. Americans differ in race, age, gender, sexual orientation, religious belief, language, nation of birth, education, physical characteristics, and more. There is growing diversity in the United States as African Americans, Hispanics, and Asians accounted for approximately 30 percent of the 291 million population in 2003, while the White, non-Hispanic population accounted for 68 to 69 percent of the population. The Hispanic population is growing rapidly and is now slightly larger than the African American population.[49] Labor force statistics, which count both individuals over the age of 16 who are employed along with those who are unemployed but available for work, show some interesting trends. By the year 2010, when the U.S. labor force is projected to reach 158 million people, 48 percent of women are projected to be in the labor force, which is up from approximately 38 percent in 1980. In contrast, by 2010, approximately 73 percent of men are projected to be in the labor force, which is down from approximately 77 percent in 1980.[50] People who were born in another country make up a rapidly growing component of the U.S. labor force as almost 14 percent are foreign-born.[51] In addition, older people are remaining in the labor force—in 2003, people over 55 years of age accounted for more than 15 percent of the labor force, up from slightly less than 12 percent in 1995.[52]

DIVERSITY

Diversity in individuals can both unite and separate. Organizations also have cultures: systems of shared values, beliefs, experiences, habits, norms, and expectations that give them a distinct identity. An organization usually has a dominant culture that shapes and is shaped by its members' attitudes and behaviors. The greatest influence comes from the people in charge—their values, norms, and beliefs. But an organization has subcultures as well, shared by groups of employees that influence and are influenced by the organization's culture. Thus, organizations nearly always have diverse cultures. **Cultural diversity** exists when two or more cultures co-exist within an organization.

diversity
differences among people and groups that serve to both unite and separate them from others

Motorola has an outstanding reputation for world-class products and is truly a global business. "But the key to Motorola's success is a culture that fosters candid internal debate, the vigorous competition of ideas and individual business autonomy."[53] Other leaders in diversity include Abbott Laboratories, Allstate Insurance, Citigroup, Colgate-Palmolive, PepsiCo, Staples, and Turner Broadcasting System.[54]

cultural diversity
the co-existence of two or more cultural groups within an organization

Valuing diversity in people and their diverse cultures is a relatively recent development in business. Today, businesses, such as Motorola, Du Pont, Avon, and Levi Strauss, are realizing that employees have a right to their own identity within and separate from that of the organization. Diversity is increasingly viewed as a source of strength—providing pools of people with different and complementary skills, competencies, and beliefs that should be valued and can be drawn on to provide what an organization needs. At Levi Strauss diversity means that the company "values a diverse workforce (age, sex, ethnic group, etc.) at all levels of the organization. . . . Differing points of view will be sought; diversity will be valued and honestly rewarded, not suppressed."[55]

Nonetheless, examples such as Home Depot's $65 million settlement for discrimination against female employees and Texaco's $176 million settlement remind us that supervisors must be vigilant to eliminate racism or sexism.[56] In addition, although much progress has been made, supervisors must prevent discrimination against the aged and disabled. The software industry has been criticized for age discrimination.

Your job as a supervisor is to help all of your people reach their potential. Allowing your biases to influence your judgment will not only hurt your employees' performance, it will also reflect badly on you as a supervisor.

Despite shortages of programmers, software companies have been reluctant to hire older workers. For example, "a year-and-a-half search has netted Alan Ezer, 45, just one job interview, despite 10 years' experience and a nifty demonstration on the Internet of his self-taught virtuosity."[57]

Businesses—like the United States as a whole—now realize that they are not melting pots through which people and cultures fuse and lose their identities. They are mosaics, tapestries, and salad bowls in which individuals and groups retain their identities but work with others to yield something greater than the pieces could yield on their own. The supervisor's role in valuing diversity is an important one.

INCREASING LEVELS OF EDUCATION

According to the U.S. Census Bureau, almost 85 percent of Americans over 25 years of age currently have completed high school, and more than 27 percent have completed four or more years of college. College enrollments continue to be high: Over 65 percent of high school graduates from the class of 2002 enrolled in college. Women appear to be taking a significant lead in higher education as more women from this class enrolled in college (over 68 percent) as compared to men (approximately 62 percent).[58] There is a striking difference in educational attainment in the 25 to 34 age cohort as 42 percent of women have degrees relative to only 36 percent for men.[59]

The growing educational level of the U.S. workforce has brought brighter, more demanding employees to the ranks of both workers and management. Increasingly, people want a voice in planning and executing their work. They bring competence and skills to the workplace, and they desire growth through challenging work and meaningful tasks. They want to be listened to and respected as individuals with their own specific needs and goals.

Countering the influx of more highly educated people is a substantial influx of people who lack adequate reading skills. According to the National Institute for

Literacy, "50 percent of the U.S. population reads below the eighth-grade level, and about 90 million adults are functionally illiterate."[60] The problem of illiteracy cuts into U.S. productivity, with the costs being estimated as high as $60 billion per year. Furthermore, the problem has been exacerbated by a decline in the percentage of employers who provide remedial training.[61]

As a supervisor, you may find both highly educated and illiterate adults in your employee mix. Both groups present challenges that you and your organization must be prepared to deal with if you are to create quality products and productivity improvements.

Increasingly, we are becoming a lifetime learning society. No longer can any of us rely on one employer or one career during our working lives. Because of downsizing and mergers, people are expected to make several job and career changes within their lifetimes. "According to a survey . . . by the executive search firm of Robert Half International, Inc., [it isn't until] a worker [makes] five job changes in a 10-year period [that he or she] is at risk of being labeled a job-hopper."[62] Today's younger workers are demanding opportunities to learn new skills that will make them employable in the future. They recognize that it is unlikely that they will be employed by one organization for their entire career. Instead of demanding lifetime job security, they want employability.[63]

DIFFERENT WORKFORCE INVOLVEMENT

Permanent part-time workers usually work for small companies that do not have enough work for a full-timer to perform. Part-time work may be for any number of hours and days per week, up to 35 hours. Older individuals, such as those who may have retired from other jobs, provide a source of reliable employees who may be interested in permanent part-time work.

permanent part-time workers employees who wish to work less than 40 hours per week

Temporary workers or contingent workers fill millions of jobs in the United States each year. The U.S. Bureau of Labor has estimated, using a broad definition of "contingent workers," that 4.4 percent of the employed population consists of contingent workers.[64] A somewhat lower estimate is provided by the CEO of Manpower who has estimated that 2.5 percent of the U.S. workforce is made up of temporary workers.[65] Temporary work agencies provide people to work part time for clients who need temporary help. Most come well trained for their jobs and work in skilled areas such as computer services, secretarial services, manufacturing, and accounting.[66] Another view of the broad presence of temporary workers in the workforce is provided by the president of a temporary help firm that provides temporary employees to such employers as Sun Microsystems and Silicon Graphics: "There's not a single major company in the United States that doesn't have a substantial percentage of the workforce as contingent workers."[67]

temporary workers workers employed by a temporary work agency to provide labor for other employers

DIFFERENT WORK ARRANGEMENTS

Today's workforce is mobile, middle aged, and increasingly made up of other than full-time workers. In addition, between 2.7 and 6 million workers are contingent.[68] Furthermore, a growing number of contingent workers are accounting, engineering, and health care professionals.[69] Even a chief information officer at Burlington Northern Santa Fe was hired to fill the role for a limited time period. Contingent or contract work arrangements may become increasingly important to older workers. With increasing life spans, people are working longer although their needs typically differ from those of younger employees. Older workers, who may have retirement income from their previous jobs, often pursue second careers on a more flexible basis as contractors, part-time workers, or temporary employees.[70]

Several other trends are in evidence: flextime, job sharing, job splitting, permanent part-time workers, telecommuting, and employee leasing. Companies are increasing their use of these flexible approaches to work. For example, Merck has reported increased use of flextime, telecommuting, and job sharing. The composition of Merck's workforce is also illustrative of trends for the future, as women make up 52 percent of its U.S. employees while minorities account for 24 percent. More significantly, in its U.S. operations 32 percent of the company's managerial positions are held by women while minorities account for 16 percent.[71] All of these trends present unique challenges and opportunities for supervisors.

flextime
a work schedule with flexible starting and ending times

Flextime allows people to vary their starting and ending times. A company may specify a core time, requiring all employees to be on the job from 10:00 A.M. until 1:00 P.M., but some may start as early as 6:00 A.M. or as late as 10:00 A.M. Some may go home as early as 1:00 P.M. Flexible scheduling appeals to working parents with school-age children and to a growing number of self-managing information workers. But such work schedules make it difficult for one supervisor to manage people who work over a span of 10 or more hours. **Compressed work weeks** of four 10-hour days also help organizations meet the needs of employees. At Lockheed-Martin Aerospace, many of the company's employees work on a 9/80 compressed work schedule in which they have every other Friday off. With this schedule they work nine hours per day for four days and then eight hours on Friday. The next week they work nine hours per day for four days and then have Friday off.

compressed work week
a work week made up of four 10-hour days

The Bechtel Group, a construction and engineering firm, has 27,800 employees worldwide. It offers a flexible schedule to its employees in Houston, Texas. Under the plan, which is similar to that of Lockheed-Martin, employees work nine-hour days, Monday through Thursday each week. Each Friday, about half the employees work eight hours, and the other half have the day off. All employees work 80 hours in nine work days. Management initially feared that longer work days would mean lower productivity, but productivity has improved. Employees seemed to be scheduling more of their personal business for their off time.

job sharing
splitting the hours of a job between two or more employees

Job sharing allows two or more people to work at one full-time job. A growing number of people want to work part time, and a growing number of businesses want more part-time employees. The employer benefits in several ways. It gets double the creativity for each shared job. It may also cut benefit costs, which often add 30 to 40 percent to an employee's salary. People come to work refreshed and eager to perform and experience less fatigue and stress. Boring jobs can be more attractive when performed for fewer than 40 hours each week.

telecommuting
working at home through telecommunications

Telecommuting allows a full- or part-time employee to work at home while remaining connected to the employer by telecommunications devices such as computers, e-mail, the Internet, and fax machines. Estimates of the number of telecommuters in the United States vary widely, with numbers ranging from 9 million to 24 million. More than half of the *Fortune* 500 companies reported that 1 to 5 percent of their employees are involved in telecommuting, and some companies have large numbers of telecommuters. For example, Merrill Lynch has 3,500 telecommuters.[72] Nortel, one of the pioneers in this area, had 3,600 telecommuters at one point.[73] In addition, AT&T has announced a telecommuting day, encouraging and making arrangements for any worker who can to telecommute.

Telecommuters can increase their quality of life by living in geographic areas that are long distances from their offices and combining work at home with childcare arrangements. In addition, major disasters quickly isolate people from their jobs and places of employment. The terrorist attack on the World Trade Center on September 11, 2001; Hurricane Katrina, which flooded New Orleans in 2005; and earthquakes have highlighted the value of telecommuting—within hours, companies whose physical plants were in ruins were making alternative arrangements to meet their customers' needs, thanks to cellular communications. On the other hand, some companies have encountered difficulties with the complexities involved with telecommuting and have discouraged the practice. While employees operating in different locations are able to e-mail files to each other and interact via e-mail, more face-to-face interactions are often required for teams that must respond quickly with innovative outcomes.[74]

OTHER TRENDS AFFECTING SUPERVISORS

TILIZATION OF TEAMS

Increasingly, businesses are turning to the use of teams—some self-managing, others not. It is common in many different types of organizations to find teams "that recommend things, teams that make or do things, and teams that run or manage things. . . . Teams are a means to an end. And that end is performance superior to what team members would achieve working as individuals."[75] Furthermore, many teams are *cross-functional,* meaning that workers from such areas as marketing, production, and accounting may work on a team to solve a problem.

As was stated in this chapter's introduction, when supervisors work with and through teams of employees, they become team facilitators. They share responsibility with a team for "cost, quality, and on-time delivery of the product. So [supervisors] must train their teams to manage the production process, including work assignments, and to solve problems that crop up along the way, rather than provide solutions themselves."[76]

Team facilitators make certain that the team has the resources it needs when they are needed, arranges the meetings where information is passed along and ideas are put to use, represents the team's views and concerns to outsiders, and helps resolve disputes between and within teams. To be an effective team facilitator, you must be skilled at presenting your ideas in a group setting, at running different kinds of meetings, at sharing your skills and knowledge willingly, at turning decision making into a learning experience for all team members, and at taking control in a crisis.[77]

To work in teams effectively, people must be trained and empowered. Supervisors **empower** their employees when they equip them to function on their own, without direct oversight and constant supervision. Empowering others requires supervisors to give their people opportunities to contribute knowledge and expertise, and to encourage them to take on new tasks and to improve their capabilities. It means allowing

empower
to equip people to function on their own, without direct supervision

Workers commonly meet to discuss issues such as quality.

people to participate in planning their work, making decisions, and solving problems. In short, empowering others means sharing the traditional roles and responsibilities of the supervisor with employees.

This chapter's feature on supervising teams describes how teams operate in a successful financial services company.

OFFSHORING AND OUTSOURCING

outsourcing
contracting with outside vendors to perform work that was previously performed in-house

offshoring
outsourcing work to vendors in other countries or shifting work to a company-owned facility in another country

Companies are increasingly **outsourcing** work to contractors, which was previously performed in-house. When such work is sent to contractors or company-operated facilities in other countries, this practice is called **offshoring**. Manufacturing work has been moving steadily to lower wage countries for many years, but in recent years, there has been a marked increase in the amount of services work, such as computer programming, data entry, claims processing, and call center work, that is being performed offshore. With such work, the product can be transmitted electronically without delay and can be timed in some cases to be performed overnight in overseas locations. Supervisors will need to develop the skills required to coordinate and integrate the work of employees or contractors located at overseas facilities. In addition, they will need to manage and motivate local employees who are worried about job security because of concerns that their work will be offshored or outsourced. In the long term, the key for their job security will be to increase their knowledge and skill levels for the future. It has been argued that new knowledge and skills will be required to create the new products and services that will result from demand generated by higher wages in countries that perform the offshored work.[78] Supervisors will need to help their employees prepare for the future with increased training and development.

SUPERVISING TEAMS

Many supervisors are managing **virtual teams** in which the members are located at different geographic locations. In some cases, team members may be located in two or more different countries. For example, information technology enables a human resources team leader for American Express, who is based in London, to work on a virtual team with other specialists based in such distant locations as Buenos Aires or Tokyo.[79] Virtual teams, which are made possible by today's information and communications technology, are becoming more important because of the global nature of business, the need for diverse skills, and the necessity for different organizational units and functions to be represented in the work of the teams. The Learning and Education Department of PriceWaterhouseCoopers, which has employees in 70 different offices throughout the United States, makes extensive use of virtual teams.

The success of virtual teams appears to rest heavily on the establishment of rules for team operations. For example, at PriceWaterhouseCoopers, team members have committed to respond to e-mails from each other in less than 24 hours. Another key to the success of virtual teams is to encourage frequent communication and to establish trust among the members. Team members also try to operate with a positive assumption about the intentions of teammates. Such assumptions are important because communications via e-mail and telephone do not allow team members to see each other's facial expressions and body language, which otherwise would communicate positive intentions. In addition, experienced managers recommend a face-to-face meeting, whenever possible, in order to provide a good start for a new team. Other suggestions for improved virtual team operations include the utilization of technology, such as videoconferencing and web-meeting software, which allows on-line demonstrations. There are some disadvantages to virtual teams, such as members' lack of personal information about each other that comes from social interactions. As a result, it takes more time to determine the level of confidence that can be placed in a team member's judgment. Nonetheless, many of the problems can be overcome and it appears that virtual teams will become a permanent part of the lives of many supervisors.

Sources: Jon Katzenbach and Douglas Smith. "Virtual Teaming," *Forbes.com* (May 21, 2001): 48–51. Jack Gordon, "Do Your Virtual Teams Deliver Only Virtual Performance?" *Training* (June 2005): 20–25.

INFORMATION AND TECHNOLOGY

The work of managers can now be streamlined with manager self-service software (MSS), that has applications, which perform such tasks as optimizing the vacation scheduling process, tracking travel requests, and projecting compensation expenses. These systems, which increase the productivity of supervisors, also allow them to generate their own reports for analysis and without waiting on the staff in the human resources department to respond to their requests.[80] More broadly, the power of computers is now at our fingertips or voice commands. Wireless handheld computers, Internet tablets, wireless e-mail, wireless browsers, notebook computers, and full-feature communicators with data organizers, video cameras, Bluetooth technology, and video recording features are information technology tools used by both supervisors and employees.[81] Many automobiles are

virtual teams geographically disbursed teams, which rely on electronic communications technology to coordinate their work

equipped with voice-activated cellular telephones, computers, printers, and fax machines. The portability of technology frees managers from their desks and provides them with greater mobility. Meetings can take place as videoconferences in which television signals are transmitted over telephone lines and through communication satellites.

Other information technology has affected the way work is performed in fundamental ways. For example, **electronic data interchange** (EDI) transfers of business-to-business (b-to-b) transactions allows for instantaneous transfer of electronic data between points, eliminating communication delays between suppliers and purchasers or retailers, engineers and product design teams, and professionals and clients. Wal-Mart is recognized as the EDI innovator in retailing, which allows just-in-time store replenishment and lower distribution costs. The Limited, which established EDI links to Asian suppliers, is an EDI innovator in the retailing of clothing. Flexible data formats, such as XML and VCML (value chain markup language), offer potential for greater use of such data transfer systems in more industries and smaller firms.[82]

The most competitive manufacturers have put the power of computers to use through computer-aided manufacturing (CAM), which offers their best hope for future increases in quality, competitiveness, productivity, and profits. CAM has come to mean computer control of production tools and machines. Both can be programmed and reprogrammed to work at a variety of tasks, providing users with dependable, predictable output at speeds no skilled person can match. Robots are CAM machines that are capable of working every hour of every day with great speed and reliability. They have been used for work that is toxic, dangerous, repetitive, boring, or extremely precise. Robots have become our nation's "steel-collar workers," demanding sophisticated supervision by a new breed of supervisors and workers with the latest in high-tech education and skills.

Flexible manufacturing—producing a variety of products and product variations (customization) simultaneously and in sequence with computer-integrated manufacturing (CIM)—is the current goal for many manufacturers. CIM links all the activities, materials flow, and machinery involved in manufacturing to a centralized computer control system, allowing for maximum efficiency and coordination. A good example of flexible manufacturing is provided by Honda America's plant in East Liberty, Ohio. The flexible system has improved worker satisfaction, increased safety, and reduced the amount of repair work needed before cars can be released from the factory. "The heart of the flexible system is a body-weld line that allows Honda to switch from vehicle to vehicle with the flip of a switch. It also shortened subassembly lines in the factory and installed quality assurance points at several spots through the assembly process."[83]

Along with being flexible, manufacturing is becoming lean—using fewer workers and adding temporary help during peak load periods. **Lean manufacturing** integrates a number of productivity enhancing and cost-savings techniques, including just-in-time processes, optimal plant layouts, and the utilization of work teams. Such approaches to manufacturing provide a number of important benefits including lower levels of inventory, waste reduction, and more efficient use of physical space.[84] **Just-in-time delivery systems** are an important feature of lean manufacturing and other manufacturing approaches, which eliminate expensive inventories of components needed for manufacturing products. Sophisticated information systems indicate times when components will be needed, and the components are delivered from suppliers

electronic data interchange
a paperless business-to-business approach, which relies on electronic communications technology for the transmission of orders, invoices, and other business transactions

flexible manufacturing
a computer-based manufacturing approach that quickly shifts production from one product to another

lean manufacturing
an integrated approach, which combines several manufacturing approaches, such as just-in-time methods, to reduce costs

"just in time." This drive to take the fat out of operations has led many companies to outsource—to allow more cost-effective businesses to provide needed work. When just-in-time companies expand their operations to new geographical areas, their suppliers follow. For example, OSI Industries, which supplies hamburger to McDonald's, also supplies OSI's global chain of restaurants and OSI's other partners throughout the world. The food processing and distribution firm has over 60 food processing plants in its global operations. Interestingly, OSI's successful use of cross-functional teams has been a key to the company's success.[85] These trends have led to better service for customers.

> **just-in-time delivery systems** information systems that indicate times when components will be needed with components being delivered "just in time"

QUALITY AND PRODUCTIVITY IMPROVEMENT

Businesses in the United States exist and compete in a global economy. Their products and services must compete with the best that the world community has to offer. To be competitive, businesses must be lean and constantly strive to improve their efficiency and effectiveness. But it is not enough simply to produce efficiently. Products and services must have quality as good as, or better than, those provided by the competition. Many companies have adopted **six sigma** approaches to quality improvement. These approaches rely on sophisticated statistical techniques, simulations, and experiments to decrease variation in outputs as a means of eliminating waste. Ford Motor Company applied the approach to solve problems with the hoods on Ford Mustangs. By using six sigma techniques the company was able to solve the problems with better-designed brackets and attachments of hood latches.[86] Bell Helicopter has relied heavily on six sigma and utilizes employees who have such skills to help redesign manufacturing processes and business practices as well as to help increase customer satisfaction.[87]

> **six sigma** a statistics-based approach for reducing variance in manufacturing or service outcomes with the goal of improving quality and reducing waste

Productivity may be defined as the measurement of the amount of input needed to generate a given amount of output. It is the basic measurement of the efficient use of resources and processes. By calculating how many products are produced by the investment of hours of human labor or by the use of machines, an organization can compare these measurements to those from the past and determine gains or losses.

> **productivity** the amount of input needed to generate a given amount of output

The quality of management obviously is a key determinant of the productivity of an organization's workforce and of the organization as a whole. Accordingly, good management provides a competitive advantage when it enables the organization to obtain greater productivity from its workforce. For example, financial managers have been able to increase productivity in their firms by attending to small issues that in combination can produce meaningful gains. These gains are sometimes related to the adoption of best practices obtained from exemplary companies, which is called **benchmarking**. The adoption of such practices can enable managers to improve productivity by as much as 10 to 30 percent in finance or support units after a few weeks or months even without the implementation of new information technology. More specifically, by examining the processes involved in the monthly financial closing process, which can involve approximately 200 activities, less time may be required to correct errors if the sources of errors can be eliminated. Fewer errors and less time for corrections are possible when departments report by entering data directly into electronic data warehouses. When employees are well-managed and feel a commitment to the goals of the unit, they can help identify numerous ways to increase productivity.

> **benchmarking** identifying better practices and processes by making comparisons with top performing companies

SUPERVISORS AND PERFORMANCE

When someone mentions good coaching, the first thought that comes to the minds of most people is probably the coach of a successful sports team. While such coaches have wonderful skills and have managed to survive under the pressure of big-time athletics, they are not the only talented coaches. Outside of the limelight of collegiate and professional sports, when adults are asked about those who had a major influence in their lives they often mention one of their coaches while they were still in school. Aside from athletic coaches, great supervisors make up another group of talented coaches, although few people except those who work with them are aware of their skills. These supervisors practice their coaching skills every day while working with customer service teams, groups of production workers, groups of service technicians, or health care professionals. While their coaching skills may be unknown outside of where they work, such skills are critically important to the performance of their organizations and to the employees who are the recipients of the coaching.

Good coaching cannot be taken for granted, and there are indications that many supervisors are not particularly good at this important role. Indeed, Development Dimensions International has found that most managers act more like referees than coaches. Nonetheless, coaching can be taught, and there are practices that supervisors can follow in order to improve their skills. For example, good coaches are proactive in that they initiate contact with employees who need to improve quality or adopt a different approach to a task. They also do not let employees struggle too long before they provide guidance. On occasion, such coaches assign tasks to employees even when they are uncertain whether the employee can handle the assignment in order to provide a developmental experience. Good coaches also monitor progress on a regular basis and, as a result, are able to praise employees when they observe good practices instead of focusing on feedback when something goes wrong. Furthermore, such coaches invest more time up front by providing explanations and guidance before the employee begins a task or assignment. They also structure assignments so that employees have ownership and feel responsible. Finally, they orchestrate the assignments and developmental opportunities so that employees will have lots of successes.

Source: Jim Councelman, "Blowing the Whistle on the Boss," *Training* (February 2005): 15.

quality
the totality of features and characteristics of a product or service (or process or project) that bear on its ability to satisfy stated or implied goals (requirements of producers and customers)

Examples such as this one, when combined with several other small practical improvements, can result in large increases in productivity.[88]

Quality means different things to different people. Its result is a satisfied customer. Throughout this text, we define quality as the totality of features and characteristics of a product or service (or process or project) that bear on its ability to satisfy stated or implied goals (requirements of producers and customers).[89] To possess quality, products and services must be designed with the customers' needs in mind. Companies such as Motorola and Toyota consult with customers throughout the design phase of their product development to ensure that their customers' needs will be met.

Customers are the receivers and users of what is produced; they exist inside and outside the organization. *Internal customers* are employees who receive output from other employees. It is common practice today in major companies to assess employees' performance through what is called a 360-degree performance review or 360-degree feedback. Each manager or team member is evaluated by her boss, associates, and peers—all users of any outputs generated by the manager, team member, or her associates.

This chapter's special feature on supervisors and performance deals with coaching skills, which are important to increasing employee performance and organizational productivity.

FOREIGN OWNERSHIP OF AMERICAN BUSINESSES

Each year foreign businesses invest billions of dollars both to acquire existing companies or establish their own operations in the United States. U.S. businesses follow the same approach, investing billions of dollars to acquire companies in other countries. Examples of foreign-owned companies that have substantial operations in the United States include the following: 7 Eleven (Japan), BP (United Kingdom), Bayer (Germany), BMW (Germany), Cemex (Mexico), CompUSA (Mexico), DaimlerChrysler (Germany), GlaxoSmithKline (United Kingdom), Honda (Japan), Michelin (France), Nestlé (Switzerland), Nokia (Finland), Nortel (Canada), Shell (United Kingdom), Siemens (Germany), and Toyota (Japan). Today companies from the following countries, beginning with those having the largest investments, are: (1) the United Kingdom, (2) Japan, (3) Germany, (4) Netherlands, (5) France, (6) Switzerland, and (7) Canada. According to federal government estimates, almost 6 percent of U.S. workers owe their jobs to a foreign-owned company, more than at any time in the past. Industries in which foreign-owned firms account for high employment include manufacturing, wholesale trade, and finance or banking.[90]

DIVERSITY

Foreign owners often bring different philosophies, methods, and traditions to the workplace. Supervising in a foreign-owned business may require changes in the attitudes, roles, and skills derived from training in the United States or abroad. Supervisors may have to adapt to different methods and values that come from a different cultural background. However, despite important cultural differences, many management practices of large multinational corporations are similar. The fact that in 2005 an American, Howard Stringer, became the CEO of Sony, the dominant company in the global consumer electronics industry, as well as a leading media and entertainment company, provides one indication of the potential for substantial similarities.[91]

Learning Objective Number Six

SOURCES OF SUPERVISORY PERSONNEL

In most companies, the person who aspires to become a supervisor—to move from worker to management—must take on the responsibility of preparing himself for such a promotion. Exhibit 1.5 lists the changes that have occurred in the skill requirements for a supervisor in an example supervisory position in the textile industry. Take a few minutes to study it. Aside from the technical features that are unique to the textile industry, think about whether you possess some of the more general skills, such as the

EXHIBIT 1.5	Changing supervisory skill requirements: Line supervisors in the textile industry.

OLD PROGRESSIVE BUNDLE SYSTEM	NEW FLEXIBLE MANUFACTURING TEAMS
PEOPLE SKILLS	
• Acts as messenger for the manager • Supervises individuals • Represents power and control as an authority figure	• Accepts initiative for decision-making • Coaches teams • Shares power and control as a communicator, motivator, coordinator
PRODUCTION/TECHNICAL SKILLS	
• Thoroughly understands selected operations but has little understanding of overall operations • Has basic sewing skills • Is an experienced production operator • Has limited production responsibility • Is a recorder of daily production • Polices equitable work distribution • Is a bundle handler • Repairs defective garments • Has knowledge in line balancing • Ensures that proper production methods are being used • Verifies that work meets quality standard	• Understands methods and techniques used in all operations and how each affects the final product • Understands work measurement and techniques used • Understands cost control • Understands quality control • Knows operator training techniques • Administers safety regulations and ergonomics • Assigns work fairly • Is an expert in line balancing • Ensures proper productions are being used • Has knowledge of various garment styles, fabrics, and machine adjustments • Can calculate production and payroll • Understands industry terminology
REASONING SKILLS	
• Is limited to following instructions	• Must have problem-diagnosing skills • Must have problem-solving skills
ADMINISTRATIVE SKILLS	
• Has little control over hiring, orientation (works with human resources department) • Has little control in policy making • Has little control over labor cost (management's job)	• Has a more direct role in employee hiring, orientation, training, and discipline • Must handle absenteeism • Participates in policy making • Has more control over labor cost

Slight modification of materials from "Supervisors Must Face Changes," *Apparel Industry* (October 1995): 72. Reproduced with permission.

people, reasoning, and administrative skills. If you need to improve on various skills, schools can help and a job change may be a good step you can take to improve a skill or gain an attribute.

Many employers prefer to hire some or all of their supervisory personnel from the ranks of community or four-year college graduates. After some preliminary training and understudy, these people are installed as functioning supervisors. The practice of hiring supervisors from outside the company may infuse new ideas and approaches into the organization. Nonetheless, some well-managed companies such as Service-Master, Whole Foods Markets, Southwest Airlines, Hewlett-Packard, AES, and Lincoln Electric promote only from within their ranks and hire only at entry level.[92]

A major disadvantage of the practice of going outside the organization for new supervisors fresh from college is that they may lack the firsthand experiences and technical skills needed to supervise the company's workers. They may also be resented by more experienced workers not promoted to supervisor. One of the major complaints of employees is having supervisors who do not understand their work. A number of companies such as the SAS Institute, which produces statistical analysis software, try very hard to avoid such situations.[93] Another example is Nordstrom, where all new employees—including those with advanced degrees—must begin by working on the sales floor.[94]

Some of your associates may not wish to be promoted to the ranks of management. Several may be convinced that the extra prestige is not worth the extra time, problems, and responsibilities that go along with a supervisory position. In addition, the attitude of the company toward supervisors may make many workers shy away from a supervisory role. In far too many companies, supervisors are given lip service as managers but are not treated with the respect, pay, and benefits that employees in other levels of management receive.

INSTANT REPLAY

1. The three most important types of skills for any manager to possess are interpersonal, technical, and conceptual. All are required for success, but different levels of management need them to different degrees.

2. Supervisors are responsible to three groups: their peers, their employees, and their superiors. Each group represents a source of support, demands on the supervisor's time, and potential problems or challenges for the supervisor.

3. Each organization attempts to define a supervisor's role through the creation of a job description and through the demands that various groups and individuals place on the supervisor. Problems can result from role conflict and role ambiguity. The supervisor can be "caught in the middle" between the demands of her managers and the workers she supervises.

4. Current trends that affect supervisors include changes in information and technology, the drive for improvements in both quality and productivity, the growth in both highly educated and illiterate adults in

the workforce, increasing international ownership of American businesses, the growing effort to value diversity, shifts in the traditional scheduling and performance of work, and the growing use of teams.

5. Supervisors emerge from two sources: from inside and outside the organization. Organizations prefer to hire those who are ready to move up; this places the burden for training on the individual who aspires to move into management.

QUESTIONS FOR CLASS DISCUSSION

1. Can you define this chapter's key terms?
2. What are the essential management skill areas that supervisors must have and apply? Give an example illustrating the application of each skill area.
3. What are the three groups to whom supervisors have responsibilities? Give an example of a responsibility to each group.
4. How do the concepts of effectiveness and efficiency apply to a supervisor's performance?
5. What are the current trends in the U.S. economy that affect the supervisor?
6. What are the sources of supervisory personnel for a business?

ASSESS THIS SITUATION

Purpose: To discover how many trends discussed in this chapter are part of your current work environment.

Your Task: Answer each of the following as completely as you can using your current or most recent job environment as your model. Where parenthetical choices are given, choose one. In all other questions, written responses are required. Share your results with your class.

1. I work/have worked in a team. (yes) (no)
2. My team has/had the following basic duties:
3. I am/have been a team leader. (yes) (no)
4. As a team leader my duties are/were:
5. I am/have been a team facilitator/supervisor. (yes) (no)
6. As a team facilitator, my duties are/were:
7. My company employs contingent workers. (yes) (no)
8. The contingent workers perform the following duties:
9. My job requires/will require technical skills. (yes) (no)

10. My company cares about quality. (yes) (no)

11. My company cares about productivity. (yes) (no)

12. My company shows it cares about quality and productivity by:

13. My company is foreign-owned. (yes) (no)

14. The foreign ownership has required me to change by:

15. The dominant culture in my organization stresses:

16. The subcultures existing in my company are based on:

17. Subcultures are (tolerated) (welcomed) at work.

18. My employer offers these nontraditional work options:

SKILL BUILDING EXERCISE 1.1

It is often observed that supervisors are placed in a difficult position of being at the first level of management and, therefore, have the responsibility of representing the organization's point of view. As such, they must look out for the welfare of the organization in the decisions they make. While managers at all levels have the same responsibility to represent the interests of the organization, the pressures are most acute at the supervisor's level because they also have the obligation to look out for the welfare of employees. Their employees expect them to represent the interests of employees as they deal with higher-level managers. The following are issues on which employees and higher-level managers may differ:

   a. overtime
   b. vacation scheduling
   c. seniority
   d. promotions
   e. merit pay
   f. training
   g. layoffs
   h. outsourcing
   i. disciplinary action

   Your Task: Work in a small group or work alone to: (1) Describe the views that employees would typically have on each of these issues. (2) Describe the views that higher-level managers could be expected to have on each of these issues. (3) Describe the conflicts that these differences pose for supervisors and how they should deal with such differences.

SKILL BUILDING WRITING EXERCISE 1.2

In recent years, a few reality-based television programs have followed supervisors and employees as they interact on a day-to-day basis in small company settings. These programs provided viewers with opportunities to observe real supervisors and managers in action. While some of the televised scenes tend to highlight more extreme interactions for their entertainment value, they provide viewers with rare opportunities to observe real supervisors and managers as they perform their jobs. Some examples of such programs include *Orange County Choppers*, which was originally aired on the Discovery Channel, and *American Hot Rod*, also originally aired on the Discovery Channel. Information on these or similar television series may be found on the websites of the Discovery Channel: *www.discovery.com* and the Learning Channel: *http://tlc.discovery.com*.

Your Task: Watch several episodes of these or similar television shows and prepare written assessments of the supervisors and managers with respect to their (1) leadership skills, (2) interpersonal skills, (3) relationships with subordinates, (4) conflict resolution skills, (5) negotiation skills, (6) utilization of teams, (7) ethics, and (8) communication or information dissemination skills. Provide specific examples in each of these areas. In addition, comment on any positive aspects of the performance of these supervisors or managers that may offset their weaknesses.

CASE 1.1   Southwest Microwave Communications, Inc.

Carla Martinez, a senior electronics technician, was filling out the forms to obtain reimbursement for last month's travel expenses. Her job as a senior electronics technician required her to be out of the office about 90 percent of the time on jobs installing transmitters in microwave towers. While in the office, the technicians usually use the time to read technical bulletins, to work in the electronics lab on repairs to the specialized testing and calibration equipment, to go through technical training, or to make travel arrangements. Carla was working in a common area the electronics technicians use as an office while not in the field. It was about 20 minutes to five, and she was almost finished with the last form.

Carla looked up from her paperwork to see Faye Griffin, her new supervisor, rush in with several file folders. Faye looked around the office and then spotted Carla and said, "I'm in a hurry and need you to complete these unit staff utilization forms for the regional office. The forms are self-explanatory, and you shouldn't have any trouble figuring out what to do. I'm just too overloaded with work and my schedule is a nightmare. Just leave the forms on my desk and I'll have them faxed to the regional office the first thing in the morning." Before Carla could say anything, Faye had turned and walked out of the office.

Carla couldn't believe that Faye had just asked her to do part of the work for which Faye was personally responsible. Faye had been the supervisor for six months, but Carla had little contact with her because she had been in the field so much. Carla and the rest of the technicians were so busy with installations that for the past six weeks they regularly put in 55- to 60-hour work weeks. After getting herself composed enough to sit down and look over the files, Carla began to figure out how to complete the forms. Two hours later, when she discovered that she didn't have all of the information she needed, she went down the hall to Faye's office to ask her some questions. To her surprise, she found that Faye was not in and that the janitor was cleaning her office. The janitor said that Faye had gone home at 5:00 and volunteered that he always cleaned Faye's office first because she was seldom in after five. Carla returned to the work room and filled out the rest of the forms the best that she could. She then wrote a note to Faye explaining that she didn't have the information to complete everything but that 90 percent of the forms were complete. She then put the forms in Faye's mail slot as she left for the evening at 7:45.

The next day as Carla was working in the electronics lab, she saw Faye come in a couple of times to talk to technicians or check on the progress of repairs. To her surprise, Faye never thanked her for her work or even mentioned it. Later in the afternoon, Carla told a couple of her technician friends, Tim Kelly and Ivan Ward, about what had happened. Tim just shook his head and said that the same thing had happened to him last month. He too had needed to stay until 8:00 to do some of Faye's scheduling. Ivan then recounted his experiences with Faye on his last installation job. When he and two other technicians arrived at the job site and started installing the transmitter, the customer's project engineer told them that they needed different equipment specifications. The engineer had called Faye three weeks before, and she said that she would make sure that the technicians ordered the right components. When Ivan called Faye at the office, she told him that he should have coordinated with the customer himself, that he needed to take on more responsibility, and that she couldn't be expected to handle details for him.

The next week, Carla and several other technicians were attending a technical training session. During the breaks in training, Faye was a common topic of discussion. Most of the technicians had similar experiences to Carla, Tim, and Ivan. One of them said that he had even confronted Faye about the fact that she gave him work to do that was obviously supervisory paperwork. Faye told him, "I'm responsible for the performance of this unit and routine paperwork is low on my priority list. You technicians will have to learn to help out when you're in the office. We all have to work as a team here."

Another technician said that he had gone in to see Faye about changes in purchasing policies. She told him that she was too busy to talk to him because she was frantically preparing for a presentation the next day that she had volunteered to do for the regional director. He then wrote out three proposed approaches for dealing with the changes and left the proposal on her desk. After a week, he tried to talk to her again, but she put him off again. Last Thursday, when he had to have an answer, he went in to see Faye, but her secretary told him that she was off for a long weekend. Because he could wait no longer to order components, he contacted purchasing and resolved the situation the best way he knew how. The next week, Faye stormed into the equipment lab where he was working with three other technicians. She told him, "Don't ever go over my head again. I was going to handle the problem with purchasing and now you've let them dictate the rules."

Questions

1. Which supervisory attributes has Faye failed to exhibit? Give examples from the case to support your choices.

2. Do you think Faye's employees need to change to adapt to her supervisory style? Why or why not?

3. How will Faye need to change if she is going to be a successful supervisor? Do you think she will be able to make these changes? Why or why not?

CASE 1.2   Walnut Grove Inn

Shelby Taylor had started her new job supervising desk clerks, housekeepers, and the bookkeeping staff for the Walnut Grove Inn. The Inn, which had 60 guest rooms, was in an attractive location in a medium-sized city. Unlike many hotels and motels, the Inn was independently owned. Because of its location and the attractiveness of the Inn, the business had been profitable, although not at the level expected by its owner. Shelby was excited about the opportunity to improve the performance of the Inn and looked forward to her first opportunity to be a supervisor. During her initial days on the job, she soon realized that she would have to develop an effective supervisory style for dealing with employees. In discussions with the owner about her first experiences on the job, the owner made several recommendations about how she should supervise the staff. He suggested what he called a "no-nonsense" approach. With this approach, employees would be treated impersonally and without regard for their feelings. Employees would be reminded regularly that they could be easily replaced if their performance was not up to standard. Furthermore, employees were to be motivated by the use of contests that placed them in competition with each other.

Although Shelby had not been a supervisor before, she had some very different views about the type of supervisory style that should be used. She wanted to adopt an approach that placed emphasis on respect for each employee. Shelby also wanted to utilize teamwork and to instill a spirit of cooperation among employees. She believed that by helping each other, employees could increase the quality of service and make each guest's stay at the Inn more enjoyable. Furthermore, it was clear to Shelby that the previous supervisor's approach was essentially the "no-nonsense" approach described by the owner. Shelby examined the Inn's employment records and found that turnover was higher than the average for the hotel industry. After looking through employee files and talking to some of the more experienced staff, she found that there were several problem employees. She also found out that a number of employees had low expectations of an acceptable level of performance. It appeared to her that the "no-nonsense" supervisory approach probably had a de-motivating effect on the staff.

Shelby began to implement her supervisory approach by meeting with small groups of employees. At these meetings, she told employees about her ideas for teamwork. She told employees that their tasks were interdependent like the spokes in a wheel. Without communication and coordination among the staff, there would be missing spokes and the wheel couldn't carry a load. Then, she told the employees that they were important to the organization. "Without effective housekeepers, helpful desk clerks, and careful bookkeepers the Inn won't survive. We have to work as a team and depend on each other to make each guest's stay an enjoyable experience." She then outlined increased performance expectations and expressed confidence that each employee could perform at these levels. In addition, she explained to employees that she wanted them to make more decisions on their own. She stressed the importance of doing quality work in which they could take pride. Shelby also started the practice of holding birthday parties and celebrations of national holidays in order to make the work atmosphere more family-like and to make employees feel more accepted. In addition, she implemented a reward system based on accomplishment of performance goals.

At the end of the first three months, there was an increase in employee productivity, and Shelby was gratified that her approach seemed to be working. Nonetheless, Shelby began to see problems, as some employees seemed to be taking advantage of her. Only a few employees were meeting their performance goals. Some employees began to ask favors, such as making exceptions to work schedules. After she would make an exception for one employee, other employees would then demand the same exceptions and claim that Shelby was being unfair when she denied such requests. She also found that some employees were not doing quality work and that they were not performing all their duties. In some instances, rooms were not being cleaned as carefully as they should be, and housekeeping supplies began to disappear. In addition, when employees could not come to work, some called in too late for her to make accommodations in work assignments. When she confronted some of the worst offenders, they offered numerous excuses for their late call-ins, absenteeism, and poor performance. Many told her that she was just being two-faced about her managerial style. In essence, they told her that if she really had respect for them as she claimed, she wouldn't be confronting them about performance and would accept their excuses.

As Shelby sat in her office one day, she wondered what she should do to get things back on track. She wondered if her supervisory approach would work or whether she should adopt the "no-nonsense" approach suggested by the Inn's owner.

Source: This case is based on a management brief written by Stoney White. Reproduced with permission.

Questions

1. What mistakes do you see in Shelby Taylor's approach?

2. Do you think that housekeepers, desk clerks, and bookkeepers will be responsive to the supervisory approach Shelby used? Why or why not?

3. What does Shelby need to do to solve these problems? What should she retain from her initial approach?

REFERENCES

[1] Berry, Leonard L. *Discovering the Soul of Service*, New York: The Free Press (1999): 238.

[2] White, Erin. "To Keep Employees, Domino's Decides It's Not All About Pay," *Wall Street Journal*, (February 17, 2005): A1–A9.

[3] Ibid.

[4] Tulgan, Bruce. "Trends Point to a Dramatic Generational Shift in the Future Workforce," *Employment Relations Today* (Winter 2004): p. 28.

[5] Bridges, William. "The End of the Job," *Fortune* (September 19, 1994): 62–64, 68, 72, 74.

[6] Katzenbach, Jon, and Smith, Douglas K. *The Wisdom of Teams*. New York: HarperCollins Publishers, 1994.

[7] Katz, Robert L. "Skills of an Effective Administrator," in "Business Classics: Fifteen Key Concepts for Managerial Success," *Harvard Business Review* (1975): 23–25.

[8] *Inc.*, "Asking Workers What They Want" (August 1994): 103.

[9] Ibid.

[10] Katz. "Skills of an Effective Administrator."

[11] Marrelo, Pete. "Intel's Staffing Plans," presentation to the Fort Worth Human Resource Association (November 1997).

[12] Glunk, Ursula, Wilderom, Celeste, and Ogilvie, Robert. "Finding the Key to German-Style Management," *International Studies of Management & Organization* (Fall 1996): 93–99.

[13] U.S. Census Bureau, *Statistical Abstract of the United States, 2001.* Washington, D.C.: *www.census.gov/statab/www*, 2002.

[14] Kirk, Randy. "It's About Control," *Inc.* (August 1994): 25–26.

[15] Nauman, Matt. "Job Well Done," *Chicago Tribune* (September 18, 1994): sect. 17, 3.

[16] Ingrassia, Paul. "A Long Road to Good Labor Relations at GM," *Wall Street Journal* (June 30, 1998): A18.

[17] Hill, Linda. *Becoming a Manager*. Boston: Harvard Business School Press, 1992.

[18] Taylor III, Alex. "GM's $11,000,000,000 Turnaround," *Fortune* (October 17, 1994): 54–56, 58, 62, 66, 70, 74.

[19] Ibid.

[20] Daft, Richard L., and Marcic, Dorothy. *Understanding Management,* 2nd ed. Fort Worth, Texas: Dryden Press, 1998.

[21] Kahn, R. L., Wolfe, D. M., Quinn, P. R., Snoek, J. D., and Rosenthal, R. A. *Organizational Stress: Studies in Role Conflict and Ambiguity.* New York: John Wiley & Sons, 1964. Miner, J. B. *Management Theory.* New York: Macmillan, 1991.

[22] Slater, Robert. *Jack Welch and the GE Way: Management Insights and Leadership Secrets of the Legendary CEO.* New York: McGraw-Hill, 1999.

[23] Feldman, Joan M. "Southwest Keeps Moving," *Air Transport World* (November 2001): 48–49. Colvin, Geoffrey. "What's Love Got to Do With It?" *Fortune* (November 12, 2001): 24.

[24] Freiberg, Kevin, and Freiberg, Jackie. *Nuts! Southwest Airlines' Crazy Recipe for Business and Personal Success.* Austin, Texas: Bard Press, 1996.

[25] Kidder, Rushworth. "The New Director Qualification: A Passion for Integrity," *Directorship* (December 2002): 12.

[26] Kidder, Rushworth. *How Good People Make Tough Choices: Resolving the Dilemmas of Ethical Living*, New York: Simon & Schuster, 1996. Kidder, Rushworth, "Ethics and the Bottom Line," Institute for Global Ethics, Address to the Graduate Management Admissions Council, Dallas, Texas (June 18–21, 2003).

[27] Weiss, Joseph W. *Business Ethics: A Stakeholder and Issues Management Approach*, Mason, Ohio: Thomson-Southwestern, 2003.

[28] Kidder, "Ethics and the Bottom Line." Trevino and Brown, "Managing to Be Ethical." Davis, Gary W. "Digging Into Ethics," *Association Management*, (October 2003): 26–33.

[29] Kidder. "The New Director Qualification," p. 14.

[30] First Do No Harm," *Economist* (November 27, 2004): 12.

[31] Gibson, Devin. "Excuses, Excuses: Moral Slippage in the Workplace," *Business Horizons 43*(6) (2000): 65–72.

[32] Trevino, Linda K., and Brown, Michael E. "Managing to Be Ethical: Debunking Five Business Ethics Myths," *Academy of Management Executive*, (2004): 69–81.

[33] Gibson. "Excuses, Excuses: Moral Slippage in the Workplace."

[34] Ibid.

[35] Ibid., 70.

[36] Gibson. "Excuses, Excuses: Moral Slippage in the Workplace."

[37] Burger, Katrina. "Righteousness Pays," *Forbes* (September 22, 1997): 200–201.

[38] Ibid., 200.

[39] The Guardian. "How Do I Prevent the User of Illegal Software in the Office?" *The Guardian* (October 24, 2005).

[40] Hou, Chua Hian, "Many Small Firms Still Using Illegal Software," *The Straits Times* (November 1, 2005).

[41] Mikolajczk, Sigmund J. "Mitchell 1 Getting Tough on Pirates of Its Software," *Tire Business* (June 9, 2003).

[42] Tulgan. "Trends Point to a Dramatic General Shift in the Future Workforce," p. 23.

[43] Smola, Karen Wey, and Sutton, Charlotte D. "Generational Differences: Revisiting Generational Work Values for the New Millennium," *Journal of Organizational Behavior* (2002): 363–382.

[44] Ibid.

[45] Loughlin, Catherine, and Barling, Julian. "Young Workers' Work Values, Attitudes, and Behaviours," *Journal of Occupational and Organizational Psychology* (2001): 543–558.

[46] Loughlin and Barling, "Young Workers' Work Values," 545.

[47] Loughlin and Barling, "Young Workers' Work Values," 548.

[48] Howe, Neil and Strauss, William. *Millennials Rising*, New York: Vintage Books, 2000, 4.

[49] McKinnon, Jesse. "The Black Population in the United States: March 2002," *Current Population Reports*, U.S. Department of Commerce, Economics and Statistics Administration, U.S. Census Bureau (April 2003). Ramirez, Roberto R. and de la Cruz, G. Patricia, "The Hispanic Population in the United States: March 2002," *Current Population Reports*, U.S. Department of Commerce, Economics and Statistics Administration, U.S. Census Bureau (June 2003). U.S. Census Bureau, "USA Statistics in Brief—Race and Hispanic Origin," (January 18, 2005), *www.census.gov/statab/www/racehiisp.html.*

[50] Devens, Richard. "New Employment Projections Released by BLS," *Industrial Relations* (July 2002): 477–479.

[51] U.S. Census Bureau, *Statistical Abstract of the United States: 2004–2005*, Last Revised August 1, 2005 [on-line version, accessed September 18, 2005].

[52] U.S. Census Bureau, *Statistical Abstract of the United States: 2004–2005*, Last Revised August 1, 2005 [on-line version, accessed September 18, 2005].

[53] Lee, William. "The New Corporate Republics," *Wall Street Journal* (September 26, 1994): A12.

[54] Sherwood, Sonja, and Mendelsson, Jonny, "Marriott Goes Far Beyond the Numbers," *DiversityInc* (October 2005): 29–34. Sherwood, Sonja and Mendelsson, Jonny, "Pepsico's Reinemund Takes His Faith in Diversity to a New Level," *DiversityInc* (October 2005): 32–52.

[55] *Business Week.* "Managing by Values."

[56] *Fort Worth Star Telegram.* "Home Depot Discrimination Lawsuit Settled for $1 Million" (December 6, 1997): A5. *The Oil Daily.* "Judge OKs Texaco Settlement" (March 27, 1997): 59.

[57] Lardner, James. "Too Old to Write Code?" *U.S. News & World Report* (March 16, 1998): 39–45.

[58] U.S. Census Bureau, *Statistical Abstract of the United States, 2004–2005*. Washington, D.C.: *www.census.gov/prod/www/statistical-abstract-04.html* (last revised October 6, 2005).

[59] Francese, Peter. "Brains & Gender," *American Demographics* (September 2004): 40–41.

[60] Baynton, Dannah. "America's $60 Billion Problem," *Training* (May 2001): 50.

[61] Baynton, Dannah. "America's $60 Billion Problem," 50–54.

[62] *Chicago Tribune.* "How Many Switches It Takes to Be Viewed as a Job-Hopper" (September 19, 1994): sect. 6, 5.

[63] Kanter, Rosabeth M. *When Giants Learn to Dance: Mastering the Challenge of Strategy, Management, and Careers in the 1990s.* New York: Simon & Schuster, 1989.

[64] Hipple, Steven. "Contingent Work: Results from the Second Survey," *Monthly Labor Review* (November 1998): 22–35.

[65] *U.S. News & World Report.* "Meet the 'New Economy' Temps" (August 30, 1999): 50.

[66] Brownstein, Vivian. "As the Job Market Heats Up, Can Inflation Stay Cool?" *Fortune* (August 22, 1994): 23.

[67] *U.S. News & World Report.* "Meet the 'New Economy' Temps."

[68] Novack, Janet. "What Exploitation," *Forbes* (February 24, 1997): 161.

[69] Bloom, Jennifer Kingston. "'Portable Executives' Find Top-Level Work as Temps," *American Banker* (January 28, 1997): 1–2.

[70] Drucker, Peter F. "New Trends in Management," *Executive Excellence* (August 2003): 8–9.

[71] Merck & Co., Inc. *1997 Annual Report,* 1997.

[72] Wells, Susan J. "Making Telecommuting Work," *HR Magazine* (October 2001): 34–45.

[73] Morrissey, Jane. "Switching on Telecommuting," *PC Week* (June 15, 1998): 135.

[74] Herr, Judith M. "Trends in Management: Observations of a Sig Manager," *Intercom* (January 2004): 14–42.

[75] Katzenbach, Jon. "The Right Kind of Teamwork," *Wall Street Journal* (November 9, 1992): A10.

[76] Klein, Janice A., and Posey, Pamela A. "Good Supervisors Make Good Supervisors—Anywhere," *Harvard Business Review* (November–December 1986): 126.

[77] Ibid.

[78] Friedman, Thomas L. *The World Is Flat: A Brief History of the Twenty-First Century,* New York: Farrar, Straus and Giroux, 2005.

[79] Katzenbach, Jon, and Smith, Douglas. "Virtual Teaming," *Forbes.com* (May 21, 2001): 48–51.

[80] Roberts, Bill. "Empowerment or Imposition?" *HR Magazine* (June 2004): 157–166.

[81] Nokia website (November 17, 2005): *www.nokiausa.com/phones/compareandbuy*. Research in Motion website (November 17, 2005): *www.blackberry.com/products/new_handhelds/index.shtml*.

[82] Bacciocco, Dana. "EDI Fit to Survive in Competitive Retail Energy Markets," *Electric Light and Power* (October 2001): 24. Borck, James R. "Say Goodbye to EDI," *InfoWorld* (October 22, 2001): 57. *Economist*, "Stores of Value," (March 4, 1995): 5–8. Meehan, Michael, "Aerospace Group Backs New EDI-to-XML Bridge," *Computerworld* (October 2001): 14.

[83] Chappell, Lindsay. "Honda's New Elasticity Has Reduced Costs," *Automotive News* (August 13, 2001): 6.

[84] CONNSTEP, Inc. "Lean Manufacturing," (November 17, 2005): *www.connstep.org/web/frames.nsf/pages/leanmanufacturing*.

[85] Serwer, Andrew. "McDonald's Conquers the World," *Fortune* (October 17, 1994): 103–104, 106, 108, 112, 114, 116. Young, Barbara. "Global Marketing Pursuits," *National Provisioner* (September 2000): 18–25.

[86] Wisconsin Manufacturing Partnership, "Lean & Six Sigma," (February 2, 2004): *www.wmep.org/artman2/publish/article_54.shtml*.

[87] Bell Helicopter website (November 17, 2005): *www.bellhelicopter.com/en/employment/viewJobs*.

[88] Heitman, William; Spencer, Philip; and Hagey, Richard. "Productivity: Small Changes Add Up," *Financial Executive*, (October 2004): 34–38.

[89] Johnson, Ross, and Winchell, William O. *Management and Quality*. Milwaukee, Wisconsin: American Society for Quality Control, 1989.

[90] U.S. Census Bureau, *Statistical Abstract of the United States, 2004–2005*. Washington, D.C.: *www.census.gov/prod/www/statistical-abstract-04.html* (last revised October 6, 2005).

[91] Sony website (November 13, 2005): *www.sony.com/SCA/bios/stringer.shtml*.

[92] Pfeffer, Jeffrey. *The Human Equation: Building Profits by Putting People First*. Boston: Harvard Business School Press, 1998.

[93] Florida, Richard, and Goodnight, Jim. "Managing for Creativity," *Harvard Business Review*, (July–August 2005): 125–131.

[94] Pfeffer, Jeffrey. *Competitive Advantage Through People: Unleashing the Power of the Work Force*. Boston: Harvard Business School Press, 1994.

2

CHAPTER

"I'm guilty of doing too much, and I'm guilty of not seeing mistakes coming. What I'm not guilty of is making the same mistake twice."

Michael Dell[1]

Objectives

After reading and discussing this chapter, you should be able to do the following:

1. List and define the essential elements of any formal organization.
2. List and explain the steps involved in delegating.
3. Identify the levels in the management hierarchy and describe the activities of each.
4. Identify the major functions performed by all managers.
5. Explain the steps in this chapter's decision-making model.
6. Specify the kinds of decisions that require your group's involvement.
7. Recognize the decision traps that can lead to poor outcomes.

Morale Issues at the Department of Homeland Security

The attacks on the World Trade Center and the Pentagon on Sepetember 11, 2001, drove home the point that the United States was quite vulnerable to terrorists acts and heightened awareness that more coordination and focus would be needed to prevent such threats in the future. As a result, the Department of Homeland Security was formed to provide such protection and to provide assistance for natural disasters. Personnel from various federal agences, such as the Coast Guard, Customs Service, Federal Emergency Management Agency, and the Secret Service were brought together under this new department, which became operational in 2003. Mergers and reorganizations are typically difficult to manage under the best of circumstances. There are often conflicts in the organizational cultures and values of the merging organizations, as well as related management problems, which sometimes take years to resolve. In this case, personnel from 22 governmental agencies were brought together in the new start-up department, which has approximately 180,000 employees.[2]

Management
Concepts

Given the conditions under which the department was formed and the urgency of its mission, it would not have been difficult to predict that there would be management problems. This is indeed the case as a management survey, conducted by the U.S. Offfice of Personnel Management, which included over 10,000 responses from the department's personnel, has revealed serious morale and management issues. An analysis and comparison of the survey data by Scott Lilly from the Center for American Progress found that the department compared unfavorably to the 30 other federal agencies and departments included in the survey.[3]

Some of the particularly critical results are as follows:

Only 3 percent [of the respondents] said they were confident that in their department, personnel decisions were "based on merit." Fewer than 18 percent said they felt strongly that they were "held accountable for achieving results." And just 4 percent said they were sure that "creativity and innovation are rewarded." . . . The morale at the Department of Homeland Security was far worse than at the agency where the survey showed morale to be next lowest, the Small Business Administration . . . in answer to the question "how would you rate the overall quality of work done by your workgroup?" only 22 percent of Homeland Security employees answered "very good." Only 20 percent strongly agreed that "my work gives me a sense of personal accomplishment." Only 27 percent strongly agreed that "people I work with cooperate to get their job done," and 13 percent strongly agreed that "my job makes good use of my skills and abilities."[4]

In contrast to these resuts, the majority of the respondents from the department felt that their work was important:

The department finished in the top half of the 30 departments and agencies on only one question. More than 56 percent strongly agreed with the statement "The work I do is important." That placed Homeland Security employees second only to those at the Department of Veterans Affairs.[5]

Source: Quoted material from Rosenbaum, David E. "Study Ranks Homeland Security Dept. Lowest in Morale," New York Times, (October 16, 2005) Copyright © (2007) by the New York Times Co. Reprinted with permission.

Questions for Thought

1. What are some organizational concepts that must be mastered in order to avoid problems with employee morale?
2. What are some of the decision-making concepts that must be mastered in order to build employee confidence in the quality of supervision?

Introduction

Learning Objective Number One

Everyone needs to be able to take charge of his own life. Each of us must be able to plan our daily activities, control our use of resources, interact with others to get jobs done, and accumulate the resources necessary to accomplish tasks and to reach our goals. Management is both an art and the application of known, proven principles. Through the practice of management, we become better people. Because the work of supervisors is sometimes quite challenging, it is especially important that we also learn from our mistakes. All that we share together in this book will help make you a better manager of your social relationships, family, career, and advancement in life.

DEFINING MANAGEMENT

management
the process of planning, organizing, directing, and controlling human, material, and informational resources for the purposes of setting and achieving stated goals; also, a team of people making up an organization's hierarchy

formal organization
an enterprise that has clearly stated goals, a division of labor among specialists, a rational design, and a hierarchy of authority and accountability

Management is an activity that uses the functions of planning, organizing, directing, and controlling to apply human, informational, and material resources for the purposes of achieving stated goals. The word *management* may also refer to a team of people that oversees the activities of an enterprise in order to get its tasks and goals accomplished with and through others.

The term **formal organization** is used here to make a distinction from other types of organizations—for example, social or informal organizations. A formal organization is one created by design and a rational plan, such as a business or industrial union. A formal organization is basically the coming together of people for the accomplishment of stated purposes, in which the tasks to be performed are identified and divided among the participants and a framework for decisions and control is established.

The essential elements of any formal organization are as follows:

1. A clear understanding about stated purposes and goals
2. A division of labor among specialists
3. A rational organization or design
4. A hierarchy of authority and accountability

Each of these elements is related to the others. We will look at each separately in order to understand all of them better.

STATED PURPOSES AND GOALS

Every business enterprise is established to make a profit. How each organization intends to make its profit is stated in its **mission.** The mission states in words—backed up with both plans and actions—the organization's central and common purpose, its reason for existing. The mission acts as a unifying force, giving all personnel a common purpose and direction. To create a proper mission, top management needs two things: a recognition of what the organization does best—its core competencies—and a continuing focus on the future. According to professors and consultants Gary Hamel and C. K. Prahalad, "Our experience suggests that to develop a . . . distinctive point of view about the future, a senior management team must be willing to spend 20% to 50% of its time over a period of months. It must then be willing to continually revisit that point of view, elaborating and adjusting it as the future unfolds."[6] Both individuals and teams in all parts of the organization need their own missions as well. "Teams develop direction, momentum, and commitment by working to shape a meaningful purpose . . . Most successful teams shape their purposes in response to a demand or opportunity put in their path, usually by higher management."[7] The following example from Whole Foods Market provides a good example of a comprehensive mission statement:

> Our Company mission is to promote vitality and well-being for all individuals by supplying the highest quality, most wholesome foods available. Since the purity of our food and the health of our bodies are directly related to the purity and health of our environment, our core mission is devoted to the promotion of organically grown foods, food safety concerns and sustainability of our entire ecosystem.[8]

The mission statement of Southwest Airlines provides an example that recognizes the importance of how employees are treated and, in turn, the importance of providing superior customer service:

> The mission of Southwest Airlines: dedication to the highest quality of Customer Service delivered with a sense of warmth, friendliness, individual pride, and Company Spirit.[9]
>
> We are committed to provide our Employees a stable work environment with equal opportunity for learning and personal growth. Creativity and innovation are encouraged for improving the effectiveness of Southwest Airlines. Above all, Employees will be provided the same concern, respect, and caring attitude within the organization that they are expected to share externally with every Southwest Customer.[10]

The mission statement of Starbucks Coffee provides another example of a comprehensive statement, which includes important principles or values:

> To establish Starbucks as the premier purveyor of the finest coffee in the world while maintaining our uncompromising principles as we grow. The following six Guiding Principles will help us measure the appropriateness of our decisions:
>
> - Provide a great work environment and treat each other with respect and dignity.
> - Embrace diversity as an essential component in the way we do business.
> - Apply the highest standards of excellence to the purchasing, roasting and fresh delivery of our coffee.

mission
the expression in words—backed up with both plans and actions—of the organization's central and common purpose, its reason for existing

- Develop enthusiastically satisfied customers all of the time.
- Contribute positively to our communities and our environment.
- Recognize that profitability is essential to our future success.[11]

manager
a member of an organization's hierarchy who is paid to make decisions; one who gets things done with and through others, through the execution of the basic management functions

vision
a statement of what kind of company the organization wants to be in the future and the direction in which it will go

Each day, an organization's **managers** must ask two basic questions: What is our business? What should it be? As time progresses and circumstances change, an organization's managers must continually reassess where they are and where they want to be.

In addition to the mission statement, chief executives also continually communicate their *vision* of where the company will go, what it will be in the future, and how it will change. Professor John Kotter provides the following explanation of **vision**:

> *Vision* refers to a picture of the future with some implicit or explicit commentary on why people should strive to create that future. . . . [A] good vision serves three important purposes. First, by clarifying the general direction for change, by saying the corporate equivalent of "we need to be south of here in a few years instead [of] where we are today," it simplifies hundreds or thousands of more detailed decisions. Second, it motivates people to take action in the right direction, even if the initial steps are personally painful. Third, it helps coordinate the actions of different people, even thousands and thousands of individuals, in a remarkably fast and efficient way.[12]

The organization's chief executive establishes a vision for the entire organization. Top management sets specific goals and plans for its achievement. With these in mind, managers of each division and department establish for themselves both short- and long-range goals and plans for achieving the vision. Insight into the vision of the top management team at Wyeth Pharmaceuticals is provided in the following communication:

> Our vision is to lead the way to a healthier world. By carrying out this vision at every level of our organization, we will be recognized by our employees, customers and shareholders as the best pharmaceutical company in the world, resulting in value for all.
>
> We will achieve this by being accountable for:
>
> - Leading the world in innovation through pharmaceutical, biotech and vaccine technologies
> - Making trust, quality, integrity and excellence hallmarks of the way we do business
> - Attracting, developing and motivating our people
> - Continually growing and improving our business
> - Demonstrating efficiency in how we use resources and make decisions[13]

A DIVISION OF LABOR AMONG SPECIALISTS

We live in a world of specialists. In government, the professions, and business, men and women are asked to choose areas in which to specialize so that they can become experts in their fields. Any formal organization is set up to make good use of the special talents and abilities of its people. Each person is assigned tasks that he is best qualified to

A team of supervisors meets to discuss goals for their firm. After agreeing on their overall goals, each supervisor must decide how her own workers will be utilized to meet the goals.

complete through the application of specialized knowledge. Through the coordination and teaming of these specialists—each of whom contributes a part to the whole job—the entire work of the organization is planned and then carried out.

In many of today's businesses, specialization is achieved by grouping individual experts into cross-functional teams that take ownership of a project or a process—such as designing a new product or improving customer billing. Highly educated specialists or knowledge workers, such as software engineers and market research experts, routinely work in cross-functional teams with other knowledge workers. The goals of cross-functional teams are to save time, save money, and improve products or services through both incremental and radical change.

Unfortunately, teams sometimes get derailed and fail to perform as expected. This chapter's feature on teams discusses some of the problems for which supervisors need to be alert.

TEAMS

A RATIONAL ORGANIZATION OR DESIGN

Formal business organizations must have designs that properly facilitate their missions and activities. Organizational designs or structures must be tailored to provide for the proper flow of needed information to all individuals, teams, and units. They must allow for the coordination and oversight of essential operations. Above all, they must be flexible enough to meet new challenges and opportunities.

A HIERARCHY OF AUTHORITY AND ACCOUNTABILITY

The term **hierarchy** refers to the number of levels in an organization and the group of managers who occupy those levels and make the necessary plans and decisions that allow it to function. From the chief executive to team facilitators and team leaders, they must plan, organize, direct, and control the many activities that have to take place if the organization's goals are to be reached.

hierarchy
the management levels and people who staff an organization's positions of formal authority

SUPERVISING TEAMS

Although teams offer the potential for high performance, they often do not reach their potential because they suffer from various team diseases. Some of the diseases that afflict teams include the following:

Collective Amnesia. This disease occurs when top executives implement teams in work situations where there is no compelling need for teamwork. For example, when employees individually perform their work and the group leader integrates their individual contributions, there is no need for teams or teamwork. Inappropriate implementations of teams sometime occur in situations where executives have uncritically decided to use teams without having a good understanding of their limitations and inefficiencies. Furthermore, even when there is a need for teams, they sometimes fail because instead of real teams there are only employee work groups. Teams differ from groups in that their members hold each other accountable for performance.

Chronic Cantankerousness. With this disease team members face recurring quarrels within the team, cannot agree on even the smallest of details about how the team should function, and have at least one member who does not follow the rules. If the team proceeds without dealing with such issues, these disagreements can escalate into full-blown conflict. A preventive measure for this disease is for the team to write up a set of responses that it will use when members break the rules. An example of this preventive approach involves writing the responses on cards, which are then played when each rule is broken.

Leadership Phobia. This disease results from the absence of leadership within the team. Prevention of this disease involves making sure that the team has members that can play three different roles: team designer, team midwife, and team coach. Each of these roles is critical in different phases of the team's evolution. Designers help ensure that teams are set up correctly with clear tasks, responsibilities, and reward systems. Midwives assist with the development of team goals and work procedures as the teams make progress toward deadlines. Coaches begin to apply their skills after teams have reached their performing phase and are most effective when used sparingly at break points, such as when new projects begin or at various milestone points.

Source: Mark Fischetti. "Team Doctors, Report to ER," *Fast Company* (February 1998): 170.

authority
a person's right to give orders and instructions to others and to use organizational resources

Authority. **Authority** is the right to give orders and instructions to others and to use organizational resources. Every manager needs authority in order to mobilize resources required to accomplish tasks. Authority allows team facilitators and team leaders to make a decision or take action that affects the organization and its associates. All managers have the authority of their offices or positions. This kind of authority is often called positional or formal authority because it resides in a job or position and is there to be used by the person who holds that job or position.

Formal or positional authority is usually described in a formal written document, called a *job description,* that outlines the specific duties that the position holder is expected to execute. Managers' job descriptions usually give them the right to assign work to employees or team members, to oversee the execution of work, to appraise employees' and team members' performances, to use various kinds of capital equipment, and to spend specific amounts of budgeted funds. As a supervisor, team facilitator, or team leader, you must act within the limits of your authority.

Power. **Power** is the ability to influence others so that they will respond favorably to the orders and instructions they receive. Power may come from several sources. In general, power comes to a person through his or her position (formal job description), personality traits and character (attractiveness to others), knowledge and experience base (expertise), and relationships with other powerful people. Power that flows to a manager from the position held is called *legitimate* or *position power*. It consists of the right to punish and reward—sometimes called *coercive power*. Your attractiveness to others is the basis for friendship and professional relationships. It is usually referred to as your *charisma*. Your influence over others because of what you know and are capable of doing is called *expert power*. Finally, you have influence over others because they see you as a person who is well connected—a person with powerful associates. All sources of power are important to you if you want to be a truly effective manager. Authority alone is not enough. You must be the kind of person others respect and want to follow. In addition, you must not abuse your power and engage in unethical behaviors. This chapter's feature on ethics deals with conflicts of interest.

Responsibility. **Responsibility** refers to each employee's obligation to execute all duties to the best of her ability. Because all employees have the authority of their job descriptions, they all have responsibility. The concept of responsibility tells us not only that we must perform our duties but also that we must do so in line with the instructions and limits we receive from above.

Accountability. **Accountability** is having to answer to someone (your superior or teammates) for your actions or failure to act. All employees in any organization have duties and, therefore, authority, responsibility, and accountability.

WORKFORCE FLEXIBILITY

Although job descriptions provide a basis for authority, power, responsibility, and accountability, many organizations recognize that job descriptions can also limit the **flexibility** of their workforce. When employees rigidly adhere to their job descriptions by performing only those tasks they enumerate, the organization's performance declines. Organizations need flexibility because work flows are often uneven. Where there are light work flows for some tasks and heavy work flows for others, supervisors need the flexibility to move employees where they can be fully utilized. When unions represent employees, greater emphasis is often placed on performance of only those tasks outlined in the job description. This is because different wage rates are negotiated for the various jobs, and the union does not want the employer to be able to assign lower-paid workers to perform higher-wage jobs. In order to obtain greater flexibility, some companies have limited the number of different jobs and have made their job descriptions very broad. For example, Chaparral Steel, which has very high workforce productivity, has only two job descriptions for its factory jobs—production worker and maintenance worker. Many employees respond favorably to broader job descriptions when they are linked with greater responsibility, empowerment, and higher compensation.

power
the ability to influence others so that they respond favorably to orders and instructions

responsibility
the obligation each person with authority has to execute his duties to the best of his ability

accountability
having to answer to someone for your performance or failure to perform to standards

flexibility
the ability of members of a workforce to perform different tasks

*Learning
Objective
Number Two*

SUPERVISORS AND ETHICS

Conflicts of interest are a common source of ethical problems in many organizations. Such conflicts arise when managers or employees make decisions or take actions, which provide benefits for themselves at the expense of their employers. Because such conflicts can so easily arise whenever there is discretion in decision-making, supervisors must be continually vigilant to avoid such conflicts in their own decisions and actions as well as in the actions of the employees for which they have responsibility. In addition, supervisors must avoid engaging in actions that even create the impression of conflicts of interests because their employees look to their conduct for examples of acceptable behavior. A case involving Boeing and the U.S. Air Force reveals how costly conflicts of interest can be and the devastating consequences of such ethical lapses for employers and those who engage in such behaviors.

Darleen Druyun, a high-ranking civilian Air Force procurement official who was working on a $23 billion lease arrangement for Boeing 767 planes that would be used as tankers, entered into inappropriate confidential conversations with Boeing officials about future employment opportunities. At the time she had these conversations, she was still representing the Air Force, and eventually she went to work for Boeing in 2002 as a vice president. While still working on the deal for the Air Force, she also sold her Virginia home to an attorney who also worked for Boeing. Because she did not withdraw from her representation of Air Force interests for some period of time after having these discussions, she became mired in very serious ethics and legal issues. After an investigation, she entered a guilty plea to a charge of conspiracy and entered into a cooperative arrangement with prosecutors for the federal government.

As the investigation continued and additional documents were discovered, more problems came to light as it was found that additional senior Boeing executives were aware of her attempts to obtain employment with the company and Boeing's overtures to her. The fallout from this ethical lapse was significant as Boeing's chief financial officer, who was expected by knowledgeable observers to take over the company at some point in the future, was fired. As a result of these developments, a few days later, Boeing's CEO resigned his position.

Sources: J. Lynn Lunsford and Andy Pastor. "Former Boeing Official Pleads Guilty to Conspiracy," *Wall Street Journal*, (April 21, 2004): A1–A9. Anne M. Squedo. "Air Force Ex-Official Had Ties to Boeing During Contract Talks," *Wall Street Journal*, (October 7, 2003): A1–A16.

DELEGATION

delegation
the act of passing formal authority by a manager to another

Delegation is the act of passing part of one's authority to another. Only people possessing authority over others, such as managers, team leaders, and team facilitators, can delegate. When you accept a duty through delegation from your boss, you accept new authority and the responsibility for it, and you agree to be held accountable for your performance of the new duty. When you as a supervisor delegate authority, you agree to be held accountable for your decision to delegate (the way you have chosen to handle your responsibility) and for the execution of the delegated duty by your employees. The act of delegation, therefore, creates a duality of both responsibility and accountability related to the same task or duty and its execution. If this were not so, any manager could pass a tough job to an employee and escape from it entirely, with no adverse consequences. But the concept of accountability tells us that delegation is simply the manner in which a manager has chosen to execute a task—the way the manager has chosen to handle responsibility for the task. Delegation does not eliminate the supervisor's need to justify the decision.

Consider this example. Suppose you are going away from your job next Tuesday for personal business. You have one task that must be executed during your absence, and you decide to delegate it to an employee. You take your day off. When you return, you discover that the task was not performed. Your boss will want to know why, and you will be asked to answer for the failure to execute the task. You, in turn, will want to know what went wrong and why. Both you and your employee are accountable for the ways in which you chose to handle responsibility for the same task. But you, as supervisor, shoulder the primary burden of accountability in the eyes of your boss.

WHY YOU MUST DELEGATE

Delegation is a tool that allows you to train team members and associates. By introducing your most capable employees to bits and pieces of your job, you prepare them for advancement. Unless you have a trained successor to fill your shoes, it will be very hard for you to get promoted. Your boss will not want to create a hole in the operation by letting you move up if it means leaving behind a leaderless group.

Second, by delegating, you can free yourself from time-consuming routines and other duties that might be better performed by employees. Until you create some free time for yourself, you will not be able to accept delegation from your boss. Like yourself, your boss wants to meet your need to grow by letting you experience greater responsibilities, thereby grooming you for promotion.

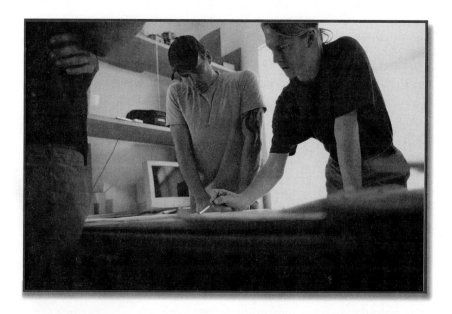

Part of delegating is making sure your employee understands the job. Although you may delegate the work, you are still accountable for its outcome. Decision-making is an important time to involve employees. Ask for their opinions. When explaining the decision, take the time to explain why the decision was made.

Third, delegating empowers your associates. For the majority of people, empowerment adds interest, challenges, and opportunities for growth. By empowering your people, you are making a clear statement about your trust and faith in them. You are helping improve your operations by tapping into your associates' uniqueness and creativity. You also will be aiding their search for job satisfaction by giving them more say and control over their activities and decisions.

Some managers fear the delegation process because they do not want to give up any of their authority. They fear that an employee cannot do the job as well as they can or that they will lose control over the execution of their authority once it is in the hands of another. They may fear that once employees know their bosses' jobs, they will be a threat to their job security. But fearing the act of delegation is no excuse for not doing it. You must recognize that you will have no other choice. Your boss expects it, employees may demand it, and you will be away from your job at times because of illness and vacations. Keep in mind that delegation frees you from any task that your employees can do, helps you identify the employees that you can depend on, and lets you spend more of your time on things that only you can do or that you do best.

HOW TO DELEGATE

Seven steps are involved in the decision to pass some of your authority to another person:

1. *Decide on the task(s), limits, and support to provide.* Spell out in as much detail as is necessary exactly what you want your associate to do, the limits that you are placing on the execution, and the support you have to offer.
2. *Choose the employee.* The person you choose may be one in need of the experience, one who is capable of doing the job already, or one who wants exposure to the task. You may want to choose more than one person so that several people get the training or exposure. This will give your people more flexibility and will allow you to be less dependent on any one person.
3. *Give the assignment.* Let the person know what you want done, the limits, and the support. Explain why the task is necessary and the kind of results you expect. Ask the employee for feedback. Find out if there are any misunderstandings. When the employee can restate the assignment and limits accurately and knows how to perform the task(s), you are ready for step four.
4. *Provide resources.* Provide the tools and materials needed for the task or information on where the employee can obtain these resources.
5. *Provide skill enhancement.* Take time to make sure that the employee knows how to perform any new tasks. If the task is new, use this assignment as an opportunity for teaching opportunities and skill development. Be prepared to provide more assistance during the learning phase.
6. *Specify authority and responsibility.* Be sure to clearly specify the authority that the employee will have in the performance of this task as well as the level of accountability and responsibility.
7. *Stay in touch.* Even so-called simple tasks are not so simple when an inexperienced person has to perform them. Keep track of the person's

progress by checking with her periodically. You may ask for periodic reports of progress if the task is to stretch over several days or weeks.

When the task is accomplished, let the employee know how you evaluate her efforts. You may want to reward the person with praise and point out what went well and what could be improved.

WHAT YOU DO NOT WANT TO DELEGATE

In general, you should not delegate a task that you do not understand or know how to perform. If you do, you will be unable to offer any support when trouble arises, and you may not be able to evaluate the results fairly. As a supervisor, you should not delegate the authority to punish or reward. People work to please those who have this authority. Delegation should never strip you of these rights and duties. Finally, if you have no one who is capable of taking on the task, you must either prepare someone to take it or keep the task for yourself.

Learning Objective Number Three

THE MANAGEMENT HIERARCHY

We have concluded that, among other things, managers make up a team of decision-makers charged with operating the formal organization of a business. You will recall that one of the characteristics of a formal organization is that it has a hierarchy of authority and accountability. We will now examine this hierarchy. The simple pyramid shown in Exhibit 2.1 is a basic model for a management hierarchy. In most organizations, this

The pyramid of the management hierarchy.　　　　**EXHIBIT 2.1**

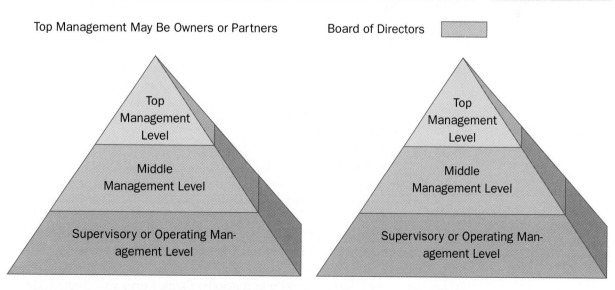

Top Management May Be Owners or Partners　　　Board of Directors

Privately Owned Firms, Sole Proprietorships, and Partnerships

Corporations

pyramid is divided into three levels: top management, middle management, and the supervisory or operating level of management.

As a result of downsizing during the 1980s and 1990s, the pyramid model has changed. Most organizations have a relatively smaller proportion of middle managers than in the past. In addition, in many organizations the pyramid has become flatter with fewer levels between top management and rank-and-file employees. Because computer information systems now handle much of the information dissemination and coordination performed by middle managers in the past, there is less need for such managers. In addition, in order to reduce labor costs many organizations have adopted lean staffing approaches in which smaller numbers of first-level managers each supervise a larger number of employees. This involves granting managers a broader **span of control.**

span of control
the number of employees over which a manager has direct supervisory control

Steeper pyramids are typical of the traditional structure often found in large organizations in stable industries with stable competitive environments, and in government. Companies in less stable industries and environments will need a different, more flexible structure.

Many sole proprietorships and partnerships have only one or two managers who must, out of necessity, direct more than one specialized area. Most sole proprietorships and partnerships are extremely small in terms of the number of people they employ. Their operations are usually not complex enough to require more than one or two levels of management. The examination that follows uses a business corporation as its model. Nonetheless, much of the discussion applies to sole proprietorships and partnerships as well. An exception is that a corporation is the only type of business organization to have a board of directors. The board of directors is outside and above the corporate management pyramid, and is represented graphically above the second pyramid in Exhibit 2.1.

THE TOP MANAGEMENT LEVEL

top management
the uppermost part of the management hierarchy, containing the positions of the chief executive and immediate subordinates

Occupying only the small topmost portion of the pyramid, the **top management** level is the location of the chief executive or president and immediate subordinates (vice presidents or their equivalents). In a sole proprietorship, the owner is usually the chief executive. In a partnership, the role of the chief executive is usually shared between or among the managing partners, each of whom concentrates on his own specialty.

In a corporation, the top management is made up of the officers of the company: a president, one or more vice presidents, a treasurer, and a secretary. Any two (or more) offices may be held by the same person, except the offices of secretary and president.

The chief executive's role. The chief executive officer (CEO) has several major responsibilities. She must articulate a mission, vision, core values (quality, integrity, and employee participation, for example), and guiding principles for the entire company. The mission, values, and guiding principles become part of the organization's corporate climate and must govern the actions of its team leaders, facilitators, and associates.

The CEO must also sense when change is called for and initiate the change. This was the case when Dick Brown came to EDS. Shortly after he became CEO of EDS, Brown "quickly laid off one-third of the sales force and cut $2 billion in annual costs, yet has landed $89 billion in multi-year contracts, double the previous sum."[14] By continually focusing on the future and reexamining organizational strengths and weaknesses, the CEO is able to develop and initiate major organizational objectives and strategies (grow the company by adding new products, increasing market share). The chief executive is the one manager who must be able to observe and comprehend the entire operation. Like the captain of a ship, the chief executive is responsible for his own decisions and is accountable for those of all other managers. Sometimes the CEO has to make very tough decisions, such as closing down a plant or laying off employees. Many companies also have a president, who takes on major responsibilities for the organization. The president reports directly to the CEO. In addition, companies in which operational responsibilities are significant may have a chief operating officer (COO) who reports directly to the CEO or president.

The vice president's role. Vice presidents are the immediate subordinates of the chief executive. In a typical bureaucratic–mechanistic organization, they are charged with the overall operation of the company's functional areas:

- Marketing—sales and all sales-connected activities
- Production—manufacturing and procurement of raw materials
- Finance—managing the company's financial resources and access to capital
- Human resource management—staffing, development, compensation, and employee relations duties

Other business activities, such as engineering, research and development, and procurement or supply chain management, may fall under one or another of these headings, or they may be led by their own specialized members of top management. Further, many companies combine this functional approach with other approaches, such as organizing by product or customer groupings. In many companies, vice presidents are in charge of strategic business units (SBUs). These are often autonomous and organized around product groups or customers served. Such is the case at IBM, Ford, and Xerox. The vice presidents must plan, organize, direct, and control the general operation of their departments, units, or divisions. Their subordinates are usually middle managers.

THE MIDDLE MANAGEMENT LEVEL

Middle management occupies the middle area of the pyramid. The middle management level is the location of all managers below the executive level ranks of president and vice president. Each functional area has many specific tasks to be performed. Exhibit 2.2 illustrates the hierarchy of a grocery chain. The company's regional and store managers are middle managers. They are not specialists, but all of their subordinate managers are. Each must carry out the operation of a specific part of the store's activities. Like those of all managers, the middle manager's functions are to plan, direct, control, and organize.

middle management
the members of the hierarchy below the rank of top management but above the rank of supervisor

THE OPERATING MANAGEMENT LEVEL

Shown at the lower part of the management pyramid, is the first-level management area where the assistant store managers and department managers are located. It should be noted that in some grocery chains department managers are essentially lead persons, who simply direct the work. Frequently, they do not have the full authority of supervisors and are not actually supervisors. In such cases, the assistant store managers may

operating management
the level of the hierarchy that oversees the work of non-management employees (workers)

| EXHIBIT 2.2 | A grocery retailing organization showing the different levels of management. |

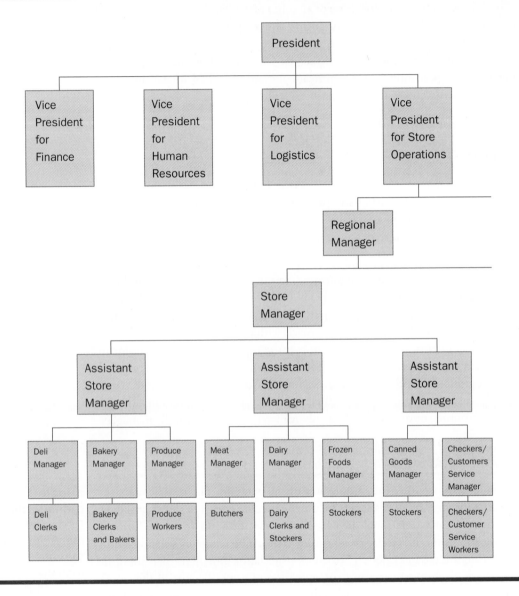

Note: Only one store in the region and only one region are depicted. None of the managers and workers reporting to the vice presidents of finance, human resources, and logistics are shown.

worker
any employee who is not a member of the management hierarchy

be the actual supervisors. Managers or supervisors direct the work of non-management **workers**, individually or in teams. If a manager directs the work of other managers, he does not belong on this level.

In many organizations the supervisor is evolving into a team leader or facilitator, aiding the efforts of the group she heads. Typically, both the leader and the facilitator assist teams by providing training and support to team members. A team leader may even rotate on a regular basis, allowing other members of the team to gain managerial experience.

Pindar Set, a small company in the United Kingdom that typesets yellow page directories, is an outstanding example of a company that utilizes teams very effectively. The company's award-winning application of teams was prompted by pressures for shorter delivery times, desire for greater responsiveness to customers, and tighter margins. The company's approach to teams and the role of team leaders is described as follows:

> The company set about training all its unskilled staff to do skilled jobs, phasing out unskilled text-inputting jobs completely. All the unskilled workers upgraded as planned . . . Remedial training was provided where necessary. Employees were also trained to follow a job through from start to finish, reducing the internal "pipeline" from 80 processes to one. And team working was introduced . . . This meant creating new team-leader roles. Previously senior operators had supervised work, but had still retained hands-on tasks. The company also recognized it needed a pool of new team leaders to respond to future growth. Team leaders were given more responsibility for financial operations and people management than before. They now run their sites as semi-autonomous businesses, with their own profit and loss accounts. This also required training and a team-leader programme was introduced.[15]

More will be said about team leaders and team facilitators throughout this text.

Exhibit 2.1 depicts only the management team. The majority of workers in an organization form the base of the pyramid, the group of people on whom managers depend to execute plans and to achieve goals. Exhibit 2.3 shows a more complete picture of a typical business corporation.

A corporation's management pyramid showing the functional areas and base of workers.

EXHIBIT 2.3

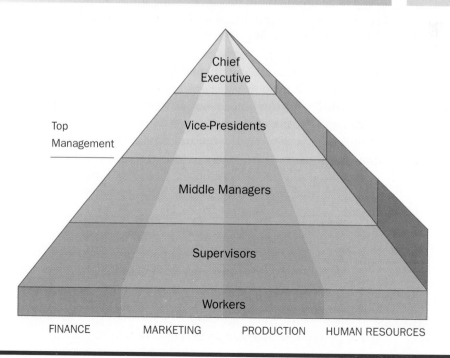

LINE AND STAFF AUTHORITY

line authority
a manager's right to give direct orders to subordinates and appraise, reward, and discipline those who receive those orders

Line authority allows its holder—a traditional manager, team leader, or team facilitator—to exercise direct supervision over his subordinates. Managers who have line authority can give direct orders to, appraise, reward, and discipline those who receive their orders.

The managers in the organization hierarchy who manage activities or departments that directly influence the success (profitability) of a business are called *line managers.* Their departments make direct contributions toward achieving the company's goals. Since line activities are identified in terms of the company's goals, the activities classified as line will differ with each organization. For example, a manufacturing company may limit line functions to production and marketing, whereas a department store, in which buying is a key element, will include the purchasing department and the sales department in its line activities.[16]

When an organization is small, all positions may be line roles; staff roles are added as the organization grows and as it becomes useful to devote specialists' time to assist the line members in doing their primary jobs.

staff authority
the right of staff managers to give advice and counsel to all other managers in an organization in the areas of their expertise

Staff authority, like line authority, is a kind of formal authority. It is distributed throughout the organization to various managers at any level who advise and assist other managers. Staff managers are specialists who supervise activities or departments that help others achieve the company's major goals. The staff managers' primary mission is to support all other managers who need their specialized knowledge.

The concept of staff is relevant only as applied to the relationships between managers. A manager is a staff manager if his job is to advise, counsel, assist, or provide service to another manager. You can tell if managers are staff or line managers by observing their relationships to the other managers. Since staff managers are linked to the top of an organization, they receive line authority also. If they have subordinates, they direct, appraise, and discipline those subordinates, just as any line manager does with her subordinates. When staff managers direct the work of their associates, they are using line authority. But when staff managers give advice or assistance to other managers, they are acting as staff managers.

Exhibit 2.4 is an abbreviated organization chart of a management hierarchy that shows both line and staff positions, as well as the relationships of authority. Note that staff and line managers appear at both the top and the middle of the hierarchy. The broken lines show advisory relationships. The solid lines show the flow of line authority.

Organization charts are just one of several tools used to show the part that each person or section plays in the entire enterprise. They should show the following things:

- Who reports to whom
- The flow of authority and accountability
- Formal positions of authority and their titles
- Lines of communication
- Lines of promotion

Organization chart showing staff positions and the flow of both line and staff authority.

Exhibit 2.4

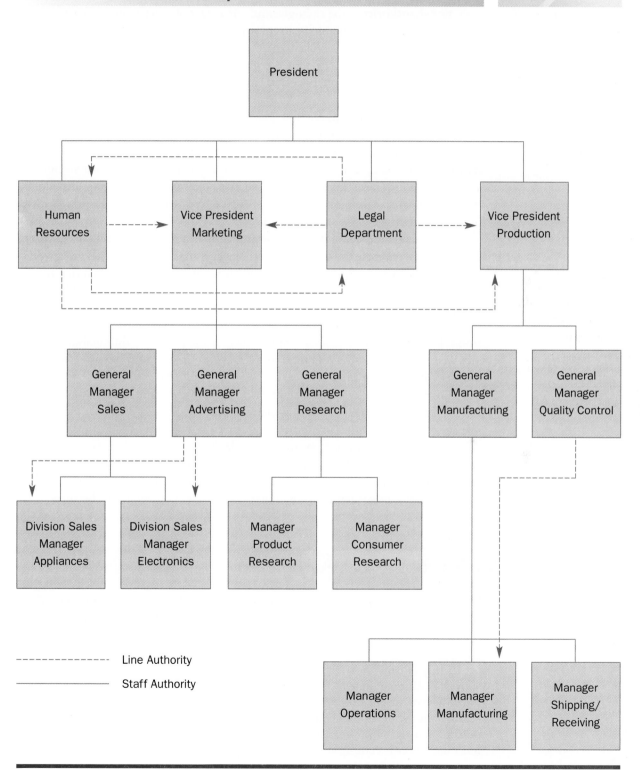

FUNCTIONAL AUTHORITY

functional authority
the right that a manager of a staff department has to make decisions and to give orders that affect the way things are done in specific functions in another department

Functional authority is the right given to a manager of a department (usually a staff department) to make decisions that govern the operation of another department in specific functions. Exhibit 2.5 illustrates the flow of functional authority from the staff managers to the other managers in an organization. The lines of functional authority indicate a measure of control by a staff manager over a line manager and her people and their activities.

The normal practice (where functional authority is not used) is for a line manager to have complete control over his area of responsibility and relative freedom to make his own decisions. Staff managers have been installed to help the line as well as other staff managers but usually only when called on to do so. Under this arrangement, a staff manager may never be consulted. Line managers must take full responsibility for their actions when acting on staff advice. After all, they could have ignored the advice of the staff manager.

For this and other reasons, many companies make use of the concept of functional authority. This concept holds that if a staff manager makes a decision about her functional area (such as marketing, finance, human resources, or legal affairs) that has application to the area of another manager, the manager of that other area is bound by the staff manager's decision. For example, the payroll department issues a directive stating that henceforth all payroll data from each department must be submitted electronically in a specific format by a certain date. If the managers throughout the business wish to get themselves and their people paid on time and in the correct amounts, they had better follow the directive.

Learning Objective Number Four

Functional authority seems to subject a manager to the will of many bosses. But does it? Isn't a company merely removing many important, but nonessential, areas from a manager's concern in order to promote uniformity and efficiency? When many routine decisions about problem areas are made outside the department, each manager is freed of the responsibility for these matters. As a result, the manager has more time to devote to her specialized, essential tasks. The loss in autonomy is more than compensated for by an increase in efficiency and economy in the overall operation of the business.

THE MANAGER'S FUNCTIONS

We will now briefly explore the four major functions of management. By major functions we mean the most important and time-consuming activities common to all managers. These functions consist of planning, organizing, directing, and controlling.

Planning. Planning is the first and most basic of the management functions. Through planning, managers attempt to prepare for and forecast future events. Planning involves the construction of programs for action designed to achieve stated goals through the use of people and other resources. Planning is also a part of the other functions of management: organizing, directing, and controlling. It is the first thing you must do, before executing any of these functions.

The flow of functional staff and line authority in a manufacturing business.

EXHIBIT 2.5

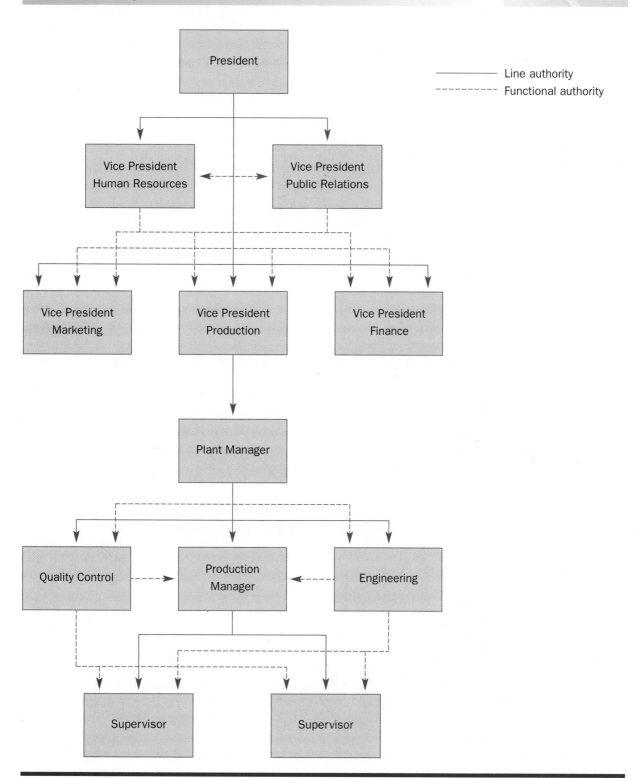

Organizing. The organizing function determines the tasks to be performed, the jobs or positions required to execute the tasks, and the resources needed to accomplish the organization's goals. Organizing is directly related to and dependent on planning.

Directing. The directing function includes the activities of overseeing, facilitating, coaching, training, evaluating, disciplining, rewarding, and staffing. Staffing is concerned with adding new talent to an organization, promoting or transferring people to new jobs and responsibilities, and separating people from the organization.

Controlling. The controlling function is concerned with preventing, identifying, and correcting deficiencies in all phases of an organization's operations. Through controlling, standards of performance are established, communicated to those affected by them, and used to measure the operation and performance of individuals and the entire organization.

These four functions apply to all managers, but each level of management spends different amounts of time performing each (see Exhibit 2.6). Although top management spends most of its time on planning, supervisors (operating management) spend most of their time on directing.

Three other sets of activities are related to each of the four major management functions. First, it is impossible to consider any of the functions without recognizing the need to communicate. Communicating is the ability to get your ideas across to others by means of the spoken or written word. Second, it is impossible to carry out your duties without interacting with others. This fact tells us that a second set of activities is needed to coordinate what you do with others in your organization. By coordinating, teams and team members attempt to synchronize their activities with other groups and individuals. By working to maintain good relationships and through regular communication with employees, peers, and superiors, you promote cooperation and facilitate coordination. Along with being good communicators, supervisors need to have good interpersonal skills.

The example of Jacques Nasser, who was forced out as the CEO of Ford, provides an example of the problems that can result from a lack of good interpersonal relations.

EXHIBIT 2.6	**Proportions of time spent on the management functions by the three management levels.**

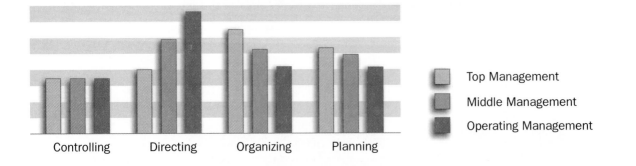

SUPERVISORS AND
PERFORMANCE

Supervisors are increasingly faced with the dilemma of how to obtain increased productivity with the same number of employees. Unfortunately, in many instances employees are being required to work longer hours. Recent reports indicate that large numbers of employees in the United States are working more than 50 hours per week and a large number of U.S. workers do not take vacations. Furthermore, between 2001 and 2004 the percentage of U.S. workers who reported that they were being overworked increased from 28 to 44 percent. This situation stands in stark contrast to practices in European countries, such as Belgium and France, where workers take five or six weeks of vacation each year.

It has been observed that U.S. productivity is high solely because employees spend more time on the job. There is now evidence that when productivity is computed on an hourly basis, the productivity of workers in Belgium and France is higher. The challenge for supervisors is to enable employees to work smarter rather than longer. Improvements in productivity will help offset declines in morale caused by long hours and enable workers to devote more time to their personal lives. Many employees, especially women, have been sending the message that more time for their personal lives is important as they are leaving companies that require long hours. A large number of U.S. employers have responded to demands for more balance in employees' professional and personal lives by allowing employees to have flexible work schedules so they can meet childcare and other responsibilities.

The recent experiences of Best Buy provide an example of potential solutions to some of these problems. Best Buy has been conducting an experiment involving 3,500 employees in its Minneapolis headquarters with a new flexible work practices approach that provides better work and life balance. More employees are working from home and teams are meeting less frequently. When they do meet, they are more productive and there is less chit-chat. Employees communicate with each other more by e-mail, cell phone, or telephone and there are fewer casual drop-in visits in the office. Much of the flexibility in new work arrangements has been made possible because of the trust that supervisors and managers have in their employees. The results of the initial pilot test with 300 employees were impressive as turnover dropped from 14 percent to zero, job satisfaction increased by 10 percent, and performance indicators for teams increased by 13 percent.

Sources: Chuck Salter. "Solving the Real Productivity Crisis," *Fast Company*, (January 2004): 37. Jyoti Thottam. "Reworking Work," *Time*, (July 25, 2005): 50–55.

Nasser, who was perceived on occasion as abrasive while also being somewhat isolated, had not established solid relationships with Ford's employees or its network of dealers. As a result, he lacked allies when he attempted to streamline the company's bureaucracy and could not retain his position in the face of mounting pressures from the aftermath of litigation and bad public relations related to faulty Firestone tires on Ford Explorers.[17]

The pressures for performance, which Nasser was seeking with these measures, have also been reflected in longer work hours for many employees. This chapter's feature on supervisors and performance deals with such demands.

PERFORMANCE

Learning
Objective
Number Five

DECISION-MAKING

You have been making decisions all of your life. You have already made many today. As a supervisor, team facilitator, and team leader, you are paid to make them to the best of your ability. As we have already seen, you have a responsibility to make them and are accountable for the results. A decision in its most essential form is a conclusion that you reach by making judgments. Most of us have a decision process, but we may never have put it in writing. It's simply there in our minds and serves us each time we try to answer questions and make a decision. The approach described next can help you make difficult decisions rationally. This approach will remove a great deal of uncertainty and will give you a method for problem solving that will help you avoid making many bad or mediocre decisions.

A RATIONAL MODEL

The rational model in Exhibit 2.7 has six steps. None of them is really new to you, but all are essential. They simply put what you have been doing all of your life into a systematic framework that will help you make better decisions. We will work through the sequence of steps by using an example.

Define the problem. A problem exists when a situation is not as it should be. Symptoms are usually the first signs of a problem. Your toaster keeps burning your bread or your television's channels are all snowy.

Ed, the supervisor of data control, has noticed several analysts sitting idle. All should be working. What is the problem? Lazy workers? Local area network (LAN) is

EXHIBIT 2.7   **Steps in the rational decision-making process.**

1. *Define the problem.* The effort here is to define the difference between what is and what should be. Avoid the pitfall of defining symptoms. Dig beneath the symptoms to make sure you have identified the underlying cause.

2. *Identify your restraints.* Your restraints are such resources as time, money, and talent. Anything that limits your ability to solve a problem as you would like is a restraint.

3. *List your alternatives.* Alternatives are possible solutions. List as many as you can without regard for their good and bad points. Involve the ideas of others if they can be of assistance.

4. *Evaluate your alternatives.* Go back to step two and consider each alternative with your restraints in mind. List the advantages and disadvantages of each course of action.

5. *Decide on the best alternative(s).* Pick one or a combination of two or more that have the fewest serious disadvantages and the most important advantages.

6. *Implement the decision and follow up.* This is the action step that tries out your solution. Learn from the application and be prepared to fall back to another solution if the one you have chosen does not give positive results.

down? Without further investigation, Ed will not be certain. He first talks with the operators to discover the source of their idleness. His investigation tells him that a necessary set of figures from the accounting department has not arrived on schedule. What is the problem now? Missing data from accounting? Ed calls the accounting supervisor and discovers that the data were sent over two hours ago. Ed conducts a search and his secretary discovers the data attached to an e-mail message on her computer buried among other messages that arrived later.

Ed started with symptoms and moved to an investigation that led him to the discovery that vital information was getting lost in his own department on his own desk. This discovery tells Ed that his problem is related to the way in which information from outside his office is received and filed. Ed now frames the problem as a question: "How can information flowing to us from the outside be properly handled to avoid losing it?" Having defined his problem, Ed is now ready to proceed to step two.

Identify your restraints.   Restraints are limiting factors that affect your efforts to make a decision. Restraints generally fall under several headings, such as _who, what, when,_ and _where._ Who will be involved in the decision? Is it a decision that needs the group's support and input? If so, the group must be involved in the process. "Who" also asks us to consider who is affected by the problem and whether or not the affected people have a role to play in solving it. What is involved? What resources may be affected and may have to be committed in order to implement the decision? Money, time, and other resources will surely be involved in some way. When must a solution be delivered? By what date must a decision be made? Finally, where is the solution needed and best implemented?

Ed has decided that he must make the decision and that the others will simply be informed about it after they give him their ideas about handling the problem. Ed has further decided that few resources will be needed. Time is the primary resource he and others must expend to make a decision. Ed thinks that the "when" is best answered with "as soon as possible." He assigns the highest priority to dealing with the problem. Ed is now ready for step three.

List your alternatives.   Alternatives are the courses of action that may solve your problem. Lists of alternatives should be developed without criticism, as they are offered. The merits and drawbacks can be dealt with in step four. In developing the list, be as creative as you can, and seek counsel from others. All of your alternatives should represent possible ways to correct the difficulties you are experiencing.

Ed consulted his workforce, and over a period of several hours put together a list of four solutions:

1. Do little since this is the first time the problem has occurred. Ed should merely instruct his secretary to check her e-mail more often.
2. Have all incoming work e-mailed directly to Ed.
3. In Ed's absence, have all work e-mailed to his secretary.
4. Have all data sent directly by e-mail to the analysts with information copies to Ed and his secretary.

Ed is now ready to evaluate his alternatives.

Evaluate your alternatives.   This step asks you to look critically at the list of alternatives and to focus on their relative merits and disadvantages. In doing so, you must consider the restraints you have identified in step two. For some merits and disadvantages, you may wish to assign a relative point value to give either a higher or a lower importance to each.

Ed evaluates his first alternative as follows. The problem is new but could recur. It resulted from the fact that through habit, people have always e-mailed their items to Ed's secretary, not to Ed. She checks her e-mail regularly, but there are blocks of time when she is out of the office. For this reason, the first alternative is rejected.

Ed realizes that the alternatives require cooperation from people in other departments if they are to work. The fourth alternative is advantageous in that neither he nor his secretary need be present for the system to work. However, its major disadvantage is that all analysts would have to check their e-mail regularly for their work instead of getting it directly from Ed as in the past. The major disadvantage to the second and third alternatives is that a person must be present. If Ed and his secretary were absent, the current problem might then recur. Ed is now ready to move to step five.

Decide on the best alternative(s). At this step, the best alternative or combination of alternatives is chosen. The relative merits and disadvantages of each are considered, and the alternative offering the fewest serious disadvantages and the most merits is chosen. Keep in mind that after deciding and implementing, you may find that the problem still persists or that a new problem has arisen. For this reason, you may want to set up a contingency plan and be ready to implement other methods.

Ed has decided to go with his fourth alternative. It overcomes what Ed feels is the biggest disadvantage of the other two alternatives—that the physical presence of either himself or his secretary is required for them to work. Even though he will have to get outsiders to change their routing procedures, Ed feels that they will cooperate with little opposition. It will take little adjustment on their part.

Implement the decision and follow up. Without implementation, a decision helps no one. Everyone involved in the decision must be informed in advance of his individual roles and responsibilities. People must know what is expected of them and what is new and different. In addition, they must be committed to their roles if the solution is to work. After the decision is enacted, the results must be monitored.

Ed has contacted the heads of the various departments that supply his work and has been assured that the new procedure will be made known. Ed has instructed his analysts to check their e-mail for data files. Both Ed and his secretary will make it a habit to check on the analysts' receipt of e-mail data attachments. Ed sets the time when the new procedure will be implemented and arranges to monitor the results.

COMMON ELEMENTS IN DECISION-MAKING

Most supervisors are new to formal decision-making. Before you become a member of management's team, you have specific goals and orders, resources provided by your boss, and a problem solver represented by the boss. You may or may not be consulted when decisions have to be made. But once you become a manager, you soon realize the need to consult with others before, during, and after the period when a decision is made.

Most decisions share the following common elements:

- A situation that demands action
- Time pressures created by things getting steadily worse

- Incomplete information
- Some uncertainties that force you to take some risk
- The likelihood of costly consequences if your decision is wrong
- The likelihood of benefits from an effective decision
- The existence of at least two alternatives[18]

Given these elements, you have to gather what input you can from whatever sources are available in the time allotted for your decision. Keep in mind that others may have been down this path before you. Your boss, your peers, and your associates may have the experience and ideas that you lack. Use whatever help you can to avoid as many traps as possible. Your aim is to make the best decision you can given the resources and restraints that exist.

INTUITION IN DECISION-MAKING

In addition to employing rational approaches to decision-making, supervisors also need to consider their intuitions in some situations. This does not mean that supervisors should abandon rational analysis and rely on intuition for decision-making. Instead, supervisors should be aware that decision-making in some circumstances may benefit from an appropriate reliance on intuition. Interestingly, there is evidence that as one moves up the managerial hierarchy, the relative importance of intuition in decision-making tends to increase. While these skills are of greatest value at executive levels, supervisors also need to refine such skills as a part of their development. The value of intuition in decision-making has been recognized at the same time there has been dissatisfaction with excessive reliance on rational decision-making processes. Rational decision processes are less satisfactory where there is great need for speed, overwhelming masses of information, and a desire for creative solutions to problems.[19] These findings may be summarized as follows:

> Over the years, various management studies have found that executives routinely rely on their intuitions to solve complex problems when logical methods (such as cost-benefit analysis) simply won't do. In fact, the consensus is that the higher up on the corporate ladder people climb, the more they'll need well-honed business instincts.[20]

The former CEO of Johnson & Johnson, Ralph Larsen, has summarized the importance of such skills as follows:

> Very often, people will do a brilliant job up through the middle management levels, where it's very heavily quantitative in terms of the decision-making. But then they reach senior management, where the problems get more complex and ambiguous, and we discover that their judgment or intuition is not what it should be. And when that happens, it's a problem; it's a *big* problem."[21]

The role of intuition as a potentially valuable component of decision-making is better understood when it is considered that intuition involves thought processes that occur subconsciously. More specifically, intuition may be viewed as having origins in two sources. One source is expertise or tacit knowledge built up over time with experience. With such expertise, decision-makers may recognize similarities or patterns as a result of knowledge obtained from past experiences. The other source of intuition is attributed to gut feel or a sense of awareness, which is difficult to articulate.[22] The following definition of intuition incorporates these two sources:

> Knowledge of intuition has made significant advances in recent years, and it can now be understood as a composite phenomenon involving interplay between knowing (intuition-as-expertise) and sensing (intuition-as-feeling) . . . Intuition is a capacity for attaining direct knowledge or understanding without the apparent intrusion of rational thought or logical inference . . . some psychologists are now arguing that much, if not most, of cognition occurs automatically outside of consciousness.[23]

The appropriateness of intuition in decision-making varies according to the decision context as research indicates little need for intuition in decision-making on matters dealing with finance, capital expenditures, and operations. On the other hand, research indicates a role for intuition in decisions on such matters as human resource development, marketing, public relations, and research and development.[24] Nonetheless, supervisors should be cautious about the extent to which they rely on intuition to make decisions or substitute such processes for rational analysis. Intuition should play an important role in decision-making when time and resource limitations preclude more explicit analysis.[25] Furthermore, senior executives have emphasized the importance of not ignoring their instincts. For example, Ralph Larsen attributes a few of his bad decisions to circumstances when he did not consider his instincts. Similarly, Richard Abdoo, the former CEO of Wisconsin Energy Corporation, advises decision-makers to develop the ability to rely on their intuition instead of prolonging the decision until virtually all uncertainty has been removed because the decision will be too late by that time.[26]

Supervisors would be well advised to recognize that their gut feelings will often be wrong, and that they will need to develop a sense of the accuracy of their instincts. Such instincts are subject to errors of overconfidence, which will be discussed in the following section.[27]

ERRORS IN DECISION-MAKING

anchoring trap
a decision-making trap that places inordinate emphasis on the first information of which the decision-maker becomes aware

status-quo trap
a decision error that presumes that past conditions will remain in the future and places too much weight on maintaining the status quo

While this chapter has presented a rational model for decision-making, supervisors should also be aware that psychological traps can have profound effects on decisions. One such trap is called **anchoring,** which refers to a tendency for decision-makers to place inordinate emphasis on the first information of which he or she becomes aware related to the issue. For example, a purchaser of a used car is affected by anchoring if he or she prepares a counteroffer for the car almost entirely on the basis of the seller's asking price as opposed to the value of the car. Smart negotiators are well aware of the anchoring trap, and supervisors need to guard against the trap by obtaining information from many sources. Another countermeasure applies to the advice obtained from others. Supervisors should refrain from voicing their initial views because such views may anchor the positions suggested by advisors, and the advice will be confounded. Supervisors should also have developed their own initial ideas on the decision before seeking advice in order to prevent the advisor's view from serving as an anchor.[28]

Another threat to decision-making is called the **status-quo trap,** which presumes conditions existing in the past will continue in the future and that the status quo should be maintained. Interestingly, as decision-makers are provided with more alternatives, they tend to make decisions even more inclined to favor the status quo. **Sunk-cost traps** can have serious consequences as they prevent supervisors from discontinuing a course of action that is leading to poor results instead of writing off the investment as a loss or acknowledging the failure of the decision and moving on. The desire to avoid sunk-costs sometimes causes decisions-makers to irrationally escalate their commitment to a losing course of action. For example, you may have continued to repair an automobile because you want to recoup your previous investments in a new transmission, engine work, and so on. When all repairs are totaled, you recognize that you could have purchased a much better automobile if you had mentally written off your prior costs and had gotten rid of the car. Supervisors can avoid sunk cost traps by seeking guidance from associates and peers who had nothing to do with the previous decision as they can be objective.[29] "Remember the wise words of Warren Buffet: 'When you find yourself in a hole, the best thing you can do is stop digging.'"[30]

Decisions are also influenced by the **confirming-evidence trap** in which the decision-maker seeks advice for a decision, which he or she feels will be consistent with his or her inclinations. In order to avoid this trap, decision-makers need to pursue all evidence with the same effort, use a respected colleague to act as a devil's advocate to challenge your thinking on the intended decision, and avoid the use of leading questions when obtaining advice about a decision. **Framing,** which is also used as a means of persuasion, can also serve as a decision trap. Essentially, the context in which a decision is placed or framed can affect the decision. For example, if the cost of a piece of equipment is framed as a small percentage of the operating budget instead of actual dollars, a supervisor may be more inclined to authorize the expenditure. To guard against the framing trap, supervisors need to frame the decision in different fashions than it was posed, as the frame can be expected to have been carefully crafted by the person advocating a particular alternative.[31]

Finally, supervisors need to be aware of **estimating and forecasting traps** as most people assume that they are more accurate in such matters than the facts would warrant. The reason for this discrepancy between assumed accuracy and reality is that there is little feedback for most decision-makers on such forecasts. A related error is called the **overconfidence trap** in which decision-makers fail to set a sufficiently broad range for the minimum and maximum conditions of future events while they are confident that events will fall within a much narrower range. Supervisors need to devote careful consideration to the minimum and maximum conditions that could occur.[32]

Sharing the Decision Process

You should involve members of your work group in a decision if they have valuable input to give, if they are going to have to implement it, or if their commitment to the decision is essential to make it work. Probably the easiest way for a supervisor to get in trouble is to make decisions without the input of people who will be affected by the decision or who have expertise on the matter. This is a common mistake that causes a great deal of grief for both supervisors and employees.

One of the keys to good decision-making is to recognize that you will frequently have incomplete information for making the best decisions and that your associates may have critical information or may ask key questions in a group decision-making session that can

---

sunk-cost trap
failure to stop a course of action because of a reluctance to write off costs and acknowledge a previous mistake in making a decision

confirming-evidence trap
seeking information about a decision that is expected to align with one's initial inclinations

framing traps
being overly influenced by the context of the decision, which may have been crafted by an advocate to guide the decision-maker toward a preferred alternative

estimating and forecasting traps
assuming greater accuracy in one's estimates and forecasts than warranted

overconfidence trap
failure to anticipate a sufficiently broad range for the outcomes of a forecasted event

Learning Objective Number Six

lead to a superior decision. Supervisors sometimes make the mistake of deciding what to do and then simply go through the motions of seeking inputs from employees to make them feel that they were involved in the decision. In addition to being dishonest with employees, the supervisor has not taken advantage of information that may have affected the decision and the eventual outcome of the decision. Good supervisors understand that their promotion to a management role did not make them intellectually superior to their associates and that they need the input and best thinking of their employees for superior decisions. In addition, good decision-making often requires debate and conflict and unless employees understand that their inputs are valued, the best decisions will not be forthcoming. Conflict, debate, and questions are descriptive of the decision-making processes at well-managed companies, such as Gillette. In addition, it has been noted that questions from associates are very important to decision quality, and that higher ratios of questions to statements is a good indicator of a high-quality decision process.[33]

It is important to note that many decisions occur in a context of uncertainty, and supervisors are better prepared for such uncertainty when they make good decisions about the people that will be in their groups or teams. It has been observed that some of the best decisions are related to these staffing decisions. A good example of this is the response from Dick Cooley, who was the CEO at Wells Fargo, during the period leading up to major changes in the regulatory environment of the banking industry. There was so much uncertainty about what would occur that Cooley prepared by putting together a talented group of executives who would have the ability to make superior decisions in the future about what the bank should do after information became available.[34] It is difficult to understate the importance of having the right group of people who have the right attitudes to help move the unit forward.

> You are a bus driver. The bus, your company, is at a standstill, and it's your job to get it going. You have to decide where you're going, how you're going to get there, and who's going with you. Most people assume that great bus drivers (read: business leaders) immediately start the journey by announcing to the people on the bus where they're going—by setting a new direction . . . In fact, leaders of companies that go from good to great start not with "where" but with "who." They start by getting the right people on the bus, the wrong people off the bus, and the right people in the right seats . . . if you begin with "who," you can more easily adapt to a fast-changing world. If people get on your bus because of where they think it's going, you'll be in trouble when you get 10 miles down the road and discover that you need to change direction because the world has changed.[35]

Exhibit 2.8 offers some additional insights into when others should be involved in decisions. Note that the exhibit makes no recommendation to involve others when the problem stems from the behavior of a person and only that person's corrective action will solve the problem. In addition to the errors discussed in the previous section, groups are also vulnerable to other decision-making errors and biases.

DECISIONS ABOUT VALUING DIVERSITY

Most of us work in a culturally diverse workforce. To prosper in such a workforce, you must prepare yourself by valuing your own uniqueness and the diversity in others.

EXHIBIT 2.8	**When to involve others in decisions that you have to make.**

Involve others in the decision under the following conditions:

1. There is time for discussion and analysis; the decision does not have to be made immediately.

2. The decision affects the personal or business lives of the employees; their input and feedback will help you make a mutually acceptable decision.

3. Collective discussion would yield a better solution than simply mulling it over on your own.

4. The group should share responsibility for the decision with no individual being blamed if the decision produces an unsatisfactory result.

5. Others have information needed to solve the problem or their expertise will help you solve the problem.

6. Implementation requires group commitment and effort.

7. The members of the group need to develop their decision-making skills.

Supervisors, managers, and the organizations in which they work value diversity when they treat everyone fairly and with dignity and utilize their skills and abilities to the fullest extent. Diversity is given more than lip service when people from all races and genders feel accepted and are included at all levels in the organization's social and managerial hierarchy. Such treatment of all people who work in the organization satisfies ethical, moral, and performance rationales. In regard to the performance rationale, it is helpful to find evidence showing where diversity efforts have led to increased revenue or decreased costs.[36]

DIVERSITY

Here are five guidelines to help you with your efforts to value diversity:

1. *Know yourself and your own cultural background.* Identify any preconceived notions you hold about others, where these notions came from, and how they affect your interactions with others who are different from yourself.

2. *Work to identify negative stereotypes.* Identify inflexible sets of beliefs about groups of people, usually obtained through the hearsay of others rather than gained through your own experiences. Once they are identified, work to release yourself from the constraints these beliefs place on your thinking and interactions with others.

3. *Get to know your associates at work as individuals.* Learn from them about their cultures—their values, customs, and traditions. Attend workshops and seminars on cultural diversity. Read all that you can on the topic. Note the differences as well as the similarities between your culture and those of others with whom you work.

4. *Avoid being judgmental.* Approach each person as an individual and seek an understanding of what that person values and why. If you are uncertain about how to approach someone, ask her how best to do so. In everyday matters, the new golden rule is simple—treat people as they want to be

treated. As a team facilitator and team leader, your job is to get the most from all your associates and team members.

5. *Remember the Pygmalion effect.* The essence of the Pygmalion effect is that the subconscious performance expectations a manager has for employees will often affect the employees' performance. Accordingly, when supervisors have expectations that their employees will perform at a high level, the supervisors are likely to treat their people in a manner that facilitates high performance. Conversely, when supervisors have expectations that their employees will not perform well, they will probably treat them in a manner that causes poorer performance.[37] In the context of diversity, some supervisors may have performance expectations of new employees based solely on race or gender. Because such supervisors may feel that a female or minority employee will not perform as well as others, it is important for them to develop and periodically conduct a mental review of profiles of individuals from the stereotyped group who are outstanding performers.

MANAGING YOUR TIME

We all have the same amount of time in each day. We vary only in how we use that time. Studies have indicated that most of us waste time on the job in a variety of ways. We may make or accept personal phone calls. We may regularly stretch breaks by several minutes. We may fail to plan our work, reacting to things as they come, without giving the work to be done a timetable or priority. If you often find yourself working late, taking work home, and rushing to meet deadlines, you have a time management problem. People who use time well have enough time for their tasks, are able to train employees and delegate, can take on additional duties, and have time for themselves. Using time well gives us a sense of pride, whereas wasting it gives us a sense of guilt and frustration.

A good way to improve your use of time is to start keeping a record of how you use your time at present. Record your use of time at work by stopping each hour (or after each task is completed) to record how much time you just spent and on what you spent it. This record will let you know very quickly at the end of each day where you wasted time and where you used it productively.

KEEPING A TIME LOG

A daily time log provides an easy way for you to list the activities you perform each day, to record the time each activity took, and to classify each activity as regular, recurring, or one that is unexpected or unusual. The regular activities routinely make up a part of each working day: evaluating associates, planning your work schedule, attending planned-for meetings, and preparing regular reports. The unexpected activities include unscheduled visitors (drop-ins), unexpected telephone calls, and crises—problems that could not have been foreseen. After a few days, some interesting patterns will emerge. You will have a clear understanding of how you are using time, and you will then be ready to start planning in a realistic way for using it more efficiently.

CATEGORIZING WORK

By dividing your work into categories, you can more effectively execute tasks and assign priorities to them. For example, consider the pile of work on your desk each morning. There is probably work left over from preceding days: the mail, e-mail, memos and work generated by others, and various notes that you have left for yourself. Divide this work into three categories: read (then file or discard), to be delegated, and must do. Each task on your desk will fall into one of these categories. Memos sent to keep you informed belong in the first category. Work you want others to act on belongs to the second. Work only you can do belongs to the third. For the work to be assigned to others, determine a due date based on when it must be completed. Assess your third category from two points of view: how much time each task will take and by what date it must be completed. Then block out the time you will need on your calendar, working ahead as time allows and planning early completions where possible.

ELIMINATING INTERRUPTIONS

Your time log will list the unnecessary interruptions that have taken place. Consider what to do about them. For most supervisors, unexpected phone calls are among the most frequent sources of interruption, second only to unplanned-for visitors who drop by to shoot the breeze or seek your assistance. If you have a secretary, let him screen your calls. Calls can be classified in three ways: deal with now, I'll get back to you, or leave your message. Ask people to leave brief memos in writing or on your voice mail or e-mail instead of using the telephone. Drop-in visitors can be asked, courteously, to book an appointment, at a mutually acceptable time and place, so that you will have enough time to deal with their concerns. Social visits can wait for breaks and lunch.

USING DAILY PLANNERS

The use of a daily planner and time log can help you start getting your time at work under control. In addition to paper planners, various computer software packages can also help you manage your time. Pocket-sized computers called personal information managers (PIMs), personal data assistants (PDAs), and smart phones (combinations of cellular phones and PIMs) can perform a variety of tasks, such as automatic scheduling of appointments, maintaining address lists, sorting lists, establishing priorities, displaying task lists, providing access to e-mail and stock market reports, storing telephone numbers, and printing calendars.[38] By keeping a time log and reviewing it each day, you will learn how realistic your planning of time and activities has been and how you can make it more accurate in the future. It won't be too long before you are blocking out time in your head, as well as on paper, and making better use of it. Then you can eliminate the log and rely on your choice of planning tools to manage your time.

USING SPARE TIME

Use your previously unproductive time productively. You can employ time spent traveling to and from work in your car or on a train to catch up on essential, work-related tapes or reading. You can make notes with a notepad and pen, on a portable digital recorder, or with a PIM. Some computerized devices allow you to write on a hand-held computer and may offer a pager, address book, fax, and phone. Capture and store your good ideas as they occur to you. When you anticipate having to wait for an appointment, take work with you. By doing these things, you will become more accomplished and will look good to others as well as to yourself. These suggestions will also help you preserve sufficient time for your life away from work and achieve a balance between work and family life. An anthropologist studying work behavior in the Silicon Valley has reported an example of poor balance. In a play on words, he reported the actions of an executive who "quit his family to spend more time at work."[39]

INSTANT REPLAY

1. Management is an activity that uses the functions of planning, organizing, directing, and controlling human and material resources for the purpose of achieving stated goals.

2. A manager is a member of a team of paid decision-makers who gets things done with and through others by executing the four management functions. Managers occupy positions of formal authority in an organization.

3. Managers work for formal organizations, which have clearly stated purposes and goals, a division of labor among specialists, a rational structure or design, and a clearly defined hierarchy of authority and accountability.

4. Power flows to a person from two sources: the job she holds and the skills, experience, and personality she possesses.

5. The management hierarchy consists of three levels inherent in most businesses: top, middle, and supervisory or operating.

6. Staff managers may exercise functional authority over many other managers.

7. There are many decision traps, which supervisors should try to avoid when making decisions.

8. Managing time is as important to a supervisor as managing a career. Time, like other resources, must be used effectively and efficiently.

QUESTIONS FOR CLASS DISCUSSION

1. Can you define this chapter's key terms?

2. What are the essential elements of any formal organization and the definition of each element?

3. What are the steps you should take to delegate?

4. What are the levels of the management hierarchy and the activities performed by each level?

5. What are the major functions performed by all managers?

6. What are the steps in this chapter's decision-making model, and what happens in each step?

7. What is the role of intuition in decision-making?

8. In general, what kinds of decisions require the involvement of your employees?

9. What are the various decision traps of which supervisors should be aware?

10. How can you use a time log and a daily planner to help you improve your use of time?

ASSESS THIS SITUATION

Purpose: To assess your decision-making skills.

Your Task: Take the following quiz by agreeing or disagreeing with each statement, based on you experiences in your organization.

Agree	*Disagree*	
○	○	1. When making a difficult decision, I generally seek advice from peers and associates with whom I get along with the best.
○	○	2. When negotiating a purchase, I tend to decide my counter-offer on the basis of the seller's initial offer as opposed making a more extreme lower counter-offer.
○	○	3. After being put on hold for a long time while making a telephone call, I decide to stay on the line because I have already invested a long time waiting on hold.
○	○	4. When making a forecast of a future event, there is typically a relatively small difference between my worst case and best case scenarios.
○	○	5. My usual approach to decisions about possible changes is to rely heavily on the premise that the present way of doing things will probably not need to be changed in the future.
○	○	6. When making decisions, I prefer not to consult with the employees in my unit because it is too time consuming to have discussions with them.

○	○	7. I try to disourage conflict and debate in group decision-making sessions.
○	○	8. I tend to exclude those who march to a different drummer from group decision-making sessions.

If you disagreed with these statements then you are on your way to developing better decision-making skills.

SKILL BUILDING EXERCISE 2.1

Juanita Alvarez is a relatively new supervisor at the management consulting firm of Furman & Associates. She was promoted because of her expertise in computer programming—she was considered the best of seven department members—and is now overseeing the work of six former coworkers.

Juanita prides herself on her continuing efforts to stay current in her field, believing that maintaining her expertise is the best way to influence her associates. She is reluctant to delegate high-profile jobs to her associates because she fears they will not be able to do them as well as she can. She is afraid of the consequences that can result from a job poorly done, especially on projects assigned by top management.

Her employees are all young, well trained (by Juanita's predecessor), and eager to grow in their fields. All are specialists to some extent, but most recognize that they need a wide variety of programming experiences in order to advance their pay and careers. When asked by her associates for a role in the tougher assignments, Juanita usually turns them down. When asked for assistance on a project, she prefers to give her associates only as much as she feels they need to complete a project.

Your Task: Work by yourself or in small groups to identify the problems that Juanita is likely to encounter with her current approach. Compare her actions with the principles discussed in this chapter. What are the ethical issues for Juanita and her associates? If you were her boss, what advice would you have for her? Develop an action plan for Juanita that will (1) address the underlying concerns that are motivating her behavior and (2) steps she needs to take to remedy the situation.

SKILL BUILDING WRITING EXERCISE 2.2

As discussed in this chapter, supervisors have several sources of power, which reside in their formal position in the organizational hierarchy, the power that comes from their personal attributes, such as charisma, and the power that comes from their expertise and capabilities. One of the key determinants of a supervisor's effectiveness hinges on whether the supervisors' employees, peers, and higher managers sense that he or she has power. Those supervisors who have power can use it to influence people and the allocation of resources for the good of the organization and its employees. Also, supervisors can use their power for their personal benefit or self-gratification.

Your Task: Visualize the behaviors of several different supervisors or managers in which there appears to be an application of power. Use these mental pictures to: (1) Describe several indicators of power that signal that a supervisor has a substantial amount of power. (2) Describe several indicators of a lack of power. (3) Identify behaviors or actions that are applications of a supervisor's power for the good of the organization and employees. (4) Identify several behaviors or actions that appear to be intended only for the self-gratification of a supervisor.

CASE 2.1   Welcome to KVM

Carl Foster looked forward to starting his new job as director of the headquarters systems support department at KVM Snack Foods. He was excited about the job because he had finally made it into the managerial ranks. In his previous company, REM Investments, he had been in a similar department but had been unable to advance beyond a senior systems coordinator position. He told several of his old colleagues about getting the job and said, "I think I'm going to like being a director at KVM. I'll have a big office, a reserved parking place, and my own secretary."

On his first day as manager at KVM, Carl met with his boss, Wes Taylor, the vice president for corporate information services. One of the things Wes told him was, "We need to place more emphasis on introducing leading-edge systems here. Your predecessor, Betty Carson, did a good job, but we need to move forward. I like the ideas you talked about during your interview for introducing new technology. You're going to have to get the word out that our priorities have shifted a bit."

In the following weeks, Carl met with all the members of departments using the systems his unit supported. After telling them how delighted he was to be on board and a bit about his background, he told them that fewer services would be offered by his department because it would concentrate on more important activities. While the people who attended the meetings were happy to have Carl on board and wanted to make him feel welcomed at KVM, they were not pleased to hear that his department would be supplying fewer services. No one actually voiced a complaint at the meetings, but after Carl made the announcements about changed priorities and his department's intention to provide fewer "hand-holding services" the meetings generally became unusually quiet.

A few days after the last of his meetings with the departments, Carl was walking down the hallway when Gil Smith, one of the more experienced members of the marketing group, approached him. Gil said, "I'd like to talk to you about getting some support for adapting software. We want to use this software on laptop computers in focus groups that need to be run over the next few weeks." Carl said, "Just call my secretary for an appointment, and I would be happy to meet with you." Gil was fuming as he returned to his office and passed Bill Kelly in the suite. He said to Bill, "Can you believe this one. I just told Carl Foster that I needed to see him about getting some help with software for focus groups and he told me to make an appointment!" Bill said, "This is not good news. It's not like they're overwhelmed with people walking in down there. I wish Betty Carson hadn't retired."

A couple of weeks later, on Tuesday, Luis Ortiz, another member of the marketing staff, went down to see Carl. Luis was worried about a problem in setting up the group decision support system (GSS) for some supermarket executives the next day. Carl's secretary was not in, and Luis walked into Carl's office. Luis said, "Carl, the GSS isn't working like it should. I made prior arrangements for support from your department, but the system isn't working right. It has to be working tomorrow morning for the meeting with the supermarket executives." Luis was surprised when Carl responded, "I'm too busy preparing for a briefing for the Executive Committee on Friday. Have Jim help you." Unfortunately, Carl's assistant, Jim Frazier, was out and did not return to the office until almost 5:30. Jim was able to help for only 30 minutes before he had to leave for the airport. Luis and two other non-technical people from marketing worked until 11:30 that night. Fortunately, they were able to get most of the features of the GSS working for the 8:00 A.M. session the next day.

After the session with the supermarket executives, Luis was fuming as he walked into the office of his boss, Sharon Armstrong, the vice president of marketing. Sharon said, "What's wrong?" Luis said, "We were really lucky. The GSS held together until the last task. I'm absolutely exhausted. What are you going to do about Carl Foster? We need help, and he's not providing it." Sharon replied, "I understand. I've been hearing from others about him as well. We've got a real problem with him. He's going to have to change how he deals with other units. I don't know why he didn't help you. Carl only has five people to manage, and one of them is his secretary! Wes told him three weeks ago that he would be making a briefing to the Executive Committee. Unfortunately, Wes seems to think only about the needs of information services, and Carl appears to be heading in the same direction. I'm going to talk to Carl today."

Questions

1. Evaluate Carl's performance and his approach to supervision.

2. How could this situation have been avoided? Identify any actions of others that may have contributed to the problem.

3. If you were Sharon Armstrong, what would you do? What authority issues are involved here?

4. How do you think Wes Taylor will react after Sharon visits Carl?

CASE 2.2   It's Not Easy Riding on the MTA

Ellsworth Carpenter, the new director of the Metropolitan Transit Authority (MTA), thought about what he should do next to turn things around. He had been a star performer for the city and had succeeded in turning around bad situations, the most recent being the Water Line Maintenance Department. As a result of his past successes, the city manager asked him to take over the MTA. Ellsworth had just returned from a meeting with Greg Williams, the MTA's operations manager; Pat Dowling, the head of MTA's maintenance unit; Trisha Moore, the head of MTA's accounting and purchasing section; Jennifer Ho, the assistant city manager; and Harvey Jones, the business agent for the Amalgamated Transit Union.

Right from the start, the meeting had been acrimonious. The subject had been low morale among the MTA's bus drivers and the increasing complaints by customers about discourteous drivers. Early in the meeting, Harvey Jones said, "If things don't get better quickly, the drivers will picket at several locations throughout the city, including in front of City Hall. We're also going to demand 10 percent raises!" Greg Williams, the operations manager, fired back that the drivers were to blame for much of the situation. He felt that the supervisors should be stricter with the drivers, that they needed to put in more controls, and that they should fire the discourteous drivers. In response Harvey Jones said, "Haven't you guys here at the MTA learned that organizations that treat their drivers well find that the drivers then treat the customers well? This is not rocket science we're dealing with here. Why don't you try treating the drivers better?"

Jennifer Ho then said that the city manager was getting lots of complaints about driver discourtesy and bus breakdowns. At that point, Pat Dowling became defensive and said, "The drivers are too hard on the buses. If they would be more careful, the buses wouldn't break down! Besides, my guys can't get repair parts quickly enough because of all the red tape imposed on us by accounting and purchasing." Trisha Moore then shot back, "The maintenance people never file reports on time and sometimes their papers are so smudged with grease that we can't read them. Furthermore, their requisitions are usually incorrect and everything is submitted as a rush job. Don't you guys ever plan ahead?" Pat Dowling countered by saying, "My guys are too busy supervising repairs. They don't have time for paperwork. You ought to come out of your office and see what it's like in the shop." The bickering continued for several minutes until Ellsworth called the meeting to a halt. He told the group that they would reconvene in three days.

Ellsworth knew there were problems with the MTA, but he was surprised by the magnitude of what he found. He had been in the job only two weeks, but he had spent most of the time walking around and talking to drivers, mechanics, schedulers, and supervisors. He found numerous symptoms of bad management. For example, one of the more irksome practices required drivers to show their driver's licenses to their supervisors each day before they left on their routes. There were no exceptions, even for bus drivers who had worked for the MTA for 25 years. Another driver showed Ellsworth the MTA rule book. He said, "Do you know that there are 156 rules in this book that tell us such things as not to spit on the floor, not to watch portable televisions while driving the bus, and to get the passengers off the bus if it catches on fire? They must think we're idiots! How would you feel if someone treated you like this?" Later, Ellsworth asked Greg Williams about the rules. Greg said, "Each one of the rules was put in the book because we've had drivers do exactly those things! Three years ago, a bus caught on fire and the driver just jumped off without trying to help the passengers. And during the World Cup last year one driver was watching it on his portable TV while he was driving!"

There was also a problem with overtime. The city's auditors and the local newspaper had found that approximately 25 of the 500 MTA drivers made over $60,000 last year because they worked so much overtime. Since this amount was far above the average driver's salary, Ellsworth knew that there were serious problems somewhere. In addition, the drivers felt that their supervisors acted more like police officers than managers. For example, supervisors regularly drove to points on the routes to check on whether the buses arrived and departed on schedule. Ellsworth had asked Greg Williams about this practice, and Williams said that every city bus operation does the same thing. He said that drivers tend to "run hot" (early) before quitting time if they are not monitored and that this is a particularly serious problem because passengers may arrive at the bus stops after buses have already departed.

Source: A few of the features of this fictitious case are based on conditions reported in an article by Curtis Howell. "Many Bus Drivers Are Unhappy with DART," *Dallas Morning News* (April 8, 1997): 1A, 4A.

Questions

1. How do you think the typical MTA supervisor views the bus drivers?
2. What supervisory and managerial deficiencies are likely causes of the MTA's problems?
3. How are the MTA's organizational structure and its line and staff authority contributing to the problems?
4. What do you recommend that Ellsworth do next?

REFERENCES

[1] *Forbes,* "Thoughts on the Business of Life," (October 10, 2005): 34.

[2] Rosenbaum, David E. "Study Ranks Homeland Security Dept. Lowest in Morale," *New York Times,* (October 16, 2005).

[3] Ibid.

[4] Rosenbaum, David E. "Study Ranks Homeland Security Dept. Lowest in Morale," *New York Times,* (October 16, 2005) Copyright © (2007) by the New York Times Co. Reprinted with permission.

[5] Ibid.

[6] Hamel, Gary, and Prahalad, C. K. "Seeing the Future First," *Fortune* (September 5, 1994): 64, 66–67, 70.

[7] Katzenbach, Jon R. "The Discipline of Teams," *Harvard Business Review,* (July/August 2005): 162–171.

[8] Whole Foods Market, Form 10-K for fiscal year ending September 25, 2005 (December 8, 2005): p. 3.

[9] Southwest Airlines, Form 10-K for fiscal year ending December 31, 2004 (February 4, 2005): p.3.

[10] Southwest Airlines website (October 16, 2005): *www.southwest.com/about_swa/mission.html.*

[11] Starbucks Coffee, *Starbucks Coffee Fiscal 2004 Annual Report,* p. 4.

[12] Kotter, John P. *Leading Change.* Boston: Harvard Business School Press, 1996: 68–69.

[13] Wyeth website (October 15, 2005): *www.wyeth.com/about/mission.asp.*

[14] Weinberg, Neil. "Scare Tactics," *Forbes* (March 4, 2002): 84.

[15] Crabb, Steve, and Johnson, Rebecca. "Press for Success," *People Management* (November 9, 2000): 30.

[16] Stoner, James A. F. *Management.* Englewood Cliffs, NJ: Prentice Hall (1982): 310.

[17] Hymowitz, Carol. "In Times of Trouble, The Best of Leaders Listen to Dissenters," *Wall Street Journal* (November 13, 2001): B1.

[18] Uris, Auren. *The Executive Deskbook,* 2nd ed. New York: Van Nostrand Reinhold (1986): 66.

[19] Sadler-Smith, Eugene, and Shefy, Erella. "The Intuitive Executive: Understanding and Applying 'Gut Feel' in Decision-Making," *Academy of Management Executive* (November 2004): 76–91.

[20] Hayashi. Alden M. "When to Trust Your Gut," *Harvard Business Review,* (February 2001): 60–61.

[21] Hayashi. "When to Trust Your Gut," 61.

[22] Hayashi. "When to Trust Your Gut."

[23] Sadler-Smith and Shefy, "The Intuitive Executive: Understanding and Applying 'Gut Feel' in Decision-Making," 76–78.

[24] Sadler-Smith and Shefy. "The Intuitive Executive: Understanding and Applying 'Gut Feel' in Decision-Making."

[25] Miller, C. Chet, and Ireland, R. Duane. "Intuition in Strategic Decision Making: Friend or Foe in the Fast-Paced 21st Century?" *Academy of Management Executive,* (February 2005): 19–30.

[26] Hayashi. "When to Trust Your Gut," 61.

[27] Hayashi. "When to Trust Your Gut."

[28] Hammond, John S., Keeney, Ralph L., and Raiffa, Howard. "The Hidden Traps in Decision Making," *Harvard Business Review,* (September/October 1998): 47–58.

[29] Ibid.

[30] Hammond, Keeney, and Raiffa, "The Hidden Traps in Decision Making," 52.

[31] Hammond, Keeney, and Raiffa, "The Hidden Traps in Decision Making."

[32] Ibid.

[33] Useem, Jerry. "Jim Collins on Tough Calls," *Fortune* (June 27, 2005): 89–94.

[34] Useem. "Jim Collins on Tough Calls."

[35] Collins, Jim. "Good Great," *Fast Company,* (October 2001): 90–99.

[36] Gilbert, Jacqueline A., and Ivancevich, John M. "Valuing Diversity: A Tale of Two Organizations," *Academy of Management Executive* (February 2000): 93–105.

[37] Thomas, David A., and Wetlaufer, Suzy. "A Question of Color: A Debate on Race in the U.S. Workplace," *Harvard Business Review* (September–October 1997): 118–132.

[38] *Fortune,* "It's a Phone! It's a PDA! But Wait, There's More!" (March 5, 2001): 240. *InfoWorld,* "The New Shape of Mobile Communication" (April 23, 2001): 65–66.

[39] Kaplan, David A. "Studying the Gearheads," *Newsweek* (August 3, 1998): 62.

3

CHAPTER

"The secret of managing is to keep the guys who hate you away from the guys who are undecided."

Casey Stengel
Manager, New York Yankees[1]

Objectives

After reading and discussing this chapter, you should be able to do the following:

1. List and briefly explain the steps in the planning process.
2. Contrast the bureaucratic/mechanistic organization to the organic organization.
3. List and briefly define the principles of organizing.
4. List and briefly explain the steps in the organizing process.
5. List and briefly explain the specific activities that are part of directing.
6. List and briefly explain the essential steps in the control process.
7. List and briefly describe the kinds of controls used by managers.
8. Describe ways in which a supervisor can coordinate his or her operations.

Management Problems at the Federal Emergency Management Agency

In late August 2005, Hurricane Katrina hit New Orleans and the surrounding Gulf Coast region, including Louisiana, Mississippi, and Alabama, with devastating Category 4 winds and huge tidal waves. The hurricane's destructiveness made it one of the worst natural disasters, in terms of the breadth and magnitude of damage, in U.S. history. The death toll was in the thousands and families were broken up and scattered throughout several states in the confusion of the evacuation. Most of New Orleans was under water after the levees broke on August 29, and entire towns were wiped out. Hundreds of thousands of people lost their homes, and businesses were destroyed. Cities lost their sources of revenues and had to lay off employees because there were no sales of goods on which taxes were paid.[2]

One of the failures revealed by this national tragedy was the ineffectiveness of the Federal Emergency Management Agency (FEMA), which failed to act until

Management
Functions

several days after the hurricane struck. FEMA's glaring failures resulted from fundamental lapses in management functions, such as coordinating, directing, and planning. While such failures extended to the very top level of the organization and far beyond the supervisory level, they indicate how the managerial basics, which are essential for supervisory effectiveness, were not being addressed even at the top levels of the organization. Millions of Americans and television viewers from throughout the world saw thousands of citizens of New Orleans trapped at the New Orleans Convention Center without food, water, medical care, or any of the essentials of life. Dead bodies were left on the streets for days in plain view of millions of televisions viewers.[3] Large numbers of buses, which the local governments could have used to transport thousands of evacuees out of the city, sat ruined in perfect alignment in flooded parking lots.[4] Incredibly, FEMA officials claimed that they were unaware of the situation at the convention center until it was brought to their attention by television viewers.[5]

Interesting, FEMA had been planning for exactly the situation, which occurred with Katrina, because in 2004, the agency paid $1 million for a study of the expected consequences of a Category 3 hurricane in southeast Louisiana. A report from the study stated that local governmental authorities would be unable to cope with the massive damage:[6]

Floodwaters would surge over levees, creating high casualties and forcing a mass evacuation. It said that hundreds of thousands of homes would be destroyed, a half-million people left homeless, and "all 40 medical facilities in the impacted area isolated and useless," according to The Associated Press.[7]

Unfortunately, the failure of FEMA to implement planning on a timely basis reveals a lapse in one of the other basic functions of management—follow-up. Finally, there was confusion during the hurricane relief efforts as to who was in charge. Workers received contradictory orders from various authorities and relief was delayed as a result of the confusion. This confusion revealed another failure in one of the organizing principles of management—unity of command, which means that there needs to be a clear understanding of who is in charge.[8]

Questions for Thought

1. What are the actions that supervisors must take to ensure that plans are implemented or that workers take effective action when the unexpected occurs?
2. What are some of the activities that are required for effective coordination?

Introduction

The four major functions of a manager are planning, organizing, directing, and controlling. These represent the major sets of activities performed daily by all managers and autonomous teams. In this chapter, we examine these functions in detail with an emphasis on how you as a supervisor, team facilitator, or team leader can execute each. Planning prepares for the future, whereas organizing establishes a structure through which the decisions you and your people make can be implemented. Directing and controlling activities put resources and decisions into action. These activities also involve monitoring performance and evaluating results.

Three sets of activities—decision making, communicating, and coordinating—are part of every manager's and team's daily routines. You do these activities simultaneously, as you perform each function. Although our analysis treats each function separately, keep in mind that all the functions are interrelated and interdependent. For example, planning is at the heart of the other functions; you must think ahead, set objectives, and determine needed resources as the first step in planning, organizing, directing, and controlling.

PLANNING

planning
the management function through which managers decide how they will proceed toward future goal accomplishment

You must first decide where you want to go and what you want to achieve before you commit any of your resources to the journey or the quest. **Planning** is the management function through which managers decide what they want to or must achieve and how they are going to do so. The goals to be achieved may be set by individual managers or teams, or higher-level managers may set them. We will examine the flow and parts of planning in a formal organization next.

PHILOSOPHY OF MANAGEMENT

The ways in which the management of a company thinks about and acts toward people and business events are known as its philosophy of management. An organization's

Development of a new General Motors vehicle involved cross-functional teams and a strong commitment to quality.

Aflac's principles and values.	EXHIBIT 3.1

Guiding Principles

- Offer quality products and services at competitive prices and use new technology to better serve our policyholders.

- Build better value for our shareholders.

- Supply quality service for our agents.

- Provide an enriching and rewarding workplace for our employees.

Values

- Treat individuals with care, respect, dignity, and fairness.

- Provide security and peace of mind.

- Promote a positive environment, caring culture, and team spirit that extends to the community.

- Offer opportunities for growth and advancement.

- Encourage camaraderie and fun.

Source: Extracted from Aflac's website, (January 22, 2006), www.aflac.com/us/en/aboutaflac/missionandvalues.aspx.

management philosophy is largely determined by the attitudes, values, and guiding principles held by the managers with the most influence—usually top management. The philosophy results in predictable approaches to executing each of the management functions. All managers have a philosophy that affects their thinking and behaviors. Exhibit 3.1 highlights guiding principles and values at Aflac, which is frequently on the lists of the best companies for which to work. The principles in Exhibit 3.1, which describe the positive way in which employees will be treated, reflect Aflac's management principles and values.

Like organizations, you have a personal philosophy of management. You have developed, through your experiences, predictable patterns of behavior that are based on your attitudes toward people, your job, your company environment, and your perception of your roles in your company. Your individual ways of approaching people, problems, and events make you unique as a person and as a manager. Your philosophy colors all of your judgments and, therefore, your decisions and their results.

Our values and beliefs about various individuals and groups, whose backgrounds are different from our own, form our philosophies and affect our ways of thinking about and interacting with them. Equal employment opportunity laws, business practices,

DIVERSITY

and America's population mix bring diversity to the workplace. The job of team leaders and team facilitators then becomes one of creating pluralism—allowing each person to maintain identity and then finding ways to celebrate and effectively utilize the uniqueness of each person.

Mission and Vision Statements

Every organization needs a mission: the formal statement about the central purpose behind its existence—its reason for being. Top management articulates the corporate vision of where the organization is headed and to what it wants to commit its resources in the short and long run.

Once these statements have been constructed, all the people in the organization must know about them and subscribe to them. Before you and your associates engage in any activities, make certain that what you plan to do conforms to your organization's vision and mission. Furthermore, supervisors and employees must understand how the mission should be translated for their units and circumstances. The following situation encountered by Norman Chambers, former CEO of the marine construction firm Rockwater, is illustrative:

> Shortly after distributing . . . [the] mission statement, Chambers received a phone call from a project manager on a drilling platform in the middle of the North Sea. "Norm, I want you to know that I believe in the mission statement. I want to act in accordance with the mission statement. I'm here with my customer. What am I supposed to do? How should I be behaving each day, over the life of this project, to deliver on our mission statement?" Chambers realized that there was a large void between the mission statement and employees' day-to-day actions.[9]

Goals or objectives serve as the mechanism for translating the mission into day-to-day actions.

Goals

goal
the objective, target, or end result expected from the execution of programs, tasks, and activities

From an organizational perspective, **goals** are defined as "a desired future state that the organization attempts to realize."[10] Thus, the outcomes that managers decide to work to achieve are known as their goals or objectives. A typical goal for a company might be to reduce expenses by 10 percent over the next two months. This goal meets important criteria of being both time-specific and quantifiable. The company-wide goal must be translated into divisional, departmental, team, and individual goals. Thus, another criterion for effective goals is specificity. As goals are being formulated, the resources needed to achieve them should be determined. There is little point in setting goals that are beyond the capabilities of a company, group, or individual to achieve.

As a supervisor, many of your goals and those of your team are determined for you by higher levels of management. The other goals you set must not contradict those set at higher levels. Your goals determine the roles you and your associates will play in achieving upper management's goals. In addition, your unit's or team's goals must be coordinated with the goals set in other areas of the company to avoid duplication of effort. Once your goals have been determined, they should be precisely stated, communicated, and kept constantly in mind by all concerned until they are achieved.

Two goals on which you must constantly focus are quality improvement and productivity. A case in point relates to the quality and productivity achieved by auto industry suppliers. Ford Motor Company has been challenged by quality problems, recalling several vehicles for safety concerns, such as with the Ford Explorer. The company also had to recall another Ford model five times for safety reasons. Because of such problems Ford has imposed tougher quality standards on its suppliers and requires them to meet a monthly quality score. The company plans to raise these quality standards on an annual basis in the future.[11] In order to help its suppliers meet the new and tighter quality standards, Ford has sent its own engineers to its suppliers' plants to help with manufacturing processes, just as Toyota and Honda have done in the past.[12]

POLICIES

The broad guidelines for management action that have been formulated by members of top management are known as policies. They are based on top managers' philosophies and the company's mission and vision. **Policies** are used to coordinate and promote uniformity in the conduct of the business and in the behavior of associates. Policies tell managers what top management wants to encourage or what it hopes to achieve, such as promoting diversity and empowerment. The following excerpt from ExxonMobil's employment policies and practices provides an example of such policies.

> In addition to providing equal employment opportunity, we also undertake special efforts to:
>
> - Create and support educational programs and recruiting sources and practices that facilitate employment and career development of minorities and women;
> - Develop and offer work arrangements that help to meet the needs of the diverse workforce in balancing work and family obligations.
> - Foster a work environment free from sexual, racial, or other harassment;
> - Make reasonable accommodations that enable qualified disabled individuals to perform the essential functions of their jobs; and
> - Emphasize management responsibility in these matters at every level of the organization.[13]

Policies affect your role as a supervisor because you must act within their limits when carrying out your duties. For instance, the company policy on recruiting and hiring presented in Exhibit 3.2 requires supervisors to consider all applicants equally and seek a wide diversity in applicants.

RULES

Inflexible guides for the behavior of employees at work are known as the company **rules**. They are specific directions that govern the way people should act on the job. Many are prohibitions, such as no smoking while on the job or in certain locations; others are

policy
a broad guideline constructed by top management to influence managers' approaches to solving problems and dealing with recurring situations

DIVERSITY

rule
a regulation on human conduct at work

EXHIBIT 3.2	**A policy prohibiting discrimination.**

There shall be no discrimination for or against any applicant or for or against any current employee because of his or her race, creed, color, national origin, sex, sexual orientation, marital status, age, or handicap or membership or lawful participation in the activities of any organization or union or because of his or her refusal to join or participate in the activities of any organization or union. Moreover, the company shall adhere to an affirmative action program with each functional division's hiring, promotions, transfers, and other ongoing human resource activities.

simply instructions, such as "turn lights off when they are not in use." Rules promote safety and security; they are aimed at conserving resources and preventing problems from arising during the company's operations. Examples of rules that come from a labor agreement include those that cover assigning overtime and disciplinary procedures.

Supervisors find that employees tend to obey reasonable rules while they tend not to obey those that are unreasonable. In general, rules are reasonable when they are needed for safety or to promote operational efficiency. Unfortunately, organizations sometimes have unreasonable rules. They sometimes have too many rules as well—a condition that contributes to rule violations. Unnecessary rules result when managers are reluctant to confront individuals about unreasonable behavior. Instead of dealing with the individual, managers sometimes issue new rules prohibiting the behavior and then apply them to all employees. Employees who follow rules then have more rules to obey. Unfortunately, the individual whose behavior prompted the new rules may not follow them unless carefully monitored.

When there are too many rules employees typically learn that some are outdated and that others are simply not enforced. While supervisors sometimes deny that their organizations have too many rules, when asked if any rules are unenforced they generally agree. Upon reflection they often conclude that indeed, their organization has too many rules. When there are too many rules, employees observe instances when rules are not enforced. Inconsistent rule enforcement leads to perceptions of unfair treatment and makes it difficult for employees to distinguish between important rules that should be obeyed and those that are unimportant.

Nordstrom has a reputation for good management. One of its distinctive management practices is that the company has few rules. In fact, its employee handbook consists of one small card. In addition to reaffirming that the company's "number one goal is to provide outstanding customer service," the card also specifies the rules. The company's only rule is the following: "Use your good judgment in all situations."[14] Nordstrom is able to rely on its employees' good judgment because the retailer is highly selective in its hiring practices, it invests heavily in training, and it has a strong organizational culture that serves to guide employee behavior in the absence of rules.

Mars, Incorporated, the candy maker, is a $14 billion dollar business with factories in 28 countries and over 30,000 employees. The company is another example of a company that strives to minimize rules. It also has a strong organizational culture that provides guidance for appropriate behavior. In spite of its size, Mars has "only two human resources people at corporate headquarters. It has a culture of the utmost fairness, not because of corporate-wide rules, regulations and red tape, but simply because the division heads are expected to treat people with respect."[15]

In addition to company rules, various local, state, and federal laws determine rules for the workplace. Such is the case with the Occupational Safety and Health Act (OSHA). It is the source of many rules related to both safe and healthful conduct at work.

PROGRAMS

Once goals are established for each department or for the entire organization, plans must be developed to achieve them. A **program** is such a plan. It starts with the goal to be achieved (the "what" of the plan); identifies the tasks required; and specifies the who, when, where, how, and how much that are needed. The required people, time allowed, methods to be employed, and dollars that are allotted are all pieces of a program. Most programs are single-use plans. Your budget is but one example. It is created to guide you for a specific period and is replaced by a new one when its time frame expires. Other programs, called *standing plans,* deal with ongoing activities such as hiring, payroll preparation, and customer service. These must be periodically evaluated and revised as circumstances dictate.

program
plan listing goals and containing the answers to the who, what, when, where, how, and how much of the plan

PROCEDURES

Procedures are the "how" in programs. They are the ways or methods chosen to carry out the tasks that a person or group must perform to reach a goal. Like programs, some procedures are for single use, whereas others are ongoing. Organizations often have sets of procedures that should be followed under different routine circumstances. These sets of procedures are often called **standard operating procedures (SOPs)**. New programs may call for the creation of new procedures. Some procedures within your department are left to you and your associates to create and change as necessary. But before you change a procedure, consider who will be affected and consult with those people before you make the change. The people closest to a task or problem are often the best source of information about it. They can help you develop effective procedures. Well-designed and well-understood procedures can provide the basis for competitive advantage. For example, Marriott, one of the best-managed companies in the hospitality industry, has extensive procedures manuals that are described as follows:

procedure
general routine or method for executing day-to-day operations

standard operating procedure (SOP)
set of procedures providing guidance for decision making given different routine circumstances

> We are sometimes teased about our passion for the Marriott Way of doing things. If you happen to work in the hospitality industry, you might already be familiar with our encyclopedic procedural manuals, which include what is probably the most infamous of the bunch: a guide setting out sixty-six separate steps for cleaning a hotel room in less than half an hour.[16]

As this example from Marriott illustrates, such procedures help ensure uniformly high quality. Detailed procedures may be needed for less-skilled employees, particularly in industries characterized by high turnover. Nonetheless, procedures or SOPs should not be unnecessarily rigid or burdensome.

> Even the most maniacally detailed procedures can't cover every situation, problem, or emergency that might arise. . . . What solid systems and SOPs

---

| EXHIBIT 3.3 | Procedure for staffing a new position. |

1. Develop a job description describing all major tasks to be performed.

2. Develop a job specification describing the minimum qualifications for the position.

3. Complete a request for authorization of staffing (Form 101-B).

4. Submit Form 101-B, the job description, and the job specification to the Division Vice President.

5. After obtaining the Vice President's approval, submit the approved Form 101-B, job description, and job specification to Human Resources.

6. After approval by Human Resources, advertise the position in appropriate media.

7. Acknowledge applications and keep records of all applications.

8. Screen applications for qualifications.

9. Conduct interviews of remaining applicants.

10. Conduct background check of remaining applicants.

11. Arrange for drug test of applicant selected.

12. Make offer of employment to applicant.

13. Inform Human Resources when applicant accepts offer.

14. Complete affirmative action documents (EEO-1 and Form 108).

---

do is nip common problems in the bud so that staff can focus instead on solving the uncommon problems that come their way.[17]

Exhibit 3.3 shows a company's procedure for staffing a new position.

OUTCOMES

Learning Objective Number One

The main reason for establishing procedures, programs, rules, and policies is to reach goals in an effective and efficient way. The results of efforts to achieve goals and execute programs are called *outcomes*. In large measure, teams and their facilitators are judged on how effectively they achieve outcomes.

STEPS IN PLANNING

Every manager has an approach to planning that has been developed over time and refined by experience. But just about everyone can improve his planning efforts. The five steps shown in Exhibit 3.4 can help you become a better planner. As you read

Steps in planning (the planning process).	**EXHIBIT 3.4**

Step 1: Setting Objectives (Goals)

      Establish targets for both the short and the long term.

Step 2: Determining Your Alternatives and Restraints

      Build a list of possible courses of action that can lead you to your goals and a list of the limits within which you must live.

Step 3: Evaluating Your Alternatives

      Measure each alternative's advantages and disadvantages in order to choose the alternative with the fewest serious defects.

Step 4: Implementing Your Course of Action

      Place your plan in the hands of those who will carry it to completion.

Step 5: Following Up

      Monitor progress toward accomplishment of the goal.

---

about each in the sections that follow, consider how they are related to the steps in decision-making. After all, planning involves a series of decisions, as do the other management functions.

STEP 1: SETTING OBJECTIVES (GOALS)

Some of your goals and those of your team are set for you through the planning of others. Your boss may instruct you to reduce operating costs by 5 percent by the end of the month. How you do it may be left to you to decide. However, most of your goals will require consultation and cooperation with others, such as the union steward, fellow supervisors, employees, team members, or various staff managers.

Some companies such as Goodrich, are attempting to make major performance improvements by continuous improvement and setting goals or targets, which the company interprets in a more reasonable fashion than some companies in the past. While the company calls these stretch targets, they are designed to stimulate new ideas and are not unreasonably high standards.[18] Tim Dumbauld, a Goodrich vice president and general manager says,

> "It's not that we're expecting X millions of sales; it's X-plus to get people thinking. We don't expect to meet 100% of all of them because they're stretch. If we do 80%, that's meeting expectations; if we do 100%, we've exceeded expectations." . . . employees are starting to understand "that continuous improvement [is] . . . everyone's job."[19]

The Kellogg Company has also eschewed unrealistic goals and now emphasizes the importance of setting reasonable goals.[20]

Kellogg's new management team was committed to restoring realism to its financial forecasts . . . [according to Vice President for Investor Relations John Renwich] "changing this goal had a huge impact for us. Business units were now able to pursue realistic goals. We didn't have to do self-defeating things in order to achieve exaggerated goals that could only be achieved a single time . . . The mentality that's needed to have 'stretch targets,' to stretch organizations in ways that are questionable, can be so destructive."[21]

This chapter's feature on supervisors and performance deals with goal setting.

STEP 2: DETERMINING YOUR ALTERNATIVES AND RESTRAINTS

Your alternatives are the feasible courses of action (sets of tasks) that enable you to reach your goals. Together, they make up a program for action. As with your goals, external factors can limit and influence the courses of action available to you. When you know your limits and the restraints of budgets, policies, union agreements, and so on, you are ready to make a list of possible courses of action. As you construct your list, tap in to the diversity around you for new and unique suggestions for ways to deal with any issue. Your peers may have faced similar situations in the past, and you can benefit from their experiences.

STEP 3: EVALUATING YOUR ALTERNATIVES

Create a list of advantages and disadvantages for each of your alternatives. Consider what each alternative calls for in resources such as time, labor, and materials. Keep your company's mission, vision, values, and policies in mind as you evaluate alternatives. Using your conceptual skills and personal code of ethics, consider the impact of your alternatives on your group, on other sections, and on your company as a whole. You will have to work with and through those other people and sections in the future, so avoid any loss of their goodwill. You do not want to incur any negative side effects that can be avoided.

STEP 4: IMPLEMENTING YOUR COURSE OF ACTION

Having weighed the relative merits and disadvantages of each of your alternatives and having chosen one that has the fewest serious problems, you are now ready to move from the thinking phase into the action phase of planning. Meet with those who will share responsibility for executing your program. Explain your course of action in detail, emphasizing the limits and means available. Set completion dates for various operations and establish checkpoints between the present and the completion dates. Explain the help available to all and stand ready to assist them in times of difficulty. Most important, let them know that you want to be kept informed of their progress.

SUPERVISORS AND PERFORMANCE

A critical process in obtaining high quality and performance is setting goals that are specific, relevant, capable of being monitored, and challenging yet attainable. Although the process of goal setting often appears relatively simple, it can be difficult to develop good goals that provide motivation for quality and performance. A number of practitioners have shared their views on goal setting. Establishing expectations of desired performance turns out to be critical: "'We want everybody to know what to expect, and that what we expect is measurable,' said Gary Geisel, president of Provident Bank in Baltimore. The use of measured performance based on specific goals helps create a climate where results are clearly expected, he adds. 'It makes you sit down and say 'define it'—to take management practices and identify them in a definable way.'"

A key to effective goal setting is the establishment of accountability. "The use of 'deliverables' in measuring performance makes everyone accountable, says Colleen O'Neill, practice leader for talent management at William M. Mercer in Atlanta. 'You see real, significant increases in financial returns for those organizations that have a formal system of communicating goals and expectations, and regular feedback,' O'Neill said. 'You see a difference on sales per employee, net revenue and other measures you can connect to shareholder value.'"

Other keys to effective goal setting are the clarity and the credibility of the process. "Clear goals and benchmarks stated in advance make reviews more credible too, she [O'Neill] says. The rewards of going over and above those goals also motivate workers and managers to work smarter and harder." Providing a clear target for employees is absolutely critical: "The hardest thing is that companies still struggle with the 'I'll know it when I see it' approach rather than being clear about performance goals, O'Neill said. Rather than set goals, many firms still use open-ended reviews, she says. 'They wait until someone has performed, and then tell someone they didn't do their job well.'"

In addition, it is not enough to set good goals, as monitoring progress toward them is vital. "Carol Bartz, CEO of Autodesk, in San Rafael, Calif., is well known for monitoring results closely. She expects bad news at her software firm to come out quickly. That way, changes are made right away before any damage is done." Finally, using several different measures in goals is important. "Bartz uses a variety of gauges to see how her people deliver. Some are based on hard data, like revenue goals. Others are benchmarks based on specific projects. Geisel says Provident varies its goals based on an employee's rank and how much his or her job can directly affect bank profits. The seven positions that report to Geisel are graded against corporate objectives. Rank-and-file people are gauged on individual goals. For those in between, a ratio of corporate to individual goals is crafted, Geisel says. Where an employee can affect earnings more directly, corporate goals carry a higher weight."

Source: Quoted material from Antonio A. Praco, "Give Your People Specific Goals and They're More Apt to Deliver," *Investor's Business Daily* (October 31, 2001):A1. Reproduced with permission.

STEP 5: FOLLOWING UP

You chose or helped to choose the goals and the courses of action to reach them, so you bear the primary responsibility for execution. Do not rely on your employees to come to you with problems. Check with them periodically, allowing yourself and them time to make adjustments and to avoid surprises. Be sure to recognize good performances and demonstrate sincere concern for problems. Your reputation and success depend on your employees' efforts, and you will need them to execute your future plans.

We are now ready to examine the organizing function.

ORGANIZING

Organizing consists of four primary tasks:

Learning Objective Number Two

1. Determining and grouping the tasks to be performed.
2. Assigning work to people or people to work.
3. Establishing a framework of authority and accountability among the people who will accomplish the tasks.
4. Allocating appropriate resources to accomplish the tasks and reach the targets.

TYPES OF ORGANIZATION

What is the best way to organize a company in a specific industry and competitive environment? The answer may result in a pyramid-type structure or a more flexible structure. Two contrasting types of organizations exist today: the *bureaucratic* (sometimes called *mechanistic*) and the *organic*. The bureaucratic/mechanistic organization usually looks like a pyramid or cone, with several layers of management. The organic

Supervisors in all fields need good organizational skills. Directors and writers like Larry David must organize both the technical aspects of their operation and the actors' performances.

Bureaucratic/mechanistic organization structure contrasted with the organic organization structure.

EXHIBIT 3.5

BUREAUCRATIC/MECHANISTIC	ORGANIC
1. Focus on functions	1. Focus on process using cross-functional teams
2. Centralized decision-making	2. Decentralized decision-making
3. Tall structure, several layers	3. Flat structure, few layers
4. Distinctions between line and staff	4. Both line and staff represented in teams
5. Narrow job definitions	5. Broad job definitions
6. Heavy reliance on rules and procedures	6. Heavy reliance on innovation
7. Emphasis on vertical communication	7. Emphasis on horizontal communication
8. Conformity to dominant culture	8. Cultural diversity
9. Emphasis on individuals	9. May place emphasis on teams
10. Focus on maintaining stability	10. Focus on change

is flatter by comparison and can change its shape more quickly to meet new challenges and opportunities (see Exhibit 3.5).

The bureaucratic/mechanistic organization makes use of vertical layers of narrowly defined jobs, usually within several functional areas such as production, marketing, finance, and human resource management. It usually concentrates decision-making at the top, imposes severe constraints on risk taking, and unintentionally discourages innovation at the lower levels. It calls for reliance on specific vertical channels for communication. Such organizations usually find that it is quite difficult and time-consuming to respond to external changes or to change their structure.

The organic structure usually focuses horizontally and often uses teams when appropriate. Organic structures facilitate cross-functional communications and encourage decision-making, innovation, and risk taking at the lowest, most appropriate levels through various means of empowerment. Think of organic structures as living organisms capable of changing their shape and purpose as needed to respond to the new and different. This chapter's feature on supervisors and teams deals with very creative teams.

TEAMS

Bureaucratic and organic organizational structures have their place under differing sets of circumstances. In general, bureaucratic structures are appropriate in stable industries; gas companies, electric companies, and governmental agencies are three

SUPERVISING TEAMS

Teams have been able to accomplish some remarkable feats in business and in sports. Perhaps less well known are the successes of some remarkable teams in the arts and entertainment. Some of the best examples of such accomplishments are provided by the teams that created *West Side Story* and *Your Show of Shows*, a live television show from the 1950s. These teams were not the typical teams, but were instead, virtuoso teams that differed in almost every respect and which required very different supervisory skills.

The team, which was led by comedian Sid Caesar, that wrote the scripts for *Your Show of Shows* had remarkably talented writers, such as Woody Allen, Mel Brooks, Carl Reiner, and Neil Simon. Interestingly, on initial review, there is little about the operation of this team that appears appropriate for the supervision of other teams. The writers were tremendously competitive with each other and big egos were prevalent. Their relationships may be described as follows:

> They may have been the best comedy writers in America—but they weren't the nicest . . . The tension among team members led Caesar to describe the competitive atmosphere as one filled with "electricity and hate"; two other virtuosos translated Caesar's descriptions into terms of "competition" and "collaboration."

The operation of virtuoso teams is very different than other teams in which individualism is sacrificed for the team and collaborative relations. Indeed, the virtuoso team, which wrote *Your Show of Shows*, was characterized by internal tensions and highly competitive relationships among their members. However, over time the "individual stars harness themselves to the product of the group." Interestingly, even with such competitive relationships, close physical proximity was critical to the success of the *Your Show of Shows* team as they were forced to work under very crowded conditions in frequent contact with each other. As a result of such proximity, messages were communicated to the appropriate persons very quickly.

> Impassioned dialogue becomes the critical driver of performance, not the work itself. The inescapable physical proximity of team members ensures that the right messages get to the right people—fast. As a result, virtuoso teams operate at a pace that is many times the speed of normal project teams.

Some of the lessons from the success of virtuoso teams are the following: (1) Selection is the key—these teams can have great success because they have great people. (2) Close physical proximity and a fast pace are critical. (3) Creativity is more important than efficiency. (4) A high flow of ideas within the team is essential. (5) Individual egos are accepted as a tradeoff for high quality contributions.

Source: Bill Fischer and Andy Boynton. "Virtuoso Teams," *Harvard Business Review* (July–August, 2005): 117–123.

examples. Organic structures work best in unstable, rapidly changing industries and competitive environments, such as those in consumer electronics and computer software. *Network* and *cellular* organizations, which are very organic, provide maximum organizational flexibility and are likely to become more prominent in the future. Exhibit 3.6 discusses such organizations and the managerial characteristics they will require. More will be said throughout this text about the different types of structures.

Managerial requirements for twenty-first-century network and cellular organizations.	**EXHIBIT 3.6**

Network Organizations—core organizations linked to other independent organizations throughout the world providing manufacturing, marketing, and other services. The core organization in the network often performs a broker function. Membership of non-core organizations in the network may be stable or dynamic.

Skills Required in Network Organizations
- Referral skills
  Directing problems to appropriate network components
- Partnering skills
  Conceiving mutually beneficial outcomes
  Negotiating solutions
  Implementing solutions
- Relationship management
  Sensitivity to the needs of customers and partners

Cellular Organizations—loosely structured organizations made up of small companies employing technical professionals who also function as entrepreneurs. For a specific project, one company within the cellular organization provides project leadership in working with an external technology-based company and a customer company providing financial resources. Another company within the cellular organization may join the project to provide additional skills or to obtain knowledge. The cellular organization has characteristics of classical guilds and professional associations.

Skills Required in Cellular Organizations
- Technical knowledge
- Cross-functional experience
- International experience
- Collaborative leadership
- Self-management
- Flexibility

Source: Brent B. Allred, Charles C. Snow, and Raymond E. Miles. "Characteristics of Managerial Careers in the 21st Century," *Academy of Management Executive* (November 1996): 17–27.

ORGANIZING PRINCIPLES

Six basic principles govern the execution of the organizing function: unity of command, span of control, chain of command, homogeneous assignment, flexibility, and centralization versus decentralization. Each of these principles will help prevent the

Learning Objective Number Three

designer of any organization from falling victim to the most common pitfalls of organizing. Keep them in mind as you plan an organization, evaluate an existing one, or attempt to redesign one.

Unity of command. Unity of command requires that there be only one individual responsible for each part of an organization. In each organization, each element of the organization should be under one chief. Each individual throughout an organization should have only one boss. This principle helps prevent conflicting orders and instructions and makes control of people and operations easier. Unity of command and departures from such unity, which sometimes occur after organizational mergers, are described in the following account from the health care industry:

> Unity of command is an age-old organizational concept that calls for a straight line of authority down through the organization. That is, for each task to be done or each responsibility to be fulfilled, one person is responsible: for each group of workers, there is one supervisor, and for each supervisor or manager, there is a higher manager to which they report, and so on. Split-reporting relationships were felt to violate unity of command, as was having multiple individuals responsible for portions of a task, group, or area. In the merged organization, however, unit of command is no longer inviolate; it has given way to expediency and necessity. It is now common, for example, to find a manager with responsibility for a function that serves multiple locations and now is partially answerable to managers at several locations—as though a halfway organizing effort had resulted in a matrix or project-management organization partially overlaying a traditional functional organization.[22]

matrix organization
an organizational structure in which there are dual reporting relationships, which commonly involve functional and project reporting relationships

Clearly, organizational structures based on expediency are not likely to provide clarity in reporting relationships. As noted, there are exceptions, such as **matrix organizations,** in which dual reporting relationships are desired. For example, matrix structures are common in aerospace firms because of the complexity of the technology used, the high level of coordination that is necessary, and the project nature of the work. In a matrix organization, an employee, such as a cost estimator, may temporarily report to a manager on one project while having a more permanent or core functional reporting relationship with a different manager in finance. Matrix organizational structures are also used in other industries as well. For example, the organizational structure of some elementary schools may have a matrix form with reporting relationships to grade level coordinators, such as for the first, second, and third grades, and reporting relationships to functional coordinators, such as science, music, and art.

Exhibit 3.7 provides a very simplified view of a matrix organizational structure at Lockheed Martin Aerospace. The exhibit shows three major projects, the F16, the F22, and the F35 fighters. Employees, ranging in numbers from hundreds to thousands, work on each of these three projects and report to numerous managers and supervisors. Employees who work on these projects come from several functional areas such as engineering, finance, information systems, materials management, procurement, program management, and production and operations. In addition, each of these employees has a functional or core area manager to which he or she also reports. Some of the advantages of the matrix structure are better information flows, enhanced technological innovation, and stronger employee focus on company-wide efforts. Some of the weaknesses of the

| Simplified example of Lockheed Martin Aeronautics matrix structure. | | | Exhibit 3.7 |

FUNCTIONAL OR CORE AREA MANAGERS	F16 "FIGHTING FALCON" PROJECT MANAGERS	F22 "RAPTOR" PROJECT MANAGERS	F35 "JOINT STRIKE FIGHTER" PROJECT MANAGERS
Engineering	X	X	X
Finance	X	X	X
Information Systems	X	X	X
Materials Management	X	X	X
Procurement	X	X	X
Program Management	X	X	X
Production and Operations	X	X	X

matrix form are, as indicated earlier, violations of unity of command as well as unclear responsibilities, ambiguous authority, conflict, and increased costs for administration.[23]

Span of control. The span of control concept recognizes that there is a limit to the number of individuals a supervisor, team leader, or team facilitator can manage effectively. Many variables can influence the span of control. Two of these variables are the complexity of the tasks performed by the employees and the degree of experience and expertise the associates possess. In bureaucratic structures, the highest levels of the management hierarchy contain the smallest number of employees. In organic structures, this principle is usually concerned with how many people should be in a team and how many teams a team facilitator should manage. Jon R. Katzenbach and Douglas K. Smith, consultants who have worked with many teams in numerous companies, offer the following counsel:

TEAMS

> Virtually all the teams we have met, read, heard about, or been members of have ranged between two and twenty-five people. . . . A larger number of people, say fifty or more, can theoretically become a team. But groups of such size more likely will break into subteams rather than function as a single team. . . . Thus groups much bigger than twenty or twenty-five have difficulty becoming real teams.[24]

Chain of command. The chain formed by managers from the highest to the lowest is called the *chain of command.* Managers are the links in that chain. In bureaucratic structures, they must communicate through the links of the chain to which they are connected. Links may be skipped or circumvented only when superiors approve and there is real need to do so. In organic structures, command is usually vested in team leaders who head up process, project, or other types of autonomous work teams. These people run their own shows: they "own" their processes and projects and carry within their teams the functional expertise needed to do their tasks.

It is important to have an accurate understanding of the pace at which organic organizations are evolving and the extent to which they are actually displacing bureaucracies. More concisely, reports of the death of bureaucracy appear to be premature. On the other hand, there is evidence of a movement toward an intermediate level where there is less bureaucratic organizational structure instead of a widespread shift to organic structures. In evolving bureaucratic-lite structures, the jobs of managers are changing as the vertical dimension of administrative structures has been compressed and there are fewer levels between the supervisor and the chief executive. However, many of the rules of the bureaucracy have been retained and managers are being held more accountable to outcome measures of performance. Organic and network organizational structures are not yet the predominant mode, and managerial work is likely to retain much of its command and control orientation. In short, although there are important examples of organic and network organizations and movements in this direction, decentralization and empowerment are not expected to become the dominant themes in most organizations, at least in the near term.[25]

TEAMS

Homogeneous assignment.

Homogeneous assignment is the major reason companies organize by functions, as in the typical bureaucratic structure. Similar or related functions—advertising, selling, and sales promotion, for example—give rise to related problems and require coordinated efforts by teams and individuals with similar levels of experience and types of expertise. In organic structures, the focus is on a process such as developing a common scheme for evaluating project bids. In such cases, homogeneous assignment means equipping a team with all needed expertise that bears on each process or project so that it can be managed from its beginning to its end.

The development of Hewlett-Packard's financial services center provides insights into the advantages that can be gained with networked and self-directed teams. Because of the high processing expenses for financial transactions ($60 million on an annual basis) the company sought to cut these costs by half over a period of five years. By employing a combined approach that drew on leading-edge technology, partners from different geographic locations, and self-directed teams, Hewlett-Packard reduced these costs by 75 percent in an eight-year period. This accomplishment is more impressive when it is considered that the company's revenues during the period increased from $16.4 to $47 billion.[26]

Flexibility.

Flexibility means that an organization, like Hewlett-Packard, is able to react quickly to changing conditions. It can change to take advantage of new challenges and opportunities. Nonetheless, when there are decisions to be made about structural changes, which presumably accompany strategic decisions by the firm's top-level management team, it is important to choose the appropriate one.[27]

Even two similar firms, competing in the same industry with a similar set of products, technologies, and markets, may find that a structure that works for one firm may need some modification in another. Choosing the right structure is critical because switching from one structure to another is a laborious and costly process. As the very word *structure* suggests, moving from one broad type to another is like moving and relocating the pyramids of Egypt—you have to do it piece by piece, brick by brick—which is why senior management needs to understand how to select a structure that best fits and accommodates the firm's strategy.[28]

Once any organization is established, managers at all levels must regularly plan to embrace the new and review the organization's relevance and adaptability to changing situations. Most important, an organization's structure is dictated by the operations it was designed to accomplish. Attention should be given to the subtle changes worked out by an organization's autonomous units and teams. They often make changes that add greater efficiency and effectiveness to their units and might well do so for the organization as a whole when adopted by others.

Centralization versus decentralization. Everything an organization or manager does to reduce the importance of an individual employee's role leads to centralization of authority. *Centralized* organizations, like bureaucracies, place the responsibility for decision-making at higher levels, concentrating both authority and power at the top.

In contrast, everything an organization or manager does to increase the importance of the individual is a move toward *decentralization,* which places decision authority in the hands of individuals and teams who are closest to a problem or who manage a process. Decentralization occurs through delegation of authority and empowerment. It speeds up decision-making by reducing the number of people and hours needed to make a decision and usually results in an organic organization.

There is a great deal of benefit to be gained from decentralization, which empowers employees to act quickly to solve customers' problems and which gives them the authority and responsibility to make decisions when they have the best information. High performance companies, such as Southwest Airlines, which have strong organizational cultures that guide employee behavior and decisions, have benefited enormously from highly trained, empowered employees who know what to do. Nonetheless, there is also a downside to decentralization from a broader organizational structural view. Louis Gerstner, who led a successful turnaround at IBM, has voiced the following concerns about decentralized structures:

> The prevailing wisdom has been that small companies are fast, entrepreneurial, responsive, and effective. Large companies are slow, bureaucratic, unresponsive, and ineffective. This is pure nonsense. It isn't a question of whether elephants can prevail over ants. It's a question of whether a particular elephant can dance. If it can, the ants must leave the dance floor . . . There's a lot to be said about the power of this construct . . . However, I believe that in the 1980s and 1990s it was carried to an extreme in many companies, with unproductive and, in many cases, highly disruptive results . . . Decision-making was, in fact, fast if the decision touched on a single decentralized unit. However, when multiple segments of the enterprise had to be involved, the highly decentralized model led to turf battles and inadequate customer responses because of incompatible systems in the bits and pieces of the enterprise.[29]

Supervisors should be aware that there are both positive and negative consequences from decentralization and that its affects differ according to the organizational level at which decentralization occurs.

*Learning
Objective
Number Four*

As a supervisor, one of your most rewarding tasks will be training your subordinates to reach their potential. Just as your supervisor once gave you the training to get where you are today, you too have the opportunity to affect someone's career in a positive manner.

STEPS IN ORGANIZING

The organizing process involves the five steps discussed here and listed in Exhibit 3.8.

Step 1: Determining the tasks to be accomplished. The tasks (collections of activities) to be accomplished in your unit will be, in large measure, dictated by goals and responsibilities assigned by upper management and by the design of jobs in your unit. Your unit's goals will dictate the tasks your unit must execute. Step one illustrates the link between planning and organizing. Planning sets goals, both short and long term, and determines the programs needed to reach them. Programs constructed at various levels set forth what is to be done and by whom and determine what resources are to be expended. Tasks must then be broken down into the specific activities required.

Step 2: Subdividing major tasks into individual activities. Staff specialists can help individual unit supervisors break unit tasks down into specific activities. Existing and familiar tasks usually present no particular problem. Units and unit personnel are already equipped to deal with them. When new tasks are assigned or created, however, a job analysis must be done to determine what each task will require in the way of personal skills, knowledge, and abilities.

Step 3: Assigning specific activities to individuals. The specific skills needed to perform worker activities can generally be broken down into data processing, interpersonal, and technical skills. Once these skills are identified as being a part of an activity, individuals who possess the skills required can be assigned to execute the activity. Workers are matched by their particular skill levels to the activities that must be executed. Testing provides one means for matching workers with job activities and there is evidence that the use of testing is increasing. A recent survey indicates that the most common tests are those used to access literacy and mathematical skills.[30] Where tests of skills or aptitudes are available to assess and identify skills for such matching, it is critical that employees feel that they are valid predictors of ability to perform important job activities. The use of invalid tests or tests in which the results do not correlate with job

The steps in constructing an organization (the organizing process).

EXHIBIT 3.8

Step 1: Determining the Tasks to Be Accomplished

Tasks are identified and included in programs, which then become the specific responsibilities of organizational units to accomplish.

Step 2: Subdividing Major Tasks into Individual Activities

Through analysis, tasks are broken down into specific activities, which can then be assigned in part or in total to individuals who possess the needed skills, knowledge, and abilities.

Step 3: Assigning Specific Activities to Individuals

The skills, knowledge, and abilities needed to execute specific activities are identified, and individuals who possess them are assigned activities. Where existing personnel cannot adequately handle the activities, training, new people, or outside assistance may be required.

Step 4: Providing the Necessary Resources

In order to accomplish their assignments, individuals and units may need additional people, authority, training, time, money, or materials.

Step 5: Designing Organizational Relationships

A hierarchy must be designed, or the existing one adapted, to provide the arrangement of authority and responsibility needed to oversee the execution and completion of assignments.

---

performance, is simply poor management and also exposes the employer to charges that the test discriminates against employees on the basis of race, age, and so on. Trial periods provide another means for matching workers to job activities. With trial periods, workers have the opportunity to demonstrate their skills while actually performing the job for a period of time. An important advantage of trial periods is that they are not subject to validity challenges and have widespread acceptance because of their fairness.[31]

Step 4: Providing the necessary resources. Additional demands on people may tax them beyond their capabilities. If the existing workforce cannot absorb the activities, new people may have to be obtained, or the work may have to be outsourced. Where employees do not have the expertise or levels of skills required, additional training may be needed. Talent from other areas may be temporarily assigned to assist with the execution of specific activities. Additional funds and authority may be needed to accomplish all the tasks given to a particular individual or unit.

Step 5: Designing organizational relationships. The existing structure of management positions may or may not be adequate to oversee the execution of operations. When it is not, a new design—temporary or permanent—may have to be established. Enough authority must be in the hands of those designated to execute the various tasks. Everyone involved must have clear knowledge of who is to do what, by what time, and to what standards. The principles of organizing will help you design relationships that can function properly. The end result can be shown in graphic form as an organization chart.

DIRECTING

directing
the supervision or overseeing of people and processes

Directing may be defined briefly as supervising or overseeing people and processes. It includes the specific activities of staffing, training, offering examples of appropriate behavior, evaluating performance, rewarding, coaching, counseling, and disciplining. One example of what it means to direct comes to us from theatrical and motion picture directors. These people remove obstacles that may stand in the way of individual and group performance. They attempt, through coaching and by giving examples, to bring out the best performances their actors have to give. Directors are teachers, facilitators, and cheerleaders. So should you be.

*Learning
Objective
Number Five*

Directing employees individually and in teams is the most demanding and time-consuming function for all supervisors. The responses of your employees to your efforts to direct them will either make or break your career. This is why directing employees is the primary focus of this book. All the remaining chapters will help you become an effective director, team leader, and team facilitator.

STAFFING

Staffing involves adding new people to the organization, promoting people to higher levels of responsibility, transferring people to different jobs, and separating people from their employment. It is based on human resource planning—the analysis of the organization and its present and future needs for people with particular talents. An inventory of existing personnel is taken to determine who is now at work, what their skill levels are, how long they are likely to remain in the organization, and who among them is qualified for larger responsibilities. Existing personnel are matched to the organization's present and future needs in order to determine what kinds of people will be needed in the future. Specific staffing activities are defined as follows:

1. *Recruiting* is the search for talented people who might be interested in the jobs that the organization has. It occurs inside as well as outside the organization. Announcements about job opportunities may be posted on Internet websites and bulletin boards, or placed in newspapers or trade journals. Everyone who responds is considered a potential employee until the decision to hire is made.

2. *Selecting* screens potential employees and job applicants to determine who among them is most qualified. Tests, interviews, physical examinations, and records checks are used to eliminate the less qualified. The applicants are narrowed down to the most qualified. Selection is often considered a negative process because the people hired have the fewest deficiencies for the job opening.

3. *Placement and orientation* follow as soon as a new employee is hired. It involves introducing the person to the company—its people, the jobs, and the working

environment. The new employee is given the proper instructions and equipment needed to execute the job for which she has been hired. Once work rules are explained and coworkers are introduced, the break-in period begins.

4. *Promoting* involves moving people from one job in the organization to another that offers higher levels of pay and responsibility. Promotions usually require approval by two levels of management and the assistance of the human resources department, where one exists. As a supervisor, your continual concern should be to qualify yourself for promotion and to prepare one or more of your employees to take your job.

5. *Transferring* moves people from one job to another, either temporarily or permanently. A transfer does not usually carry with it an increase in pay or responsibilities. Most transfers are lateral moves; they facilitate training and are often used to move people from one career path to another.

6. *Separating* people from their employment can be done on a voluntary or an involuntary basis. Voluntary separations include quits and retirements. Involuntary separations include firings (terminations due to disciplinary actions or unsatisfactory performance) and layoffs (terminations due to downsizing and economic slowdowns).

TRAINING

Training teaches skills, knowledge, and attitudes to both new and existing employees. It can be provided through classroom or on-the-job instruction. Although the supervisor of each trainee has the primary duty to train, the actual instruction may be done by any person who is qualified to train. Often the human resources department assists supervisors in training by providing training materials or by teaching them how to train their employees. In some cases, supervisors delegate the authority to train to an experienced employee while retaining accountability for the training.

OFFERING INCENTIVES

Incentives are things that the company hopes will have a strong appeal to their employees. Those who desire incentives offered by their employer will be encouraged to give the kind and quality of performance required to earn them. The kinds of incentives most businesses offer include raises, bonuses, promotions, better working conditions, greater challenges and responsibilities, and symbols of status in the organization. Status symbols can be as small as a phone on the desk, as large as an executive suite, or anything in between. Which one, if any, appeals to a given employee at a given time depends on the individual—including such factors as his current level of job satisfaction and financial condition.

EVALUATING

Evaluating requires each supervisor to make periodic appraisals of each employee's on-the-job performance. The primary purpose of performance evaluation is to improve job performance. Before supervisors can conduct performance evaluations, they must

Informal encounters with your subordinates are an important part of management. Sharing and spreading the enthusiasm of your subordinates is paramount to your own success.

have precise guidelines and standards to follow. Employees must be evaluated on the performance standards for the job instead of on factors that are often irrelevant to the job, such as personal appearance.

Supervisors evaluate their employees informally each day through regular observations of their work. In contrast, formal appraisals are usually done only once or twice each year. Supervisors who lack intensive knowledge of their employees' performance will find it impossible to conduct fair appraisals.

DISCIPLINING

Disciplining requires supervisors to deal with employees' mistakes and shortcomings on the job. *Positive discipline* demands that employees be informed about and understand the rules that govern their behavior, the standards that guide their output, and the expectations their bosses have of them. The emphasis is on preventing trouble through the creation of an educated, self-disciplined employee. *Negative discipline* is concerned with handling infractions, usually through reprimands or more severe penalties.

MANAGEMENT BY WANDERING AROUND (MBWA)

Management by wandering around (MBWA) is a principle of management that encourages managers to get out of their offices regularly so that they can touch base with customers, suppliers, and others in their own organizations. MBWA encourages managers to listen, empathize, and stay in touch with people who are important to their operations and their mission.[32]

Most supervisors can practice MBWA each time they meet another person at work or make contact with outsiders during their business activities. When you meet customers, you should interact with them to find out how they like your products and services. If you uncover any complaints or criticisms, take them to the people who should know and can do something about them.

MBWA with suppliers is especially important if quality is uncertain. Before most procurement or purchasing agents decide on a supplier, they visit various suppliers' facilities and talk with those who will be responsible for creating what they need. If suppliers are making your life and the lives of your employees more difficult, practice a little MBWA with them.

Your most frequent use of MBWA will be with your associates. Casual and informal meetings, as well as formal encounters, create lots of opportunities to interact with them. You and they can then catch up on what is happening in your lives. You get a chance to see them in action—to watch and to listen. In addition, your employees want you to see them perform well. There is probably no better way to spend most of your time at work than with your people—those who make or break your own reputation and on whom you depend for the execution of your plans and instructions. Most of the activities we examine in later chapters depend on your practice of MBWA. A good example of MBWA is provided by J.W. Marriott Jr., the CEO of the Marriott Corporation:

> The time I spend on the road—actually, some 150,000 air miles a year—visiting Marriott locations is invaluable to me. One of the most important things it allows me to do is counter the notion that big corporations are faceless machines. If you're in the service business and your name is above the door, it's important for people to be able to link a face to the name. I want our associates to know that there really is a guy named Marriott who cares about them, even if he can only drop by every so often to personally tell them so. I also want to show our team in the field that I value their work enough to take the time to check it out.[33]

Some other important purposes are served by MBWA. For example, when managers practice MBWA late at night, on weekends, or during a difficult time, they often provide positive reinforcement and motivational boosts to heroics-in-progress. The impact of MBWA is important for all managers but is especially effective when practiced by high-level executives. An executive's visit to the workplace of a research and development team working late at night can send an invaluable message that the team's efforts are valued. Similarly, MBWA can reinforce the core values of the organization, such as when the former CEO of Southwest Airlines greeted passengers as they got on the planes, when Michael Eisner, former CEO of Disney, took time to help pick up trash at Disney World, or when Bill Marriott helps Marriott guests carry their luggage into one of the hotels. Likewise, MBWA enables leaders at all levels to demonstrate their humility. The former

management by wandering around (MBWA)
a leadership principle that encourages supervisors to get out of their offices regularly so that they can touch base with their employees and customers

CEO of Harley-Davidson used MBWA for this purpose, which he felt was important in the organization's creativity and adaptability to change. In addition, MBWA enables leaders to provide important role modeling. Carl Sewell, the CEO of a large company of automobile dealerships, demonstrates the importance of customer service when he takes time to go to the service areas and get under the cars with his mechanics.[34]

CONTROLLING

controlling
the management function that sets standards for performance and attempts to prevent, identify, and correct deviations from standards

standard
a definition of acceptable performance levels for people, machines, or processes

benchmarks
performance levels or best practices of the most exceptional companies in an industry

Controlling involves preventing, identifying, and correcting deficiencies in the performances of both people and processes. It begins with an assessment of the need for control, what types of controls are best (prevention efforts, monitoring ongoing operations, or after-action reporting on measures of outputs), and the establishment of various standards for measurement.

STANDARDS

A **standard** is a device for measuring or monitoring the behavior of people or processes. Standards can be quantitative, qualitative, or a mixture of the two. Those for controlling people include policies, rules, and procedures. Standards set for the control of processes often include upper and lower control limits that form a boundary around acceptable output. Various measurements and observations are necessary throughout the performance of any operation to determine if standards are being met. Organizations sometimes use **benchmarks** for standards. Benchmarks are standards of performance, such as levels of defects, or practices that are characteristic of the best companies in a given industry. Companies often set benchmarks by studying the products or practices of the best companies in their industries, and sometimes in unrelated industries as well. Nonetheless, setting ambitious performance standards is insufficient for the attainment of outstanding performance. The company must also provide support systems, such as training and equipment that will enable employees and units to meet these standards. In addition, the company must consider how a standard or benchmark fits with other organizational priorities.[35]

THE CONTROL PROCESS

Learning Objective Number Six

Exhibit 3.9 summarizes the control process in any formal organization. Systems of controls should establish standards, measure performances against those expectations, detect deviations from standards, analyze causes for the deviations, and initiate corrective action.

1. *Establish standards.* Standards provide the who, when, why, what, and how of a process. Qualitative and quantitative standards need to be established for all key activities (those directly affecting goal achievement). People must know their limits and what is expected of them.

2. *Measure performance against expectations.* If managers are going to prevent, identify, and correct deviations from standards, they must be able to compare performance to established standards. It is only through comparisons that the terms good or bad become meaningful. For example, the comparison of planned

The control process in a formal organization.	**EXHIBIT 3.9**

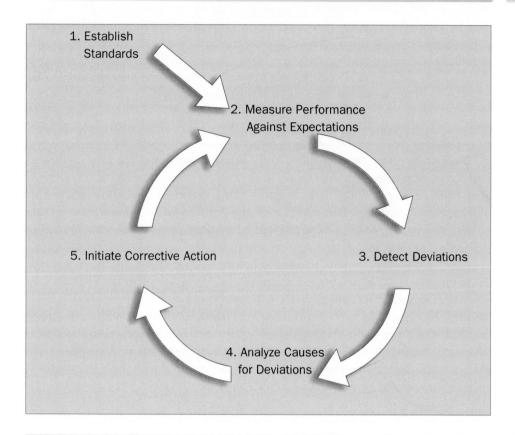

production levels to actual levels of production output will let a manager know if the actual is in line with the desirable.

3. *Detect deviations.* Through comparisons, managers can detect and note deviations. For example, a worker is supposed to generate 15 parts per hour for each of the last four hours. The supervisor compares output to this standard and discovers that the worker is five parts short of the goal. To do this, a supervisor needs accurate and timely information about each worker's production output. Both the worker and the supervisor need to know the standard and how it is applied.

4. *Analyze causes for deviations.* When a supervisor notes deviation, such as poor quality, an investigation must be conducted to determine why the deviation has taken place. What is not functioning as planned? Through the decision-making process, the supervisor determines possible remedies.

5. *Initiate corrective action.* Additional training or more explicit instructions and supervision may be needed. Problems with machines, equipment, supplies, or raw materials may call for changes in maintenance procedures, workflow, sources of materials, and more.

Learning Objective Number Seven

The control process may tell managers or an organization that its standards are inappropriate—either too loose or too strict. Further, the need for additional standards may be uncovered when a supervisor investigates the causes of deviations. New controls may be required to monitor other operations. The board of trustees for a Midwestern community college district discovered that its chief financial officer had invested $10 million of college funds in risky, speculative, long-term investments that earned no interest. The board had no control mechanism to prevent the poor decision so the employee had full authority to do this without board approval.

TYPES OF CONTROLS

Preventive controls are familiar to all of us. Safety devices on a machine or firearm, a lock on a door to prevent unauthorized entry, safety locks on medicine containers to keep children from opening them, and the various checklists throughout this text are all examples of preventive controls. It is usually better to prevent trouble than to have to deal with it. If all of our problems could be foreseen, organizations would need no other types of controls.

Diagnostic controls attempt to identify trouble when it occurs. Ideally, they should do so immediately. Just as a physician cannot prescribe a treatment for an illness until its cause is identified, a manager needs to know why something has gone wrong in her department before taking corrective measures. Some familiar examples of diagnostic controls are warning lights, meters, and gauges. Personal observation and taking note of abnormal sounds and sights are daily routines that managers use to detect trouble. Once you detect problems, you must identify their causes and deal with them effectively.

Therapeutic controls are usually automatic in their operation. They are designed to deal with and correct deficiencies once the causes are known. Thermostats that regulate the operation of heating and cooling systems are a good example. A safety valve that opens to release excess steam when the pressure reaches a certain level is another example.

All these controls are necessary for most operations and should form an integrated approach to controlling. No one type is completely adequate. Managers usually need to use combinations of controls to control resources and activities effectively.

A budget and the budgeting process effectively illustrate the three types of controls. A budget is a preventive control because it prevents (or helps prevent) unauthorized expenditures of funds. It is a diagnostic control because it helps monitor the funds as they are spent and matches actual expenditures against planned expenditures. When budgeted funds prove insufficient to meet required expenditures, an investigation should be made to determine why. If the budgeting process is at fault, changes can be introduced to make it more realistic. Budgets have a built-in therapeutic control. When more money is requested than has been authorized, it cannot be spent without higher approval.

This chapter's feature on supervisors and ethics deals with employee dishonesty.

GLOBAL

CONTROL CHARACTERISTICS

Controls may have one or more of the following characteristics:

1. *Acceptance* by members of the organization who must enforce them and over whom they are enforced. That they are established and enforced in consultation and with the consent of the governed is the hallmark of effective controls.

SUPERVISORS AND ETHICS

Recent survey data indicate that employees may be increasingly more likely to lie about work-related issues. One study found that of those who call in sick, 60 percent are simply taking time off for errands or personal time while another found that 36 percent were well when claiming to be sick. Dishonesty is also creeping in academic credentials, as 12 percent of résumés have some component of fabricated information. For example, the CEO of Radio Shack was recently forced to resign because he falsely claimed to have an undergraduate degree, which he did not have. The culture of organizations has an impact on the truthfulness of employees, and the ethics of the top executives has a pervasive effect. In addition to culture and leadership influences, experience and position in the managerial hierarchy also impacts ethics. Interestingly, there is a difference in the likelihood that employees will report misconduct. Of those who observe such ethical lapses, 28 percent of managers indicate a reluctance to report such conduct while 44 percent of rank-and-file employees indicate a similar reluctance.

Some of the misconduct appears to be a consequence of pressures resulting from major organizational changes such as mergers and acquisitions. Untruthfulness also appears to be related to the complications of personal lives, such as lying about the need to avoid a business trip because of a need to mend a relationship with a spouse in order to avoid a divorce. Interestingly, an increasing feeling of entitlement also appears to be the cause of some untruthfulness. Observers have reported abuses of the Family and Medical Leave Act resulting from bogus claims of illness or family demands. For example, one extreme abuser of the act has requested leave for the death of the employee's father on three different occasions at different companies.

Unfortunately, in addition to the adverse impact on the employer, untruthfulness and acts of dishonesty exact a toll on the employee who runs the risk of not knowing where to draw the line before becoming involved in more serious acts of dishonesty.

Source: Sue Shellenbarger. "How and Why We Lie at the Office: From Pilfered Pens to Padded Accounts," *Wall Street Journal* (March 24, 2005): D1. Barry Shachter, "Few Surprised by Departure," *Fort Worth Star Telegram* (February 21, 2006).

2. *Focus* on critical points that affect individuals' and the organization's ability to achieve goals. Critical points include essential areas of marketing, financial, production, and human resource activities.

3. *Economic feasibility.* Controls must be cost-efficient—the benefit they provide has to be worth their cost of installation and operation. Too much control can be worse than too little. Appropriateness is the key.

4. *Accuracy.* Controls must provide information about operations and people in sufficient quantity and quality to enable managers to make meaningful comparisons to standards. Too much information can be worse than too little.

5. *Timeliness.* Information needed for comparisons has to be in a manager's hands in time for him to take effective action.

6. *Clarity.* Controls and their applicability to specific situations must be communicated clearly to those responsible for implementing them and to those who will be controlled by them.[36]

All these characteristics are important, but a control need not have all of them to do the job for which it is designed.

To illustrate these characteristics, we will look at a tool room situation. A supervisor wants to control the use of his department's tools. He starts by locking them up in a tool room. Next, he assigns to one person the task of issuing and accounting for each tool. Then he issues an ID card to each employee and sets up a procedure whereby tools are exchanged for these cards. Finally, he establishes records of the condition the tools are in and fixes responsibility for changes in their condition.

This may or may not be a good control system depending on the circumstances. It may be too expensive depending on the value of the tools he is safeguarding. It may be inadequate and impractical if, in the absence of the tool room supervisor, no one can get a tool. It may be inappropriate if only one or two workers ever need the tools. In short, all of the six control characteristics may be necessary; if any one of them is missing, the controls may accomplish something less than is desired.

Ricardo Semler, head of Semco in Brazil, has written about his experiences with the company in a book entitled *Maverick*. The company, in which control is based on mutual trust and respect between managers and workers, is radically different from the company he inherited—a traditional bureaucratic organization run by rules, procedure, and manuals. Essentially, the company moved to three levels of management and employs a set of concentric circles of coordinators and worker teams that execute most tasks. Controlling is everyone's job, and each person does what is necessary to control his or her own behavior and outputs.[37]

Because the company's performance was disastrous when Semler took over, he knew dramatic action was needed. Essentially, he eliminated much to the executive hierarchy, and moved to a more responsive flatter organizational structure, which has only three levels including workers at the bottom level. Few job titles were retained and even the CEO's position is rotated among six top managers on a six-month schedule. He gave control for all important decisions to the employees and adopted an open compensation system in which the pay for all jobs is public information within the company. Semler's approach was to create the most radically managed company in the western hemisphere. As he likes to say, he created an environment in which employees are treated like adults.[38] The following comment provides perspective on Semler's approach:

> All workers set their own hours . . . Workers choose their managers by vote and evaluate them regularly, with the results posted publicly. Obviously it's all insane, except that it seems to work.[39]

Semler's approach has been very successful: His company has been growing at a rate of 24 percent per year since he wrote his book. In addition, Semco has expanded from industrial machinery manufacturing into some service businesses such as property management and equipment maintenance and has joint ventures with such well-established companies as Johnson Controls. Not surprisingly, Semler's unorthodox views of control and management have prompted the Harvard Business School and the Sloan School of Management at MIT to conduct case studies of Semco.[40] Semler's views about control are also reflected in his comments about the limitations of some of the world's most important leaders:

> Managers overrate knowing where they are going, understanding what business they are in, defining their mission. It is a macho, militaristic, and self-misleading posture. Giving up control in exchange for freedom,

creativity, and inspired adaptation is my preference. . . . Bad leadership is personified to me by the Pope, Fidel Castro, Bill Gates, and Lee Iacocca, all wonderful figures, brilliant strategists, and historic giants. They created enormous value and transformed the entities they led into some of the most important symbols of our age. But because they couldn't rise above their egos, they failed to create organizations that could flourish in spite of them, not because of them. Because they all overstayed their welcome, they have presided over declining creativity, freedom, innovation, and success.[41]

MANAGEMENT BY EXCEPTION

The recognized principle of **management by exception (MBE)** applies most directly to controlling. A manager should spend his time only on areas that demand personal attention. Routine matters should be delegated to others, and procedures should be established to deal with them. When exceptions occur, they are usually situations for which there are no precedents. Then the manager's attention is warranted. Where controls reveal exceptions for which there is no prescribed cure, the manager must take action. The theory underlying management by exception is illustrated in Exhibit 3.10, which identifies a few of the everyday demands on a supervisor's time and tells how the supervisor should handle each of them. Competent employees usually appreciate management by exception because it suggests that the manager has confidence in them.

management by exception (MBE)
a management principle asserting that managers should spend their time on those matters that require their particular expertise

MANAGEMENT BY OBJECTIVES

Objectives are goals or targets to be achieved or reached within some specific time. **Management by objectives (MBO)** requires each manager (and sometimes each worker) to sit down periodically with her boss and work out goals on which they agree. These goals will, when achieved, result in a more efficient and economical operation

management by objectives (MBO)
a management principle that uses performance objectives to guide, evaluate, and reward employee behavior

An illustration of management by exception.			**EXHIBIT 3.10**

TASK	KEEP	DELEGATE	OTHER
Appraisals of employees	X		
Interviewing applicants for job vacancies	X		
Handling regular reports to higher-ups		X	Read before sending
Answering correspondence	Those only supervisors can answer	Those others can do as well or better	Read before sending
Attending meetings and conferences	When your expertise is needed	When your input is not required	Have substitute brief you

for a section or department. Such goals can be set only after a clear understanding is reached about what a department's weaknesses are and what its capabilities seem to be. Goals set by any manager must be in line with—not contradictory to—those of his superiors and those of departments with which the manager must coordinate.

If MBO is to work efficiently, those participating in it must set clear, specific, and realistic goals for both the short and long term. Once goals are set, progress in reaching each goal is monitored by both the person who set the goal and her superior. The goal-setter's reputation and performance appraisals will be based in large measure on her efforts and success in reaching the established goals. MBO reduces the need for close supervision by involving employees in setting their own sights on specific targets and then having them work out the methods by which each goal is to be reached. In such a system, results are what really matter.

COORDINATING

Learning Objective Number Eight

Coordinating is the managerial task of making sure that the various parts of the organization all operate in harmony with one another. It involves integrating all the details necessary for reaching the company's goals. Each activity must be executed without interference from other activities in order to have a unified effort in both the planning and the execution phases of every operation. The coordinating function should happen simultaneously with all the others. Through it, the manager attempts to foresee potential conflicts or to deal with existing ones. For example, the organization may have to be redesigned for better efficiency, or plans may have to be modified to include a better mix or balance between people and events. Lack of coordination means chaos.

KINDS OF COORDINATION

There are two kinds of coordinating: *coordination of thought* and *coordination of action.* A manager coordinates thought by making certain, through effective communication, that all parties involved in planning an operation have the same concepts, objectives, and overall understanding. He coordinates action by including in his plans for a project the steps to be taken in its execution, the sequence of those steps, the roles that each person must play, and how all the persons involved are to cooperate. As these definitions suggest, coordinating is both an aid to planning and an objective to be realized through planning.

Coordination of thought and coordination of action are best provided for by fixing responsibilities. Each person should have an up-to-date, clear definition of her duties in general, as well as of her particular role in each project in which she becomes involved. In this way, everyone's efforts are directed toward common purposes with as little wasted effort and overlap as possible. Coordination is the thread that stitches an entire operation together.

COORDINATION TECHNIQUES

Organizational units can coordinate their operations through programs, procedures, schedules, vertical feedback, and horizontal interaction. Horizontal interaction requires teamwork and occurs regularly when individuals and groups from different departments touch base with each other through a variety of means and for a variety of purposes. The larger the organization, the greater the need for these efforts at coordination.

As a supervisor, you can adopt the following measures to help coordinate your operations:

- Enforcing company policies
- Enforcing departmental procedures
- Regularly meeting with people who share responsibilities for projects
- Practicing management by wandering around—communicating regularly with those who feed you work, those who do your department's tasks, and those to whom you feed work or output
- Using the organization's established lines of authority and channels of communication
- Sharing information with those who need it through e-mail and regular routing of bulletins, newsletters, memos, and copies of pertinent documents
- Being available to those who need you; letting people know where you are and how they can reach you both on and off the job
- Rotating responsibilities in order to cross-train your people
- Playing your management roles of liaison, monitor, disseminator, spokesperson, disturbance handler, and negotiator
- Constantly focusing yourself and others on the mission

INSTANT REPLAY

1. Planning is often called the first management function because it is a part of every other function.

2. Organizing requires managers to determine tasks, break them into activities, identify the skills needed to perform them, and assign them to qualified people.

3. Directing requires managers to staff their operations and to train, offer incentives and examples, evaluate, and discipline their employees.

4. Staffing involves human resource planning, developing, recruiting, selecting, promoting, transferring, and separating people from their employment.

5. Controlling establishes standards to govern people's conduct and output at work, measures performance and conduct against those standards, detects deviations, finds the causes for the deviations, and implements appropriate remedies.

6. Preventive controls rely on methods to prevent problems, diagnostic controls signal the occurrence of deviations, and therapeutic controls deal with deviations as they occur.

7. Controls should be accepted by those who must use them and should be focused on critical points in vital operations.

8. The principle of management by exception tells a manager to spend time on only those matters that demand her personal attention and expertise.

9. Management by objectives requires bosses and employees to set goals that will become the standards by which their performance is measured.

10. Supervisors must take steps to coordinate the thoughts and actions of those who affect their operations so as to avoid confusion, waste, and duplication of effort.

QUESTIONS FOR CLASS DISCUSSION

1. Can you define this chapter's key terms?

2. What are the steps in the planning process, and what happens in each step?

3. What are the principles that govern the organizing function, and what does each principle mean?

4. What are the steps in the organizing process, and what happens in each step?

5. What are the major differences between the mechanistic and the organic types of organization?

6. What is a matrix organization and what are its advantages and disadvantages?

7. What activities belong to the directing function, and what is involved in each activity?

8. What are the steps in the control process, and what happens in each step?

9. What are the major ways in which supervisors can coordinate their actions and operations within and outside their work units?

ASSESS THE SITUATION

The following table provides a list of the titles of managers and executives, which commonly form the managerial hierarchy in major U.S. corporations employing tens of thousands of employees. In addition, the table provides the managerial hierarchy in a small company, which has 35 employees. Compare these managerial hierarchies and explain how the jobs of managers or supervisors in these different organizations are likely to be similar or different with respect to the following aspects. Because smaller organizations are typically less bureaucratic than larger ones, explain how the form of the organization is likely to affect the supervisor's job.

- Goal setting
- Policies
- Rules

- Unity of Command
- Flexibility
- Controlling
- Coordinating

Major U.S. Corporation with Several Thousand Employees	Small Privately Held Company with 35 Employees
Chief Executive Officer	President
Chief Operating Officer, Chief Financial Officer, and Chief Information Officer	Chief Operating Officer
Executive Vice Presidents	Managers/Supervisors
Senior Vice Presidents	
Vice Presidents	
Assistant Vice Presidents	
Directors	
Managers	
Supervisors or Team Leaders	

SKILL BUILDING EXERCISE 3.1

As discussed in the chapter, bureaucratic organizations are a common organizational form and are often very appropriate for the purposes they serve, in spite of the negative connotation of bureaucracy as it is used in everyday conversation. As noted, such bureaucratic organizations do not typically respond well to rapidly changing competitive environments. An example of a bureaucracy would be the U.S. Postal Service. For many years the U.S. Postal Service has provided reliable service on a massive scale for millions of customers. Currently, it provides message service to 141 million homes and businesses on a daily basis.[42] Many Americans take good postal service for granted, and the organization probably has not received the credit that it deserves. Nonetheless, as with many large organizations, there have been difficulties in employee relations at the U.S. Postal Service and its employees have become highly unionized. In the past, there have been instances of violence in the workplace and the U.S. Postal Service places emphasis on workplace dispute resolution.

Work in small groups or by yourself and perform the following tasks. (1) Identify the rules and procedures that may be in place for postal workers, which supervisors are expected to enforce. (2) From your own experiences with the U.S. Postal Service, identify areas in which you see good performance and areas in which improvements may be needed. (3) Provide explanations for any good and poor performance, which you have observed. (4) Identify ways in which supervisors could improve the performance of some postal employees who provide service to patrons in post offices.

Information about the U.S. Postal Service can be found at the following website: *www.usps.com/about/organizationinformation.htm.*

SKILL BUILDING WRITING EXERCISE 3.2

Assume that you are a supervisor of 15 maintenance technicians in a manufacturing company based in Chicago, Illinois. Your company has purchased and installed new production equipment, which is manufactured by a company in Stuttgart, Germany. While the equipment has been installed and is up and running, there are frequent jams or overloads, and the rate of defective products is high. It is clear that the technicians are not able to calibrate the equipment properly and do not understand several features of its sophisticated control systems. Clearly, the equipment is not operating at peak efficiency.

The German manufacturer of the equipment provides training in which maintenance technicians learn how to optimize the operation of the equipment. When the equipment was purchased, your company declined the manufacturer's recommendation that the maintenance technicians should be trained in Germany because of the costs involved. The training itself is not the issue because it is provided at no charge by the German company. Nonetheless, the travel expenses and lost work time make the training an expensive proposition, because it takes two weeks and is conducted only in the company's plant in Stuttgart. You have persuaded your boss that the technicians should receive the training. She is still concerned about the costs and is worried about not having enough maintenance technicians on the job while others are away being trained.

Your task will consist of the following: (1) develop plans and procedures for the performance of maintenance work while some of the operators are in Germany, (2) develop detailed plans and procedures for taking the operators to Germany, (3) develop a budget for the training including transportation and accommodations in Germany, and (4) set objectives for the training outcomes, which will enable you to demonstrate to your boss that the training was effective and that you stayed within the budget. You should also be aware that none of the technicians you supervise has ever traveled outside of the United States.

The following websites may be helpful for the travel components of your task.

- Travelocity
  www.travelocity.com

- U.S. State Department, Passport Services Office
  http://travel.state.gov/passport/passport_1738.html

- Stuttgart Tourism and Marketing Office
  www.stuttgart-tourist.de

CASE 3.1   Balancing Work and Family Obligations

Stephanie Barr is a computer technician at Mercury Industrial Design. She is a specialist in computer-aided design (CAD) and produces computerized designs for

Mercury's design engineers. Stephanie has an associate's degree in computer technology and is very knowledgeable about state-of-the-art CAD software. She works well with the engineers and is respected for her skills and the quality of her work. Stephanie enjoys her work, and market demand for her skills is strong. She occasionally receives job inquiries from other companies but likes her current employer and the proximity of the office to her home, her mother's house, and her children's school.

Until six months ago, Stephanie loved working at Mercury. She enjoyed her work, liked her supervisor, and had several good friends in the office. In addition, the pay and benefits package was very attractive. Unfortunately, things changed when her supervisor, Lucinda Ortiz, was transferred to one of the firm's other locations. Lucinda's replacement, Angelo Farris, began to make changes in the way work was scheduled. Because business was booming, the company had several new contracts, and Angelo began asking Stephanie and the other CAD operators to work overtime when there was a rush job. After a couple of months, Angelo began to schedule Stephanie for 50 to 60 hours of work every week. Overtime was no longer used only for rush jobs. It was simply built into the regular work schedule for each week.

After it became clear that the amount of overtime was not going to decline, Stephanie discussed the issue with Angelo. Stephanie said, "I don't mind working overtime on occasion when there is a rush project or an emergency. But I have two young children and obligations outside of work. My husband Cliff is a sales representative for an industrial products company and he's on the road at least two nights every week. So Cliff does not help much with the kids. Please don't schedule me for 10 to 20 hours of overtime every week." Stephanie was surprised by Angelo's response: "Stephanie, you have to understand that we have to get the work done that the engineers bring in here. I don't have any choice about overtime and I don't like to work a lot of overtime either. But the engineers like your work and the company is making a lot of money. Don't forget, the company's mission is to make money." Stephanie then said, "Well, why don't you hire more CAD technicians? We have more than enough work to justify more people." Angelo replied, "You know as well as I do that the market is so tight that we can't find good CAD technicians."

The situation continued for a few more weeks and Stephanie had one or two more conversations with Angelo about getting some relief from the amount of overtime. Finally, Angelo said, "Look, Stephanie, you have three options: work the overtime, transfer to another unit, or quit." Later, while Stephanie was talking with some coworkers about her conversation with Angelo, one of them said, "Angelo has been telling people that you are just trying to get more money." Stephanie was disappointed by this news and sought advice from friends away from work about her situation. All of them advised her to go to work elsewhere and said that she could find another job very quickly.

A few days later, Stephanie inquired in the human resources office about getting a transfer. She was told that she could apply but that there were no guarantees that she would obtain one. Stephanie then went to see Angelo. Stephanie said, "Angelo, I've just talked to the people in HR and I'm going to request a transfer." Angelo then said, "Stephanie, we need you here. We have three major new projects coming in and the company is going to make half a million dollars on each one." Angelo then laid out the plans he had for Stephanie and the other CAD technicians. After listening a few more minutes Stephanie said once more, "Angelo, I'm going to request a transfer."

Questions

1. Why is Angelo handling the issue with Stephanie in this manner? What do you think about Angelo's planning skills?

2. How should a supervisor balance the demands of the company's mission of generating profits with an employee's family obligations? What do you think about Angelo's view of the company's mission?

3. What should a company be willing to do when an employee says that family obligations are interfering with work?

4. How much can a company reasonably expect from its employees? What would you recommend as a reasonable accommodation?

CASE 3.2	**Channel 66 Community Cable Television**

Channel 66 Community Cable Television is located in a large metropolitan area. Cable subscribers receive this community service channel as a part of their basic cable package. The station provides local public service shows, such as city commission meetings, athletic events at local universities, high school football playoffs, minor league hockey games, and special events in the community. The station operates with a much smaller budget than commercial television stations since its revenues come from the cities and the local cable TV company. Nonetheless, the station takes pride in the quality of its programming and does frequent shoots at remote locations. Joe Washington is the producer/director for most of the remote shoots. Part of his responsibilities involves staffing the audio and video crews for every shoot that he produces and directs. The majority of the crew members are freelancers. Because the pay for experienced professional freelancers is high, Joe hires people at lower rates who have only minimal experience to do the video and audio work on these shoots. Many of these video and audio people are motivated by the desire to gain television experience so that they can eventually obtain jobs at commercial stations. Unfortunately, a few months ago the city and cable company lowered their contributions to the station and most of Joe's more experienced crew members left for higher-paying jobs.

As a result of these staffing problems, the shoots sometimes lack quality and take more time than they should. Furthermore, some of the freelancers are unreliable and shoots sometimes have to be completed without a full crew. Joe says, "If we could raise our pay rates, we could start requiring things like personal references and videotaped work samples. If my employees were getting really good pay, I could treat them a lot differently. But since they're not, I have to be more accommodating with schedules and behavior." Furthermore, Joe has found that the varying experience and competency levels require him to adapt his supervisory style to the individual members of his crews. Joe says, "When you offer such low pay, you almost have to take people fresh out of college. A lot of them have never been on a sports crew before, and if they don't take the initiative to learn and help out, it can set everyone back. Some have worked out and some haven't." Joe also stated, "Sometimes I even find that these people are unfamiliar with our equipment, and I have to drop everything and pitch in to get the work done. And a lot of the time when the crews arrive at the site of the shoot, they discover that they don't have all of the equipment, and I have to load up the van and make a special run." Although Joe tries to spend some time at every shoot, he says that he is spread too thin on other projects to be on site as much as he would like. He says, "When I have to leave, I ask someone on the crew to make sure the job gets done. It usually works out, but we've had some real problems."

This case is based on a management brief written by Daniel Baham. Reproduced with permission.

Questions

1. How can Joe improve his situation without more money to increase the pay for his crews? How would you evaluate his staffing practices?
2. What planning issues exist?
3. What directing issues exist?
4. What control issues exist?

REFERENCES

[1] Reeves, Jim. "Rangers in Debt to Buck," *Fort Worth Star Telegram* (August 25, 2005): 1D.

[2] Editorial Desk. "Actually It Was FEMA's Job," *New York Times* (October 2, 2005). Cable News Network (CNN), Network Coverage. [various dates]. MSNBC Network Coverage. [various dates].

[3] Cable News Network (CNN), Network Coverage. [various dates]. MSNBC Network Coverage. [various dates].

[4] Coale, Phil. Associated Press, photograph taken on 1 September 2005. *www.snopes.com/katrina/photos/buses.asp.*

[5] Cable News Network (CNN), Network Coverage. [various dates]. MSNBC Network Coverage. [various dates].

[6] Editorial Desk. "Actually It Was FEMA's Job."

[7] Ibid.

[8] Cable News Network (CNN), Network Coverage. [various dates]. MSNBC Network Coverage. [various dates].

[9] Kaplan, Robert S. and Norton, David P. *The Balanced Scorecard: Translating Strategy into Action.* Boston: Harvard Business School Press, 1996: 24–25.

[10] Daft, Richard L. *Management,* 5th ed. Fort Worth: Dryden Press, 2000: 206.

[11] Connelly, Mary. "Ford Suppliers Risk Losing New Business," *Automotive News Europe* (October 22, 2001): 12.

[12] Connelly, Mary. "Ford Works with Suppliers to Ensure Quality Standards," *Automotive News* (April 30, 2001): 36.

[13] ExxonMobil, "Employment Policies and Practices," (January 21, 2006): website: *www.exxonmobil.com/Corporate/Citizenship/CCR4/2004_ccr_csr_employment. asp.*

[14] Nordstrom. *Nordstrom Employee Handbook* (undated card furnished to one of the authors in 1997).

[15] Statistics: Mars Incorporated website: *www.mars.com*, 2002. Quote: Cantoni, Craig J. "A Waste of Human Resources," *Wall Street Journal* (May 15, 1995): A18.

[16] Marriott, J.W., Jr., and Brown, Kathi A. *The Spirit to Serve.* New York: HarperCollins Publishers (1997): pp. 5, 16. (©) 1997 by Marriott International, Inc. All rights reserved. Reprinted with the permission of Marriott International, Inc.

[17] Ibid.

[18] Carter, Rick. "Running Lean, Flying High," *Production Technology News* (February 2005): 26–28.

[19] Carter, "Running Lean, Flying High," 27.

[20] Fraser, Jill A. "A Return to Basics at Kellogg," *MIT Sloan Management Review*, (Summer 2004): 27–30.

[21] Fraser, "A Return to Basics at Kellogg."

[22] McConnell, Charles R. "The Manager and the Merger: Adaptation and Survival in the Blended Organization," *Health Care Manager* (September 2000): 1–11.

[23] Sy, Thomas, and D'Annunzio, Laura S. "Challenges and Strategies of Matrix Organizations: Top-Level and Mid-Level Managers' Perspectives," *Human Resource Planning* (Vol. 28, No. 1, 2005): 39–48.

[24] Katzenbach, Jon R., and Smith, Douglas K. *The Wisdom of Teams.* Boston: Harvard Business School Press, 1993.

[25] Hales, Chon. "Bureaucracy-Lite and Continuities in Managerial Work," *British Journal of Management* (March 2002): 151–166.

[26] Hutcherson, Norman B. "The Power of Networked Teams (Book Review)," *Library Journal* (May 1, 2001): 102.

[27] Pitts, Robert A., and Lei, David. *Strategic Management: Building and Sustaining Competitive Advantage*, 2nd ed., New York: South-Western College, 2000, 329.

[28] Pitts and Lei, *Strategic Management*, 329.

[29] Gerstner, Louis V. *Who Says Elephants Can't Dance?* New York: Harper Business, 2002, 242–244.

[30] *Personnel Today*, "Selection Test Increase," (March 11, 2003).

[31] BNA Editorial Staff. *Grievance Guide*, 10th ed., Washington, D.C.: Bureau of National Affairs (2000).

[32] Peters, Tom, and Austin, Nancy. *A Passion for Excellence.* New York: Warner Books, 1985.

[33] Marriott, J. W., Jr., and Brown, Kathi A. *The Spirit to Serve.* New York: Harpercollins Publishers (1997), p. 5. (©) 1997 by Marriott International, Inc. Reprinted with the permission of Marriott International, Inc.

[34] Bell, Chip R., and Heerwagen, Judith H. "Managing by Wandering Around," *Journal for Quality and Participation* (Winter 2000): 42–44.

[35] Kaplan and Norton. *The Balanced Scorecard:* 24–25.

[36] Drucker, Peter R. *Management Tasks, Responsibilities, Practices.* New York: Harper & Row (1974): 489–504.

[37] Semler, Ricardo. *Maverick.* New York: Warner Books, 1993.

[38] Colvin, Geoffrey. "The Anti-Control Freak," *Fortune* (November 26, 2001): 60.

[39] Ibid.

[40] Ibid.

[41] Semler, Ricardo. "Personal Histories: Ricardo Semler," *Harvard Business Review* (December 2001): 36. Reproduced with permission.

[42] U.S. Postal Service, *www.usps.com/postalhistory/welcome.htm.*

CHAPTER 4

"The most important thing in communication is to hear what isn't being said."

Peter Drucker[1]

Objectives

After reading and discussing this chapter, you should be able to do the following:

1. List the major goals of communication.
2. Outline the steps one should take in planning a communication.
3. List the basic components in the communication process.
4. Explain the barriers that can inhibit your efforts to communicate at work.
5. Describe the purposes of a management information system (MIS).
6. Explain ways to improve your listening skills.
7. Explain ways to improve communication within small groups.

French Feedback

A survey of French workers by the Gallup organization has found a remarkable level of dissatisfaction. A comparison of the results to those of U.S. workers indicates that the proportion of disgruntled workers in France was 26 percent relative to 16 percent in the United States. A similar disparity was found in positive results with only 6 percent of French workers reporting that they were engaged or happy with their work while 30 percent of U.S. workers were happy or engaged. Interestingly, French workers do not have to work as long as U.S. workers, as their workweeks are only 35 hours long and they also receive five weeks of vacation. One explanation for such results is based on differences in communication and the reluctance of managers in France to provide positive feedback: "It burns our throats to say good things to people." The supreme compliment is "ce n'est pas mal." Which means "not bad."[2]

The survey results probably present an overly critical statement about French workers, as there are productivity indicators that contradict such a pessimistic view. More specifically, French productivity has been at the top of European countries. Furthermore, other observers are very positive about French workers. For example, Kosuke Shiramizu, who has headed up Toyota's

Communication

operations in France, has pointed out that French workers were substantially more productive than their equivalents in North America.[3] Nonetheless, the consequences of poor communications are difficult to overstate, such as the impact of a supervisor's failure to share positive feedback with workers who are performing well, and there are French workers, and North American workers alike, who are under-performing because of the poor communication skills.

Questions for Thought

1. What are the actions that supervisors should take to ensure that their associates receive appropriate feedback?
2. How does a supervisor's ability to communicate effectively affect productivity?

Introduction

The importance of communication to you as a traditional supervisor, team leader, or team facilitator cannot be overstated. You must routinely give orders and instructions and relay information and ideas to and from your subordinates, associates, team members, superiors, and peers. Your plans can come to fruition only through effective communication.

Communication is the transmission of information and understanding from one person or group to another through the use of common symbols. **Information** is defined as facts, figures, or words in a usable form—the result of processing data. By **understanding,** we mean that all parties to a communication are of one mind as to its meaning and intent. The understanding that you should seek when receiving a communication is the exact perception of what the other person or group is trying to convey or transmit to you.

Communication can flow downward (vertically or diagonally), upward (vertically or diagonally), or horizontally (left or right). You will remember from our previous discussions of organization charts that the lines connecting the various blocks of the management hierarchy indicate, among other things, formal and routine business

communication
the transmission of information and common understanding from one person or group to another through the use of common symbols

information
any facts, figures, or data that are in a form or format that makes them usable to a person who possesses them

understanding
all parties to a communication are of one mind regarding its meaning and intent

*Learning
Objective
Number One*

communications. By using these lines of communication, managers help to plan, organize, direct, control, and coordinate their operations.

GOALS OF COMMUNICATION

The goal of your communication is to produce one or more of the following responses:

- To be understood—to get something across to someone so that he knows exactly what you mean
- To understand others—to get to know their exact meanings and intentions
- To gain acceptance for yourself or your ideas
- To produce action or change—to get the other person or group to understand what is expected, when it is needed, why it is necessary, and how to do it

All these goals point out the two-way nature of communication. There must be a common understanding; that is, each person must know the other's meaning and intent. One or both parties may have to ask questions to determine exactly what the other person means. Whether you are the initiator of or the target for a communication, you have the duty to seek common understanding—to be understood and to understand.

When you initiate communication, you should attempt to give the other person or group your exact perception and meaning. Communicating requires a two-way effort. Ideally, all parties to the process should be active participants; unfortunately, this is not always the case. Before you can listen attentively to another person, the area surrounding you must be free of distractions. Both parties must concentrate on the ideas under discussion. After someone speaks to you, try rephrasing what the person has said. Put what you think the person said into your own words and ask if that is an accurate restatement. Rephrasing is important because it forces you to listen for meaning as well as to words. Once you understand the words, try next to understand what the person intends as well. We examine techniques for effective listening later in this chapter.

*Learning
Objective
Number Two*

PLANNING COMMUNICATION

No matter to whom or why you feel the need to communicate your ideas, planning must precede the act of communication. The following checklist will serve you well as a sequential list of questions to answer as you prepare to communicate:

1. What are the objectives I wish to achieve by communicating? Do I want action? Understanding? Acceptance?
2. What are the essential facts? Do I know them, and am I able to express them properly?
3. Are my thoughts outlined? Whether your outline is mental or written, keep it brief and to the point.
4. Have I considered my receivers? What are their needs, and how can I sell my message to them? Do I know their backgrounds and frames of reference for this message?

5. Have I chosen the right symbols? Whether words, pictures, or some other symbols, are they correct for this communication? (Remember that words take on meaning both from the context in which they appear and in the minds of the people involved in the communication process.)

6. How should I communicate this message? Face to face? In writing? If in writing, should I use a memo? A letter? Is there time for formal channels, or should I go directly to my intended receivers?

7. When should I communicate? How receptive are my receivers? When will the environment be most free of anticipated disturbances?

8. Have I allowed for questions? Will I be able to judge my receivers' reactions, and will they be able to seek further information from me? How will I be sure my message has been received and properly interpreted?

Learning Objective Number Three

THE COMMUNICATION PROCESS

There are several major components or variables in the communication process: (1) the **transmitter** (sender), (2) the **message** (the sender's feelings, intent, ideas, and their meaning), (3) the **medium** (the message carrier), (4) the **receivers** (intended audience), and the (5) **feedback** (efforts by either sender or receiver to clarify the meaning and intent of a message). The interaction and mix of these can result in effective or ineffective communications.

THE TRANSMITTER

As this chapter points out, the effort to communicate is quite complex. Before you attempt to engage in it, you must be certain of its intended purpose(s). Who should receive your message? What is the best way (in person or in writing) to communicate the message? Only after you answer these and related questions will you be ready to outline your thoughts and convey them to others. The emotional content and sense of urgency of your message are also important to the ideas contained in its content. Your attitudes reflect your predisposition toward a subject and will affect the tone of your message. Receivers will know by listening to or reading your messages how you feel about their content.

THE MESSAGE

Your message consists of your feelings, intent, ideas, and the meaning of all these that you want to communicate. The objective of your communication dictates, in part, your choices regarding the other five components. The choice of words will be influenced in part by your intended receiver's point of view with regard to the subject matter of your message. How much you have to include, as well as how you will phrase your message, depends in part on what your receiver already knows about the subject and its importance.

transmitter
the person or group that sends a message to a receiver

message
the ideas, intent, and feelings that you wish to communicate to a receiver

medium
a channel or means used to carry a message in the communication process

receiver
the person or group intended by a transmitter to receive the message

feedback
any effort made by parties to a communication to ensure that they have a common understanding of each other's meaning and intent

THE MEDIUM

Your choice of medium may be dictated by your choice of receiver. If the receiver is a team leader or team member, oral conversations in person with individuals and teams are usually adequate. Your boss, however, may require written correspondence. This is especially true when the contents have historical significance and relate to her evaluations of your unit's progress. Written communication provides specific evidence that can confirm later just what was communicated, when, by whom, and to whom. Complicated messages are best transmitted in writing.

PowerPoint presentations. Some information is best presented in tables, charts, graphs, or pictures. Such visual media can communicate ideas at a glance that would otherwise take many paragraphs to explain. The PowerPoint medium allows presenters to incorporate charts and graphs, which amplify understandings of the major points of their messages. Unsurprisingly, because of the power of the medium, presentation skills are becoming increasingly important for supervisors as well as professionals with whom they work. By adhering to a few guidelines, supervisors can improve the quality of their presentations. For example, it is important to know your audience so the presentation can be tailored to their needs and level of awareness of the subject of the presentation. The presentation should not underestimate or overestimate the knowledge of the audience.[4] In addition, it is recommended that any bad news should be positioned early in the presentation so that those in the audience do not arrive at such a conclusion before it is presented. Similarly, major points, conclusions, or requests for action should be positioned early.[5] Another general guideline is that presenters should know the material well enough that they aren't tempted to read from the slides and should maintain eye contact with the audience.

Presentations can be improved by following a few specific guidelines. For example, only a limited number of slides should be included in the presentation, such as one slide for every three minutes of the presentation.[6] Many presenters do not understand this point, as they tend to overwhelm the audience with large numbers of slides. The old adage that less is more, applies to presentations. Another guideline is to follow a 10/30 rule for presentations in which there will be questions from the audience. For a 30-minute presentation, your prepared comments should cover approximately 10-minutes while questions and answers can be expected to take 20 minutes. With such a presentation, approximately three slides would be appropriate although backup slides should be prepared for greater detail if requested.[7]

Several technical guidelines should be followed. Bullet points should be short enough to fit on one line. In addition, numerical and tabular data should be converted to graphs and pie charts to facilitate comprehension. In general, no more than three colors should be used, other than those that make up the background. An exception is that critical information may be highlighted with one or two additional colors. A final suggestion is that the use of red should be minimized because it cannot be seen as well as other colors at longer distances.[8]

groupware
software enabling group members to work together without close proximity

Electronic communication technology. It is important to use the technology at hand in your organization as it best applies to your purposes and needs. Of particular note are e-mail, voice mail, voice messaging, networking, and **groupware** software packages. E-mail sends messages and documents instantaneously. However, both e-mail and voice mail must be used appropriately:

> In e-mail, express sincere appreciation for the work of the group by using words that fit your character. If you're effervescent, use demonstrative words. If you're not, don't use words that are totally out of character. If you are sending a voice mail, the right tone is more important than the words you use. If you get a voice mail that you must forward, hold on to it for review before broadcasting it to managers or staff. If the tone isn't right, you might want to recast the message in more appealing tones. Always remember this: Tone isn't simply part of the message; it is the message.[9]

E-mail etiquette. While e-mail is a wonderful tool that can enhance a supervisor's ability to communicate and coordinate quickly with large numbers of people, it can lead to problems when simple rules of etiquette are not followed. For example, sensitive issues should not be handled with e-mail. Instead, face-to-face communication, which provides a richer form of communication with facial expressions, tone of voice, and body language, should be the medium for conversations involving sensitive matters. In contrast to e-mail, personal conversations demonstrate vastly more consideration for the other people involved and leave less room for misunderstanding. An often-ignored rule for e-mail etiquette is to make sure the addressees are correct before sending the message. Sending e-mail messages to the wrong people can be very embarrassing and damaging.[10]

Several other etiquette suggestions are worth noting. For example, one should avoid sending long e-mail messages. If the message is long, then it should be discussed in person. In addition, it is important to ensure that the tone is appropriate. The tone should not be too informal nor should it be too impersonal. By taking a little time to examine the message from the perspective of the people who will read it, one can usually avoid using the wrong tone. By all means, never send an e-mail when you are angry or frustrated because emotions are typically amplified in writing and you cannot get the message back after you have calmed down. Some other suggestions are not to waste other people's time by copying them or using the reply to all parties function if they do not need the information. Similarly, you can save recipients time by providing a clear subject line for the message. A good time management suggestion is to keep e-mail from driving your schedule. Supervisors can manage their time better if they block off times to attend to e-mail rather than responding quickly to all messages.[11] On the other hand, it is good etiquette to reply in a timely manner, typically within 24 hours, when a message needs a response.[12]

Finally, supervisors need to be aware of, and make their employees aware of, the types of materials that should not be sent through e-mail. Many companies have found that inappropriate e-mails have led to lawsuits.[13] E-mail records of companies are being subpoenaed with greater frequency today and can put an employer at a disadvantage in lawsuits.[14] As a general rule, one should assume, when deciding on the appropriateness of content to be sent in an e-mail, that it may be read by anyone. An attorney has provided the following advice, "Don't put anything in an e-mail that you wouldn't shout down an office hallway."[15]

Virtual teaming. As noted earlier in this text, the global nature of business and advances in Internet and groupware technology, which facilitates group interactions, have led to the development of geographically dispersed **virtual teams.** Because of the

TEAMS

virtual team
a geographically disbursed team that utilizes various forms of telecommunications and computer-based technologies to coordinate its activities

importance of communications to virtual teams some of the special communication issues will be addressed in this discussion. Although they have little face-to-face contact, members of virtual teams work together by communicating with one another through computer groupware, such as Lotus Notes, e-mail, and video conferencing. An example of a virtual team is provided by an engineering team at Lockheed-Martin in which members of the team are located at the company's different plants in Palmdale, California; Fort Worth, Texas; and Marietta, Georgia. Members of virtual teams have discovered that they have to learn new skills before their teams can perform well. As with other teams, there must be a compelling purpose for the team to perform, clearly defined objectives, accountability, and commitment.[16]

A major difference between virtual and traditional teams is that some special rules are necessary. For example, the team needs to have solutions to problems when some members are not participating, the team should be small (no more than 12 to 16 members), and it should agree on "netiquette," such as the acceptability of some good-natured flaming. The team also has to resolve the issue of leadership because a team leader is not present in real-time. In addition, it is important that the members of virtual teams have the opportunity to meet face to face in order to form stronger relationships. At such meetings, the goals and purpose of the team can be clarified.

STMicroelectronics and American Express found that a benefit of such teams is that they can apply the best talent to the task instead of forcing the company to rely on the people who are at a particular physical location. In addition, virtual teams offer quality-of-life advantages in that team members do not have to travel as much and can be at home with their families at night.[17] Despite the advantages of virtual teams, team experts Jon Katzenbach and Douglas Smith point out that virtual teams do not provide as rich of a form of communication as personal contact:

> Note Katzenbach and Smith, "E-mail and threaded discussions, for all their virtues, cannot simulate a firm, friendly handshake, can't grin disarmingly and pat a colleague on a shoulder. Humans don't communicate by words alone." And, "Teaming only works with small groups, yet technology makes it too easy to keep adding members to the team."[18]

Telecommuting. The number of telecommuters (teleworkers) who work for governments and such businesses as IBM, AT&T, Du Pont, American Express, and Pacific Bell is increasing. In the United States, there are at least 28 million workers who telecommute.[19] Telecommuting, which is made possible by today's information technology, is growing because of quality-of-life considerations and environmental concerns about reducing work-related vehicle use. More specifically, reasons for increased telecommuting include reduced commuting time, improved work-family life balance, fuel savings, accommodation of workers with disabilities, reduced costs for offices, and compatibility with virtual organizations.[20] Surprisingly, many Silicon Valley technology firms have lagged other companies in telecommuting. Telecommuting is particularly attractive to employees of such firms because of the area's crowded highways and expensive housing. Because the average cost of homes in the area is very expensive, it is not possible for many employees to live within a short distance of their companies. Intel has recently opened satellite facilities that save on commuting time for employees. For example, one of its satellite offices in downtown San Francisco is equipped with 103 workstations. The company's recent support for telecommuting is in contrast to its previous view. "The old Intel mentality was that if you weren't in your cubicle, you weren't doing your work."[21] Not all Silicon Valley companies have been slow to adopt telecommuting; Hewlett-Packard and 3Com have longstanding telecommuting policies.[22]

Other media. Different media have different effects on receivers. Most people are used to seeing company bulletins, memos, and newsletters because they are routinely used to carry information. As a result, these media lose their ability to capture people's attention and gain their interest. They are read casually, if at all, and may be set aside during busy times to be read at a later date. Further, using two or more media either sequentially or simultaneously can add emphasis and help ensure that reception takes place. Unusual media should be used to carry only unusual messages.

THE RECEIVERS

Your own experience tells you that some subjects are received with more enthusiasm and interest than others. Some subjects touch off emotional responses and can inhibit reason and understanding. Try to determine your receiver's prior knowledge and predisposition toward the subject about which you wish to communicate before you attempt to do so. Delicate subjects, such as those requiring reprimands or punitive measures, are best handled in person, one on one, and in private. By anticipating how your receivers are likely to view your message, you can tailor your message's words, tone, and method of delivery to fit the circumstances.

Communicating with associates. Your associates want to know what you expect from them. They expect and need information from you on their progress, successes, and shortcomings. You should pass e-mail, memos, bulletins, and reports from others to them on an as-needed basis. Your practice of management by wandering around allows you ample opportunity to find out what is on their minds, what they are feeling, and what they are thinking about. Their activities and goals must be coordinated with those of your other subordinates.

A new management approach called **open book management** addresses many communication issues. Essentially, open book management says there are no secrets. All employees are entitled to be informed about the company's financial status so that they will be able to make decisions that support the company's performance. The Bradshaw Group in Richardson, Texas, provides a good example of open book management that relies on sharing financial information with employees as a means of becoming more competitive.

open book management
sharing all financial information with employees so that they can make informed decisions and earn a share of increased profits

> "Everybody makes decisions," he [the CEO] says. . . . "If they make them in a vacuum of information—or with what little information you eke out, or maybe even under a false impression of the truth—how can you expect them to make the right decisions for the result you want?" . . . Rather than go it alone, he decided 55 heads were better than one. So everything has been laid out in black and white. The only info kept under wraps is individual salaries.[23]

Because most of its employees did not understand accounting and financial terms, the Bradshaw Group taught employees the basics of these subjects. Brown-bag lunches involving humorous presentation styles were used to teach these subjects. The incentive for employees is that they share 10 percent of the company's profits if it reaches its profit goal.[24]

SUPERVISORS AND ETHICS

A telephone conversation of five minutes is not something that would typically be viewed as a behavior that could constitute both an ethics violation, as well as a legal violation, serious enough to end one's career and result in a 30-month sentence in a federal prison. Nonetheless, Daniel Bayly, 30-year employee at Merrill Lynch who previously headed up Merrill Lynch's investment banking operations, found himself in exactly such a situation. The telephone conversation in question, which was held with Enron's CFO, Andrew Fastow, concerned a purchase of barges from Enron. Government prosecutors maintained that the deal, concluded during the conversation between Bayly and Fastow, constituted a crime because of a guarantee from Fastow that either Enron or another buyer would purchase the barges at some point in the future. Prosecutors argued that Merrill Lynch entered into the deal in order to obtain investment banking business from Enron in the future. A jury eventually convicted Bayly and three other executives at Merrill Lynch on charges of fraud and conspiracy. Bayly and his former colleagues appealed their convictions on several grounds.

It is ironic that Bayly had an enviable reputation for high standards of ethics over many years with Merrill Lynch. He was even referred to as "Eagle Scout Bayly" by some colleagues at the firm because he had rejected deals that did not conform to ethical standards he upheld. Furthermore, the CEO of Merrill Lynch served as a character witness for Bayly.

While Bayly was a high-level executive, the lessons learned from his experience are relevant to supervisors. This chapter has emphasized the importance of accurate, timely, and persuasive communications. Nonetheless, in some environments within complex organizations, communications about some topics are legally prohibited because they can create conspiracy and fraud. Supervisors simply cannot assume that private conversations or unwritten agreements are permissible. Whenever they have the slightest doubt about the ethical or legal propriety of communications, they should obtain clear and unambiguous guidance from the firm's ethics and legal officers.

Source: Landon Thomas, Jr. "Deals and Consequences," *New York Times* (November 20, 2005).

Communicating with peers. Your peers consist of all managers who are on the same level of the company's hierarchy as you are. Touching base with peers regularly allows you to build friendships, share information, coordinate operations, and teach as well as learn. Open and honest communication with peers builds the teamwork and mutual commitment to values, goals, and strategies so essential to good working relationships.

Communicating with others. Others you must communicate with regularly include your boss, staff managers, and outsiders such as customers and suppliers. The boss wants to be kept up to date on your progress and on that of your section, without having to ask for updates. Staff people want to be consulted so that they can share their expertise. They need to know your progress on problems they have been asked to help you solve. They want to find you receptive to their suggestions and assistance.

As you read this chapter's Supervisors and Ethics feature, think about the care that supervisors must exercise in communications involving sensitive matters.

THE FEEDBACK

Feedback allows both the sender and receiver to discover if they are of one mind as to the meaning and intent of a message. If the receiver does not engage in feedback, the sender must do so. Asking a receiver to restate a message in her own words is a good start. Anticipate where misunderstanding might take place and quiz the receiver about those areas. Only when both sender and receiver have the same understanding has communication taken place.

Supervisors should seek feedback and provide feedback on a timely basis. A common flaw of supervisors is that they sometimes wait too long to provide feedback to their employees and then they provide a historical account of how things could have been handled better. Such an approach is demoralizing to employees and is unlikely to accomplish what the supervisor had in mind. An improved approach for giving feedback is to direct the feedback toward the future by providing suggestions for how the employee can handle an issue or task when it comes up the next time.[25] Another suggestion for feedback is to provide analysis instead of opinions or feedback based on matters of taste. For example, instead of telling an employee that you would have priced something differently than he or she has, provide the employee with information on the success of products that have been priced differently and inquire about the employee's rationale. Finally, do not be a miser with positive feedback or save it up for a future occasion. Pass it on to the employee because it will be appreciated and because the positive comments provide the employee with a good sense of the direction for the future.[26]

The word *feedback* has other meanings in communications. Giving individuals and teams praise, constructive criticism, and measurements of their performance is often referred to as **scoreboarding.** More specifically, scoreboarding is an effort to:

> Set up a game designed to change [a] situation. It has an easily measurable goal [usually quantifiable]. . . . It has rules that everybody understands. At the end there's some kind of payoff for a win. . . . Teach everybody to track [the] numbers. Show employees how what they do affects the figures. Then put up a big scoreboard and watch what happens. Oh, yes—pass out bonuses if employees hit monthly or quarterly targets.[27]

scoreboarding
providing feedback on individual and team efforts to reach goals

More will be said in later chapters about scoreboarding. It has the power to energize people and gain their commitment to a project.

The Supervisors and Performance feature for this chapter deals with conditions that provide challenges to supervisors and the ways in which they can succeed in such situations.

DOWNWARD, UPWARD, DIAGONAL, AND HORIZONTAL COMMUNICATION

As a traditional supervisor or team facilitator, you will most frequently send your communication in an upward or downward **direction.** You will be communicating most often with associates, team leaders, or your boss. You also will be using diagonal communication to communicate with staff specialists. Diagonal communication can occur outside formal channels, leaving your boss out of the flow. This is often the case when

direction
in communication, the flow or path a message takes in order to reach a receiver

SUPERVISORS AND PERFORMANCE

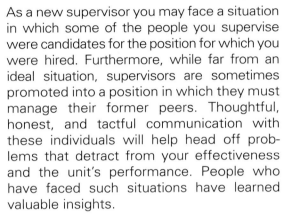
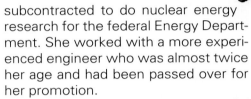

As a new supervisor you may face a situation in which some of the people you supervise were candidates for the position for which you were hired. Furthermore, while far from an ideal situation, supervisors are sometimes promoted into a position in which they must manage their former peers. Thoughtful, honest, and tactful communication with these individuals will help head off problems that detract from your effectiveness and the unit's performance. People who have faced such situations have learned valuable insights.

When Amy Pearl interviewed in 2001 for an engineering director's role with a communication device company based in Santa Clara, Calif., she knew that one of the managers interviewing her had been rejected for the position. So she addressed it in the interview itself. "I frankly and nicely told her that I knew that she had been interested in the job, and that I hoped I had something to offer her as a boss," Ms. Pearl said. "When she was grilling me about how I viewed and handled some particular engineering management issue, I got to talk to her about her experience and problems she encountered. Then I gave her some concrete advice."

Ms. Pearl, who landed the job, says the contender was a loyal supporter because Ms. Pearl had demonstrated her usefulness as a supervisor early on.

Another example of how to handle such sensitive situations is provided in the following account:

Susan Sorstokke . . . was transferred to . . . manage a technical department of a *Fortune* 500 company that subcontracted to do nuclear energy research for the federal Energy Department. She worked with a more experienced engineer who was almost twice her age and had been passed over for her promotion.

"I was always very, very respectful of his depth of experience," Ms. Sorstokke said. "That went beyond just acknowledging his direct input to the way I interacted with him. For example, I never, in the entire three years that we worked together, called him to my office. If I wanted to meet with him, I always went to his office. I was very careful of never pulling a power play." As a result of her deference, she said, the engineer was never a problem.

Such situations may also involve performance issues, which supervisors cannot ignore. A final example is illustrative of such a situation.

Beth VanStory . . . ran into a problem after she joined the Internet division of a television channel . . . Despite numerous overtures to build a positive relationship, she said, a manager in her department was sulking more than performing because she had not gotten Ms. VanStory's job. Ms. VanStory said she felt that this could have an impact on the team, so she issued an ultimatum: "I told her it was up to her. 'I'll work with you on a development plan to get your work here back on track, or I will work with you on a search plan for your departure.'" The manager chose the development plan and turned her performance around.

Source: Cheryl Dahle, "Office Space: Career Couch; A Co-Worker Wanted the Job You Got," New York Times (May 1, 2005). Copyright (©) (2007) by the New York Times Co. Reprinted with permission.

staff managers possess functional authority. It is wise, therefore, to keep appropriate records of such communication and to check with your boss before answering or reacting to staff orders or requests. A simple e-mail message or memo can keep your boss informed of actions that you eventually take.

As a traditional supervisor and team facilitator, you use horizontal paths to communicate with peers. As a team leader, you use them to coordinate your team's operations with those of other team leaders. Team members communicate horizontally on a regular basis. You also use horizontal paths to resolve conflicts and mutual problems between and among groups. The following advice applies to teams that rely heavily on electronic forms of communication:

> One of the key early lessons [of virtual teams with members in different locations] is that for collaboration to work well, it has to be between people, not just machines. Management experts say digital workspaces can't completely replace more traditional interactions, especially in the creative process. In-person communication is important for training, building relationships, and riding herd on a difficult project. Nistevo [a software company] addresses that by mixing tech wizardry with old-fashioned meetings. Palacios of Land O'Lakes says companies participating in Nistevo's . . . project build trust and sort out their problems by meeting face-to-face every quarter.[28]

When communicating upward to their bosses and higher level managers, or executives, supervisors should exercise care to ensure that their communications, either verbal or in writing, do not waste the time of the listener or reader. While the jobs of supervisors are typically fast paced, higher level positions usually have even greater time pressures and a broader scope of responsibility. A supervisor who can get the point across quickly or get a question answered quickly will be greatly appreciated. The author is aware of a situation in a large U.S. corporation, which has a daily operations conference call involving top executives and a fairly large number of geographically dispersed operations managers. The executives have expressed frustrations at how frequently the operations managers take far too much time in these daily briefings as they seem to provide far too much verbiage in their reports and explanations.

Learning
Objective
Number Four

COMMUNICATION BARRIERS

The essential ingredients in the communication recipe are the transmitter, the message, the direction, the medium, the receiver, and the feedback. If any of these ingredients is defective in any way, clarity of meaning and understanding will be lacking. Communication barriers can arise that will spoil these ingredients and, therefore, the communication process. The following sections describe seven major barriers to successful communication.

UNCOMMON SYMBOLS

Words, such as *feedback*, take on meaning only in the context of the message they compose. Similarly, facial expressions can be misinterpreted. Gestures viewed out of context can take on entirely different meanings than were intended. Every child knows the blank expression that his slang expressions can evoke on the face of a parent. Every employee knows the discomfort and confusion that can arise when the boss exhibits unfamiliar or contradictory behaviors.

Example: Sally, the supervisor of a data-processing section, has an established pattern of communication. Each morning on entering her section, she greets each of her seven associates warmly and inquires about their well-being and work. Today, she entered the office and went straight to her desk, ignoring all of her subordinates. What do you think might happen in the minds of her subordinates? What might the impact of her behavior be on today's work output?

Communication problems arise when a message in one language must be translated into another. Translating is becoming increasingly necessary for many team leaders, team facilitators, and their companies. In addition to the operational necessities for translating language, there are safety issues as well. In the construction industry, where approximately 18 percent of the workers speak Spanish, there have been inordinate fatalities with such workers as they account for one-third of fatalities. Companies such as DPR Construction and Devcon Construction are addressing this issue with classes, which teach safety terms in Spanish.[29] Many companies that experience an influx of foreign-born employees have created English as a Second Language (ESL) programs. In tight labor markets, temporary help agencies, such as Select Personnel Services in California, have entered into cooperative arrangements with important clients to provide language training for large immigrant groups such as Hispanics and Asians.[30] Interestingly, many Hispanics who become managers of newly immigrated Hispanic workers now need to learn to speak Spanish because they grew up in the United States speaking only English.[31]

IMPROPER TIMING

Unless the receiver is in the right frame of mind and tuned in to the proper channel, he will not hear your message. Likewise, the sender can be upset, agitated, or improperly prepared to communicate. We all know the regrets that go with speaking in haste while we are in the heat of emotion or not thinking clearly. And when we are distracted, we may hear words but not their intended meanings.

ENVIRONMENTAL DISTURBANCES

The communication environment should be as free as possible from *noise*—any thing or condition in the physical environment that interferes with the transmission and understanding of information. Such conditions as static on a cell phone, the din of machines on the shop floor, and the simultaneous conversations of people in groups create background noise that inhibits communication. When people must shout to be heard or receive too many messages at one time, they experience noise. When noise exists, you must either remove it or move to an environment more conducive to the communication process.

Example: A team leader had no sooner begun to interview a job applicant in her office when the phone rang. After handling the call, she resumed the interview.

Five minutes later, a change in shift occurred, creating noise and confusion outside her office. How successful do you think this interview was for either person?

IMPROPER ATTITUDES

An unfavorable predisposition toward the subject, the sender, or the receiver will interfere with understanding. In fact, it may provoke emotional and harmful responses in place of the desired ones. Poor attitudes held by the sender or the receiver will confuse rather than clarify.

Example: One of your subordinates, Shirley, comes to ask you again today if she has gotten the pay raise you recommended for her two weeks ago. She has been asking you about it for the past five days, and you have told her that, as soon as you know, you will tell her. Since you have not heard anything yet, you answer her tersely, "No! Now don't bother me!" Have you created problems for yourself by such a response? How do you think Shirley will react?

BACKGROUND DIFFERENCES

A lack of similar backgrounds for the sender and the receiver may hinder receptiveness to a message and prevent a proper reaction to it. Deborah Tannen, author and professor, notes that the majority of men and women "learn to speak particular ways because those ways are associated with their own gender. And individual men or women who speak in ways associated with the other gender will pay a price for departing from cultural expectations."[32] When a newcomer attempts to give advice to the old-timer, the latter may react with irritation. These and many similar situations arise every day at work and often interfere with communication efforts.

Communication problems caused by language can be alleviated through education. Some companies offer on-site English as a Second Language (ESL) courses, like this one at Ore-Ida Foods. Ore-Ida Foods also offers tuition reimbursement for those willing to learn Spanish.

Example: Allen, age 25, is being trained by Arthur, who is about to retire. Arthur is teaching Allen his job. While certain established procedures are being discussed, Allen recommends a change he feels will speed things up. Instead of evaluating Allen's proposal, Arthur shuts him off by stating, "Who's the expert here, you or me? This is the way I have always done it, and it works." What do you think will be Allen's reaction? What are the potential negative effects for the company?

Communicating with people who differ significantly from you can be a challenge. One big problem is that most of us group people and use labels for them—Hispanics, blacks, whites, Asians, career women, handicapped, and so on. These labels can separate people and may be offensive to those to whom they are applied. The key to communicating with others is to determine what they want you to do and how they wish to be addressed—what they feel comfortable with—and to avoid generalizations and stereotypes.

Two examples serve to highlight the importance of personal communication with a boss, subordinate, or peer. When you ask a member of the Navajo people "How are you?" you are implying that the person has been sick. This question is not an everyday greeting. It is an inquiry about how a person is doing on the road to recovery. In like fashion, if you ask a disabled person if he or she needs help, that person may view your inquiry as an insulting expression of doubt about his ability to function independently. Most people with physical limitations will ask for assistance if they need it. They want to be treated like anyone else—on an individual and personal level.

Workshops with the physically challenged yield the following tips for communicating with handicapped subordinates or team members:

- Treat them with the same respect and trust as any other employee or coworker
- Ask them what they need to succeed, and empower them with the needed items and assistance
- Don't expect anything less from them than you would expect from able-bodied subordinates in the same job
- Don't wait for them to experience problems in their physical environment; be proactive and seek to identify and remove barriers to their mobility and productivity

Educate yourself on the attitudes and problems typically encountered on the job by people facing physical challenges. One supervisor who had a subordinate with impaired hearing took the time to learn sign language and now communicates in this way or in writing with that person. Another supervisor quickly realized that her vision-impaired subordinate's productivity could be improved with the simple addition of a large magnifier lens affixed to a flexible arm attached to her desk. It greatly enhanced the readability of the text with which she had to work.

SENDER-RECEIVER RELATIONSHIPS

Potentially conflicting functional relationships, such as between line manager and staff manager or between engineer and accountant, can hinder communication. Suspicion on the part of one about the other's intentions or doubt about her ability to communicate about the other's specialty can block the transmission of information. Unequal

Communicating in a noisy environment interferes with the transmission and understanding of information.

positional or status relationships, such as between supervisor and subordinate or between skilled worker and apprentice, can cause one to tune out the other.

Example: A production supervisor is told by the director of human resources that the production section will be reorganized into autonomous teams and that he is being assigned to training for a team leader position. Since the production manager resents being told by an "outsider" that he will have to learn to share authority with former subordinates, the supervisor resists the training assignment and begins to plot to sabotage the efforts at team building. What are the possible consequences? How could they have been prevented?

Non-Questioning Associates

Without conflict and discomfort, little meaningful change occurs in people and organizations. The saying "If it ain't broke, don't fix it" is often an excuse to maintain the old, familiar, and comfortable ways of doing things and may cause teams and their leaders to wait too long before reexamining their performance. A total quality management philosophy demands that all persons and their organizations commit to continual and often radical efforts to improve. It requires a commitment to a never-ending journey.

In everyday organizational life, there are those who promote and those who object to change. Resistance, no matter what its motivation, is to be expected and helps promoters become aware of any flaws in their thinking—anything they may have overlooked that could spell disaster. When you and your team members propose the new and different, you should welcome disagreement and arguments both for and against proposals. In addition, resistance is often a code for fear that the individual cannot successfully cope with the change.

Often the first response people give you is not the true resistance. You need to explore their reactions deeply. For example, your plan to automate procurement procedures won't work because software development will be far too expensive. It could be that "costs too much" is a fact and that listening to the resistance may save you headaches and dollars. . . . Slowing down, going deeper lets you get at the real resistance. Perhaps people fear that they lack the skills to work sophisticated programs. Go deeper: perhaps they fear they are expendable. . . . To even hope to get people in sync with your plans, ideas, or dreams, you must listen and hear their concerns and fears—both rational and emotional. You must listen to the messages that come from their heads, hearts, and bodies. Let yourself be influenced by what you hear.[33]

When you don't receive any disagreement, you should suspect that "yes men and women" surround you. "If your [associates] haven't been disagreeing with you very much or very hard, you may need to do a bootlicking reality check. You may even need to reexamine your organization's incentive structure."[34] Beware, also, of those among your associates who make proposals that they believe will please you and agree with yours. Such people rarely report unpleasant developments and may act to hide them from your view. According to research by economist Candice Pendergast at the University of Chicago, "companies unwittingly create a culture of yes men [and women] when they rely on subjective performance evaluations of workers . . . the more the worker's pay is tied to the manager's opinion of [the worker], the more powerful [the worker's] incentive to say what the manager wants to hear."[35]

Example: This story is told about the founder of a company who held a meeting with his team facilitators to discuss a radical reorganization plan. The meeting went something like this:

FOUNDER: I trust all of you have read my proposal?
TEAM FACILITATORS: (Responses and nodding of heads in the affirmative.)
FOUNDER: Do you have any questions or objections?
TEAM FACILITATORS: (Silence and shaking of heads in the negative.)
FOUNDER: This meeting is adjourned and will reconvene when you all have both.

All barriers have the same effect on communication—they limit mutual understanding. Knowing that these barriers exist is half the battle. The other half is working to tear them down or to minimize their effects.

This chapter's feature on supervising teams provides an example of how leaders help their teams obtain a high level of performance.

MANAGEMENT AND INFORMATION

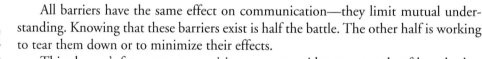

Learning Objective Number Five

All managers and their teams exist to make decisions. To make them, they need a steady flow of many kinds of information. Information originates with data (raw facts and figures) that are then gathered, analyzed, and placed into appropriate formats. This information can then be delivered to those who need it. Specialized departments and activities exist in larger organizations to accomplish these activities.

SUPERVISING TEAMS

Dean Smith, the former legendary basketball coach at the University of North Carolina for more than 36 years, is the most successful coach in collegiate basketball history in terms of games won. During his coaching career at North Carolina his teams won 879 games and lost only 254. Coach Smith has always been known as a "class act" for the manner in which he treats his players as well as other coaches and their teams. His calm demeanor, even in the most intense moments of games, inspired his players' confidence. He stood out among competing coaches for the respectful manner in which he treated his players instead of screaming at them for mistakes. In addition, he was a developer of talent, with 51 of his players, such as Michael Jordan, going on to play in the National Basketball Association and Roy Williams becoming a highly successful and respected coach at the University of Kansas and at the University of North Carolina.

Smith's coaching provides many examples that are relevant to supervisors and work teams. One is that team members need to acknowledge each other's contributions and reinforce successful team behaviors. As an example of such reinforcement of teamwork, Smith originated the practice in which a player who scores then acknowledges the contribution by pointing to the player who provided the assist. Smith, who grew up in Emporia, Kansas, watching teams coached by his father, Alfred Smith, learned the importance of teamwork and discipline. In one incident, his father found out that four of his five starting players had broken curfew one night. Even though the game on the following day was a critical one, Alfred suspended the four players and replaced them with substitutes. Because of superb teamwork of the substitute players, the team was able to win the game by one point. The lesson was not lost on Dean Smith, who made teamwork the hallmark of his coaching philosophy. Smith also stressed unselfishness in his coaching philosophy. He felt that when individual players received attention for their play, the other players would lose their intensity and care less about winning.

Source: Michael Richman, "Basketball Coach Dean Smith: Emphasis on Teamwork Netted Him Record Number of Wins," *Investor's Business Daily* (January 8, 2001), A3.

MANAGEMENT INFORMATION SYSTEMS

In most large businesses, a systems approach is needed to manage the inflow, processing, and outflow of both data and information. A *management information system (MIS)* is a formal organizational effort to make information of the right quality available to all decision-makers. An organization's MIS should provide usable and needed information to the right people, at the right time, in the right amount, and at the right place. It may or may not use computers.

The first step in designing an MIS begins with a study or survey to determine who needs what kind of information, when, and in what quality and form. Information users help determine how the system will operate and what it will generate. Both users and data processors must cooperate to ensure that the system produces only what is needed—no more and no less—at a reasonable cost.

An example of a computer-based MIS is found in many supermarket chain stores. Their checkout lanes are equipped with cash registers and electronic sensing equipment linked directly to a central computer. Most items in these stores' inventories have data stored in universal product codes (UPCs)—the panels on the products that contain patterns of black lines and numbers below them. The UPCs are sensed at the checkout counter, and the data they contain are sent directly to a computer. In this example, the checkout system is only one part of the chain's MIS, but a vital one. It provides both data and information to the checker, the customer, and the store's and the chain's managers. The UPC data are needed to keep track of the store's inventory and sales, to assist in consolidated purchasing by the chain, and to carry out routine accounting activities for both the store and the chain.

The following describes a new and sophisticated form of MIS in which answers to questions about the buying patterns of retail customers can be found:

> Data mining . . . is the process of discovering interesting patterns in databases that are useful in decision making. Data mining is a discipline of growing interest and importance, and an application area that can provide significant competitive advantage to any organization by exploiting the potential of large data warehouses. The task of finding patterns in business data is not new. Traditionally, it was the responsibility of business analysts, who generally use statistical techniques. The scope of this activity, however, has recently changed. Widespread use of computers and networking technologies has created large electronic databases that store business transactions. Retailers, like Wal-Mart Stores, capture millions of sales transactions through their point-of-sale terminals. Transactions can be analyzed to identify buying patterns of individual customers as well as customer groups, and sales patterns of different stores.[36]

THE SUPERVISOR AND THE MIS

As a traditional supervisor, team leader, or team facilitator, you are part of your organization's MIS. Whether it is a formal, planned system using sophisticated computers and software or not, you send data to it and receive information from it. After you determine your information needs, you should consult with MIS specialists about meeting these needs. For example, are you receiving too much information, information in the wrong form, outdated information, or not enough information? If so, take action now to improve your situation. Stop the flow of unneeded information. Help create a flow of information you lack. Let those who generate your information know how well they are meeting your needs. If your organization lacks an adequate MIS, investigate what you and your peers can do to create one.

While the MIS has made massive contributions to improved operations in most organizations and is of substantial value to supervisors and managers, MIS has not made the same contribution to the jobs of top managers. While this text is concerned with the subjects of supervision and management, it is important to understand that MIS does not provide much of the information top managers need. All managers, especially top managers, need information about the external environment.[37] Management scholar Peter Drucker provided an interesting perspective on the information needs of top managers and how information available in MIS can distract top executives from an external focus on opportunities and threats. The availability of information from such systems tends to cause top executives to shift their emphasis to internal matters, such as costs and measures of effort. As a result, Drucker concluded that such systems have had a negative impact on top management.[38]

COMPUTERS AND COMMUNICATION

Computer technology is having an immeasurable impact on managers' jobs. Leading-edge applications are affecting the work of managers in myriad ways. For example, Blockbuster maintains a sophisticated customer database that has allowed the company to increase same-store sales in a declining industry. Another example is Detroit Edison, which uses an information system to deploy its employees in advance of forecasted storms. The system is so precise that when a utility pole is knocked down by a storm, it signals the location so that repair crews can be dispatched. Duke Energy, which is pursuing an aggressive acquisition strategy, uses PeopleSoft to quickly include the employees of acquired companies into its payroll and benefits systems.[39] Keebler Foods provides another example of excellent information systems. The company has an information system to which its "five regional offices, 12 plants, 14 shipping centers, and 54 distribution centers are connected, allowing Keebler to efficiently manage inventory, sales, and costs and to maintain a two-day delivery cycle to grocery stores."[40]

Probably the best example of the impact of computerized information systems on managerial communications is provided by Wal-Mart, America's largest and most successful retailer. Before he died, Sam Walton saw to it that Wal-Mart's stores and managers were connected to his companies' suppliers. Through interfacing computer networks, store managers track sales by inventory item, keep in touch with suppliers, keep tabs on the progress of orders, and allow suppliers to tap in to their computer

Laptop computers, PDAs, and other technology continue to improve employee flexibility, mobility, and efficiency.

memories. Such instant communication and monitoring allows the organization to respond to any trends and changes in consumer preferences within a few hours. Stores can communicate with the home office, each other, and their suppliers with the touch of a few keys on their computer keyboards. Vendors stay on top of the trends that may be developing and are able to respond to the buyers' needs within hours. The company, which spends $500 million each year on information technology, now has a database that is exceeded in size only by the U.S. government.[41]

Computers can make work faster and more efficient. They can eliminate paperwork, make information flow more freely, put information into more useful forms, and reduce costs. Unfortunately, they can also create more stress for the people who use them. As with so many other things, the manner in which computers are used can mean either that work will be more efficient or that it will be more tedious. If people are not taught how to use their computer technology properly, they will fear and misuse it. If people see computers as another way that management can keep track of them and monitor their work, they may resent management.

Many companies are now providing managers with a wider variety of computer-based communication devices including the following:

- Laptop and notebook computers with wireless capability and handheld computers along with personal data assistant (PDA) phones and smart phones, are important tools for supervisors and manager. These devices, many of which are very compact, provide a wide range of capabilities that enable managers to read their e-mail, access the Internet, receive instant messaging, and access large contact databases.[42] Such devices, along with compact printers and faxes, enable supervisors and managers to have almost the entire functionality of an office in their briefcases.
- Teleconferencing through either cable, satellite communication links, or Internet allows people in different locations to see, hear, and speak to one another. Companies, such as PepsiCo, use videoconferencing for training and to cut back on the amount of travel required for its top executives.[43] W.R. Grace & Company, which has approximately 6,000 employees throughout the world, reduces travel by conducting from 40 to 60 videoconferences per month.[44]
- Computer voice recognition systems now allow people to converse with computers for a wide variety of tasks that previously required manual human interaction. Voice recognition software allows computers to handle routine interactions with exceptions being handled with human interaction. The accuracy of voice recognition has been steadily improving and now has high accuracy even with strong accents. In addition, sophisticated voice recognition systems provide added security by making a record of the caller's voice. When a subsequent call occurs, the system verifies whether the caller is who he claims to be. Needless to say, such systems promote cost savings because they eliminate the need for human data entry via keypad.[45]

Do what you can now to become familiar with how you and your company can put these and many other innovative methods and tools to effective use in managing your tasks, people, and information.

SPOKEN COMMUNICATION

All successful managers have two basic qualities in common: the ability to think logically (analyze and problem solve) and the ability to communicate effectively. The most frequently used form of communication for a supervisor is oral. The ability to express yourself effectively through the use of spoken words is the most important tool at your disposal.

Effective speaking is much more than knowing correct grammar. You must know your audience. Your way of talking to Juanita is probably different from your way of talking to Elle, even though your subject is the same with both. Elle requires key concepts cemented to several application examples (a kind of show and tell), whereas Juanita requires that you link your message to her experiences. Furthermore, the communication that takes place involves much more than speaking. Communication experts explain that words account for only 7 percent of communication, while tone of voice conveys 38 percent and body language conveys 55 percent.[46] Therefore, you should make sure your total approach to the conversation is appropriate for the information you wish to share.

As you speak, watch your listeners' facial expressions and body language. Give your listeners time to ask questions. If they do not, ask some of your own in order to check their understanding and keep their attention.

Tailor your message to your audience. Choose your words carefully. Use the minimum number of words possible to get your point across. Be honest and open, and your message will be welcomed. Stick to the facts and leave out personal opinions. If your listeners ask for more information than you have, do not bluff. Tell them you will get it and give it to them as soon as you can; be sure to do so.

BASIC INGREDIENTS

An effective oral presentation to individuals or to groups usually contains three stages: the introduction, the explanation, and the summary. Each part has a definite purpose and specific ingredients.

The introduction. The introduction or beginning of your oral presentation should attempt to do three things: (1) get the listener's attention, (2) arouse interest, and (3) introduce the subject matter and purpose of the communication. The introduction can help you gain the listener's attention through a number of devices. These include a statement designed to startle or amaze, a quotation from a famous source, an anecdote, a story with a moral, or a question that will be answered later in the oral communication (see Exhibit 4.1). To convey the subject matter and the purpose of the communication, you as speaker can simply state what you intend to talk about, why the communication is necessary, and what goals and responses you have in mind. To obtain and keep the listener's interest, you need to say why the communication is necessary and how the message will affect your listener. Try to relate the oral presentation to your listener's experience, job, or special interests. If a PowerPoint presentation is appropriate, integrate the suggestions provided earlier in this chapter with your approach.

The explanation. The explanation follows the introduction and should also be well organized. It should flow logically from one key point to another. To make sure

| Exhibit 4.1 | Guide to planning your oral presentation. |

INTRODUCTION

- Gain the listener's attention
- Arouse the listener's interest
- Introduce your purpose
- Introduce your idea

EXPLANATION

- Develop your idea with logic and examples
- Link your idea to the listener's interests
- Use language your listener will understand
- Keep it brief and on track
- Use illustrations and graphics whenever possible
- Invite questions when and where appropriate

SUMMARY

- Restate your idea and its advantages to your listener
- Call for questions and be prepared to ask some of your own to check the listener's understanding of the topic
- State the specific actions you desire

that it does, you must (1) identify the key points or ideas, (2) group them in a sequence that makes sense, and (3) present them in that sequence to your listener.

Transitions from one point to another should carry your listener logically from one point or idea to the next. Use emphasis to help your listener define in her own mind what the key points are and why they are worth knowing and remembering. Some devices for adding emphasis include repetition, voice tone and inflection, specific wording such as "this is really important," visual aids, and specific questions. When speaking, use these devices to fix important ideas in your receiver's mind.

The summary. Use a summary at any stage in an oral presentation where it might be helpful to restate important points you have been making. Frequent summaries aid the memory and add emphasis. Any oral communication should conclude with a comprehensive summary of all the key ideas, as well as a statement of the responses expected from your listener. This final summary is your opportunity to reemphasize major points, to clarify the message through questions, and to leave a lasting impression with your listener. It should restate the goals and actions that you expect as a result of the communication, echoing how they were first stated in your introduction.

THE INFORMATIONAL MEETING

Informational meetings provide opportunities to disseminate various kinds of information to your people. Usually, you will use the lecture format to communicate information about such topics as status reports on work (scoreboarding) and new projects or programs in progress. You may also use the lecture format to explain changes taking place elsewhere in the company that will affect your department and its members. Many teams hold such meetings fairly regularly since meetings provide a means for efficient communication and an excellent opportunity to relate to teammates.

Informational meetings promote cooperation among group members by fostering individual growth, keeping people informed, and conveying the reasons behind changes that will be necessary in the future. These meetings work best when they permit the supervisor and group members to accomplish the following purposes:

1. Keep informed about what is going on in all areas of the company and in their division, department, or section
2. Obtain observations and information from people outside their group—for example, from higher management authorities, guest lecturers, or consultants
3. Report on decisions and changes that have been made or will be handed down from a higher level of the hierarchy

Informational meetings benefit employees greatly by helping them understand more fully how each part of the company contributes to the whole. They are reminded that they are members of a team and are kept informed and up to date on individual and group progress. Although the format is usually a lecture, time should be set aside for questions so that misunderstandings can be identified and resolved. Exhibit 4.2 points out a number of things to think about before you decide to hold such a meeting.

Learning Objective Number Six

LISTENING

"From listening comes wisdom, and from speaking repentance."[47]

—Chinese Proverb

Research indicates that the time spent in communication activities at work, is distributed in the following descending order: listening, speaking, reading, and writing.[48] For supervisors good listening skills are absolutely critical because it is through listening that we find out what is really bothering an employee, what is important to an employee who needs to improve his or her performance, how we can convey to employees their importance to us and the organization, and so on.

Unfortunately, not as many supervisors and managers are as good at listening as they should be. They are not alone in this skill deficiency as it has been observed that the efficiency with which people listen is quite low, approximately 35 percent.[49] Some other studies have found even lower levels of listening efficiency. More specifically, research indicates that we operate at a 25 percent level of efficiency when listening to a 10-minute talk.[50] A classic study of the communicative efficiency of 100 businesses found that 37 percent of information passed from the board of directors to vice presidents was lost. By the time the information had been relayed to supervisors, 70 percent

| EXHIBIT 4.2 | Guide to planning your meetings. |

- In advance, notify all who are invited of the meeting's purpose, starting time, ending time, and place

- Reserve facilities and equipment

- Prepare notes for the meeting, and rehearse your presentation

- Prepare and distribute a written agenda for the meeting

- Start the meeting on time

- Keep the meeting on its agenda

- Gather input from all attendees

- End the meeting once the purpose is achieved or at the scheduled ending time

- Record significant contributions

- Summarize the meeting's results before and after adjournment

- Make certain that all participants know their new roles or the changes that arise from the meeting

- Follow up on the results of the meeting

had been lost. Workers ultimately got 20 percent of what had been initiated by the board.[51] A similarly depressing account of listening effectiveness goes as follows:

> In fact, research indicates that we hear half of what is said, listen to half of what we hear, understand half of it, believe half of that, and remember only half of that. That means in an eight-hour work day, you spend about four hours *listening.* You hear about two hours' worth. You listen to one hours' worth. You understand 30 minutes of that hour. You believe only 15 minutes' worth. And you remember just under eight minutes' worth.[52]

Most of us speak at a rate ranging between 100 to 125 words per minute, but most of us can think at between 400 and 500 words per minute. This difference allows us time to criticize and to let our minds wander off on tangents while listening.[53] Our criticisms can be of the speaker, the delivery, or the content. Being critical, judgmental, approving, or disapproving of a speaker's message takes us away from our primary goals: to perceive the other person's point of view, to know how that person feels, and to understand his frame of reference. Wandering off on mental trips during listening shuts down our hearing and perceptions.

BARRIERS TO EFFECTIVE LISTENING

Remember the following: "A wise man once explained, 'We never learn anything with our mouth open. We can only learn by reading, *by listening,* by observing, and by doing.'"[54] Many things (including our own attitudes and desire to talk) stand in our way when we attempt to listen to another person. Here are the major barriers to effective listening:

- Interrupting the speaker or finishing his or her sentences[55]
- Wanting to talk more than we want to listen
- Prejudging what the speaker is going to say, based on what we know about the speaker's knowledge of the subject, experience, and point of view
- Letting the speaker's less-than-perfect delivery turn us off to the ideas and words
- Taking exception to a speaker's remarks as they are made and thus not listening to the message that follows those remarks
- Allowing events and those around us to distract our attention from the speaker
- Labeling the speaker or the subject dull or boring
- Dealing only with the speaker's facts and not listening for the speaker's emotional content
- Tuning out the speaker because she disagrees with what we "know" is right
- Mentally preparing arguments to refute what the speaker is saying
- Making assumptions about anything we are not certain of—filling in the blanks with what we think the speaker or writer means

ACTIVE LISTENING

Supervisors who are active listeners have a major advantage in that they not only obtain information that would be missed in passive learning, but they also convey a message to the persons to whom they listen, that the speakers are important to them. It takes more energy to be an active listener, but the investment is well worth the effort. **Active listening** avoids the barriers noted earlier by not interrupting the speaker and not thinking ahead to how he or she will refute or rebut what the speaker is saying. More importantly, active listeners use techniques that draw the speaker out to ensure that they obtain a good understanding, such as by seeking information by asking questions. For example, the listener might say, "So you are concerned that the quality testing may be flawed? Tell me some more about the testing issues." The active listener will also seek clarification of what the speaker is saying, such as by saying, "Are you saying that you do not feel appreciated when you call Joe's attention to the machine settings that result in more defective products? Can you clarify how these conversations occur and how Joe responds?"

Active listening, which is sometimes called **empathetic listening,** also involves the use of some other important techniques. The term empathetic listening conveys the importance of having a caring attitude about the speaker. More specifically, active listeners reflect what the speaker is saying like a mirror by summarizing what the speaker is saying. By periodically summarizing and asking whether their summary is accurate, active listeners ensure that they have a good grasp of the speaker's message and force themselves to focus on the speaker's content. In addition, the active listener tries to understand the speaker's needs because such knowledge can lead to permanent solutions for problems. Furthermore, active listeners are not judgmental. They see their responsibility as one of helping the speaker and understand that if they were to begin offering

active listening
listening that clarifies, restates, and summarizes in order to obtain a deep understanding of the speaker

empathetic listening
active listening with a purpose of understanding the speaker's real needs

judgments, they will prematurely cut off the discussion. Active listeners also encourage the speaker to continue with intermittent reinforcements, such as by saying "I understand" or "tell me more."[56] Active listeners also attempt to gain a good understanding of the speaker's emotions. They probe to find out how the speaker really feels about something and do not settle for statements that everything is okay. Finally, they maintain eye contact with the speaker approximately 80 percent of the time.[57]

Keep in mind that listening is not a passive activity. It requires mental alertness and skills. Use every opportunity to seek clarification of the speaker's subject, feelings, and frame of reference. Questions are the key, as they set the stage for listening.

DIALOG

In addition to the value of communicating effectively with coworkers, peers, and associates, effective communication also enables organizations to increase the level of customer satisfaction or the satisfaction of clients within the organization. Dialog is an important aspect of communication that deserves greater emphasis in the work environment in which supervisors must operate. In a practical sense, the process of dialog develops mutual understanding, and an outcome of dialog is enhanced relationships. Interestingly, Daniel Yankelovich has observed that the reduction of power residing in organizational hierarchies and in formal authority and its horizontal redistribution has increased the need for effective dialog. Because of these changes there is more reliance on dialog to solve problems as people must create shared understandings. Furthermore, as global competitive pressures have created needs in many organizations in the United States and other developed countries, to compete on a basis other than cost, there has been a need for more creativity or innovation. Such creativity and innovation also require more dialog within organizations as well as with customers and vendors.[58]

Suggestions for improvement of the quality and effectiveness of dialog with others are presented in Exhibit 4.3. Mastering these techniques will help supervisors reach shared understandings and improve relationships.

LISTENING EFFECTIVENESS

Exhibit 4.4 is a short quiz to help you determine the effectiveness of your listening efforts. In addition to taking this quiz yourself, you should encourage your subordinates or team members to take it. The maximum score is 30. A rating of 24 or more indicates that you are an above-average listener. A score of 18 to 23 is average. Below 18, your listening skills need improvement.

A recent study has examined listening effectiveness using an instrument called the Listening Styles Inventory (LSI). The LSI, which comprises items similar to the active listening techniques discussed earlier, measures the extent to which listeners perceive that they are concerned with the speaker's motivation, their degree of understanding, and the degree to which they were unfocused or detached. The study, which analyzed self-report perceptual data for professionals, found that managers of nurses appeared to be better listeners than audit managers and other managers. The study also found that supervisors can improve the effectiveness of their listening skills when they participate in multiple training sessions.[59] Thus, if your listening effectiveness is not as good as it should be, you can improve with training.

*Learning
Objective
Number Seven*

Suggestions for improving the effectiveness of dialog.	**EXHIBIT 4.3**

- Accept communications from others at face value.

  This means that you should not attempt to read between the lines, search for ulterior motives, or assign a different meaning to the words.

- Use questions to promote two-way communications.

  By using questions to probe for understanding you can convert a conversation that is dominated by one party to a real opportunity to communicate.

- Exercise care not to talk too much.

  People who talk too much prevent others from communicating and spend little time listening. Unfortunately, an explanation for their excessive talking may be that they may be overly concerned about themselves. By asking questions you can keep from talking too much and can shift your orientation toward the other person rather than yourself.

- Look for opportunities to establish relationships and enhance trust.

  Trust is typically weak when you perceive that the other person is not really listening to you. Likewise trust is often lacking when there has not been a conveyance of understanding.

- Do not engage in unfair arguments.

  Examples of unfair argument include the use of labels, such as "bean counters" to refer to accountants who are legitimately concerned about costs or straw man techniques in which it is argued that if something is done for a person, he or she will come back with more demands.

Sources: Stephan Menallack, *You Can Communicate: PR Secrets for Personal Success*, Frenchs Forest, N.S.W.: Pearson Education Australia, 2002. Christine Uber Grosse, "Managing Communication within Virtual Intercultural Teams," *Business Communication Quarterly*, (December 2002): 22–38. Jane Thomas, *Guide to Managerial Persuasion and Influence*, Upper Saddle River, N.J.: Pearson Prentice Hall, 2004.

SMALL GROUP COMMUNICATION

High performing small groups are characterized by extensive sharing of information. Employees in such groups do not hoard information and instead there is free-flowing communication. An example of such communications is provided by Toyota. At Toyota, group members make use of frequent small group collaborations in which they deal with only one topic. As a result, they may have multiple short meetings each day. Leaders of high performing small groups communicate clear goals and handle traditional leader tasks, such as resolving conflicts. A side effect of the free flow of information in the group is that high levels of trust are established.[60] A good communications practice for supervisors is to regularly check with employees to determine whether they are satisfied with the amount of information they are receiving. Supervisors should place great value on the importance of keeping their employees aware of developments.[61]

EXHIBIT 4.4	**Measuring your listening skills.**

Read the questions below and rate yourself according to the following:
Always = 3 points   Usually = 2 points   Rarely = 1 point

③②① 1. Do I let speakers deliver their messages without interrupting them?

③②① 2. Do I take notes, recording the most important points made by a speaker?

③②① 3. Do I try to connect the speaker's points with my past experiences to help me remember them?

③②① 4. Do I try to restate the speaker's points to make certain that I understand them?

③②① 5. Do I give the speaker my undivided attention, blocking out any noise or distractions?

③②① 6. Do I keep my emotional reactions to the speaker in check, not allowing them to distract me?

③②① 7. Do I keep my emotional reactions to the speaker's message in check, not allowing them to distract me?

③②① 8. Do I keep listening even if the message is boring or uninteresting to me?

③②① 9. Do I try to get at the speaker's intended meaning by listening to more than the speaker's words?

③②① 10. Do I formulate questions to ask about any unclear messages in the speaker's words?

Informal meetings with subordinates provide an important avenue for communication. When group meetings involve decisions to be made, the supervisor should typically be the last person to offer views on the issues because his or her views will often affect the direction of the discussion. Employees should feel free to disagree and challenge alternatives so that the best decision can be obtained. A good suggestion for the conduct of such meetings is to emphasize the successes of the group instead of letting them deteriorate into complaint sessions. When bad news needs to be communicated, it should be done with honesty and should include an assessment of the impact on the group. Whenever possible, the supervisor should communicate the actions that the organization will take in the future to deal with the issue.[62]

Aside from communications that occur within the small group, leaders of small groups sometimes have responsibilities to communicate about major issues or initiatives that come down through the organizational hierarchy from the top executives. Often times there is a desire by the senior leadership team for supervisors to persuade their employees to embrace the initiative. Unfortunately, attempts on the part of

The grapevine is the channel of communication for informal groups. Informal groups form at lunch, after work, or any time coworkers get together on a casual basis.

supervisors to sell such ideas to their employees typically do not work. When there is a selling approach, employees feel that their intellectual abilities are not respected and that they are being treated like children.[63]

A better approach for the supervisor or team leader is to communicate the idea to employees and then to listen to the concerns of the group. By listening to such concerns, the supervisor develops an understanding of employees' concerns and acknowledges their importance. By informing employees of the major issues and responding to their concerns, supervisors are better able to communicate a clearer understanding of the issues within the group. As a result, the group is more likely to develop a good understanding of their objectives and role in the initiative. At some point, group members will draw their own conclusions about the merits of the initiative. In essence, supervisors of small groups can communicate better if they focus on developing understanding rather than attempting to gain acceptance for the initiative.[64]

THE GRAPEVINE

Transmission media or channels of communication can be formal or informal. *Formal* channels are those specifically set up for the transmission of normal business information, instructions, orders, and reports. The organization chart of a business outlines formal channels. *Informal* channels—the **grapevine**—are not specifically designated for use in the dissemination of information, but nearly every employee uses them for this purpose.

Informal channels exist because of the natural desire of employees to be "in the know" and to satisfy their curiosity. Because employees mix and socialize frequently during and outside their normal working relationships, they tend to speculate and invent "information." Often, the less they know about something, the more they invent.

grapevine
informal channels at work that transmit information or misinformation

At coffee breaks, during lunch, or at social events, people often share things they have heard and seen even though they may not have a complete story to tell.

The grapevine can give managers a clue about what is bothering their people and where the need for immediate or future action lies. Although it is generally a means by which gossip and rumors about the company are spread, managers should be tuned in to it. Do not, however, use the grapevine for disseminating orders or instructions to your people. It is no substitute for formal channels.

Gossip can sometimes serve you in your role as a supervisor by acting as an early warning system. When you hear a rumor, ask yourself what you would do if it were true. Gossip also alerts you to where the leaks are and who may be letting confidential communications get into circulation.

To prevent the grapevine from yielding a crop of sour grapes, satisfy your people's need to know what is happening in their department by applying the following rules to your daily situation:

1. Tune in on their informal communications.
2. Combat rumors and gossip with the facts.
3. Discredit people who willfully spread improper information.
4. Be available to and honest with your people.
5. Know when to remain silent.

By applying these rules, you create in your subordinates a feeling of confidence about what is true and what is not true. You also strengthen your personal reputation as a source of sound information, and you foster better morale and cooperation. As a result, you can lessen resistance to change and soften its impact.

WRITTEN COMMUNICATION

Probably the most difficult form of communication is the written form. Yet nothing will mark you more clearly as a poor manager than an inability to write your thoughts effectively and correctly. A badly written, poorly constructed piece of writing can quickly discredit you.

Just what is good writing? It is writing that transmits an idea or information clearly to the intended reader in accordance with the rules of grammar and proper sentence construction. Effective writing, like effective oral presentations, must accomplish several things. It should especially be gauged to accomplish the following purposes:

- *Command the reader's attention.* Something in your writing or its appearance has to get the reader to read.
- *Arouse interest.* The writing's appeal must be aimed at the reader's specific interests. The "what's in this for you" should be up front. A benefit can be promised, or a potential loss or cost can be cited.
- *Specify the needed action.* The basic purpose of most business correspondence is to get a favorable response or an acceptance from the reader.

Written summaries and reminders make effective follow-ups to oral communication. The combination of the two forms of communication helps add importance and emphasis to key points, prevent misunderstandings, and provide evidence that communication about a subject has taken place. It is also a good practice to take time for verbal **follow-up.** When supervisors take the time to check with employees to insure that the message was received as intended and to involve employees in any decisions to be made, many misunderstandings can be easily cleared up and employees are more likely to be committed to a desired course of action. Many managers fail to understand that a well-written e-mail or memo is not sufficient to get people moving in the same direction on an issue. They must take the time to follow-up verbally.[65]

follow-up
checking with others to ensure that a message was received and that action is being taken

Effective writing amounts to talking on paper or a computer screen. Effective writers make their points clearly, using ordinary language that is familiar to the people they are trying to reach. Your writing should read well—sound good to the ear when read aloud. As you write, say what you are writing to yourself. When polishing your writing, read it aloud to catch any awkward phrases or sentences, and any disconnected or unclear thoughts.[66]

Writing effectively is not easy. But you can make it a lot less difficult for yourself if you lay a proper foundation before you try to write. First, you should have a specific objective in mind. Next, you should gather your facts (this may involve searching your files or consulting with others). Then, you should make an outline—that is, a simple breakdown of your major points. Expand each major point by writing beneath it the minor ones that you wish to use to support it. Arrange your points in the order best suited for a logical presentation. Then write using simple, familiar, and concrete words.

When you review your writing, be sure that you clearly understand the words you have used. Then ask yourself: "Will my readers understand my words? Will they get the same meaning that I do?" Some words pose little danger of any misunderstanding. For example, the word *book* means much the same thing to all of us. Other words, however, may have wide differences in meaning for various people.

If you want your written communication to have impact, use short sentences. Professional writers know that writing is easier to read and remember if most of the sentences and paragraphs are brief. However, you should not use short sentences all the time because such writing tends to strike readers as choppy and monotonous. Try to alternate a long sentence with one or two short ones, and try to keep sentences to 15 or 20 words.

Try to limit each paragraph to a single topic. As a rule, start each paragraph with a topic sentence that tells what the paragraph is about. Use transitional devices to tie both your sentences and your paragraphs together. The final sentence in a paragraph can either emphasize the points you wish to get across or lead the reader to your next subject. The introductory paragraphs in a piece of writing tell what the writing is about. The paragraphs that make up the body of a communication state the writer's case (facts, figures, and so on). The closing paragraph or paragraphs recommend an action or summarize the important points of the paper.

Exhibit 4.5 shows an actual memo (Memo A) sent by Jane, a middle manager, to her subordinate managers. Read it first, and then read Memo B, which is a suggested improvement. Do you believe that Memo B carries the basic message intended by the author of Memo A? Which memo would you prefer to receive if you were one of Jane's subordinates?

EXHIBIT 4.5 **Two memos compared: Memo A (the original) and Memo B (a revision).**

MEMO A

TO: ALL SECTION SUPERVISORS
FROM: Jane Barton
DATE: June 20, 2010

The newly designed personal data sheet—Form 14A—has a necessary, essential, and vital purpose in our organization. It provides the necessary and statistically significant personal data required by the human resources department to be kept on file for future references regarding promotions, transfers, layoffs, and more.

During our recent relocation efforts from the rented facilities at Broad Street to our present location here at Cauley Boulevard, files were lost, damaged, or misplaced, necessitating the current request for replacement of vital personal data on each and every manager in this department. It is also the company's policy to periodically update personal data on file through periodic, personal perusal of one's own records—updating and adding new information as required and deleting obsolete or outdated personal data on file.

Therefore, please complete the attached personal data sheet at your earliest possible convenience but no later than Thursday, June 24, and return it to me by the close of the business day on the 24th.

MEMO B

TO: ALL SECTION SUPERVISORS
FROM: Jane Barton

Attached is our company's revised edition of the personal data sheet. Please fill it out completely and return it to me no later than the close of business on Thursday, June 24. Thank you.

ROOM FOR IMPROVEMENT

Unfortunately, despite the critical importance of written communication as well as verbal communication skills, employers continually express concerns about the quality of these skills exhibited by high school and college graduates. Results of a study by the National Commission on Writing, which involved a survey of large U.S. companies, found the following:

> Despite what seems to be a generally positive picture, a significant proportion of responding firms (about one-third) report that one-third or fewer of their employees, both current and new, possess the writing skills companies value.[67]

The study also found that companies are spending large amounts of money on training employees whose writing skills need improvement.[68] The poor state of students' communication skills is not unique to the United States. In the United Kingdom, a survey indicated that only that only 30 percent of responding managers found graduates of institutions of higher education to have impressive communication skills. Only 23 percent gave high ratings to their presentation skills.[69] Similarly, an Australian study of employers' evaluations of recent college graduates revealed that oral business communication was one of the major skill deficiencies.[70]

The message is clear. Students need to work on their writing, speaking, and presentation skills because these are critical determinants of professional success. Interestingly, there is good software that can help you improve your writing. By regularly using the grammar check on Word you can learn how to eliminate errors in grammar and to clarify your sentence structure. In addition, software is available for reviewing electronic files for excessive use of jargon.

INSTANT REPLAY

1. The major goals of the communication process are to be understood, to gain understanding, to gain acceptance for yourself or for your ideas, and to produce action or change.

2. A management information system (MIS) is a formal method for making accurate and timely information available to management to aid the decision-making process and the execution of management and organization functions.

3. Communication barriers interrupt the flow of information and inhibit understanding. Communication efforts should be planned to limit or eliminate the effects of barriers.

4. Delivering a speech or a lecture usually involves providing an introduction, an explanation, and a summary.

5. Listening takes up nearly one-half of our days. It is a skill that can be learned and improved by techniques such as anticipating a speaker's next point, identifying the speaker's supporting elements, and making mental summaries.

6. The grapevine consists of the transmission of information or misinformation through informal channels in the working environment.

QUESTIONS FOR CLASS DISCUSSION

1. Can you define this chapter's key terms?

2. What are the possible goals behind efforts to communicate? Which do you think are part of every effort to communicate?

3. What does a management information system do for (a) managers and (b) the organization?

4. What are the basic components of the communication process? How might the choice in one category influence the choices in others?

5. Suppose you are getting ready to communicate to your subordinates about a change in a safety procedure. What should you do before you attempt to relay your message?

6. What are the barriers to effective communication? Can you give an example of each from your experience?

7. How can you improve your listening skills and your ability to retain more of what you hear?

ASSESS THIS SITUATION

Purpose: To help identify ways in which managers and companies use the Internet to facilitate communication.

Your Task: Review the Web pages of the companies listed below. Identify the ways in which these Web pages facilitate communication with managers.

Alcon Laboratories: www.alconlabs.com
Chubb Corporation: www.chubb.com
Ford Motor Company: www.ford.com
General Electric: www.ge.com
3M: www.mmm.com
Motorola: www.motorola.com
Nokia: www.nokia.com

SKILL BUILDING EXERCISE 4.1

Supervisors of employees who have contact with customers, clients, or the public need to ensure that they make a good impression in their interactions with these people. Unfortunately, the manner in which employees sometimes communicate with the public often leaves much to be desired. For example, a customer may have been impressed by the manner in which an employee handled a transaction and then expressed appreciation by saying "thank you." Some employees respond to such expressions of appreciation by saying "no problem." Saying "no problem" in response to a kind comment may make the customer feel that he or she has not been treated respectfully for making a kind comment. The "no problem" response may be taken literally by the customer as an indication that the employee saw no problem with the customer's kind response for the assistance received.

A better response would have been for the employee to say "you are welcome." With this response there is a clear message that the employee appreciated the kind words from the customer. Ritz Carlton Hotels, which often appears on the lists of some of the best companies to work for in the United States, trains its employees to respond to such expression of appreciation by saying, "it was my pleasure."[71] Regardless of the customer's age or background, such a gracious response has a much greater chance of making a favorable impression. Another problematic expression may be "have a good one" instead of "have a good day" or "have a good evening." Again, the employee has created an ambiguous impression with the customer instead of a highly predictive positive experience.

Your Task: Working alone or in a small group, (a) identify expressions that are likely to disappoint, offend, or fail to impress customers, (b) identify expressions likely to impress the customer or make him or her feel as if he or she has been treated with respect, (c) discuss techniques that supervisors might use to get employees to communicate more responsibly with customers, clients, and the public, and (d) identify how various expressions may cause very different reactions depending on characteristics of the customer or client.

SKILL BUILDING WRITING EXERCISE 4.2

Consider the following three examples of poor verbal and written communication:

(A) A marketing executive described his firm's rationale for acquiring another firm. He explained that the objective was to:

> "create an integrated marketing platform that allows for multichannel marketing on a real-time basis and sunsets the current modality of episodic marketing campaigns."[72]

(B) A mutual fund manager might provide the following account of his fund's performance:

> "These last few months have proven to be a good challenge for some market participants and, in particular, our equities fund displayed negative correlation with an increasing benchmark index."[73]

(C) A representative of a call center provided the following account of a performance problem:

> "Although we strenuously continue to easily outclass our competitors on an enterprise-wide level of actionability, our global customer care

agents are experiencing a skill gap in terms of their abilities and knowledge in the area of satisfying customers, particularly when their first call response rate is measured against industry benchmarks and their call resolution rate is compared to rates achieved by other entities in this space."[74]

Your Task: Provide a brief written analysis that (1) describes the intended message of the statements, (2) identifies what the parties hearing or reading these messages were likely to infer from them, and (3) speculate about the reasons why someone would speak or write in such manners.

CASE 4.1	Is Anyone Listening?

Four Star Financial operates a national chain of retail loan offices that make loans based on homeowners' equity. The retail loan offices process loan applications, compile documentation of collateral, and then send the applications and documentation to the home office. The collateral section in the home office then verifies the documentation and wires funds for the borrower's loan to the retail offices. After receiving loan documentation from the collateral section, Four Star's treasury department then sells most of the loans to other financial institutions. Victor Lopez, a loan resale specialist in the treasury department, has become concerned about documentation verification practices in the collateral department and has approached his boss, Kim Hoffer, about his concerns.

VICTOR: "Kim, I'm worried that some of the collateral documentation specialists are not verifying all of the information before they send the loans on to us for resale. I've spot checked a few and found lots of missing documents. Some of the borrowers are going to default on their loans and the financial institutions that bought the loans are going to accuse us of misleading them about the quality of the loans."

KIM: "What do you mean they aren't verifying the information? They have loan documentation procedures to follow, and the verifiers know what they're doing. Listen Victor, we've got enough problems of our own to worry about."

VICTOR: "I know that they have procedures and that they are easy enough to understand. But they have some people who are cutting corners and don't seem to care about doing good work. If I was a manager, I'd do something about their work."

KIM: "I don't think this is a big problem. There are always going to be some loans on which they miss some information. The financial institutions that buy our loans know that a few are going to be bad. We and the banks have good projections of expected default rates. and interest rates are set high enough to allow for this."

VICTOR: "But that's what I'm talking about. When the workload gets heavy like it has been this year, some of the collateral people just pass on loans without actually verifying the documentation. They just fill out the checklist like they really completed the verification and send them on. Unless you actually go back and do the work yourself, you can't tell if they've actually done the verifications. I've checked a few and have sent them back to collateral, but I don't have time to check them all!"

KIM: "Victor, this isn't the first time we've had a conversation about this subject. I know you have been in this business a long time, but I think you are overstating the seriousness of this problem. Quit worrying so much. Anyway, business is good and the company is making money. You'll probably get a good bonus this year. And you're not the collateral manager, so it's not your problem."

VICTOR: "But business won't always be good, and when some of these loans go bad, people are going to find that there isn't good documentation for a lot of these loans. I know that these are high-interest loans, but the extra income won't be high enough to offset a large number of defaults. What are you going to do about the problem?"

KIM: "Well, what would you have me do? The collateral people don't report to me. Why should you be concerned about this? You know as well as I that if I go over to tell the head of collateral verification that we don't think they are doing a good job, we'll just make them mad at us. And that will just make things worse in the future. Listen, Victor, you get too worked up about things. You know what your problem is? You don't know how to go with the flow. If you get loans with inadequate collateral, just send them back. Is there anything else on your mind? If not, I've got a lot of work to do."

Questions

1. How do you think Victor feels about his conversation with Kim?

2. What is the likely impact on Victor's future interactions with Kim? How likely is it that Victor will tell Kim about problems in the future?

3. How could Victor have communicated more effectively? What could he have done to obtain a more favorable response from Kim?

4. How should Kim have responded to Victor's concerns?

CASE 4.2   Baker-Allison

Judy Whitmire is a product manager for Baker-Allison, a company based in a town with a population of 9,000 in a Midwestern state. Baker-Allison manufactures disposable surgical gowns and drapes that are used in operating rooms. The surgical team wears the gowns, and the drapes are used to cover the patient while the surgery is performed. The company also manufactures a few other products used in medical care. The use of disposable drapes and gowns has become widespread because of concerns about the likelihood of infection when non-disposable materials are reused and because of the cost of sterilizing reusable materials.

A new line of surgical gowns and drapes, for which Judy is the product manager, provides surgeons and nurses with greater protection from accidental infection from viruses. In addition, their prices are very competitive even though the company's profit margin on the line is substantial. As a result, sales of the new gowns and drapes have been exceptionally good and will exceed $40 million this year.

Needless to say, the company's reputation for quality and its high standards for maintaining sterile products are critical to the company's sales. A major factor helping to control costs is the low cost of labor in the rural area in which the company is based. All manufacturing takes place in a clean environment in a new plant built specifically for this purpose. In addition, the gowns and drapes are sterilized with cobalt radiation. Because an exact amount of radiation is required for sterility without excessive radiation effects, the radiation equipment must be certified frequently for proper calibration. State regulations require Baker-Allison to conduct and report self-tests of the equipment on a monthly basis and have the equipment tested four times a year by a certified testing firm. Without such testing, Baker-Allison cannot be confident that its surgical supplies are sterile or that they have not been subjected to too much radiation.

Today when Judy was compiling an internal report, she went down to the sterilizer room to get information about the certification of the radiation equipment. The head of the sterilization section was not in so Judy picked up the equipment certification logs and began to take notes on the information she needed. Much to her surprise, Judy realized that the latest certification test results appeared to have been falsified. She concluded that it would not have been possible for the certification to be performed on the date indicated. She had been working across the hall during the whole week and was certain that the sterilizer had not been shut down that week. Judy feels that the head of the section probably falsified the self-test records because the test requires the equipment to be shut down for a day and the sterilizer section was under severe time pressures caused by the high volume of production. As a result, the company cannot be certain of the sterility of all of the surgical supplies produced over the past month.

On the other hand, despite the careful regulation and required testing of the radiation equipment, there is only a small probability that the equipment is not properly calibrated. In fact, industry-wide test results report that only a few sterilizers need recalibration each year. As a result, several manufacturers have begun lobbying the regulatory agency for more liberal certification requirements. The manufacturers have argued that the equipment needs to be self-tested only twice a year and recertified by an independent testing firm once a year.

There are several potentially negative consequences of the problem that Judy has uncovered. One is the action that the state agency may take when it learns that the certification report filed by Baker-Allison was based on phony test results. Another is the potential danger to surgical teams and patients using Baker-Allison products. Because the gowns and drapes may not have been sterile, Baker-Allison may have liabilities related to any infections caused by their surgical products. The situation is made even more difficult by financial pressures on the company resulting from declining sales of some of its other products that are being undercut by imports. In fact, if it were not for the sales of the new line of products, 375 of the company's 750 employees would have been laid off last month.

Judy was shaken as she walked back to her office. She walked into her office and stared out the window as she thought about what she should do.

Questions

1. What issues should Judy consider when making her decision?
2. What action should Judy take?
3. What issues should she take into consideration in making her decision?

4. Whom should she communicate with about her concerns?

5. How should she communicate her concerns?

REFERENCES

[1] Michael Moncur's Quotations, (November 6, 2005): Website: *www.quotationspage.com/quote/32975.html.*

[2] Jones, Del, and Know, Noelle. "2 Executives Praise French over U.S. Workers: But Gallup Survey Shows Many in France Dislike Jobs," *USA Today* (March 6, 2003): 1B.

[3] Ibid.

[4] Reingold, Jennifer. "Behind the Curtain," *Fast Company,* (October 2004): 101–104.

[5] Gilbert, Rick. "Presentation Advice for Boardroom Success," *Financial Executive,* (September 2005): 12. Marton, Betty. "How to Construct a Winning Presentation," *Harvard Management Communication Letter,* (April 2000): 5–6.

[6] Gilbert. "Presentation Advice for Boardroom Success."

[7] Ibid.

[8] Marton. "How to Construct a Winning Presentation."

[9] Curtin, Leah, and Simpson, Roy L. "Conveying an Effective Message in Voicemail or E-Mail," *Health Management Technology* (February 2002): 52.

[10] Hughes, Liz. "E-mail Etiquette: Think Before You Send," *Women in Business,* (July/August 2003): 29.

[11] Ibid.

[12] Manecksha, Ferina. "Advancing with E-mail Etiquette," *New Straits Times,* (March 11, 2004).

[13] Ibid.

[14] Lenckus, Dave, and Ceniceros, Roberto. "Employees' E-mails Seen as Posing Professional Liability Risk," *Business Insurance,* (December 12, 2003): 10–18.

[15] Lenckus and Ceniceros, "Employees' E-mails . . . ,": 10.

[16] Nucifora, Alf. "Virtual Teams Are Viable Under the Right Circumstances," *Fort Worth Business Press* (August 31, 2001): 21. Katzenbach, Jon and Smith, Douglas, "Virtual Teaming," *Forbes* (May 1, 2001): 48–50.

[17] Ibid.

[18] Nucifora. "Virtual Teams": 21.

[19] Expansion Management. "Telecommuting on the Rise, Seen as a Cost Saver," *Expansion Management* (August 2003): 2.

[20] Crandall, William R., and Gao, Longge. "An Update on Telecommuting: Review and Prospects for Emerging Issues," *SAM Advanced Management Journal*, (Summer 2005): 30–37.

[21] Tam, Pui-Wing. "Silicon Valley Belatedly Boots Up Programs to Ease Employees' Lives," *Wall Street Journal* (August 29, 2000): B1.

[22] Ibid.

[23] Hall, Cheryl. "An Open-Book Policy," *Dallas Morning News* (June 28, 1998): 1H–2H.

[24] Ibid.

[25] Goldsmith, Marshall. "Leave It at the Stream," *Fast Company*, (May 2004): 103.

[26] Godin, Seth. "How to Give Feedback," *Fast Company* (March 2004): 103.

[27] Case, John. "Games Companies Play," *Inc.* (October 1994): 46–47.

[28] Keenan, Faith, and Hamm, Steve. "The New Teamwork," *Business Week* (February 18, 2002): EB 16.

[29] "Language Barriers Hike Safety Risks," *Industrial Safety & Hygiene News* (June 2, 2003): 12.

[30] Sheridan, John H. "Partnering for Personnel," *Industry Week* (July 6, 1998): 11–12.

[31] Schuster, Karolyn. "Speaking the Language," *Food Management* (April 2000): 24.

[32] Tannen, Deborah. *Talking from 9 to 5.* New York: William Morrow (1994): 15–16.

[33] Maurer, Rick. *Beyond the Wall of Resistance: Unconventional Strategies That Build Support for Change.* Austin, TX: Bard Books Inc. (1996): 153–154.

[34] Norton, Rob. "New Thinking on the Causes and Costs of Yes Men (and Women)," *Fortune* (November 28, 1994): 31.

[35] Ibid.

[36] Bose, Indranil, and Mahapatra, Radha K. "Business Data Mining—a Machine Learning Perspective," *Information & Management* (December 2001): 211.

[37] Drucker, Peter F. "The Next Information Revolution," *Forbes ASAP* (August 24, 1998): 47–58.

[38] Ibid.

[39] *Forbes ASAP.* "America's Best Technology Users" (August 24, 1998): 63–86.

[40] Ibid., 68.

[41] Ibid., 63–86.

[42] PC World. "Going Mobile," *PC World*, (February 2005): 76–77.

[43] Savvas, Antony. "Videoconferencing Saves PepsiCo Executives Travel Time and Costs," *Computer Weekly*, (December 7, 2004): 16.

[44] Kontzer, Tony. "Victory for Videoconferencing," *Information Week*, (December 15, 2003): 58.

[45] Maselli, Jennifer. "Voice Recognition Aims to Lower Call-Center Costs," *Information Week* (October 22, 2001): 63.

[46] Patti Hathaway, "Building Rapport," Executive Excellence (July 2001): 13.

[47] Ibid.

[48] Burley-Allen, Madelyn. "Listen Up," *HR Magazine*, (November 2001): 115–120.

[49] Ibid.

[50] Nichols, Ralph G. "Listening Is Good Business," in *Readings in Management,* ed. Max D. Richards. Cincinnati: South Western Publishing (1982): 111.

[51] Ibid.

[52] Hathaway, Patti. "Building Rapport," *Executive Excellence* (July 2001): 13. Reproduced with permission.

[53] Nichols. "Listening Is Good": 111.

[54] Rega, Michael E. "Developing Listening Skills," *American Salesman* (May 2000): 3–7.

[55] Fuimano, Julie. "Sharp Listening Skills Point Staff in the Right Direction," *Nursing Management*, (May 2004): 12.

[56] Burley-Allen. "Listen Up."

[57] Raphael, Todd. "Listening Trumps Schmoozing," *Workforce* (October 2002): 96.

[58] Yankelovich, Daniel. *The Magic of Dialogue: Transforming Conflict into Cooperation.* New York: Simon & Schuster, 1999.

[59] Pearce, Glenn C., Johnson, Iris W., and Barker, Randolph T. "Assessment of the Listening Styles Inventory," *Journal of Business and Technical Communication,* (January 2003): 84–113.

[60] Evans, Philip, and Wolf, Bob. "Collaboration Rules," *Harvard Business Review*, (July–August 2005): 96–104.

[61] Haeuser, Jamie L., and Preston, Paul. "Communication Strategies for Getting the Results You Want," *Healthcare Executive* (January/February 2005): 16–20.

[62] Haeuser and Preston, "Communication Strategies for Getting the Results You Want."

[63] Mindszenthy, Bart, and Roberts, Gail. "Team Leaders and the Communication Loop," *Strategic Communication Management,* (December/January 2001): 28–31.

[64] Mindszenthy, "Team Leaders and the Communication Loop."

[65] Goldsmith, Marshall. "Don't Just Check the Box," *Fast Company* (February 2005): 89.

[66] Weiss, Donald. *How to Write Easily and Effectively.* New York: Amacom (1986): 49–50.

[67] Kerrey, Bob. "Writing: A Ticket to Work . . . Or a Ticket Out,*" Report of the National Commission on Writing* (September 2004): 13.

[68] Ibid.

[69] *Personnel Today*, "Graduates Lack Basic Skills," (May 7, 2002): 7.

[70] A.C. Neilsen Research Services. "Employer Satisfaction with Graduate Skills," Research Report, (February 2000): *www.dest.gov.au/archive/highered/eippubs/EIP99-7/exesum99_7.htm* [accessed November 23, 2005].

[71] Neiderhauser, Steve. "The Shakespeare Economy," *Musings About Strategy, Marketing and Creativity,* (December 28, 2004): *http://sneiderhauser.typepad.com/blog/2004/12/the_shakespeare.html.*

[72] Magill, Ken. "Sunset Your Modality, Please," *Direct* (October 15, 2005): 24.

[73] Bruining, Nick. "Weasel Words: The Knock Out Blow," *Money Management* (April 28, 2005): 26.

[74] Dolezalek, Holly. "The Clarity Challenge," *Training* (September 2005): 28–33.

5
CHAPTER

*"I was often misquoted. I was supportive of my managers,
even though they all may not think so."*

George Steinbrenner[1]
Owner, New York Yankees

Objectives

After reading and discussing this chapter, you should be able to do the following:

1. List and briefly explain the purposes of positive human relations.
2. Describe the application of each of the roles in the relationships between supervisors and their employees and peers.
3. Describe how a middle manager's job is different from a supervisor's job.
4. Describe how supervisors can create and maintain good relations with their bosses.
5. Identify several ways in which supervisors can appropriately manage conflict.
6. Identify the causes or antecedents of conflict.

Building Relationships at Hewlett Packard

Soon after replacing Carly Fiorina as CEO of Hewlett-Packard, Mark Hurd immersed himself in learning all he could about the giant multi-national so that he could develop a plan for handling some of the challenges facing the organization. While many of his actions are pertinent to only top executives, he also engaged in actions that provide good lessons for supervisors. Unlike some other CEOs, Hurd prefers to obtain information about the company by talking to managers and employees instead of relying on consultants. His approach, when talking to groups of managers, is to ask them questions about how they would handle various aspects of the business if they were the CEO. Managers have responded with insightful and forthright information. He has also held informal sessions or coffee talks with groups of employees so that he can obtain information not mentioned by the managers. Unsurprisingly, he found that employees who have the biggest personalities tend to take up most of the "air time" in these

Building Relationships
and Managing Conflict

meetings. Interestingly, he found that he was getting insightful two-page e-mails afterwards from employees who said nothing in the meetings.[2]

Hurd's experiences are not uncommon. In general, extroverted employees tend to make their views known at meetings while their more introverted colleagues are likely to reflect on the issues and share their thoughts later. Supervisors need to remember that they need to be proactive in obtaining information from all employees and that those who do not make their views known in meetings may have valuable suggestions. Hurd clearly saw the value in employee input and invited e-mail suggestions from employees. In addition, he asked them to call him. At one point, he was receiving over 300 e-mail messages per day. He found that the richer communication from the phone calls have been helpful because he has been able to comprehend the important issues and the emotions involved.[3] Aside from the valuable information that Hurd received, he also made a great start establishing relationships with employees and managers.

Questions for Thought

1. How should a supervisor go about strengthening relationships with employees?
2. What are the important issues involved in developing strong relationships with peers?

Introduction

This chapter explores how you as a supervisor can build good working relationships with each individual with whom you work. Relating successfully to others is the key to your growth and advancement. Solid individual relationships produce the cooperation and assistance you need to reach your goals.

The development and maintenance of sound on-the-job relationships with associates, peers, and superiors is referred to as **human relations.** From the moment you first meet another person at work, a relationship begins. How you relate to each person with whom you must work is largely up to you. Because none of us works in a vacuum, the quality of your interpersonal relationships will determine just how effective and efficient you will be. We all must depend to some extent on others. Consider the following example of the

human relations
the development and maintenance of sound on-the-job relationships with subordinates, peers, and superiors

undesirable outcomes of poor interpersonal relations in two plants, one that manufactures automobile parts and another that assembles televisions, in the United Kingdom. The researcher found that workers resented attempts to speed up production and the style of supervision. Poor interpersonal relations resulted in the following:

> A quality inspector thought of as a management lackey was tied up and dumped in a rubbish bin . . . one of his colleagues was put into a bin of parts headed for Birmingham, and found only at a gate inspection.[4]

Learning Objective Number One

Obviously, interpersonal relations have reached a low ebb when such activities take place in the workplace. This chapter is designed to help you develop effective working relationships, for sound working relationships are at the heart of building teams, leading, staffing, training, appraising, and disciplining.

GOALS OF HUMAN RELATIONS

The wide range of ages, backgrounds, and experiences in many work groups increases the difficulty of building sound human relations. After a brief look at the goals of human relations, we examine some major roles you must play to build relationships on the job. Keep the following goals in mind as you approach the task of building sound human relations:

- To help each individual obtain satisfaction in the work environment
- To increase each individual's effort and commitment to the job and the company
- To foster a spirit of cooperation between you and your subordinates, peers, and boss
- To help each individual be himself or herself while on the job
- To know and understand each person as an individual
- To treat each associate as an individual deserving of respect

Good employee relations is now being recognized as one of the critical determinants of success in many successful companies. Richard Branson, the founder of Virgin Atlantic Airways and Virgin Records, emphasizes the importance of treating employees well so that customers will be treated well. FedEx recognizes the same relationship and emphasizes employee development.[5] A similar approach is used at Enterprise Rent-A-Car in that there is no double standard in how people are treated because there is no distinction between the treatment of non-managers and managers. In addition, the newest employee in the organization has access to the company's top executives.[6] These companies, which all compete in the service industry, recognize the importance of treating employees well. An executive of O.C. Tanner, a company that sells employee recognition products,[7] summarized the importance of employee relations as follows:

> "If you want employees to . . . treat your customers the right way, you have to set the example by making sure they have that message and they're treated with the same care and respect you want them to demonstrate to customers."[8]

SUPERVISORS AND ETHICS

In the fast-paced world of the Silicon Valley, it might be assumed that people do not have sufficient time to ensure that their decisions regarding the treatment of employees, customers, and vendors reflect the highest standards of integrity. Such an assumption would be false for many Silicon Valley companies, and when employees are asked to tell their favorite stories about their companies, the themes of the stories often deal with integrity. Furthermore, integrity is often defined in such basic terms as whether one keeps his word.

One example concerns CenterBeam, a company that specializes in the installation of wireless networks. The firm had been hiring extensively and had made an offer to a candidate. Before the candidate accepted, the firm received a résumé from an overwhelmingly impressive individual. When the firm's managers asked CenterBeam's CEO whether they could rescind the offer, the CEO said no. He replied that the firm had to keep its promises in order to be a company that people will trust. In another incident, the firm had received an order of equipment, but before its engineers unpacked the equipment they found that another vendor could supply the same equipment for a savings of over 18 percent. Some of the engineers asked whether they could send the equipment back to the original vendor so that they could take advantage of the lower prices with the other vendor. CenterBeam's executives said no, but they did ask the original vendor to replace the order with less expensive equipment, which produced a savings of over 8 percent.

A common problem in many start-up "dot com" firms was that the companies exaggerated their potential financial performance. When they could not deliver on their extravagant promises, investors became disappointed and stock prices took a dive. The same kind of exaggerations were often used to recruit employees. When employees see their firms present exaggerated promises to outside stakeholders and job candidates, they become cynical and distrustful of their employers. On the other hand, companies that are honest in their promises build reputations of trustworthiness and get positive referrals to other potential customers.

Source: George Anders. "Honesty Is the Best Policy—Trust Us," *Fast Company* (August 2000): 262.

TREATING PEOPLE WITH RESPECT

Allowing employees to be themselves is an important practice of many top-ranked companies. An employee at Southwest Airlines, which has been in the top five of *Fortune's* top-ranked companies to work for on multiple occasions, said the following: "They treat you with respect, pay you well, and empower you. They use your ideas to solve problems. They encourage you to be yourself."[9] An employee at TDI Industries, which has been ranked in the top ten of Fortune's best companies, said the following: "This company makes you feel like a human being again."[10] At Microsoft, "Bill (never Mr. Gates) personally answered all e-mail from employees."[11]

COMMUNICATING SUPPORTIVELY

All of your efforts at developing sound human relations involve communicating by both words and actions with your associates and those outside your immediate sphere of influence. The ways in which you communicate can cause others to be open and honest or closed and defensive. If your words and deeds are supportive of the feelings and efforts of others, you encourage open and honest two-way communication. This two-way communication process should firmly bridge your relationships with your associates, peers, and superiors. The following are guidelines for communicating in a manner that will maintain or improve employee relations.

- Avoid responding to employees in a sarcastic or insulting manner.
- Provide explanations for actions and do not rely on company policy as an excuse.
- Provide a consistent message but adjust terms or level to the individual.
- Wait to cool off before communicating if you have been angered.
- Communicate in plain language without waffling on tough messages.
- Do not make employees wait on information that they need to hear.
- Tell the truth and do not compromise your message with half-truths.[12]

Take the short quiz in Exhibit 5.1. Any "rarely" responses indicate a need to improve your communication efforts.

DEVELOPING SOUND RELATIONSHIPS WITH EMPLOYEES

You should have a personal commitment to do what you can to help all of your associates and teams reach their potential. The ideal on-the-job relationship should result from your understanding, mastering, and executing four fundamental roles. These roles relate to and depend on one another.

Learning Objective Number Two

1. Educator—a builder of skills and developer of potential
2. Counselor—an adviser, director, cheerleader, and coach
3. Judge—an appraiser, mediator, and dispenser of justice
4. Spokesperson—a message carrier for both associates and superiors

YOUR ROLE AS EDUCATOR

Your role as an educator is usually the first one you play in relation to a new associate. Before new associates arrive, you have assessments of the training they need in order to adjust to their duties. This initial training is vitally important; it communicates the manager's expectations, the company's standards for performance, and the skills, knowledge, and attitudes required in the individual. Through training, new employees discover what the company stands for (its core values), and they become more closely aligned with the company.

Training, when properly planned and executed, does much to remove the initial fears we all have as we begin something new. It convinces trainees of our interest in and

EXHIBIT 5.1	How supportive are you when communicating with subordinates or team members?

USUALLY	RARELY		
○	○	1.	I make time to listen to my people's problems.
◉	◉	2.	I greet my people warmly and sincerely express my interest in their well-being.
○	○	3.	I give my people the information they need to perform effectively.
◉	◉	4.	I encourage my people to come to me with their ideas and suggestions.
○	○	5.	I am slow to criticize any idea given to me and try to look for its good points first.
◉	◉	6.	I use humor when appropriate in my communications.
○	○	7.	I share any praise I receive when part of it is due to the efforts of my subordinates or team members.
◉	◉	8.	I take the chance, whenever possible, to talk with my people, one on one.
○	○	9.	I express sincere interest in my people's families, inquiring as to their health and well-being.
◉	◉	10.	I consider my people's feelings and circumstances before attempting to judge or criticize their actions.
○	○	11.	I take every opportunity to compliment people for any job that is well done.
◉	◉	12.	I give quick feedback to my people on all matters that are of importance to them.
○	○	13.	I try to keep people from waiting on me.
◉	◉	14.	I offer explanations for my actions and decisions.

concern for them. They should emerge from training with a clear understanding of what is expected of them and how they are supposed to achieve it. Through training, team leaders, team facilitators, and supervisors demonstrate their commitment to helping trainees perform well and reach their potential.

In order to perform this role well, supervisors need to be aware of approaches that increase the likelihood that employees will learn needed skills while building their confidence and desire to make a good impression on their supervisor. Supervisors who lack the skills to train others tend to be impatient and have a tendency to start to do the work themselves. Instead of being patient and offering pointers they begin to do the work, and since they know the job well, they can perform it very quickly. Those being trained see the speed at which the supervisor can do the work and may become

In your role as educator, you demonstrate your commitment to helping your subordinates reach their potential. After your training sessions, workers should understand what is expected of them and how they can achieve it.

discouraged or feel inadequate. When this occurs, employees reach a point at which they neither respect nor like the supervisor. In contrast, good supervisors find that employees respond better to training when they are congratulated for making progress and are shown real respect. Employees must feel free to ask questions and this requires that supervisors take time to be good listeners.[13]

By understanding your role as an educator, mastering the knowledge and skills you wish to teach others, and executing this role in accordance with established training principles and procedures, you will be well on your way toward promoting your own success by fostering success in others.

YOUR ROLE AS COUNSELOR

counselor
the human relations role in which a supervisor is an adviser and director to subordinates

When performing the **counselor** role well, good supervisors want to know the subordinate's individual needs, aspirations, and desires. They listen and sometimes provide advice on how realistic the person's thinking is. Sometimes they suggest solutions to problems. They do not suggest solutions to personal or emotional problems;

instead they may suggest talking with a specialist—an authority trained to help in that particular area.

One of the critical requirements of being a good supervisor is that employees must feel that their supervisor notices them and that she really cares about them. Taking the time to coach employees sends a strong message that you are aware of subordinates and that you have their welfare in mind. While supervisors are always pressed for time, good supervisors find the time to coach their subordinates. Here is a three-step approach for coaching in relatively short amounts of time on a day-to-day basis:

> *Recognize:* Notice what the employee likes and dislikes, when he looks excited about his work and when he looks like he's bored silly. Has he recently shown a new skill or interest? Has he asked for your feedback on a task he has done? Is he having trouble with some aspect of his job? Has he indicated that he is interested in changing or expanding his responsibilities?
>
> *Verbalize:* Strike up a conversation. Let the employee know that you notice. If he has demonstrated a new skill, you might say, "Hey, do you really like doing that? What do you like about it? Would you like to do more of it?" Establish rapport. Show your interest in his current job satisfaction, and help him explore ideas for his long-run career development.
>
> *Mobilize:* All the talk in the world does no good if you are not prepared to take action. An employee who talks to you about his job is not just seeking sympathy. He wants advice, guidance, and the opportunity to pursue his goals. How can you help him find those opportunities within his current job? How can you help him prepare for future challenges? Show the sincerity of your support by helping to remove obstacles that prevent his further development.[14]

On the other hand, you should help solve problems or recommend solutions when problems are job-related and beyond the capability of subordinates. Nonetheless, you should not solve all problems, as this may retard the development of the problem-solving skills of your subordinates. When problems must be resolved at higher levels, ensure that they are referred to the correct authority. Follow up by checking on their disposition, and make sure that your subordinate is informed of the decision. Even if the results do not satisfy the individual, you have tried to help. You have done the best you could, and a subordinate will know it. You will have passed a major test.

Staying aware. Many supervisors ignore counseling until a problem arises. Then, they call a hasty conference and belittle, berate, or chew out the subordinate who is in trouble. Very soon subordinates get the message that the only time they see or hear from the boss is when she is unhappy or upset about their performance. Some supervisors claim that they do not have the time or that the time spent on counseling could be better spent on other things. The plain fact is that if supervisors do not counsel their people, they will have plenty of fires to put out and very little time for counseling. But if they invest the time necessary to touch base with each person periodically, they will be able to spot potential difficulties and prevent future problems or the necessity of corrective measures such as discipline or punishment.

Doing something. The value of learning from mistakes is a point we have touched on before, and it applies to coaching as well. Good coaching can come from

To be effective in your role as counselor, you must practice active listening. When you have discussions with subordinates, do more listening than talking.

team members as well as the team leader. The former director of the British Athletics Federation stresses the importance of coaching by team members and has made the following observation: "One person's experience is a learning opportunity for the team. What is the point of making a mistake if no one is going to learn from it?"[15]

An analogy can be drawn between the supervisor's role in the motivation of subordinates and the theater director's role in bringing out the best in actors. A director, like a supervisor, knows that the actor's motivation comes from within, and many influences can interfere with a superior effort. But the director knows that she can do much to provide the climate and incentives that may spark an inner drive within the actor. She may remove distractions that interfere with concentration, make certain that the actor has done the necessary homework, and confer with the actor to determine his perceptions of the role. The director also is able to set the stage with props and lighting that will allow the actor to perform to the best of his ability. Last, throughout the rehearsals and the performances, the director offers advice and criticism. Coaching and sincere concern often provide the spark the actor needs to give a superior performance. By sensing the actor's needs, strengths, and weaknesses, the director can provide advice and trigger the actor's commitment to excel.

YOUR ROLE AS JUDGE

Serving as judge successfully involves being proficient at four important tasks:

1. Enforcing company policies and regulations
2. Evaluating each subordinate's performance
3. Settling disputes between your people and teams
4. Dispensing justice

Enforcement. To enforce company policies and regulations, you must first be aware of them. You have to know what they say, as well as their proper interpretation. Consistency of enforcement is the key to gaining acceptance of company policies and management decisions. You must do the same with regard to your department's procedures and practices. Do people know about them? Do they understand them? Are they following them? All these questions are usually answered through various controls you design into your operation. Proper induction and training should go a long way toward ensuring that the department's procedures and practices are properly interpreted and utilized.

Evaluation. Evaluating subordinates is one of your most important and time-consuming tasks as a supervisor. You must use the performance criteria of the standards for each job and make objective and honest evaluations of each person's output and contributions. Is he meeting production standards? Is he correcting or trying to correct deficiencies noted in previous appraisals? Is he cooperative? Do his behaviors interfere with the efforts of other workers in the department?

Appraisals take place daily. In routine visits with your people, you have an excellent opportunity to note their successes and question their deficiencies. This will allow you to catch an error when it first appears and take corrective action. At the same time, you are letting your people know regularly how they stand with you. Your being with them routinely gives them the opportunity to ask questions and to clear up misunderstandings. When the time finally rolls around for a formal semiannual or annual review, there should be no surprises. You have kept your people informed on a daily basis.

Your day-to-day coaching and less frequent performance appraisals blend nicely with your role as a counselor. When your observations tell you that a worker's attitude probably causes a deficiency in her output or conduct, try to find the real causes for the behavior. You will recall that it is only when people see their attitude as improper that they are willing to reject it.

Settling disputes. Part of your role as a judge is to act as a peacemaker. People problems are the most persistent and frequent problems you have to deal with each day. Inevitably, two or more individuals or groups of subordinates will do battle with each other. Sometimes the causes are hidden from your view and only surface under stress with an open display of hostility. When you witness such disturbances, begin an investigation to uncover the causes on both sides. Analyze your evidence, and make a decision. Try to avoid treating the symptoms, but concentrate your energies on the disease. When you have reached a conclusion about the merits on both sides, confront the participants with your findings. Work toward a reconciliation that will not leave any scars as lasting reminders of the battle. Avoid any emphasis on who was at fault (chances are, both sides share the blame), but point out why the problem got started and how it can be avoided in the future.

Dispensing justice. Justice, in a supervisory sense, means seeing to it that each of your subordinates gets what she deserves. When your people are doing a good job, they deserve your praise. When they break a rule or violate a procedure, they must be shown the error of their ways. Rest assured that people want to know the limits of what they will be allowed to do. Once these limits are explained, people expect them to be enforced and usually anticipate some admonishment for each of their infractions. This admonishment may simply be a verbal warning, but in the case of repeated offenses, it may take the form of some other disciplinary action.

Improper or unacceptable conduct on the job cannot be tolerated. To prevent it, your company installs you as its chief enforcement officer in your department and gives you power to discipline violators. To many people, discipline simply means punishment. This is the negative side of a much broader concept. The positive side is the one that emphasizes informing organization members ahead of time about acceptable conduct. It places the emphasis on self-control and mutual trust. When new employees are hired, you should inform them of the rules on the very first day. You should clarify the meaning of acceptable and unacceptable behavior and performance. Soon after you become the supervisor of a section, you should inform your associates of your standards and expectations. When rule infractions occur, take action. To do otherwise would ultimately undermine your formal authority and your integrity. You will find that it is much better to start out tough than to try to become so later. It is difficult and unpleasant to impose discipline for infractions of rules that you failed to explain.

When punishment is necessary, you must be certain that it fits the offense. Quite often, when dealing with unionized workers, the manager's disciplinary powers are limited by the union contract. Be certain that you have the power to take a specific action before you do so. And keep in mind that subordinates expect you to act equitably—to be impartial and fair. An example of the importance of being impartial is provided by Texas Tech's basketball coach, Bobby Knight. While some of his actions have been the subject of substantial controversy, he gets high marks in the area of discipline. Knight has demonstrated courage in disciplining his players. Probably the most difficult test for Knight, while he coached at the University of Indiana, was when he removed his own son from the team for rules violations.[16]

YOUR ROLE AS SPOKESPERSON

Your superiors expect you to represent management's point of view adequately to your subordinates. You are the only manager who can translate management's plans into

In your role as spokesperson, you represent management's point of view to your subordinates and keep higher authorities informed of your team's progress.

action. Your boss, in particular, is counting on you to defend and to reinforce management's position. But you must be a **spokesperson** for your work group as well.

You must back up your subordinates when they are right—or when they are wrong because they executed your orders. If they believe that a policy or regulation is unfair, relay their feelings to those in a position to change it. You can do much to protect your people from harassment and from getting shortchanged. Just as you hope for their loyalty, they need yours. In addition, as the spokesperson for your team or unit, you must keep higher authorities informed of your team's progress.

You must respect the confidences of both your superiors and your subordinates. Sometimes your people will request an answer to a question, and you know the answer, but you may not be able to disclose it. Information given to you in private with a request for your silence must be respected. If you betray a confidence, you will soon find yourself ostracized from the group or excluded from opportunities to obtain information. Interestingly, with increasing diversity in the workforce and changing societal norms, people are more likely to talk about issues that were considered too sensitive to discuss at work in the past. Nonetheless, with the discussion of such matters there is greater likelihood someone will be offended. Furthermore, there have been instances in which supervisors and employees have discussed personal issues, such as their treatment for depression, and these matters have been used against them. On the other hand, when employees share personal issues with their supervisors or supervisors share something personal with their boss there may be an increase in trust.[17]

As a team leader or team facilitator, your spokesperson role also involves interacting with staff to acquire the appropriate support for your team. You may obtain such support by networking with your team's internal and external customers and suppliers. You also have information needs that may be served by interactions with external sources in your spokesperson role. Finally, as your unit's spokesperson, you arrange for cross-training to expand your team's skills and understanding of the needs and functions of others.

If you properly execute your role as spokesperson, your superiors and your subordinates will learn to trust you and to rely on you more in the future. This will strengthen your relationships with them and promote harmony and cooperation in your department. Take the quiz in Exhibit 5.2 to assess how well you are playing your four human relations roles with subordinates.

spokesperson
the human relations role through which a supervisor represents management's views to workers and workers' views to management

DIVERSITY

MAINTAINING YOUR RELATIONSHIPS WITH EMPLOYEES

So far we have discussed how to build a sound relationship with your individual employees. How can you preserve such relationships once they are established? The answer lies in persistence. As it is with personality formation, on-the-job relationships are also continuous processes. Like any other living thing, human relations need constant attention. Each day brings about changes in the parties involved so that what worked well yesterday may not today. Recognition of this dynamic aspect of people and their relationships dictates the need for maintenance. Establishing a sound relationship with each person is only a beginning. If the relationship is to grow and be mutually beneficial, maintenance must be scheduled and performed.

The relationship between supervisor and subordinate advocated in this chapter is distinctly different from the relationship between two people called *friendship*. At the base of sound human relations are common interests (effective and efficient operation

EXHIBIT 5.2	Assess how well you are playing your human relations role with subordinates.

EDUCATOR ROLE

USUALLY RARELY

○ ○ 1. I make certain that my actions do not contradict my words and instructions.

○ ○ 2. I carefully construct a program for training my people, being certain to set specific objectives.

○ ○ 3. I make certain that my people have the information and resources they need to do first-class work.

○ ○ 4. I assign work to people based upon their willingness and their abilities to perform it.

○ ○ 5. When I find an attitude in a subordinate that is interfering with performance, I work on changing it.

JUDGE ROLE

USUALLY RARELY

○ ○ 1. I look for causes behind any failures by my people to meet the standards set for their performance.

○ ○ 2. I withhold any criticism until I have all the facts and am aware of all the circumstances surrounding an issue.

○ ○ 3. I try to discipline without emotion.

○ ○ 4. I recognize that circumstances should temper any approach to discipline.

○ ○ 5. I know that it is better to forewarn and forearm subordinates about the expectations I and the organization have for them than to punish their failing to meet standards.

COUNSELOR ROLE

USUALLY RARELY

○ ○ 1. I make time for anyone who wishes to see me about a personal or work-related problem.

○ ○ 2. I make certain that any counseling I do is in private and free from interruptions.

○ ○ 3. I give the person seeking my help my undivided, sincere attention.

○ ○ 4. I recognize that I cannot solve every problem and should not try to give people all the answers.

○ ○ 5. When I cannot help someone solve a problem, I will try to refer him to another person with more expertise.

SPOKESPERSON ROLE

USUALLY RARELY

○ ○ 1. I take seriously every complaint or gripe I hear from subordinates.

○ ○ 2. I listen carefully to subordinates' suggestions and ideas and try to use them.

○ ○ 3. When I cannot solve any problem my people give me, I take it to a higher authority for resolution.

○ ○ 4. When my people experience success, I make certain others higher up hear about it.

○ ○ 5. I try my best to reflect management's points of view accurately, defending them and enforcing their decisions.

Each "rarely" response indicates that you need to improve your conduct.

SUPERVISING TEAMS

The performance of teams is determined by several variables, such as the degree to which the right mix of people and skills is present. While having the right people is obviously important, the ability to staff the team with exactly the right people is unrealistic in many circumstances. Team leaders must often get the job done with the people they have. On the other hand, team commitment and having a real challenge for the team to rally around may be the most important determinants of team performance in many realistic circumstances. Some of the most impressive team performances have come from circumstances in which the magnitude of the challenge was so great that it could not be met with incremental efforts. Instead, the teams have had to make a quantum change in how they do their work. The experiences of Ruston Gas Turbines, which is based in the United Kingdom, are instructive. The company faced strong compeitive threats, costs were high, production was slower than it should have been, and market share was declining. Furthermore, the community in which the company was located was higly dependent on the company and jobs were at stake. Almost inconceivably, the company's managing director, Paul Baron, challenged his team to increase productivity, revenue, and profits by a factor of two in less than five years.

Baron's team at Ruston Gas Turbines was successful because the challenge was motivating and because team members were committed to the cause. In addition, individual team members benefitted from sucesssful accomplishment of the overall goals. In order to work through the difficulties that teams encounter while accomplishing such challenges, it is important that supervisors develop and maintain positive working relationships within the team. It is especially important to work on relationships given that team members may not have the ideal representation of either job skills or interpersonal skills. Conflicts and disagreements are a natural part of teamwork and supervisors need to be able to manage and channel the energies of team members towards productive resolution that contributes to the accomplishment of the team's goals.

Source: Harvey Dubin. "Building High-Performance Teams," *Chief Learning Officer,* (July 2005): 46–49.

of the department, for example), mutual respect, and a concern for the other person's welfare. This is or should be true about your relationships with your friends, as well. But you should try to prevent a true friendship from emerging out of sound human relations with your subordinates.

If you allow a friendship to form between yourself and a subordinate, you do so at your own expense. How easy is it to give orders to a friend? Do you appraise your friend's performance and freely offer criticism? How about the times when you have to pass out an occasional dirty job? Would you consider your friend objectively as a candidate for it? You cannot form friendships with all of your subordinates, so aren't you opening yourself to criticism about playing favorites?

Your honest answers to these questions should alert you to the inherent dangers of friendship with subordinates. The subordinate you befriend is open to criticism, too, and that person's relationships with peers may be in jeopardy. Choose your friends from among your peers.

TEAMS

This chapter's Supervising Teams feature notes the importance of interpersonal relations within teams.

DEVELOPING SOUND HUMAN RELATIONSHIPS WITH PEERS

Your peers are the other managers on the same level of the management hierarchy. You work more closely with some than with others, but situations can change rapidly in business. The most important reasons for establishing good human relations with your peers are these:

- To know and understand them as individuals
- To approach and cooperate with them as individuals
- To assist them in achieving satisfaction from their jobs
- To foster a spirit of cooperation and teamwork among them
- To tap their diverse base of knowledge, skills, and experience

Your success as a manager is linked to your peers and what they think of you as a person and as a supervisor. Your personal and professional reputation with them is important for a number of reasons. If they think highly of you, they will expend their time and energy on your behalf and help you with advice. How you measure up with them and how they react when your name is mentioned are factors that may influence your boss as well. When your boss looks at his subordinates—you and your peers—for someone to delegate responsibility to or to train for a higher position, he will compare you to them. If you cannot get along with or are avoided by your peers, your boss will know it.

Your peers represent an enormous pool of talent and experience that is yours to tap and to which you can contribute. For this reason, if no other, it is to your advantage to cultivate their friendship. In many ways, you need each other, and all of you stand to benefit from a partnership or alliance based on mutual respect. If you are off in your own little world and are unwilling to share your knowledge, you deny yourself the advice and experience your peers are ready to provide. You may be branded as uncooperative or antisocial and destined, at best, for a career as a supervisor. Higher positions have no need for isolates. You will find, if you have not already done so, that the more you give of yourself, the more you will receive from others.

This chapter's feature on supervisors and performance discusses situations in which a newly promoted manager must supervise former peers.

YOUR ROLE AS EDUCATOR

The two-way nature of your role as educator includes assisting your fellow supervisors in their growth and development and enlisting their help on your own behalf. You have a great deal to give your peers. You have talents and skills that may be developed to a greater degree in you than in some of them. You have knowledge about human nature, your job, and management in general that can be beneficial to others. You have attitudes and a personality that can be the basis for friendship and that can sustain a fellow supervisor when she needs help.

Most people have experienced the joy that comes with helping a less experienced person solve a problem. Besides the momentary joy you feel when you share your knowledge and your tricks of the trade, you get something much more lasting: a good

SUPERVISORS AND PERFORMANCE

While not an optimal situation, it is not uncommon for a newly promoted supervisor to be placed in charge of former peers. Such assignments are particularly difficult when some of the employees are close friends. An engineer at the National Institute of Standards and Technology faced such a situation when he became a supervisor. One of his close friends in the unit was excessively tardy and needed to change his behavior. The new supervisor reasonably assumed that others in the unit were interested in seeing how he would respond to the tardiness. Fortunately, he responded appropriately by visiting privately with his friend. After telling his friend that he needed to be to work on time, his friend accepted the direction and agreed to change his behavior.

New supervisors do not always handle things as well, and they make the common mistake of focusing too much on maintaining the friendship at the expense of their credibility as a supervisor. They also go too far in establishing their authority and are too tough on their former peers. In addition to these mistakes in supervising former peers, new supervisors also tend to avoid providing honest feedback, are often too impatient to develop the skills of employees, and personally perform the work. Furthermore, they often fail to provide sufficient direction for employees. Unfortunately, while many of these mistakes could be avoided with training, there is evidence that companies are allocating fewer resources for supervisory training. As a result of insufficient training budgets, students who have mastered these lessons and who go on to become supervisors, will be asked to provide advice to new supervisors.

Source: Erin White. "Learning to Be the Boss," *Wall Street Journal*, (November 21, 2005): B1–B5.

reputation. Psychologically, all of your peers who profit through your efforts on their behalf are in your debt. They may not always show overt appreciation (and you should not always expect it), but they will find it hard not to reciprocate, to share what they have with you. When you need a favor, a bit of advice, or a helping hand, your colleagues will respond if they are able to do so.

Your peers' advice and know-how cannot be found in books. In a relatively short span of time, you may receive (if you are wise enough to ask) what might take you years to discover on your own. Which is easier and more fun: reading about how to do something difficult or having someone who knows how to do it show you? Your peers probably feel the same way about this as you do. The better your peers know you, the greater the quantity of help available to you. Give what you have, and take advantage of what others have to give. Do not bury your talents, and do not let others bury theirs.

YOUR ROLE AS COUNSELOR

Counseling involves a mutual exchange of ideas and opinions. Counselors are people to whom you go for advice and to try out your ideas. They provide you with guidance and a plan in the absence of one of your own. The key to counseling your peers is empathy—the intellectual and imaginative understanding of another's feelings and state of mind. From this develops a mutual respect and appreciation.

As with subordinates, just being available and favorably predisposed toward your peers may give them what they need at precisely the moment they need it—a sympathetic ear. By listening to others who have difficulties, you provide emotional first aid. By responding when asked and when qualified to do so, you may give people the support they need to resolve their difficulties.

When a friend asks you for advice and you have empathy for that person, speak your mind freely. Without empathy (which usually means without friendship), you should confine your guidance to work-related matters. Steer clear of personal advice unless you know the person well.

For the give and take of counseling between friends and associates to work, we must have open communication channels. Do your best to avoid arguments and displays of temper with your associates. Do not burn any bridges so that you cannot return to a pleasant relationship once a momentary storm passes. If for a time you alienate a peer, stand ready to apologize when you have been in the wrong. Be quick to forgive a colleague who has injured you. You do not have to call all of your peers your friends, but you should not call any of them enemies. By sharing the successes of others, you enrich the returns to them. By sharing the sorrows of others, you capture their friendship. So it is also when they reciprocate.

YOUR ROLE AS JUDGE

The role of judge is closely allied with the counseling role in human relations. You have four specific duties to attend: enforcement, settling disputes, evaluation, and criticism.

Enforcement. The duty you have to enforce company policies and regulations affects your peers as well. There is an urgent need for all supervisors to be uniform in both the interpretation and the application of these policies and regulations. You probably have experienced the unhappy situation that results when one supervisor is lenient and another is severe. Imagine a situation in which you are trying to get your workers to arrive and leave on schedule, whereas the supervisor in the adjacent department allows his people to come and go as they please. How much more difficult has this supervisor made your job? Where two managers interpret or enforce the same regulation or policy in different and conflicting ways, a wedge is driven between them. This wedge acts as a barrier to both communication and cooperation.

Settling disputes. When you find yourself at odds with a peer over an interpretation of policy or of how to enforce a rule, get together with that individual and work it out between you. A meeting and a polite discussion are all that it takes to resolve the difficulty. If you two cannot work the matter out, get together with your bosses. Do not let the conflict continue any longer than necessary. Take action as soon as you are aware that a problem exists.

Periodically, you may be called on by circumstances to serve as a peacemaker. For example, two of your associates are engaged in an argument, and their emotions have taken over. As a witness to the dispute, you may be able to intervene with a calmness and logic that the others lack. Do so when you find yourself in such a situation. It does managers no good to squabble, especially in public. Workers read all kinds of things into such events. You may save a friend or associate from the embarrassment of looking foolish.

Evaluation. Study your peers for an understanding of their management techniques. All of them have their unique characteristics and methods. Hold your standards up to theirs and see how they compare. Where you discover significant differences, make every effort to determine which is the better set to follow. Both your and their techniques could prove to be inferior to yet another set of standards.

Your peers make excellent working models to observe and evaluate. Try out your theories and applications on your associates, and get their reactions to them. Watch how they handle themselves in difficult as well as routine matters. Test your attitudes against theirs and see if you can refine your viewpoints and pick up some of their methods.

Criticism. When you observe a peer engaged in improper or forbidden conduct, you owe a bit of friendly correction. Others, especially workers, who observe a supervisor's improprieties draw conclusions that inevitably harm that supervisor's reputation and your own. You are all in this together.

When a peer's actions and objectives are contrary to yours, you must confront her with your observations. Let her know, in a tactful and sincere manner, what you know. After all, if you know what she is up to, it is quite likely that others also know— including the boss. Of course, you must still discuss the matter in private. You may find more often than not that a peer is unaware that she is doing anything wrong and will appreciate your drawing attention to the matter.

You, in turn, must stand ready for constructive criticism. We all need it occasionally and, in fact, stop growing without it. Contentment and smugness creep in, and a false sense of security takes over. We begin to believe that we are consistently right and gradually close our minds to the new and different. The strongest kind of friendly correction you can exert is your own good example. By promoting the things you believe in and by opposing the things you believe to be wrong, you take a stand and exhibit principles for others to see and admire.

We all tend to cover for a friend or peer in trouble. But in the long run, you stand to lose far more than you could ever gain. You will identify yourself as an ally of improper conduct and demonstrate wholly unacceptable attitudes for any manager to hold. You do not hold a position of power and trust in order to shield your friends from earned discipline. Nor should you punish; that is a middle manager's duty. You need not inform on a peer since, in time, things have a way of surfacing and getting to those who should know. However, if a peer is violating the law or a policy that places the company at risk, senior management needs to be informed. Confront your peer with the information you have. If your suspicions are confirmed, give the person a short time to inform senior management. If he fails to notify senior management, then you have an obligation to do so. Do not compromise your own position of trust and personal integrity to help anyone.

YOUR ROLE AS SPOKESPERSON

You owe loyalty to your peers, but only when they are in the right. Allegiance to someone is a precious gift, not to be given lightly. It must be earned as well as respected.

Loyalty implies mutual trust and confidence. When these things are not mutual, they cannot persist.

You should never spread a rumor about anyone. But when you hear one, it is your job as a spokesperson to refute it if you can. If you cannot, ask the other person to substantiate the statement. Inquire about the source. The person will know what you are thinking—that he is spreading gossip. When this bit of gossip relates to a peer, let that individual know its content and its source.

When an untrue rumor pertains to you, and you view its content as serious—such as an attack on your character—defend yourself. Trace it to its originator, and confront that individual with your knowledge. Control your temper but make your point as forcefully as you feel is necessary. Then bury the incident and try not to carry a grudge. If a rumor is minor and not related to your character, let it go. You do not have the time to track down all rumors, nor should you try to do so.

Respect legitimate demands for your silence, as when you converse about personal matters with a friend. Information revealed to you by a peer that pertains to that person alone should not be a topic of conversation with others. If you reveal a secret or break a confidence, your peer is sure to find out about it. What will happen to your reputation then?

The role of spokesperson also pertains to spreading good news or praising the ideas, contributions, and accomplishments of your peers. Giving credit where it is due and expressing your appreciation for benefits received, especially in public, is a pleasant duty one manager or friend owes another.

Finally, remember that you are also a spokesperson for your subordinates. When another supervisor interferes with them or their work, make it clear that the interference is inappropriate. Such an action challenges your authority. You must shield your subordinates and yourself from outside interference and conflicting orders or instructions.

COMPETITION WITH YOUR PEERS

Keep in mind that although you should maintain good relations with your peers and develop cooperation with them, you are still in competition with them. In much the same manner as a professional athlete, you have to maintain a balance between individual displays of talent and ability and the need for team play. All great athletes achieve their greatness in this way. You must be willing to take a back seat now and then and let another manager's talents come through. The best way to maintain good human relations is to develop yourself into the best person and manager you have the potential to become. You will gain expert and charismatic power in so doing, which will draw people to you. Use the checklist shown in Exhibit 5.3 as a guide to evaluate your human relations efforts in dealing with your peers. Any "rarely" responses indicate a need to make an adjustment.

GETTING ALONG WITH STAFF SPECIALISTS

Probably dozens of times each week your department is affected by the actions or policies of staff specialists. A large percentage of the e-mail replies, forms, and reports you generate are destined for them. The advice and service you receive from staff specialists can save you hours of agony and independent research. These people form

		EXHIBIT 5.3
Evaluate how well you are playing your human relations roles with peers.		

USUALLY   **RARELY**

USUALLY	RARELY	
○	○	1. I carry my own weight.
○	○	2. I lend a hand when and where needed.
○	○	3. I have the best interests of my peers in mind.
○	○	4. I am loyal to my peers.
○	○	5. I respect the privacy of things told to me in confidence.
○	○	6. I refrain from engaging in negative gossip.
○	○	7. I share my expertise and experiences with peers.
○	○	8. I try to earn the respect of peers.
○	○	9. I show my peers common courtesies and respect.
○	○	10. I share information with peers.
○	○	11. I avoid passing the buck.
○	○	12. I am a team player.
○	○	13. I defend my peers' actions in their absence.
○	○	14. I do not bear any grudges.
○	○	15. I try to avoid making any enemies.

Any responses of "rarely" indicate a need for improvement.

---

an invaluable group of counselors on professional matters. Do everything you can to take advantage of their labors and to foster a cooperative and receptive atmosphere. At times, they may appear to you as prying eyes or fifth wheels. But over the long run, your success as a supervisor—as well as that of all other managers—depends on your seeking and using their advice. And as the concept of functional authority suggests, you may have no choice.

Learning Objective Number Three

GETTING ALONG WITH YOUR BOSS

Before we get into specifics about your relations with your boss, we will discuss how your boss's job resembles yours and how it differs.

Since you are a supervisor, your boss is a middle manager. He is accountable for your actions. Your boss is similar to you in that he is both a follower and a staff or line manager. He executes all the functions of management and is evaluated on the basis of his subordinates' performances. Your boss, like you, must develop sound working relationships with subordinates, peers, and superiors. He probably served an apprenticeship as a supervisor, so you can probably count on him to understand your situation.

Compared to a supervisor, however, a middle manager has more differences than similarities. As the following list shows, your boss has a number of duties and interests that are unlike yours. Your boss:

- directs the work of other managers.
- exhibits strong pro-management attitudes.
- spends more time on planning than you do.
- spends less time with subordinates.
- spends more time with peers and superiors.
- is more of an adviser than a director.
- has more freedom of action and flexibility.
- has more information and a broader perspective.
- is less concerned with procedures and tactics and is more concerned with planning and strategy.
- is more concerned with tomorrow than with today.
- is more concerned with the organizational impact of management actions than individual effects.

As to the last item on this list, supervisors and subordinates often evaluate a management decision on the basis of its effect on them. Suppose that higher management has recently reduced the plant budget for overtime. This decision is translated at your level into less overtime and production flexibility for the department and less income for the workers. Your people see this as a reduction in their potential earnings. Your boss probably participated in the decision and the objectives it was designed to achieve. For instance, lower overtime expenses may conserve income, allow your company to price its

Employees with disabilities must be treated with respect and dignity. They often have superior productivity and attendance records. Here, a supervisor at Dell Computers confers with an employee who is visually challenged.

line more competitively, and reduce overall expenses. Your boss sees the decision as logical and supports it. Once you know the reasons behind a decision, you should support the decision as strongly as your boss does. Give what facts you can to your subordinates to soften the blow. Emphasize that the conservation of income may prevent layoffs and save jobs. You must be flexible enough to meet rapidly changing situations such as this.

*Learning
Objective
Number Four*

YOUR BOSS'S EXPECTATIONS

Most middle managers expect their subordinate managers to be loyal followers. Your boss, like you, needs the respect and support of subordinates. She must be able to count on your willingness and ability to enforce company policies and standards. She is relying on you to carry out decisions with the proper attitude. Do not let any of your actions or remarks jeopardize your boss's reputation.

Your boss expects you to get along well with your peers and with the company's various staff specialists as well as with your subordinates. If you are able to resolve your disputes on your own, without arguments and displays of temper, you are demonstrating resourcefulness. Initiative is another extremely important characteristic for any manager to possess. Are you the kind of manager who waits for orders or instructions before acting? If you do, you lack this essential quality. When you have the authority to act in a situation and know what must be done, you must not be afraid to respond.

Finally, your boss expects you to keep her informed. Share your knowledge about essential operations with your boss. Nothing can injure you quite as effectively as for the boss to be surprised—to find out about something secondhand. You can make your boss look bad if you fail in your duty to keep her abreast of developments. Share what information you have with your boss, without betraying any confidences.

WINNING YOUR BOSS'S CONFIDENCE

If you meet your superior's expectations, you are well on your way toward gaining his confidence. In addition, try to learn from your mistakes, as each one may have a lesson to be learned. Study your errors to avoid repeating them. Bring your efforts at self-development to your boss's attention. The courses you take in school and recent articles or books you have read that have been helpful in your work are all worthy topics of conversation with your boss. Additional ways to improve your supervisory abilities are described below.

FINDING A BETTER WAY

As a manager, you should give methods improvement a high priority. No matter how smoothly an operation is running, there is usually room for improvement. Turn your attention to the costliest operations first. That is where you stand to realize the greatest savings. Then, systematically work your way through the rest of your operations. Five magic words related to methods improvement have proved to be valuable to many supervisors and those aspiring to supervision. All are related to reengineering: (1) combine, (2) eliminate, (3) rearrange, (4) reexamine, and (5) simplify. Look at a plan, program, procedure, or practice with these words in mind.

Do not keep your successes to yourself. Share them with your peers and superiors. Others can profit from your innovations. The time, effort, and money that can be saved are important, but the effect on your reputation and career is also important. Just be certain that an idea is yours before you take credit for it. Where you receive help, give credit to that individual.

KEEPING YOUR PROMISES

A can-do attitude is great if you really can do what you promise. Before making a promise, be as certain as possible of the resources at your disposal and the limits on your operations. If, in your best judgment, you have what it will take to get the job done, commit yourself and your people to the endeavor. It is better to be a little bold than to be too cautious. If circumstances change dramatically for reasons beyond your ability to foresee, let your boss know. He will understand and adjustments can be made. However, if you should have known about or suspected changes that would make your promise invalid, your reputation will suffer.

SPEAKING POSITIVELY OR NOT AT ALL

Whatever the topic of conversation, be sure that what you say is positive. Resist the temptation to engage in gripe sessions and to put another person down. Such displays are clearly negative and completely without redeeming qualities. If your gripe is justified, reveal it to those who can act on it. If the person you wish to criticize is a subordinate, approach that person in private, and keep your comments constructive. No one, especially not a boss, benefits from associating with a person who is always negative. Few activities are as futile as gripe sessions. Names are dropped and things are said that all too often you later wish you could retract or forget. If you have nothing positive to say, you are better off saying nothing.

Constructive criticism, whether of an individual or of an idea, is not negative, and you are perfectly right to engage in it as long as the environment is correct. When an argument is put forth that favors a course of action and you see a disadvantage to it, you must air that point if the advocate of the proposal fails to do so. When the boss or anyone else puts forth a proposal in your presence, she wants your honest reactions.

TAKING A POSITION

You must be a contributing member of the management team—carrying your own weight and standing ready to help teammates. If you want the respect of others, you must have convictions. These convictions or beliefs tell others who you are and where you stand. However, before you take a stand on an issue, make sure that you think it through and anticipate the possible drawbacks, as well as your supportive arguments. Then prepare your defense.

When you take your stand and find it untenable, do not be reluctant to yield to superior forces. Bullheadedness is not a quality that endears you to anyone, while reasonableness *is* such a quality. You want to be thought of as a person of principle—one who thinks things through and fights for what he or she believes. The corollary to this is equally important: You must oppose things you believe to be improper or wrong.

Involving Your Boss in Major Decisions

Just as you stand ready to help a subordinate or peer with a problem, your boss is ready to help you. When you have a problem with which you have wrestled but to which you have no certain solution, set up a meeting with your boss, explaining in advance what you wish to discuss. Assemble your research and facts. Construct a list of alternatives you have considered. What the boss wants most is to see that you have considered the matter and given it your best effort. She will not make your decisions for you, except when you have reached an impasse. Even then, most bosses offer only suggestions and direct your attention to additional items you may have overlooked. That method may be a little frustrating, but the learning experience is invaluable to you.

Each contact you have with your boss should be as professional as you can make it. Be yourself, but be prepared.

Obtaining Some of Your Boss's Authority

Learn your boss's needs, ambitions, strengths, and weaknesses. You can learn from a strong boss and may be able to help a weak one. The boss, like you, is probably looking for subordinates who can attend to time-consuming details and assume routine tasks. By delegating them, the boss creates time for more important tasks—the ones he alone must tackle. Your boss also gains time to take on a larger portion of his own boss's duties and thus prepares for advancement. So it goes from supervisor to chief executive. Through delegation, each trains another. A manager who has not trained a subordinate to take her place may be unable to advance. Her lack of mobility acts as a ceiling on those with ambition and ability below.

Your boss will begin to delegate duties to you when you have proved that you are worthy of respect and confidence. You will get details and routine tasks at first. If you handle them well, you can look forward to increased responsibilities. The increased duties may become yours permanently, enlarging your job description and serving as justification for increases in pay, status, and a possible change in title.

If your boss is reluctant to delegate, you should urge him to do so. First, you must free yourself from your details and routines in order to make time available. Then go to your boss with time on your hands and a plea for additional duties. You may not be successful at first; old habits die slowly. But you have planted a seed, and a good manager will not let it die. Your boss will be disturbed by your idleness and impressed by your initiative. If you persist, your boss will respond.

Do not assume any of your boss's duties or anyone else's without consultation. There is a tendency for a bright and eager young supervisor to spot something that needs doing and do it. This is fine as long as you have jurisdiction over the matter. But when the duty you perform belongs to another, you are guilty of grabbing power from that person. This will be interpreted to your disadvantage.

Do not get yourself into a position where your boss becomes too dependent on you. If the boss views you as indispensable, she may consciously or unconsciously restrict your chances for advancement. She will fear losing you, through promotion or transfer, and the corresponding disruption of the status quo this may represent. Your best defense is to train a successor. When the opportunity arises and the time is right, you can then point with pride and confidence to that subordinate as your logical and well-trained successor.

Exhibit 5.4 provides some suggestions that can help you maintain a good relationship with your boss.

Exhibit 5.4	**Suggestions for managing your boss.**

- Analyze your boss's job, leadership/operating style, and needs system to gain a better feel for his or her perspective.

- As a consequence of this analysis, you should understand the boss's aspirations, goals, and plans, concerns, problems, and priorities, and so perform to increase the likelihood of your boss's success.

- Recognize that the boss is a human being and thus has need for support, encouragement, attention, and sincere praise, as well as for the expected technical assistance. Avoid backing him into a corner with possible loss of face.

- Keep the boss fully informed as to progress on and problems with assignments and, above all, avoid embarrassing the boss with surprises.

- Present solutions to problems as opposed to merely highlighting the problems.

- Function in a positive and facilitating manner, but don't hesitate to challenge the boss and offer constructive criticism when needed.

- Ensure that the boss gets the credit for success and thus is made to feel and look good.

- Should you get a new boss, show him or her how indispensable you are and that you intend to remain so.

- In all transactions involving the boss, ask yourself: "Will my action strengthen or weaken my boss's perception that I am an understanding and supportive subordinate?"

- To the extent possible, develop strategies to cope with the less attractive aspects of the boss's behavior.

- Use "I messages" when it is essential to confront your boss regarding behaviors you find inconsiderate or possibly punishing.

- Use positive "self-talk" to bolster your feelings about your supervisor, avoiding self-sabotaging messages ("can't," "don't know how," "it's too hard"). A good verbal guide: "What you say is what you get!"

- Change yourself because your ability to change your boss, who has the power, is necessarily limited. *Example:* Assume your boss is a slow decision-maker. Shift your self-talk from "That guy dreads making a decision," to "Hey, this gives me a lot of freedom to fill that void."

YOUR EXPECTATIONS OF YOUR BOSS

Besides mutual respect and trust—which are prerequisites for a working relationship—your boss should provide you with the following:

- Constructive criticism
- Fair evaluations
- Essential guidance
- A constant flow of necessary information
- Recognition for jobs well done
- An appropriate management style
- Training for growth and development
- A good example

Where one or more of these items is lacking, look first at yourself for the cause. Something in you or your performance may be missing. If you do not give respect or loyalty, you have none coming. If you do not respond well to criticism, you may not receive it. If you do not think your boss's evaluations of your performance are fair, why did you accept them without protest? You may not be receiving guidance because you have not asked for any. Is the guidance you seek really essential? If you do not get information, maybe it is because you cannot keep a secret or have no need to know. If your boss's management style with you is not to your liking, have you discussed it with him? You may find, as many management students do, that the more you learn about management principles and practices, the more critical of people in authority you become. If this is happening to you, do not be alarmed. You are experiencing what all children growing up experience: the realization that the adult who occupies a position of trust and authority is really just a human being.

The beauty of all this is that you will know when something goes wrong and why. How you react to your new knowledge and act on it determines whether you remain always a freshman or become a senior and graduate. Knowledge is power, and power needs controls on its use. As you mature, you will discover flaws where you saw none before. An inadequate manager often provides a better learning situation than one who is a real professional. When things run smoothly, you often do not know why. But when things go sour, you have a chance to ask and determine why. That goes for your own mistakes as well as for those of the boss. Your analysis of your boss's shortcomings can prevent them from plaguing your own efforts. Most of the cases in this book (and in every other management text) portray managers with flaws and inadequacies for just this reason.

According to a study by professors and psychologists Robert Hogan and John Morrison, the average subordinate thinks that her managers are competent between 60 and 75 percent of the time. In another study done by Personnel Decisions International of Minneapolis, a human resource consulting firm, 56 percent of the 800 people surveyed thought their bosses were "top-notch"; only 8 percent thought that their bosses treated them unfairly.[18]

RECOVERING FROM A MISTAKE WITH YOUR BOSS

It is likely that at some point you will make a mistake that will potentially cause a problem for your boss. While the strength of your relationship and trust that have been

Exhibit 5.5	**Suggestions for developing a better relationship with your boss.**

- Stay attuned to performing the things that your boss wants you to do.

- Initiate regular conversations or e-mails with your boss that deal with productivity improvement and direction.

- Develop ideas for improvement of processes or activities, put them in writing or presentation form, seek input from your boss, allow time for consideration, and work to obtain approval.

- Prevent negative impressions from forming by exhibiting a positive commitment to resolving difficult issues and by not getting involved in altercations.

- Commit to being loyal, courteous, and forgiving in your interactions with your boss and others.

- Tell the truth in all dealings with your boss and others.

- Acknowledge your boss's accomplishments and express sincere appreciation.

- Work overtime on a voluntary basis, come to work early and leave late.

Source: "How to Improve Your Relations with the Boss," *Supervisor* (January 2003): 15.

Learning Objective Number Five

established to that point will determine much of how your boss will respond, there are some ways in which you can improve the chances of a successful recovery. One suggestion is to begin restoring his or her trust by offering an immediate and sincere apology. This should be followed with an acknowledgment that you take responsibility for your actions and how you will ensure that the incident will not be repeated in the future. It may also be helpful to ask for your boss's suggestions for how you should proceed in the future or how the consequences of your actions can be ameliorated. Your attempts to correct any problems created by your mistake are likely to help shore up your relationship with your boss.[19]

Exhibit 5.5 provides some suggestions for improving your relationship with your boss.

MANAGING CONFLICT

Supervisors and managers spend a substantial amount of their time dealing with conflict that occurs between employees and associates, between organizational units, with other units, vendors, and so on. It is critical that supervisors have the skills needed for resolving conflict as well as the knowledge and skills to use it for constructive purposes.[20] Unfortunately, some supervisors are uncomfortable with conflict and tend to avoid dealing with the issues while hoping that the conflict will go away. In addition, others suppress conflict and view it as destructive. On the other hand, other supervisors probably cause more conflict than is necessary.

Over the years, different views of conflict have evolved. Until a few decades ago, the **traditional view** of conflict maintained that all conflict is dysfunctional or symptomatic of bad management and that conflict resolution should be emphasized. In the 1960s a **behavioral perspective** evolved in which it was recognized that in complex organizations conflict is inevitable and as a result, conflict is not necessarily symptomatic of bad management. Later, it was recognized that some level of conflict is important to high quality decision-making. This view of conflict, which is called the **interactionist** perspective, maintains that some conflict is necessary and that managers should attempt to manage conflict at an optimal level.[21]

Antecedents of Conflict

There are many antecedents of conflict. One cause is ill-conceived reward systems that create competition between employees or teams in situations in which the work could be performed better with cooperation and information sharing. Another cause is scarcity of resources, which leads to competitive interactions. Ambiguous organizational boundaries and responsibilities are other sources of conflict along with breakdowns in communication and destructive criticism. In addition, a greater range of individual differences in the work environment, such as cultural background, age, race, and gender, are likely to set the stage for increased conflict.[22]

The character and personalities of supervisors, managers, and executives who provide leadership for an organization also provides antecedent conditions for conflict. Peter Frost has described toxicity in the workplace and has called attention to managers who are emotionally unintelligent. Just as there are emotionally intelligent managers, there are also managers on the other end of the scale. One of the key features of **emotionally unintelligent managers** is ignorance of the manner in which their emotions affect others and an absence of empathy for employees and peers. While having only one toxic manager is not good, when there are several in an organization, the results can be devastating. Other types of **toxic managers** include micromanaging control freaks, indecisive managers, those who act with malice, and those who mislead employees into performing at high levels when they have no intentions of following through with promised rewards.[23] The following describes a toxic manager:

> Ryan was a senior manager who kept two fishbowls in the office. In one were goldfish; in the other a piranha. Ryan asked each of his staff to pick out the goldfish that was most like themselves (the spotted one, the one with a deeper color, and so forth). Then when Ryan was displeased with someone, he would ask the person to take his or her goldfish out of the bowl and feed it to the piranha.[24]

Constructive Conflict

Supervisors should not attempt to suppress all conflict because **constructive conflict** is often needed for improved decision quality.[25] Such conflict often results in problem solving because it clarifies issues and alternatives.[26] It is also an important impetus for change because it causes us to search for ways to solve problems. On the other hand,

traditional view
a view that all conflict is dysfunctional or symptomatic of bad management and that conflict resolution should be emphasized

behavioral perspective
a view that in complex organizations conflict is inevitable and as a result, conflict is not necessarily symptomatic of bad management

interactionist
view that some conflict is necessary and that managers should attempt to manage conflict at an optimal level
Learning Objective Number Six

emotionally unintelligent managers
managers who lack empathy and are oblivious to the effect of their emotions on others

toxic managers
manipulative managers who lack emotional intelligence and tend to be over-controlling

constructive conflict
conflict that results in problem solving because it clarifies issues and alternatives

destructive conflict
conflict that is emotion laden, may involve attacks of a personal nature, often includes insults, and may lead to retaliation

avoiding style
not addressing the conflict by ignoring it

accommodating style
allowing the other party to satisfy his or her needs

competing style
pursuing your own needs at the expense of the other party

change also leads to conflict as change involves various adjustments, such as shifts in power and resources, which typically cause conflict.[27]

DESTRUCTIVE CONFLICT

While constructive conflict is sometimes necessary to ensure that differing views receive sufficient attention and that necessary changes are made, not all conflict is constructive. **Destructive conflict** is often emotion laden, may involve attacks of a personal nature, often includes insults, and may lead to retaliation.[28] Such conflict detracts from workplace morale, undermines group cohesion, undermines teamwork, and leads to turnover. Individuals who are abusive, selfish, and inconsiderate also cause destructive conflict.[29] Unfortunately, as noted earlier, there are a few people in most organizations who cause destructive conflict because they lack basic interpersonal skills. These people often leave a trail of strained or broken relationships.

APPROACHES FOR DEALING WITH CONFLICT

Most managers deal with conflict in a somewhat characteristic manner or style or have tendencies to approach conflict in the same manner. Our characteristic styles and flexibility in using other styles can be determined with the use of instruments, such as the widely used Thomas-Kilmann Conflict Mode Instrument (TKI) developed by Kenneth Thomas and Ralph Kilmann.[30] As the TKI indicates, different styles are appropriate in different situations, although some approaches are ineffective in many circumstances. There are five basic styles or approaches for handling conflict.[31]

Avoiding. Instead of dealing with the conflict, the supervisor tries to ignore or deny that such a situation exists.[32] In some instances involving minor or temporary issues, conflicts are likely to resolve themselves. For example, employee complaints may occur when people are in crowded work environments during office or plant renovations. These are likely to be temporary as are conflicts that occur when temporary contractors are on site for short periods of time. However, in most instances, avoidance is a poor approach for dealing with conflict because it does not address the root causes of the conflict or the underlying issues. If it is not dealt with, it may become more severe and difficult to resolve. If supervisors or managers tend to avoid conflicts, their employees will probably lose confidence in their willingness to address concerns. When this happens, employees run the risk of being perceived as weak or unresponsive.

Accommodating. With this style, the supervisor chooses to approach the conflict from a cooperative perspective and makes no attempt to be competitive or assertive.[33] This style is more relevant to conflicts that supervisors encounter with peers, higher-level managers, other organizational units, customers, and vendors. By accommodating, the supervisor defers to the other parties and lets them implement their preferred solutions or satisfy their needs. Typically this would be appropriate when one has a weak position and more value can be gained from accommodating on this round than competing. By being reasonable in this situation and letting the other party win, the supervisor has created an obligation for the other party to reciprocate in the future.

Competing. With the competing style, the parties rely on power to force a solution favorable to themselves but not as favorable for the other side.[34] Such a style is appropriate in some circumstances, such as when an employee keeps performing an activity in the wrong way or when an employee is violating a company policy. In this approach to conflict resolution, the supervisor directs the employee to follow the correct procedure or to not violate policy. On the other hand, some supervisors rely on this power or forcing approach in other circumstances and attempt to win when there is room for all parties to win. Because the approach can undermine situations in which all parties can satisfy their needs with innovative or integrative solutions, the style can lead to more conflict in the future. Too much reliance on this style has the potential for creating strained relationships with employees, peers, and other units because they may see little chance that their concerns will be addressed in a cooperative manner.

Compromise. With this style or approach, the parties obtain a resolution to the conflict by adopting an intermediate level of cooperation or assertiveness and competition.[35] The compromise style is appropriate when there is insufficient means to pursue a collaborative approach or when it is unlikely that the parties are willing to share their real underlying needs in a conflict situation. Because compromise does not identify the underlying needs of the parties, there may not be a long-term resolution to the conflict. With compromise, the parties typically obtain less than they desire, and there is incomplete satisfaction with the resolution. Nonetheless, compromise is a valuable conflict resolution procedure and is particularly appropriate when there are severe time pressures or where an intermediate solution can help the parties get by with a temporary solution.

compromising style
an approach for resolving conflict in which each party gives up some need satisfaction

Collaborating. When the parties collaborate, they identify needs and work to satisfy their own needs as well as the other party's needs in a win-win solution.[36] Collaboration does not imply that the parties are not assertive or that they are easy bargainers. Instead, they actively and cooperatively pursue a resolution of the conflict that satisfies their needs as well as the other parties' needs. With such approaches, the parties are often said to be tough on problems or that they attack problems while they are soft or easy on people.[37] With collaborative approaches to conflict, the parties form an integrative and long-lasting solution, which addresses the underlying problems. This approach to conflict resolution is time consuming and does not work well where there is long-lasting hostility or an absence of trust. Nonetheless, it is clearly an approach that the parties should pursue as an ideal when the circumstances are appropriate.

collaborative style
pursuing mutual need satisfaction in the resolution of a conflict

Exhibit 5.6 illustrates the relationships among the five styles of dealing with conflict. As can be seen in the exhibit, the vertical axis signifies distribution and the horizontal axis signifies integration. These five conflict resolution styles are categorized by the extent to which they are distributive or integrative. For example, the competing style represents an assertive approach that emphasizes favorable distribution of resources for satisfying one's own needs. In contrast, the accommodating style represents an integrative or cooperative approach in which the emphasis is on satisfying the other party's needs. As indicated in the exhibit, the collaborative style has maximum concern for satisfaction of both one's own and others' needs.[38]

INSTANT REPLAY

1. Human relations involves the development and maintenance of sound on-the-job relationships with subordinates, peers, and superiors.

2. Supervisors must relate to people at work by perceiving them as they perceive themselves—as members of diverse groups that influence their attitudes and behaviors.

EXHIBIT 5.6	Conflict resolution styles.

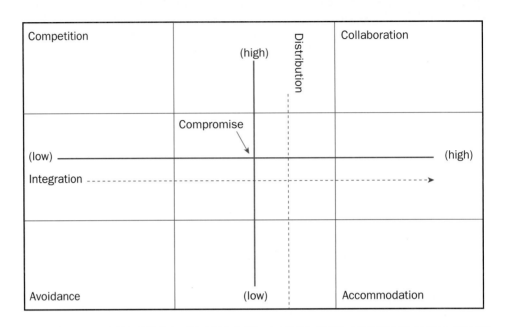

Source: Greenburg, Jerald, and Baron, Robert A. *Behavior in Organizations,* 7th Edition, © 2000. Adapted by permission of Pearson Education, Inc., Upper Saddle River, NJ.

3. Building human relationships requires you to play fundamental roles as educator, counselor, judge, and spokesperson.

4. As an educator, you share your knowledge, skills, and experiences with others.

5. As a counselor, you provide advice, service, direction, and a sympathetic ear.

6. As a judge, you evaluate the performance of subordinates, enforce rules and standards, settle disputes, and dispense justice.

7. You win your peers' respect by lending a hand when and where you can and by being a friend.

8. As a spokesperson, you represent subordinates to higher authority and management to subordinates.

9. You win your boss's respect and confidence by meeting expectations and by playing your roles as they are prescribed.

10. You learn your boss's job by creating time in which to help perform some of the boss's tasks. You train your replacement through delegation of duties.

11. There are several approaches for dealing with conflict, but they must be used appropriately.

QUESTIONS FOR CLASS DISCUSSION

1. Can you define this chapter's key terms?
2. What are the major purposes of human relations?
3. How should a supervisor play the basic human relations roles with subordinates? With peers?
4. How is a middle manager's job different from a supervisor's?
5. What is involved in creating and maintaining a good working relationship with one's boss?
6. How do the compromise and collaboration approaches to conflict resolution differ?
7. What are the various antecedents for conflict?

ASSESS THIS SITUATION

Purpose: To help you identify cultural differences between yourself and others.

Your Task: For each aspect of culture listed, write out a summary statement for yourself and another person at work or in your class who is different from you in some major way. Then discuss the similarities and differences.

You	Another Person	Aspect of Culture
◯	◯	1. Importance of being on time
◯	◯	2. Command of the English language
◯	◯	3. Openness to meeting new people
◯	◯	4. Conversational style
◯	◯	5. Age
◯	◯	6. Educational background
◯	◯	7. Work ethic
◯	◯	8. View on importance of family
◯	◯	9. Gender
◯	◯	10. Favorite foods
◯	◯	11. Willingness to conform
◯	◯	12. Respect for others

SKILL BUILDING EXERCISE 5.1

One of the realities of organizational life is that people sometimes find themselves working for a person who is a bully or jerk. Supervisors are not immune from such treatment as they may find themselves working for such a manager or executive.

Bullies tend to engage in a number of behaviors that are very demeaning and demoralizing to the recipient of such treatment. More specifically, they commonly use sarcastic language to demean and intimidate people, often under the guise of humor. They are also amazingly inconsiderate, rude, and unprofessional. They also break promises, may undermine you with critical comments or untruths about you to others, and treat you as if your time is completely unimportant compared to theirs. In many cases, there is no way you can do your job well enough to avoid the bully's attacks because he or she can always claim that you could have done better. Eventually such conduct causes even the best employee to lose confidence and to begin to have doubts about her own abilities and performance. In addition, it is not uncommon for bullies to engage in sneaky and manipulative behavior. If you complain about their attacks to them, you may run the risk of being labeled as being too sensitive. Such experiences are often exasperating because people who are being abused by such people sometimes conclude that they lack the insights or enough power to change the situation.

Your Task: Work in a small group or work alone to identify (1) how you should behave in the face of such treatment, (2) how you could obtain help from peers, (3) how you could determine whether the bully's behavior is driven by his or her own fears, (4) how you could obtain help from higher-level managers, and (5) what you should do to document the abusive treatment.

Sources: Ben Leichtling. "Bullies in the Workplace," *OfficePro*, (June/July 2005): 10–12. Martin Couzins, and Scott Beagrie. "How to Deal with a Bad Boss," *Personnel Today* (September 27, 2005).

SKILL BUILDING WRITING EXERCISE 5.2

Consider the following statements that are likely to cause or intensify existing conflict:

- "You must—" "You have to—" "You will—"
- "If you don't—" "You'd better or else— " "You'll pay a big price—"
- "It's only right that you should—" "You ought to—" "You'll pay a big price—"
- "What you should do is—" "Here's how it should go—" "It would be best if you—"
- "You are argumentative (lazy, stubborn, dictatorial . . .)." "I know all about your problems." "You'll never change."
- "It's all your fault." "You are the problem here."
- "You lied to me." "You started this mess." "You won't listen."
- "You're being unrealistic (emotional, angry, hysterical . . .)—" "This is typical of you—"

- ■ "You always—" "Every time this happens you do the same thing—" "You never—"
- ■ "Don't you think you should—" "To really help you should—"

Your Task: (1) Provide a one-word descriptive label for each set of these phrases. (2) Rewrite these phrases so that the meaning is communicated in a manner that is less likely to lead to conflict.

Source: Resolving Conflicts at Work: A Complete Guide for Everyone on the Job, Kenneth Cloke and Joan Goldsmith, pp. 67–68. Copyright © (2000 Jossey-Bass Publishers). Reprinted with permission of John Wiley & Sons, Inc.

CASE 5.1   Short in Stature

Kirby walked into Nancy's office and said, "I need to talk to you." He then closed the door and said, "I didn't appreciate it when you challenged my new production scheduling plan in the meeting a while ago. If you had real concerns, why didn't you wait to talk to me in private? It is embarrassing to have someone trash my ideas, and I don't want it to happen again."

Nancy, taken by surprise by Kirby's response, replied, "Well, I'm sorry if I embarrassed you. It was certainly not my intention. I just have some strong feelings about the schedule and simply said what I felt. It looked to me like at least two others felt the same way because it seemed to me like they were really biting their tongues when you outlined the plan."

Kirby said, "I don't think that's true. You were the only one who objected to the schedule. Besides, your tone of voice indicated that you were dismissing the plan as ridiculous. You're not going to get away with being disrespectful to me."

Nancy then said, "I'm sorry you feel that way. You really caught me by surprise with the plan for a new production schedule."

Kirby then responded, "I will not let you undermine my attempts to improve the way we do things around here. Nancy, you've got a bad attitude and you need to change it. If you're that unhappy around here, then you need to leave. We can't tolerate any people who aren't cooperative." Kirby then opened the door and left.

Nancy couldn't believe what had just happened. She felt terrible about Kirby's reaction. Just then, Irene stuck her head in the door. She said, "I'm sorry, but it looks like Little Napoleon had another temper tantrum. Was he in here chewing you out?"

Nancy said, "Yes, that's what happened. I should have known better than to challenge his ideas in the meeting. I just feel awful."

Irene said, "I know it was no fun for you, but I really appreciate the fact that you shot down his idea. Everybody knows that his proposed new schedule would be a disaster. Besides, he's so insecure that even the slightest objection by anybody gets misconstrued as a personal attack. People are afraid to say anything."

Nancy said, "I don't know what to say anymore. We all have more experience than Kirby and have a pretty good idea about what will work with our production facilities. These meetings never go well anymore because we can't disagree with anything Kirby wants to do."

Just then Cary walked in and said, "Wow! I just saw Little Napoleon walking down the hall from this direction. What did he say to you?"

Nancy described the conversation again and Cary said, "That sounds like him. I think that you'd be a great supervisor, but this organization is so male-dominated that even someone like Kirby is tolerated. I know you're upset, but thanks for saying what you did. This new scheduling plan of Kirby's sounds about as bad as the rest of his ill-conceived ideas. Because we've been a good unit in the past and still care about this place, we perform in spite of his incompetence. So it's not clear to me that upper management knows how bad he is."

Thirty minutes later Kirby went to see his boss, George Master. "George, I've had it with Nancy. She's really got a bad attitude and is poisoning the well with her negativity. Every time I try to introduce a new change, I've got to deal with her. I want to start laying a paper trail to get rid of her. She's got some friends in the department, and they tend to take her side on most things. If we get rid of her, the rest will fall in line."

Questions

1. How should Kirby have attempted to gain acceptance of his plan for a new production schedule?

2. How should Kirby handle his differences with Nancy? With some of the other associates?

3. What do you think George Masters will want to know about the situation?

4. What advice do you have for Kirby? For Nancy? For George?

CASE 5.2   Feedback from the Boss

Sandy had asked Ed, one of eight project managers who reported to her, to come by to talk about issues related to the project Ed's group had just completed at Blue Valley Manufacturing.

SANDY:"Ed, thanks for coming by. I wanted to share some feedback from the last project your group just completed. You're just starting your group's next project and there's some information that may be helpful. We received some feedback from Francis Drummond, the contract manager at Blue Valley, that they were a little dissatisfied with the amount of cooperation they received from your group."

ED: "I'm not surprised to hear that Francis complained. He seemed to be determined, even from the first day, not to like anything we did for them."

SANDY: "Why didn't I know about any problems you were having with Francis? You didn't tell me about any difficulties."

ED: "Well, we never really worked with Francis very much except for the first week of the project. After a week, two other people at Blue Valley took his place as contacts for our group, and he faded into the background. They were good people to work with, although I gather that they were taking a lot of abuse from Francis for various things. Evidently he's one of those people who is never satisfied with anything, and I understand that he is not well-liked over there."

SANDY: "Francis said that you and your group were difficult to work with and that he had serious reservations about ever working with us in the future."

ED: "I don't know why he would say that. We did good work for them, and their people were delighted with the inventory system we installed."

SANDY: "I know that you and your group do good work. Your group is one of our best, and we've received good feedback from clients in the past. But Blue Valley is an important client to us. They have work for us to do, and there is a lot more competition now. In the future, whenever your group is having any difficulty with a client, I need to know about it."

ED: "Well, we really never had a problem with anyone except Francis, and he seems to be such a grouch that their people provide a buffer between him and outside contractors."

SANDY: "I understand your point about Francis, but I didn't know there were any problems at Blue Valley."

ED: "Well, I didn't think there *were* any problems. Our guys work well with everyone. They're the most congenial group around. The clients we work for are always asking us to do more jobs because they like us and the work we do."

SANDY: "Ed, I don't think you're hearing what I'm trying to tell you. I just found out this morning that it will be difficult to get more jobs with Blue Valley because Francis is unhappy with us, and I didn't know anything about it."

ED: "There are always some minor issues with any job. I always thought that as the project manager I would be trusted to deal with them. I dealt with them, and we got the job done. Furthermore, we got along really well with the people we worked with over there. It seems to me that we always do good work, our jobs are never late, and we're never over budget."

SANDY: "Ed, I appreciate the good work you and your group do. I just need to be informed any time there's a problem. That's all I'm asking for. Just keep me informed better on the next job."

ED: "Sandy, I've got to tell you. I'm really surprised by your reaction to whatever Francis told you. We really knocked ourselves out on that job. We made money for our company, and we worked around a real jerk to get the job done. And the feedback I seem to be getting is not 'thanks for doing a tough job.' Instead I'm being told that you don't trust my judgment in dealing with clients. Do you want us to call you all of the time with everything that comes up on the job?"

SANDY: "That's not what I'm saying, Ed. All I'm asking you to do is to tell me when there is a problem with the client."

ED: "Look, I feel really bad that Francis is saying that Blue Valley isn't going to give us any more business. But Francis is a jerk and everybody over there knows it. Our guys really took a lot of guff from him during that first week. He was really abusive to our people. Finally I told him, in a calm and quiet manner, that he had to quit abusing our people if he wanted us to get the job done. I was very professional in dealing with him, and he has no reason for dissatisfaction. It just surprises me that you don't seem to believe what I'm telling you."

SANDY: "One more time, Ed, and listen closely. Tell me when there are problems with any client in the future."

Questions

1. What is the likely outcome of this session between Sandy and Ed?
2. How could Sandy have done a better job of providing feedback to Ed?
3. What do you think of how Ed handled the feedback from Sandy?
4. How well is Ed managing his relationship with Sandy?

REFERENCES

[1] Brainy Quote (November 6, 2005): *www.brainyquote.com/quotes/quotes/g/georgestei227569.html.*

[2] Tam, Tui-Wing. "Rewiring Hewlett-Packard," *Wall Street Journal,* (July 20, 2005): B1–B4.

[3] Ibid.

[4] *Forbes.* "Labor Relations," citing *The Economist* (July 27, 1998): 32.

[5] Martin, James. *Cybercorp: The New Business Revolution.* New York: American Management Association, 1996.

[6] Berry, Leonard L. *Discovering the Soul of Service,* New York: The Free Press (1999).

[7] O. C. Tanner Website (November 27, 2005): *www.octanner.com.*

[8] Odell, Patricia. "Thank You Counts," *13th Annual Sourcebook 2006* (2005): 20–21.

[9] Levering, Robert, and Moskowitz, Milton. "The 100 Best Companies to Work for in America," *Fortune* (January 12, 1998): 84.

[10] Levering, Robert, and Moskowitz, Milton. "The 100 Best Companies to Work for in America," *Fortune* (January 8, 2001): 148–159.

[11] Ibid.

[12] Ramsey, Robert D. "20 Ways to Be a Better Communicator," *Supervisor* (January 2002): 10–12.

[13] Friley, Edmond. "Today's Training," *Supervisor,* (September 2005): 18–19.

[14] Chase, Nancy. "Coaching on the Run," *Quality* (September 1999): 80. Copyright ©. Reprinted with permission.

[15] "Catch the Coach at Least 8 Times a Year," *People Management* (November 9, 2000): 18.

[16] Martin, Donald E. *Team Think.* New York: Penguin Books USA, 1993.

[17] Shellenbarger, Sue. "Ovulating? Depressed? The Latest Rules on What Not to Talk About at Work," *Wall Street Journal,* (July 21, 2005): D1.

[18] Winokur, L. A. "Well, They Say There Are Lies, Damn Lies, Statistics and Bosses," *Wall Street Journal* (January 10, 1991): B1.

[19] Lublin, Joann S. "How You Can Survive the Dumbest Thing You Did to Your Boss," *Wall Street Journal,* (August 30, 2005): B1.

[20] Collins, Sandra D. *Managing Conflict and Workplace Relationships,* Mason, Ohio: Thomson-Southwestern, 2005.

[21] Robbins, Stephen P. *Managing Conflict: A Nontraditional Approach,* Prentice Hall, 1974. Filley, Alan C. *Interpersonal Conflict Resolution,* Glenview, IL: Scott Foresman, 1975. Collins. *Managing Conflict and Workplace Relationships.*

[22] Greenberg, Jerald, and Baron, Robert A. *Behavior in Organizations: Understanding and Managing the Human Side of Work,* 7th ed., Upper Saddle River, NJ: Prentice Hall, 2000.

[23] Frost, Peter J. *Toxic Emotions at Work: How Compassionate Managers Handle Pain and Conflict,* Boston: Harvard Business School Press, 2003.

[24] Ibid., p. 35.

[25] Collins. *Managing Conflict and Workplace Relationships.*

[26] Berstene, Thomas. "Conflict and Change: Conflict Can Be Managed to Create a Positive Force for Change," *Journal for Quality and Participation* (Summer 2004): 5–9.

[27] Ibid.

[28] Collins, *Managing Conflict and Workplace Relationships.*

[29] Godin, Seth. "Send in the Clowns," *Fast Company,* (May 2004): 105.

[30] Thomas, Kenneth W., and Kilmann, Ralph, H. *Thomas-Kilmann Conflict Mode Instrument,* Palo Alto, CA: Xicom.

[31] Much of this discussion is informed by a broad range of sources on conflict resolution. Some of these sources are the following: Robbins, Stephen P. *Managing Conflict: A Nontraditional Approach,* Prentice Hall, 1974. Filley, Alan C. *Interpersonal Conflict Resolution,* Glenview, IL: Scott Foresman, 1975. Lewicki, Roy J., Litterer, Joseph A., Saunders, David M., Minton, John W. *Negotiation: Readings, Exercises, and Cases,* 4th ed., Homewood, IL: Richard D. Irwin, 2003. Fischer, Roger, Ury, William, and Patton, Bruce.

Getting to Yes: Negotiating Agreement Without Giving In, New York: Houghton Mifflin, 1981.

[32] Kilmann, Ralph H. (December 3, 2005): Website: *www.kilmann.com/conflict.html.* Greenberg and Baron, *Behavior in Organizations.*

[33] Ibid.

[34] Ibid.

[35] Ibid.

[36] Ibid.

[37] Fischer, Ury, and Patton. *Getting to Yes: Negotiating Agreement Without Giving In.*

[38] Greenberg and Baron. *Behavior in Organizations.*

6

CHAPTER

"All I want is a warm bed, a kind word and unlimited power."

Ashleigh Brilliant

Objectives

After reading and discussing this chapter, you should be able to do the following:

1. List and give examples of the common needs that humans share.
2. List and give an example of each of Herzberg's maintenance factors.
3. List and give an example of each of Herzberg's motivational factors.
4. Describe the expectancy theory of motivation.
5. Describe the reinforcement theory of motivation.
6. Describe the equity theory of motivation.
7. Describe how goal setting can impact motivation.
8. Discuss how supervisors can improve quality and productivity.

Motivation at Burt Rutan's Scaled Composites

TEAMS

In July 2004, Burt Rutan's tiny firm, Scaled Composites, won the $10 million Ansari X-Prize by sending a man into space 62 miles above the earth's surface two times in a seven-day period. Rutan's firm, which has only 125 employees and is located in the Mojave Desert, had accomplished the unthinkable. With a very small budget, Rutan's firm had designed and developed the small rocket ship, SpaceShipOne, which was carried to a 46,000 foot altitude by a slightly larger jet-powered aircraft called the White Knight, which was also designed and developed by Rutan's firm. It may be speculated that NASA or one of the large aerospace companies would have required a vastly larger budget to accomplish the same feat. In contrast to the ups and downs of the aerospace industry, Rutan's firm has been profitable for 88 consecutive quarters and has created 26 different airplanes over the past three decades.[1] In addition to the remarkable success of winning the Ansari X-Prize, Rutan's firm has accomplished other extraordinary aerospace feats. In the 1986 his company's plane, the Voyager, did something never done before when its crew of two pilots flew the plane in a nonstop flight around the world without refueling.[2]

Motivation

Rutan's approach to management and the motivational impact of his approach is fascinating. He selects employees who have a passion for aircraft design and empowers them to get the job done. Rutan also prefers that his engineers work as generalists instead of specialists and tackle assignments that allow them to do a wide variety of work. Because of the breadth of their responsibilities and assignments, they go through an incredible learning experience. As a result of such empowerment and responsibility, his employees take on a sense of ownership in their work. The work environment is also unconstraining as Rutan prefers to minimize rules although safety is a primary value at the firm. In contrast to the work environment of many organizations, at Scaled Composites when an employee makes a mistake and calls others' attention to it, they receive applause rather than admonishment. Rutan also sets a great example by maintaining active involvement in projects and helping his teams as a designer. Clearly, his employees are motivated by their passion for what they are doing, instead of the monetary rewards, as pay and benefits are not emphasized and there is no retirement plan.[3]

Questions for Thought

1. What are some of the ways that supervisors can motivate employees without relying on financial rewards?
2. What are the potential motivating factors in a job that are likely to provide the greatest sustained effort and performance?

Introduction

People are the most complex, difficult-to-manage resource that any business has. We bring our hopes and ambitions to work, along with our problems and defects. Most of us want our jobs and careers to provide us with many things. Some of us view our jobs as a source of the money we need in order to live the kind of life we feel is important. Some of us want a challenge, work that we can take pride in, and a sense of progress and accomplishment.

Most employers recognize that their employees are complex creatures who expect more than a paycheck from their employment. Employers know that dissatisfied, unhappy workers are generally poor performers. They know that satisfied workers often produce above the standards set for their jobs. Knowledgeable employers recognize,

Worker recognition enhances self-esteem. Here, a supervisor at Xerox presents a service award based on length of service. The presentation is held in front of coworkers to enhance self-esteem.

therefore, that it is in their best interests to attempt to provide their employees with the kinds of satisfaction they seek on the job.

This chapter explores human needs and their relationship to our behavior. It introduces you to popular theories of human motivation and describes what you and employers can do to help others get more from their jobs than simply a paycheck. Finally, it links motivation with the all-important concepts of quality and productivity.

MOTIVATION DEFINED

motivation
the drive within a person to achieve a goal

TEAMS

Motivation is the drive within a person to achieve a goal. It is an internal process that takes place in all human beings, influenced by their perceptions and experiences as well as external variables. People are motivated by a variety of causes that can and do influence their behaviors. For example, Jamal's wife is expecting a baby. Consequently, he has become very eager to work all available overtime hours to earn more income. Maria is asking for additional duties from her supervisor and has returned to school to enhance her chances for a promotion. But as soon as both people achieve their objectives, their behaviors will usually cease to be motivated by these objectives.

As a supervisor, team leader, or team facilitator, your primary responsibility is to influence behaviors in order to increase the effectiveness and efficiency of your employees and operations. You must maintain an environment that supports your employees' motivated behavior. To achieve this, supervisors have to make sure that their diagnosis of performance problems is accurate before they attempt to increase the motivation of their employees. The following incident involving legendary football coach Bear Bryant illustrates such a misguided attempt:

> The University of Alabama was playing the University of Arkansas. Coach Bear Bryant was in a rage because the game was scoreless at halftime. In the locker room he went from player to player, telling them they were playing

like dogs. When he came to player Henry Clark, he grabbed him by the shoulder pads, lifted him up, shook him, put him back down, and said, "Henry, you ain't playing worth a damn." Clark looked up and said, "Hell Coach, I ain't even been in the game yet."[4]

As author and consultant Tom Peters puts it: "The average person, age 18 or 58, comes to the workplace fully endowed with motivation. Our primary role as 'leaders' is to clear the silly B.S. out of the way—and let the troops get on with the job."[5] Terry Neill, a management consultant, believes that "Genuine empowerment . . . is not the things you do to or for people: it's the impediments you take away, leaving room for folks to empower themselves."[6]

This chapter examines several basic, interrelated theories about motivation—why people do what they do. All will help you visualize and interpret the causes behind your own and your employees' behavior.

Learning Objective Number One

HUMAN NEEDS

When people work for subsistence-level wages, as most Americans did until the late 1940s, they concentrate on surviving. Their primary concern is for employment that will give them the money to furnish themselves and their families with the necessities of life. They live in fear of losing their jobs and, therefore, tolerate nearly any kind of working conditions and environment. People who observed the industrial economy of the United States in the early years of the twentieth century found little joy in its workers' hearts. While it is difficult to grasp the severity of the Great Depression, which left most Americans at a subsistence level, some indication is provided by the fact that the stock market's Dow Jones Industrial Average declined 90 percent between 1929 and 1932.[7] Unsurprisingly, many companies and their managers believed that people worked primarily for money, and they were partially correct in those beliefs.

THE HAWTHORNE STUDIES

Since the 1920s, businesses have studied their employees in efforts to find out more about them. Probably the most important study—one that launched intense interest about and research into employee behavior and motivation—was the Western Electric Company's study in the 1920s. In 1927, engineers at the Hawthorne Plant of the Western Electric Company near Chicago conducted an experiment with several groups of workers to determine the effect of illumination on production. When illumination was increased in stages, the engineers found that production increased. To verify their findings, they reduced illumination to its previous level. Surprisingly, even after illumination was reduced, production increased again! Perplexed, they called in Elton Mayo and his colleagues from Harvard to investigate.

THE FIRST STUDY

The Harvard researchers selected several experienced women assemblers for an experiment. Management removed the women from their formal group of assemblers and had them work in another area. The women were compensated on the basis of the output of their group and received no direct supervision as they had before, only indirect supervision from several researchers in charge of the experiment. Next followed a series of environmental changes, each discussed with the women in advance of its implementation. For example, breaks were introduced and light refreshments were served, the normal six-day week was reduced to five days, and the workday was cut by one hour. Each of these changes was accompanied by an increase in the group's output.[8]

To verify the assumptions that the researchers made, the women were returned to their original working conditions. Breaks were eliminated, the six-day week was restored, and all other conditions that had prevailed before the women were isolated were reinstated. The results were that production again increased!

In the extensive interviewing that followed, Mayo and his group concluded that a team spirit had been created, quite by accident, when management singled out these women to be the study group and then consulted with them before making each change. The women felt that they were something very special, both individually and collectively. Their isolation as a group and their proximity at work provided an environment for the development of close personal relationships. The formal group had been transformed into an informal one—a clique.

TEAMS

The supervising teams feature for this chapter provides several examples of motivation as applied to team settings.

THE SECOND STUDY

To test the researchers' findings, a new group of workers was selected and isolated. This time the researchers chose a group of men. Several of them were involved in wiring equipment, whereas others soldered the wired connections. Several important events happened in this formal group. The men eventually split into two separate informal cliques because one group felt its work was more difficult than the other's and its members adopted a superior attitude. This left the remainder of the workers to form another clique. Both cliques included wirers, solderers, and an inspector, and each group also engaged in setting standards of output and conduct. The members of the group that considered itself superior mutually agreed on production quotas. As intergroup rivalry developed, the output of the other group began to decline. The superior group became superior in output also, which caused additional condescending behavior and a still greater decrease in morale and output in the other group. Even though each man was to share in a bonus based on the formal group's total output, informal group conflict resulted in a decline in production.

These two experiments revealed that people work for a variety of reasons—not just for money and subsistence. They seek satisfaction for more than their physical needs at work as they also seek to satisfy their social and esteem needs.

A HIERARCHY OF NEEDS

The Hawthorne studies and many more that followed have given us a much wider view of why people work and what they expect from work. Well-known psychologist

SUPERVISING TEAMS

Methods for motivating teams are provided in the following examples from three leading companies: Motorola, General Electric, and Medrad.

Motorola

One of the most impressive examples of empowered teams that we have seen was in our visit to a Motorola microchip-making plant in the Philippines. With team names such as the Last Maverick, Path Finder, Revival X, and Be Cool, the Filipino teams have been consistent finalists (appropriately referred to as the "Magic 10") in Motorola's worldwide team recognition program, the Total Customer Satisfaction (TCS) showcase. Winning teams are flown, all expenses paid, to locations such as Disney World in Florida to display and discuss examples of how they achieve breakthrough results. Team accomplishments are regularly reported in an in-house quarterly magazine. As a result of this "publicity," teams at other Motorola facilities around the world can learn about and incorporate these valuable team ideas.

General Electric

General electric offers a good example. Its corporate process requires that the supply chain teams in every GE company are held accountable for achieving strict cost-takeout targets, with their results widely reported at a corporate level. Other leading companies also post team goals and progress on an intranet so they are visible across the organization.

Medrad, Inc. (Schering AG)

Performance excellence driven by a team culture is the blueprint for success and a Malcom Baldrige quality award . . . "He's [the CEO] built a culture where everyone at the company has a voice in the way things are done.". . . Teamwork and sharing of communication are detailed as paramount . . . This loyalty was earned by Medrad executives who retained and retrained workers when the company automated its sterile disposables operation . . . 87% of employees responded affirmatively when asked if they understood their relationship between what they do and Medrad's goals and objectives . . . Medrad executives pointed to frequent formal and informal communication, interaction with key stakeholders and participation in training, and employee recognition as key reasons for its success . . . Target efficiencies for each production line are assigned visual indicators, for example a frown or a smiley face, and posted so that the workers know if they are meeting goals.

Sources: Motorola section excerpted from Bradley L. Kirkman and Benson Rosen. "Powering Up Teams," *Organizational Dynamics* (Winter 2000): 54–55. General Electric section excerpted from Robert J. Trent. "Making Sure the Team Works," *Supply Chain Management Review* (April 2005): 35. Medrad section excerpted from Larry Adams. "Medrad Works and Wins as a Team," *Quality* (October 2004): 42–46.

Abraham H. Maslow identified five universal human needs that act as fuel for our internal drives to change or achieve. Exhibit 6.1 shows this hierarchy of needs as levels or steps in an upward progression from the most basic to the highest psychological need.[9]

EXHIBIT 6.1	**Maslow's hierarchy of human needs.**

SELF-REALIZATION NEEDS	JOB-RELATED SATISFIERS
Reaching Your Potential	Involvement in Planning Your Work
Independence	Freedom to Make Decisions Affecting Work
Creativity	Creative Work to Perform
Self-Expression	Opportunities for Growth and Development

ESTEEM NEEDS	JOB-RELATED SATISFIERS
Responsibility	Status Symbols
Self-Respect	Money (as a measure, for some, of self-esteem)
Recognition	Merit Awards
Sense of Accomplishment	Challenging Work
Sense of Competence	Sharing in Decisions
Sense of Equity	Opportunity for Advancement

SOCIAL NEEDS	JOB-RELATED SATISFIERS
Companionship	Opportunities for Interaction with Others
Acceptance	Team Spirit
Love and Affection	Friendly Coworkers
Group Membership	Team Inclusion

SAFETY NEEDS	JOB-RELATED SATISFIERS
Security for Self and Possessions	Safe Working Conditions
Avoidance of Risks	Seniority
Avoidance of Harm	Fringe Benefits
Avoidance of Pain	Proper Supervision
	Sound Company Policies, Programs, and Practices

PHYSICAL NEEDS	JOB-RELATED SATISFIERS
Food	Pleasant Working Conditions
Clothing	Adequate Wage or Salary
Shelter	Rest Periods
Comfort	Labor-Saving Devices
Self-Preservation	Efficient Work Methods

THE NEEDS-GOAL MODEL OF MOTIVATION

Human needs provide the basis for our first theory of motivation. Our definition of motivation—the drive within a person to achieve a goal—tells us that motivation is an internal process. It is something we do within ourselves, not something we do to others. The term *drive* in our definition denotes a force that is fueled by human needs common to all of us. These needs, both physical and psychological, provide motives for our actions and behavior. To achieve our goals, we must take actions. Our actions toward achievement are efforts, both mental and physical, that we feel are necessary to attain our goals.

Our goals may be tangible or intangible. We may want a new car or a job with higher status. The specific forms our goals take are a result of our personal makeup and desires at given moments in time. They are shaped in part by our experiences, individual perceptions, and current environments.

According to the needs-goal theory of motivation, a person who is motivated is in a state of unrest because she feels or believes that something is lacking—the goal. It is the unfulfilled need that creates the state of unrest. And since our needs can never fully be satisfied, we are continually setting goals. It is in our nature to want more—to continually strive to progress, to improve our conditions, and to acquire something new. As a result, we engage in courses of action to achieve these goals, which result in satisfaction. Failure to achieve these goals results in frustration.

Supervisors who wish to understand the drive to work may wish to consider the following assertions about human needs and motivation:

human needs
physiological and psychological requirements that all humans share and that act as motives for behavior

- An unsatisfied need is a strong motivator.
- People can be influenced by more than one unsatisfied need at any given time.
- Needs can never be fully satisfied. They may cease to motivate behavior for a time, but they can and will return to act once again as motivators.
- People who seek satisfaction in one need area and do not find it will experience frustration and may try to compensate by overemphasizing another need.
- The perception of what we need at any given time is shaped in part by our experiences, by external influences on us, and by our capabilities to change our situations.

TYPES OF HUMAN NEEDS

Physiological Needs

Physiological or bodily needs are at the base of the need hierarchy. Unsatisfied physiological needs can influence behavior, whereas satisfied physiological needs are not motivators. For example, when we are hungry, we desire food of a type and in a quantity necessary to satisfy our hunger. Once we have eaten our fill, our hunger dissipates and no longer motivates our actions. New needs surface and take over as motives for our actions. But as we all know, hunger will return.

Safety Needs

The second level of human needs—safety needs or physical security—is our next concern. Having satisfied our physiological needs for the moment, we are concerned about providing for their satisfaction in the future. Once we have achieved an economic position that provides the means necessary to secure our physical maintenance, we want to protect this condition. A person who gets a job is anxious to keep it. He is concerned with preventing its loss and the accompanying loss of the ability to provide for physical needs. The person may, as a result, join a union to gain this kind of security. Like his physical needs, the person's need for security will weaken as a motive for actions once the individual reaches an adequate degree of satisfaction. But if his job is threatened, the need for security may once again become an active motivating force.

Social Needs

With the satisfaction of safety or security needs, the desire to satisfy social needs may become preeminent. These needs include a desire for human companionship, for affiliation with people and groups, for love and affection, and for a sense of belonging. Once we have achieved an adequate measure of satisfaction, our social needs begin to wane, and the fourth level of need stimulates our behavior.

Esteem Needs

The need for esteem is two-sided. First, we wish to be appreciated for what we are and for what we have to contribute—to be respected by others. Second, we need to have a feeling of self-esteem—to know we are worth something to ourselves and to others. We need a positive self-image. From this need comes the desire for praise and for symbols that reflect our self-approval and others' appreciation of our efforts. We seek prestige and status positions among our peers. We behave in ways that are pleasing and acceptable to others whose opinions we value. We wish to master the tasks given us, thus becoming competent performers. We want fair and equitable treatment from others.

Self-Realization Needs

Finally, our need for self-realization (sometimes called self-actualization) takes over when we achieve some measure of satisfaction in the previous four levels. We begin to experience a need to fulfill our potential and to be creative. To some, this means striving for higher levels in company management and obtaining the added authority and prestige that such positions provide. To others, it means being the best machinist, computer programmer, violinist, or supervisor that they have the potential to become. The need for self-realization causes people to pursue interests and knowledge for their own sake and for the joy of the pursuit.

All these needs are common in all of us to some degree. At any given moment, one or more of them are active, while the others lie dormant. When we feel satisfied in one or more areas, those areas will cease for a time to motivate our behavior. However, enough satisfaction for some may be too little or too much for others. In general, no need is ever completely satisfied, and none can ever cease completely to be a motivator. It is the unfulfilled need that is the strongest motive for human behavior.

MCCLELLAND'S ACQUIRED NEEDS THEORY

In addition to the needs described above, D. C. McClelland has identified three important needs that commonly serve to motivate employees: *achievement, power,* and *affiliation.* McClelland says that employees acquire such needs from their experiences in life. Because the strength of these needs varies across employees, supervisors must determine the dominant needs for each employee in order to understand how to motivate her. Interestingly, he found that achievement is a dominant need for only 10 percent of the U.S. population.[10] Although such individuals constitute only a small proportion of the workforce, they are important for company performance. Supervisors need to know how to channel their need for achievement through valuable work activity.

McClelland's work also provides good insights into the motivations of managers, particularly in the area of needs for power. McClelland found that most good managers have a strong need for power that is oriented toward the institutions they serve, where they want to have influence and make an impact. Interestingly, managers with high needs for power and who have high inhibitions (high self-control) often use their power in an altruistic manner on behalf of others. McClelland developed the term **institutional managers** for those managers who have high needs for this type of power, are high on inhibition measures, and have low needs for affiliation. He found that institutional managers feel responsible for their organizations, like to work, tend to sacrifice some of their own interests for the good of the organization, and have high regard for justice in the sense that they want employees to be rewarded for their hard work and sacrifices.[11]

Institutional managers provide a dramatic contrast to managers McClelland calls **personal power managers.** These managers have stronger needs for power than affiliation but, in contrast to the institutional managers, they have low inhibition (low self-control), and their power is often directed toward self-gratification. Personal power managers exhibit a number of unfortunate behaviors, such as being rude to others, engaging in sexual exploitation, and surrounding themselves with symbols of their power, such as big offices and fancy cars. McClelland also identified a third type of manager as **affiliative managers,** whose affiliation needs are greater than their power needs. Unfortunately, affiliative managers, who have a strong desire to be liked, are the least effective of the three types of managers. These managers often disregard organizational procedures, and their employees do not feel personal responsibility and do not take pride in their work groups. They also do not know how their managers feel about them.[12]

Strong needs for achievement are not necessarily consistent with good management. McClelland and Burnham describe the relationship as follows:

> While it sounds as if everyone ought to have the need to achieve, in fact, as psychologists define and measure achievement motivation, the need to achieve leads people to behave in ways that do not necessarily engender good management. For one thing, because they focus on personal improvement and doing things better by themselves, achievement-motivated people want to do things themselves. For another, they want concrete short-term feedback on their performance so that they can tell how

institutional manager
a manager who has a high need for power, high inhibitions, and low need for affiliation

personal power manager
a manager with strong power and affiliation needs and low inhibition

affiliative manager
a manager with affiliation needs greater than power needs

well they are doing. Yet managers, particularly in large, complex organizations, cannot perform by themselves all the tasks necessary for success. They must manage others to perform for the organization. And they must be willing to do without immediate and personal feedback since tasks are spread among many people.[13]

In a later section we explore how managers can apply their knowledge of needs in order to obtain motivated work behavior.

ALDERFER'S EGR THEORY

EGR theory
motivation theory based on existence, growth, and relatedness needs

Alderfer's **EGR theory** explains that motivation in the work environment may be explained by three types of needs: existence, growth, and relatedness. Existence needs in EGR theory encompass both physiological and safety needs, which Maslow's theory treats as separate needs. Examples of existence need satisfiers include job security and safe working conditions. Similarly, growth needs in EGR theory is a broader need, which comprises both esteem and self-actualization needs in Maslow's theory. Examples of growth need satisfiers include having a challenging job, responsibility and autonomy in how the job is performed. Finally, relatedness needs in EGR theory are similar to social needs in Maslow's theory. Examples of relatedness need satisfiers include teamwork and social recognition. EGR theory maintains that while there are basic needs, there is no rigid order in which the three needs may become the dominant motivator of behavior.[14] EGR theory also differs from Maslow's theory in that it explains that more than one need may be activated or operational at the same time. It also differs from Maslow's theory in that it explains that when a person's pursuit of satisfaction for a specific need is blocked, the person may revert to actions directed at satisfying a more basic need.[15]

Recent empirical research has found support for ERG theory and provides guidance for supervisors and managers. This research has found that the performance of frontline employees is affected by their needs for relatedness. More specifically, when such employees feel acceptance, belongingness, and respect from their peers, they are more likely to perform at a higher level. The research also indicates that supervisors and managers should have a good understanding of their employees' personalities, particularly self-esteem, in order to determine how various satisfactions of needs can affect productivity. Interestingly, for front-line employees pay does not improve performance through a linkage with improved self-image. Instead, the linkage is more direct in that front-line employees need to feel that their pay is fair and that productivity gains from their efforts are shared with them. Empirical research also shows that for executives, satisfaction of their growth needs, such as through challenging work, opportunities for innovation, or autonomy are critical for retention.[16]

Companies such as Southwest Airlines understand that employees' relatedness needs can be satisfied by social activities that create fun and enjoyment. Exhibit 6.2 presents ways in which supervisors can create opportunities for employees to have fun at work.

Creating opportunities for fun.	**EXHIBIT 6.2**

- Establish a "Fun Committee" that has responsibilities for creating fun events.

- Set up a bulletin board for humor and jokes.

- Create an understanding that professionalism does not require constant seriousness.

- Establish the limits on what is fair game and what is potentially harmful.

- Find ways for customers to participate.

- Begin the process of creating more fun with a few activities and build over time.

- Find ways to develop games that are linked with production or service.

- Kick off meetings with a fun activity or a joke.

- Establish theme days when people wear costumes to work.

- Set up social events for evening trips to sporting events or the theater.

- Hire an actor portraying a humorous character who mingles with employees.

Source: Jody Urquhart. "Creating a Fun Workplace," *Healthcare Registration* (August 2005): 3–5. Andy Moore. "He's Having a Laugh," *Personnel Today* (September 28, 2004): 29. "Smile Guru Is Far from Conventional," *Employee Benefits* (September 2002): 14.

SUPERVISORS AND HUMAN NEEDS

What does all this mean to you as a supervisor? A major goal for every organization is to help individual associates reach their goals while they help the organization reach its goals. You know that our common needs provide the motives for human behavior and that each person's personal goals may be quite different from those of her peers. As a supervisor, you are in a unique position to assist your employees and to provide them with some of the satisfactions they are seeking. You can be most helpful with regard to their safety, social, and esteem needs, as we shall now see.

When your employees joined your department, chances are that you assessed their strengths and weaknesses and got to know as much about them and their abilities as possible. Then, you determined their specific needs for training so that they might improve their performance and skills. The end result is that you provided them with the knowledge, skills, and attitudes they needed to keep their jobs. You increased their sense of security and helped them remove some of their initial fears. You taught and enforced safety on the job. Your actions helped them achieve a measure of satisfaction for both their physical and safety needs.

TEAMS

You also helped your employees with their need for affiliation when you introduced them to their new jobs and work groups. Your effort to know them has made you aware of their individual needs for affiliation and has enabled you to identify those employees who are satisfied and those who are frustrated with regard to social needs. You did all you could to help the isolated individuals gain acceptance by fostering a team spirit and by making them all feel part of a larger group. The process of turning individuals into team players is difficult and time consuming. People need to learn a variety of skills to make the transformation, and teams are not for everyone or for every task. But where they do apply and when they function properly, they provide satisfaction for team members' need for affiliation as nothing else at work can.

In regard to your employees' esteem needs, you have several key roles to play. When you do performance appraisals, you provide the raw material they need for self-insight and improvement. You pass out praise if they deserve it and note the specific areas they must work on to gain your continued praise and acceptance. You also have authority that, if delegated, can enrich their feelings of importance and give them a way to learn certain aspects of your job. They know that this is an important sign of your faith and confidence in their abilities. When one of your people makes a good suggestion, you use it and give the credit to the source of the suggestion. If the idea is not suited to the operation, you tell the employee the reason, improving his understanding of the operation.

Various incentive systems can encourage employees to submit suggestions. Haworth, Inc., an office furniture manufacturer, has reinvigorated suggestion systems by eliminating a common flaw in such systems—dismissal of the suggestion by the employee's supervisor. At Haworth, supervisors may make comments but are not allowed to dismiss suggestions because employees submit their suggestions for evaluation by a committee.[17] Keys to successful suggestion systems are quick acknowledgment of the suggestion and a timely response indicating whether the suggestion will be adopted or the reason why it will not be adopted. At American Axle and Manufacturing, Inc., 50 percent of employees now submit suggestions, and in a recent six-month period the company saved $37,000 and paid employees $73,000 for their suggestions.[18]

General Motors (GM) is also using employee suggestions in attempts to make its plants more productive. Aside from employee self-esteem needs served by the suggestion system, significant financial awards are available for teams of workers that make valuable suggestions. The suggestion system has generated a great deal of interest among employees: In a recent quarter the company received 44,000 suggestions. The savings produced by the suggestion system have been substantial. For example, employee suggestions in GM's Metal Fabricating Division enabled the company to save $10 million in a recent year. While the company is making improvements with such innovations and other managerial initiatives, it faces severe competition from international automobile manufacturers. Although GM has attempted to be more competitive and has cut costs by closing plants and reducing the size of its workforce, many of its competitiveness issues are a result of high health care costs.[19]

As pointed out earlier, a small but important percentage of the U.S. population is motivated by the need for achievement. Achievement needs for such individuals can often be fulfilled by placing them in sales work or in positions in which they can act as entrepreneurs. Interestingly, while the need for achievement is high for managers, it tends not to be dominant for them.[20]

Supervisors can also provide greater responsibility to employees who are motivated by their need for power. For example, supervisors can allow such individuals to plan and exercise greater self-control over their work.[21] An example of expanding control would be to allow the workers to do the final inspection of their own work. A newspaper advertisement for machinists in the Miami facility of Rolls-Royce included such an inducement by stating that "Selected applicants will work in an innovative environment and be responsible for inspection and superior quality of all products they help manufacture."

You may become frustrated when you attempt to discover which need is a conscious concern to each individual employee at any given time. This is difficult knowledge to gain because when you observe your people, you do so in a fragmented way. You see them at work under the influence of many forces from within and outside the company. Even if you know each of your people well, you can be fooled by your observations. In observing the actions of others, we seldom see the motives for them. You, like your associates, tend to play roles at work that mask your true feelings and motives. Yet every supervisor, team leader, and team facilitator must attempt to determine what needs are most important to herself and her employees.

MAINTENANCE AND MOTIVATION

We can understand motivation better by examining the contributions of Frederick Herzberg, whose work on motivation in business demonstrated some applications of Maslow's hierarchy of human needs. Herzberg and his associates found that two sets of factors must be provided in the working environment to promote motivation.

Learning Objective Number Two

MAINTENANCE OR HYGIENE FACTORS

First, Herzberg argued that there is a set of factors he labeled **maintenance factors** or hygiene factors. These conditions or factors are *extrinsic*—not connected to the work we do—and will not cause employee motivation in the great majority of people. But a lack of them can cause dissatisfaction, thus preventing or inhibiting motivation. Herzberg argued that these environmental conditions, when provided in the right mix, can only prevent dissatisfaction and remove barriers to motivated behavior. The best a business can hope for by providing these factors is that the average employee will put forth an average commitment in time and effort at his job. Maintenance factors Herzberg identified are:[22]

maintenance factor
a factor that can be provided in order to prevent job dissatisfaction

1. economic—wages, salaries, fringe benefits, and the like.
2. security—grievance procedures, seniority privileges, fair work rules, company policy, and discipline.
3. social—opportunities to mix with one's peers at work and at company-sponsored events such as parties, outings, and the like.
4. working conditions—adequate heat, light, ventilation, and hours of work.
5. status—privileges, job titles, and other symbols of rank or position.

Herzberg viewed money as a maintenance factor because, for the majority of people he studied, it is extrinsic to one's job and of little help in satisfying our higher-level psychological needs—esteem and self-realization. When people are working in jobs they hate, or under conditions that hurt psychologically or physically, money cannot make them work with a personal commitment to excel. (We include economic incentives such as bonuses and suggestion awards in the category of money.) Money or the promise of it can motivate us in the short term, but once obtained, it ceases to motivate. When people feel that they have enough money it becomes less important to acquire more. (For each of us this is an individual perception.)

The quest for money often masks a search for what money cannot buy. "If your workers are complaining about their pay, it's usually a sign that something else is missing. . . . People will work for less (not less than a fair wage . . .) if they enjoy their work and feel as if they're being treated fairly."[23] For most people, money cannot offer intrinsic satisfactions—those directly connected to work and the performance of it. Consider, for example, *Fortune's* 2005 listing of the 100 best large companies to work for in the United States. Beginning with the top 10, these companies are Wegmans Food Markets, Starbucks, Valero Energy, Cisco Systems, Whole Foods Market, Baptist Health South Florida, Amgen, Goldman Sachs, American Express, and Synovus.[24] While some of these companies place more emphasis on compensation than others, the role of money in the overall scheme of things at Whole Foods Market is not unusual for top performing organizations:

> It's all about equality at this natural-foods grocery chain: A wage disclosure report lists everyone's gross pay (execs included) and a salary cap limits compensation to 14 times the average total of all the company's full timers.[25]

An analysis of an earlier listing of *Fortune's* top 100 companies revealed the following insights about the role of money in such companies:

> But here's the part that may surprise you: Nobody mentioned money. That is not because the 100 best companies necessarily pay better than their peers. Rather, it's that—pay being equal—most humans seem to need a better reason to get up in the morning. You no doubt dimly recall this concept from Psychology 101: Once people reach a certain level of material comfort, they care more about self-actualization...being interested in what they actually do all day.[26]

According to psychologist C. J. Cranny, "the most important factor in creating an atmosphere that workers find satisfying is whether employees find their work 'intrinsically interesting.'"[27] This can only happen through what Herzberg called *motivation factors.*

Lapses in maintenance factors, such as failure to attend to ethical standards, can undermine motivation. This chapter's feature on ethics describes price fixing, which is an illegal act for which supervisors must be alert.

Motivation Factors

Motivation factors, the second set of factors, are *intrinsic*—directly related to the work we do. For the great majority of us they provide the incentive to make a better-than-average commitment to our efforts. Motivation factors provide the means by which individuals can achieve greater job satisfaction. When provided in the proper quantity and quality, they have the potential to satisfy employees' needs and cause an increased commitment of time and energy. Herzberg identified seven motivation factors:[28]

Learning
Objective
Number Three

SUPERVISORS AND ETHICS

Patrons of Sotheby's Holdings and Christie's International, auction houses for very expensive artwork, were shocked by revelations of a price-fixing scandal. Federal prosecutors charged that high-level executives of the two firms colluded on the commissions they charge for sales. The former chief executive for Sotheby's pled guilty and testified at the trial that she was directed by her boss, the chairman and controlling shareholder of the firm, to engage in price-fixing with Christie's. Prosecutors also charged that Christie's previous chairman gave the same instructions to his employees. A lack of personal accountability was evident as executives testified that they engaged in illegal behavior because their bosses told them to do so. As with many failures in ethics, the price for their mistakes was high, as Sotheby's former chief faced a three-year sentence.

Not surprisingly, this incident of flawed behavior has become the subject of a Home Box Office film with actress Sigourney Weaver playing the role of the former Sotheby's chief executive. While the film was expected to generate viewer interest because it provides a view of the flaws and lifestyles of some of the world's most wealthy and influential people, the moral lesson is the same for supervisors and production workers. The consequences of lapses in business ethics can be professionally and personally devastating to individuals and the organizations that employ them.

Source: **Kathryn Kranhold. "Auction Scandal Will Come Back as A TV Movie,"** *Wall Street Journal* **(November 21, 2001), B11.**

1. *Challenging work.* The average person wants to view his job as offering an avenue for self-expression and growth. Each person needs something to tax his abilities.
2. *Feelings of personal accomplishment.* The average employee gets a sense of achievement and a feeling of contributing something of value when presented with a challenge that she can meet.
3. *Recognition for achievement.* The average employee wants to feel that his contributions have been worth the effort and that the effort has been noted and appreciated. Money awards, for some, help here.
4. *Achievement of increasing responsibility.* The typical employee wants to acquire new duties and responsibilities, either through expansion of her job or by delegation from the supervisor.
5. *A sense of individual importance to the organization.* Employees want to feel that their personal presence is needed and that their individual contributions are necessary. Higher-than-average compensation can help here for some people.
6. *Access to information.* Employees want to know about the things that affect them and their jobs; they want to be kept in the know.
7. *Involvement in decision-making.* Today's employees desire a voice in the matters that affect them and a chance to decide some things for themselves. They need freedom to exercise initiative and creativity.

motivation factor
a factor that has the potential to stimulate internal motivation to provide better-than-average performance and commitment from those to whom it appeals

Exhibit 6.3 provides several examples of specific ways in which jobs can be made more challenging and interesting.

EXHIBIT 6.3	Examples of challenging and interesting work that can increase motivation.

- Creating a task force on a pressing business problem
- Handling a negotiation with a customer
- Creating a new system
- Integrating systems across units
- Supervising product, program, equipment, or systems purchases
- Supervising the liquidation of a product, program, equipment, or system
- Presenting a proposal to top management
- Going off site to deal with a dissatisfied customer
- Supervising the furnishing of offices
- Serving at a trade show booth
- Working short periods in other units
- Managing a renovation project
- Launching a new product or program
- Managing the visit of a VIP

Source: Extracted from Bob Nelson. *1001 Ways to Energize Employees.* New York: Workman Publishing (1997): 68, 69, 70.

Several of these seven factors, such as those involving increased responsibility and greater involvement in decision-making, can be designed into the structure and operations of a business. When companies make the commitment to empower employees, they give individuals and teams the authority to make their own decisions, solve their own problems, and achieve greater control over their work. In short, associates and colleagues achieve greater autonomy—a key motivating factor in Herzberg's research. Since Herzberg's work, many organizations have empowered their employees in order to produce greater operational efficiencies and to capture the motivational impact of empowerment. There are typically three major components of such empowerment initiatives, which include increased autonomy, greater information sharing, and the replacement of some organizational hierarchy with teams. However, with such empowerment, employees must understand that there will be greater accountability on their part and that they will be held responsible for results.[29]

An understanding of empowerment may be obtained by reviewing practices at companies that have empowered their employees. At a clothing retailing company, employees at all levels of the organization have access to a comprehensive new information system. Employees can access real-time information on sales, returns, client histories, or any other information that will help them do their jobs better. They can

SUPERVISORS AND PERFORMANCE

One of the results of the move to a global economy, offshoring, and outsourcing is that logistics has become an increasingly important business. Supply chain management, which encompasses logistics, is now a key determinant of whether a company will be profitable or not. In addition, just-in-time manufacturing, which minimizes inventory levels, requires sophisticated logistics systems that can provide timely deliveries. These developments provide the context for the challenges faced by supervisors and managers who work in warehousing and logistics. Warehousing facilities have become huge, and the operations have been pushed to breakneck speeds. The number of different products that are housed in such facilities requires sophisticated tracking systems and a knowledgeable workforce. Large, specialized third-party logistics operations, such as ODW Logistics, Inc., and Penske Logistics, have taken on the logistics activities that have been outsourced by manufacturers and retailers.

The companies that have outsourced these activities are now the customers of logistics firms such as ODW and are placing increasingly high demands for quick service. The task of these firms has been described by the *Wall Street Journal* as a "daily high-wire act." Lead-time is disappearing as orders for next-day delivery have migrated from noon to 4:00 P.M. in some cases. Given the pressures for speed, it is no surprise that the people who work in such facilities face intense pressure. Unsurprisingly, logistics firms have experienced high employee turnover, and there are shortages of truck drivers. Other indicators of workforce problems include theft of merchandise by employees. Furthermore, during peak-periods logistics facilities must sometimes operate on a 24-hour basis. Another challenge for logistics supervisors is that as much as 90 percent of the work, such as that performed by drivers, is performed out of their sight.

Given the pressures for speed in such environments, the ability to provide appropriate motivation is critical. The pace of change and the level of innovation that is required for such change indicate that supervisors may obtain desired performance and innovation by empowering employees, giving them autonomy, and allowing them to take risks (other than those related to safety). In addition, it is important to develop appropriate measures of desired performance and reward such behaviors appropriately. Furthermore, as discussed elsewhere in this chapter, goal setting provides a very robust motivational approach that has the potential to increase performance in a wide variety of settings, such as in logistics operations.

Sources: Kris Maher. "Global Goods Jugglers," *Wall Street Journal*, (July 5, 2005): A11–12. Matthew B. Myers, David A. Griffith, Patricia J. Dougherty, and Robert F. Lusch. "Maximizing the Human Capital Equation in Logistics: Education, Experience, and Skills," *Journal of Business Logistics* 24, 1, (2004): 211–232. Donald J. Bowersox, David J. Closs, and Theodore P. Stank. "Ten Mega-Trends That Will Revolutionize Supply Chain Logistics," *Journal of Business Logistics* 21, 2 (2000): 1–16. Claudine Soosay and Paul W. Hyland. "Driving Innovation in Logistics," *Creativity and Innovation Management* (March 2004): 41–51.

also enter comments into the system in order to share lessons learned with other employees. With such information available to all employees, they are more empowered to provide better service. Employees at Disney World are also empowered to take action, consistent with the company's values of courtesy and safety, that will make the guests' experience a memorable one.[30] The Container Store provides another example

EXHIBIT 6.4	What employees desire from their supervisors and managers.

- Greater sharing of information so employees do not have to rely on the grapevine

- Greater availability from supervisors and managers for meaningful, informal discussions

- More praise instead of a more frequent focus on criticism and correction

- More freedom to disagree in an informal discussion rather than a dictatorial edict

- More consistency between a manager's words and his or her real attitude

- Better feedback about employees' performance

- Better responses to employee complaints

- Greater opportunities for advancement

Sources: Kerry Liberman. "What Employees Want," *Credit Union Management* (January 2004): 44–46. Al Tuttle. "What Employees Want," *Industrial Distribution* (May 2003): 63–66. Ted Pollock. "What Employees Want," *Automotive Design and Production* (March 2002): 10–12.

PERFORMANCE

of employee empowerment as clerks have wide latitude to correct problems for customers. In most retail companies only managers have such latitude.[31]

Some employees do not desire all or even a few of these factors and the opportunities they represent. This may be true because, for the moment at least, they lack ambition and do not feel the need to change. Still others, because of mental or emotional limitations, may lack the potential to take advantage of these factors and to master higher job responsibilities. For those who, in the manager's opinion, can take advantage of these factors but do not do so, some standards and goals must be set to prod them to keep growing. The manager should make it clear to these employees that more is expected of them and that they can receive more rewards in return for increased effort. In short, the supervisor, team leader, or team facilitator must try to get such employees oriented toward making progress.

Exhibit 6.4 presents several responses, reported in trade journals, to questions about what employees desire from their managers and employers. While these survey findings are informal, industry-specific, and do not provide general results, they provide an indication of issues that are frequently of concern to employees. As the exhibit reveals, several responses indicate potential issues with maintenance factors while some deal with motivating factors.

We point out that Herzberg's theory has limitations in that a substantial number of people may not be motivated by the factors he identified as motivators. Still, his work provides the basis for the concept of job enrichment, which is discussed later in this chapter.[32] Thus, for employees who have the potential and the drive to achieve something greater, supervisors have a duty to provide a work environment that provides motivation factors. If they are made available, like different kinds of fine foods on a buffet, the "hungry" people in any group will select among them according to their needs. Furthermore, Herzberg's theory builds on some of Maslow's theory in that hygiene or maintenance factors generally help us satisfy our physical, safety, and social needs, while motivation factors generally help us satisfy our esteem and self-realization needs.

Unfortunately, Maslow's and Herzberg's work has caused some misunderstanding about the role of money in motivation. When used inappropriately, such as when employees feel that they are being bribed or manipulated, money can undermine motivators or intrinsic aspects of work.[33] Nonetheless, research by Jason Shaw and Nina Gupta shows that properly designed compensation systems are not incompatible with intrinsic factors that underlie job enrichment.

> Our meta-analysis explored whether the relationship between financial incentives and performance was stronger for *extrinsic* (i.e., dull and boring) tasks than for *intrinsic* (i.e., challenging and interesting) tasks. Presumably, if financial incentives erode intrinsic motivation, we would find them to be negatively related to performance for intrinsic tasks. The data show otherwise. It doesn't matter what kind of work people are doing—incentives improve performance. . . . Taken together, then, the hard data are unambiguous—financial incentives improve performance quantity; they *do not* erode intrinsic motivation.[34]

ADDITIONAL THEORIES OF MOTIVATION

EXPECTANCY THEORY

The development of expectancy theory is credited to Victor Vroom, a renowned management scholar at Yale University. Expectancy theory goes beyond the identification of needs and describes the process by which workers make decisions about motivated behavior. Accordingly, many management scholars call expectancy theory a *process theory.* Expectancy theory explains that workers are concerned about three important questions:[35]

Learning Objective Number Four

1. How much effort, diligence, care, and so on, should I devote to my work?
2. If I perform well as a result of my effort, diligence, care, and so on, will I obtain desired outcomes to satisfy my needs?
3. Does my employer provide work outcomes that satisfy my needs?

The first question is important to supervisors because it means that their employees should expect to be high performers if they exert high effort. If, on the other hand, their employees do not have the necessary skills for the job or, for example, the supervisor fails to provide the proper materials to perform the job, they will not expect to be high performers regardless of their efforts. One's belief that efforts will result in productivity is called **expectancy.**[36] Therefore, supervisors must provide training and coaching so that their employees will have a strong expectancy of high performance given high effort.

expectancy
belief that effort will result in performance

According to expectancy theory, when training an employee in a task, you must communicate exactly what, how, when, and where you want it done. Reaffirm that the worker understands what to do before delegating the task.

The second question also is important because it deals with reward systems and associates' perceptions of reward systems. In other words, if associates perceive that high performance is not rewarded with desired outcomes, such as promotions, they will not perceive performance as *instrumental*. The perceived linkage between performance and desired outcomes is called **instrumentality.**[37] Supervisors need to examine the rationality of the reward system when their associates have low perceptions of the instrumentality of performance. For example, the supervisor would need to determine whether promotions are based on performance or on the basis of political factors such as friendship with the boss. Even if promotions are actually based on performance, if associates *perceive* that they are based on politics there will still be low instrumentality and low motivation to perform. In such situations, the supervisor will need to communicate the real reasons for promotions and do a better job of explaining promotion procedures.

instrumentality
belief that performance will result in desired outcomes

The third question also is important because it assesses the attractiveness of the potential outcomes that an employee might obtain. The attractiveness of outcomes, such as promotions or raises, varies across employees because they have different needs. The attractiveness of outcomes is called **valence**.[38]

valence
the value or attractiveness of an outcome

The usefulness of expectancy theory is that it tells supervisors that high motivation is likely only when employees perceive that (1) high effort will lead to high performance (high expectancy), (2) high performance will lead to outcomes (high instrumentality), and (3) outcomes are highly desirable (high valence).[39] Expectancy theory provides supervisors with a diagnostic tool for assessing the motivation potential of the work situation for each of their employees. Thus, expectancy theory tells us that people will do what their supervisor wants them to do if she makes sure the following conditions exist:[40]

1. Knows what outcomes her employees value
2. Has identified the behaviors that she wants from her employees

3. Provides sufficient training and facilitates the work so that her employees can reach desired levels of performance
4. Arranges the work such that high effort produces outcomes large enough to be motivating
5. Examines the reward system periodically to make sure inequities are eliminated

As a supervisor, you can influence all of these conditions directly. However, in regard to motivation and rewards, the individual's perception of the desirability of the reward is largely beyond your ability to influence in any meaningful way. Research has demonstrated that supervisors need to consider more factors, such as individual personality differences, in order to determine whether an employee is likely to be motivated in a given situation.[41] We look next at the ways in which you can apply expectancy theory.

ENHANCING PERCEIVED EXPECTANCY

You must spell out in as much detail as possible what you want people to do. Your employees must have a clear understanding of the task, the standards that will be used to evaluate their performance, and the level of quality expected. In a team, team leaders and team members have a say in all these things. Employees or team members must also feel that they are capable of performance. If not, it is likely they will turn down or at least resist the assignment. Here are some ways of influencing your employees' perceptions about their capabilities to perform:

- During the hiring process and when forming teams, try to match the person's experiences and skills to the needs of the job and team.
- Provide training for the skills needed for a task before assigning it.
- Try to redesign the job so that employees will be asked to perform only those tasks that they feel capable of performing. After a person has self-confidence and a feeling of competence, he will be willing to tackle bigger and more demanding tasks.

When you have an employee who knows what is being asked of her and feels capable of performing to the level expected, then outcomes or rewards become critical.

ENHANCING PERCEIVED INSTRUMENTALITY

Supervisors need to be certain that rewards are given to high performers and not to employees who deliver less. If a person works hard, delivers the level of performance called for, and gets no significantly greater reward than that received by mediocre performers, instrumentality will be low. You will have an unhappy, unmotivated employee on your hands. This is one reason companies are shifting their compensation focus to rewards based on results, not simply seniority and increases in the cost of living. In addition, make sure that the performance being rewarded is under the complete control of the employee and is not dependent on some factor over which the person has no control. Control over performance, fair evaluations, and rewards can stir people out of complacency and into a motivated state.

Learning Objective Number Five

REINFORCEMENT THEORY

Reinforcement theory has its foundation in research performed by B. F. Skinner. This theory holds that one can encourage desired behaviors by focusing on the consequences of those behaviors.[42] Simply stated, desired behaviors should be rewarded while undesired behaviors should not be reinforced. If a manager or a company wants to modify employee behavior, timely and appropriate rewards should be provided.

Positive reinforcements should occur as soon as possible after the desired behavior, so that such behavior will be connected with rewards. Good performance can be rewarded through praise, pay increases, promotions, and special favors within a manager's power to dispense. When it is followed by positive reinforcement, rewarded behavior tends to be repeated.

Negative reinforcement involves withholding a punishment if the employee engages in a desired behavior. In this manner it rewards desired behaviors. For example, you may tell an employee that if her work is completed according to the production schedule, you will not engage in micro-management.[43]

Punishment attempts through fear and sanctions to discourage repeat performances. Punishment may include denial of privileges, reprimands, and loss of pay or opportunities. As with positive reinforcement, the quicker the punitive action occurs and the more appropriate it is, the greater will be its impact. Unfortunately, a disadvantage of punishment is that its results are less predictable because employees learn only what *not* to do. They still do not know what they should do. Punishment may also lead to revenge and other undesired consequences.[44]

Certain performances need no reinforcement. Actions that are undesirable but have small (if any) consequences may often be ignored. Temporary, non-serious misbehavior may simply be noted and go unpunished. Supervisors are often required to make a judgment about the cause of the behavior and the intent behind it. Most people lose their tempers now and then, and all of us make minor mistakes fairly regularly. Save your punishment for serious offenses, and punish people in private. Pass out your rewards publicly and take time to help celebrate positive contributions.

As a supervisor, team leader, or team facilitator using this theory, keep the following points in mind:

1. Keep your people aware of what is expected and of the consequences for failing to meet expectations.
2. Rewards and punishments must be tailored to the behavior they are intended to reward or punish. Consider the consequences, intent, and seriousness of the behavior.
3. Don't reward mediocre or poor performance.
4. Don't punish inconsequential instances of misbehavior.
5. Don't fail to reward desired behavior.
6. Don't fail to punish behavior you want eliminated.

Companies fail sometimes because their leaders fail to walk like they talk. They emphasize in words certain concepts and then contradict them with their actions. "They preach the importance of teamwork—then reward individuals who work at standing out from the crowd. They encourage risk taking—then punish good-faith failures. . . . Corporate leaders can scuttle a reengineering effort quite quickly if they pump up their own bonuses and order a new fleet of company jets while telling the troops to tighten belts."[45] When your walk contradicts your talk, your associates label you a hypocrite and take their example from your walk.

EQUITY THEORY

Another important theory considers motivation from each person's unique perspective. Equity theory holds that people contribute or withhold their contributions based on individual perceptions of their equity ratios. People compare the ratio of their rewards (outcomes) to their contributions (inputs) with the ratios of relevant comparison groups, to determine the equity of their work situations. Such comparisons may include coworkers or people at other companies. The ratio of outcomes divided by inputs yields a psychological perception of the equity or fairness at work.

When your employees perceive that their equity ratios are smaller than the ratios of others, they will experience *negative inequity* and will be dissatisfied with how they are being treated. Common responses to such perceived inequities with comparison groups are to reduce inputs, such as effort or quality of work, and to attempt to change outcomes, such as by seeking a pay raise. Other potential responses include cognitive distortion of the inputs or outcomes of others or changing comparison groups. It is possible to experience *positive inequity*, in which your ratio of outcomes to inputs is more favorable than those of people you use for comparison. In cases of extreme overpayment, individuals sometimes increase their inputs in order to restore their perceptions of equity.[46]

How people perceive their ratios is more important than how their managers or facilitators perceive them. When people lose their enthusiasm and appear to be slacking off, supervisors should consider employees' perceptions of their equity ratios. Sit down and discuss their perceptions with them. Ask if they believe anything in the working environment is inequitable or unfair. Quite often you will find a misconception. Sometimes you will find that employees have untrue information or that other unmotivated people are influencing them. In such cases, you must do what you can to remove their feelings of inequity.

GOAL SETTING

Goal setting can provide remarkable results in a wide range of workplace settings and motivational contexts.[47] This approach to motivation has the advantage of being simple to understand and typically does not require large outlays of resources. Goals provide two critical components for motivation as they identify both a target and the level of intensity needed to reach the goal. In order to be effective, goals need to be specific about what is to be accomplished, and they need to be sufficiently difficult to inspire performance. In addition, employees need to accept goals, and this often means that they should participate in developing the goals that they should strive to accomplish. With participation and acceptance there is likely to be employee commitment to the goals. When employees are committed to difficult and specific goals and accept them as legitimate targets for their efforts, organizations can obtain meaningful improvements in performance.[48]

An example of Weyerhaeuser's application of goal setting to the loading of trucks provides evidence of the power of goal setting. In this example, employees were told to try to reach a goal of loading log trucks at a specific percentage of the legal limit. Even though no financial rewards were attached to the goal accomplishment, employees vastly improved the load levels of trucks, and their improved performance was sustained in the long run.[49] Another example from the logging industry demonstrates the power of goal setting. In this example, loggers, who were compensated according to the number of trees that they cut or by piece-rate, were given high goals by their supervisors and provided with tally meters for tracking their performance. The performance of those logging crews that were assigned goals far exceeded the crews that were simply told to "do their best." With the setting of goals, the loggers saw purpose and challenge in their work. As a result of reaching these goals they bragged to their peers and families about their performance. In addition, their attendance also increased dramatically.[50]

Goal setting has a motivational impact because of several reasons. First of all, challenging goals have the ability to energize. Goal setting also focuses effort and attention on activities related to the goal and draws attention away from those that are unrelated. Furthermore, challenging goals encourage persistence, and those with demanding deadlines encourage faster work. Finally, goals encourage the application of knowledge or knowledge discovery.[51]

MANAGING MOTIVATION

Employees' beliefs, attitudes, and values affect how they perceive their world and the demands that are made on them. All of us look for jobs that offer a fit between what we want from work and what our organizations want from us. The closer the fit, the more likely it is that we will find job satisfaction and the means to achieve our personal and professional goals. As Herzberg's theory tells us, job satisfaction comes from the work itself, not from things external to it. Without job satisfaction, we will find it difficult if not impossible to become or to stay motivated—to give our best effort to our performance at work.

Employees become dissatisfied for a variety of reasons. They may enter a job expecting too much. In other cases, people may be hired for jobs that are too difficult or too easy. Applicants for employment are often desperate and take the first job offer that comes their way because they need money. Once on the job, people find boredom, unsafe conditions, inadequate training, and uncooperative coworkers. All these situations add up to problems for the new employees and their employers. Most job dissatisfaction can be prevented, but both employees and employers have to work at prevention.

A question frequently asked is whether high morale or happy workers result in improved financial performance. Although this question has been the subject of numerous studies, the evidence is not clear. There are obvious counterexamples in which a company's economic environment prevents good financial performance regardless of the fact that it has satisfied or happy workers.[52] On the other hand, if managers treat talented employees so badly that they leave or refuse to exert themselves, then high performance is impossible. A study based on a survey of 55,000 employees found several positive relationships between employee attitudes and company profits. These attitudes were that: (1) they were allowed to perform tasks best suited to their strengths, (2) they perceive that their opinions matter, (3) they perceive a commitment by their peers to quality, and (4) they perceive a relationship between their jobs and the organization's mission.[53]

Nonetheless, while many factors such as involvement and empowerment impact performance, the reward system must be rational before we can expect performance to be sustained at high levels. And while behavior and rewards must be linked, the cost of rewards does not have to be high. Steve Kerr, a noted management scholar, makes the following comments about rewards and performance:

> Distributing rewards without regard for how well people have performed makes little sense in general and has a particularly negative impact on high performers. Rewards are among the most powerful tools an organization has to thank high performers for past efforts; noncontingent rewards don't do this. Rewards can also play a major role in stimulating future performance; noncontingent rewards don't do this either . . . Twenty years of studying reward systems has convinced me that there is virtually no relationship between the power of rewards and their cost.[54]

Learning Objective Number Eight

QUALITY

Employee motivation is a critical determinant of the quality of products and services that an organization will be able to produce. Attempting to improve quality before dealing with motivational issues is unlikely to accomplish desired results. Nonetheless, feeling that they are producing a quality product or service is important to an employee's motivation. Accordingly, a discussion of quality issues is included in this chapter on motivation.

In this text we have defined quality and noted its link to the customer or user of a product or service. Quality, in the final analysis, is measured by the ability of a product or service to meet the needs of the internal or external customer. An internal user may be any person or group in the company who receives output from another employee or group. Exhibit 6.5 highlights four major dimensions of quality.

When a company decides to emphasize quality, it often adopts a *total quality management* (TQM) approach.

> TQM involves the application of quality management principles to all aspects of the business, including customers and suppliers. Total quality

---

Dimensions of quality.

EXHIBIT 6.5

1. *Performance characteristics.* A product's operating features and the final outcomes that they produce.

2. *Users' perceptions.* The ways in which a product feels, looks, and performs—its fit and finish.

3. *Useful life.* The length of time that the product can be expected to deliver performance that is in line with user expectations.

4. *Serviceability.* The manufacturer's willingness and ability to furnish quick and reliable repairs—how well the producer backs up the product and its users.

management requires that the principles of quality management should be applied in every branch and at every level in the organization. It is a company-wide approach to quality, with improvements undertaken on a continuous basis by everyone in the organization. Individual systems, procedures, and requirements . . . will pervade every person, activity and function of the organization [and will] . . . require a broadening of outlook and skills and an increase in creative activities . . . The spread of the TQM philosophy would also be expected to be accompanied by greater sophistication in the application of quality management tools and techniques and increased emphasis on people.[55]

six sigma
a quality approach having a goal of no more than 3.4 defects in a million units

Six sigma programs, which have a goal of no more than 3.4 defects per million units, are an outgrowth of TQM and require suppliers to also pursue high-quality approaches. The high emphasis on training in both the TQM and six sigma approaches is evident in the black belt and green belt titles that are bestowed on managers and employees who have acquired expertise in six sigma methodology.[56] TQM and six sigma mean a never-ending quest by every member of an organization to improve people and processes. Everyone must be committed to and participate in the effort to improve quality. Your job as a supervisor is to instill this concept into your people and teams. Make a commitment to quality your personal philosophy. Unless you and your people see quality as your responsibility, such approaches will not work.

TEAMS

Quality leaders such as Toyota, Caterpillar, Dow Chemical, GE, and the Dana Corporation recognize that quality is a never-ending journey, not a destination.[57] Providers who are in close touch with their customers create high-quality products and services—they know what customers want and need. These producers design quality into their end products and processes and set precise performance standards for all of their component parts. From the product design teams to the engineering and production teams, concern for quality dominates the efforts of all concerned. Once the suppliers are chosen (in part for their reputations for and commitment to quality), contracts are drafted. Close contact is then maintained to ensure that all the parts produced meet standards. Cross-functional teams are sometimes used, with members from marketing, production, and design, as well as vendors, working on the projects from beginning to end. The Honeywell Corporation provides an example of this approach—creating a cross-functional team to facilitate communication and participation at all levels of the organization.[58]

PERFORMANCE

PRODUCTIVITY

Productivity is usually expressed as a ratio measure of outputs divided by inputs, yielding a *productivity index* (PI). A PI can be calculated for most clerical or production activities. Inputs may be tons of materials, hours of machine time, dollars of invested capital, or hours of labor invested to produce the output. Outputs are the units realized through the investment or application of inputs. The value of such indexes is in their comparisons over time. By continually calculating a PI for each of your people, teams, and operations, you can measure progress or setbacks.

THE QUALITY, PRODUCTIVITY, AND PROFITABILITY LINK

Quality and productivity are two sides of the same coin. Improvements that lead to better quality also must lead to increased productivity. When this occurs, profitability will increase as well, thus assuring the continued existence of the organization. W. Edwards Deming—the man who taught Japanese companies and many in America much of what they know about quality—believed that when quality improves, costs decrease.[59] Companies have less need to scrap materials and rework their outputs. With less waste and fewer mistakes, productivity improves through the more efficient use of resources. Customers are satisfied, more jobs are provided, and companies ensure their future.

> It's no secret that many manufacturers have succeeded in linking cost-cutting with quality improvement. Toyota, for instance, expects a 3 percent reduction in costs each year from its supplier firms, says Dan Cavanaugh, plant manager at Dana Corp.'s automotive frame plant in Stockton, Calif. . . . Workers at the plant, which performs 115 ft. of welds on each 300-lb. frame, are constantly looking for ways to improve quality and reduce costs. Each worker is expected to come up with three ideas per month, and in a recent month the average was 3.8, Cavanaugh says.[60]

Most efforts to improve quality also will help increase productivity. As with quality improvements, productivity gains begin with a commitment from top management to make improving productivity a priority. The efforts required for productivity must be funded. Goals need to be stated, and corporate environments must be modified to take on the new challenges and changes required. Standards must be set, gains and losses measured, plans created, tools and techniques chosen and used, and people rewarded for their efforts.

Productivity can be improved by producing the same outputs with fewer inputs or by increasing outputs with the same or fewer inputs. Either approach implies more efficient use of resources. People are a main ingredient in the constant search for improvements in productivity. The more motivated and satisfied the individuals, the more productive they are likely to be. On the other hand, people suffering from job stress and job dissatisfaction tend to produce less than their satisfied, low-stress counterparts.

A look at the symptoms typically exhibited by dissatisfied workers should tell you how they affect productivity in a negative way. The typical symptoms are tardiness, absenteeism, delayed work, shoddy work, and time lost to gripes and complaints about their station in life. There also may be theft and shrinkage, or employees may actually damage company property or engage in sabotage simply to vent their frustration. Over time, dissatisfied employees may become emotionally and physically ill, further reducing their productive capacities. If they decide to leave, their replacements will need training and production time will be lost.

The Property and Casualty Division of United Services Automobile Association puts its philosophy about productivity this way:

> Productivity improvement isn't just working harder, it's working smarter. It means devising a method to get the best return on our investment in people, facilities, equipment and other resources. . . . Improving productivity . . . means finding better ways to do more with the resources

we have. . . . In short, we need to provide quality products through distribution systems that are customer-convenient and operator-efficient.[61]

Note that the company, though discussing productivity, makes clear references to quality.

People are both the cause and the cure for problems in quality and productivity. Today's emphasis on empowering workers requires them to be proficient in the four *R*s— reading, 'riting, 'rithmetic, and responsibility. The Ritz-Carlton Hotel Company empowers all employees, without higher approval, to "spend up to $2,000 to fix a guest's problem. . . . [Its] new focus on employee involvement has helped cut turnover from 80 percent to 45 percent, saving nearly $12.5 million."[62] When you and your company give people more authority, you are asking them to think and decide more—to depend more on their own abilities and judgment than they have in the past. "As long as you let everybody in on the facts—budgets, cost data, customer-satisfaction feedback—these independent decisions will usually be good ones."[63] Exhibit 6.6 offers some suggestions to help you and your people improve your organization's quality and productivity.

TEAMS

This chapter has covered several useful models that help you understand how to motivate your associates. With appropriate motivation, good training, and a TQM approach, managers can expect high quality from productive associates. Nonetheless, the manager's own behavior can undermine otherwise favorable conditions for high motivation. The following excerpt explains—in contrast to mere lip service—how a manager's actions have real impact:

> Every manager's best remembered teachings come at unexpected times— a compassionate hand on a shoulder; a supportive comment when the politically safe course is silence; a word of encouragement when criticism might easily be justified; a selfless distribution of credit in front of people who make a difference.[64]

QUALITY OF WORKING LIFE

quality of working life (QWL)
a general label given to various programs and projects designed to help employees satisfy their needs and meet their expectations from work

Improvements in the **quality of working life (QWL)** may be obtained through a variety of programs. Typical QWL programs include a variety of EAPs, training programs, team-building activities, labor-management committees, flexible work schedules, and pay for performance. These programs attempt to "give employees greater opportunities to participate and a larger say in decision making."[65] Such programs are most effective when every manager, team leader, and team facilitator is committed to their success, and when those they are designed to play a meaningful role in their design and implementation.

WORKER PARTICIPATION TECHNIQUES

Many organizations have discovered that the best way to improve operations is to empower employees, both individually and in teams. "To empower people is to make them virtually autonomous, to inform them, to invest them with authority and then trust them to use it."[66] Giving people access to needed information is vital to making empowerment succeed. Many companies use a variety of techniques to do so: general information-sharing sessions, various kinds of scoreboarding activities, company newsletters, computer training, and committees for dealing with a variety of work-related issues.

Suggestions for improving both quality and productivity in your operations.	EXHIBIT 6.6

1. Be committed to improving quality and productivity. Constantly demonstrate your commitment in every action you take.

2. Once you have defined a problem, seek suggestions from employees closest to the problem about how to solve it. Diverse people yield diverse suggestions.

3. Give your people all the information they need and the reasons for changes in procedures before you attempt to implement them. You need your people's cooperation and support to make the changes effective and efficient.

4. Whenever possible, show and demonstrate rather then simply tell people why changes are necessary.

5. Keep the trust and respect of employees, and do what you can to break down any barriers to effective communication and cooperation.

6. Encourage your people to look for ways to improve everything they do and to share their ideas with you and their coworkers. Then reward them when they do so.

7. Let employees and team members know why quality and productivity are important to them and their organization. Explain and demonstrate with real examples the costs of poor quality and lagging productivity—for example, how a defective product lost a customer and wasted resources.

8. Make it clear that each person is accountable for quality and productivity gains. Make employee quality and productivity improvements part of each employee's regular evaluations.

9. Share productivity and quality improvements with other supervisors and get them to share their discoveries with you.

MOTIVATION AND JOB DESIGN

Job Rotation

The term **job rotation** is used in two ways. In one type of job rotation, people are moved to different jobs, usually on a temporary basis, to give them additional experience, understanding, and challenges. It is most frequently used to cross-train people and to give them a better appreciation for the importance of jobs and their interrelationships. Employees who participate in job rotation are usually more valuable to themselves and to their employers because they can perform competently in more than one job. From this, supervisors gain more flexibility and can deal with absences more effectively. In another type of job rotation, employees rotate the performance of tasks

job rotation movement of people to different jobs, usually for a temporary period, in order to inform, train, or stimulate cooperation and understanding among them

on a relatively short cycle, such as every set number of hours or days, in order to relieve the boredom of repetitive tasks. This is a common practice in production line settings to prevent boredom from affecting motivation.

Job Enlargement

job enlargement
increasing the number of tasks or the quantity of output required in a job

Job enlargement increases the number of tasks a job includes or the amount of output expected from the jobholder. It does not increase the number of responsibilities or the level of personal involvement the jobholder experiences. It usually requires people to do more of the kinds of tasks they are already doing regularly. Since job enlargement can add challenges for some, it can aid motivation and spark a renewed interest and enthusiasm for work. And for some, a sense of competence can arise from being able to produce more, both in quantity and quality.

Job Enrichment

job enrichment
providing variety, deeper personal interest and involvement, greater autonomy and challenge, or increased responsibility on the job

Today, manufacturers are turning many highly specialized, hazardous, and routine assembly-type tasks over to robots. In contrast, for human workers, the emphasis now is strongly on **job enrichment**—enriching a job by providing the jobholder with variety, greater autonomy, and an increased amount of responsibility and challenge. Essentially, job enrichment attempts to build in more of the motivators that Herzberg found.[67] Job enrichment establishes client relationships for the jobholder, includes more responsibility (vertical loading), forms natural work units, combines tasks, and opens feedback channels. Those employees respond best in enriched jobs who have a stronger desire to grow or develop skills on the job.[68] However, job enrichment is not for everybody. While job enrichment has many benefits, many production-line workers prefer their repetitive, specialized tasks. Their reasons are many. Some do not want a challenge and the additional effort it represents. Others are working to their capacities with the current configuration of their jobs and could not adjust to more duties. Still others do not like the new responsibilities or the ways in which their jobs will be enriched.

Workers develop organizational commitment and identify more closely with the organization when they participate in group activities.

INSTANT REPLAY

1. The Hawthorne studies of the 1920s demonstrated the social and esteem needs that people have and the natural tendencies of workers to form their own groups or cliques.

2. Abraham Maslow ranked human needs in a hierarchy that progresses from physical needs through four psychological needs. Each can act as a motive for human behavior.

3. Managers and their organizations have the power to assist employees in their search for satisfaction in every need category.

4. Herzberg identified two sets of factors that can either prevent dissatisfaction or promote motivation in employees. These are called, respectively, maintenance factors and motivation factors.

5. Expectancy theory holds that people will exert effort if they believe that performance is likely and that performance, in turn, will lead to desired outcomes.

6. Reinforcement theory states that desirable behavior will be repeated if rewarded and that undesirable behavior can be discouraged through withholding rewards or administering punishment.

7. Equity theory states that individuals' perceptions of equitable treatment are based on comparisons with relevant people and groups. Inputs are compared with outputs to determine if equitable treatment exists.

8. Goal setting can increase performance in a wide variety of conditions even in the absence of financial rewards.

9. Productivity and quality go together. Efforts to improve one must also act to improve the other. Efforts to improve both must never end.

QUESTIONS FOR CLASS DISCUSSION

1. Can you define this chapter's key terms?

2. What are the needs we humans have in common? What are some examples of satisfactions that are available to us through our work?

3. What are the motivation factors identified by Herzberg? What is their purpose in an organization?

4. What are the maintenance factors identified by Herzberg? What is their purpose in an organization?

5. What is the expectancy theory of motivation? How has it been demonstrated in your own experience?

6. What is the reinforcement theory of motivation? How has it worked in your own experience?

7. What is the equity theory of motivation?
8. How can goal setting be used to increase performance?
9. What can supervisors do to promote improvements in both quality and productivity?

ASSESS THE SITUATION

Purpose: To assess the motivational climate at work for both you and your employees.

Your Task: Take the following quiz. Tally your responses as follows: for each "yes" response, 2 points; for each "no" response, 1 point. A score of 20 or higher indicates that you work in a highly motivating climate. Let your employees or team members take this quiz. The results may help you create more stimulating environments and jobs for employees.

Yes	No	
○	○	1. My boss knows me as an individual to include what I do for recreation and something about my family.
○	○	2. I have easy access to the information I need to perform my job.
○	○	3. Company incentives encourage my intellectual growth.
○	○	4. I have served or am now serving on a team.
○	○	5. I am often commended for doing a good job.
○	○	6. I am proud of my company and the products or services it produces.
○	○	7. I receive regular feedback on my performance at work.
○	○	8. My company allows time to deal with family and personal problems.
○	○	9. I recommend my company to outsiders as a great place to work.
○	○	10. My pay is linked to my performance.
○	○	11. It is okay to make a mistake as long as I learn from it and am more careful in the future.
○	○	12. I have a great deal of latitude in how to perform my job.
○	○	13. People who work here would probably do so even if the pay was a little less attractive and they had other opportunities.

SKILL BUILDING EXERCISE 6.1

Exhibit 6.3 presented several different suggestions for increasing the performance of employees by enhancing the motivating potential of their work. Such suggestions can be very helpful to supervisors who are searching for ways to improve employee performance. Rewards can also be used at another level to help build motivation. The use of appropriate rewards can reinforce desired behaviors, provide recognition, and say thank you to employees for a job well done. Small rewards or prizes are sometimes administered on the spot to employees. However, better results are obtained when supervisors ask their employees about their preferences for such rewards. Recognition constitutes a reward that typically has great value for the recipients and is of low cost to the organization. Interestingly, while reward schemes, such as those that involve contests in which employees can win prizes or trips to exotic locations tend to have short-term impact, it is important to work on emotional values for long-term results. For example, actions that enable employees to feel like they are important to the organization have substantial long-run impact.[69]

Your Task: Work in a small group or work alone to identify rewards that can be used to help motivate employees. More specifically your task is to: (1) Identify 10 different low-cost rewards that you can obtain for less than $50 each. (2) Note the specific needs to which each reward is targeted. (3) Describe the specifics of how you would implement these rewards in a place where you have worked to obtain maximum impact. (4) Identify any problems that may occur and conditions that may limit the motivational impact of these rewards.

SKILL BUILDING WRITING EXERCISE 6.2

As discussed in this chapter, the intrinsic motivation that resides within the job itself often has important implications for performance. As a result, savvy companies often strive to increase the motivating potential of many of their jobs through the process of job enrichment, which builds in such features as autonomy, responsibility, meaningful work, and knowledge of results through direct feedback from clients. Greater awareness of the potential for intrinsic motivation may be obtained by reviewing job postings. Some companies describe motivation potential in their job postings because they recognize its importance and understand its appeal to many desirable applicants. On the other hand, other companies provide no such detail and in some cases they may not be taking full advantage of the potential intrinsic motivation in their jobs.

Your Task: (1) Review on-line job sites such as Monster.com or CareerBuilder.com for job postings from leading companies and search for specific features of the job and work environment that indicate intrinsic motivators. (2) Compile a list of 10 companies that address such job features in their postings, the job titles, and the conditions that you consider to have intrinsic motivating potential. (3) Compile a similar list of 10 companies that appear not to be taking advantage of such opportunities to call attention to such motivating potential in their jobs. List job titles for these companies. (4) Describe any differences between the two sets of companies, such as the industries in which they operate, the types of jobs that they post, and their reputation as employers.

CASE 6.1	Lighting a Fire Under the Sales Force

Kelly Morton owns a small chain of shoe stores. The stores sell medium- to higher-quality shoes for both men and women, and the sales force is paid on commission. Over the past six months sales have been flat. Kelly has brought in the store managers for a group meeting in order to seek their advice on how to get the sales people to generate more sales. Because the stores are relatively small, the store managers are the direct supervisors of their sales people. Kelly started the meeting by reviewing sales figures and then asked the store managers how to improve sales.

Lou was the first to speak. Lou said, "I think the solution is simple. We've always done well with commissions. Because we pay straight commission, we get good sales people and they tend to stay with us. Our sales people make more than those at other stores who get paid an hourly wage. I think we're getting some competition from the larger retailers that are beginning to carry lines of shoes similar to some of our higher-quality merchandise. We need to bite the bullet and increase the percentage for commissions. It'll cost more, but we'll make up for the extra cost with volume."

Chris spoke up next. "I disagree with Lou. We've always paid commissions, but sales are still flat. Something has changed, and it's not just the competition from big chains. That tells me that we need to add something else. Let's have an awards dinner where we give out plaques to our top sales people. We can post their pictures in each store. You know, sort of a Wall of Fame. And we could have a professional athlete come in and make a motivational speech that will fire everybody up for next year. Money is not the answer because these people already make good money. What's a bigger commission or a cash award going to mean to them? I think that people want to see themselves standing up in front of their peers receiving the top sales person award for the year and hear the applause. They can visualize that, and it's real to them."

Lou said, "I disagree. Plaques don't mean much because everybody gets them. The next time you go to your insurance agent's office look at the line of plaques on the wall. Those insurance people aren't all superstars, but they all have plaques. If we want more sales, we need to get out the checkbook."

Cary said, "I think you're wrong, Lou. But I don't know whether an awards dinner is the answer. I try to create a warm environment where the sales people like to come to work. In our store we all like each other, and I try to tell people when they've done a good job. This causes the sales people to treat the customers well and we get repeat business. Sure, the money's important, but our sales are flat because not enough of our people know that we appreciate their efforts."

Lynn spoke next. "I don't think praise and pats on the back are going to increase sales. They might work with kids' soccer teams, but they won't work with adults. Why don't we have a contest where the sales person having the highest sales next quarter gets an all-expenses-paid trip for two to Hawaii. It will be January then, and it will probably be about 5 degrees here with a cold wind blowing off the lake. Our sales people will work harder to try to sell the most shoes because they know they could be sitting on the beach in Maui. My sister is an insurance agent, and her company has contests all the time. Last year she got to go to Bermuda because of one of those contests."

Pat responded, "Our sales people are very competitive and like to win at anything they do. It's like a game with them, and they keep score of whether they're winning by the dollar amount of their sales. But I disagree with Lynn. People want cash prizes based on their sales instead of trips. Lots more people could get rewards that way. If we only send the top sales person on a trip to Hawaii and we have 50 sales people, there is only a two percent chance of winning. I don't think our sales people are going to connect hard work with a trip. As a result, most of them are going to blow it off. Why work hard if only one of us is going to get a trip?"

Lou said, "Look, I don't think we need any fancy gimmicks to make sales increase. Everybody knows how it works. If you work hard, you make money. My go-getters work hard and generate sales. The lazy people who don't work hard don't make much money, and they leave after a few months. There are two kinds of people in this world: the go-getters and the couch potatoes. The go-getters are going to work hard because they can make good money, and it's not worth our time dealing with the lazy people because they aren't going to change. All we have to do is pay more for commissions. Selling is becoming harder, and we need to pay more."

Finally Kim spoke up. "Look, I hate to be negative, but we're going to waste a lot of money with all of these ideas. I think we simply have some people who need to be reminded that everybody has to sell hard if they want to keep their jobs. Let's give everybody a sales quota and then rank everybody by sales at the end of the next quarter and fire the bottom 10 percent. They'll get the point."

Questions

1. What theories of motivation are represented in the different store managers' comments?

2. If you were Kelly Morton, what would you do?

3. What does this case reveal about human motivation?

CASE 6.2   Slow Motion

Fernando, Morrie, George, and Isaac were standing next to the service manager's office as a woman drove her car out of the shop. Fernando, the service manager, turned to Morrie, the shop supervisor, and said, "She's the third customer this week who has complained about the work we did on her car. She said that we took twice as long to fix the car as we promised. It seems like we are either too slow or don't do good work. Other times we can't even figure out what's wrong with the car. I don't know how many people are bringing their cars back multiple times before we get them repaired correctly, but it's a lot. Why can't we fix the cars right before they send them out?"

Morrie said, "Cars are a lot more complicated today than they were 20 years ago. The mechanics have to know how to use computer diagnostic equipment, and they have to be able to repair the computers and electronics on the cars. They have to be able to fix cars that have a lot more moving parts than the old ones. We used to be able to keep someone's car longer to fix it, but now customers really get upset if we have to keep their cars overnight. Another problem is that it's really hard to find and keep good mechanics. Many of our people are inexperienced, and turnover is high. And you wouldn't believe the number that apply but flunk the drug test."

George, one of the best and most experienced mechanics, said, "I think some of the younger mechanics don't care about their work like we used to. It used to be that when you worked in a garage you saw the customer and knew whose car you worked on. Now, I don't even know who owns the car. There's just a number on the windshield, and I never see the customer. When I started doing this work in the 1970s, sometimes a customer would come back and say "thanks." That made me really feel good. Other times they would come back and tell you that their car wasn't fixed right. You could see that you had really let them down if their car broke down on the road after you worked on it. I really learned something from that. But now I just work back here in the shop and don't see anybody but mechanics all day long. Sometimes I feel like I'm just working in a factory."

Isaac, a well-trained young mechanic, said, "George, you old guys always think that things were better in the old times. But seriously, I'll bet you didn't have to work under so much pressure. We get told to do it right, but the customers always want us to do the work in less time than we really need. And we're supposed to be learning how to use the latest diagnostic computers just to keep up with the new cars. Why bother? Some of the guys are just taking their time to do the jobs. I try to work hard in order to get the car out quickly. But then one of the runners will bring back another car, and I'll start working on it while the other guys are still working on the same car. I'm taking courses at the community college at night in bodywork and am saving my money so that I can open my own body shop some day. That's where the real money is."

Morrie said, "I think that's part of the problem. We're losing too many guys like Isaac. And the guys like George are going to be retiring someday. Most of these young mechanics don't take any pride in their work anymore. I think most of this younger generation doesn't care about doing a good job. George is right, things were better in the old days."

Fernando said, "These young people tell me that they don't want to be mechanics. They want white-collar jobs even though they may not make more money than good mechanics or plumbers. I understand, though, because I used to be embarrassed when people asked what I did for a living or when people would see grease under my fingernails. I feel a little better about the kind of work that we do now because of those shows on TV, like "American Hot" and "Rides." Now it doesn't bother me as much. Besides, I just do paperwork now and deal with the customers. But if I lived in Germany I would go back to being a mechanic because I could work on those great cars all the time. Those German mechanics are really good. And they get to wear those uniforms that say BMW or Mercedes. I'd really like that."

George said, "Do you think they pay mechanics in Germany with an incentive for fixing more cars or a monthly salary? That would make a difference to me. I like to get paid on an incentive basis like we get paid here. But these younger guys don't seem to respond to it. Most of them are just slow, dumb, and sloppy."

Fernando said, "Well I still don't know what to do. Maybe I should ask the owner of the garage to hire some more mechanics."

Questions

1. What is causing the problems in the shop? Will hiring more mechanics help?

2. What motivational theories seem to apply to this case?

3. What would you do to improve the situation?

4. Are age differences relevant to the problems?

5. What else could be causing the problems? What motivates Fernando, Morrie, George, and Isaac?

REFERENCES

1 Freeman, David H. "Burt Rutan Entrepreneur of the Year," *Inc. Magazine* (January 2005): 59–66.

2 Stevens, Tim. "Just Plane Smart," *Industry Week* (December 15, 1997): 91–58.

3 Freeman, "Burt Rutan Entrepreneur of the Year."

4 Martin, Don. *TeamThink.* New York: Penguin Books USA (1993): 96. Herskowitz, Mickey. *The Legend of Bear Bryant.* New York: McGraw-Hill (1987): 95–96.

5 Peters, Tom. "To Be the Best You Can Be, Forget About the Boss," *Chicago Tribune* (December 5, 1994): sect. 4, 2.

6 Peters, Tom. "Managers Need Surprise Tactics, Front-Line Thinking to Route Competition," *Chicago Tribune* (October 3, 1994): sect. 4, 5.

7 Franklin, Stephen. "90% Collapse of 1929–32 Was Worst U.S. Bear Market," *Fort Worth Star Telegram* (September 1, 1998): A9.

8 Mayo, Elton. *The Social Problems of an Industrial Civilization.* Boston: Division of Research, Graduate School of Business Administration, Harvard University (1945): 68–86.

9 Maslow, Abraham H. *Motivation and Personality,* 2d ed. New York: Harper & Row, 1970.

10 Marx, Robert, Jick, Todd D., and Frost, Peter J. *Management Live: The Video Book.* Englewood Cliffs, NJ: Prentice Hall, 1991.

11 McClelland, David C., and Burnham, David H. "Power Is the Great Motivator," *Harvard Business Review* (January 2003): 126–139.

12 Ibid.

13 Ibid., 117–118.

14 Greenberg, Jerald, and Baron, Robert A. *Behavior in Organizations,* Upper Saddle River, NJ: Prentice Hall, 2000. Dunham, Randall B. *The Manager's Workshop V3.0,* Upper Saddle River, NJ: Prentice Hall, 2004.

[15] Hersey, Paul, Blanchard, Kenneth H., and Johnson, Dewey E. *Management of Organizational Behavior: Leading Human Resources*, 8th ed., Upper Saddle River, N.J.: Prentice Hall, 2001.

[16] Arnolds, C. A., and Boshoff, C. "Compensation, Esteem Valence, and Job Performance: An Empirical Assessment of Alderfer's ERG Theory," *International Journal of Human Resource Management* (June 2002): 697–719.

[17] DuPont, Dale K. "Eureka! Tools for Encouraging Employee Suggestions," *HR Magazine* (September 1999): 134–138.

[18] Ibid.

[19] Durbin, Dee-Ann. "GM Is Cutting 30,000 Jobs," *St. Louis Post-Dispatch* (November 22, 2005): A1.

[20] Marx, Jick, and Frost. *Management Live.*

[21] Ibid.

[22] Herzberg, Frederick. "One More Time: How Do You Motivate Employees?" in *Business Classics: Fifteen Key Concepts for Managerial Success.* Boston: Harvard Business Review (1975): 13–22.

[23] Caggiano, Christopher. "What Do Workers Want?" *Inc.* (November 1992): 101.

[24] Levering, Robert, and Moskowitz, Milton. "The 100 Best Companies to Work For," *Fortune* (January 24, 2005): 61–90.

[25] Levering and Moskowitz. "The 100 Best Companies to Work For."

[26] Fisher, Anne. "The 100 Best Companies to Work for in America," *Fortune* (January 12, 1998): 69–70.

[27] Caggiano. "What Do Workers Want?"

[28] Herzberg. "One More Time."

[29] Randolph, W. Alan, and Sashkin, Marshall. "Can Organizational Empowerment Work in Multinational Settings?" *Academy of Management Executive* (February 2002): 102–115.

[30] Randolph, W. Alan. "Re-Thinking Empowerment: Why Is It So Hard to Achieve? *Organizational Dynamics,* (Fall 2000): 94–107.

[31] Lei, David, and Greer, Charles R. "The Empathetic Organization," *Organizational Dynamics* (May 2003): 142–164.

[32] Champoux, Joseph E. *Organizational Behavior: Integrating Individuals, Groups, and Processes.* Minneapolis: West, 1996.

[33] Kohn, Alfie. *Punished by Rewards: The Trouble with Gold Stars, Incentive Plans, A's, Praise, and Other Bribes.* New York: Houghton-Mifflin, 1993. Kohn, Alfie. "Why Incentive Plans Cannot Work," *Harvard Business Review* (September–October 1993): 54–63.

[34] Gupta, Nina, and Shaw, Jason D. "Let the Evidence Speak: Financial Incentives Are Effective!" *Compensation and Benefits Review 30*(2) (1998): 28, 30.

[35] Weiss, Joseph W. *Organizational Behavior and Change: Managing Diversity, Cross-Cultural Dynamics, and Ethics.* Minneapolis: West, 1996.

[36] Ibid.

[37] Ibid.

[38] Ibid.

[39] Ibid.

[40] Kreitner, Robert, and Kinicki, Angelo. *Organizational Behavior,* 5th ed. Boston: Irwin McGraw-Hill, 2001.

[41] Kanfer, Ruth. "Motivation," in Cary L. Cooper and Chris Argyris, eds., *The Concise Blackwell Encyclopedia of Management.* Oxford, UK: Blackwell (1998): 422–426.

[42] Skinner, B. F. *Contingencies of Reinforcement: A Theoretical Analysis.* New York: Appleton-Century-Crofts, 1969.

[43] Weiss. *Organizational Behavior.*

[44] Ibid.

[45] Labich, Kenneth. "Why Companies Fail," *Fortune* (November 14, 1994): 52–54, 58, 60, 64, 68.

[46] Champoux. *Organizational Behavior.*

[47] Locke, Edwin A. "Guest Editor's Introduction: Goal-Setting Theory and Its Applications to the World of Business," *Academy of Management Executive 18*(4) (2004): 124–125.

[48] Dunham. *The Manager's Workshop V3.0.*

[49] Dunham. *The Manager's Workshop V3.0.*

[50] Latham, Gary P. "The Motivational Benefits of Goal-Setting," *Academy of Management Executive 18* (4) (2004): 126–129.

[51] Ibid.

[52] Grant, Linda. "Happy Workers, High Returns," *Fortune* (January 12, 1998): 81.

[53] Ibid.

[54] Kerr, Stephen. "Organizational Rewards: Practical, Cost-Neutral Alternatives That You May Know, But Don't Practice," *Organizational Dynamics* (Summer 2000): 66, 70.

[55] Barrie, Dale. "Quality," in Slack, Nigel (ed.), *The Blackwell Encyclopedic Dictionary of Operations Management.* Cambridge, MA: Blackwell (1997): 166.

[56] Schmitt, Bill. "A Slow Spread for Six Sigma," *Chemical Week* (February 13, 2002): 34–35.

[57] Bartholomew, Doug. "Cost vs. Quality," *Industry Week* (September 2001): 34–41. Schmitt. "A Slow Spread for Six Sigma."

[58] Boyle, Richard J. "Wrestling with Jellyfish," *Harvard Business Review* (November–December 1992): 14.

[59] "William Edwards Demming and TQM," *Workforce* (January 2002): 40.

[60]Bartholomew. "Cost vs. Quality," 40.

[61] Belcher, John G., Jr. *Productivity Plus.* Houston, TX: Gulf Publishing (1987): 27.

[62] Austin, Nancy K. "What's Missing from Corporate Cure-Alls," *Working Woman* (September 1994): 16–19.

[63] Ibid.

[64] Mullen, James X. "Actions Speak Louder Than Speeches," *Wall Street Journal* (July 10, 1995): A12.

[65] Schuler, Randall S. *Managing Human Resources,* 5th ed. New York: West (1995): 9–10, 676–677.

[66] Austin. "What's Missing."

[67] Weiss. *Organizational Behavior.*

[68] Oldham, Greg R. "Job Enrichment" in Cary L. Cooper and Chris Argyris, eds., *The Concise Blackwell Encyclopedia of Management.* Oxford, UK: Blackwell (1998): 340.

[69] McGarvey, Robert. "Right-Sized Reward," *American Way* (June 15, 2003): 74–77.

"My center is giving way, my right is in retreat; situation excellent. I am attacking."

Marshal Ferdinand Foch[1]
Commander in Chief of Allied Forces, World War I

Objectives

After reading and discussing this chapter, you should be able to do the following:

1. List and give examples of this chapter's principles of leadership.
2. Briefly define the contingency models of leadership.
3. Provide an explanation of emotional intelligence.
4. Describe the behaviors of a Level 5 leader.
5. List and give situations in which each of the management styles would be appropriate.
6. Explain the steps involved in charismatic leadership.
7. Explain the steps involved in becoming a leader.
8. List and briefly explain the leadership indicators.

Leading a Turnaround at Beth Israel Deaconess Medical Center

Beth Israel Deaconess Medical Center (BIDMC) was in a state of rapid decline and was on the verge of being sold. The hospital, which previously enjoyed a reputation for excellence in patient care, research, and teaching, had not performed well after a merger. Heavy financial losses were incurred, and the hospital's medical staff and its administration did not have effective working relationships. Unsurprisingly, employee morale was poor, cost containment efforts had failed, and the hospital struggled to develop effective approaches to deal with the competitive health care environment. A new CEO, Paul Levy, who had successfully engineered a highly visible turnaround under difficult circumstances, was brought in as the new CEO. While he did not have a medical background, he had leadership skills that enabled him to quickly gain the respect and trust of the staff.[2]

Levy's approach to the turnaround at BIDMC provides lessons for supervisors, as the leadership skills evident in this situation are directly applicable.

Leadership and Management Styles

Levy's approach with the turnaround began with efforts to create an understanding of the imperative for change and a commitment from the staff to doing things differently. He acquainted employees with his open management approach and interacted frequently with employees by walking throughout the hospital, interacting with them in hallway conversations, and asking about their concerns. Levy also communicated frequently with employees through various mediums and did not sugarcoat the bad news about the changes—including layoffs—that would be required. When it was necessary to conduct layoffs, he was supportive and sensitive of the mood of remaining employees after the layoffs. As he moved forward with the turnaround, Levy encouraged employee involvement in turnaround plans and educated the staff on collaborative decision-making. When people failed to work collaboratively or pursued self-interests instead of the welfare of the organization, he took decisive action and made it clear that such behavior was unacceptable. Furthermore, when there was improvement and movement in the right direction, Levy was quick to congratulate employees for their good work. As a result of his leadership over a three-year period, the hospital went from a $58 million loss to a $37.4 million net gain from operations, and turnover of nurses declined to 3 percent from the previous 15 percent annual rate.[3]

Questions for Thought

1. What are the aspects of a leadership approach that are critical to successful turnaround situations?
2. How does a flexible leadership approach produce good results?

Introduction

Authority is the right to give orders and instructions while power is the ability to influence others—to get them to subject their wills to yours. In this chapter, we will see that leadership is based on both power and authority but depends most heavily on power. Although all managers need authority—the ability to punish and reward that rests in their formal positions—manager–leaders need both power and authority. It is possible to be a manager and yet not be a leader. Exhibit 7.1 relates these two concepts. On the left, we find managers having only management ability, who rely solely on formal authority to influence people. On the right, we find non-managers who possess leadership ability and have power from other sources to influence people. In the

EXHIBIT 7.1　　**The relationship between managers and leaders.**

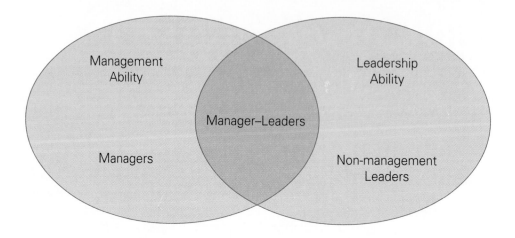

middle, we find manager–leaders—those managers who couple their formal authority with their personal power.

LEADERSHIP VERSUS MANAGEMENT

There are several important differences between leaders and managers, although both roles are critical to all organizations. The major underlying theme for leadership is change, while management is more concerned with efficiency of operations and implementation. Nonetheless, both functions are critical and successful supervisors and leaders display both leader and manager skills and behaviors. The leadership role facilitates and serves as a catalyst for change in three distinct ways that differentiate the role from management.[4]

The first difference is that the leadership role involves the process of articulating and communicating a compelling vision that shows the direction in which the unit or organization needs to move in the future. As such, it is more concerned with the future or more distant future than management. In contrast, management is more concerned with such functions as planning and budgeting processes or implementation of the vision. Without such planning and organizing, today's complex organizations could not perform their missions or operate with any degree of efficiency.[5]

A second distinction is that leadership is concerned with aligning the organization's personnel with the roles and performance needed to move in the desired direction. Such alignment is produced by the leader's credibility and ability to communicate the vision such that employees make the necessary changes. In today's dynamic and competitive economy, employee empowerment is typically required for the future envisioned by leaders. In such envisioned future states, organizations respond quickly to customer or client demands with actions resulting from decisions made quickly by employees at lower levels in the organization. In contrast, management is concerned with such matters as staffing, delegation, and procedures needed for implementation of the vision.[6]

A third distinction is that the leader serves in an inspirational and motivational role in which he or she obtains the support of others in order to make the desired changes. The leader provides such motivation by identifying needs that employees can satisfy by performing the desired activities and changing how they perform their jobs. For example, leaders may gain employee commitment by showing employees how they will be able to gain recognition or a sense of achievement by helping the organization make the desired changes. In contrast, management is concerned with problem solving, establishing controls for the efficient use of resources, and achieving key results.[7]

To summarize, without sufficient leadership, there may be inattention to the purposes of the organization and needs for change, while without sufficient management, initiatives may fail because they lack practicality.[8] Exhibit 7.2 presents several critical leadership behaviors although many of them are also required for management.

LEADERSHIP AND POWER

One source of power comes from one's position. As a manager, you have the right to punish and reward. Power also originates in your personality, competencies, interpersonal relationships, and reputation at work. People look up to authorities who have the expertise they lack. People respect others who are fair and honest. They want to be with and work for others whom they can trust. But trust must be mutual. If you don't trust your people, they will find it difficult to trust you. Trust in your people comes from knowing them well—their abilities, goals, and values.

You demonstrate it in what you say and do each day. How you treat others sets the tone for your interrelationships and encourages others to use it as an acceptable model for their own behavior. **Leadership by example** is a powerful way to lead.[9]

In contrast, some members of the board of New York's Metropolitan Transit Authority, which operates the city's subway and bus systems, provide an example of failure to lead by example. Recently, reporters staked out board members to see how they traveled to the authority's monthly meetings to see whether these officials actually use subways and buses themselves. Most officials used the mass transit system to travel to the meeting, although there were notable exceptions, such as the chairman of the board who used a limousine to travel the short distance from the meeting to his office. Some others drove their SUVs or used the authority's pool vehicles. The large photograph, which appeared in the *New York Times,* of the chairman getting into his limousine after the meeting should provide a reminder to supervisors that their actions will be observed by others, and that they need to "walk the talk."[10]

Similar behaviors caused problems for Carly Fiorina, who served as CEO at Hewlett-Packard, until she was ousted. While there were a number of reasons for her departure, she did not seem to appreciate the expectations of the company's culture and did not always lead by example. For example, although egalitarianism was a strong

leadership by example
modeling the way for others to act, such as a supervisor who sets high standards for her own performance

EXHIBIT 7.2   **Critical leadership behaviors.**

- Clarifying what is important
- Building consensus on what is important
- Determining direction and a vision for the future
  - Negotiating agreement
  - Building commitment
- Integrating the contributions of contributors
  - Developing and maintaining teamwork
- Resolving conflicts
  - Mediating disputes among contributors
- Persisting while being willing to alter one's direction when appropriate
- Developing knowledge of contributors that enables new behaviors
- Building trust and a reputation for integrity
- Acting on the basis of concern for others
- Drawing personal motivation from a compelling purpose
- Developing the courage to pursue the correct course of action
- Engaging in self-sacrifice
- Developing accurate self-awareness
  - Obtaining feedback on how others perceive you
  - Understanding your strengths and weaknesses
- Placing appropriate emphasis on management issues such as practicality, efficiency, and stability

Sources: Bruce J. Alolio and Fred Luthans. *The High Impact Leader: Moments Matter in Accelerating Authentic Leadership Development.* New York: McGraw-Hill (2006). John P. Kotter. *A Force for Change: How Leadership Differs from Management.* New York: The Free Press (1990). Jeswald W. Salacuse. *Leading Leaders: How to Manage Smart, Talented, Rich, and Powerful People.* New York: American Management Association (2006). Robert E. Quinn. *Building the Bridge As You Walk On It.* San Francisco: Jossey-Bass (2004). Gary Yukl. *Leadership in Organizations.* Upper Saddle River, N.J.: Pearson – Prentice Hall (2006). Gary Yukl and Richard Lepsinger. *Flexible Leadership: Creating Value by Balancing Multiple Challenges and Choices.* San Francisco: Jossey-Bass (2004).

cultural value at Hewlett-Packard, she negotiated a huge compensation package, which involved a $3 million signing bonus and a stock deal valued at $65 million. In addition, she requested that the company take on the expense of shipping her 52-foot yacht to the San Francisco area.[11]

LEADERSHIP

Leadership is the ability to get work done with and through others while winning their respect, confidence, loyalty, and willing cooperation. The first part of our definition is true of management as well. It is the second half of the definition that distinguishes a leader from a non-leader. It is likely that though you may be a leader to some of your employees, you may not be to others. The goal is to be a leader to all of your employees. Leadership is an art that can be acquired and developed by anyone with the motivation to do so.

leadership
the ability to get work done with and through others while winning their respect, confidence, loyalty, and willing cooperation

LEADERSHIP PRINCIPLES

Established principles or guidelines should govern the exercise of your informal and formal authority. Exhibit 7.3 lists 15 principles of leadership presented by Gordon England, when he was Secretary of the Navy, to the midshipmen at the U.S. Naval Academy. Prior to becoming Secretary of the Navy, England served many years as a senior executive in the aerospace industry.

Each of these principles provides sound advice for leaders in any position. They serve as concise reminders and as a checklist to which you should frequently refer. They constitute a handy guide to help you assess your practice of management and the exercise of authority over others. If you understand their meaning and make an honest effort to act in accordance with their wisdom, you can avoid many errors and problems.

*Learning
Objective
Number One*

LEADERSHIP TRAITS AND SKILLS

Since the early 1900s, attempts have been made to discover a list of traits that would guarantee leadership status to their possessor. The U.S. Army surveyed all levels of soldiers exiting the service in the late 1940s to determine what traits were possessed by the commanders who were perceived to be effective leaders. Although a list of 14 traits emerged from the survey, no commander had all the traits listed, and many famous commanders lacked several. A typical list of leadership traits appears in Exhibit 7.4, which was prepared by the U.S. Small Business Administration. The basic traits in the exhibit are ones based on Raymond Catell's research from the 1950s of military leaders.[12] The other traits were added for conditions faced by today's leaders. Because the list is extensive, it is unlikely that any manager–leader would possess all of them. Research has failed to give us a final list of traits that guarantee leadership status to those who possess them. Certain traits may be considered indispensable, whereas others may be a plus

EXHIBIT 7.3	Principles of leadership.

1. Provide an environment for every person to excel.

2. Treat every person with dignity and respect—nobody is more important than anyone else.

3. Be forthright, honest, and direct with every person and in every circumstance.

4. Improve effectiveness to gain efficiency.

5. Cherish your time and the time of others—it is not renewable.

6. Identify the critical problems that need solution for the organization to succeed.

7. Describe complex issues and problems simply so every person can understand.

8. Never stop learning—depth and breadth of knowledge are equally important.

9. Encourage constructive criticism.

10. Surround yourself with great people and delegate to them full authority and responsibility.

11. Make ethical standards more important than legal requirements.

12. Strive for team-based wins, not individual.

13. Emphasize capability—not organization.

14. Incorporate measures and metrics everywhere.

15. Concentrate on core functions and outsource all others.

Source: Gordon R. England, Secretary of the Navy. "Principles of Leadership," United States Naval Academy's Forrestal Lecture Series, November 20, 2002. *www.chinfo.navy.mil/navpalib/people/secnav/eng-principles.html.*

but not essential. All the traits and skills listed can be developed and perfected through developmental programs emphasizing education, training, and leadership experiences.

FUNDAMENTAL PRACTICES OF LEADERSHIP

In contrast to the lists of traits in Exhibit 7.4, recent research on leadership has identified five fundamental leadership practices (behaviors) that are necessary for exemplary leadership. Contradicting some of the leadership literature of the past, this research finds no support for the notion that leaders should be charismatic or that the position of leaders is lonely. Instead, the research indicates that exemplary leaders are heavily involved with their followers, about whom they care deeply and to whom they are committed. Research by James Kouzes and Barry Posner has identified five basic practices, which are enduring and universal that define leadership excellence. These

	EXHIBIT 7.4
Leadership traits.	

BASIC TRAITS	OTHER TRAITS
Compulsiveness	Charisma
Conscientiousness	Empathy
Dominance	High Energy
Emotional Stability	Intuitiveness
Enthusiasm	Maturity
Self-assurance	Team Orientation
Social boldness	
Tough-mindedness	

Source: United States Small Business Administration, Managing Your Business, "Leadership Traits," November 5, 2005. *www.sba.gov/managing/leadership/traits.html.* The seven basic traits are attributed to early research by Raymond Cattell.

practices include: (1) a willingness to seek out better ways of doing things, departing from the status quo and taking risks; (2) sharing a vision of a desired future state that engages the aspirations of others, (3) sharing power through delegation and trust; (4) leading by example or walking the talk; and (5) providing encouragement and recognition.[13]

Another fundamental component of leadership is demonstrated by how leaders deal with adversity and how they develop from the challenges of failure and bad times. Exhibit 7.5 identifies several key behaviors that have been exhibited by leaders who have dealt successfully with adversity and who have used it for the benefit of their organizations, others, and themselves.

This chapter's feature on supervisors and performance warns against over-controlling supervisors or **micro-management.**

LEADERS OF DIVERSE WORKFORCES

Leaders routinely rely on a participative leadership style. But leading a diverse workforce calls for leaders who truly value diversity. **Pluralistic leaders** help create work environments that invite everyone's involvement by promoting cooperation and mutual respect.[14] Here are two suggestions to help you become a pluralistic leader.

First, uncover barriers. You need to know what problems, if any, exist for the individuals under your influence. Do company policies, customs, rituals, ceremonies, and procedures block their progress? Do they ridicule or ignore anyone's ethnic background or personal condition? If so, what can be done to eliminate the barriers? Are

micro-management
close supervision, which leaves little room for employee discretion

pluralistic leaders
leaders who capture the benefits of diverse workforces by seeking input from all employees

EXHIBIT 7.5	Dealing with adversity.

- Approaching difficult situations in an honest and open manner

- Demonstrating personal sacrifice

- Listening to everyone who is affected by the situation

- Learning from one's failures and recognizing their role in learning

- Protecting those who fail for the right reasons from developing a fear of failure

- Persisting after failures and recognizing change will have setbacks

- Recognizing the signals from adversity for the need to change

- Confronting adversity by honestly collecting and analyzing the facts

- Understanding that failures by oneself and others are not incompatible with leadership

Sources: Bruce J. Alolio and Fred Luthans. *The High Impact Leader: Moments Matter in Accelerating Authentic Leadership Development.* New York: McGraw-Hill (2006). Cy Charney. *The Leader's Tool Kit: Hundreds of Tips and Techniques for Developing the Skills You Need.* New York: American Management Association (2006). Jim Collins. *Good to Great.* New York: Harper Collins Publishers (2001). Morgan W. McCall, Jr. *High Flyers: Developing the Next Generation of Leaders.* Boston: Harvard Business School Press (1999). Jeffrey Pfefer and Robert I. Sutton: *The Knowing-Doing Gap: How Smart Companies Turn Knowledge into Action.* Boston: Harvard Business School Press (2000). Robert E. Quinn. *Building the Bridge As You Walk On It.* San Francisco: Jossey-Bass (2004).

diverse individuals and groups able to communicate and work in harmony with one another? If not, why not? Is your company's management really committed to valuing diversity and empowering women, the differently abled, and minorities? You should examine your own attitudes for any biases, values, stereotypes, and actions that inhibit your ability to value and lead people who are different from you. You can use personal interviews, group meetings, an anonymous survey, or a combination of these to help you.

Second, make personal commitments. You need to have an honest commitment to encourage two-way communication between you and individuals different from you. Through such communication you gain new knowledge and perceptions that help you better understand each individual for whose working life you are responsible. You must have a personal commitment to eliminate unequal and unfair treatment based on an individual's age, sex, sexual orientation, physical limitations, race, nation of origin, or religion. Make a commitment to train, coach, and empower your diverse employees to

SUPERVISORS AND
PERFORMANCE

Some supervisors or managers are described as having a "hands on" style. While such a description can have a positive connotation when it refers to someone who is energetic and who pitches in to help with the work, it often refers to a style of micro-management, which has a very different meaning. Supervisors who micro-manage reduce the descretion of associates by providing detailed instruction, eliminating autonomy, and limiting the range of issues over which employees can make decsions. Micro-managers, who also may be referred to as controlling, can cause employees to feel dependent and as if they are being treated as children. Other manifestations of this style are very close supervision, short time spans of discretion, or a supervisor's penchant for "hovering" in close promixity while employees attempt to perform their jobs.

Clearly, such a supervisory approach is likely to lead to employee frustration and poor morale. Employees spend more time creating paper trails because they expect to be second-guessed and as they spend time creating protection for themselves, productive time is lost. The organization's creative people are also likely to leave as they see no future within such a controlling environment. In addition, the lack of trust conveyed by micro-management has other serious consequences because performance is positively associated with the degree of trust within the organization. When supervisors and managers trust their employees and vice versa, decisions are made more quickly and problems are dealt with at lower levels within the organization. In the absence of trust, the opposite effects are evident. A sense that employees are incapable of performing may become part of the unit's culture and lead to a self-fulfilling downward spiral.

Aside from these unfortunate effects, micro-management also tends to retard the development of employees because they have few opportunities to exercise independent decision-making and judgment. With a micro-managing supervisor, employees are less likely to take the initiative to solve problems because of fear that they will be criticized by the supervisor for not obtaining approval before responding. Furthermore, micro-managers tend to spend so much of their time focusing inward on details within the unit, they have less time to devote to planning or for more strategic issues, such as scanning the external environment for developments that may impact their units in the future. In addition, while micro-managers often justify their over-contolling approaches with cost savings or efficiency rationales, their approaches may be more costly to the organization because of the inefficiences and associated costs.

Sources: Jared Sandberg. "Overcontrolling Bosses Aren't Just Annoying; They're Also Inefficient," *Wall Street Journal* (March 30, 2005), B1. Robert Galford and Anne Seibold Drapeau. "The Enemies of Trust," *Harvard Business Review* (February 2003), pp. 89–95.

draw the best from them. "It's not enough to hire for diversity; you must also plan for the development of your nontraditional workers."[15] When an organization cannot keep its diverse employees, it usually means that the organization is sending clear signals that success is not possible for these people.

GLOBAL

TRENDS IN APPROACHES TO LEADERSHIP

The earlier description of General Cota's leadership by example was from a command-and-control military setting. Leadership by example is a timeless leadership principle that all supervisors should keep in mind as a continual reminder of ideal leadership behavior. On the other hand, with the exception of military and emergency services organizations, which are also changing to allow more honest upward feedback, **command-and-control leadership** approaches are being replaced with newer power sharing approaches. Leadership approaches are changing in other countries as well. For example, Japanese electronics companies are beginning to select chief executives for their managerial skills instead of in-depth knowledge of engineering and operations. Atsutoshi Nishida, who is the CEO of the Japanese company Toshiba, exemplifies this trend as he was pursuing a doctoral degree in history when he came to work for the company 30 years ago.[16]

Changing leadership styles are evident in the following description of leadership by David Gergen, the director of the Center for Public Leadership at Harvard University. Gergen, who was an advisor to four U.S. presidents, describes how leadership is changing to a new model and the role that women, as well as men, play in leadership:

> The old [leadership] style was top-down, command-and-control, and directional. If you see the movie *Patton* with George C. Scott, you will spot it instantaneously. There are many other examples . . . "Chainsaw Al" Dunlap as CEO, Bobby Knight on the basketball court . . . Today that kind of command-and-control leadership has given way to a new approach, often called an influence model of leadership. Instead of picturing a leader at the top of a pyramid, we envision her in the middle with spokes extending outward. Instead of hurling thunderbolts from atop Mount Olympus, the new leader persuades, empowers, collaborates, and partners. The best leader, we are finding, is one who identifies top talent and nurtures them to become leaders in their own right—a leader of leaders.[17]

This new model of leadership is well suited to some of the unique strengths of women who are steadily taking on more leadership roles.

command-and-control leadership leadership that emphasizes power based on authority and obedience to a supervisor's directives

DIVERSITY

MEN, WOMEN, AND LEADERSHIP

There is a substantial amount of research on the differences in leadership approaches that are associated with gender. Before examining the differences, it is good to remember that regardless of whether there is a slightly greater likelihood that a man or woman will exhibit a particular leadership or managerial behavior, there will always be both men and women who exhibit behaviors predicted for the other gender. Accordingly, we should not expect to be able to predict, with much precision, how someone will lead based on gender. Nonetheless, there are some interesting differences that hold promise for improved leadership in the future.

Some of the most interesting findings have been identified as a result of differences in the thought processes of women and men. One difference is that women process information differently than men, as they tend to integrate details more rapidly while men compartmentalize data and ignore material deemed to be extraneous. Such differences may be related to physiological differences in the brains of women in that they have a larger number of nerve connections between the left and right parts of their brains. Hormonal differences may also come into play as male testosterone has the effect of focusing attention while the lower levels of testosterone present in women may be associated with broader viewpoints. These differences may provide women with the advantage of broader vision, thinking in terms of systems, and greater tolerance for ambiguity. Furthermore, some of these differences appear to provide women with stronger intuitive skills, which have advantages for decision-making.[18]

There are also gender-related differences that are more directly reflected in leadership and managerial approaches. More specifically, women tend to have greater mental flexibility, better verbal skills, and better social skills. In addition, they tend to be better than men in collaborative efforts, the ability to empathize, power sharing, and networking. When all of these skills are considered along with those noted earlier, women have some natural advantages for the collaborative leadership environment that is likely to evolve in the future.[19]

Unfortunately, the natural talents of women are not always utilized in many organizations and in the larger society in which we live. For example, Gail Evans, the first female executive vice president at CNN, and a prolific writer on women leaders has observed that women likely take on responsibilities even when they are not provided with the authority that would normally accompany such responsibilities. However, when problems occur and there is a need for authority, women sometimes are subject to blame when there is no successful resolution.[20]

Supervisors need to keep these differences in mind as they utilize the talents of their employees and help them develop their leadership skills.

LEADERSHIP BEHAVIORS

Research has revealed that there are essentially three major categories of specific leader behaviors. These categories include specific behaviors directed toward tasks, relationships with people, and change. These categories and examples, which were developed by Gary Yukl, are presented in Exhibit 7.6. These specific behaviors enable us to recognize what leaders do and help us see such behaviors in our own daily lives. Since these behaviors are quite specific, they can help you identify how to be a better leader. As you study the categories and specific examples, rate yourself on how many of them you put to use regularly. Try to relate each to your knowledge of human motivation. Finally, consider how each ties in with your roles as educator, counselor, judge, and spokesperson.

Learning Objective Number Two

CONTINGENCY MODELS OF LEADERSHIP

Several researchers have attempted to explain leadership effectiveness with contingency models. These models draw on a small number of key factors to explain how the effectiveness of leadership approaches varies across different situations. The research underlying these models shows that leadership can be improved in specific situations by assessing the leadership characteristics of leaders, evaluating the extent

| **EXHIBIT 7.6** | **Examples of task-, relations-, and change-oriented behaviors.** |

TASK-ORIENTED BEHAVIORS

- Organize work activities to improve efficiency.
- Plan short-term operations.
- Assign work to groups or individuals.
- Clarify what results are expected for a task.
- Set specific goals and standards for task performance.
- Explain rules, policies, and standard operating procedures.
- Direct and coordinate work activities.
- Monitor operations and performance.
- Resolve immediate problems that would disrupt the work.

RELATIONS-ORIENTED BEHAVIORS

- Provide support and encouragement to someone with a difficult task.
- Express confidence that a person or group can perform a difficult task.
- Socialize with people to build relationships.
- Recognize contributions and accomplishments.
- Provide coaching and mentoring when appropriate.
- Consult with people on decisions affecting them.
- Allow people to determine the best way to do a task.
- Keep people informed about actions affecting them.
- Help resolve conflicts in a constructive way.
- Use symbols, ceremonies, rituals, and stories to build team identity.
- Recruit competent new members for the team or organization.

CHANGE-ORIENTED BEHAVIORS

- Monitor the external environment to detect threats and opportunities.
- Interpret events to explain the urgent need for change.
- Study competitors and outsiders to get ideas for change.
- Envision exciting new possibilities for the organization.
- Encourage people to view problems or opportunities in a different way.
- Develop innovative new strategies linked to core competencies.

CHANGE-ORIENTED BEHAVIORS

- Encourage and facilitate innovation and entrepreneurship in the organization.

- Encourage and facilitate collective learning in the team or organization.

- Make symbolic changes that are consistent with a new vision or strategy.

- Encourage and facilitate efforts to implement major change.

- Announce and celebrate progress in implementing change.

- Influence outsiders to support change and to negotiate agreements with them.

Source: Yukl, Gary A., *Leadership in Organizations,* 6th Edition, © 2006. Adapted by permission of Pearson Education, Inc., Upper Saddle River, NJ.

to which leadership situations differ in terms of these factors, and matching leaders with situations.[21] Some of the better known of the contingency theories are Fred Fiedler's contingency theory of leadership, the path-goal theory of leadership effectiveness developed by Robert House, and the life-cycle theory developed by Paul Hersey and Ken Blanchard.[22]

FIEDLER'S CONTINGENCY THEORY OF LEADERSHIP

Fred E. Fiedler and others have speculated that the effectiveness of a group or organization depends on two main factors: (1) the leader's personality and (2) the leadership situation. As a consequence of their personalities, leaders tend to be either task oriented or relationship oriented. The situation determines the leader's authority and power and places limits on his or her ability to get things done through others. Fiedler's situational factors include leader-member relations, task structure or nature of the task, and the leader's positional authority to punish or to reward.[23]

LEADERSHIP PERSONALITIES

According to Fiedler's contingency model (sometimes called *situational leadership*), leaders are primarily motivated by their tasks or their interpersonal relationships with their followers. Whether one or the other is an appropriate focus depends on the leader's situation. Task-oriented leaders seek accomplishments that fortify their sense of self-esteem and competence. Relationship-oriented leaders seek the admiration and respect of their followers to meet their social and esteem needs. Both types of leaders need to be able to play both kinds of roles. The task-oriented leader may, as the need arises, adopt the relationship orientation. A relationship-oriented leader may focus on getting the job done when a crisis arises and time is short. But each will then return to her former orientation. This flexibility marks a true leader who is destined to achieve higher authority. Not all people have this flexibility. [24]

PERFORMANCE

THE LEADERSHIP SITUATION

According to Fiedler's contingency model, a leader's situation has three variables: (1) the degree to which the leader is or feels accepted by followers, (2) the degree to which the task to be accomplished is structured or defined, and (3) the extent of the leader's power—her job description and the influence over others in the organization. The greater the leader's power and acceptance by followers and the more highly structured the task, the easier it is for the leader to control a situation.[25] Research into the contingency model shows that task-oriented leaders perform best when they have either high or low concentrations of power, control, and influence over their situations. Relationship-oriented leaders perform best with moderate power, control, and influence.[26] Leaders should be matched to the situation that calls for their favored approach or orientation. Instead, organizations often require managers to adjust to a variety of situations calling for different approaches.

HOUSE'S PATH-GOAL THEORY OF LEADERSHIP

Path-goal theory is a complex contingency leadership theory, which maintains that there are four leadership behaviors: directive, supportive, participative, and achievement-oriented, which depict a range in styles from task orientation to people orientation As with other contingency theories, the theory is applied by matching leader behaviors with the leadership situations according to the nature of the work setting (environmental factors) and characteristics of employees (subordinate factors).[27] Although researchers have tested the model many times, its complexity has provided challenges in the assessment of its ability to explain leader effectiveness. Researchers have found that the model is less useful in predicting leader effectiveness when there is uncertainty about effort requirements, uncertainty about goals (likelihood of performance), and under stressful conditions.[28] With these limitations in mind, it can be stated that various combinations of leader, job, and employee characteristics determine the effectiveness of different leadership approaches and that successful leaders are sensitive to the problems encountered by employees and have the flexibility to adapt their styles to these different conditions.[29]

HERSEY AND BLANCHARD'S LIFE-CYCLE THEORY

People need different styles of supervision and leadership at different times. Paul Hersey and Kenneth Blanchard have given us a theory that explains the importance of adapting one's leadership approach to differences in employee experience. The life-cycle theory maintains that the new or less experienced employee needs a high amount of direction or task focus. Accordingly, the leader would use a telling approach in which he or she tells the employee what to do. As the employee acquires new knowledge and skills and demonstrates competence, she requires a more supportive relationship with the supervisor and somewhat less emphasis on direction and the task. With this focus, the supervisor would use a selling approach, which involves persuading the employee to do something. As the employee becomes even more experienced, but may lack confidence to take on a new task, the leader maintains a supportive relationship but reduces the amount of direction even further. This is essentially a participative approach in which the employee makes the decision about what actions to take. With employees who have matured in both tenure and capabilities, the supervisor can move to a low direction approach. For these types of employees, the supervisor does not need to provide support and uses a delegating approach that leaves the decision about what to do to the employee's discretion.[30] Some researchers have noted that the models' predictions may not be valid for all types of employees.[31]

Learning Objective Number Three

EMOTIONAL INTELLIGENCE

Daniel Goleman has developed a concept called **emotional intelligence,** which appears to be a critical characteristic of effective leaders. Goleman has found that there are five components of emotional intelligence: self-awareness, self-regulation, motivation, empathy, and social skill. *Self-awareness* essentially refers to one's understanding of how pressures and influences from others affect one's own behavior toward others. For example, leaders with high self-awareness who know that they may react poorly toward others when facing a tight deadline focus on preparation and lead-time to avoid the pressures of deadlines. Another example is that they ask for help when overloaded.[32]

emotional intelligence a multidimensional theory of leadership behavior based on personal skills and knowledge associated with maturity

Self-regulation pertains to controlling one's emotions. For example, when a team the leader is supervising has performed poorly, she would not lash out at the team or engage in a display of anger and bad temper. Instead, the leader would calmly and carefully provide feedback regarding the poor performance without judgment and then analyze the reasons for the poor performance, including her own role. The leader would assemble the team, describe the performance, provide an analysis of the causes, and offer a solution or involve the group in development of a solution. Self-regulation is in stark contrast to the impulsiveness of leaders whose fiery temper and outbursts are sometimes described as components of charismatic leadership. Goleman's research has found that such impulsiveness typically limits the effectiveness of leaders at higher organizational levels.

Motivation in terms of emotional intelligence means that the leader has a greater desire to achieve than to obtain an impressive title, big salary, or status. Instead, leaders with high emotional intelligence have a passion for the work they do and want creative challenges. They are also committed to the organization. Interestingly, they enjoy keeping score of how they are doing and continually raise the bar of performance.

Empathy allows leaders with high emotional intelligence to factor in employees' feelings when they make decisions. They spend time listening and are attuned to how others are feeling. Goleman provides the following strong support for the importance of empathy:

> In what is probably sounding like a refrain, let me repeat that empathy doesn't get much respect in business. People wonder how leaders can make hard decisions if they are "feeling" for all the people who will be affected. But leaders with empathy do more than sympathize with people around them: they use their knowledge to improve their companies in subtle but important ways.[33]

The final component of emotional intelligence is *social skill,* which enables leaders with high emotional intelligence to maintain good interpersonal relationships. Such skills enable leaders to find common ground with a variety of people, establish rapport, and understand others.

EXAMPLE OF EMOTIONAL INTELLIGENCE

A supervisor who has high emotional intelligence will deal with an employee who has become involved in a conflict with another employee by calmly listening to the employee's description of the situation and how he or she perceives the issues. Employees of an emotionally intelligent supervisor will probably have developed some skills for resolving conflicts from vicarious observations of the supervisor's approaches in the past. However, occasionally employees will not be able to resolve the situation on their own and will seek help from the supervisor. The emotionally intelligent supervisor will demonstrate empathy by making time available to talk to the employee, by listening carefully, and by asking questions to make sure that he or she understands the situation. Such questions commonly help the employee gain insights into the causes and solutions for the problem. The supervisors may also recall a past incident in which she dealt with such a similar conflict and will help the employee work through potential approaches to the problem.

Learning
Objective
Number Four

On the other hand, if the employee takes no responsibility for resolving the conflict or wants to hand off the problem, the supervisor will encourage the employee to take responsibility for resolving the issue by herself. In other cases, the supervisor will make a determination that she needs to become involved in resolving the conflict. In such cases, the supervisor will use the same calm and empathetic approach in talking to and gathering information from the other person. She will be well aware that there are always two or more sides to an incident, and that it will do no good to prejudge the situation. Most likely at some point in the conflict resolution process, the supervisor will visit with both employees, find a way for each one to save face, and discuss how the conflict can be avoided in the future.

LEVEL 5 LEADERS

Jim Collins and his research team studied companies that made the transition from being only good to great. They classified companies on the basis of their stock returns over a period of 30 years and identified 11 companies that met the criterion of reaching a transition point after which they obtained stock returns at least three times the level of the market for a period of 15 years. When they examined the difference between a comparison group of companies and great companies, they found that outstanding leadership was one of the factors that made the difference in their success. As a result of their studies of great companies, they developed a concept called *Level 5 Leadership.*

Level 5 leaders
fiercely competitive
leaders who
combine humility
and personal
sacrifice with high
performance
expectations and a
commitment to the
organization

Collins and his team found that **Level 5 leaders** are characterized by personal humility, in that they are modest and not boastful; they attribute their company's success to other people and not to themselves. They also have fierce resolve and a quiet determination. Their determination has been described, as "an unwavering resolve to do whatever must be done to produce the best long-term results, no matter how difficult."[34] They motivate others with high standards instead of personal charisma. When things go wrong, they look in the mirror to assign blame, but when they assign credit for successes, they look out the window toward others. Their ambition is typically manifested in a desire for the company to flourish in the future, instead of personal ambition. Examples of Level 5 leaders include Alan Wurtzel, former CEO of Circuit

City, and the late Darwin Smith, a previous CEO of Kimberly-Clark.[35] The research results of Collins and his team illustrate the importance of having the right people in place. Their results indicate that Level 5 leaders started with getting the right people in place instead of beginning with a vision or strategy:

> We expected that good-to-great leaders would start with the vision and strategy. Instead, they attended to people first, strategy second. They got the right people on the bus, moved the wrong people off, ushered the right people to the right seats—and then they figured out where to drive it.[36]

ETHICS

This chapter's feature on ethics provides a reminder of the importance of the leader's actions because of the signals they send others about appropriate behavior.

EXAMPLE OF LEVEL 5 LEADERSHIP

A supervisor who is operating at Level 5 may do the following. He consults with employees to ask how a problem should be solved and is genuinely interesting in their inputs. As a result, the employees understand that their ideas and knowledge are important. When employees perform well, the supervisor takes time to tell them what a great job they are doing. Employees know that the Level 5 supervisor has high standards of performance so they understand that good feedback and compliments are sincere and carry great meaning. In addition, the supervisor is quick to give the credit for the good performance of the unit to the employees and does not want to take credit from employees. Furthermore, the supervisor foregoes personal benefits so that more resources will be available to his employees. For example, when new computer equipment is made available, a Level 5 supervisor will probably insist that he not receive any until all employees in the unit receive new equipment.

MANAGEMENT AND LEADERSHIP STYLES

Four main styles of management are available to you: bureaucratic, autocratic, democratic, and spectator. All but the bureaucratic style are leadership styles. Each can have either a positive or a negative impact on your employees, depending on their characteristics and the situation. As we will see, each has its place and, when used appropriately, can help you motivate people and create an environment that fosters both quality and productivity. As a leader-supervisor, you must be able to use all three leadership styles as the need for each arises.

With the autocratic style, managers hold most of the formal authority. The manager–leader may announce a decision or ask for feedback on it before it is implemented, but the decision is made by the manager–leader. A manager who takes the middle position, the democratic style, asks employees to play a part in making the decision. They may be asked to help define a problem, come up with alternatives, or evaluate alternatives. Finally, with the spectator style, the manager delegates to employees the authority they need to make their own decisions, individually or through teams.

Learning Objective Number Five

SUPERVISORS AND ETHICS

The ethical standards of supervisors are revealed in relatively small matters, such as those that involve small amounts of money. Relatively routine actions of supervisors take on greater importance than those of individual contributors because their employees or associates look to them for guidance on appropriate behavior. Even relatively private matters that are not likely to be observed by employees are often revealed to them through informal communications with employees in other organizational units. For example, if a supervisor cuts corners and overstates expenses when filing for reimbursement, information is likely to get back to employees from such sources as friends who work in claims processing or administrative assistants who process the claims. Supervisors can be assured that extravagant or dishonest claims will become a hot topic of employees who typically are not likely to have significant opportunities for travel. Because the character and ethical standards of supervisors and managers are revealed in the smallest of such actions, supervisors must not be tempted to take liberties in such matters or resort to expedient approximations that may undermine the importance of accurate reporting in other matters.

It is somewhat ironic that one of the largest public accounting firms in the United States was recently involved in an ethics incident and litigation related to the costs of travel charged to its clients. The firm had engaged in the practice of billing its clients for the full costs of travel while it was also obtaining volume discounts and rebates from airlines and other firms in the travel industry. These funds were not returned to the firm's clients nor were their clients told of these discounts.

Source: Jonathan Weil. "Pricewaterhouse Coopers Partners Criticized Travel Billing," *Wall Street Journal* (September 30, 2003): C1-C9.

THE BUREAUCRATIC STYLE

bureaucratic style a management style characterized by the manager's reliance on rules, regulations, policies, and procedures to direct employees

The **bureaucratic style** is typified by the manager's reliance on rules, regulations, policy, and procedures. To him, they represent authority and certainty. It is management by the book. Through the exercise of this style, the manager adopts the posture of a police officer religiously enforcing rules and depending on superiors to resolve problems not covered in the manual.

Unlike the other three styles, the bureaucratic style cannot really be a leadership style, because managers who practice it are not really directing their people in a personal way. Instead, they are directing them through regulations, procedures, and policies.

Prerequisites. There are three major prerequisites for the use of the bureaucratic style:

1. All the other styles must be inappropriate for use.
2. Employees subjected to this style must need it.
3. There is no latitude in decision-making or in deviations from procedures.

The bureaucratic style of management is appropriate in organizations where strict rules and regulations are required. Although bureaucratic managers must adhere to these rules, they must also show empathy toward their employees who must obey those rules.

Limitations*.* This style is appropriate for some governmental agencies, some military services, and some nonprofit enterprises, such as public hospitals. It has very little value in businesses, and if used improperly, it can be devastating to anyone with ambition and creativity who is subjected to it.

Employee reactions*.* This style does little to build motivation in employees. Employees tend to adopt an indifferent attitude toward their peers and their work. The supervisor becomes rather unimportant to employees and is perceived by them as a watchdog rather than a manager.

THE AUTOCRATIC STYLE

Leaders of the **autocratic style** keep power to themselves and do not delegate to their employees. The making of a final decision is reserved for the leaders alone. They keep their employees dependent on them for instructions, and they allow their employees to act only under their direct supervision.

Prerequisites*.* The necessary prerequisites for using the autocratic style are the following:

1. You are an expert in the practice of management, as well as in the handling of your employees' jobs.

autocratic style
a management and leadership style characterized by the retention by the leader of all authority for decision-making

The autocratic style of management lends itself to situations where you need short-term, high-quantity production out of your staff. Supervising repair and damage from a ruptured storm drain in New York City is one such situation.

2. Your employees need this approach.
3. You wish to communicate primarily by means of orders and detailed instructions.

Limitations. In general, you should restrict your use of this style to the following situations:

- When you are dealing with new employees who are unfamiliar with the tasks and methods they are expected to perform
- When time is short or when there is an emergency situation that does not allow you to explain the reasons for your orders
- When you are directing a stubborn or difficult employee who does not respond favorably to requests or the other styles of supervision
- When your authority is directly challenged

You should restrict your use of this style of supervision to the situations outlined. If you lack the prerequisites, you cannot use it effectively. Once the situation changes, you should shift to another leadership style. Keep in mind that the autocratic style is both a management style and a leadership style.

Employee reactions. People subjected to the autocratic style will generally be high-quantity producers, but only for the short run. They will tend to be tense and somewhat fearful of you. If the style is used too long—that is, after the need for it has ceased—employees will become resentful and withhold their normal contributions to the job. It is not a style that builds team players or encourages strong ties among workers. It also causes employees to become dependent on their leaders.

THE DEMOCRATIC STYLE

Managers of the **democratic style** adopt a "we" approach to their work and to their employees. They play the role of coach, drilling their teams on fundamentals and sharing decision-making authority with them. They make frequent use of problem-solving meetings. They delegate freely to employees who have earned their confidence, as well as to members of the group in general. They attempt to build a strong team spirit and to foster mutual respect with members of the team and with peers.

This style of supervision often goes by other names, such as the consultative, general, or participative style. It is a leadership style very much in use today.

Prerequisites. The following conditions are needed before you implement the democratic style:

1. You should have support from your boss to use it.
2. You should be willing to accept a certain number of mistakes and delays in the early stages of its implementation.
3. You should have a personal commitment to this style and a strong belief in its ability to motivate people. Once you extend this style to your employees, you will find it difficult to shift to a different style.
4. You should have carefully prepared your employees by means of initial delegations of some of your authority and be willing to consult with your employees on small matters during early use of the new style.
5. You should have a high degree of patience and time for group decision-making meetings.
6. You should be prepared to accept less-than-optimum solutions to problems.

Some supervisors may feel threatened by this style. If so, they should not attempt to use it until they have been trained in its use. An employee who has never before been asked for the time of day, let alone an opinion on new procedures, might become suspicious at sudden attempts to obtain her participation in matters affecting the department.

Limitations. This style is best used in the following situations:

- When your workers are highly skilled or highly experienced at their jobs
- Where time is sufficient to permit employees to participate as individuals or as a group
- When preparing groups or individuals for changes
- When attempting to solve problems common to the group, and when group support is needed to implement solutions
- When attempting to air gripes or otherwise relieve workers' tensions

Employee reactions. The great majority of today's workers are educated enough for the democratic style of leadership. They can achieve and sustain a high quality and quantity of output for extended periods when supervisors are democratic. Supervisors who use this approach are employee centered rather than work centered, and employees know it. They appreciate the trust and freedom that the supervisor gives them. This style strongly promotes cooperation and group spirit and gives morale a corresponding boost. Under

democratic style
a management and leadership style characterized by a sharing of decision-making authority with employees

If you supervise using the democratic style of management, you will share decision-making responsibility with your employees. This style works well with highly skilled or experienced workers.

TEAMS

the democratic style, workers tend to understand the contributions of their peers to a greater degree, and they get to know each other better than under the other two styles.

The transition at the Levi Strauss & Company plant in Murphy, North Carolina, points out the value of both democratic and spectator styles. The plant moved from a traditional, top-down autocratic style of management to a team-based mix of democratic and spectator styles.

> Tommye Jo Daves, a 58-year-old mountain-bred grandmother . . . is responsible for the plant which employs 385 workers and turns out some three million pairs of Levi's jeans a year. . . . [Through management training] . . . two lessons stuck with Daves: "You can't lead a team by barking orders, and you have to have a vision in your head of what you're trying to do." . . . She and her line supervisors have since been converting their plant . . . to team management, in which teams of workers are cross-trained for 36 tasks instead of one or two and thrust into running the plant, from organizing supplies to setting production goals to making personnel policy.[37]

The results? She and her team reduced the company's policy manual from 700 pages to 50. Quality and customer-response time improved, whereas costs and rejects declined. Nonetheless, the transition was not an easy one. Daves reports that she finds it difficult to refrain from being directive by telling team members what to do. Instead, with teams she asks for team members' ideas on how things should be done. She has found that even though she may have better insights, there is value in the learning that takes place when team members make their own decisions.[38]

THE SPECTATOR STYLE

The **spectator style,** sometimes called the *free-rein style,* is characterized by treating employees as independent decision-makers. The manager or manager–leader develops

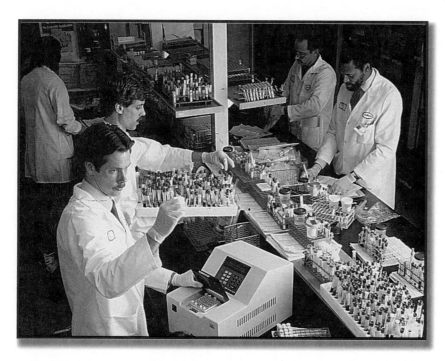

The spectator style of management is useful when your workers are experts in their field and enjoy working independently. Lab technicians are one such example. What could you do as a supervisor to motivate such workers?

a strong independent spirit in individual employees and teams and relies on their skills, knowledge, experience, and initiative. Employees, individually or in teams, perceive themselves to be professionals—that is, experts in their specialties.

spectator style
a management style characterized by treating employees as independent decision-makers

The supervisor becomes a facilitator, coach, and consultant. He remains available to employees and will intervene when asked to do so or when it is deemed necessary. Supervisors are generally physically removed from direct and frequent contact with employees, but continue to stay in touch through meetings, reports, and records of output. This style of leadership is usually the last phase in the evolution of the supervisor's approach to handling employees. This chapter's feature on supervising teams and the life-cycle theory of leadership both emphasize this point.

Prerequisites. The prerequisites of the spectator style of leadership are as follows:

1. Since workers are treated as experts, they must be highly experienced and skilled in their crafts.
2. Controls other than direct and frequent observations must be established to monitor the performance and interactions of both individuals and teams.
3. Workers, individually and collectively, must possess pride in themselves and their abilities as well as the qualities of endurance and initiative.

Limitations. The use of the spectator style should be restricted, as a rule, to the following groups or situations:

■ When your employees are highly skilled, experienced, and educated
■ When you are using outside experts, such as staff specialists, consultants, or temporary skilled help
■ When you as the boss are new at your job or lack personal experience in the work being performed by your employees

Employee reactions. Workers who work under the spectator style perceive themselves as being in business for themselves; that is, they adopt a somewhat independent air and see their boss as a kind of staff assistant who stands ready to help if needed. This style generally promotes high levels of individual output for indefinite periods. It fosters pride and morale better than the other styles. But if the boss becomes too remote or inaccessible, insecurity may set in, along with resulting stress, fears, and frustrations. All the workers are pretty much on their own and strongly feel the need to prove themselves to their boss and their peers. Consequently, people working under this style need constant reassurance that they are performing up to standard and that they are appreciated.

As a supervisor, team leader, or team facilitator, you must be familiar with all four management styles. You will be faced with employees, associates, and situations at one time or another that will call on you to use each of these styles.

During the training of a new employee, you should probably rely on the autocratic style, the bureaucratic style, or a blend of the two. Once the newcomer has been placed in his job and is performing up to standard, you should switch to one of the other styles of leadership. If you do not, your worker may rebel, and you will have contributed to his eventual termination.

If you try to use a style that is wrong for a specific employee, she will probably let you know it. Changes in an associate's attitudes and behavior are the first sign that you may be using an improper style of leadership. Selecting the proper style for individual workers is easy once you acquire some experience as a supervisor, but it may involve a bit of trial and error. Do not hesitate to switch if the style you are currently using fails to get the desired results. And don't forget that a lot of help is available to you through the advice and counsel of your peers and your superiors.

TEAMS

You may not be entirely free to select your own styles of leadership. Your boss may frown on the use of one or another of them. You also may feel inadequate in your understanding of how to implement one or more of the styles. Your tendency might be to use the one with which you feel most comfortable for all of your people. This is almost always a mistake. You should stand ready to offer the style each employee needs. Practice and study can enable you to feel confident enough to use all four styles successfully.

This chapter's feature of supervising teams provides some examples of how leading companies have been able to use teams for creativity.

Learning Objective Number Six

CHARISMATIC LEADERS

charismatic leaders
leaders who excel at communicating a vision for the future and in persuading others to become committed to achieving the vision

Leaders may be classified by whether they are charismatic or non-charismatic, although effective leaders do not have to be charismatic. **Charismatic leaders** have special qualities that enable them to move their followers beyond the status quo toward radical change. Leadership researchers Jay Conger and Rabindra Kanungo have found that there are three stages in the charismatic leadership process. In stage one, charismatic leaders assess the status quo in order to identify areas in which major changes are needed. They also determine the extent to which their followers' needs are being satisfied by the status quo. After examining resources and constraints, they develop long-term goals for improvement and advocate radical change from the status quo. In contrast to charismatic leaders, *administrators* either maintain the status quo or make only incremental changes.[39]

SUPERVISING TEAMS

Robbie Bach, a senior vice president at Microsoft, has established a reputation as someone who can provide leadership that results in good teamwork. More specifically, he has developed skills that enable him to harness the capabilities of groups that are frequently in conflict. These skills were refined earlier in his career while he worked in Europe with local units that were not united in their efforts and later in his work with Microsoft Office in which he consolidated the efforts of various marketing entities. More recently he has been tasked with creating a team that will be responsible for Microsoft's music products, including the use of the Xbox in digital music applications. In the past, some of Microsoft's initiatives in music products have trailed the competition because multiple units failed to work as part of a unified team effort.

While Microsoft has not always been successful with its teams, some other much smaller firms have prospered because of their effective use of teams. Under Steve Jobs' leadership, Apple Corporation, which is dwarfed by Microsoft's resources, has dominated the music player market with its iPod. At Apple, which is known for world-class innovation and risk taking, a team of 35 engineers created the iPod under the leadership of Tony Fadell. This wildly successful device was developed in only six months, which was the quickest important product development in Apple's history. IDEO is another world-class innovator that makes use of effective multidisciplinary teams to design new products. At IDEO, team members have different roles, such as the experimenter who facilitates the development of prototypes and the collaborator who helps members from different disciplines work together. IDEO relies extensively on brainstorming processes and its leaders minimize negativity during these sessions.

Sources: Robert A. Guth. "Microsoft Taps Xbox Leader for Music Fix," *Wall Street Journal* (June 14, 2005): B1–B3. John Markhoff. "Oh Yeah, He also Sells Computers," *New York Times* (April 25, 2004). Robert D. Hof, Peter Burrows, Steve Hamm, Diane Brady, and Ian Rowley. "Building an Idea Factory," *Business Week* (October 11, 2004): 194–200. Bruce Nussbaum. "Innovation at a Team Sport," *Business Week* (October 24, 2005): p. 144.

In stage two, charismatic leaders formulate their vision of what the situation will be like after the radical change. The manner in which charismatic leaders communicate their vision of the future often inspires their followers to action. Conger and Kanungo offer the following rich description of how leaders communicate their vision:

> Using expressive modes of action, both verbal and non-verbal, they manifest their convictions, self-confidence, and dedication to materialize what they advocate. In the use of rhetoric, words are selected to reflect their assertiveness, confidence, expertise, and concern for followers' needs. These same qualities may also be expressed through their dress, their appearance, and their body language. Charismatic leaders' use of rhetoric, high energy, persistence, unconventional and risky behavior, heroic deeds, and personal sacrifices all serve to articulate their high motivation and enthusiasm, which then become contagious among their followers.[40]

In stage three, charismatic leaders show their followers the tactics and behaviors that will enable them to achieve the vision. They work also to build trust with their followers. For example, they take great personal risks such as by putting their own wealth at risk, taking risks of being fired, or making personal sacrifices on behalf of their followers. Greater trust is established when leaders make greater personal sacrifices. Other important criteria for building trust are that the leader must be willing to work tirelessly on behalf of the vision and must be perceived to have great expertise in the area.[41]

Leadership researchers Robert House, James Woycke, and Eugene Fodor have used evaluations of historians to classify U.S. presidents into charismatic and non-charismatic categories. Those categorized as charismatic leaders include the following: Jefferson, Jackson, Lincoln, Theodore Roosevelt, Franklin Roosevelt, Kennedy, and Reagan.[42]

Unfortunately, there also is a dark side to charismatic leadership. The charismatic leader's total commitment to the vision may prevent the leader from recognizing problems that can derail its accomplishment. Because of their personal commitment of time and energy to the fulfillment of the vision, charismatic leaders sometimes become blind to better ways of accomplishing desired change. In essence, the charismatic leader's remarkable commitment to the vision can become his Achilles' heel. Charismatic leaders then become less effective because they dismiss valid criticisms or reject good suggestions provided by others.[43] Jay Conger points out how even Thomas Edison's strengths became a source of weakness:

> Thomas Edison, for example, so passionately believed in the future of direct electrical current (DC) for urban power grids that he failed to see the more rapid acceptance of alternating power (AC) systems by America's then-emerging utility companies. Thus the company started by Edison to produce DC power stations was soon doomed to failure. He became so enamored of his own ideas that he failed to see competing and, ultimately, more successful ideas.[44]

Learning Objective Number Seven

BECOMING A LEADER

CHANGING LEADERSHIP STYLES

Mort Myerson, a well-known and highly capable executive, helped Ross Perot build EDS into a giant of the information systems industry. In the 1980s, EDS merged with General Motors, and eventually Perot and Myerson left EDS. Several years later, Perot formed Perot Systems and asked Myerson to take over as CEO. Myerson found, after returning to a high-level leadership position, that his views on leadership had changed since leaving EDS and that the leadership environment had changed as well.[45] Myerson explained the change as follows:

> What I realized after I left was that I had also made a lot of people very unhappy. Our people paid a high price for their economic success. Eighty-hour weeks were the norm. We shifted people from project to project and simply expected them to make the move, no questions asked. . . . In terms of priorities, work was in first place; family, community, other obligations all came after. . . . We asked people to put financial performance before everything else, and they did. [46]

Myerson held extensive conversations with employees and customers during his first six months at Perot Systems and found examples of leadership, such as the following:

> I listened to some of our senior leaders talk about how they handled people on teams who didn't perform. I heard talk of "drive-by shootings" to "take out" nonperformers; then they'd "drag the body around" to make an example out of them.[47]

As a result of what he learned, Myerson became determined to change leadership at Perot Systems. He and his colleagues worked to change managers who were abusive to their employees and coached them toward improvement. Those who could not make the change were asked to leave. Myerson and his colleagues also concentrated on making the organization more humane and encouraged their employees to spend time on community programs and causes. They worked to develop greater concern for the welfare of both their employees and their customers. Myerson himself led by example by being accessible to employees and established honest, open, and direct communications.[48]

Another example of Myerson's leadership at Perot Systems and the values he displayed are illustrated in an incident related to the company's annual Christmas party. The Christmas party became an issue when Myerson realized that the company would be spending $360,000 for the party. When he asked about the rationale for the expenditure, he was told that employees enjoyed dressing up in tuxes and having a good time. Myerson's response was a directive to cancel the party:

> "Now, since I'm Jewish, that wasn't too . . . it wasn't received well—I'll put it that way. I said, 'Look, this has got nothing to do with being Jewish or Christian, this has got to do with the spirit of the holidays. I hereby cancel the party, and here's what we'll do.'
>
> "I said, 'We'll take the $360,000 and buy food and clothes and toys, and we will get our employees to take those things personally and deliver them to the inner city, to people who don't have anything'—which we did.
>
> "The result was, first, outrage that we canceled the party, then depression, then recognition that we were doing something different, and then elation for those who actually took those things."[49]

DEALING WITH MISTAKES

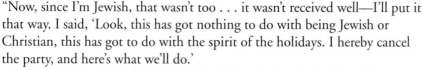

The manner in which leaders deal with their employees' mistakes reveals much about their style and the kind of persons they are. Similarly, the way organizations deal with mistakes speaks volumes about their cultures and the value they place on their employees. While supervisors and organizations may claim to value their employees, mistakes provide a critical test of leadership and fundamental supervisory values. In addition to the impact on the employee making a mistake, other employees observe the consequences of mistakes, and their future behavior is affected by their perceptions of the events.

An incident personally reported to one of the authors provides a good example of how mistakes should be handled. This incident involves a mistake by a plant manager in a leading company. The plant manager had been pressured by the higher-level corporate sales staff to make a million-dollar shipment of one of its products before he was absolutely certain of its quality. Unfortunately, the plant manager gave in to the pressure and shipped the product before he had sufficient assurance that all quality standards had been met. The shipment turned out to be flawed and had to be recalled, causing a million-dollar loss.

The plant manager's superiors decided that, although the company's financial performance for the year would be adversely affected, the manager had potential to develop in the future. Therefore, his bosses decided that they would not terminate or penalize him. They advised him of the seriousness of his mistake and stressed that he had to stand firm even when pressured by others in the organization. In the future he would have to make decisions that he knew were right. This incident, and the leadership demonstrated by the plant manager's superiors, have become part of the folklore of the company. As an interesting aside, the plant manager's superiors have said that they did not terminate him because the company had just invested one million dollars in his development! This investment paid off; the manager became one of the company's best plant managers.

This example shows how the values of the company's leaders guide their decisions about how to deal with a mistake. The leaders were convinced that the plant manager would learn from his mistake and that he deserved another chance. The plant manager's treatment undoubtedly increased his loyalty to the company and to his superiors. Perhaps more importantly, other employees in the organization became aware of the manner in which the mistake was handled. As a result, they have more confidence that they are valued by the organization and are more likely to feel that they will be treated fairly when they make mistakes.

The manner in which leaders handle mistakes also has an impact on the speed with which mistakes are reported to superiors. Some supervisors have a reputation of "shooting the messenger" who bears bad news. A railroad executive told one of the authors of an incident involving a train wreck. In this incident, lower-level employees knew of a correctable problem that could lead to a train wreck. Because the lower-level employees feared executives' reactions to bad news, they did not report the problem. Unfortunately, such examples are all too common, and in some instances such behavior may be representative of how employees perceive the organization's leaders and its culture.

When employees fear leaders' reactions to mistakes, they are less likely to admit their mistakes, request timely assistance, or call attention to problems. Mistakes are then more likely to be covered up or hidden. As a result, there will be less opportunity to correct problems in a timely manner. Consequently, the costs of dealing with the results of mistakes may become more severe. Poor leaders spend too much time placing blame for mistakes when their efforts should be focused on determining how such mistakes can be avoided in the future. Blaming employees may also lead to perceptions of unfair treatment because in some instances the fault for the mistake may lie squarely with the supervisor as a result of a failure to provide adequate instruction or training. There is a great deal of wisdom in the adage that leaders should reduce their efforts to "fix blame" and spend more time on "fixing problems." This does not mean that when employees repeatedly disregard established procedures, and make mistakes as a result, that there should be no adverse consequences. In such cases the supervisor must use progressive discipline, to change the employee's behavior, with termination being the final step if improvement is not forthcoming.

Supervisors should consider the following suggestions when dealing with mistakes. The most important is that the supervisor should focus on determining how the mistake can be avoided in the future. This requires an accurate diagnosis of the situation and answers to several questions. Were circumstances within the control of the employee? Did the employee have adequate instruction? Was the employee adequately trained? If the supervisor's diagnosis reveals that the employee's mistake occurred because the organization's reward system encouraged the wrong behaviors, then supervisors must work to make the system consistent with desired behaviors.

Supervisors have to recognize that employees are human and that even the best employees occasionally make mistakes. However, when supervisors fail to confront mistakes, other employees may view their failure to act as evidence that procedures, product quality, customer service, and so on, do not matter. Honest mistakes may be handled in a number of ways. One of the core ideologies of 3M, a highly effective, visionary company, is toleration of honest mistakes.[50] It is important that confrontations about mistakes occur in private. There is wisdom in the U.S. Navy's guideline that one should "praise in public, penalize in private."[51] Employees may be embarrassed or humiliated if coworkers overhear such discussions. Furthermore, coworkers may be embarrassed by the discussion and therefore feel that they have also been punished. Group admonishments should also be avoided because they punish the innocent.

THE BASIC STEPS TO BECOMING A LEADER

Based on his experience as an IBM marketing manager, Buck Rodgers offers the following nine steps for becoming an influential manager:[52]

1. *Establish who's in charge.* Each person in a unit within an organization must be clear about her authority, responsibility, and accountability.
2. *Know what you want to accomplish.* Define your goals, short and long term. Map out your priorities for each day. Monitor your use of time, and check on your progress regularly.
3. *Know what you want each person you manage to accomplish.* Set specific goals for a person to achieve, and let that person know the quality of performance expected. Judge performance on achievements, not on style.
4. *Let the person know what you expect.* Don't let people guess at what you want from them or about how they are doing. Communicate regularly with each individual about what you expect and about what will happen when those expectations are met, exceeded, or not met.
5. *Find out what your employee wants for himself.* Insist that each subordinate spell out goals, aspirations, and expectations.
6. *Find out what your employee expects of you.* What is expected in terms of help—more frequent or less frequent contact with you? More responsibility?
7. *Take being a role model seriously.* Subordinates do as you do more often than they do as you say they should do. Your example provides the psychological and performance models for your group.
8. *Expect others to be self-motivated, but don't count on it.* People have their peaks and valleys. You may need to intercede on occasion, helping subordinates to improve, grow, and prosper.
9. *Understand that the quality of your leadership is determined by the methods you use to motivate others.* What you use and apply to others will be used and applied to you. Open, honest, and sensitive communication builds mutual trust and respect.[53]

*Learning
Objective
Number Eight*

In addition to Rodgers' nine steps, another step is vital to becoming a leader. This step in leader behavior is increasingly important because companies continue to place greater emphasis on treating the customer or client as if he or she is always right, sometimes at the expense of the employee. This step is to be prepared to back up your people when they are abused. Southwest Airlines has been extraordinarily successful in part because of its legendary customer service. Nonetheless, Herb Kelleher, former CEO of Southwest Airlines, backs up his people and believes in firing a customer before an employee. As Kelleher has said, "The customer is frequently wrong . . . We write them and say, 'Fly somebody else. Don't abuse our people.'"[54]

ASSESSING YOUR LEADERSHIP ABILITY

You can rely on four major indicators as you attempt to determine the effectiveness of your leadership with your people: morale, group spirit, proficiency, and self-discipline. Each of these can help you measure the impact you are having on your formal group members, individually and collectively.

Morale

People's attitudes toward all the individuals, things, and events that affect them at work constitute their morale. *Morale* can be defined as an individual's state of mind with regard to his job, supervisor, peers, and company. Through the actions and statements of people, you can effectively measure their morale. If your employees are positive individuals who take pride in their work, they reflect favorably on you and your group. If they are absent frequently, fail to attend to their duties, or dwell on negative factors, you can assume that your leadership needs improvement.

Group Spirit

What are the major attitudes reflected by the members of your formal group and any informal groups associated with it? Are they positive and supportive, fostering teamwork and harmony, or are they negative and destructive? Both individual and group attitudes are shaped in large measure by your human relations efforts.

Proficiency

How good are you at your job? How good are your employees? Are you making an effort to improve both your own level of competence and theirs? Are you aware of any efforts of theirs to seek a higher level of competence? Are you fostering their growth and development? This indicator is tied directly to morale and group spirit. If these are below normal or negative, your employees will usually demonstrate low levels of proficiency.

Self-Discipline

Can your shop or office function in your absence? Do your people respond promptly and positively to your instructions? Do they readily accept honest criticism? Have you had to reprimand more often than praise? Do your people know the reasons behind what they are expected to do? Can they be trusted? If not, what are you doing about these problems?

You can rate yourself by using these indicators at any time. Chances are that your boss is doing so regularly. If you are placing the kind of emphasis that you should on your human relations, you should experience little difficulty in these general areas.

INSTANT REPLAY

1. Leadership is based on a person's formal authority and other sources of influence, such as one's personality, skills, knowledge, and personal relationships with others.

2. Not all leaders are managers, and not all managers are leaders. People who can get work done through willing followers who respect them are leaders.

3. Leaders vary in their traits, such as enthusiasm, tact, and endurance. No one set of traits is common to all leaders.

4. The contingency model of leadership holds that the effectiveness of a group or organization depends on the leader's personality and the leadership situation.

5. In general, the degree to which leaders should focus on tasks or people depends on their own abilities, their employees' abilities, and the situation they face at any given time.

6. Charismatic leadership is often required to implement radical change.

7. The manner in which leaders deal with employees' mistakes reveals much about their style and the effectiveness of their leadership in the long run.

8. Leadership effectiveness may be evaluated by assessing the morale of individual followers, their levels of proficiency, their self-discipline, and team spirit.

QUESTIONS FOR CLASS DISCUSSION

1. Can you define this chapter's key terms?

2. What are the components of the contingency model of leadership?

3. What are the four basic management styles? Which is not a leadership style? Why?

4. What style of supervision would you use in each of the following situations, and why would you use it?

   a. A new employee with two years' experience in a similar job

   b. An old-timer who appears to be an informal leader of one of the cliques in your department

   c. A neurotic employee, with a good deal of experience, whose neurosis is interfering with job performance

   d. An employee, with many more years experience than you have, who resents you and your authority

ASSESS THIS SITUATION

Purpose: To emphasize the differences between leadership and management.

Your Task: Read each listing, and indicate if it is unique to management (M) or leadership (L).

M	**L**	1. Creating a vision for the company or company unit
M	**L**	2. Engaging in day-to-day planning
M	**L**	3. Sensing the need for and producing the strategies for change
M	**L**	4. Setting the path for reengineering the company or its units
M	**L**	5. Setting up an organization structure
M	**L**	6. Controlling and problem solving
M	**L**	7. Inspiring and energizing people to overcome barriers
M	**L**	8. Producing a degree of predictability and order
M	**L**	9. Creating policies and procedures

SKILL BUILDING EXERCISE 7.1

Ray is a traditional supervisor of a toy department in a major chain of discount stores. After the store closed last night, he spent two hours setting up discount signs on various "specials" throughout his department that offered customers up to 25 percent discounts on several very popular items. The discounts he posted were faxed to him yesterday by company headquarters and were to remain in effect for the next seven days.

Shortly after opening the store this morning, one of his cashiers notified Ray that a customer was complaining about the scanner's price not matching the store's sale price for an item. Ray scanned the item and discovered that the new sale price was not recorded. Instead, the older, higher price was still in the computer's memory. Ray immediately told his cashier to honor the sale price and reported his finding to the store manager, Ukare Shimito.

Shimito seemed somewhat unconcerned, dismissing the problem as an "oversight" on her part, and told Ray that the sale price would be entered shortly. She gave Ray this advice: "If the customer discovers a price difference at checkout, honor the sale price you posted by the merchandise."

Throughout the day, cashiers notified Ray of several other price differences. All but one was in the store's favor; prices were higher than the sale placards advertised. By closing time, the sale prices still had not been entered into the computer.

What do you think of the store manager's response to Ray? If you were in Ray's position, what would you do now?

Your Task: Work in a small group or by yourself to develop answers for the following questions: (1) What do think of the store manager's response to Ray? (2) How is the manager's decision likely to affect the behavior of cashiers and other employees? (3) If you were facing Ray's situation, what would you do? (4) Develop a plan for Ray that includes the specific action steps that he should take in resolving this problem and predict the likely short- and long-term consequences.

SKILL BUILDING WRITING EXERCISE 7.2

Unfortunately, not all leaders are good people, and some have been described as being toxic. Indeed, some very effective leaders have been terribly flawed individuals. When leaders go astray, it is not uncommon to see their bad behaviors manifested in abuses of power. What makes matters worse is that people often find it difficult to resist terribly flawed or toxic leaders who do great damage to employees, citizens, companies, and organizations. Interestingly, toxic leaders sometimes gain control of others by misleading them into thinking that they can provide the means of satisfying their needs, such as those for success or safety.

When supervisors or employees are faced with a situation in which their leader is truly toxic and destructive, they may need to take actions to replace the leader. Some suggestions for dealing with such extreme situations include investigating and documenting the leader's past history and then passing on such information to colleagues, developing a coalition of credible others who have had similar experiences with the leader, and confronting the leader with the coalition asking for changes in his behavior. It is recommended that individual confrontations without witnesses should be avoided. More drastic measures involve the coalition's presentations of concerns to higher-level executives with calls for the leader's replacement.[55]

Your Task: Work alone or in a small group and identify a toxic leader with whom you or your group may have knowledge. If you or someone in your group does not know such an individual, find an example by talking to others outside your class, reading newspapers, or by conducting an Internet search. Write out answers to the following questions: (1) Describe the troublesome behaviors of the toxic leader and the impact on employees. (2) Provide a description of how the leader's behaviors have developed over time. (3) Offer potential explanations for the leader's behavior, such as his or her needs that may be satisfied by these behaviors. (4) If there has been a change in the leader's behavior or if he or she has been replaced or moved to another assignment, describe the conditions leading to the change.

CASE 7.1 Leadership at Malden Mills

Malden Mills, a family-owned textile company employing approximately 3,000 employees, is located in Lawrence, Massachusetts. During the early 1980s, the 90-year-old company went through bankruptcy but then recovered by placing heavy emphasis on research and development. Research efforts resulted in the development of two new textile products, Polartec and Polarfleece. These products, which are used in coats sold by such retailers as L.L. Bean and Patagonia, enabled the company to become profitable again. Unlike most of its competitors, Malden Mills retained its production facilities in the United States, paying approximately $11 per hour for wages ($15 including benefits) versus $2 to $3 per hour it could obtain with production in lower-wage countries. The company's high-tech products and equipment set it apart from labor-intensive textile manufacturers, and its emphasis on quality provides a competitive advantage.[56] The company's CEO, Aaron Feuerstein, says that "The quality of our product is paramount . . . and it's the employee who makes that quality. If the quality slips, the employee is in a position to destroy your profit."[57]

On December 11, 1995, the company had a fire that destroyed most of its production facilities. "Structural losses were enormous: 750,000 sq. ft. of manufacturing and office space in three buildings were destroyed . . ."[58] Feuerstein, who was 70 years old at the time, could have retired and collected the insurance money. Instead of retiring, he did the unthinkable and paid wages totaling almost $15 million. Two days after the fire, Feuerstein gave each employee a $275 Christmas bonus, and then he paid the entire workforce a full month's pay for December. In January, he paid employees again, even though the plant was still unfinished. And then he paid the employees again for a third month. Employee reactions to Feuerstein's actions were as follows:

> "When he did it the first time, I was surprised," said Bill Cotter. "The second time was a shock. The third . . . well, it was unrealistic to think he would do it again." Nancy Cotter finished her husband's thought: "It was the third time that brought tears to everyone's eyes."[59]

A majority of the company's workforce was back at work on a full-time basis by March. Incredibly, productivity reached 230,000 yards per week only a few weeks after the fire—it had produced 130,000 yards per week prior to the fire. Feuerstein explained that "Our people became very creative. They were willing to work 25 hours a day."[60] A few months later, 85 percent of the workforce was back on the job, although 400 others were still not on the job. Feuerstein covered their health insurance costs and promised employment with the company in 1997 after the company's new plant became operational. By 1997, all but 70 employees had been re-hired and the company's production facilities have been expanded to include state-of-the-art equipment.

Mr. Feuerstein, a deeply religious individual, said the following:

> I have a responsibility to the worker, both blue-collar and white-collar. . . . I have equal responsibility to the community. It would have been unconscionable to put 3,000 people on the streets and deliver a death blow to the cities of Lawrence and Methuen. Maybe on paper our company is worth less to Wall Street, but I can tell you it's worth more. We're doing fine.[61]

These actions related to the fire are not the only ways in which Feuerstein has demonstrated concern for his employees. He has a reputation for looking out for the interests of his people, such as by enabling employees to obtain heart bypass operations and by providing free soft drinks on the production lines when temperatures get too high.

Finally, there were other positive developments after the fire:

> Another type of loyalty figures in the Malden story: fidelity of the retail customer. In the first weeks after the fire, more than 10,000 letters poured in from retail customers vowing to buy Malden's products and nothing else. Brand identification, an integral part of Malden's rise to success in recent years, remains a driving force after the fire.[62]

Malden Mills Update[63]

Malden Mills filed for Chapter 11 protection from its creditors in November 2001. The fire at the company's facilities kept it out of the fleece market for two years, which allowed competitors to enter and take a sizeable share of the market. Unfortunately, some of Malden Mills' customers did not return after the company went back into production. A contributing factor to the company's financial difficulties was the general slowdown of the economy. Aaron Feuerstein emphasized that he is still convinced that paying his employees after the fire was the right thing to do. Feuerstein's commitment to his employees appears to have been validated as the firm came out of bankruptcy in the later part of 2003.

Sources: Ryan, Michael. "They Call Their Boss a Hero," *Parade Magazine* (September 8, 1996): 4–5. © 1996 Michael Ryan. Reprinted with permission. All rights reserved. John McCurry. "Loyalty Saves Malden Mills," *Textile World* (February 1997): 38–42. *All Things Considered.* National Public Radio (November 30, 2001). *Boston Business Journal,* "Malden Mills Emerges from Bankruptcy," (October 17, 2003).

Questions

1. What aspects of leadership do you see in the actions of Aaron Feuerstein?
2. Why did productivity at Malden Mills increase after the fire?
3. Why don't more leaders act like Aaron Feuerstein?

| CASE 7.2 | Winston Churchill |

Successful leaders often have the experience of prevailing in the face of adversity and learning from earlier failures. Leaders' skills also must match the circumstances. Winston Churchill's career provides a classic example.

Churchill began his remarkable political career in 1901 when he became a member of the House of Commons at the age of 26. Prior to his entry into Parliament he had seen combat as a cavalry officer in India, Cuba, and the Sudan and was awarded several medals for valor.[64] He rose quickly in politics and governmental service, becoming the First Lord of the Admiralty (civilian head of the British Navy) in 1911. One of Churchill's decisions about deployment of naval forces in 1915 during World War I resulted in failure and marked the end of his fast-track career. Churchill returned to combat, serving as an infantry officer in 1917. After World War I, Churchill returned to public office but was essentially relegated to the sidelines of politics. His calls for rearmament, warnings about the intentions of the Nazis between 1933 and 1939, and criticisms of the government's attempts to appease the Nazis were ignored. When things looked the worst in May 1940, the country turned to the 65-year-old Churchill for leadership as Prime Minister.[65] It is said that Churchill "stood out as the one man in whom the nation could place its trust."[66]

In June 1940, Britain had been at war with Germany for a year. British soldiers had been driven out of France and narrowly escaped capture through an evacuation from Dunkirk. France surrendered on June 22, and the United States had not yet entered World War II. The Battle of Britain, which involved heavy bombing of Britain's major cities, was about to begin, and it appeared that Germany would invade Britain. The outcome looked bleak.[67] In June 1940, Winston Churchill made the following speech to the British Parliament:

> I have, myself, full confidence that . . . we shall prove ourselves once again able to defend our island home, to ride out the storm of war, and to outlive the menace of tyranny, if necessary for years, if necessary alone . . . we shall not flag or fail. We shall go on to the end, we shall fight in France, we shall fight on the seas and oceans, we shall fight with growing confidence and growing strength in the air, we shall defend our island, whatever the cost may be, we shall fight on the beaches, we shall fight on the landing grounds, we shall fight in the fields and in the streets, we shall fight in the hills; we shall never surrender.[68]

Aside from speeches such as this, Churchill's hats, cigars, and two-fingered "V" for victory signs were distinctive, as well as symbolic, and endeared him to his followers.[69] There were other qualities about Churchill as well that made him well-suited for the challenges of leadership during these difficult times. Two specific examples of his personal risk-taking are described as follows:

> Churchill as Prime Minister frequently and deliberately ran terrible personal risks. But the people admired him for it, and loved his offhand disregard for danger. Once, when a German bomb landed near his car and nearly tipped it over, he joked, "Must have been my beef that kept the car down"—a reference to his pudginess.[70]

Winston Churchill . . . liked to leave his underground air-raid shelter in Whitehall for the streets the moment bombs began falling. Attempts were made to stop him, because the risk of getting one's head blown . . . "I'll have you know," thundered Churchill, "that as a child my nursemaid could never prevent me from taking a walk in the Green Park when I wanted to do so. And, as a man, Adolf Hitler certainly won't."[71]

At the end of World War II in 1945, Churchill lost his bid for reelection because he was unresponsive to the needs for social change after the war. He returned to office again as Prime Minister from 1951 to 1955, but his performance was limited by age and health problems. In general, his service as a peace-time Prime Minister did not measure up to his service during war time.[72]

Sources: John Keegan. "Churchill," *Time* (April 13, 1998): 114–118. Leonard Mosley. *The Battle of Britain,* Alexandria, VA: Time-Life Books, 1977. C. L. Mowat. "Sir Winston Leonard Churchill," in the *World Book Encyclopedia,* Vol. 3, Chicago: Field Enterprises Educational Corporation (1960): 424–426. Winston Churchill. Speech to the United Kingdom House of Commons, June 4, 1940. Brian L. Blakeley; "Sir Winston Leonard Spencer Churchill," *Encarta Encyclopedia,* Vol. 97. Microsoft Corporation, 1996.

Questions

1. What aspects of charismatic leadership were displayed in Churchill's speech to the Parliament?

2. Categorize Churchill's specific leadership actions in terms of the three stages of charismatic leadership described in this chapter.

3. Which of the leadership theories presented in this chapter explains why Churchill was a better leader during war than during peace? Explain.

4. Explain how Churchill was prepared to take on the leadership challenges of serving as Prime Minister.

REFERENCES

[1] "Thoughts on the Business of Life," *Forbes* (November 1, 2004).

[2] Garvin, David A., and Roberto, Michael A. "Change through Persuasion," *Harvard Business Review* (February 2005): 104–112.

[3] Ibid.

[4] Kotter, John P. "What Leaders Really Do," *Harvard Business Review,* (December 2001): 85–96. Kotter, John P. *A Force for Change: How Leadership Differs from Management,* New York: The Free Press (1990). Zimmerman, E. L. "What's Under the Hood? The Mechanics of Leadership Versus Management," *Supervision* (August 2001): 10–12.

[5] Ibid.

[6] Ibid.

[7] Ibid.

[8] Yukl, Gary, and Lepsinger, Richard. *Flexible Leadership: Creating Value by Balancing Multiple Challenges and Choices.* San Francisco: Jossey-Bass (2004).

[9] Chan, Sewell, and Newman, Andy. "Mass Transit Chiefs, Traveling Without the Masses," *New York Times* (November 19, 2004): A22.

[10] Rivlin, Gary, and Markoff, John. "Tossing Out a Chief Executive," *New York Times* (February 2005): C1, C4.

[11] United States Small Business Administration, Managing Your Business, "Leadership Traits," November 5, 2005. *www.sba.gov/managing/leadership/traits.html.*

[12] Kouses, James M., and Posner, Barry Z. *The Leadership Challenge: How to Keep Getting Extraordinary Things Done in Organizations.* San Francisco: Jossey-Bass (1995).

[13] Kouses, James M., and Posner, Barry Z. *The Leadership Challenge: How to Keep Getting Extraordinary Things Done in Organizations,* San Francisco: Jossey-Bass (1995).

[14] Loden, Marilyn, and Rosener, Judy B. *Workforce America!* Homewood, IL: Business One Irwin (1991): 180–194.

[15] Nelton, Sharon. "Winning with Diversity," *Nation's Business* (September 1992): 18–22, 24.

[16] Dvorak, Phred. "Toshiba's New CEO Is an Innovation: A Manager," *Wall Street Journal,* (August 25, 2005): B3–B4.

[17] Gergen, David. "Foreword: Women Leading in the Twenty-First Century," in Linda Coughlin, Ellen Wingard, and Keith Hollihan, Eds., *Enlightened Power: How Women Are Transforming the Practice of Leadership,* San Francisco: Jossey-Bass (2005): p. XIX.

[18] Fisher, Helen E. "The Natural Leadership Talents of Women," in Linda Coughlin, Ellen Wingard, and Keith Hollihan, Eds, *Enlightened Power: How Women Are Transforming the Practice of Leadership,* San Francisco: Jossey-Bass (2005): 133–140.

[19] Fisher. "The Natural Leadership Talents of Women."

[20] Evans, Gail. "Are We Looking After Each Other," in Linda Coughlin, Ellen Wingard, and Keith Hollihan, Eds. *Enlightened Power: How Women Are Transforming the Practice of Leadership,* San Francisco: Jossey-Bass (2005): 143–150.

[21] Turner, J. Rodney, and Muller, Ralf. "The Project Manager's Leadership Style as a Success Factor on Projects: A Literature Review," *Project Management Journal* (June 2005): 49–61.

[22] House, Robert J., and Aditya, Ram N. "The Social Scientific Study of Leadership: Quo Vadis?" *Journal of Management* (Issue #3, 1997): 409–473.

[23] Fiedler, Fred E. "The Contingency Model—New Directions for Leadership Utilization," *Journal of Contemporary Business 3*(4) (Autumn 1974): 65–80.

[24] Ibid.

[25] Ibid.

[26] House and Aditya. "The Contingency Model . . ."

[27] Turner and Muller. "The Project Manager's Leadership Style . . .". House and Aditya. "The Contingency Model . . ."

[28] House and Aditya. "The Contingency Model . . ."

[29] Wofford, J. C., and Liska, Laurie Z. "Path-Goal Theories of Leadership: A Meta-Analysis," *Journal of Management*, (Issue #4, 1993): 857–876.

[30] Paul Hersey, Kenneth H. Blanchard, and Dewey E. Johnson. *Management of Organizational Behavior for Leading Human Resources*, 8th ed., Upper Saddle River, NJ: Prentice Hall, 2001, p. 196. House and Aditya. "The Contingency Model . . ."

[31] House and Aditya. "The Contingency Model . . ."

[32] Goleman, David. "What Makes a Leader?" *Harvard Business Review* (November–December 1998): 93–102.

[33] Ibid., 101.

[34] Collins, Jim. "Level 5 Leadership: The Triumph of Humility and Fierce Resolve," *Harvard Business Review* (January 2001): 73.

[35] Ibid., 67–76.

[36] Ibid., 71.

[37] Huey, John, and Sookdeo, Ricardo. "The New Post-Heroic Leadership," *Fortune* (February 21, 1994): 44, 48.

[38] Huey and Ricardo. "The New Post-Heroic Leadership," 42–50.

[39] Conger, Jay A., and Kanungo, Rabindra N. "Behavioral Dimensions of Charismatic Leadership," in Jay A. Conger, Rabindra N. Kanungo, and Associates, *Charismatic Leadership: The Elusive Factor in Organizational Effectiveness*. San Francisco: Jossey-Bass (1988): 78–97.

[40] Ibid., 87.

[41] Ibid.

[42] House, Robert J., Woycke, James, and Fodor, Eugene M. "Charismatic and Noncharismatic Leaders: Differences in Behavior and Effectiveness," in Jay A. Conger, Rabindra N. Kanungo, and Associates, *Charismatic Leadership: The Elusive Factor in Organizational Effectiveness*. San Francisco: Jossey-Bass (1988): 98–121.

[43] Conger, Jay A. "The Dark Side of Leadership," *Organizational Dynamics* *19*(2) (1990): 44–55.

[44] Ibid.

[45] Myerson, Mort. "Everything I Thought I Knew About Leadership Is Wrong," *Fast Company* (April–May 1996): 71–79.

[46] Ibid., 72.

[47] Ibid., 72.

[48] Ibid.

[49] Colvin, Geoffrey. "Value-Driven: Think About This As You Don Your Tuxedo," *Fortune* (December 18, 2000): 74. Fortune, Geoffrey Colvin, © 2005 Time Inc. All rights reserved.

[50] Collins, J. C., and Porras, J. I. *Built to Last: Successful Habits of Visionary Companies,* New York: HarperCollins, 1994.

[51] Ricks, Thomas E. "Deep Trouble: A Skipper's Chance to Run a Trident Sub Hit Stormy Waters," *Wall Street Journal* (November 20, 1997): A6.

[52] Rodgers, Buck, with Levey, Irv. *Getting the Most Out of Yourself and Others,* New York: Harper & Row (1987).

[53] Source: "The Basic Steps to Being a Leader", pp. 122–127 (9 headers; text not reprinted) from Getting The Best Out of Yourself and Others by Buck Rodgers and Irv Levy. Copyright © 1987 by Francis G. Rodgers and Irving N. Levey. Reprinted with permission of HarperCollins Publishers.

[54] Peters, Tom. " 'Fountain of Youth'—And Low Fares," *Chicago Tribune* (September 26, 1994): sect. 4, 5.

[55] Kellerman, Barbara. "Leadership: Warts and All," *Harvard Business Review* (January 2004): 40–45. Lipman-Blumen, Jean. "The Allure of Toxic Leaders: Why Followers Rarely Escape Their Clutches," *Ivey Business Journal* (January/February 2005): 1–8.

[56] Ryan, Michael. "They Call Their Boss a Hero," *Parade Magazine* (September 8, 1996): 4–5. McCurry, John. "Loyalty Saves Malden Mills," *Textile World* (February 1997): 38–42.

[57] Ryan, Michael. "They Call Their Boss a Hero," *Parade Magazine* (September 8, 1996): 4–5. © 1996 Michael Ryan. Reprinted with permission. All rights reserved.

[58] McCurry. "Loyalty Saves Malden Mills," 38–42.

[59] Ryan, Michael. "They Call Their Boss a Hero," *Parade Magazine* (September 8, 1996): 4–5. © 1996 Michael Ryan. Reprinted with permission. All rights reserved.

[60] Ryan, Michael. "They Call Their Boss a Hero," *Parade Magazine* (September 8, 1996): 4–5. © 1996 Michael Ryan. Reprinted with permission. All rights reserved.

[61] Ryan, Michael. "They Call Their Boss a Hero," *Parade Magazine* (September 8, 1996): 4–5. © 1996 Michael Ryan. Reprinted with permission. All rights reserved.

[62] McCurry. 41.

[63] *All Things Considered.* National Public Radio (November 30, 2001).

[64] Keegan, John. "Churchill," *Time* (April 13, 1998): 114–118. Mowat, C. L. "Sir Winston Leonard Churchill," in the *World Book Encyclopedia,* Vol. 3, Chicago: Field Enterprises Educational Corp. (1960): 424–426.

[65] Keegan. "Churchill." Brian L. Blakeley. "Sir Winston Leonard Churchill," *Encarta Encyclopedia,* Vol. 97, Microsoft Corp., 1996.

[66] Keegan. 116.

[67] Mosley, Leonard. *The Battle of Britain,* Alexandria, VA: Time-Life Books, 1977.

[68] Churchill, Winston. Speech to the United Kingdom House of Commons, June 4, 1940.

[69] Mowat. "Sir Winston Leonard Churchill." Mosley. *The Battle of Britain.*

[70] Mosley, 60.

[71] Ibid., 148.

[72] Keegan. "Churchill." Blakeley. "Sir Winston Leonard Churchill."

8

"The power of technology . . . to build . . . and destroy . . . is such . . . that it is likely . . .
few of us have ever heard . . . the name of what will be the
world's largest company in 2020."[1]

Juan Enriquez

Objectives

After reading and discussing this chapter, you should be able to do the following:

1. Explain how people form their attitudes.
2. List and briefly explain the techniques available to change people's attitudes.
3. Explain how to implement change.
4. Describe the barriers to change.
5. List and briefly explain the basic steps you can take to change a person's attitude.
6. Describe how to use persuasion to facilitate change.

Changing Leadership at the New York Times

The New York Times *has been a veritable icon in the newspaper publishing business for many decades. The newspaper's reporters have been some of the most widely read and admired newspaper people in the world, and in 2002 alone* Times *reporters won seven Pulitzer prizes. Nonetheless, like all organizations, the* Times *has not been resistant to the pain of management problems nor immune from the need to change. In the 19-month period, beginning in 2001, during which Howell Raines served as executive editor, the newspaper was rocked by a plagiarism scandal and deteriorating morale. The scandal involved Jayson Blair, a young reporter with questionable experience that Raines had favored and protected. The paper's credibility was threatened when it was found that Blair, who was allowed to work with little supervision, had fabricated or plagiarized 36 or more stories. The management style of Raines, who billed himself as a change agent on a mission to shake up a complacent staff, has been described as tyrannical, self-aggrandizing, and arbitrary. Raines also*

Leading Change

tended to share power with only a small group of insiders and was not tolerant of dissent. In July 2003, Times publisher Arthur Sulzberger Jr. terminated Raines and replaced him with Bill Keller, who had served previously as managing editor.[2]

Under Keller's leadership, the newspaper has made substantial changes that were needed to restore its credibility and the communal culture of its work environment, which had been damaged during Raines' leadership. Keller, who has a more gracious style, has been an effective change agent, making widespread structural and personnel changes and instituting reforms to prevent another scandal. He has also eliminated the favoritism from Raines' operations, which has restored the newspaper's communal spirit and culture. The Times still faces serious competitive challenges and will undoubtedly need future changes, but it has demonstrated that effective leaders can be successful in implementing needed changes.[3]

Questions for Thought

1. How should a supervisor approach a turnaround situation to produce major changes in how things are done?
2. What are conditions that create employee resistance to changes? How can such resistance be overcome?

Introduction

The quote by Juan Enriquez tells us that we probably cannot imagine the degree of change that will occur in the work environment by 2020. For supervisors, the message is clear, as there will be ample opportunities for them to participate in change initiatives. Nonetheless, change is not easy. Woodrow Wilson, the twenty-eighth president of the United States, said that "If you want to make enemies, try to change something."[4] President Wilson's conclusion from the early years of the previous century tells us that there is nothing new about the challenges leaders face when trying to implement change. Wilson's insights remain valid because changes in organizations potentially redistribute power, status, and resources.[5] Resistance to change is often strong because the losses to individuals are relatively certain and identifiable. Those interests of individuals and units facing potential losses can become concentrated and thereby create a strong barrier to change. On the other hand, the benefits for those who may gain as a result of a change are less certain and potentially more diffuse or dispersed. Accordingly, there is often less concentration of interest and a lower source of support for the change.[6] The enduring challenges to change provide an important test of a supervisor's abilities, as a key to his eventual success lies with her ability to initiate and implement change.

It is difficult to overstate the necessity for change as Harvard Professor John Kotter has identified the need for behavioral change of individuals as the most critical issue in times of organizational turbulence.[7] The reality of readiness for change has been described as follows:

> People don't change when you tell them they should. They change when they tell themselves they must. Or as Johns Hopkins foreign affairs professor Michael Mandelbaum puts it, "People don't change when you tell them there is a better option. They change when they conclude that they have no other option."[8]

The *New York Times* example of a successful turnaround demonstrates that organizations and individuals can successfully navigate difficult challenges in order to make significant changes that are needed for survival in increasingly competitive environments.[9]

In the future, supervisors will be required to help lead massive changes, which must be implemented in much shorter time frames. Thomas Friedman, an insightful observer of change, has written about forces that have had dramatic impacts on the way that business is conducted throughout the world. He has observed that the playing field for competition has been leveled and there are now several billions of workers who are now producing goods and services that are very competitive in world markets. One of the forces Friedman has identified includes such developments as the fall of the Berlin Wall in 1989 and the subsequent influx of citizens from former communist countries into the world economy. He has also pointed out the effect of technology forces, such as the tremendous expansion of the power and utilization of the Internet made possible by the first successful web browser, Netscape in 1995; software applications that can communicate with each other and open source software and associated collaboration. Friedman has also called our attention to the effects of advances in supply chain technology, which is reflected in Wal-Mart's requirement that its suppliers must have radio frequency identification microchips (RFID) on their merchandise.[10]

Friedman also includes the powerful force of shifting production to offshore facilities or offshoring to low wage countries such as China. These and other forces have created an imperative for countries, such as the United States and other developed countries, to find ways to become much more competitive. For example, it has been argued that entirely different ways of competing will be needed to overcome the low wages, productivity, and high quality that are now available in China, as well as other previously developing economies.[11]

While some companies have moved production overseas, many U.S. industries are responding to the challenges of foreign producers by increasing their use of automation and computer-driven machines. They are also redesigning jobs to put more decisions into the hands of those who know the work best, creating teams, and reengineering their processes for greater efficiency. Because people are the key to better quality and productivity, work attitudes, values, and beliefs are critical to the organization's success.

ATTITUDES, BELIEFS, AND VALUES

This chapter looks at attitudes, beliefs, and values and how they form and influence individuals' productivity in the workplace. It also discusses how you as a supervisor can influence individuals to become or to remain good producers. Finally, it offers advice on how you can manage change in yourself and in others.

Learning
Objective
Number One

ATTITUDES

An **attitude** is a consistent predisposition—either favorable or unfavorable—toward a specific stimulus. While attitudes are very stable, general attitudes are more susceptible to change. Research indicates that the degree to which more general attitudes can be changed is related to phases of adulthood. General attitudes are most stable for people in middle adulthood, while they are more amenable to change in early and late adulthood because people tend to be less self-assured and are more open in these phases of their lives.[12]

attitude
a person's manner of thinking, feeling, or acting toward specific stimuli

Behavior and attitudes influence each other. While it is intuitive to conclude that changes in attitudes drive behavior, research indicates that the reverse is true—changes in behavior drive changes in attitudes. When we get an employee to change her behavior, we should find that she experiences some movement in her attitudes toward alignment or conformity with her change in behavior.[13]

Examples abound at the Toyota–GM assembly plant (NUMMI) in Fremont, California. The attitude of one team leader, Lee Ledbetter, is that team leaders work for the team members, not the other way around. "Communication between workers and managers and among the workers is the key to NUMMI's success. Good products and a good process are important . . . but it's the ability to correct mistakes, to stop the line that makes for top-quality cars."[14] A key to the success of the NUMMI plant has been the participation of workers in improving production processes. Recently, in one year alone, NUMMI workers made 27,000 suggestions for improvements and 90 percent of their suggestions were put into place. In addition, there is enough trust between the United Auto Workers union and GM that managers can do some of the work at this plant, whereas the union's contracts at other GM plants prohibit such actions.[15]

Motorola is another company that is recognized as one of the leading companies providing training for its employees. The nature of the electronics industry requires the company to invest heavily in training in order to cope with changing technology and the competitive environment. The company, which follows a principle of lifelong learning for employees, provides 40 hours of employee training each year. In addition, the typical employee who works in information technology receives between 100 and 150 hours of training each year. Motorola faces great challenges in providing timely training because of the fast-paced, rapidly changing nature of the electronics industry. Motorola's operations are also distributed throughout the world—the company has information technology people in business units in more than 50 countries. The geographic dispersion of Motorola employees has prompted the company to conduct some of its training through the Internet and with CD-ROM technology.[16] Quest faces similar challenges in training its technical employees because of their geographic dispersion. The company has used a training consulting firm to provide technical training to almost 4,000 employees, who speak 12 different languages, in 31 countries.[17]

BELIEFS

Our work experiences and the people we have worked with have created changes in us at various stages in our lives. Our experiences have taught us our individual sets of beliefs. A **belief** is a perception based on a conviction that certain things are true. Beliefs also are based on what seems to be true or probable in one's own mind. This latter kind of belief is often called an *opinion*. Beliefs shape our attitudes, and our attitudes, when made known to others, display our beliefs.

When you are confronted with new people or concepts, you are usually not predisposed in any specific way toward them. You lack definite attitudes, opinions, and beliefs about them. It is at this point that you are most open and impressionable about the new contacts. Initially, you try to make your own observations, gain some insights, and draw your own conclusions. Think back to the time when you were seeking employment with your present employer. You probably applied based on its reputation, as relayed to you by others whose beliefs and opinions you respected. A friend who spoke well of the company may have suggested that you apply. You were willing to put your future in the hands of an employer on the basis of another's beliefs. As a new applicant, you made your own observations during the selection process and received answers to specific questions. Your beliefs about your new employer were taking shape, and when you accepted the job, you had probably formed a positive set of attitudes toward both your employer and your new job. Your beliefs, therefore, had a definite influence on your behavior.

belief
a perception based on a conviction that certain things are true or probable in one's own mind

VALUES

One set of beliefs that we all have is our values. **Values** include judgments about what are important and acceptable behaviors. Values are often expressed as wants and as worthwhile objectives. Having a high-paying job or working for a respected and admired employer are examples of values. Insights on values may be gained by considering the work values that mentors and their protégés might share. When both

values
judgment about what is right or wrong and important or unimportant

Your workers' attitudes will be a direct reflection of your attitude toward them. The worker pictured here receives recognition and words of encouragement from his supervisor. Wouldn't you work harder knowing your supervisor really cares about you?

hold similar work values there is greater likelihood for a harmonious relationship. The following are examples of work values that are relevant to such relationships: innovation, attention to detail, supportiveness, team orientation, aggressiveness, and decisiveness.[18]

Like attitudes, values are learned throughout life. Usually, values are more difficult to change than attitudes. Unfortunately, people are often quick to make assumptions about a person or group's values based on the person's or group's ethnic or racial background, religious affiliation, place of birth, gender, or age. Their assumptions, which are often inaccurate, may change as they discover the real values of others through interactions in the workplace. For this reason it is essential for each supervisor to develop an understanding of the values of each of his employees. Greater workforce diversity brings greater diversity in values and a challenge for managers to balance the majority's values "with the need to recognize and value individual differences."[19]

DIVERSITY

PEOPLE'S ATTITUDES ABOUT WORK

Southwest Airlines is well known for placing heavy emphasis on attitude or temperament when the company hires employees. The company typically places high value on work ethic, team spirit, energy, self-confidence, sense of humor, and a desire to interact with people. One of the company's screening practices is to ask groups of applicants to describe an incident in which they used humor to work through a situation or to tell about their personal motto. The company takes cues from responses to such questions as an indicator of applicants' thought processes and their coping styles. After the screening process, Southwest then probes more deeply with behavioral interviewing questions.[20] **Behavioral interviews** ask applicants to describe how they have coped with a past situation, such as solving a crisis with a vendor, or how they would act in a hypothetical situation. Such questions often provide very realistic indicators of a good match with a job. The following description of mismatches between employee attitudes and those desired, highlight the need for change and the critical role of employee attitudes:

> Click the employment site of almost any large retailer and you're likely to
> see these words plastered across the screen; friendly, helpful, motivated,
> enthusiastic and self-starter. Yet from Best Buy to Lowe's, McDonald's
> to Target, unfriendly, unknowledgeable employees and poor customer
> service are all too often the reality. Obviously management's thinking
> that a company has a particular culture or approach doesn't make
> it true.[21]

behavioral interview
interview in which interviewees are asked to describe how they have coped with a past situation, or how they would act in a hypothetical situation

THE WORK ETHIC

People's attitudes about work—their **work ethic**—can be grouped into three areas: the importance of working, the kind of work a person chooses or is required to perform, and the quality of the person's efforts while performing work. As a supervisor,

work ethic
a person's attitude about the importance of working, the kind of work he chooses, and the quality of his efforts while performing work

team leader, and team facilitator, you can influence the experiences of your associates and, therefore, help shape their attitudes about work and their individual work ethics. DaimlerChrysler wants employees who have "not only aptitude, but the right attitude. Teamwork is a must, along with the ability to use math, computers and statistics to identify, analyze and solve quality and cost problems . . . "[22] Although it has no requirement that applicants have high school diplomas, nearly one-fourth of its employees on the third shift (600 people) in its plant at Windsor, Canada have a college degree. Like NUMMI, to stay competitive the company needs teams of empowered individuals committed to quality and productivity improvement.

As a supervisor, you need to be aware of your own work ethic and the work ethic of each of your associates. You need to know why people are working for you and your company, what they think of their work, and the quality of their performance. Only then can you understand them as individuals. Unfortunately, some behaviors are the antithesis of those needed for a positive work environment. Furthermore, such behaviors occur more frequently than might be expected. Consider the following examples of behaviors, the type of work ethic they represent, and the impact they are likely to have on the workplace: "talk loudest and don't listen to other people . . . talk behind people's backs . . . over-promise and under-deliver . . . don't help anybody else . . . and take the credit for other people's efforts."[23]

This chapter's feature on supervisors and performance deals with pressures for increasing performance in many organizations.

THEORIES X AND Y

Douglas McGregor, a former professor of management at MIT, developed two theories about managers' views of human nature and motivation. These theories describe opposing perspectives that seem to provide an explanation of how many managers treat their employees. **Theory X** managers tend to have the following views of human nature:

Theory X
a set of attitudes traditionally held by managers that includes assuming the worst with regard to the average worker's initiative and creativity

1. The average person has a natural dislike for work and will try to avoid it.
2. The average person has to be threatened, controlled, coerced, and punished to give a fair day's work.
3. The average person avoids responsibility, lacks ambition, and needs constant direction.[24]

Unfortunately, results from a recent survey revealed that Theory X was alive and well:

Nearly half of companies monitor E-mail, up from 38% last year, according to a recent American Management Association survey, while Internet monitoring increased to 62.8%, up from 54.1% . . . Another study by the nonprofit Privacy Foundation shows that Internet and E-mail use of one out of three employees is monitored daily. Big Brother is watching more employees, more closely, and more often than in the past.[25]

While monitoring may indicate Theory X assumptions about employees, such as they need to be closely controlled, some electronic monitoring by employers is motivated by concerns about legal liability and the improper use of e-mail and the Internet for sexual harassment.[26]

SUPERVISORS AND
PERFORMANCE

As a result of increasingly competitive markets, companies have been forced to continuously search for ways to squeeze out further gains in performance and productivity. U.S. companies have become very productive as a result of such efforts. While a number of factors explain these gains in productivity, one important influence has been the successful harnessing of the power of information technology, such as through vendor information sharing and supply chain tracking systems. Supervisors have taken on responsibilities involved with the reorganizations and the employee retraining that is necessary to capture payoffs from advances from technology. The utilization of other technology, such as radio-frequency identification (RFID), has also involved substantial changes in operations and supervisory attention. Initiatives such as these highlight the need for supervisors to be effective in managing change.

Companies have also attempted to obtain gains in productivity through **downsizing,** even though such efforts have not produced positive results in a substantial number of cases. Nonetheless, in some situations there are few alternatives to downsizing because there is a mismatch between the level of business activity and the organization's workforce. General Motors' announcement in 2005 that it would reduce its workforce by 25,000 employees by 2008 provides an example of such downsizing. In an increasing number of cases, companies have moved production operations off-shore while retaining only selected operations in original locations.

Unfortunately, downsizing and **offshoring** create some real management challenges for supervisors. One of the challenges involves dealing with the aftermath of downsizing among survivors. With downsizing the same amount or even more work remains for remaining employees to perform, and there are usually declines in morale along with concerns about job insecurity among surviving employees. One of the keys to effectiveness in such situations is to persuade remaining employees that there will be career opportunities for them in the company in the future. These efforts require honesty and frequent communication to explain what is happening and the actions that are likely to occur in the future. In some extreme cases, employees and managers have even been required to take cuts in pay in order to preserve their jobs. At Marlow Industries, 600 of 800 jobs were off-shored to China, more automation was introduced, the jobs of mid-level managers were eliminated, and the pay of employees was reduced by 5 percent. Marlow's president, Barry Nickerson, cited heavy emphasis on communication with employees as the key to the firm's ability to cope with these changes. Needless to say, such severe conditions make the task even more difficult for supervisors, who are also probably concerned about their own job security. Nonetheless, trust in supervisors and honest communication are necessary requirements for retaining good employees during major organizational changes.

Sources: Jon E. Hilsenrath. "Adventures in Cost Cutting," *Wall Street Journal* (May 10, 2004): R1–R3. Joseph B. White and Lee Hawkins, Jr. "GM Plans to Cut 25,000 Jobs by '08 in Restructuring," *Wall Street Journal* (June 8, 2005): A1–A6.

offshoring
shifting manufacturing or services work to other countries.

downsizing
reducing the size of a workforce

Theory Y
a set of attitudes held by today's generation of managers that includes assuming the best about the average worker's initiative and creativity

On the other hand, McGregor has found that **Theory Y** managers have views of human nature that reflect the findings of recent research on human behavior and motivation. Theory Y includes the following propositions:

1. The average person desires work as naturally as play or rest.
2. The average person is capable of self-control if committed to a goal.
3. The average person is committed to goals for which achievement is rewarded.
4. The average person desires responsibility and accepts it willingly.
5. The average person possesses imagination, ingenuity, and initiative.
6. The average person is intellectually underutilized in the typical industrial setting.[27]

Team leaders who hold Theory Y beliefs about their associates will take an entirely different approach toward them than will leaders who adhere to Theory X. Theory Y managers assume the best, expect no less, and demand the best from each individual. Theory Y managers also demand the best from themselves. According to management consultant and author Tom Peters: "Front-line people have been secretly champing at the bit for decades: Give them the same information the boss gets. Give them access, at any time, to any kind of training they desire. And then let them have at it. 'They' will respond."[28] Theory Y assumptions about human nature are revealed in the success of Julia M. Garcia and her team members at Frito-Lay who have a broad range of accountability that ranges from the potato inputs to keeping the machinery operating properly. The team is furnished with regular data on cost, quality, and service metrics [scoreboarding] as well as its standing in comparison to teams at Frito-Lay's other plants throughout the country. The team's receipt of such data facilitates its ability to improvise methods for creating production and logistics efficiencies. It also, "determines crew scheduling and even interviews potential employees for the department—once the sole domain of management."[29]

Countless companies have had similar experiences once they tapped the inherent diversity and willingness to do well in most human beings. Look around you at work. You will probably find many examples of men and women, both in and out of management, who are putting forth a mediocre effort. Such mediocre behavior often occurs because their managers expect nothing more from them. Employees learn to give what is expected. A mediocre employee is usually the reflection of a mediocre manager.

THE SUPERVISOR'S ATTITUDES

It is often said that supervisors are "caught in the middle" because they are concerned most directly about the welfare of their employees and associates and at the same time must share and fortify management's authority. Needless to say, this fence straddling can be uncomfortable and demanding at times, but it is necessary. Truly, supervisors, team leaders, and team facilitators are positioned between the needs of their employees and associates and the needs of their superiors. Supervisors must be able to empathize with the perspectives of both their employees and upper management. Supervisors get in trouble when they identify too closely with either group and become labeled as having extremely "pro-worker" or "pro-management" attitudes. In such cases, supervisors are likely to lose the trust and cooperation of the other group.

Beware of accepting the attitudes or opinions of others as your own. We all have a tendency to fill a void in our knowledge by the quickest means available, but this can be a dangerous practice. When you first became a supervisor, you may have heard from your boss or predecessor, "Watch out for Al; he's a sneak," or "You sure are lucky to have Juana; she's a peach." Dismiss these "insights" and wait to form your own attitudes and opinions through your firsthand observations.

THE PYGMALION EFFECT

George Bernard Shaw's play, later made into a film, about an English flower girl in the slums who is groomed to become a lady of English society was called *Pygmalion*. From the book and film we have deduced what has become known as the ***Pygmalion effect:*** Assuming the best about people will often result in their giving their best; assuming less will often yield less in their performance. In short, people learn to give what they are expected to give. Students and trainees often learn in accordance with what their teachers and trainers expect of them.

One real tragedy of Theory X is that it is a self-fulfilling prophecy. If a manager really believes what this theory holds about employees, she will treat them in an authoritarian and suspicious manner, threatening them and exercising close control.

Pygmalion effect a self-fulfilling prophecy in which a supervisor's high expectations for an associate result in high performance because of the manner in which the supervisor treats the employee and the resultant response

The Pygmalion effect describes the performance effects of self-fulfilling prophecies. Think how motivated you would be if your manager and colleagues had strong beliefs in your ability to perform. What could your employees accomplish with your belief in them?

New employees who have something fresh and creative to offer will soon learn that their ideas, initiative, and drive are not respected or rewarded. They will learn to behave in the ways the boss expects. Soon the employees will adopt the what's-the-use attitude that their boss assumed existed from the beginning. Then the boss can smile and say, "See, I told you so." What Theory X does not say, but implies, is that only a small minority of people possess the attitudes, values, and beliefs necessary to manage others.

An article by Susan White and Edwin Locke provides us with the following insights and suggestions about the Pygmalion effect:

1. Leaders' expectations of their employees' performance have subconscious effects on both the leaders' behaviors toward employees and the performance of employees.
2. Employees' self-efficacy (confidence in one's own ability to accomplish a task) can be improved when their managers set up opportunities for them to have a series of small wins.
3. Studies generally demonstrate that the Pygmalion effect does not work as well with female leaders and with female employees, but more research is needed.
4. Leaders should have an orientation that employees' mistakes are learning opportunities rather than delays in goal accomplishment.[30]

You should have little doubt that you as a supervisor can help or hinder a new person's adjustment to and success in your company's environment. Your attitudes will soon shape those of your employees. They will look to you for respect, guidance, and example. Your expectations of them and the examples you set by your daily behavior determine their attitudes toward you and toward their own work.

PROBLEM SUPERVISORS

Without realizing it, some supervisors may be the primary cause of an employee's difficulties. Through their actions or lack of action, supervisors influence their employees' behavior. Supervisors have the ability to aggravate their employees' difficulties or help them steer clear of problems. Your people are very conscious of your behavior and see guidelines for their own behavior in yours. How your people perceive you—what they think of you as a person and a boss—is very important to you. You need to recognize that you are seen and heard by many others. Your observers are all unique individuals with different attitudes, values, and experiences. Each will observe you at different times and under different circumstances. Therefore, each person's perception of you will be unique and unlike any other.

Consider the checklist in Exhibit 8.1. The items you answered with a "yes" response indicate potential sources of difficulty in your relationships with employees. Without positive perceptions of you, your employees will not trust and respect you. As a result you will lack power to influence them by means other than threats and punishment. In short, you will lack leadership ability. Another problem that may originate with some supervisors is their tendency to quickly stereotype or form inflexible views of employees and then subsequently ignore indicators that their performance has changed. As a consequence, employees who may be ready for further development are never given the chance while others may be given undue credit. Such inequities are

| EXHIBIT 8.1 | Determining employees' perceptions of you. |

YES	NO		YES	NO	
○	○	1. Do I like to control my people with threats?	○	○	6. Do I issue conflicting orders and instructions?
○	○	2. Do I like to keep them a little off balance and insecure?	○	○	7. Do I forget to compliment them for work well done?
○	○	3. Are my behaviors and dealings with them unpredictable?	○	○	8. Do I discipline them in public?
○	○	4. Do I make promises that I do not or cannot keep?	○	○	9. Do I carry a grudge?
			○	○	10. Do I play favorites?
○	○	5. Do I betray confidences?	○	○	11. Do I take my employees for granted?

very harmful as they detract from employee morale and cause employees to look elsewhere for opportunities.[31]

"It happens all the time," and it's one of the main causes of employee discontent and high turnover, says Brian Sullivan, the chairman and CEO of executive recruiter Christian Timbers. [32]

YOUR EMPLOYEES' ATTITUDES

Your people have attitudes about their work, the company, and you as their boss. When you first become a supervisor, your people will adopt a wait-and-see attitude about you and your abilities. They are, for the most part, open and objective, waiting for evidence on which to base their opinions. The attitudes they will eventually adopt about you are almost entirely within your power to mold. Their attitudes will surely influence their performance, their output, and the reputation of the department. One of the most demanding and important tasks for managers (and particularly for supervisors) is to identify improper or unacceptable attitudes—attitudes held by employees that interfere with their performance.

GOOD ATTITUDES VERSUS BAD ATTITUDES

Once we recognize an attitude as the source of problems, we may be able to change it. But problems arise when we must identify the attitudes of other people. First, we attempt to determine the other person's attitudes through observations of the person's actions or words. Because we cannot "see" attitudes, we can only make assumptions about them on the basis of what we see people do and what we hear them say. Second, we may be too quick to label another person's attitude as bad or improper simply because it differs from our own. Despite the difficulty, as a supervisor you need to understand your attitudes and those of your employees, and you need to discover why these attitudes exist.

Suppose, for example, that as a supervisor in a machine shop you observe an employee named Joe not wearing his safety goggles while operating a grinding wheel, in violation of safety rules. Ten minutes later you pass him again, and he is still not wearing his safety goggles. At this point, you may ask yourself why. The question should have been asked earlier. If it had been, the second infraction might have been prevented. The answer to the question lies in the worker's attitude toward wearing safety goggles. He believes that his attitude is a proper one, or he would not behave in this manner. As his supervisor, your tendency is to label his attitude bad or improper. At this point, the dialogue might go as follows:

SUPERVISOR: Joe, you know we have a shop rule about wearing safety goggles, don't you?

JOE: Yeah, I know the rule.

SUPERVISOR: Do you want to lose an eye?

JOE: Nope.

SUPERVISOR: Didn't I tell you a few minutes ago to wear your goggles?

JOE: Yep.

SUPERVISOR: Well, why don't you wear them, then?

JOE: The strap's too tight. It gives me a headache.

The lesson should be obvious. People believe their attitudes are adequate and act accordingly. Until they see a need for change or can be shown an alternative that gives them better results, they have no incentive to change. Joe was willing to accept a risk to his eye in order to avoid a headache. Why he did not complain without being asked is another problem. If he has to buy goggles out of his own money, he may be reluctant to buy another pair. If the company furnishes them, the storeroom may be out of Joe's size. There could be a dozen reasons. The point is that you must ask, what is the person's attitude and why does the person have it? When you know the answers to these questions, you can begin to change the attitudes that are the source of problems.

UNCOOPERATIVE ATTITUDES: WHY PEOPLE RESIST CHANGE

Learning Objective Number Two

Cooperation means working together to reach common objectives or goals. The primary barrier to cooperation may be your weaknesses, inadequacies, and failure to offer a good example. Look first at yourself and your management practices. If you can honestly say that the barrier to cooperation lies outside yourself, the remainder of this chapter should prove helpful to you.

At the core of a person's non-cooperation is a lack of motivation to cooperate. This means that the person has no desire at present to do so. It falls to you, therefore, to attempt to provide the climate and incentives that will foster a spirit of cooperation in each of your people.

PAST CHANGE EFFORTS AND CYNICISM

How well people accept changes may depend on how well changes have been introduced in the past. Accordingly, it is important for change to go well because unsuccessful changes can provide the fuel for greater cynicism about future change. Such cynicism then becomes a self-fulfilling prophecy because successful change depends on how well employees accept and become committed to the change. Lack of information about a change also fuels cynicism. Thus, attempts to implement change should be well thought-out and well communicated. In addition, employees can be predisposed toward cynicism. The massive downsizing of the 1980s, 1990s, and 2000s has probably contributed to such cynicism in the United States. The following suggestions may be helpful for minimizing change-related cynicism:

1. Inform employees of the when, why, and how of the change.
2. Avoid surprises.
3. Involve employees in decisions that potentially affect them.
4. View the change from the employees' perspective to understand their needs.
5. Provide employees with examples of successful change.
6. Allow employees to ventilate their frustrations about the change.
7. Admit past mistakes and provide atonement for costs incurred.
8. Explain why the change is necessary at this time.[33]

PERSONAL REASONS

If change was handled well in the past, employees should be reasonably receptive to new changes. If not, you can anticipate resistance or opposition to the change. On the other hand, people may resist changes because of the personal advantages they may lose. For example, if people know their jobs well and are successful at them, they have job security. They are using tried and proven methods, and they feel no need to make an effort to learn something new. Success also tends to make some people blind to the need to change. This may occur with individuals higher up the organizational hierarchy: "achieving success and power often encourages a misplaced belief that there is nothing left to learn—a sure ticket to derailment."[34]

Most of us have a built-in fear of change. Nearly all such fear is based on ignorance—not knowing what the changes might mean to us and to our position. We have seen people displaced through advances in technology and traditional skills and crafts eliminated. A change in methods may be viewed as a criticism of our present performance, especially when the change is enforced from outside our department. For all these reasons, the supervisor must plan for change, communicate the need for it effectively, and show employees the advantages that will accrue to them as a result of adopting the change.

In addition, some people revert to dysfunctional behavior when it comes to change. Management scholar Morgan McCall calls our attention to this human tendency that sometimes proves to be a major barrier to change. He says this "resistance to change is described in drug treatment as 'doing the same thing over and over again, expecting it to come out differently.'"[35] While the job environment is not drug treatment, some employees act exactly as McCall describes—they keep doing the same thing while expecting different results. As a result, supervisors may need to use some of the techniques described in later sections to get such employees to change.

Some of the difficulty of introducing change in the workplace can be better appreciated after considering the difficulties we face in making changes in our personal lives. One need only to reflect on failed New Year's resolutions to appreciate how difficult changes are at a personal level. If change were easy, dieting would be effective and people would exercise regularly. Unfortunately, change is probably no easier at the organizational level than at the personal level.[36]

SOCIAL REASONS

As you are well aware, most people in a business do not work by themselves. They are probably members of both informal and formal groups. Changes proposed or suspected may give rise to a fear that the worker's social relationships may be upset, either by the loss of present associates or by the need to find new ones. An individual may be in favor of a change because he can see personal advantages in the new development. The group to which he belongs, however, may be against the change. The individual can either adopt the group's viewpoint about the change and risk difficulties with the supervisor or favor the change and risk expulsion from the group. Exhibit 8.2 presents several myths and realities about changing behavior.

EXHIBIT 8.2	**Myths and reality about changing behavior.**

MYTH	REALITY
1. Crisis is a powerful impetus for change.	Ninety percent of patients who've had coronary bypasses don't sustain changes in the unhealthy lifestyles that worsen their severe heart disease and greatly threaten their lives.
2. Change is motivated by fear.	It's too easy for people to go into denial of the bad things that might happen to them. Compelling, positive visions of the future are a much stronger inspiration for change.
3. The facts will set us free.	Our thinking is guided by narratives, not facts. When a fact doesn't fit our conceptual "frames"—the metaphors we use to make sense of the world—we reject it. Also, change is inspired best by emotional appeals rather than factual statements.
4. Small, gradual changes are always easier to make and sustain.	Radical, sweeping changes are often easier because they quickly yield benefits.
5. We can't change because our brains become "hardwired" early in life.	Our brains have extraordinary "plasticity," meaning that we can continue learning complex new things throughout our lives—assuming we remain truly active and engaged.

Source: Alan Deutschman. "Making Change," *Fast Company* (May 2005): 55. Fast Company by Alan Deutschman. Copyright 2005 by Mansueto Ventures LLC. Reproduced with permission of Mansueto Ventures LLC in the format Other Book via Copyright Clearance center.

FACILITATING CHANGE

John Kotter, a professor at Harvard University, has developed a comprehensive approach for implementing change. While much of his approach is applicable to organization-wide change, some of it applies to supervisors as well. A particularly important step in his approach is to create a sense of urgency for the change. Supervisors can create such urgency through actions like having employees obtain feedback from unsatisfied customers. They can refuse to take last-minute heroic action to prevent a crisis when the old ways of doing things are no longer adequate to do the job. Supervisors can also facilitate the change process by providing rewards for short-term wins. When employees make incremental progress toward the desired change in behavior, supervisors should reward the behavior.

Examples of three approaches to change are described as follows:

> Three groups of ten individuals are in a park at lunchtime with a rain-storm threatening. In the first group, someone says: "Get up and follow me." When he starts walking and only a few others join in, he yells to those still seated: "Up, I said, and NOW!" In the second group, someone says: "We're going to have to move. Here's the plan. Each of us stands up and marches in the direction of the apple tree . . . do not run . . . When we are all there . . . " In the third group, someone tells the others: "It's going to rain in a few minutes. Why don't we go over there and sit under that huge apple tree. We'll stay dry, and we can have fresh apples for lunch." [37]

The first approach is one of attempting to force people by use of authoritarian decree. This approach generally does not work well and requires great power on the part of the boss. The second approach is one of micro-management. While it may produce somewhat better results, it is time consuming. In addition, while the manager is busy looking inward in order to issue numerous directives for micro-managing the change, she is not looking outward for environmental forces that may affect the unit. The third approach, and obviously the preferred one, involves communication of a vision for change and the benefits to all for changing. It has the advantage of overcoming many of the forces that act as barriers to change.[38]

ARRANGE CONDITIONS FOR CHANGE

There are several conditions that increase the likelihood of successful change. Unsurprisingly, the first of these is that employees must first have internalized the notion that the organization serves a valuable purpose. If employees do indeed value the organization's overall purpose, they must then receive a good explanation of how changes, in which they are being asked to participate, will enable them to make contributions to the organization. Simply directing employees to adopt new behaviors or to implement new procedures is unlikely to lead to desired results. Supervisors and other managers have the responsibility of providing such explanations so that employees understand the rationale for the change. The second condition, which is discussed later, is a reinforcement system that is aligned with the desired changes in behavior. More specifically, performance measures, performance targets, rewards, reporting relationships, and various management processes need to be aligned with desired changes. For example, if a goal of adopting cross-selling approaches is not rewarded, or bureaucratic barriers discourage cross-selling, such changes are unlikely to occur or will be short-lived. In addition, a third condition is that employees must be provided training in order to develop the skills required for the new behaviors, such as asking sales persons to be more customer oriented. Without specific training, they may not pick up on important techniques that lead to customer satisfaction. Finally, the fourth condition is that the supervisor and other managers through the organizational hierarchy must model the behaviors that are being asked of employees. Employees are quick to see any inconsistencies in what they are being asked to do whenever they see supervisors and higher-level managers reverting to previous forms of behavior.[39]

ATTEND TO THE PAYOFFS FOR CHANGE

Learning Objective Number Three

One of the problems that managers and supervisors encounter in leading change efforts is that they have not sufficiently considered the benefits for the employees who must implement the change. At some point, everyone involved in a change effort wants to know how he or she will benefit from the change. While the benefits of making changes are often very apparent for executives as they may be promoted or receive a bonus, the payoffs for other employees are not as obvious. Furthermore, supervisors have a more limited range of payoffs to offer employees and typically have very little latitude to provide financial rewards. Nonetheless, supervisors have payoffs or positive features of the work environment that can be used as rewards for change and one of these is the nature of work or team relationships. Supervisors can work to insure that the working relationships that employees value are not strained or destroyed by the changes.[40]

For example, employees often have enjoyable working relationships with others on their teams and want very much to retain them. In such instances, supervisors may be able to obtain desired changes while allowing employees to remain in close contact with each other. It is important for supervisors to demonstrate sensitivity to the maintenance of such relationships and the impact on the organization's culture. On the other hand, supervisors find that employees are interested in developing new relationships that may be possible with a change. Another related payoff may be the potential to develop a stronger relationship with the supervisor and higher-level managers. Supervisors may be able to gain employee commitment to a change by explaining the possible outcomes of such strengthened relationships but must be careful to not over-promise or mislead.[41]

Potential payoffs may include appealing to employees' sense of team spirit and pride in making valuable accomplishments that make the organization better and improve its perception by the public. The Walt Disney Company provides an example of a company that has been successful in appealing to its employees' sense of pride in their organization. New employees participate in a program that is directed toward building team spirit and a sense of pride for working at Disney. Other payoffs may include opportunities for personal and career development by providing employees with opportunities to perform challenging tasks. Interestingly, it is not uncommon for employees who are the best performers to be given such opportunities because they have an established record of getting things done. Unfortunately, for all practical purposes, the best workers often end up with more work as a result of their good performance. At the same time, other employees, who are not performing well, appear to get away with lower contributions and a sense of inequity may develop among the best employees even though they may be gaining visibility from the assignment.[42]

ORGANIZATIONAL BARRIERS TO CHANGE

Supervisors will be better prepared to lead change efforts when they understand that resistance to change is the normal reaction that they should expect. Given that resistance is normal, it follows that probably more time will be required for the change than an inexperienced supervisor might think. More specifically, employees need time to think about the change and how they have fared with past changes and how successful the supervisor and unit has been in past change initiatives. In general, it useful to focus on the benefits that will accrue from the change as opposed to an emphasis on the details of the change.[43]

As indicated earlier in this chapter, the benefits of change are usually perceived as less certain than the losses to specific persons and units. Accordingly, it is helpful to allow for greater time to communicate the benefits of the change. A lack of sufficient communication about the change may be indicated by an active **grapevine** or rumor mill, which grinds out misinformation or even worst-case scenarios. While employees differ in their needs for security and predictability, supervisors must be prepared to address these concerns with the information they have available. As the change effort unfolds and more questions arise, employees can play an important role as problem solvers and resource persons who can fill in some of the gaps in information. Supervisors also need to prepare employees for the additional effort since change typically requires learning new skills or behaviors. In addition, change typically involves additional work to prevent backsliding, once the change has been made. Successful changes are not indicated by only a short period of changed behavior but by a longer period of sustained change.[44]

Other sources of resistance to change have historical origins. As noted earlier, the organization's track record in implementing change will affect how employees perceive a proposed change and the likelihood that it will be successful. How they have been dealt with in the past by the supervisor, the leadership team, and by members of other units in the organization will also affect their level of trust. In the absence of trust, change initiatives may be perceived as opportunities for others to gain advantage. Interestingly, the supervisor's boss and others in middle management are common sources of resistance to change. Middle managers are often faced with the conflicting demands of strategic initiatives from the executive team along with cost constraints, quality standards, and time pressures as well as operational issues that flow upward from supervisors and employees. In addition, there will be greater resistance to change in organizations that punish people for mistakes and tend to emphasize blame. Finally, the role of reward systems needs to be recognized because employees may have been rewarded for the behaviors that now need to be changed.[45] For example, under the previous circumstances, maintenance personnel may have been told that controlling costs in maintenance work was more important than quick repairs, and they may have been rewarded accordingly. In order for a change to work, employees will need to see the rewards for the desired new behaviors.

Learning Objective Number Four

grapevine
gossip or informal communication in an organization that often occurs when there is inadequate information from the managerial hierarchy

CHANGING THE ATTITUDES OF EMPLOYEES

*Learning
Objective
Number Five*

A supervisor can bring about a change in an employee's improper attitude through a four-step process. After you have observed improper behavior that appears to be driven by an attitude, you should take the following steps:

1. Identify the improper attitude or behavior.
2. Determine what supports it—opinions and beliefs (root causes).
3. Weaken or change whatever supports it (root causes).
4. Offer a substitute for the improper attitude.

Consider the following example, contributed by a student. Mike was a supervisor of 30 assemblers in an electronics plant in Chicago. It was his practice to turn each new employee over to an experienced worker for training until the new person adjusted to the job and became capable of meeting both quality and quantity standards on his own. One day, Mike hired a young, recent immigrant from India named Ehri. Ehri was placed under the direction of Dave, an experienced and willing worker–trainer. However, once he was on his own, Ehri's production was marked by an unacceptable level of rejects.

STEP 1: IDENTIFY THE IMPROPER ATTITUDE OR BEHAVIOR

When you determine that an employee's behavior is improper, you must look for the attitude behind it and state it in precise terms.

Mike went to Ehri and observed him at work. Ehri was working at an almost frantic pace. Mike assumed that this was the reason for the large number of rejects and asked Ehri to slow his pace and concentrate on quality, not quantity.

Often, just by investigating the action, showing concern, and giving corrective instructions, you will be able to solve the problem. The worker may realize at this point that her behavior is unacceptable and change it to meet the demands of the supervisor. This did not happen with Ehri.

Mike had failed to identify the attitude that supported the fast pace of work. Instead, he simply identified an action, which he attempted to stop with orders and instructions. He had dealt with the symptom of an attitude, not with the opinions or beliefs that were causing the problem.

STEP 2: DETERMINE WHAT SUPPORTS IT

On the basis of your investigation and analysis, see if you can spot the roots of the attitude—the primary beliefs that both support and feed the attitude in the employee's mind. The best way to do this is to get the employee talking about his true feelings. Some frequent root causes that support and nurture incorrect attitudes include group pressures, faulty logic, and misunderstood standards.

Mike thought the problem had been solved. After all, when a supervisor lays down the law, especially to a new worker, the employee should respond. Ehri's production, however, continued to yield an unacceptable number of rejects. Next, Mike and his boss both talked with Ehri. They again emphasized quality and included an implied threat that unless the situation reversed itself, Ehri's job was in jeopardy. But still the problem persisted because Mike had not uncovered the root cause. Even though he was armed with the additional authority of his boss, Mike was still treating a symptom of the attitude. He had not yet uncovered the attitude and its root causes.

Finally, it occurred to Mike that the problem might have originated in Ehri's training. He approached Dave and related the problem of too much quantity and too little quality. After stating that Ehri's job was at stake, he asked if Dave knew how this situation might have evolved. Dave became somewhat embarrassed, and on further questioning, Mike discovered that Dave had told Ehri that quantity was all management really cared about, regardless of what they said to the contrary. Mike had finally struck pay dirt. He now knew what Ehri's attitude was and the root cause for it—misunderstood standards.

STEP 3: WEAKEN OR CHANGE WHATEVER SUPPORTS IT

Once the root causes are known, they can be analyzed and their vulnerabilities noted. A program of action can then be developed to change beliefs through the use of reason. One way is to point out flaws in the employee's assumptions or how the basis for these assumptions has changed.

Mike instructed Dave to go to Ehri and explain that he had been misinformed. Dave apologized to Ehri and made it clear that he had only been kidding about quantity over quality. Dave had the reputation of being a practical joker, and he really had meant no harm by what he did. He was only taking advantage of a novice who was naive to the ways of a skilled worker like Dave. Ehri had a language difficulty with English and tended to take things literally. Thus, he had been easy prey for a joker. Dave felt certain that once Mike talked to Ehri, Ehri would realize that he had been had. When Dave understood that Ehri had not responded to Mike's talk, he was most eager to help correct the problem.

STEP 4: OFFER A SUBSTITUTE

Dave had no trouble persuading Ehri to change his thinking because Ehri had received quite a bit of pressure by that time. Once Ehri realized (as a result of the statements of both Dave and Mike) that his attitude was based on misinformation, he became a superior worker.

You may be able to change behavior by constant harping and criticism, but like the action of water in wearing away rock, it may take too long and leave scars. In general, people will change only if they see that their behaviors are no longer worth maintaining. Threats and orders usually only suppress a natural and observable behavior and drive it underground. The person becomes sneaky and does what you say only when you are there to police your order. When you are absent, the old behavior pattern resurfaces. You must identify the root causes of the behavior and encourage the individual to question the position. Only then will you be able to initiate a permanent change in that person's behavior.

GLOBAL

TAKING DECISIVE ACTION

After appropriate information gathering, involvement of individuals affected by the change, and consideration of alternatives, it is important that a unified effort should be evident, particularly among the management team. Lou Gerstner's experiences in a large-scale change effort at IBM describe the resistance that is often associated with change and the strong stance that sometimes must be taken against those who seek to actively block the change effort.

> In one example he found that some of his communications were not being forwarded to employees in the company's European operations. After this discovery he confronted IBM's executive in charge of the European organization and sought an explanation for why his messages had been intercepted. The executive explained that he had determined that they were not appropriate for his executives and that there were difficulties in translation. At that point Gerstner took decisive action by calling him to IBM's U.S. headquarters where he made it clear that the employees were IBM employees, not the executive's and that Gerstner's messages were not to be intercepted. The executive soon left the company because he could not change his orientation from a European operation to a global one.[46]

Similarly, Gerstner found that not all employees accepted the need for timely change and took measures to insure an action orientation. During his change efforts, he found that some employees were resisting decisions even from years in the past when IBM had to make rapid changes because of decreasing market share and the company's failure to live up to customers' expectations. Because of the need to be competitive in the marketplace, Gerstner got the message out to employees that performance was critical, that he would play a role in all hiring for key positions, and that he wanted employees who were action oriented.[47]

More recently, change efforts have involved a greater focus on ethics. This chapter's feature on supervisors and ethics describes the problems that have occurred when organizations have treated employees as expendables.

TECHNIQUES FOR OBTAINING CHANGE

Fortunately, many tried and proven methods are available for reducing resistance to change and instilling a desire to cooperate. The basic techniques at your disposal for introducing changes and resolving conflicts include:

- Force-field analysis
- Effective communication
- Persuasion techniques
- Participation techniques
- Training programs
- Organizational development activities

FORCE-FIELD ANALYSIS

force-field analysis
a method for visualizing the driving and restraining forces at work within an individual so as to assess what is needed to make a change in a person's behavior

Kurt Lewin, a social psychologist, developed the technique of **force-field analysis.** It is a useful device for visualizing employees' resistance to change. Force-field analysis tells us that individuals' behavior with regard to any issue is affected by driving forces

SUPERVISORS AND ETHICS

U.S. companies practiced widespread downsizing during the 1980s and early 1990s. Reports of downsizing came so frequently that they were almost daily features in the business press. Some downsizing was necessary because it enabled U.S. companies to become extremely efficient and helped to ensure their survival. On the other hand, downsizing frequently did not deliver anticipated cost savings. Some companies that were profitable also downsized. When employees see no compelling need for downsizing, it is more difficult for them to accept the changes related to downsizing, such as increased workloads for survivors. In addition, the consequences of downsizing to those who lose their jobs can be devastating.

Al Dunlop, a CEO who acquired a great deal of notoriety because of his extensive use of downsizing, became known as "Chainsaw." His exploits as a CEO were chronicled in an autobiography entitled *Mean Business*. During his career he downsized extensively at Lily-Tulip, a disposable cup maker; eliminated 11,000 jobs (approximately one-third) at Scott Paper; and eliminated approximately one-half of the jobs at Sunbeam. In 1998, Sunbeam's stock declined from $53 in March to $11.25 in June. "In addition, shareholder suits alleged that Sunbeam had pumped up its winter-time sales by selling grills to retailers on attractive terms, with the understanding that they would be delivered later." In June 1998, Chainsaw Al received a dose of his own medicine when he was fired as the Sunbeam CEO. In August 1998, Sunbeam's stock declined to $5.13.

Sources: Martha Brannigan and James R. Hagerty. "Sunbeam, Its Prospects Looking Ever Worse, Fires CEO Dunlap," *Wall Street Journal* (June 15, 1998): A1, A14. Allan Sloan. "Chainsaw Massacre," *Newsweek* (June 29, 1998): 62. Ellen Joan Pollock and Martha Brannigan. "Mixed Grill: The Sunbeam Shuffle, or How Ron Perelman Wound Up in Control," *Wall Street Journal* (August 19, 1998): A1, A8.

and restraining forces. Driving forces encourage us to change, whereas restraining forces encourage us to resist change. Whether we are predisposed toward a change in a negative way or in a positive way depends on the nature and quantity of these forces. If the forces are balanced, we are in a state of inertia. If a change is to take place, driving forces must outweigh restraining ones, the restraining ones must be reduced, or a combination of these must take place. Exhibit 8.3 illustrates this concept.

To understand more clearly this type of analysis, let us consider an example. Assume that you want Barbara, one of your graphics specialists, to work overtime on a special project. Since overtime is never mandatory in your company, Barbara has a choice. Let us assume that you have asked her, and she has refused. The situation might appear as follows:

Driving Forces

1. Barbara will receive additional pay at overtime scale.
2. She wants to please you.
3. She enjoys the type of graphics work in this project.

| **EXHIBIT 8.3** | **Representation of force fields.** |

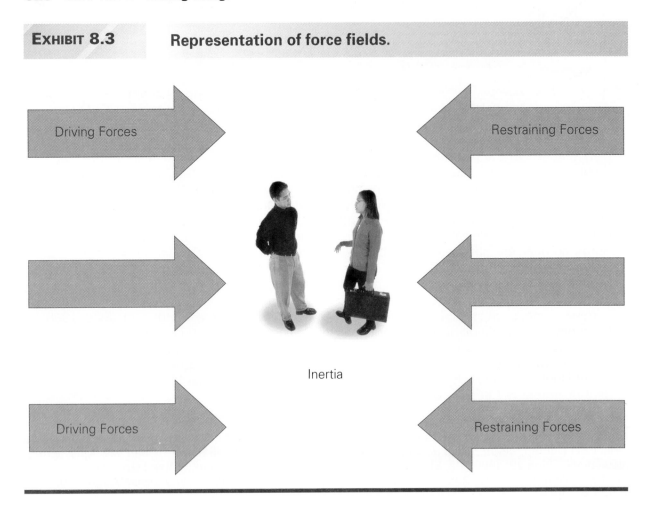

Restraining Forces

1. She will be unable to attend a play for which she has expensive tickets.
2. She is concerned about personal safety when traveling home late at night.
3. She needs to leave the deposit for a new apartment at the leasing office.

At this point, there appears to be a standoff. You cannot order her to work so you must try to reduce her restraining forces or increase the driving forces. Before attempting to do either you will need to understand the forces as Barbara perceives them. In this case, we can assume that Barbara is aware of the driving forces but that they are inadequate to overcome the restraining forces. You could increase the driving forces by offering double overtime or making a personal plea for her assistance. Such approaches are sometimes relatively unimaginative and may add to your employee's stress level.

On the other hand, you may obtain a more predictable outcome by reducing the restraining forces, and you will not add to the stress Barbara experiences. For example, in this situation you may have discretionary funds that will allow you to obtain tickets for her for another night. You also could arrange for someone to escort her safely home, such as a company driver, or you could use company funds to reimburse her for the use of a private limousine service. Alternatively, you could arrange to have a courier service deliver the deposit for her apartment to the rental office. These approaches should have a high probability of gaining the behavior you need.

EFFECTIVE COMMUNICATION

Regardless of the form of communication used, you must lay the groundwork for change and communicate its advantages before you can obtain commitment from your people. A company that is now part of Anadarko Petroleum provides a good example of an organization that used effective communication to facilitate change. The company, which changed its culture to be more responsive to competitive conditions, had a very extensive communications program. Employees were heavily involved in meetings in which action plans were developed for changing the company's culture. Furthermore, detailed timetables of the change process kept everyone informed as to when each component of the cultural change would be initiated and completed.[48]

Learning Objective Number Six

In the absence of communication about a pending change, there is a strong likelihood that the grapevine will fill in with miscommunication.[49] An example is provided by a large manufacturing firm that was changing its tuition reimbursement policy for employees. As the company carefully worked through the implications of the change and developed the new policy, rumors began to circulate among employees as to the terms of the changes. E-mails began to circulate with various interpretations of the information that had been obtained. Eventually, employees who were pursing graduate programs during the evenings started to make enrollment decisions based on these rumors even before the final policy was announced. While the company was being careful with this change in policy, the grapevine was very active, and there was the potential for miscommunication. This example is very consistent with the following observation:

> During the initial phases of the process [change] many managers try to keep things under wraps while they develop a comprehensive strategy. They try to keep everything a secret until all the answers are known. What happens when management stays quiet is that the rumor mill kicks in to supplement the information void . . . Management is naïve if it thinks anything can be kept a secret, because the organizational grapevine will provide people with speculation and answers.[50]

As a concluding comment on this aspect of the change process, it is almost impossible to communicate too much about change and such communication needs to continue to prevent a revision back to the previous state.

PERSUASION

Our discussion up to this point has revealed that the process of leading change is a challenging task at best because there are typically numerous forces, which act in concert to maintain the status quo. While many of the critical elements of the change process are well understood, there have been some recent contributions to our knowledge of the conditions that facilitate change. Recent research has found that change efforts frequently fail because leaders rely too much on rational arguments as the major thrust of the process of persuasive.[51]

It is unsurprising that leaders attempting to create change have focused on the rational aspects of change since analytical training is a hallmark of business, engineering, legal, and medical education and practice. On the other hand, research indicates that the chances for successful change are enhanced when there is greater emphasis on the emotional aspects of change or emotional persuasion. Until recently, medical researchers have been unable to understand why only a small proportion of patients make needed changes in their lifestyle behaviors following serious medical problems, such as heart attacks, even though relapses are almost a certainty without such changes. Unfortunately, the use of rational arguments, such as describing the increased risks of death if changes in lifestyle behaviors are not adopted, do not usually lead to remedial behaviors, such as increased exercise, changes in diet, or cessation of smoking. However, medical researchers have recently found that greater motivational impact can be obtained from an emphasis on the joys that can be obtained with such changes in behavior.[52]

Interestingly, while crises have frequently been viewed as optimal times for initiating change, such occurrences are also times in which strong emotions are likely to come into play. In the past, change agents may have mistakenly viewed such emotions as a side effect to be managed; they typically failed to understand the usefulness of emotion as a powerful tool for initiating change. **Change agents** sometimes mistakenly assume that the rational or cognitive aspects of change, such as logic and analytical results, are aligned with the emotional aspects, such as fear, sadness, and anger, when in fact they may be in conflict. Research indicates that such emotional aspects may be more powerful influences on change than the former. Supervisors can increase the likelihood of successful change attempts by drawing on the appropriate use of emotion with other change efforts. The next section presents several suggestions for using emotions to enhance the initiation and implementation of change.[53]

One of the keys to this new approach to change involves the use of a different frame for the needed change. In this sense, frames provide a mental structure for thinking about the desired behaviors.[54] **Framing** provides a good explanation of why people will behave in a seemingly irrational manner, such as by paying a much higher price for a bottle of beer from a resort hotel than they would for the same beer from a run-down grocery store or why they would walk several blocks to save $30 on the price of a watch costing $70 while they would not do the same when given the opportunity to save the same $30 on a much more expensive item, such as a $700 video camera.[55]

change agent
a champion or proponent who provides the driving force to implement and maintain a change

framing
placing a decision option in a background context that increases the likelihood that the option will be selected or accepted

USE OF EMOTION IN PERSUASION

An example of the effective use of emotion in facilitating change is provided by the following description of a weekly management meeting in a hospital. At the meeting, which was attended by both administrators and physicians, the participants were dealing with troublesome cases and budgetary issues related to a managed care contract. The hospital had made a mistake with a patient prior to the diagnosis and was going to incur extra expenses in order to comply with a request from the patient's wife.

Just as they are preparing to move to the next case, the surgeon who had made the diagnosis, ordinarily a taciturn man, speaks up with barely controlled intensity of feeling. "Come on, now," he says. "This guy has just been diagnosed with cancer. He's depressed and frightened. He thinks he is going to die. Shouldn't we assume that our job is to take care of the patient and not just the budget?" This comment releases a flood of sympathetic reactions as the group wrestles with the conflicting demands imposed by their managed care contract and their own feelings and ethical tradition . . . . The meeting runs into overtime. Almost incidentally, the committee reverses its earlier decisions and decides to honor the wife's requests despite the extra costs. . . . [56]

There is little doubt that the difficult issues in health care cost containment generate countless conversations of a similar nature in hospitals every day. Furthermore, this was probably not the first time that the physician and administrators involved in the incident had discussed the issue. One can easily assume that physicians routinely argue that there should be greater priority placed on patient welfare when there is a conflict over costs. Nonetheless, in this case, genuine emotion set the stage for a change, and it occurred in a constructive problem-solving process in which status differentials were not allowed to interfere with the process. Exhibit 8.4 provides some suggestions for the use of emotion in persuasive efforts.

Exhibit 8.4	**Use of emotion in persuasive efforts to initiate change.**
Core Message	Add emotional content to rational arguments, such as danger and unpleasantness in the absence of change and pleasure and comfort after the implementation of change.
Packaging of Message	Employ different modes to sensitively capture attention; such as with pictures, posters, logos, slogans, and music; to establish a link between the change and emotions. Use appropriate humor to break the tension and provide a view of the human side of the leaders of the change effort.
Leader Characteristics	The actions of change agents should match what they say, and their behavior should conform to high ethical standards.
Leader-Audience Interaction	Those leading the change effort should listen to employees' concerns, emphasize fairness, and consider all the facts before making decisions.
Setting of Interaction	Use appropriate ceremonies in appealing physical settings to mark the end of the past approach and to reinforce change and celebrate progress toward the new approach.

Source: Based on material presented in Shaul, Fox, and Yair, Amichai-Hamburger. "The Power of Emotional Appeals in Promoting Organizational Change Programs," *Academy of Management Executive* (November 2001): 84–93.

You will find that you must often use persuasion techniques to get your employees to cooperate. Always remember to put yourself in your employees' shoes. Treat them the way you wish to be treated.

PERSUASION TECHNIQUES

Each of the following persuasion techniques works well in certain situations. Which one you choose depends on your understanding of the people and events involved in the particular situation you face. Become familiar with all of them so that you will always carry with you one or more techniques that can be applied to any set of circumstances.

1. *Explain why.* Let your people know the reason behind the proposal or change. Put it in their terms and tailor your message to each individual.

2. *Show them how.* Explain how the change will affect them, how it will help them, and how it will be implemented. Appeal to their individual needs.

3. *Tell them the truth.* If the change will be painful, let them know it. If they are to be displaced, provide truthful assurances about the company's relocation services or its willingness to retrain them for new positions.

4. *Try a compromise.* You may not have foreseen all the possibilities, and people who disagree with you may have some good points on their side. In fact, skilled persuaders often incorporate the suggestions of those they are attempting to persuade into solutions that combine their views. This has a positive impact on the process because the persuader's willingness to adapt the solution to the needs of others builds trust and greater receptivity to sacrifices for the mutual good.[57]

5. *Give an example of a past accomplishment.* Tell your people about similar situations and the positive results that followed. Explain how each person benefited as a result of the change. Professor Jay Conger says that "it is critical to identify your objective's tangible benefits to the people you are trying to persuade."[58]

6. *Plant a seed.* Give your employees an idea and let it germinate in advance of the change. For example, converse with them about "How nice it would be if . . . " or "Have you guys thought about . . . " Then nurture that idea with the proper care and feeding. Your employees may come to you with the very suggestion you anticipated. Even better, they may think it is their own idea.

7. *Ask questions.* Ask questions to which the answers will yield support for a change or remove the cause of a possible conflict. When properly presented, questions can lead employees to the responses you desire.

8. *Offer a choice.* The choice you present is not *whether* to do something or reject it but rather *when* or *by whom* it will get done.

9. *Offer a challenge.* Present the idea as a goal to be reached or a standard to be surpassed. Portray the change as a test of the team's abilities and skills. Turn the event into a game or contest—a way of probing their potential.

10. *Make a promise.* If possible, give your promise that if the idea is not successful or does not yield the desired results (given an honest effort), you will retreat from your position and withdraw the directive.

11. *Try making a request.* Instead of ordering compliance and being autocratic, ask people to cooperate. You will be amazed at the difference in responsiveness to requests rather than commands. This technique has special appeal to the individual who feels insulted by demands but who bends over backward to meet an appeal for help.

12. *Use subtle appeals for change.* Conger says that autocratic, up-front hard sell approaches or "John Wayne" techniques often lead to failure. Instead, he proposes the following:

> In reality, setting out a strong position at the start of a persuasion effort gives potential opponents something to grab onto—and fight against. It's far better to present your position with the finesse and reserve of a lion tamer, who engages his "partner" by showing him the legs of a chair. In other words, effective persuaders don't begin the process by giving their colleagues a clear target in which to set their jaws.[59]

13. *Give a demonstration.* Show by your own performance the behaviors the new system calls for, how it will work, and how it will benefit the group or individual. Introduce the change with a planned and carefully executed tryout, and the doubts will fade in the light of reason. Seeing is believing.

14. *Involve them in the decision.* Using a problem-solving session, get your employees into the problem with both feet. State the dimensions of the problem and then lead them to a consensus.

15. *Establish an emotional connection with your objective.* Chrysler's Robert Marcell helped persuade Chrysler executives to build a sub-compact car in the United States rather than overseas by showing pictures of his hometown, Iron River, Michigan. The pictures showed deserted homes and boarded-up buildings, such as Marcell's high school. The town's economy had been devastated when manufacturers shifted their purchases of raw materials to foreign mining companies. The consequences to a small city of the loss of employment established an emotional connection with Marcell's objective.[60]

Before you decide to use any of these techniques for persuasion, put yourself in your employees' shoes. Identify with their needs, concerns, and attitudes. Then set

SUPERVISING TEAMS

Football fans may remember the success of the New England Patriots when the team won its first Super Bowl in 2002. Although the Patriots gained only 267 yards versus the 427 gained by the Saint Louis Rams, they won the game 20 to 17. The game statistics reveal that defense played a major role in the win because the team forced turnovers by the Rams while they had no turnovers. While the statistics tell part of the story, it is likely that the real reason for the Patriot's win was that they played as a team. Although the notion of playing as a team may be easily dismissed as a tired sports cliché, in this case the Patriots demonstrated uncommon commitment to teamwork that deserves attention. When it was time for player introductions, the entire team was introduced as a team—there were no individual names or players on the different units or any names of star players. Instead, the 53 players entered the field as a team. This had never happened before in Super Bowl history.

Georgetown University newspaper columnist Sean Gormley stated that the Patriots's team entrance provided a remarkable signal of teamwork, which stands in stark contrast to the me-first behaviors that characterize professional sports. Interestingly, while the Patriots had star players, they had the ability to keep their egos under control for the good of the team. The message sent by the team's introduction was that the players were in the game together, win or lose. The example of the Patriots applies to work situations and business organizations. When people can keep their personal interests in check for the good of team, they can accomplish great things through teamwork. Savvy business leaders understand this as they are careful to avoid taking individual credit for their accomplishments and are quick to acknowledge the contributions of others in their organizations who produced the results. Supervisors who are faced with the task of leading change need to keep these lessons in mind.

Sources: John C. Maxwell. "Check Your Ego at the Door," *Leadership Wired*, (October 2003). Website: *http://INJOY.com/LeadershipWired.* NFL's Super Bowl Website: *www.superbowl.com/ history/recaps/game/sbxxxvi* (August 10, 2005).

TEAMS

your course to deal with their driving and restraining forces. By eliminating forces that restrain desired behaviors or by adding incentives that drive people toward such behaviors, you will increase the likelihood of successful change.

This chapter's feature on supervising teams provides an example of the results that can be produced when the focus is truly on the team rather than the individual.

PARTICIPATION TECHNIQUES

Frequently, organizations fail to make changes that would improve service to customers or the quality of products. Such foregone opportunities are often a result of failures to ask employees for their ideas. Employees are the closest to the problem and often represent an untapped source of improvements that are overlooked. They are often frustrated by the poorly thought-out or obsolete policies and have to perform their work in a less efficient manner or with poorer service as a result. Interestingly, executives often fail to calculate the costs of dysfunctional policies and are unaware of the potential savings that could be obtained with appropriate ones.[61] Too often the following is the case:

> The people closest to the problem aren't given a chance to offer solutions because the boss is too arrogant to ask them, "If you were in charge, what's the first way you'd make this place work better for our customers?"[62]

Managers must use various means to involve their people in decision-making and to allow them to participate more fully in the work of the department. Disney provides an example of a company that fixed a broken practice when it implemented its Fastpass approach, which enables customers of its parks to reserve a place in line. It is interesting that the old practice had been in place since the mid-1950s.[63] It will be up to supervisors to begin asking their associates for solutions to such problems, such as those encountered by Disney.

One means for increasing employee participation is to share one's formal authority. By delegating authority to responsible employees, a supervisor can expose her employees to the complexities of her job. Such delegation also facilitates the development of her employees. Supervisors should be sincere in their efforts to obtain employee involvement in decisions about potential change. Employees are perceptive and will know when a supervisor is simply going through the motions and has no intention of implementing their suggestions or of revising a predetermined plan.[64]

A high-level executive of a grocery chain provided the author with an example of the value of such participation. His company had experienced difficulties in obtaining operational efficiencies in its produce logistics operations and was making no progress toward a solution. Finally, it occurred to the logistics center manager that he might obtain some advice from the union steward. When he asked the steward for his ideas, the steward said, "I thought you'd never ask. Here's a list of things that should help." The steward pulled out the list from his pocket and handed it to the manager, and the answers to the problems were found. The point of this example is that employees need to feel that their ideas are valued. They have a great deal of information about how things could be changed for the better but need to be invited to contribute.

Another approach for increased participation is the formation of worker teams to assist in identifying and solving problems. "At a time when companies are looking for ways to streamline operations and cut costs, managers . . . have gotten measurable results that show the best answers can come from asking those who know best—the workers."[65]

A third method of enlisting participation depends on your style of supervision. A democratic management style promotes a feeling of shared responsibility and a voice in what happens. Such a style places trust in the workers and makes the supervisor more dependent on them. The workers know this and usually act accordingly. No one wants to betray the trust of another. For the most part, people want to live up to the expectations others have of them, provided that they have the abilities and skills to do so.

Genencor, a biotech company based in Palo Alto, California, provides an example of an organization in which employees are heavily involved in decisions. When the company decided to design a new building, it involved its employees in the planning, and the result was an architecture that facilitates creativity. Aside from this example of involvement, employees at Genencor also participate in the development of practices for the work environment as well as more routine matters, such as surveys about which benefits they prefer. Genencor credits its employee involvement for increased productivity, strong employee loyalty, and an annual turnover rate of less than 4 percent, as compared to 18.5 percent for its industry. [66]

FACILITATE ACCEPTANCE OF RISK

In order to facilitate acceptance and adaptation to change, supervisors need to help associates be more comfortable with risk. There are methods for reducing risk, such as by offering additional training to help associates make a transition to new procedures. Nonetheless, not all risk can be eliminated, and employees are often rightfully concerned about their abilities to meet the requirements of a change. Supervisors must have a good understanding of the level of risk that their emloyees are comfortable with and its compatibility with the organization's culture. The necessity of accepting risk and even promoting risk-taking are probably permanent features of the rapidly changing competitive environments in which organizations now operate.

IBM provides an example of a very large company that is attempting to change by taking on new businesses. The company's approach is directed toward what it calls emerging business opportunities (EBOs). As these opportunities are identified, the company assigns top executives to lead these initiatives. These executives often have track records of leading very large units having thousands of employees. Interestingly, they are asked, in some cases, to make the transition from having thousands of employees to only one or a handful of employees in the start-up phase as IBM has realized that the innovations involved in EBOs are less likely to occur within a large organization. The company's approach encourages risk-taking and accepts mistakes as part of the cost of facilitating the learning that is required to make breakthroughs.[67]

IBM's Bruce Harreld has provided the following observation: "You want to celebrate failure because you can learn something. It's harder to do that early in your career. You need some level of security to say, 'I screwed it up,' and be comfortable that you're not going to get fired."[68]

Supervisors need to remember that associates are not going to take risks when they see that they will be penalized or punished for mistakes that occur with change.

TRAINING PROGRAMS

Training programs are formal ways in which you and your organization can teach employees skills, knowledge, and attitudes that they need to perform their present tasks. For example, when you teach one of your employees how to operate a piece of machinery, you impart the information he needs to understand the machine's performance capabilities. Through practice, the operator gradually gains the manual dexterity required for efficient operation of the machine. Finally, you impart the proper attitudes about safe operation, proper operating procedures, and appropriate maintenance. You teach it all simultaneously and with equal emphasis.

ORGANIZATIONAL DEVELOPMENT ACTIVITIES

Organizational development (OD) is typically a large-scale change process initiated to improve the performance of units or entire organizations. This process involves efforts in education and training that eventually affect everyone in an organization.

OD requires that an organization identify its strengths and weaknesses, define its objectives, identify its problem areas, establish OD goals, set up programs for achieving those goals, and evaluate progress toward improvement. Outside consultants and experts usually conduct research into the organization's operations. They then recommend and teach the implementation of OD programs for change. If OD efforts are to succeed, the commitment of top management to them is essential. Organizational changes, if they are to be lasting, must begin at the top.

Organizations that adopt OD programs must set specific goals for their entire operation and its various divisions and sub-units. The total organization may have the following goals: (1) to improve the organization's productivity, profitability, and human resources and (2) to improve the organization's efforts at communicating, promoting intergroup cooperation, and preparing for and coping with change. As a supervisor, your goals will be influenced by those of your boss and your unit or division. One goal might be to reduce waste and scrap by 10 percent. Another might be to improve the communication skills of the personnel in your department. You can then design specific programs to accomplish your goals.

OD programs include those designed to assess employee attitudes, to improve employee cooperation, and to build team spirit. OD activities need your commitment if they are to succeed. You, like all the managers above you, must be committed to them, and you must be willing and able to sell them to employees who will participate in them. Change can mean security for those who know it is coming and are prepared for it. It can mean insecurity for those who do not. You can do a great deal to reduce insecurity and stress among your people by supporting change.

> An example of wide-scale organizational development has been taking place at Levi Strauss and Company, which has historically been one of the better-managed U.S. organizations and has gone through difficult times in recent years. The company's delivery of its products had become slower than competitors and it had been losing market share. To turn the situation around, Levi dramatically changed the organization and its processes. A large task force of key employees was given the task of designing new processes for getting products to the market quicker. The task force also designed new jobs to make Levi more competitive. Employees then had to apply for these new jobs.[69]

organizational development
a planned, managed, systematic process used to change the culture, systems, and behavior of an organization to improve its effectiveness in solving problems and achieving goals

INSTANT REPLAY

1. Our experiences help shape our individual beliefs.
2. Our beliefs help shape our attitudes.
3. When supervisors observe undesired behaviors, they must act to change them.

4. To change attitudes, we must identify the supports for them, weaken those supports, offer a substitute, and sell it.

5. Techniques for changing behaviors include force-field analysis, effective communications, persuasion techniques, participation techniques, training programs, and organizational development activities.

6. Our attempts to initiate change are enhanced by the appropriate use of emotion in persuasion.

QUESTIONS FOR CLASS DISCUSSION

1. Can you define this chapter's key terms?
2. How do you form an attitude about a person, place, or thing?
3. What kinds of attitudes held by workers need changing? How would you go about changing an employee's attitude?
4. What are the techniques or tools described in this chapter that can help you change your own or other people's attitudes?
5. What are the common organizational barriers to change?
6. What are the myths and realities of changing behavior?

ASSESS THIS SITUATION

Purpose: To help you assess your receptiveness to change.

Your Task: Answer honestly the following questions. Think about your responses and what they indicate about your resistance or receptivity to change.

Agree	*Disagree*	
○	○	1. I am usually the last of my friends to adopt new fashion trends.
○	○	2. I typically focus more on the downside of a new way of doing things rather than the potential benefits.
○	○	3. Although with a few exceptions my past experiences with change have been positive, I generally feel that change involves substantial risk.
○	○	4. When faced with an increased work or school workload, I generally try to work harder rather than find a new approach for getting the job done.
○	○	5. Whenever someone tries to convince me to change the way I do something, my first reaction is to become defensive.
○	○	6. I generally need to see whether a new procedure will work before I feel comfortable trying it.

SKILL BUILDING EXERCISE 8.1

Cynicism was discussed earlier in the chapter as a common outcome of previous unsuccessful attempts to initiate change. Often cynicism is used by employees to provide some degree of self-protection or defense against what they see as attempts on the part of the organization or a supervisor to manipulate them or to exercise excessive control over their work or personal lives. Employees sometimes attempt to reveal through cynicism that they have not been fooled by the rhetoric or communication smokescreens and are well aware of what management is attempting to do to them. Cynicism may be expressed various ways such as mimicking, lampooning, developing bawdy versions of company slogans, and so on. Another expression of cynicism may be to engage in **working to the rule** by inflexibly following work procedures down to very minute details, thereby bringing production to a standstill. [70]

working to the rule
following work procedures down to very minute details, thereby bringing production to a standstill

Your Task: Work in small groups or by yourself to identify and discuss examples of employee cynicism that your classmates may have encountered in a change initiative at work. Select the best example and analyze the causes of the cynicism. Develop an approach for preventing such cynicism or dealing with it once a supervisor becomes aware of it and present your analysis to the class.

SKILL BUILDING WRITING EXERCISE 8.2

Under the Family and Medical Leave Act (FMLA), employees are entitled to take as much as 12 weeks of unpaid leave in a 12-month period. Provisions of the FMLA require employers to provide such leaves for a number of medical events, including situations in which an employee needs to provide care for a child who is experiencing serious medical problems. Under the law, employees can take intermittent leave, by notifying the employer, only a short time before they are required to report for work, of the need to take care of a child who is experiencing a health problem, such as an asthma attack.

Consider the following situation in which several employees of a small manufacturing firm are taking frequent and short FMLA leaves, such as half-day or one-day leaves, to care for children who they allege are experiencing serious health problems. For example, they are calling in only an hour before work with claims that their children are having asthma attacks. The employer understands that these chronic medical conditions are real, but it is not clear that every report of an episode or attack is legitimate. The employer is convinced that several employees are abusing the FMLA provisions because the incidence of leaves is very high on Fridays and Mondays, and it is relatively easy to falsely claim that a child is having an asthma attack.

Your Task: Use the force-field analysis technique that was presented in this chapter to identify the driving and restraining forces that are maintaining the current levels of absenteeism and FMLA abuse. Write a memo to the plant manager with your analysis of the situation. In the first part of your memo, identify potential driving and restraining forces and speculate about the possibilities of their relative strengths. Provide recommendations in the second section on specific driving forces that should be increased and restraining forces that should be reduced or eliminated. Also provide a discussion of the potential consequences of changing these driving and restraining forces and the potential for unexpected results.

CASE 8.1	**New Database Software**

Lupe Mendoza spotted Cecilia Hunter at the other side of the cafeteria and walked over to sit down at her table. Lupe said, "Have you heard the latest? We're going to change database software."

Cecilia said, "Who told you that? This isn't another of those rumors, is it? I've just recovered from the last change in software."

Lupe said, "I have a friend, Joanne Branson, who used to work in this section. She moved over to corporate procurement a couple of years ago. Anyway, last week she saw contracts for new database software."

Just then Martin Cowan and Greg Youngblood walked up to the table. Cecilia said, "Have you heard that we're changing database software again?"

Martin groaned, "Not again! I've still got a few files that I haven't converted from the previous software. Most of us have only recently learned the present software well enough to feel comfortable. How are we going to learn all of this new stuff while we take on these new accounts from the merger?"

Greg said, "I heard about this new software from a friend whose company implemented it last fall. It's so complex that it takes almost a year to really learn it well. In fact, at my friend's company a couple of people quit their jobs because of the software."

Lupe said, "This is going to be a disaster. The last time we switched software the whole system was messed up for months. The worst problem was when we found errors in the conversion and people had to go back and trace through the data to do corrections."

As the four of them walked back to their office they ran into their boss, Tommy Lance. Martin said, "We've heard rumors that we're going to change database software. Are they true?"

Tommy said, "I had hoped to keep this quiet until I could announce the change to everyone at once. Yes, it's true. The new software is much more powerful than what we're currently using, and it has new features that will really help us in the future. Besides, we're getting a good price on the software because we'll be among the first in our industry to make the changeover."

Lupe said, "But isn't it bad to be among the first to use new software? Don't some companies like to let other companies experiment first and then adopt it after it appears that everything works okay?"

Martin said, "Lupe's right. One of our old vice presidents who left for a big promotion said that it's better to be safely behind the leading edge of information technology. One of the wags around here likes to say we're on the bleeding edge of technology."

Tommy said, "This isn't leading-edge software. It's been out for a year now and lots of companies in other industries are using it. We need to get on with the change and quit dragging our heels. This software will be the new standard and we'll be better off making the change now rather than waiting until our competitors change over."

Greg said, "I agree with Cecilia. New software always sounds great on paper. But I've heard that when you start to work with the new software, the new features just make your computer run slower. And, the added features are kind of a waste because most people never use them."

Tommy said, "Listen, you can complain all you want, but it's not going to change anything. Just get used to it. We're going to have to make the change, and I think it's a good move. Telling doom-and-gloom stories about the new software isn't going to help. You need to adopt a positive attitude and embrace the new change. You'll see that we'll be better off with this new software. Besides, it's useless to try to resist new technology. I'll send out a memo about the change next week. I've got to run to a meeting with the vice president."

After Tommy left, Greg said, "Do any of you know why we have so much security where the computers that support the systems are located? Back in the 1990s one of the employees got so frustrated with the company that he threw buckets of water on the computers. Can you imagine how frustrated he was? I heard that when the police took him away he was mumbling something about changes in software."

Questions

1. Why do you think Tommy's employees are so resistant to the new software?
2. Explain how the change could have been managed more effectively.
3. How can Tommy help get his people to accept the change?
4. Why do you think Tommy did not involve his employees in the decision?

TEAMS

CASE 8.2   Another Reorganization

Betty Cooper couldn't believe the e-mail from Vice President Larry Kendall: "Effective immediately the workers' compensation claims unit and the long-term disability claims unit will be moved to the 24th floor to be located with the health insurance claims unit. All three units will report to Hal Murdoch, assistant vice president for claims. Office assignments are posted on the bulletin board in the health insurance break area. The physical relocation of files and office equipment will take place the day after tomorrow. If you have any questions about this change, consult your supervisor." Betty thought to herself, "I am a supervisor, and I don't have a clue about what's going on!" She looked up and saw her boss, Libby Wilkerson, standing at the door.

Libby said, "Betty, Vice President Kendall just called and wants us to come up to his office. In case you haven't heard, we're going to reorganize, and he wants to give us the specifics. I don't know anything more about this than you do, except that the whole thing came together very quickly at the senior executive level."

At the meeting in Vice President Kendall's office, Betty learned that Libby was being transferred to underwriting and that, indeed, Hal Murdoch would be her new boss. She had worked with Hal before and had a good relationship with him. She also learned that all three claims processing units were going to be organized in teams and that a team-based compensation system was going to be implemented. After the meeting Hal said, "What a surprise! I just found out about the reorganization myself two days ago. But let's focus on the task ahead of us. Claims processing costs have skyrocketed and senior management has told us that they want us to try teams and team-based compensation in order to improve efficiency. You'll have to get your people on board with this change in order for us to make this work."

The next day, Betty brought her employees together to explain the reorganization. She outlined what she had learned at the meeting about the reorganization. She explained that they would be working in teams and that they would be compensated on the basis of team performance. She then asked for questions.

Joanne Moore said, "Why do we have all of these reorganizations? One of the reasons costs are increasing is that they keep moving us around all of the time. We've had so many reorganizations around this place that if it weren't for the telephone book I couldn't tell where anyone works anymore. And where did this stuff about teams come from?"

Carolyn Hudson said, "Between the reorganizations and downsizing, the only people who have any job security around here are the people who do the moving for us. But aside from the move, I don't understand the need for teams or the team-based compensation. That sounds like a bad idea to me."

Jim Harper, who seemed to be upset, said, "Why do they think teams will be the answer to increasing costs? And while I respect the people in this unit, I'm not sure my pay should be determined by how well they perform as a team."

Sandy Barry said, "How big are the teams going to be, and how are we going to decide who's going to be on each team? Can we pick who we want to be on our team? Has anybody in this company actually tried to do this?"

Carolyn Hudson said, "What happens to those people who don't get picked for a team? Can we kick someone off our team if they don't perform?"

Betty said, "Hold on, we're getting way ahead of ourselves. These are good questions for which I don't have any answers at this time. And I certainly understand your concerns. Nonetheless, I would like for us to come up with our own approach to this and then get Hal's support for what we want to do."

Joanne Moore said, "Why should we waste our time trying to come up with rational ways to organize with teams? I'll bet that one of the senior executives will tell us what we're going to do regardless of what we decide. So why don't we just save a lot of time and wait for another e-mail from Vice President Kendall?"

Questions

1. What are the likely barriers to successful implementation of the changes in this case?

2. What mistakes have already been made?

3. What should Betty do to increase the likelihood of successful change?

4. What factors will help Betty implement these changes?

REFERENCES

[1] Bianco, Anthony, Rossant, John, and Gard, Lauren. "The Future of the *New York Times*," *Business Week* (January 17, 2005): 64–71. Rose, Matthew, and Cohen, Laurie P. "Amid Turmoil, Top Editors Resign at *New York Times*," *Wall Street Journal* (June 6, 2003): A1–A6.

[2] Ibid. Alan Deutschman. "Making Change," *Fast Company* (May 2005): 52–62.

[3] Enriquez, Juan. *As the Future Catches You: How Genomics and Other Forces Are Changing Your Life, Work, Health and Wealth*, New York: Crown Business, 2000, 71.

[4] Hunt, Trevor. *Presidents: Quips and Quotes from George Washington to George W. Bush*, New York: Gramercy Books, 2001, 152.

[5] Thomas A. Stewart. "Rate Your Readiness to Change," *Fortune* (February 7, 1994): 106–108.

[6] Jeffrey Pfeffer. *Competitive Advantage through People.* Cambridge, MA: Harvard Business School Press (1996).

[7] Alan Deutschman. "Making Change," *Fast Company* (May 2005): 52–62.

[8] Friedman, Thomas L. *The World Is Flat: A Brief History of the Twenty-first Century.* New York: Farrar, Straus and Giroux (2005), 462.

[9] Bianco, Rossant, and Lauren. "The Future of the *New York Times*," 64–71. Deutschman. "Making Change."

[10] Friedman. *The World Is Flat: A Brief History of the Twenty-first Century.*

[11] Ibid.

[12] Kreitner, Robert, and Knicki, Angelo. *Organizational Behavior*, 5th ed. Boston: Irwin McGraw-Hill, 2001.

[13] Burke, Warner. "Organization Change Is Not a Linear Process," Presentation to the Academy of Management Annual Meeting, Washington, DC (August 6, 2001).

[14] Nauman, Matt. "Job Well Done," *Chicago Tribune* (September 18, 1994): sect. 17, 3.

[15] Chappell, Lindsay. "GM Missed Early Lessons of NUMMI," *Automotive News* (June 7, 1999): 26.

[16] Kosan, Lisa. "Training Spans the World," *eWeek* (January 29, 2001): 54–57.

[17] Ibid.

[18] Lee, Felissa K., Dougherty, Thomas W., and Turban, Daniel B. "The Role of Personality and Work Values in Mentoring Programs," *Review of Business* (Spring/Summer 2000): 33–37.

[19] Jamieson, David, and O'Mara, Julie. *Managing Workforce 2000.* San Francisco: Jossey-Bass (1991): 27–29.

[20] Greengard, Samuel. "Gimme Attitude," *Workforce Management* (July 2003): 56–60.

[21] Greengard. "Gimme Attitude," 58.

[22] Muller, Joann. "Assembling a New Auto Worker," *Chicago Tribune* (May 29, 1994): sect. 8, 1.

[23] Browning, Guy. "How to Get Ahead by Being a Bastard," *People Management* (November 25, 2001): 154.

[24] McGregor, Douglas. "The Human Side of Enterprise" in *Classics in Management,* Harwood F. Merrill, ed. New York: American Management Association (1970): 461–475.

[25] Swanson, Sandra. "Beware: Employee Monitoring Is on the Rise," *Information Week* (August 20, 2001): 57.

[26] Ibid., 57–58.

[27] McGregor, "The Human Side of Enterprise."

[28] Peters, Tom. "Nobody Knows Nothin', So Go Ahead, Take Those Risks," *Chicago Tribune* (August 29, 1994): sect. 4, 3.

[29] Zellner, Wendy. "Team Player: No More 'Same-ol'—'Same-ol'," *Business Week* (October 17, 1994): 95–96.

[30] White, Susan S., and Locke, Edwin A. "Problems with the Pygmalion Effect and Some Proposed Solutions," *Leadership Quarterly* (Fall 2000): 389–415.

[31] Hymowitz, Carol. "Bosses Who Pigeonhole Workers Waste Talent, Contribute to Turnover," *Wall Street Journal* (May 24, 2005): B1.

[32] Ibid.

[33] Reichers, Arnon, Wanous, John P., and Austin, James T. "Understanding and Managing Cynicism about Organizational Change" in *Academy of Management Executive* (February 1997): 48–59.

[34] McCall, Morgan W., Jr. *High Flyers: Developing the Next Generation of Leaders.* Boston: Harvard Business School Press, 1998: 164.

[35] Ibid., 163–164.

[36] Atkinson, Philip. "Managing Resistance to Change," *Management Services* (Spring 2005): 14–19.

[37] Kotter, John P. *Leading Change.* Boston: Harvard Business School, 1996: 67.

[38] Ibid.

[39] Lawson, Emily, and Price, Conlin. "The Psychology of Change Management," *McKinsey Quarterly* (Special Edition 2003): 30–39.

[40] McAllaster, Craig M. "The 5P's of Change: Leading Change by Effectively Utilizing Leverage Points within an Organization," *Organizational Dynamics* (August, 2004): 318–328.

[41] Ibid.

[42] Ibid.

[43] Ibid.

[44] Ibid. Thatcher, Mandy. "The Grapevine: Communication Tool or Thorn in Your Side?" *Strategic Communication Management* (August/September 2003): 30-33.

[45] Ibid.

[46] Gerstner, Louis V., Jr. *Who Says Elephants Can't Dance?* New York: Harper Business (2002).

[47] Gerstner, *Who Says Elephants Can't Dance?*

[48] Franklin, Ann. Address to the Metroplex Human Resource Planning Society, Las Colinas, TX (Spring 1997).

[49] McAllaster, "The 5 P's of Change: Leading Change by Effectively Utilizing Leverage Points within an Organization."

[50] McAllaster, "The 5 P's of Change: Leading Change by Effectively Utilizing Leverage Points within an Organization," 322.

[51] Fox, Shaul, and Amichai-Hamburger, Yair. "The Power of Emotional Appeals in Promoting Organizational Change Programs," *Academy of Management Executive* (November 2001): 84–93.

[52] Deutschman, Alan. "Making Change," *Fast Company* (May 2005): 52–62.

[53] Fox and Amichai-Hamburger, "The Power of Emotional Appeals."

[54] Deutschman. "Making Change."

[55] Bazerman, Max H. *Judgment in Managerial Decision Making.* New York: Wiley, 1994. Bazerman, Max H., and Neale, Margaret A. *Negotiating Rationally.* New York: Free Press, 1992.

[56] Extracted from Yankelovich, Daniel. *The Magic of Dialogue: Transforming Conflict into Cooperation.* New York: Simon & Schuster, 1999, 69–70.

[57] Conger, Jay A. "The Necessary Art of Persuasion," *Harvard Business Review* (May–June 1998): 84–95.

[58] Ibid., 91.

[59] Ibid., 87.

[60] Ibid.

[61] Godin, Seth. "If It's Broke, Fix It." *Fast Company* (October 2003): 131.

[62] Ibid.

[63] Ibid.

[64] McAllaster, "The 5 P's of Change: Leading Change by Effectively Utilizing Leverage Points within an Organization."

[65] Narisetti, Raju. "Bottom-Up Approach Pushes Plant's Performance to the Top," *Chicago Tribune* (November 29, 1992): sect. 7, 13.

[66] Haley, Fiona. "Mutual Benefit," *Fast Company* (October 2004): 98–99.

[67] Duetschman, Alan. "Building a Better Skunk Works," *Fast Company* (March 2005): 68–73.

[68] Duetschman. "Building a Better Skunk Works," 73.

[69] Scheff, David. "Levi's Changes Everything," *Fast Company* (June–July, 1996): 65–78.

[70] Fleming, Peter. "Metaphors of Resistance," *Management Communication Quarterly* (August 2005): 45–66.

CHAPTER

*"Coming together is a beginning. Keeping together is progress.
Working together is success."*

Henry Ford[1]

Objectives

After reading and discussing this chapter, you should be able to do the following:

1. Explain the characteristics of work groups.
2. Describe the major features of teams and how they operate.
3. Explain how to build effective teams.
4. Describe the characteristics of effective teams.
5. Describe errors in group and team decision-making.
6. List and briefly describe the group-serving and self-serving roles played by members of a group problem-solving session.
7. List the types of cliques and give an example of each.
8. Describe how group behavior can be affected by internal group competition—what happens to the winning side and what happens to the losing side.

Using Teamwork to Develop New Products at Hypertherm

Hypertherm was selected by the Society of Human Resource Management as the fourth best small- or medium-sized company to work for in 2005. The company, based in Hanover, New Hampshire, manufactures plasma metal cutting equipment for the global market. Hypertherm is the worldwide leader in plasma cutting technology and holds more patents than any other of its competitors.[2] Hypertherm has over 600 employees and annual revenues of approximately $200 million.[3] The company, which began in 1968 in a small garage with only two employees, is noted for its high rate of innovation. In one recent year alone, the company's associates proposed 2,362 ideas for various types of improvement and 1,536 were adopted.[4]

The company's founder, Richard Couch, credits teamwork between such disciplines as marketing, sales, and engineering as a reason why it is able to

Teams and Groups

Questions for Thought

1. What are the differences in management practices and systems in organizations that rely on teamwork versus those that focus on individual contributions?
2. How do supervisors implement team-based approaches in their work environments?

Introduction

Groups are formed when two or more people come together for the purpose of achieving some mutual goal or benefit. More specifically, a **group** is two or more people who are consciously aware of one another, who consider themselves to be a functioning unit, and who share in a quest to achieve goals or obtain some common benefit. When we say that the members are aware of each other, we mean that they know something about each other, are clear about why they are together, and recognize the need to cooperate. There are two basic kinds of groups in organizations: *formal groups* that are created by management and *informal groups* created by members of the organization. This latter type of group allows its members to associate with

Learning Objective Number One

group
two or more people who consider themselves a functioning unit and share a common goal

341

team
a work group in which members feel a compelling need for teamwork, assume joint responsibility for accomplishment of the team's goals, and hold each other accountable for results

TEAMS

others who share their values and interests. As a supervisor, you must learn to work with both kinds of groups. You will also most likely work with **teams.** One of the most important distinctions between groups and teams is that teams perform interdependent work. As will be discussed later, in real teams there is also a compelling purpose for teamwork.[7] Another difference is that team members are more actively involved in decision-making, take on responsibilities for the team's performance, and hold each other responsible for results.[8]

Teams in U.S. factories and offices are having a tremendous impact on quality and the productivity of their organizations. The value of such teams is flexibility for management and motivation to excel for team members. For example, at Goldman Sachs, an enormously profitable Wall Street firm, a professional observed that "Team work here is better than on any professional sports team I've ever even seen."[9] It is no surprise that Goldman Sachs was number eight on *Fortune*'s 2005 list of the best 100 companies for which to work.[10] Similarly, furniture maker Herman Miller, an early innovator with work teams, has also been on *Fortune*'s list.[11] Teams can accomplish incredible feats. For example, teams of astronauts have repaired the Hubble telescope while it orbited the earth. The astronauts worked as a team while sharing ideas for improvement during training. The team's members helped each other and wanted each to perform with perfection.[12]

The role of the supervisor also is changing because of team structures. Supervisors may be elected members of such teams, serving on a rotating basis, or they may become more like coaches than traditional managers. This chapter focuses on how groups and teams form and how you can effectively manage and get along with them at work.

THE PERSONALITY OF GROUPS

A group, like the people who compose it, has a personality as unique and subject to change as any individual's. The group's personality is partially a composite of the personalities of its members. We say "partially" because a group is always something more than the sum of its parts. That something more comes about because of the interaction of group members, which creates energy and qualities that may not be possessed by any of the individual group members. An example would be a basic training group in the military. Individually, its members may not have the desire or the will to excel and may not know their capabilities. But in group situations, the pressure to conform and the feeling that "If they can do it, so can I" will dominate. If 20 trainees were dispatched on a 20-mile hike, one at a time at intervals of 10 minutes, very few (if any) would complete the march. When all 20 embark on the hike together, most will finish, even if their buddies have to carry some of them. Combat units often exhibit tremendous courage that individuals would not show without the support of and the commitment to their comrades.

synergy
cooperative action or force of two or more elements pulling together that yields a result greater than the sum of the results that could be achieved separately by the elements

There is a term for the fact that groups often produce at greater levels than the sum of their individual members: **synergy.** Common table salt is a chemical combination of two poisons—sodium and chlorine. Alone each is dangerous; together they are beneficial and take on properties that neither has alone.

All groups—eve
ones—have perso
Group personalities
sum of individual pers   es,
plus the synergy that is created
when those individuals work
together.

The term *synergy* applies to any combined operation or action; thus, it can be either positive or negative. Satisfied groups or group members can exhibit greater positive action than the individuals within the group could do on their own.

FORMAL GROUPS

A **formal group** may be defined as two or more people who come together by management decision to achieve specific goals. Your company, your department, your shift, and the various management committees are but a few of the many formal groups you encounter each day. Any individual, especially a manager, may belong to more than one formal group simultaneously. For instance, you are an employee of a company, working in a particular functional division and within a specific department. You are a member, therefore, of at least three formal groups. If you serve on a committee, you belong to a fourth formal group.

Formal groups may be temporary or permanent. An *ad hoc* committee—one set up to solve a particular problem and dissolved when the solution is determined—is an example of a temporary formal group. Most formal groups in your company are

formal group
two or more people who come together by management decision to achieve specific goals

SUPERVISORS AND ETHICS

The retail giant, Wal-Mart, has received a great deal of negative publicity for some of its practices as well as the actions of some of its managers and executives. The company, which has approximately 1.3 million employees in the United States, has been criticized for low pay and heath insurance coverage. More specifically, in the past, full-time employees have been required to wait six months to qualify for health insurance while part-time employees have not qualified for coverage until they have been with the company for two years. Reports indicated fewer than 50 percent of Wal-Mart employees had health insurance. In addition, the *New York Times* reported on a memorandum written by a Wal-Mart executive that discussed concerns about growing costs of employee benefits. The executive proposed that:

> To discourage unhealthy job applicants, Ms. Chambers [Executive Vice President] suggests that Wal-Mart arrange for "all jobs to include some physical activity (e.g., all cashiers do some cart-gathering)."

In addition, there have been approximately 40 lawsuits in 25 states claiming Wal-Mart has used contractors that relied on illegal immigrants to obtain cost savings, and Wal-Mart was aware of this. With these allegations about its ethical standards, it is no surprise that some more affluent customers are boycotting the retailer because they perceive that Wal-Mart employees are not being treated well. Supervisors must be careful to avoid situations in which they will be involved in unethical treatment of employees. They have to decide for themselves and cannot rely on any organization for the definitive standards of ethics.

Sources: Tracie Rozhon. "Teaching Wal-Mart New Tricks," *New York Times*, (May 8, 2005). "Be Kind to Be Cruel," *Economist* (October 29, 2005): 62. Steven Greenhouse and Michael Barbaro. "Wal-Mart Memo Suggests Ways to Cut Employee Benefit Costs," *New York Times* (October 26, 2005). Jeffrey E. Garten. "Wal-Mart Gives Globalism a Bad Name," *Business Week* (March 8, 2004): 24.

permanent although even whole divisions can be dissolved or merged into others on occasion, as the needs of the business may dictate. Formal groups may be true teams if they consist of "a small number of people with complementary skills who are committed to a common purpose, performance goals, and approach for which they hold themselves mutually responsible."[13] "The teams most popular today are of two broad types: work teams, which include high-performance or self-managed teams, and special-purpose problem-solving teams. . . . While problem-solving teams are temporary, work teams, used by about two-thirds of U.S. companies, tend to be permanent."[14]

Every formal group has a leader. The heads of most formal groups are managers who have been installed for just that purpose. The leader of a self-managed team may be elected or appointed by the team's members, and leadership may be rotated among the members over time. Either way, the formal group's leader has varying degrees of formal authority at her disposal. The higher a team climbs on the continuum, the more autonomy it has. Management teams usually have the highest degree of autonomy.

TEAMS

TEAMS

According to experts, "the task of setting up work teams among employees should begin at the top."[15] Several conditions must exist before organizations can successfully implement teams. The first is that they must have the expertise needed to form teams and a willingness to share problem solving with team members. The second is that it must be possible to change the way things get done—procedures, processes, traditions, and habits. The third is that there must be sufficient commitment in money and time to prepare people for team roles and to continue training efforts. Typical subjects of team training include decision-making, how to run meetings, communication skills, handling conflict, implementing change, using quality tools (benchmarking, statistical controls, and scoreboarding), evaluating team and team members' performances, and reengineering concepts. Before GM produced any Saturn cars, "workers got 300 to 700 hours of schooling, covering basic skills such as conflict management and problem solving. That has been followed by ongoing training in specific areas, such as interviewing techniques."[16]

Learning Objective Number Two

Most major corporations have product design teams that include engineers, market researchers, production managers, and representatives from suppliers. The multiple perspectives represented within the teams ensure, from the very beginning, that the product created is what the consumer wants and can be manufactured efficiently and with quality. Another kind of management team is the crisis team—a group of managers from various departments that can act swiftly in the face of any crisis the company may face. Such teams plan their actions before crises actually occur.

Ideally, you should be concerned with molding your people into a team or group of teams that feels an owner's concern for the organization and its goals. A true team leader or facilitator is much more than the head of a group of workers and must have both a mature personality and a sense of security.

Maturity is required so that emotions can be controlled when dealing with people who may be less mature. Security is required so that the leader does not fear sharing management authority with others and does not fear being challenged. Managers who are new to team leadership have much teaching and learning to do. They must master a participative style of supervision and be willing to teach problem solving and decision-making to team members. They also must be proficient in interpersonal skills and be able to take the time necessary to deal with delays that group approaches often involve. The qualities of patience, tact, and enthusiasm are essential. "Typically, a team leader still spends time actually performing various production or service tasks. . . . Often the team leader serves as a spokesperson for the team, coordinates team activities with other departments or teams, and devotes time to training new team members."[17]

One of the keys for good team dynamics is a solid foundation for relationships within the team. Such a foundation should include a clear mission, explicit values that are accepted by team members, ground rules that are agreed upon, and an understanding of the limits of the team's empowerment and the decisions that will be made by management. A second key is to hold face-to-face meetings periodically instead of relying too much on more sterile forms of communication, such as e-mail. Another key is to facilitate conflict resolution by training members to engage in healthy discussions of differences, to listen actively, and to avoid finger pointing and blame placing. In addition,

SUPERVISORS AND PERFORMANCE

The role of team leader on a self-directed work team boils down to being an active participant and facilitator—removing obstacles by providing training that allows team members to execute the processes and tasks that accomplish their purposes and goals. Specifically, facilitators' roles include the following:

1. Provide training and tools essential for maintaining and improving quality. Team members should be able to:
   - Identify and define internal and external customers' needs and requirements.
   - Establish quality standards for the team's and team members' performance.
   - Measure all performances and identify deviations from set standards.
   - Investigate and remove the sources of deviations from standards.
   - Make all improvements standard operating procedure.
   - Continue to search for evolutionary and revolutionary (reengineering) changes to improve quality.

2. Provide training and tools essential for team interaction and collaboration. Team members should be able to:
   - Exercise effective communication skills when conducting meetings, resolving conflicts, reaching agreements, and engaging in feedback activities.
   - Navigate through the various stages of team building.
   - Appreciate the uniqueness of each team member and value the contributions and participation of each.

3. Provide training and tools essential for team members to obtain and improve work-related skills and experiences. For example, team members should be able to:
   - Operate equipment and machinery effectively and efficiently.
   - Maintain equipment and machinery properly.
   - Engage in safe work habits and practices.
   - Execute tasks effectively and efficiently.

it is important for team members to recognize that there may be gender differences that affect group dynamics, such as in how men and women listen. A final key is that the team needs recognition in order to sustain high performance in the long term.[18]

Team facilitators (sometimes called *team advisers* or *group leaders*) "frequently play a coordinating and facilitating role. They help teams communicate with one another and serve as a conduit for information that flows from teams to other organizational departments and from these back to the teams."[19] As a leader of teams, you must learn that your major tasks are to help each team define its goals, set the limits for each team, help obtain the resources each team requires, and mold a cooperative and committed spirit in each team. The team facilitator has a blend of traditional supervisory and middle management responsibilities. Both team leaders and team facilitators often have wide spans of control—numbers of subordinates. "For example, AT&T Operator Services in Richmond, Virginia, moved from a span of control of one leader for each 12 members to one leader for each 72 members. As teams mature, it is not uncommon for six or more teams to report to a single group leader."[20]

PERFORMANCE

This chapter's feature on supervisors and performance provides specifics on how the leader can facilitate team performance.

An example of successful teamwork is provided by ABC Rail Products Corporation's Chicago Heights factory. The factory was losing money, and managers and union workers were not cooperating. One hundred twenty-five jobs were on the line when the chairman and CEO, Donald W. Grinter, met with union leaders: Either the two would work to save the plant or it would be closed. Management shared financial data, and union representatives and plant managers met to discuss their options. The importance of departmental boundaries diminished as employees and managers implemented teams to solve problems related to quality. The company worked with vendors to tighten control and quality over supplies, and a new management team was installed. Gradually, the losses diminished, profits returned, and backorders resulted.[21] The plant's general foreman says, "You ask somebody to do something extra now, they do it."[22] Says Don Grinter about the turnaround, "It was a thousand little things adding up."[23]

TEAMS

This chapter's feature on supervising teams identifies several types of the more common types of teams.

Toyota's automobile manufacturing operations in the United States have established a reputation for excellent teamwork. However, the U.S. operations of other Japanese automobile manufacturers also display excellent teamwork. For example, Honda of America provides extensive training for its employees in both problem solving and teamwork. The purpose of such training is to improve efficiency and quality by harnessing the suggestions and creativity of its teams. Honda also provides opportunities for team recognition by having the teams make presentations every six months on their quality circle results. Judges evaluate the presentations on the teams' problem-solving processes.[24]

PERFORMANCE

Team training is critical to success, and there is evidence that such training increases productivity, produces cost savings, and leads to increased customer satisfaction. At a Ralston pet food plant, team training led to a 55 percent increase in productivity and associated annual cost savings of 5 percent for six consecutive years. In addition, turnover has declined at the plant. The team environment at Ralston emphasizes empowerment of the teams, delegation of authority from managers to teams, improved communication, reduced emphasis on rank or position, and team member involvement in such matters as hiring and scheduling. Team members were trained in selection and interviewing while team leaders, who were promoted from the ranks, received negotiation training.[25]

An example of superb teamwork by Southwest Airlines ground crews is presented in Exhibit 9.1. Southwest's ground crews work with the precision of an Indy race-car pit crew. Interestingly, Southwest is one of the most highly unionized companies in the United States, with over 84 percent of its employees represented by unions. Obviously, Southwest Airlines has a very different relationship with its unions than many other companies. One difference is how the company invests in relationships. This is reflected in negotiations as Southwest's former CEO James Parker says the company tries to work with a goal of determining the most that it can pay employees rather than the least.[26]

TEAMS

In addition to teamwork in manufacturing plants and on the flight line, teams of knowledge workers also work in office environments. Unfortunately, the layout of existing office space often detracts from both teamwork and personal space. To address the intensive information requirements for knowledge workers and their need for collaborative efforts, IBM and Steelcase have developed a new, highly personalized

SUPERVISING TEAMS

Organizations may utilize several different types of teams for different purposes. The following are some common types of teams. Note that some of the types of teams may overlap. For example, a project team may also be a cross-functional team.

Cross-Functional Teams

These teams include members from different functions in order to better coordinate efforts and obtain quicker results. For example, a team tasked with product development responsibilities could include sales personnel who know customers' preferences, engineering representatives who can develop the product, production representatives who know what can be produced and the expense involved, an information technology specialist who can provide information systems support, and a finance person who can provide budgetary support.

Problem-Solving Teams

These teams, which are the most common, are tasked with finding a solution for a specific problem. After they accomplish this (their task), they are disbanded. Survey data indicate increasing use of such teams, and that over 90 percent of companies use them.

Project Teams

These teams are often formed to work on a specific project and are expected to have a limited lifespan. Their objectives are generally of a short-term nature. Since these teams usually have relatively short life spans, there is typically insufficient time for team building, they often experience communication problems, conflict, and a lack of cohesion.

Virtual Teams

Such teams include members from different geographic locations who interact with each other using computer-based communication and information technologies. They often include members who are located in different regions and countries as well as different time zones. They can be very diverse and may include members from several cultures.

Work Teams

Such teams, which are also called production or service teams, usually work on an on-going basis in a production facility or in a service capacity. As a result, they have relatively long life spans, which allows them to engage in team building and teamwork skill development. These relatively permanent teams also have a clear sense of purpose or objectives. Examples include assembly, maintenance, account, and sales teams. Because these teams remain together for extended periods of time, their leaders can implement appraisal and review procedures within the teams.

Sources: Michael West. *Motivate Teams, Maximize Success: Effective Strategies for Realizing Your Goals*, San Francisco: Chronicle Books, 2004. Jill E. Nemiro. *Creativity in Virtual Teams: Key Components for Success*, San Francisco: Pfeiffer, 2004. Thomas R Keen. *Creating Effective & Successful Teams*, West Lafayette, Indiana: Ichor Business Books, 2003.

TEAMS

computerized office environment called BlueSpace. The BlueSpace environment, which facilitates collaborative efforts while retaining personal space, has cubicles with such innovations as sensors that automatically adjust the temperature in spaces to individuals' preferences as they arrive and touch screens that enable team members to instantly determine members' locations and their availability.[27]

Teamwork by ground crews at Southwest Airlines.   EXHIBIT 9.1

MINUTE BY MINUTE AT LAX

2:45 P.M. Like a finely honed pit crew waiting for that Indy car to arrive, Rudy Guidi, Calvin Williams, Kirkland Howling, and Ricardo Perez prepare to spring into action. Rudy and Calvin go over the bin sheet, which tells the team how much baggage, freight, and mail is on the aircraft, while the rest of the team makes sure the equipment is in position to turn the plane. The ground crew is joined by First Officer Ken Brown, who is there to do a preflight check on the aircraft.

2:46 P.M. The aircraft is in sight, and Ricardo jumps up on the back of the tug to guide the plane into the jetway. Rudy and Calvin each start up a belt loader and begin to move toward the plane as it approaches the gate.

2:47 P.M. The aircraft comes to a complete stop at the gate. The jetway is already moving toward the door of the aircraft. The baggage bins of the Boeing 737 fly open. A fueler pulls up to the aircraft while crew members off-load bags.

2:48 P.M. Ken pauses for a moment from his preflight check to help Kirkland connect the pushback to the nose gear of the airplane. Provisioning crew members race through the rear door of the aircraft to stock ice, drinks, and snacks and to empty trash. Passengers begin to deplane.

2:49 P.M. The freight coordinator pulls up in his tug to ensure freight labeled NFG (Next Flight Guaranteed) makes the next flight.

2:50 P.M. First officer completes his preflight check. Flight attendants move through the cabin of the aircraft to reposition seat belts and pick up trash.

2:51 P.M. All bags are off-loaded. Ramp agents begin loading bags for new passengers. Provisioning is complete. Current flight crew (pilots and flight attendants) is relieved by new flight crew. Operations agent makes initial announcement calling for preboarders. Several adults with children and a person on crutches make their way to the plane. Fueler is pulling the hose out of the wing of the aircraft.

2:52 P.M. Operations agent begins boarding customers in groups of 30. Bags are loaded and fueling is complete. Most of the ground crew move to another gate to prepare for the arrival of the next aircraft.

3:00 P.M. Passenger boarding is complete; operations agent gives weight and balance sheet to pilot. Pilots trim the aircraft according to the load. Ramp agent connects the communication gear to talk to the pilots from the tarmac.

3:01 P.M. The jetway pulls back and the door of the aircraft closes. Pushback maneuvers the plane onto the tarmac and turns the plane toward the runway. Ramp agent unhooks the pushback from the aircraft and the plane taxis toward the runway.

Here is what this ground crew of four accomplished in 15 minutes: There was a complete change of flight crew; 137 customers came off the plane and another 137 boarded; the ramp agents unloaded 97 bags, 1,000 pounds of mail, and 25 pieces of freight weighing close to 500 pounds. The ramp agents then loaded 123 bags and 600 pounds of mail (no freight), while the fueler pumped 4,500 pounds of jet fuel into the wing of the aircraft. It's an impressive spectacle. People come out of nowhere and the entire area around the plane is abuzz. Then, in a mater of minutes, their jobs complete, the swarm of people disappears and the plane pulls away.

VIRTUAL TEAMS

As noted in the earlier discussion of communication and this chapter's supervising teams feature, virtual teams are becoming increasingly common and critical to the work performed in a number of organizations that operate in multiple geographical locations. In many cases, the team members have very little opportunity for personal interaction and rely almost exclusively on telecommunications and computer-based information technologies. Such teams allow organizations to draw on world-class talent from different countries as well as different locations in the United States to perform various projects and functions. Virtual teams also provide an advantage of allowing the use of top talent on the team, regardless of where the individuals are located, while avoiding relocation. They also allow a quick response to customer requirements and allow companies to take advantage of expanded working days when team members are located in different time zones.[28] As indicated in the communications discussion, virtual teams require various accommodations for their reliance on communication technology rather than personal contact as well as other adjustments. Exhibit 9.2 provides guidance for virtual teams on the use of videoconferencing, audioconferencing, telephone calls, and asynchronous computer meetings, such as through the use of Lotus Notes or Teamware.

Learning Objective Number Three

BUILDING TEAM AND GROUP EFFECTIVENESS

The hallmarks of a "learning organization," one that "values—and thinks competitive advantage derives from—continuing learning, both individual and collective."[29] Here is a case in point. Fred Simon, project manager for the development of a new Lincoln model, brought the car to market faster, cheaper, and with less intergroup infighting than ever before at Ford. His engineering teams learned to work together instead of jealously guarding their respective turfs.

> Simon found that the engineers who designed the air conditioning, the headlights, the power seats, and the CD player, all working separately, had each made their component such that when used simultaneously they would drain the car battery. . . . Because Simon's engineers understood [the value of working in a learning organization] they put their heads together and came up with a solution: Raise the car's idle to increase the battery's charge. Of course, that lowered fuel efficiency, and the engineers in charge of that didn't particularly like making such a sacrifice. The difference this time was that the problem got solved quickly and because it was clear the change was made for the good of the car, no one felt like a loser.[30]

Team leaders or supervisors in charge of teams need rewards to help keep teams moving in the right direction. They also need to be able to reinforce behaviors that make for good teamwork. In some organizations, the process of putting the interests of the team ahead of individual interests is such a foreign concept that it has been humorously referred to as an "unnatural act." While the ability to provide financial reinforcements

Typical applications of communication technology in virtual teams.	**EXHIBIT 9.2**

VIDEOCONFERENCING

- To conduct strategic planning sessions

- To discuss and refine problems

- To list, debate, and prioritize potential solutions

- To make straightforward (not complicated) decisions

- To state and discuss opinions on specific topics

- To provide a forum for large keynote meetings (such as speakers or company state-of-the-union addresses)

- To celebrate team success

AUDIOCONFERENCES

- To generate ideas

- To assess and review current work

- To review previous work

- To raise new issues or concerns

TELEPHONE CALLS

- To get input, feedback, or a second opinion about how to proceed

- To ask project-related questions and get answers

- To share ideas or discuss important information

- To touch base, keep in touch, or establish personal contact

- To communicate when there are technological problems with other methods

- To respond to individual team members' personal crises

ASYNCHRONOUS COMPUTER MEETINGS

- To brainstorm and generate ideas

- To generate ideas for plans and ideas about products

- To comment on products

- To collaboratively author written documents

- To collect data and discuss trends

Source: Creativity in Virtual Teams: Key Components for Success, by Jill E. Nemior, pp. 144–147, Copyright © (2004 Pfeiffer), Reprinted with permission of John Wiley & Sons, Inc.

is important in all work organizations, we know that many of the reinforcements are non-financial.[31] The following are a few suggestions for non-financial rewards:

■ Give out formal recognition for exceptional individual achievement, like "Living the Teamwork Values" awards for team members who have been caught "walking the talk" of the company's and/or team's explicitly stated values.

■ Take video shots of your team's working experiences and create a video production for use and distribution at key organizational meetings.

■ Invite senior management and key stakeholders to attend team meetings and functions in order to "showcase" the team and its members at work.

■ Take a photo of the team, or a team member, with a corporate executive or distinguished external VIP, and have it framed for all the team members and/or the VIP. Include the photo in a public recognition event, publication, or other type of "visibility vehicle."[32]

TEAMS

As a group's supervisor, you need to be a facilitator. You must clearly define the group's goals, listing the essential tasks and the degree of quality you wish to see in its performance. You also must structure the group to provide sufficient interaction among group members, monitor its performance, and when necessary, offer leadership and coaching. Finally, you must be certain that the group perceives the fact that important group outcomes depend on both individual and collective performance.[33]

PUTTING THE TEAM TOGETHER

Supervisors do not always have the freedom to assemble the team that they would ideally like to have. As such, they must work with the people that are available or who have already been assigned to them. Nonetheless, for temporary, secondary assignments, or special purpose teams there may be opportunities to be selective in assembling the team. In such cases, it is helpful to understand how team performance can be enhanced by staffing the team with people who have unique strengths and by filling the team with people who can offset the weakness of others. Aside from considering relative strengths in skills or abilities to offset weaknesses, it is important to consider how team members are likely to interact with each other.[34]

Myers Briggs Type Inventory (MBTI)
an assessment instrument that provides measures of personality components

Insights into personality differences are helpful and may be obtained by reviewing the **Myers Briggs Type Inventory (MBTI)** scores of potential team members. While scores on personality inventories may be considered confidential information in some organizations, in others such information is widely shared. In employee workshops, employees may even engage in exercises in which they wear nametags that designate their MBTI categories. Accordingly, supervisors will need to understand their organization's policies about the use of such information and obtain help from trained professionals before proceeding.[35] They should understand that the results of personality inventories, profiles, and tests have been used improperly at times in the past, and they must be careful with such information. For example, the MBTI should not be used for hiring decisions.[36] It is important to obtain help from trained professionals who understand the **validity,** which is the extent to which the instrument measures what it purports to measure, and **reliability,** which means the consistency, of any such instruments.

The MBTI is probably the most commonly used personality type indicator in work settings and can provide helpful indications of how team members will interact. Worldwide, over 2.5 million people complete the MBTI each year.[37] Another similar instrument, the **Keirsey-Bates Temperaments** system, which is a derivative of the MBTI, can be obtained on-line at *www.keirsey.com.* One of the most important applications of the MBTI is in providing insights into how team members are likely to approach problem solving in very different manners. The MBTI provides information on two dimensions that are relevant to problem solving: (1) how people obtain information for solving problems and (2) how they evaluate such information. On the information-gathering dimension, at one end is **sensing,** in which there is extensive information gathering obtained through the senses, such as by seeing and hearing. At the other end of this spectrum are those who spend much less time gathering information, and rely on **intuition,** such as through feelings and hunches. The other dimension deals with the evaluation of information. At one end of this spectrum are those who employ very rational considerations, such as logical reasoning, economic factors, costs, benefits and so on, which is called **thinking.** At the other end of the spectrum is **feeling** in which people evaluate the information in terms of their values.[38]

Cross-classification of these dimensions produces four unique problem-solving styles: sensing thinking (ST), sensing feeling (SF), intuition-feeling (NF), and intuition-thinking (NT). The ST and NF styles are polar opposites as are the SF and NT styles.[39] There are also two other dimensions on which the MBTI provides information, extraversion-introversion and judging-perceiving.[40] For example, people who are STs often get down to the details of the issue very quickly and are very pragmatic in their approach to solving the problem. It might be observed that STs may sometimes be unable to see the forest because of the trees. In contrast, the NFs, are unlikely to be concerned with details in solving problems and are more likely to be idealistic and creative in their approach. They might be considered to be a bit idealistic. When STs and NFs interact in problem-solving situations, they will likely encounter conflict. In contrast, when STs work together, they understand each other and are likely to work well together. Their answer to a problem may be quick, logical, and pragmatic, but they may not have a very imaginative solution and may miss the larger picture. On the other hand, when NFs work together, they may have a very idealistic or creative solution, with fewer details, take longer to solve the problem, and may not implement the solution very well. Like the STs, when NFs work together they tend to get along.[41]

Depending on the task at hand, supervisors may need team members with similar personality types. However, for many tasks, better decision quality and problem solving will be obtained with a mixture of personality types. The supervisor's challenge is to help these people work together and to understand each other.[42] By sharing insights about personality types within the team, the participants may be able to avoid conflict that they would otherwise experience. Even in the absence of information about the MBTI, supervisors can attempt to develop an informal sense of the personality types of potential team members and make decisions about team composition. While their judgments will be far less accurate, at least they will have a better

validity
the extent to which the instrument measures what it purports to measure

reliability
the trait of being dependable or reliable

Keirsey-Bates Temperaments
an instrument that measures personality types

sensing
a personality component that emphasizes gathering information through the senses

intuition
a personality component that emphasizes gut feelings or hunches as a means of obtaining information

thinking
a personality component that emphasizes rational thought in evaluating information

feeling
a personality component that emphasizes one's values in evaluating information

EXHIBIT 9.3	**Desired teamwork behaviors.**

- *Encouraging others.* Being friendly, warm, responsive to others, praising others and their ideas, agreeing with and accepting the contribution of others.

- *Gatekeeping effectively.* Making it possible for every member to make a contribution to the team or suggesting limited talking time for everyone so that all have a chance to be heard.

- *Standard setting.* Suggesting standards for the team to use in choosing its content or procedures or in evaluating its decisions and reminding the group to avoid decisions that conflict with team standards.

- *Following members' lead.* Going along with the decision of the team, thoughtfully accepting ideas of others, and serving as an audience during team discussion.

- *Expressing the sense of the team.* Summarizing what the feeling of the team is sensed to be and describing reactions of the team to ideas or solutions.

Source: Thomas R. Keen. *Creating Effective & Successful Teams,* West Lafayette, IN: Ichor Business Books, 2003, pp. 29–30. Reproduced with permission.

DIVERSITY

chance of putting together an effective team if they attempt to consider the mix of teammates' personalities.

Personality types are only one of the sources of the differences to be considered in developing and working with teams. Some observers have found differences in how men and women work with teams. Gail Evans, the first executive vice president at CNN, has observed that men are a little better than women at teamwork. One interesting observation that she has made is that women are less likely than men to help the weakest team member. She asserts that women tend to remove the weakest player rather than spend time helping that person improve.[43]

In addition to personality differences that impact team effectiveness, behavior of team members are also critical. Exhibit 9.3 identifies several positive behaviors that supervisors should seek to establish and maintain in their teams.

SEQUENCE OF TEAM DEVELOPMENT

group developmental sequence
phases of group development that typically include forming, storming, norming, performing, and adjourning

As indicated, teams must have a compelling purpose.[44] One of the first things needed for development of a high-performing team is a clear vision statement, which explains the team's purpose. There should also be a small set of objectives that provide focus, in applied terms, for the team's efforts.[45] Supervisors should be aware that groups and teams go through a predictable set of phases or a sequence of stages in their development. The **group developmental sequence** that was first described by Bruce W. Tuckman in the 1960s and then refined with Mary Ann Jenson in the 1970s, has been a valuable guide for team development for over four decades.[46] **Forming** constitutes the first stage in which team members determine the parameters of interpersonal relations and task behaviors.

This stage also includes orientation processes as well as testing. Dependencies with leaders and teammates are recognized at this stage. The second stage is called **storming,** as the members tend to encounter conflict with each other as they interact in the team. They may have emotional experiences as they resist pressures from the team. At the third stage, which is called **norming,** individual resistance is replaced by cohesiveness within the team. Standards become accepted and roles are understood. In the fourth stage, which is referred to as **performing,** roles are well-understood, and the interpersonal relationships provide a supporting mechanism for the performance of work tasks. The energy of the team's members is applied to the work at hand instead of on conflict and resistance activities as in earlier stages.[47] In addition, there is a fifth stage, which is called **adjourning,** in which the team dissolves. Teams that are assembled for special purposes or that have limited life spans go through this stage, which has some similarities to the mourning process. When the dissolution of the team is unexpected, members may find this stage to be stressful.[48]

Knowledge of these sequential stages of development can enable supervisors to be prepared for reactions from team members. By understanding that conflict is a normal occurrence early in a team's development, supervisors and managers will not be concerned that something has gone terribly wrong and will not make the mistake of dissolving the team prematurely because conflict was encountered. In addition, the potential value of the storming stage will be ignored if this stage is not understood. More specifically, in the storming stage, team members communicate their needs, which they may have been too reluctant to mention in the forming stage. Typically people are reluctant to talk candidly about their needs and it is only when needs and concerns are aired that the team can gain full commitment.[49] In addition, researchers have noted that some teams never proceed to the performing stage and that it may be possible for team leaders to act in a facilitating capacity to speed up the progress of teams toward the performing stage. For example, it has been hypothesized that with creative tasks, the team leader could facilitate progress of the team by encouraging a movement toward openness. More specifically, the team leader could explain the benefits of full communication among team members, stress the benefits of positive interactions, and encourage the team to question assumptions.[50]

CHARACTERISTICS OF EFFECTIVE TEAMS

One of the critical determinants of team effectiveness is a compelling purpose that requires employees to work in an interdependent manner to accomplish objectives. Without a compelling purpose and interdependent work, there is no need for a team, as group efforts will suffice.[51] Another characteristic of effective teams is that members provide support for each other. They trust each other and understand that their teammates will step up for them when needed. Communication is free flowing, respectful, and open, and members of effective teams take the time to practice active listening. Team members also participate in important decisions.[52] Teams that have the autonomy and authority to make decisions, and which are held accountable for results, are likely to be more effective.[53] Those that receive feedback on the impact of their efforts are also likely to be more effective.[54] In addition, creative teams are often characterized by diversity with people from different backgrounds and cultures contributing different perspectives and information. While there is typically greater conflict with greater diversity, the creative ideas and decisions that come out of such groups can be much better than with less

forming
the first stage of team development in which team members determine the parameters of interpersonal relations and task behaviors

storming
the second stage of team development where individuals begin thought and often have conflict

norming
third stage of team development where cohesiveness within the team is found

performing
the fourth stage of team development where roles are well-understood, and the interpersonal relationships provide a supporting mechanism for the performance of work tasks

adjourning
the fifth stage of team development where the team dissolves

DIVERSITY

Learning Objective Number Four

EXHIBIT 9.4	Characteristics of effective teamwork.

Common Goals

Leadership

Interaction and Involvement of All Members

Maintenance of Individual Self-Esteem

Open Communication

Power Within Group to Make Decisions

Attention to Both Process and Content

Mutual Trust

Respect for Differences

Constructive Conflict Resolution

Source: Extracted from Fran Rees, *How to Lead Work Teams: Facilitation Skills*, 2nd ed., San Francisco: Jossey-Bass/Pfeiffer, 2001, pp. 31–35.

diverse teams. Effective teams are able to harness the energy underlying conflict and channel it toward the team's objectives. Furthermore, effective teams conduct periodic evaluations of team performance and the contributions of individual members.[55]

Finally, reward systems that focus on team performance rather than individual performance are also associated with team effectiveness.[56] Unfortunately, survey-based research indicates that only 26 percent of companies have adopted any form of team-based rewards, and that companies continue to rely on compensation based on individual performance.[57] Such practices have the potential to undermine teamwork and until these practices change, supervisors will have to rely on non-financial rewards to reinforce team efforts. Exhibit 9.4 presents several characteristics of effective teamwork.

INFLUENCE WITHOUT AUTHORITY

Team leaders and team members have the ability to get things done or exert influence even when they have little or no formal authority. They can exert influence by providing services and other things of value to other associates or managers that create an obligation to reciprocate or return a favor. These services or things of value can serve as currencies. Currencies requiring no authority may be task related, position related, or relationship related. Task-related currencies include information sharing of both technical and organizational varieties, providing assistance, doing undesirable tasks, and various forms of cooperative behavior, such as quick responses. Position-related currencies include access to personal contacts or networks and inclusion of another person as an important insider. Relationship-related currencies include such things as acceptance or inclusion in the group, friendship, personal support, and understanding.[58]

A CONTRARY VIEW OF TEAMS

Teams are not the answer for all management problems or a silver bullet for improved performance. Unfortunately, the term "teamwork" is often misused. Sometimes it is used as a euphemism for suppressing legitimate disagreement with the manager's viewpoint or submitting to the will of others at all costs. Donald G. Smith has pointed out a number of problems with this common but dysfunctional view of teamwork.

> Positive-thinking gave business . . . the idea of the *team player,* which is a wonderful euphemism for someone who looks the other way when the Cossacks plunder the village. . . . When I entered corporate America directly out of college, I was given some invaluable advice by an older employee . . . [management] did not want to see boat rockers, and such people were immediately marked with an indelible stamp and considered unpromotable. The basic idea was to swallow one's integrity during business hours and to be a part of the "team". . . I participated in programs that cost twice as much as they should have because of mismanagement, and I slavishly followed the orders of some of the most incompetent and mentally deficient human beings I have ever encountered.[59]

The points of this discussion are that supervisors should avoid misusing the term "teamwork" and that they should not stifle constructive dissent for the purpose of teamwork. In addition, some employees do not want to take on some of the responsibilities of self-managed teams. While self-managed teams are the means by which many companies have empowered their employees, some people find that they do not fit the system. For example, self-managed team members give each other feedback. Some employees find this very stressful because other team members pay great attention to how they do their jobs.[60] In addition, with self-managed teams some employees feel that they have many bosses instead of one boss. At Eaton's plant in South Bend, Indiana, one veteran employee said, "They say there are no bosses here . . . but if you screw up, you find one pretty fast."[61] At the same plant, it has been observed that "with everyone watching everyone else, it can feel like a hundred bosses . . ."[62]

In addition to these concerns, some team members do not like to give negative feedback to other team members and find that their communication or interpersonal skills are inadequate for such functions.[63]

GROUP DECISION TECHNIQUES

In this section, we will first discuss two techniques for generating new ideas: brainstorming and the nominal group technique. An important feature of both techniques is that they prohibit evaluative comments or criticism of members' offerings during the idea elicitation phase because criticism tends to reduce the amount of new ideas put forth.[64]

Teams often make decisions through consensus. However, achieving consensus is often a challenging task. Exhibit 9.5 provides some suggestions for reaching consensus.

BRAINSTORMING

In **brainstorming** sessions, individuals are given a statement of a problem that requires their input. Members are asked to offer suggestions in the form of ideas or potential

Work teams at Saturn take responsibility for reaching quality and production goals. Because they are given decision-making tasks, workers on participatory teams often have greater self-esteem and work harder.

| EXHIBIT 9.5 | Techniques that facilitate team consensus. |

- Ask people for the rationale behind an opinion or perspective.

- Don't let people change their minds or drop out just to avoid conflict.

- Don't let the group slip into one-person subgroups, majority-rule votes, or horse-trading, unless the group consciously decides to do that.

- Don't let the group get polarized on positions or stuck in either/or decisions. Look for alternatives.

- Look for areas of agreement or common ground first, then move on to issues of disagreement.

- Ask people who are not in consensus with the majority: "What alteration of this position *could* you accept or support?"

- Poll people to determine their initial position. (Use a fist for "no support," high five for "full support," and three fingers for "needs modification.")

- After consensus has apparently been reached, ask each person individually: "Will you endorse this decision with key stakeholders when you leave this room?"

Source: Lynda C. McDermott, Nolan Brawley, and William W. Waite, *World Class Teams: Working Across Borders.* New York: John Wiley & Sons, Inc. (1998): p. 168. Reproduced with permission.

approaches that they think will be useful. Wild and unusual ideas are sought since they tend to open new directions of thought and to bring forth more new ideas. The group leader discourages criticism of the offerings in the idea-elicitation phase but allows modifications or combinations and lists them as they are put forth. Each person is encouraged to speak out on each item. Members are chosen for their ability to offer constructive and meaningful contributions. This technique is used to create advertising slogans, new uses for existing products, new products, and new approaches to existing procedures. It is also used to spark creative thinking and creative thinkers.

brainstorming group idea generation processes in which creativity is encouraged while evaluation is limited to a separate phase

NOMINAL GROUPS

Nominal groups are a variation of brainstorming. Group members are given a problem and instructed first to work alone to develop a list of ideas in writing. The group leader then goes around the group in a round-robin manner and elicits the first idea from each member. Typically, the group leader writes these suggestions on flip charts to disassociate the idea from the person who provided it. After all ideas are listed, the group then proceeds to the evaluation phase in which each idea is evaluated individually. Because each idea is disassociated from its contributor, the idea's originator is less likely to become defensive if the idea is criticized.[65]

nominal group group idea generation process in which members develop their ideas individually, and then the leader elicits all ideas for group consideration

GROUP PROBLEM SOLVING

Group problem solving is usually used for problems affecting the group. It works best in a discussion format—one that allows members to participate actively under the skillful direction of the leader. The following steps are involved in group problem-solving sessions:

1. Identify and define the problem(s).
2. List possible solutions.
3. Evaluate the positive and negative features of each solution.
4. Choose a solution or solutions.
5. Assign responsibility and authority for implementing the solution(s).

While there are advantages of group problem solving, such as involvement of your people, there are also some associated dangers. For example, if you have never included your subordinates in your decision-making process in the past, they may be suspicious of your attempt to do so now. Furthermore, participants bring to the meeting their particular interests and attitudes, which are affected by their informal groups. (We discuss informal groups later in this chapter.) Informal group leaders will be part of the meeting too so their attitudes may well affect the quality and quantity of ideas of their followers. Such leaders can promote open participation or dominate and inhibit participation. As the formal group leader, you may find your ideas and attitudes challenged openly for the first time. You may be subjected to group criticism and find yourself pitted against the informal leader or leaders.

All these problems and more can be prevented or minimized through proper planning. One point to consider during planning is whether your group is equipped to solve the problem. By soliciting concrete suggestions and taking advantage of your subordinates' involvement in these problem areas, you will be sharing your authority and enlarging your perspective.

Learning Objective Number Five

ERRORS IN TEAM AND GROUP DECISIONS

Abilene paradox
group decision-making error related to group dynamics in which group members do not press for their real needs

Unfortunately, groups and teams are prone to a number of decision-making errors of which supervisors, team leaders, and team members need to be aware. One error, called the **Abilene paradox,** results from failures of team members to communicate their real wants. Because of members' desire to get along with the group, they sometimes decide to pursue alternatives that no members really want. Thus, a group might make a decision to take an automobile trip to Abilene although no one really wants to go, as was the case in the original paradox.[66] One of the authors has an insightful colleague who has helped his department avoid bad group decisions by making timely announcements that "It looks like we're on our way to Abilene." A similar error is called *self-censorship*. This error occurs in cohesive groups in which individuals do not critically examine various alternatives because they do not want to rock the boat.[67]

groupthink
a decision-making error caused by group dynamics

Another error caused by pressures for group conformity is called **groupthink**. Conditions leading to groupthink include high pressure for conformity, strong desire to remain in the group, punishment of individuals who offer deviating input, and the presence of individuals within the group who are perceived to have extraordinary expertise. Groupthink among presidential advisers has been cited as the cause of the escalation of the Vietnam War and the disastrous Bay of Pigs invasion of Cuba. In these examples, the groups were comprised of intellectual superstars who did not want to be excluded from their high-powered groups. As a result, participants did not vigorously challenge the group even when they disagreed. This form of "collective dumbness by smart people"[68] also occurs in business. For example, several years ago groups of smart people made the decision to produce the Cadillac Allanté, a beautiful and expensive car that turned out to be a commercial failure. Such groups also approved NBC's rigging of crash tests for a sensational exposé about explosions of General Motors trucks in collisions.[69]

Several conditions cause group members to avoid critical thinking or self-limit their input when it deviates from the developing position of the group. Professors Paul Mulvey, John Veiga, and Priscilla Elsass have found that the following conditions make groupthink more likely:[70]

1. Perceptions of great expertise attributed to one or more individuals
2. A compelling argument
3. Individuals' lack confidence in their potential contributions
4. Decisions perceived as unimportant
5. Pressures for conformity
6. Disorganized and unproductive meetings

In order to offset such conditions, these researchers make a number of suggestions for reducing pressures for conformity. These include using smaller decision-making groups, minimizing status differentials among group members, clarifying the purpose of the group, emphasizing the importance of the decision, and describing the procedures to be used in the decision-making process.[71]

GROUND RULES FOR MEETINGS

If the problem-solving session is to accomplish meaningful results, rules and procedures must be established and agreed on in advance by all concerned. Imagine playing a sport in which each participant had her own set of rules. Chaos would be a certainty. Most sports need an umpire or referee whose job it is to enforce the rules and prevent infractions. This role is yours to play as the supervisor.

Essential rules are described below. Using this list as a guide while planning and conducting your meetings should prevent most problems from occurring—or at least prevent any serious conflicts.

BEFORE THE MEETING

When you have a specific problem to be solved, communicate it to the group members in advance of the meeting. Be as clear as you can be in defining the problem and in specifying the goals you want the meeting to achieve. Be certain that limits such as time, company policy, and the amount of authority the group will have are clear to the group. Is the group empowered only to recommend solutions or actually to choose them? In the latter case, you must delegate some of your formal authority to the group. If you alone have the power to decide, tell them so.

Give your members all the relevant data you have accumulated and any boundaries on solutions, such as resource limitations, imposed by management. This information will help the group adopt a realistic point of view. Let them know the order (the agenda) in which the group will consider the various issues and the time and duration of the meeting. All who have been chosen to attend should be made aware of their responsibilities to prepare for the meeting. Specifically, each member should make the following preparations:

1. Read the agenda and prepare a list of questions that he should answer, before facing the group.
2. Gather the information, materials, visuals, and so on that she will be responsible for presenting or disseminating to the group.
3. If a group member should be unable to attend the meeting for any legitimate reason, he should relay his input to the chairperson.

DURING THE MEETING

Provide name tags and assign seating when necessary. Start the meeting promptly, direct the discussion, stick to the agenda and time limits, draw out each member, list the alternatives, and summarize frequently. Maintain order and keep the meeting on the subject. Normally, you should make your comments only after other members in order to avoid inhibiting the group. In some instances, you may want to avoid making your opinions known so that the group will take greater ownership of the decision.

During each meeting, the group members have specific responsibilities that should be communicated to them in advance and briefly repeated to them at the start of each session. If the meeting is to be beneficial to all concerned, each member should be prepared to do the following:

1. Be an active participant by listening attentively, taking notes, following the discussions, seeking clarification when confused, and adding input if the group member has the expertise or experience to do so.

2. Promote discussion and input from all members by respecting their right to their opinions and attitudes and by avoiding discourteous or disruptive behavior. (The chairperson should not hesitate to call on quiet members, using specific questions and asking for opinions.)
3. Practice group-serving roles (described in the next section). From the alternatives listed and analyzed, bring the group to one mind about the best alternative or combination of alternatives to endorse. If the solution is to work, the majority must be behind it. Be ready to compromise in order to break any impasse.

Assign tasks to those affected, if need be, and put the solution into operation as quickly as possible. At the close of each meeting, the participants should be made aware of any specific duties or assignments they will have as a result of the meeting. The chairperson should not allow the members to leave until each of them is clear about her new tasks. In addition to the specific duties each person may receive, all participants have the following general obligations:

1. When the meeting concerns sensitive matters, preserve the confidentiality of the discussion.
2. Relay decisions and changes to those for whom the group member may be responsible and whom they will affect.
3. Carry out promises made and assignments received as quickly as possible.

AFTER THE MEETING

Learning Objective Number Six

After a problem-solving meeting, check on the results and on the group reactions. Follow up on individual assignments.

GROUP MEMBER ROLES

At a meeting, members of the group may play various roles; some of these will be helpful to the attainment of the meeting's goals, whereas others may hinder the group's attempts. Two broad categories of roles are *self-serving* and *group-serving*.

SELF-SERVING ROLES

Self-serving roles can have either positive or negative effects on the meeting and on group members. For example, suppose that as a group leader, you block another participant by not recognizing his raised hand. If you do so in order to get another person to speak who until then has been withdrawn, you have a positive motive and effect on the group. But if you do so in order to promote your own ideas at the expense of others' (a selfish motive), the action can have a negative effect on the group.

As chairperson, you may decide that it is best to withdraw—that is, become an observer—when one of the members begins to criticize another's suggestions. In this way, a participant may be forced to justify her proposal, new information may emerge, and others may be persuaded of the validity of an idea more readily. Why not let a participant tell her peers what you want said?

Dominating involves pushing a special interest; it may include blocking by continuing to talk and not allowing another to get into the conversation. Whether these roles go unchecked and exhibit a positive or negative influence is up to the chairperson to determine. Use your good sense and listen intently. Try to get at the motive behind the role a member is playing. If, in your judgment, the motive is positive, let him continue; if not, take action.

GROUP-SERVING ROLES

Group-serving roles are almost always positive in their effects. No matter who practices them, their purpose is to draw members together and shed light where there was darkness. They all promote unity and harmony, and each is essential in order to reach a consensus. They tend to keep a meeting on track, while systematically separating the unimportant from the relevant.

Fortifying is the process by which a member adds encouragement and insights to already aired ideas. It helps members elaborate and interpret what has been said. *Initiating* introduces ideas and major points in order to get the reactions and contributions of group members. *Orienting* tells the members where they have been and where they are at present. It may serve to add emphasis or to clarify ideas, and it keeps people from traveling again over the same ground or going around in circles. *Researching* involves fact-finding and introducing background material pertinent to the discussion so as to remove smoke from people's eyes and substitute facts for fiction.

Observe and label these activities in your group encounters. You will see various positive and negative applications of all these roles in your classes at school, as well as in meetings at work. Study your instructor and the various roles she plays. You will pick up some valuable examples of each of these roles, most of which you will be able to use at work when you find yourself a group leader or participant. Exhibit 9.6 summarizes the various roles played in groups.

PITFALLS OF MEETINGS

Problem-solving sessions may not work well if leaders fail to enforce the ground rules listed previously. In addition, other major pitfalls or traps can cause a meeting to be a sheer waste of time.

Roles played by group members.		**EXHIBIT 9.6**
SELF-SERVING ROLES	**GROUP-SERVING ROLES**	
Attention-getting	Coordinating	
Blocking	Fortifying	
Criticizing	Initiating	
Dominating	Orienting	
Withdrawing	Researching	

THE HIDDEN AGENDA

A member's hidden agenda consists of his personal feelings toward the subject discussed, the group itself, and the individuals who make up the group. We all have such an agenda whenever we attend a group session, whether with our formal or our informal group. Critical remarks toward group members or their ideas are often motivated by a dislike or distrust of those persons and their intentions—not their ideas. You must recognize that, as chairperson, you have the duty to see behind the words and get to the motives. Often, you can nullify the hidden agenda's effect simply by explaining that another person or department does not necessarily have to gain at someone else's expense.

A COMPETITIVE SPIRIT

PERFORMANCE

Competition is fine on the athletic field, but it has no real purpose among members of the team. Watch for the remark that attempts to build one person's reputation at the expense of another's. Nothing can ruffle feathers so quickly or create defensive reactions more effectively. A quick review of the second Hawthorne study should refresh your memory about intergroup competition and its dangers.

The second of the now-famous experimental studies conducted in the late 1920s at Western Electric's Hawthorne plant uncovered the formation of two informal cliques—one quite strong and the other somewhat weak. Both influenced their members in significant ways. They offered proof that workers' cliques can be positive or negative factors with respect to company standards, policies, and regulations. If they view management favorably, they are capable of achieving standards of output even higher than management may expect. If they feel negative toward management, the informal group will generate much less production than expected. If the supervisor practices sound human relations and relates positively to her group of subordinates, she can influence their behavior and productivity.

TALKATIVE MEMBERS

Have you ever tried to carry on a conversation with someone who only stopped talking to think about what to say next? It is quite a frustrating experience. Your voice only fills the gaps between his remarks. Listening is not one of that person's virtues. Members in meetings can quickly fall in love with their own voices and viewpoints. It is the chairperson's job to prevent this. Make sure that everyone has a say, and each person's views are duly noted. Chairpersons find that it is sometimes useful to avoid recognizing a talkative member's request to speak.

SABOTAGE

Group members sometimes carry on their own conversations while another is speaking; others may attempt to sidetrack the issue. These and similar tactics represent efforts to render a meeting useless. The subversive's motivation may be that failure to reach a decision will maintain the status quo. Disruptive behavior will weaken the will of the group to reach a decision and interest may wane. The chairperson must assess the

Some tips for dealing with problem group members.	EXHIBIT 9.7

1. Try a one-on-one meeting. Schedule a meeting for just the two of you. Confront the person with your observations about how he is disrupting the group's efforts. Listen for all the reasons and perceptions that unfold. See if you can turn disruptive behaviors around with force-field analysis in the meeting or afterward.

2. Let the group confront the individual. Let the individual face the group members directly. Let the members air their grievances about the problem member's behaviors. Talk about the effects those behaviors are having on the group. Avoid personal attacks. Describe the behaviors that have negative consequences.

3. Place limits on the problem member's participation. Let the group leader prescribe the level of participation allowed. For example, the leader may want to deal directly with the individual after each meeting, not during it. Or the leader may not allow the problem member to participate in group discussions when disruptive behaviors occur.

4. Separate the problem member from the group meetings. Let the individual contribute, but on an individual basis, away from the other group members. Assign work that will help the team indirectly.

---

motives and effects of conscious or accidental sabotage and must act to block it or to confront the saboteur directly. The meeting must be pulled back to its proper focus. Exhibit 9.7 gives you some alternatives for dealing with a disruptive group member.

INFORMAL GROUPS

Two or more people who come together by choice to satisfy mutual needs or to share common interests are considered an **informal group.** The feature that distinguishes formal from informal groups is the matter of choice. Informal groups or cliques form because of the mutual social needs of people. Formal groups can also be informal groups, provided that all members freely choose to associate with one another on and off the job. Every informal group has a leader. Unlike her counterpart in the formal group, the informal leader derives power through the informal means. Formal leaders of formal groups seldom have cliques of their own subordinates. This is as it should be as a manager's friends should be his peers.

informal group
two or more people who come together by choice to satisfy mutual needs or to share common interests

Learning Objective Number Seven

JOINING A CLIQUE

Once a new employee is hired, he is placed in a specific job, which makes him automatically a member of several formal groups that constitute the business enterprise. If the design of work and the working relationships permit them, informal groups or

Informal groups often form when workers share the common interest of achieving a task.

clique
an informal group of two or more people who come together primarily on the basis of social rationales

cliques will have been formed as well. The newcomer, like those who have preceded him, will naturally desire the companionship of one or more coworkers on a more or less regular basis, both during working hours and while on his own time.

The problem confronting the new arrival is that he is initially outside the existing informal groups and, although he desires membership in one of them, is not certain about which one to choose. He needs time to assess the values, attitudes, and reputation of each group. The groups, in turn, are going to be evaluating the person for prospective membership. In this sense, the new employee is similar to a person seeking admission to a fraternity or sorority. He has to look at what it stands for and get to know its members, while, in turn, its members look over the applicant.

You as a supervisor can do a great deal for new employees. If you know your people well and understand their groups, you can do all in your power to help newcomers gain admittance to a group of subordinates that will exert a constructive influence on them. You hope that all the informal cliques in your section are working with management and not against it. But if one or another is not, do your best to steer the new arrival away from that clique and into more beneficial surroundings.

Before the individual on the outside of a clique can truly become a participating member of the clique, she must go through three separate but related stages of induction: observation, transformation, and confirmation.

Stage 1: Observation. Observation is the initial stage we all find ourselves in as newcomers. By necessity, we must remain neutral toward all the informal groups we encounter until we have time to know them. As time goes on, neutrality becomes increasingly difficult to maintain, as we feel pressure to make a decision or choice. We may begin a kind of trial membership period, wherein we are invited to participate with a group. While meeting with each clique, we are somewhat passive and open to group members' opinions and attitudes, preferring to listen rather than to speak our mind.

Stage 2: Transformation.   The next step is for us to decide which group we like best. If the group honors our choice, we begin to confine our socializing almost exclusively to the new group. We mask any personal opinions that are contradictory to those the group holds as essential, and we begin to mouth agreement to these essential attitudes. Like a parrot, we begin to remember and repeat the sacred beliefs even though we may not agree with them. Without this stage, we can never really become an accepted member in a strong informal group.

Stage 3: Confirmation.   The confirmation stage is complete when we actually abandon attitudes we once held that are in direct opposition to those of the group and adopt the group's values as our own. We give up our individuality while with the group, though we may retain it on our own. The group has changed us and our attitudes in much the same way as in individual settings. The difference is that several people may have been at work on us here instead of only one.

From this point on, the group has more influence over our behavior than any other force at work. We now weigh the relative merits of proposals against the group's willingness to accept them. If the group vetoes the action, each member feels bound to support that veto.

Not long ago, one of the authors' students relayed the following story. At the start of the business day one Friday, two of George's more able workers presented him with a petition signed by all 26 of his subordinates. It requested that the workday begin and end one-half hour earlier. George was quite concerned since such a request was not in his power to grant, and he felt that the plant manager would not buy the suggestion. Wisely, he refrained from giving an immediate answer but assured the workers that he would consider the matter carefully.

Over the next two weeks, George interviewed every worker to determine just how committed each of them was to the proposed change. The results were amazing. Two men were solidly in favor of the change—the same two who had confronted George with the petition and had initiated it. Eight workers were neutral but willing to go along with the others. The remaining 16 were clearly against it. After George announced his findings, the demand was dropped, and only two people were really unhappy with the decision.

What made the other workers sign? The two men were strong personalities, and one was an informal leader of a large clique. Beginning with his clique members, starting with the weakest, the informal leader got one signature after another until nearly two-thirds of the workers had signed. The others fell into line when confronted with the sheer weight of numbers. Not wishing to obstruct the will of the majority, the few remaining holdouts also signed up.

YOU AND YOUR INFORMAL GROUP

The informal group that you choose or that chooses you will have a dramatic and lasting impact on your reputation and your future. Choose any informal group with the same caution you would exercise when choosing a friend. Pick out the ones that will have the greatest positive effect on your growth and the ones that have the most to offer. As a result, some of their luster and brilliance will rub off on you. You are judged in part by the company you keep so avoid groups bent on self-destruction.

One of the hazards inherent in membership in an informal group is the restrictions it places on your contacts with others. Once you have reached either the transformation or confirmation stage of induction, you probably have begun to confine your socializing at work to a specific few individuals. In time, you may become rather narrow and cut off from differing opinions. You may be denying yourself the valuable companionship and variety that others have to offer. Do not take yourself out of circulation. Break your routine on occasion and mix and maintain contacts with others of similar rank.

COPING WITH SUBORDINATES' CLIQUES

Several important principles can help you minimize group conflicts and tensions and maximize group cooperation and contribution:

1. *Accept your subordinates' cliques as a fact of life.* Just as you belong to one or more, so it is with them. Consider their informal groups as allies and additional forces to be won over and brought to bear on mutual problems. The trick is to learn to work with them—not to fight them or try to eliminate them.

2. *Identify and enlist the cooperation of the informal leaders.* They represent a force with which to reckon. Many of them have the potential to be tomorrow's managers. The informal power they have over others can work for you both. Practice sound human relations with them as you would with anyone in your charge. Share with the best of them (whenever you can) some of your formal authority through delegation. They are usually perfect candidates for leadership roles. They also are ambitious people who recognize the advantages that management has to offer.

3. *Prevent intergroup competition and the occurrence of a win-lose situation.* Groups in conflict tend to tear at each other and to reduce the organization's overall effectiveness. Hold out standards to be achieved and surpassed. Use past performance records as targets to hit and scores to beat.

4. *Do not force your people to choose between you and their group.* If you put it to them on an "either/or" basis, they will usually pick their group. Their loyalty to and membership in a clique does not have to be at your expense. They can be loyal and unopposed to you if you are predictable and loyal to them.

5. *Adopt a coach's attitude toward your group(s).* Foster a team spirit, and nurture the comradeship that cliques promote. Play fair and demand that your subordinates do the same. Team players know the value of rules and team play. Enlist their participation as a group and protect their self-image.

6. *Appeal to each group member and to each group's sense of competence.* We all have the urge to be good at what we do and to know that others think we are. Give your people a series of challenges that, when met, will give them a sense of accomplishment and pride.

7. *Use appropriate levers to influence people in specific situations.* Examples of levers include positive reinforcement, such as incentives, group acceptance, satisfaction of psychological needs, appeals to pride, and agreed-upon goals. The effectiveness of most of them has to do with your competence in interpersonal and intergroup relations.[72] By setting goals and helping your subordinates set their own, you will be providing incentives for excellence and ways for them to build confidence.

One example of this point involves assembly-line workers on a Corvette assembly operation. They were installing fiberglass parts provided by an outside supplier. These parts had rough edges in their openings that were designed to take dashboard instruments. The rough edges had to be filed clean before the instruments could be inserted. The supplier should have done this, not the assembly-line workers. To deal with the growing sense of frustration and irritation among the assembly workers, GM's supervisors arranged a meeting with the supplier's workers at the GM plant. The workers responsible for the rough-edged moldings witnessed firsthand how their sloppy work affected their counterparts. Moldings quickly began to arrive with smooth openings. All now knew why their work was necessary and what would happen at the other end when it was not done properly.

*Learning
Objective
Number Eight*

GROUP COMPETITION

We have seen that intergroup competition at Hawthorne caused ill will and declining productivity within the formal group. Edgar H. Schein's classic work on groups has added much to our understanding of what happens within and between competing groups. Whether we are dealing with formal or informal groups, when faced with competition, within the groups there is a tendency for members to become more cohesive and better organized. There is also increased loyalty and greater compliance with norms. In addition, members become more receptive to accept autocratic supervision and more focused on the task of the group as opposed to individual issues.[73]

All these results, at first glance, may appear to be desirable. But as we consider what happens between competing groups, the picture becomes less attractive. The groups start to perceive the other competing group as opponents and they form selective perceptions in which the positive attributes of competing groups are ignored while the negative features are emphasized. At the same time, they ignore their own group's negative attributes and emphasize the positive features. In addition, intergroup hostility intensifies while the frequency of communication and contacts decline. Negative stereotypes of the competing groups are facilitated and perceptual distortions become more ingrained. Furthermore, when there is a joint meeting of the competing groups, and their leaders address the groups, there is selective information processing as the individual groups listen to their own leaders more closely and tend to find support for their current position. In contrast, they tend to process only negative information about the leaders of the competing groups, consistent with the stereotypes they are maintaining.[74]

If this intergroup competition—whether between informal or formal groups—results in one group's emerging as the victor and the other as vanquished, the problems compound dramatically:[75] To paraphrase Schein, the winning group behaves in the following way:

- Keeps its cohesiveness
- Tends to become self-satisfied
- Loses its task orientation and reemphasizes individual needs
- Becomes reassured that its self-image must be correct and loses the incentive to question its perceptions

On the other hand, the losing group:

- becomes initially unrealistic about its perception of why it lost, tending to transfer blame to some external cause.
- tends to lose its cohesiveness.
- becomes more dedicated to tasks and winning.
- experiences less intra-group cooperation and less concern for individual needs.
- eventually reexamines its beliefs and self-image and becomes more realistic in its perceptions.[76]

It should be clear to you that intergroup competition has more disadvantages than advantages. The loser may improve, whereas the winner declines. This is not to say that competition is wrong—only that competition between groups within a company is dangerous. Competition can be a powerful tool to muster greater output and cohesiveness among your department's members if the enemy is not a group of coworkers but rather some outside force or group. If the thing to be beaten is a standard or a past record of output, the group can muster its forces in a cooperative spirit to excel and exceed its previous record.

OUTSIDERS AND INSIDERS

You are affected each day at your workplace by many factors, some of which are outside your company and some of which are inside it. The same is true for your subordinates.

OUTSIDE FACTORS

When was the last time you went to work with a personal family problem so much on your mind that your performance suffered? Your family is but one of many outside groups that can influence your efficiency. Your academic classes in management may be another example. Sometimes what you learn will bring you into conflict with your traditional beliefs or with those of your boss, putting you at odds with him when you attempt to act on your new knowledge. You may find that you know more about a particular task and the best methods for dealing with it than your boss does. The problem will then be one of your selling your idea to your boss and getting permission to implement it.

Customers and competitors can place demands on the business, in turn, directly affecting your operations. Their requests, threats, and innovations may be translated into new products, service methods, or procedures for your department. New schedules of production may be the result, with added pressures and tensions for you and those under you.

INSIDE FACTORS

The groups within the company that directly or indirectly affect your performance are your superiors, your peers, and your subordinates. Superiors construct the programs, policies, and regulations that you must enforce and translate to action. Your peers place demands on you for conformity, cooperation, and uniform approaches to problems. They form the nucleus of your friendships and place demands on your time and talents. Your subordinates, as members of your formal groups and as members of their own informal cliques, ask a great deal from you. How you cope with these groups and their demands directly relates to how well you can adjust to tension and frustration. You will be faced with many conflicts between what you think you should do and what others ask you to do. Often, you must yield completely to the demands of others. On occasion, you must work out compromises.

INSTANT REPLAY

1. A group is two or more people who are aware of one another, who consider themselves to be a functioning unit, and who share a quest for a common goal or benefit.

2. Teams have several characteristics that distinguish them from groups.

3. Effective teams have several characteristics, such as a compelling purpose and members who hold each other accountable for results.

4. Team and group decision-making can be very effective but supervisors need to be aware of the errors that can occur with such processes.

5. In group problem solving, the roles that group members play may affect the group either positively or negatively, depending on the member's motivation.

6. Various pitfalls can undermine group meetings and their results. Being aware of them and acting to render them negligible is the job of every group leader.

7. Competition has both positive and negative effects on groups. Negative effects of intergroup competition can include hostility, lack of cooperation, and outright sabotage.

8. Supervisors must recognize that informal groups exist and can wield positive or negative power. Their leaders possess strong personalities and are potential management material.

QUESTIONS FOR CLASS DISCUSSION

1. Can you define this chapter's key terms?
2. What are the features that distinguish teams from groups?
3. What are the characteristics of effective teams?
4. What are some of the common decision-making errors that teams and groups encounter?
5. As a problem-solving group's chairperson, what should you do before, during, and after a session?
6. As a participating member of a problem-solving session, what should you do before, during, and after the session?
7. What are the group-serving and the self-serving roles played by group members in meetings?
8. What happens to the winning group in intergroup competition? To the losing group? Between the groups?

ASSESS THIS SITUATION

Many people work outside the office and factory. Some, such as outside sales people, must meet with and interact with clients and customers on a regular basis. Others work at home, linked to their boss and coworkers by e-mail, fax machines, telephones, and voice mail. Such an arrangement offers many advantages to both employees and employers. Employees can stay at home with children in need of day care and avoid the time and expense of commuting to work. The company can operate in smaller spaces, providing less office furniture and equipment. But what about a team spirit linking the telecommuter to his coworkers and others at work?

Purpose: To consider team spirit issues for groups that include telecommuters and outside sales people, who normally work outside of the office or plant.

Your Task: List as many ways as you can to include telecommuting, outside sales people, and other employees who work at home in a group's efforts and activities at work. What would you do to instill the absent employees with a real spirit of teamwork?

SKILL BUILDING EXERCISE 9.1

Supervisors and their associates often complain about unproductive meetings or excessive amounts of time spent in meetings, and such problems were noted in this chapter. It is often observed that little productive work takes place in meetings. While this is a bit of an exaggeration, it is important to remember that meetings do not necessarily equate to productive time. In addition, meetings can go terribly wrong, and the group dynamics of meetings can sometimes result in flawed decision-making, such as the groupthink error mentioned in this chapter. Patrick Lencioni has even written a book entitled, *Death by Meeting.* Nonetheless, meetings are critical for coordination, information sharing, group decision-making, and many other important activities. Accordingly, while some time may be saved with teleconferences, videoconferences, or meetings using computer-based communication technology, there will always be some need for meetings. However, there is great potential for improving the efficiency and effectiveness of the meetings that are held.

Your Task: Working alone or in a small group develop a checklist that supervisors can use for improving meetings. Be sure to include the following: (1) activities before, during, and after the meeting; (2) responsibilities for the supervisors and employees; (3) any special procedures related to the purpose for the meeting; (4) guidelines; and (5) problems to avoid.[77]

SKILL BUILDING WRITING EXERCISE 9.2

As indicated in the opening discussion of this chapter, Hypertherm relies heavily on teams in its very successful operations. The company's job openings or position postings on its website confirm that it is serious about teams. More specifically, the website notes team leadership skill requirements for managerial positions and teamwork requirements for employees across a variety of different types of positions. In addition, the website provides information that enables visitors to gain a sense of the pace of innovation at the company as well as its commitment to quality.[78]

Your Task: Working alone or in a small group go to the Hypertherm website at *www.hypertherm.com/company/job* and review the company's current job postings. After reviewing the postings, provide a written summary of the following: (1) the interpersonal skills that are listed, which should be important for effective teamwork, (2) the team-related skills and responsibilities for team leaders and managers, (3) indicators of emphasis on performance, (4) indicators of quality, and (5) how teamwork can contribute to timely innovation.

CASE 9.1   Team Punishment

The module 986 motherboard team at the plant was holding a meeting to decide what to do about Theodore, one of their team members. Theodore loaded the wrong supply of resistors into the machine that assembles the boards before they are soldered. As a result, defective boards were produced for three entire days before the mistake was found. All of these boards had to be scrapped and the mistake caused a 10 percent decline in quality and productivity results for the month.

TRICIA: "Let's leave Theodore alone. He's got a lot on his mind and just made a mistake. He feels badly enough about his mistake, and we all have good days and bad days. None of us is perfect, and we shouldn't be punitive to someone who makes an honest mistake."

CAL: "No, we have to take action to let people know that we're serious about these performance standards. We don't have a boss looking over our shoulders anymore, and we won't have one as long as we manage the team ourselves. I don't like to be the bad guy either, but we're accountable for this team's performance."

CECIL: "Well, what should we do? Should we fire Theodore? This was a serious error. If we don't fire him, he's got to know that he has to really concentrate on his job when he loads those components into the assembler. After the boards go through the wave-soldering machine there's nothing we can do."

MARGE: "Let's have a team meeting tonight and vote on whether we keep Theodore or fire him. Glen's not here now, but he'll be back after lunch. He feels strongly about this and can be sort of a prosecutor and argue why we should fire Theodore. Tricia can act as the defense and tell why we shouldn't fire him. That way we'll get both sides just like in a court, and we can decide what to do. As long as Theodore gets more than half of the votes, he gets to stay."

JAN: "Wow, that sounds like a really awful thing to do to someone. I don't like this at all. Do you people realize what you are saying? How would you like to be treated this way?"

CHRIS: "Jan, we've got to do something. Nobody likes to do this, but we can't have these kinds of quality and production screw-ups. Now, let's get back to the solution we were talking about. What happens if we vote to keep Theodore? How are we going to make sure that he doesn't make the same mistake again?"

RICH: "Well, we'll make Theodore wait out in the hall while we vote. If he wins the vote, we'll go get him. Then, Theodore will have to stand up in front of us and read a formal apology. He can then tell us what he is going to do to avoid a similar mistake in the future. Now, let's decide if this is the procedure we should follow."

The team decided to return at 5:00 P.M. and vote on whether to keep or fire Theodore.

At 5:00 P.M. the team assembled to vote on Theodore. As Rich suggested, if the vote was in Theodore's favor, he would have to come into the room, read an apology, and tell the team how he would avoid making the same mistake in the future. If he lost the vote or refused to read the public apology, he would be fired.

Just as the team prepared to vote on Theodore, Julio said: "We all used to get along together before we worked with this self-directed team stuff. Now, Theodore thinks that he is being picked on because of prejudice. It looks to me like he's got a point. Of the two people disciplined by this team in the past, one was an African American and the other was Hispanic. It doesn't take much imagination to see a pattern here where most of the team is Caucasian, and it's forcing higher standards on the minority members of the team. I didn't like the old boss we had either and really got tired of her micro-managing us, but at least she wasn't biased."

MARGE: "There's nothing discriminatory about this. Theodore made a really costly error. If anyone else makes such a mistake like that, we'll vote on whether to keep him just like Theodore. Let's stop wasting time and vote."

Source: This case incorporates some ideas from an article by Timothy Aeppel. "Not All Workers Find Idea of Empowerment as Neat as It Sounds," *Wall Street Journal* (September 8, 1997): A1, A13.

Questions

1. What will be the likely long-term consequences of this team's actions?
2. How do you think the team should enforce its standards?
3. Why do you think the team is taking this approach?
4. How should the team deal with diversity issues?

CASE 9.2   Unhappy Returns

Linda Carson is the supervisor of returns at a home improvement and building materials store. Yesterday, she asked her associates to attend a meeting today before the store opens.

TOSHIRO: "I hope we're not going to have a long meeting today. Why are we meeting? I hate these early morning meetings."

LINDA: "The store manager asked us to come up with a way to reorganize the way we do returns in order to cut down on costs. Does anybody have any ideas?"

MICAELA: "Why do they want to cut down on costs in returns? Are our costs out of line with other departments?"

LINDA: "I don't know, the store manager didn't say. I don't think we need to know why or whether our costs are out of line. We're just supposed to do what the store manager asked us to do. Winfield, you've been here longer than anyone else. Do you have any ideas?"

WINFIELD: "No, but I'm flexible. I'll go along with what everyone else in the group wants."

BETSY: "I think turnover is too high."

TOMMY: "Wow, Betsy, where'd that idea come from? How's that going to cut costs? They're only paying us a little more than the minimum wage anyway. Who cares how much turnover we have?"

TOSHIRO: "Why don't we make it easier for customers to return merchandise? Right now we have to examine their receipts and then have them fill out a form that asks for lots of information. Then, we have to check the form for completeness. With an easier return policy all we would have to do is give customers their money back or give them store credits."

MICAELA: "Oh, sure, we're just going to give customers their money back. Paul, what makes you think that would work? You should have seen this guy who came in yesterday. He was trying to return this smashed electric drill because he said there was a fault in it when it was manufactured. I could see tire tracks on it where someone had run over it with a truck. So Paul, should we give money back to people who try to rip us off?"

TOSHIRO: "Well, Katy, how many great ideas do you have?"

TOMMY: "Paul's right. What does it matter if some of these people rip us off as long as overall costs go down? Right now it is costing us more to process all of the paperwork than the cost of giving some guy a new electric drill or returning his money."

MICAELA: "Do you realize how many guys would come in here every day with bogus claims on broken tools if we made our return policy that easy? Get serious."

GINGER: "Linda, why should we help the company come up with ideas to save costs? We don't get paid very much anyway. Doesn't management get paid the big bucks to solve problems like this? What's in this for us if we come up with a good answer?"

LINDA: "Well, I didn't ask the store manager. I doubt that there will be anything except an opportunity to set things up like we want."

MICHELLE: "Well, I think the problem is that it takes too long to get anyone from the departments to come to the return counter to answer our questions. They just ignore us. Why doesn't anyone do something about that problem? Some of those guys are just worthless out there. I've called ten or more times with no response on several occasions."

MICAELA: "Yeah, I hate that. Linda, why don't you get the store manager to do something about that? Why don't we fix that problem? We've complained about that before, but nobody ever does anything."

BETSY: "Hey, that's unrelated to the problem. Let's get back to my ideas about cutting down on turnover."

MICAELA: "Let's just vote on an idea and get it over with. How many in favor of Michelle's ideas about getting quicker answers from the departments?"

WINFIELD: "What are we voting on?"

LINDA: "We're not voting yet. Now, does anybody have any new ideas?"

BETSY: "I still think that turnover is the problem because there aren't enough of us who have much experience with returns."

TOMMY: "Betsy, nobody supports your idea about turnover. We're never going to reduce turnover because the work here is stressful, and they don't pay us enough to stay very long. Why don't you quit talking about turnover and let someone else come up with a new idea?"

BETSY: "Linda, I think we could cut down on turnover if we could pay everybody 30 percent more."

LINDA: "Thanks, Betsy. Paul, do you have any ideas?"

TOSHIRO: "I don't like anything I've heard so far."

LINDA: "Winfield, you've been pretty quiet, what do you think?"

WINFIELD: "I can't think of anything."

LINDA: "It looks like we're running out of time. When shall we meet again?"

GINGER: "Are you kidding? You want us to meet again?"

LINDA: "I think so. Okay, until we meet again, be thinking of some ways to lower costs."

WINFIELD: "Linda, I just thought of a suggestion. Can you get the store manager to pay for some donuts next time we meet?"

Questions

1. What steps of the problem-solving process do you see in this case?

2. Evaluate how Linda has managed the meeting and the group.

3. How should Linda handle the next meeting?

4. What are the barriers to successful problem solving in this case?

REFERENCES

[1] Quotes of the Heart Website: *www.heartquotes.net/teamwork-quotes.html*.

[2] Hypertherm Website: *www.hypertherm.com/company.htm*.

[3] Thurm, Scott. "Teamwork Raises Everyone's Game," *Wall Street Journal*, (November 7, 2005): B8.

[4] Hypertherm Website.

[5] Thurm. "Teamwork Raises Everyone's Game."

[6] Thurm. "Teamwork Raises Everyone's Game."

[7] Axelrod, Richard. "Making Teams Work," *Journal for Quality and Participation*, (Spring 2002): 10–11.

[8] *Kets, de Vries, Manfred*. "Leadership Group Coaching in Action: The Zen of Creating High Performance Teams," *Academy of Management Executive* (February 2005): 61–76.

[9] Levering, Robert, and Moskowitz, Milton. "The 100 Best Companies to Work for in America," *Fortune* (January 12, 1998): 85.

[10] Levering, Robert, and Moskowitz, Milton. "The 100 Best Companies to Work for in America," *Fortune* (January 24, 2005): 61–90.

[11] Levering and Moskowitz. "The 100 Best Companies to Work for in America" (1998).

[12] Martin, James. *Cybercorp: The New Business Revolution.* New York: American Management Association, 1996. Lozano, Juan. "Space Shuttle Captures Hubble Telescope," *Associated Press Newswires* (March 3, 2002).

[13] Katzenbach, Jon R., and Smith, Douglas K. *The Wisdom of Teams.* Boston: Harvard Business School Press (1993): 45.

[14] Dumaine, Brian. "The Trouble with Teams," *Fortune* (September 5, 1994): 86–88.

[15] McKee, Bradford. "Turn Your Workers into a Team," *Nation's Business* (July 1992): 37.

[16] Woodruff, David. "Where Employees Are Management," *Business Week*, Bonus Issue (January 19, 1993): 66.

[17] Wellins, Richard S., Byham, William C., and Wilson, Jeanne M. *Empowered Teams.* San Francisco: Jossey-Bass (1991): 135–138.

[18] Thoman, Steven. "Roadblocks to Effective Team Dynamics in the IPPD Environment," *Program Manager* (July/August 2000): 104–108.

[19] Wellins, Byham, and Wilson. *Empowered Teams.*

[20] Ibid.

[21] Maclean, John N. "Rail Equipment Company Learns ABCs of Success," *Chicago Tribune* (November 6, 1994): sec. 7, 1, 4.

[22] Ibid.

[23] Ibid.

[24] Olberding, Sara R. "Site Visit," *Journal for Quality and Production* (May/June 1998): 55–59.

[25] "Team Training Has Profound Effect on Productivity at 5 Cos.," *IOMA's Report on Managing Training & Development,* (January 2002): 3–5.

[26] Freiberg, Kevin, and Freiberg, Jackie. *Nuts! Southwest Airlines' Crazy Recipe for Business and Personal Success.* Austin, TX: Bard Press, (1996). Gittell, Judy Hoffer. "Investing in Relationships," *Harvard Business Review* (June 2001): 28–29.

[27] Ricadela, Aaron. "Office of the Future: A New Way to Work," *Information Week* (January 28, 2002): 42–47.

[28] Nemiro, Jill E. *Creativity in Virtual Teams: Key Components for Success,* San Francisco: Pfeiffer, 2004.

[29] Dumaine. "The Trouble with Teams."

[30] Dumaine, Brian. "Mr. Learning Organization," *Fortune* (October 17, 1994): 147–148, 150, 154–157.

[31] McDermott, Lynda C., Brawley, Nolan, and Waite, *William W. World Class Teams: Working Across Borders.* New York: John Wiley & Sons, Inc. (1998): 228–229.

[32] McDermott, Brawley, and Waite. *World Class Teams: Working Across Borders.* 228–229.

[33] Shea, Gregory P., and Guzzo, Richard A. "Group Effectiveness," *Sloan Management Review,* (Spring 1987): 25–26.

[34] West, Michael. *Motivate Teams, Maximize Success: Effective Strategies for Realizing Your Goals,* San Francisco: Chronicle Books, (2004).

[35] West. *Motivate Teams, Maximize Success: Effective Strategies for Realizing Your Goals.*

[36] Shuit, Douglas P. "At 60, Myers-Briggs Is Still Sorting Out and Identifying People's Types," *Workforce Management,* (December 2003): 72–74.

[37] Shuit. "At 60, Myers-Briggs Is Still Sorting Out and Identifying People's Types."

[38] Keen, Thomas R. *Creating Effective & Successful Teams,* West Lafayette, Indiana: Ichor Business Books, (2003).

[39] Hoy, Frank, and Hellriegel, Don. "The Kilmann and Herdon Model of Organizational Effectiveness Criteria for Small Business Managers," *Academy of Management Journal 25*(3) (1982): 308–322.

[40] West. *Motivate Teams, Maximize Success: Effective Strategies for Realizing Your Goals.*

[41] Hoy and Hellriegel. "The Kilmann and Herdon Model of Organizational Effectiveness Criteria for Small Business Managers."

[42] West. *Motivate Teams, Maximize Success: Effective Strategies for Realizing Your Goals.*

[43] Evans, Gail. "Are We Looking After Each Other," in Linda Coughlin, Ellen Wingard, and Keith Hollihan, eds., *Enlightened Power: How Women Are Transforming the Practice of Leadership*, San Francisco: Jossey-Bass (2005): 143–150.

[44] Axelrod, "Making Teams Work."

[45] Ibid.

[46] Smith, Mark K. "Bruce W. Tuckman—Forming, Storming, Norming and Performing in Groups," *The Encyclopecia of Informal Education*, (March 14, 2005): *www.infed.org/thinkers/tuckman.thm.*

[47] Tuckman, Bruce W. "Developmental Sequence in Small Groups," *Psychological Bulletin*, (1965): 384–399.

[48] Smith. "Bruce W. Tuckman—Forming, Storming, Norming and Performing in Groups."

[49] Patnode, Norman H. "Can't Get to Performing Without Storming," *Program Manager*, (March-April 2003): 42–45.

[50] Rickards, Tudor, and Moger, Susan. "Creative Leadership Processes in Project Team Development: An Alternative to Tuckman's Stage Model," *British Journal of Management*, (2000): 273–283.

[51] Axelrod. "Making Teams Work."

[52] West. *Motivate Teams, Maximize Success: Effective Strategies for Realizing Your Goals.*

[53] Keen. *Creating Effective & Successful Teams.*

[54] Rosen, Kirkman, L., and Rosen, Benson. "Powering Up Teams," *Organizational Dynamics*, (Winter 2000): 48–65.

[55] West. *Motivate Teams, Maximize Success: Effective Strategies for Realizing Your Goals.*

[56] Trent, Robert J. "Making Sure the Team Works," *Supply Chain Management Review*, (April 2005): 30–36.

[57] McClurg, Lucy Newton. "Team Rewards: How Far Have We Come?" *Human Resource Management*, (Spring 2001): 73–86.

[58] Cohen, Allan R., and Bradford, David L. "Influence Without Authority: The Use of Alliances, Reciprocity, and Exchange to Accomplish Work," *Organizational Dynamics* (Winter 1989): 5–17.

[59] Smith, Donald G. *The Joy of Negative Thinking.* Philadelphia: Delancey Press (1994): 93.

[60] Aeppel, Timothy. "Not All Workers Find Idea of Empowerment as Neat as It Sounds," *Wall Street Journal* (September 8, 1997): A1, A13.

[61] Ibid.

[62] Ibid.

[63] Ibid.

[64] Schuler, Randall S. "Brainstorming," in Nigel Nicholson, ed., *The Blackwell Encyclopedic Dictionary of Organizational Behavior*. Oxford, United Kingdom: Blackwell. (1995): 35.

[65] Ibid.

[66] Mulvey, Paul W., Veiga, John F., and Elsass, Priscilla M. "When Teammates Raise a White Flag," *Academy of Management Executive* (February 1996): 40–49.

[67] Ibid.

[68] Feinberg, Mortimer, and Tarrant, John J. *Why Smart People Do Dumb Things*. New York: Fireside, (1995).

[69] Ibid.

[70] Mulvey, Veiga, and Elsass. "When Teammates Raise."

[71] Ibid.

[72] Sasser, Jr., Earl W., and Leonard, Frank S. "Let First-Level Supervisors Do Their Job," *Harvard Business Review* (March-April 1980): 119–120.

[73] Schein, Edgar H. *Organizational Psychology*, 2nd ed. Englewood Cliffs, NJ: Prentice Hall, (1970).

[74] Ibid.

[75] Ibid.

[76] Ibid.

[77] Rees, Fran. *25 Activities for Developing Team Leaders*, San Francisco: Pfeiffer, (2005).

[78] Hypertherm Website.

"We take the time to find the people who fit our culture,"

Natalie Levy[1]
Controller, The Container Store

Objectives

After reading and discussing this chapter, you should be able to do the following:

1. Describe the role of the supervisor in the selection process.
2. Describe the assistance in selection normally provided by a human resources department.
3. List and briefly describe procedures and devices.
4. Describe what a supervisor should do to prepare for a selection interview.
5. List and briefly explain pitfalls of the selection process.
6. List the basic goals of an orientation program.
7. Describe the basic goals and the components of the induction process.
8. State basic questions new employees want answered.
9. Describe what takes place during a new employee's socialization process.

Using Attitudes and Personality to Select Employees at Leading Companies

A recurring theme in executives' explanations for the performance of some of the best companies is that they place great emphasis on the attitude of prospective employees. Southwest Airlines places heavy emphasis in its selection procedures on whether job applicants have positive attitudes, which are associated with courteousness, a desire to be of service to customers, and respectful treatment of coworkers. As one Southwest executive told the first author, hiring managers also observe how applicants treat office personnel, such as receptionists and other clerical employees. She said that applicants who ignore such employees or who are arrogant are unlikely to be thoughtful enough to provide the quality of customer service that is the hallmark of Southwest Airlines. For example, Southwest employees routinely help elderly passengers get off airplanes

Selection and Organizational Entry

or go out of their way to help customers. In order to obtain a good fit with the company's culture, Southwest also looks for a sense of humor, a team orientation, high energy, and confidence in one's self.[2]

In order to assess the characteristics that will determine whether an employee will have such desired qualities and fit in well with the work group and the organization's culture, companies are increasingly turning to personality testing.[3] *Personality testing that provides insights into such worker charasteristics declined and remained out of favor for many years after the U.S. Supreme Court ruling in the Griggs v. Duke Power case in 1971. This case established employer liability for the use of unvalidated tests that have a discriminatory impact.*[4] *There were also abuses of personality testing, such as administration and interpretation of test results by unqualified people, failures to protect privacy, and the use of tests for purposes for which they were not designed.*

Fortunately, employers have become more careful about their personality testing, and university researchers have been able to develop techniques for removing race and gender biases from such tests. Currently, companies such as Best Buy, DuPont, and Toyota are providing support for the development of tests that will enable them to identify applicants who have characteristics similar to the ones that differentiate their best employees from others. Some of the testing that is becoming more prevalent is directed toward identification of aspects of work that produce satisfaction and that have different motivational impacts varying across individuals.[5]

In addition to the expanding use of personality testing for selection, personality tests are being used more frequently to help executives, managers, and employees understand each other better. In a recent presentation at the first author's university, the CEO of a leading company told the group that he and his team of senior executives have the test profiles of each team member for three personality tests; the Myers-Briggs Type Indicator (MBTI),[6] *which measures personality types and predicts how people differ in their approach to solving problems; the FIRO-B, which provides insights for interpersonal relations in a work setting;*[7] *and the Kolbe, which measures instinctual strengths.*[8] *By referring to these profiles, the executives were able to understand each other and to work with each other more effectively.*

Nonetheless, as discussed elsewhere in this text, supervisors must be careful to obtain professional help before using personality tests. They should also seek assistance from human resource professionals about the best ways to assess whether job applicants have attitudes that will be compatible with job requirements and the organization's culture. Nonetheless, the good news for supervisors is that more tests are becoming available to help them make better selection decisions and that will help their employees and peers understand each other better.

Questions for Thought

1. How do most employers attempt to assess the attitudes or fit of job applicants, and why do you think that these procedures are being used?
2. What are some of the strengths or weaknesses in the approaches that you have observed?

Introduction

selection

the human resource management function that determines who is hired

Selection is a human resource management function that determines who is hired by an organization and who is not. It is the process by which applicants are evaluated so as to determine their suitability for employment. The basic aim of the selection process is to find the number and kind of employees required by a company to meet its needs for personnel at competitive cost levels. Selection begins with a description of the kind of knowledge and skills needed to fill a vacancy and ends with the decision to hire a particular person.

Selective hiring is a hallmark of successful companies.[9] Since employees are the only real source of competitive advantage for most companies, it is important that companies hire and retain the best employees possible. Careful selection practices help companies keep employee turnover at low levels as well. Simply selecting employees who have the right skills is not enough for many companies. Selecting employees who fit the organization is also important for maintaining an organizational culture in which employees work effectively in teams, cooperate with each other, and provide good customer service. For example, at MBNA, one of the largest credit card companies, the most important selection criterion is "People who like other people."[10]

After you have recruited, interviewed, tested, and hired new employees, you must begin to prepare for their arrival and initiation. Some groundwork for this procedure is laid out during the selection process. The applicant is informed of the nature of the job, the company's operations in general, and the wage and fringe benefits that go with the job. The remaining tasks involve planning and implementing an effective introduction of the employee to the company, the job, the supervisor, and the working environment.

This chapter looks at these extremely important functions from a supervisor's viewpoint. In some companies, supervisors have little involvement in hiring new workers. They are told that new people have been assigned to their departments, and they must accept that decision. This is not as it should be. Therefore, we shall turn our attention to the kind of selection process in which supervisors play a significant role.

THE PROCESS OF SELECTING EMPLOYEES

ADVANTAGES OF SUPERVISOR INVOLVEMENT

If adequate selection is to take place in a business, the decision to hire new workers should be made by the people who will become their bosses. This is because the managers have firsthand knowledge about their departments, the workforce, and the jobs that must be filled. They are best equipped to assess each applicant's suitability and potential both for performing the duties he will inherit and for getting along with the existing workforce. It makes a great deal of sense, therefore, to involve supervisors in the selection process and, in particular, to give them the power to make the final decision to hire a new employee.

Learning Objective Number One

Before you select a person for your department, you will probably look over all the applicants carefully in order to select the best from among the many individuals you interview. Since the person hired is someone you have chosen, you will feel a personal commitment to her that otherwise would be missing. You will want her to succeed because a failure will adversely affect you, your department, and the new employee. Part of your success and that of your department will be riding on your choice.

In many companies, teams are involved in the selection process. This chapter's feature on supervising teams shows how such companies share or delegate their hiring decisions.

TEAMS

THE SELECTION PROCESS

Exhibit 10.1 outlines the selection process as it occurs when a supervisor and the company's human resources department work together. In most medium to large firms, the supervisor places a request for a new worker with the human resources department as soon as the need arises. To ensure that both the supervisor and the human resources department know what kind of person they will be looking for, an up-to-date description of the job and its duties, as well as a detailed listing of the knowledge, skills, and abilities required of the jobholder, must be prepared. These two documents are called the *job description* and the *job specification*, respectively.

Learning Objective Number Two

Job Description

A **job description** is a listing of the duties (tasks and activities) and responsibilities of a job or formal position in an organization. All jobs you supervise should have such a listing. Reference to this document proves helpful in assigning work, settling disagreements, appraising subordinates, and filling vacancies. Exhibit 10.2 consists of a job description for a secretarial position. You will note that nothing in it deals with the personal characteristics desirable in the job holder. These are detailed in the job specification.

job description a formal listing of the duties that make up a position in the organization

SUPERVISING TEAMS

Supervisors can empower their teams by making them responsible for a number of functions. Here are some ways that teams can be empowered through external leadership, production/service responsibilities, human resource management, and their social structure:

External Leader Behavior

1. Make team members responsible and accountable for the work they do.
2. Ask for and use team suggestions when making decisions.
3. Encourage team members to take control of their work.
4. Create an environment in which team members set their own team goals.
5. Stay out of the way when team members attempt to resolve work-related problems.
6. Generate high team expectations.
7. Display trust and confidence in the team's abilities.

Production/Service Responsibilities

1. The team sets its own production/service and standards.
2. The team assigns jobs and tasks to its members.
3. Team members develop their own quality standards and measurement techniques.
4. Team members take on production/service learning and development opportunities.

5. Team members handle their own problems with internal and external customers.
6. The team works with a whole product or service, not just a part.

Human Resource Management System

1. The team gets paid, at least in part, as a team.
2. Team members are cross-trained on jobs within the team.
3. Team members are cross-trained on jobs in other teams.
4. Team members are responsible for hiring, training, punishment, and firing.
5. Team members use peer evaluations to formally evaluate each other.

Social Structure

1. The team gets support from other teams and departments when needed.
2. The team has access to and uses important and strategic information.
3. The team has access to and uses the resources of other teams.
4. The team has access to and uses resources inside and outside the organization.
5. The team frequently communicates with other teams.
6. The team makes its own rules and policies.

Source: Reprinted from Organizational Dynamics, Vol. 28, Bradley L. Kirkman and Benson Rosen, "Powering Up Teams," p. 56, Copyright (2000), with permission from Elsevier.

job specification
the personal characteristics and skill levels that are required of an individual to execute a job

Job Specification

Exhibit 10.3 shows the **job specification**—knowledge, skills, and abilities a person must have in order to fill the position—for the position described in Exhibit 10.2. Such factors as keyboarding speed, clerical and secretarial experience, and formal education are listed. You need this information when selecting someone to fill a job, assigning work, and determining promotions. As jobs change with the passage of time, the job

A typical selection process.

EXHIBIT 10.1

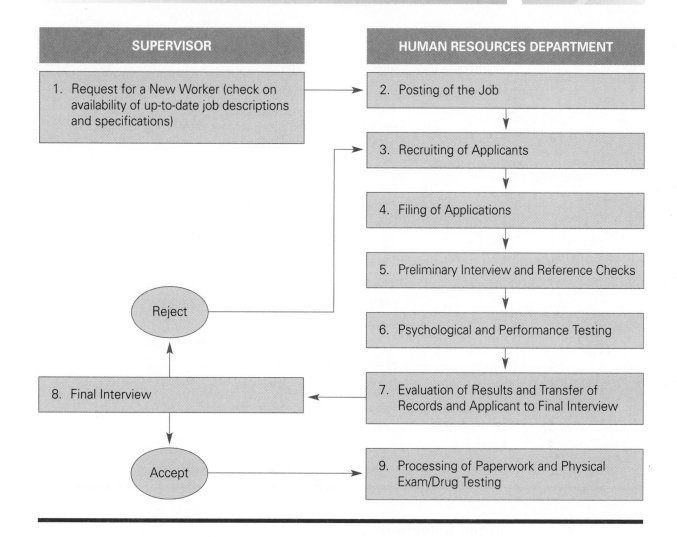

descriptions and specifications must be revised accordingly. It is standard practice to update these documents at least once every two years.

Job Posting

Steps two through seven in the selection process (as illustrated in Exhibit 10.1) are usually performed for you by your company's human resources department. Job openings are posted so that present employees will be aware of them. Posting is also a requirement in many union contracts or the employer's affirmative action program. Posting allows existing employees to apply for the vacancy and can result in promotions and transfers that will create new vacancies. In order to make sincere efforts to attract minority and female applicants, the company should advertise vacancies on a regular basis.

EXHIBIT 10.2   **Job description for personal secretary.**

Title: Secretary   Job No. C-10   Grade 4

Effective Date: 2/06

General   Perform clerical and secretarial duties involving keyboarding, correspondence and report preparation, filing, maintaining records, scheduling appointments, distributing mail. Handle confidential information regularly.

Specific Duties   Compose and keyboard routine memos and business correspondence.

Compile and keyboard routine reports.

Send and forward e-mail daily.

Send, sort, and distribute mail and faxes daily.

Maintain and set up files of memos, letters, and reports.

Obtain data and information by telephone, computer, or personal contact on behalf of supervisor.

Receive visitors.

Schedule supervisor's appointments.

Answer phone and take messages.

Handle confidential files.

Equipment   Personal computer, printer, fax, photocopier, and scanner.

Analysis by: _____   Approved by: _____

Initial Selection

DIVERSITY

After receiving and processing the paperwork that results from steps four through seven, human resources will usually send you two or more applicants for a final employment interview. As a rule, human resources will send you only applicants who qualify for and have the potential to succeed on the job. You must select the person you believe is the best qualified of the applicants you interview. Then, you turn the applicant over to the human resources department for final paperwork.

Exhibit 10.4 lists and briefly describes the federal statutes and executive orders that prevent discrimination in the selection process. In the discussions that follow, the effects of these federal laws are examined as they relate to each of the selection steps or devices. They may be summarized briefly as follows:

1. It is unlawful for an employer to fail or refuse to hire or to discharge an individual because of race, color, religion, sex, age, national origin, disability, pregnancy, or union status.

Job specification for the secretarial position shown in Exhibit 10.2.

EXHIBIT 10.3

Title: Secretary	Job No. C-10 Grade 4
Effective Date:	2/06
Education	High-school graduate or equivalent
Experience	Secretarial, including word processing
Training Period	1 month
Dexterity	Precise movement of hands and fingers required to operate keyboard at no less than 60 words per minute
Adaptability	Must be able to adjust to frequent changes in duties, such as keyboarding, filing, composing letters, handling telephone
Judgment	Must be able to follow existing procedures and establish new practices where necessary. Must be able to compose business letters, establish filing systems, and receive visitors
Specific Skills	Must have knowledge of Word, Excel, Access, PowerPoint
Contact with Others	Frequent contacts with visitors, vendors, and company managers
Physical Demands	Lifting requirements: under 10 pounds

Analysis by: _____   Approved by: _____

2. It is unlawful for an employer to limit, segregate, or classify an employee or applicant for employment in any way that would tend to deprive the individual of employment opportunities because of race, color, religion, sex, age, national origin, disability, pregnancy, or union status.

Title VII of the 1964 Civil Rights Act requires discrimination complaints to be filed within 180 days of the alleged violation and provides for remedies of reinstatement and recovery of lost pay. The Civil Rights Act of 1991 amended the act by allowing punitive damages when a company engages in discriminatory practices with malice or with reckless indifference to the law.

States and local governments also have similar statutes that cover many employers that are too small for federal coverage. In addition, many states and cities have statutes that prohibit discrimination on the basis of sexual orientation.[11]

EXHIBIT 10.4	**Federal anti-discrimination statutes and executive orders relating to selection.**

STATUTE OR EXECUTIVE ORDER	PROHIBITED SELECTION CRITERIA	EMPLOYERS COVERED
Title VII of the Civil Rights Act of 1964 (as amended by the Equal Employment Opportunity Act of 1972 and Civil Rights Act of 1991)	Race, color, religion, sex, or national origin	Employers having 15 or more employees, unions, employment agencies, and governments
Age Discrimination in Employment Act (ADEA)	Protection for applicants of age 40 or more	Employers having 20 or more employees, unions, employment agencies
Pregnancy Discrimination Act of 1978 (amendment to Title VII)	Pregnancy	Employers having 15 or more employees
Americans with Disabilities Act of 1990	Physical and mental disabilities when job duties can be performed with reasonable accommodation	Employers having 25 or more employees, unions, and employment agencies
National Labor Relations Act of 1935 (as amended by the Labor Management Relations Act of 1947)	Union status—except where pre-hire or hiring agreements are permitted	Employers have $50,000 or more annual input or output across state lines. Retailers having $500,000 or more in annual sales.
Executive Order 11246	Race, color, religion, sex, or national origin	Federal contractors and subcontractors
Rehabilitation Act of 1973	Physical and mental disabilities	Federal contractors and federal government

Sources: Charles R. Greer, *Strategy and Human Resources: A General Managerial Approach,* 2nd ed. Englewood Cliffs, NJ: Prentice Hall, 2001. James Ledvinka and Vida G. Scarpello, *Federal Regulation of Personnel and Human Resource Management.* Boston: Kent Publishing Company, 1991. Robert D. Gatewood and Hubert S. Feild, *Human Resource Selection,* 4th ed. Fort Worth, TX: Dryden Press, 1998. Herbert G. Heneman and Robert L. Heneman, *Staffing Organizations.* Middleton, WI: Mendota House, 1994.

RECRUITING

DIVERSITY

There are two sources of supply for personnel: internal and external labor markets. Companies may fill vacancies internally by promoting someone, transferring a person from one job to another (usually a permanent job change), recalling a laid-off worker, or using job rotation to fill a vacancy on a temporary basis. Consider posting your employment needs with your company's other divisions and partners.

People currently employed at your company have friends, neighbors, and relatives who might make good employees. Employee referrals are such a good source of applicants that during periods of low unemployment leading companies such as Cisco Systems, Deloitte & Touche, and Texas Instruments have paid employees for referrals who are hired.[12] Because people tend to refer people similar to themselves, if women and minorities are under-represented in your workforce, you will need to use more than employee referrals as a source of new employees. In such cases external recruiting efforts will be required. The Equal Employment Opportunity (EEO) policy may also provide guidelines for recruiting representative numbers of **minority** members and women.

Typical external sources of employees include unsolicited applications, employment agencies (both public and private), referrals from existing employees, schools, colleges, universities, temporary help agencies, unions, trade associations, and solicitation through help-wanted advertising. Employers may advertise through various electronic media, including radio and cable television programs devoted to helping local employers find workers. Internet job sites are a common avenue for listing or advertising vacancies. *E-recruiting,* the practice of using Internet sites to recruit, has become an important tool for finding job candidates. E-recruiting provides a number of benefits, such as lower costs through elimination of recruitment agency fees, speed, and access to large numbers of candidates. Unsurprisingly, the number of companies using the Internet to recruit has increased dramatically. Because of the high volumes of résumés that employers often receive, automated application evaluation tools allow employers to quickly screen applications and résumés.[13] While human resource departments usually handle such recruiting tasks, e-recruiting may be very useful for supervisors in smaller companies who may need to do their own recruiting. Exhibit 10.5 ranks recruiting sources according to their effectiveness in improving job performance and turnover/ job survival.

minority
according to the EEOC, a member of one of the following groups: Hispanics, Native Americans, African Americans, Asians or Pacific Islanders, Alaskan natives

DIVERSITY

AFFIRMATIVE ACTION PROGRAMS

The U.S. government requires companies to develop affirmative action programs (AAP) under the following circumstances: (1) they have been found guilty of discriminatory practices, or (2) they do contract work for the federal government (valued at $50,000 or more) and employ more than 50 employees. They also may develop an AAP when they recognize that they need to improve their employment record with regard to women and minorities. One important part of an AAP is a stated goal and timetable for hiring more women and minorities.

EEO/AFFIRMATIVE ACTION AND VALUING DIVERSITY

Equal employment opportunity and affirmative action are legal concepts initiated and mandated by the federal government and reinforced by numerous state and local laws. They tend to be quantitative and focus on the problem of getting employers to build and maintain workforces that are truly representative of the population from which they draw employees. In contrast, efforts to pursue diversity for cultural, moral, and economic purposes are purely voluntary, and begin where EEO and affirmative action efforts end. These are proactive efforts designed to bring change and stimulate creativity while creating working environments that welcome and utilize the unique skills

EXHIBIT 10.5	Effectiveness of recruitment sources.

MOST EFFECTIVE

- Referrals by current employees
- In-house company postings
- Rehired former employees

SLIGHTLY LESS EFFECTIVE

- Walk-ins

LEAST EFFECTIVE SOURCES

- Newspaper ads
- School placement centers
- Employment agencies

Source: Michael A. Zottoli and John P. Wanous, "Recruitment Source Research: Current Status and Future Directions," *Human Resource Management Review 10* (2000): 353–383.

of every employee. They seek to truly integrate, not assimilate. Valuing diversity means acceptance and coexistence for different cultures and values of various ethnic and social groups.

REVERSE DISCRIMINATION

Affirmative action programs are pursued when a case of prior discrimination has been established or when an employer has a significant under-representation of minority and female employees. Determinations of under-representation take into consideration the relevant labor markets from which employers can be expected to hire employees for various jobs. "Generally, minority/female promotion or hiring over white males will not be considered reverse discrimination if the company has not met its affirmative action goals."[14] On the other hand, when race or gender becomes a factor in conducting layoffs, the courts may find reverse discrimination. For example, in 1986, the U.S. Supreme Court ruled, in *Wygant v. Jackson Board of Education,* that the school board's actions were unconstitutional. The school board "attempted to preserve the racial balance of the teaching staff by laying off more senior white teachers rather than less senior black teachers."[15]

DIVERSITY

RECRUITING WOMEN

More qualified women are entering what were once male-dominated professions. For example, Meg Whitman has risen to the position of CEO at eBay. However, such successes do not guarantee that women are adequately represented in the full range of jobs in all organizations. As a supervisor in charge of hiring new workers, you must seek to recruit women from whatever sources you can. Furthermore, it may be necessary to offer childcare facilities and flexible working hours to attract some women. Another issue in recruiting women involves pregnancy. Over the next decade, more than 20 million pregnancies are anticipated among working women in the United States.[16]

As noted in Exhibit 10.4, employers cannot discriminate against women on the basis of pregnancy. As one employment lawyer says, "if pregnant workers must be reassigned because they aren't able physically to perform a job, they mustn't be treated any worse than employees with other disabling conditions."[17] Nonetheless, in 1997 3,977 pregnancy-bias complaints were filed with the EEOC, up 6 percent from the previous year. The National Association of Working Women cites pregnancy discrimination as one of the top five concerns of people who call in on its hotline.[18] Supervisors must ensure that pregnancy is not used as a reason for rejecting qualified women applicants.

ETHICS

DIVERSITY

This chapter's feature on supervisors and ethics describes some unethical recruiting practices that have emerged with the use of Internet technology.

RECRUITING MINORITIES

Minority recruiting involves development of a strategy for increasing the pool of applicants who have an interest in your job openings. Neighborhood associations, churches, community action groups, state employment offices, ethnic newspapers, and current minority employees may be able to help you, along with search firms that specialize in recruiting minorities. Schools that have large enrollments of minorities are also good sources of applicants, and the number of minority college graduates is increasing. College graduates account for 17 percent of the Black population, ages 25 and older, and for 11 percent of the Hispanic population at least 25 years old.[19] Special programs designed to increase the number of minority graduates, such as the minority engineering program at the University of Arizona, may help you find candidates. In addition, for higher-level jobs there are professional associations such as the National Association of Black Engineers (*http://www.nsbe.org/*), the National Black MBA Association (*http://www.nbmbaa.org/*), the Society for Professional Engineers (*http://www.shpe.org*) and the National Society of Hispanic MBAs (*http://www.nshmba.org/*). Internet sites also are good sources of potential applicants, as they often list résumés.

Before minorities are introduced to a workforce, current employees must be encouraged to cooperate with the company's affirmative action efforts. As with all new employees, every effort must be made to find the best qualified candidates and to ensure their early success on the job.

THE SUPERVISOR'S ROLE IN MINORITY HIRING

New minority employees, like everyone else, want an even chance for success. For those minorities who come from disadvantaged circumstances and have gaps in their educational backgrounds, employees be prepared to provide extra training. Minority employees want and need to be respected and appreciated for their good points and

SUPERVISORS AND ETHICS

Internet recruiting has rapidly become a major source of job candidates for many employers and provides great opportunities for matching applicants with jobs. The large Internet job sites, which host résumés and job listings, provide a valuable matching service to both employers and job seekers. Unfortunately, in recent years, there have also been abuses of the Internet in the area of recruiting, particularly in times of low unemployment in high-demand areas such as engineering and information technology. Because some of the best job candidates are already in the workforces of competitor companies, recruiters often target companies in their recruiting efforts. In order to find such potential job candidates, unethical recruiters hack into the private areas of company websites, where they can gain access to employee directories and home pages.

Some of the biggest abusers of Internet recruiting are freelancers who get paid by the head for quickly locating scarce talent. Since their fees are sometimes as much as 30 percent of the annual salary of the candidate, there are strong financial incentives to resort to unethical tactics. The demand for ethically borderline search skills has become so great that a few firms even provide expensive seminars that teach techniques for hacking into employers' websites. One such firm has advertised that its seminars enable one to "drive your bus right through your source company's website—loading up candidates as you go." An example of one of these techniques is flipping.

Flipping is used to find Web pages that are linked to a specific site, allowing a search within those links. This can be used to find people who create links from their home pages to their colleges, associations to which they belong, and the companies that employ them.

Unethical recruiters can use flipping techniques to enter an employer's private intranets, where they can gain detailed information about company personnel. Other similar techniques are used by unethical recruiters to obtain information from company websites not intended for public use. Because of such abuses, companies should avoid putting too much information on their websites and should build in firewalls to keep hackers from getting into information unintended for the public.

In addition to unethical recruiting practices that rely on Internet technology, there have been more traditional abuses. For example, some unethical recruiters use false identities to gain access to company sources of potential job candidates. The following example describes such a practice:

> "I know a recruiter who has called companies saying he's with the Larry King Show. He says, 'We'd like your CFO to be on our show, can you spell his name?' It's amazing, but he gets all the information he needs. And the CFO's secretary would probably send you her boss's fourth-grade report card if she thinks you're from Larry King."

Other examples of abuse include paying employees for copies of company phone directories or conning receptionists and mailroom clerks out of information on company personnel. To counter such tactics, companies need to train people in these areas to verify identities of callers and the legitimacy of their requests for information.

Source: Eilene Zimmerman, "Fight Dirty Hiring Tactics," *Workforce* (May 2001): 30–34.

As a supervisor, you play a major role in the success of minority or differently abled subordinates. With the labor force now coming from diverse groups, your company's success rests on your ability to help all employees reach their potential.

potential. They also want to carry their own weight. Supervisors must realize that in some circumstances new minority workers may arrive expecting the worst: resentment, rejection, hostility, and isolation. As a result, they may seem hypersensitive. What a non-minority worker might brush aside, a minority member may consider an insult or personal attack. Until all of your subordinates feel that they are being treated as individuals, you can expect a measure of discontent. Evaluate people on their merits, avoiding stereotypes and generalities. Get to know each person as a unique individual.

There may be a few workers, however, who try to take advantage of the situation. Some may be looking for special privileges. They may want to use the fact that they are women or minorities as a lever in an attempt to gain favored treatment. This inequity, although clearly understandable, must be prevented.

DIVERSITY

RECRUITING THE DIFFERENTLY ABLED

The differently abled or disabled are those individuals who: (1) have a physical or mental impairment that substantially limits one or more major life activities, (2) have a record of such an impairment, or (3) are regarded as having such an impairment. Two major laws protect people with disabilities: the Americans with Disabilities Act of 1990 (ADA) and the Rehabilitation Act of 1973. ADA has basically replaced the

Rehabilitation Act, although earlier court cases on the latter provide current guidance for ADA interpretation.[20] Under Section 1630.4 of the ADA, employers may not discriminate against a qualified person with a disability when they recruit, hire, determine pay and benefits, make job assignments, and grant leaves of absence. Qualified persons are defined as those who are capable of performing a job's "essential functions."[21]

The ADA protects individuals with disabilities from employment discrimination based on current or past physical and mental conditions. Examples of those protected include people with a history of cancer, heart trouble, or a contagious disease, providing that their conditions do not pose a significant risk to coworkers or render them unable to perform their work. In addition, the ADA protects people who have undergone or who now are undergoing rehabilitation for alcohol or drug dependencies.

Under both laws, employers must make reasonable accommodations that will allow employment of the disabled. Examples of inexpensive accommodations include providing wheelchair ramps, installing handrails, replacing revolving doors, installing speech-recognition aids, and lowering elevator controls.[22]

Under the ADA, physical examinations may be administered only after the applicant is given a conditional offer of employment. When the physical examination is conducted, it must be a regular part of pre-employment procedures. Furthermore, the employer can use only job-related physical conditions to deny employment. It should be noted that drug tests for illegal substances are not considered to be physical examinations under the ADA.[23]

Learning Objective Number Three

Fortunately, many employers have rejected old biases and recognize the value of the differently abled. One of the authors and two colleagues interviewed the vice president of human resources for a *Fortune* 500 company. The interview lasted over an hour while the executive outlined his views on the future of human resources and how companies can benefit from the function's evolving role. He looked at each of us, listened to our questions, and kept us spellbound with his intellect and enthusiasm. At the end of the interview, he walked us out of the departmental offices, took us down the hall to the elevators, pressed the button to summon an elevator, took us down to the main floor, escorted us to the security desk, and told the guard that we were leaving. He then shook hands with us and said goodbye. This remarkably talented man is truly an asset to his organization, and he is differently abled because he is blind.

APPLICANT SCREENING PROCEDURES

Steps four through eight listed in Exhibit 10.1 deal with several selection tools or screening devices: the application, the preliminary interview, various kinds of tests, and the final interview. These devices, like recruiting, are governed in some ways by federal, state, and local anti-discrimination legislation.

Your best defense against accusations of discrimination or bias in hiring is to be certain that any employment practice or device adheres to the following:

- It is job-related—it can predict success or failure on a specific job.
- It is a business necessity—the company must do what it does to provide for its continued existence.

- It acknowledges a *bona fide occupational qualification* (BFOQ)—for example, a licensing or age requirement.
- It honors a *bona fide seniority system* (BFSS)—a seniority system established and maintained that does not have the intent to illegally discriminate.[24]

THE APPLICATION

The application is your primary method for obtaining the key facts about a candidate for a job. The information it obtains can help you weed out unqualified people and avoid unnecessary interviews. Some companies are now using computers and sophisticated software, such as Restrac or Resumix, to scan résumés in order to eliminate unqualified applicants. Companies that use computer systems to screen résumés include Coca-Cola, Sony, IBM, Avis Rent A Car, Pfizer, Microsoft, and Shell Oil. Job applicants now are realizing that it is important that their résumés contain the key words for which such systems search, and that they must prepare their résumés in scanable formats.[25]

DIVERSITY

Examine your employer's application form. If it contains any of the inquiries discussed in Exhibit 10.6, you should be on guard. Evaluate the need for each question, and eliminate those that are not closely related to job performance or to predicting success on the job for which the applicant will be considered. In addition, include the Equal Employment Opportunity Employer notice and language explaining that the firm does not discriminate on the basis of the various prohibited criteria, such as those noted later in Exhibit 10.6 as well as criteria deemed illegitimate by company policy. Some criteria, such as sexual orientation and eligibility for partner benefits, are specific to the cities or states in which the company operates or company policy. The form should then be reviewed by a labor or employment law attorney before it is used.[26]

Learning Objective Number Four

INTERVIEWS

The **interview** can be defined as a conversation between two or more parties that is under the control of one of the parties and that has the goal of accomplishing a special objective. It must be carefully planned and skillfully executed if its special objective is to be achieved. As a supervisor, you will be using interviews to screen and hire new employees. Effective interviews require a quiet environment and extensive use of open and closed questions.

interview
a two-way conversation under the control of one of the parties

The major purpose of a selection interview is to fill in the gaps in information obtained from other selection procedures and devices such as the application, résumé, and test scores. Interviews are useful for assessing whether the applicant will fit in well and can provide a good indication of an applicant's communication and interpersonal skills.[27] Human resource experts generally agree that the interview should not be used to collect factual data since such information can be obtained more quickly and economically from an application, résumé, and so on.[28]

To encourage the interviewee to talk, you should use open-ended questions that cannot be answered with a yes or no. Open-ended questions start with such words as *why, what, when, where, which, who,* and *how.* Closed-ended questions start with such words as *can, is, do, and have.* The interviewer must always listen attentively, never interrupt, and in general refrain from expressing opinions or making snap judgments.

EXHIBIT 10.6	Pre-employment inquiry guidelines.

SUBJECT	LAWFUL INQUIRIES/REQUIREMENTS	UNLAWFUL INQUIRIES/REQUIREMENTS
Age	Whether the applicant meets the minimum age requirement set by law; if required as a bona fide occupational qualification (BFOQ); or after hire, if inquiry serves a legitimate record-keeping purpose.	That applicant state age or date of birth. That applicant produce proof of age (birth certificate, baptismal record). Specifications such as: *young*, *college student*, *recent college graduate*, and *retired person*.
Arrests and Convictions	Inquiries about convictions that bear a direct relationship to the job and have not been expunged or sealed by the courts. Consideration should be given to the nature, recentness, and rehabilitation.	Inquiries about a candidate's general arrest and conviction record.
Citizenship, Birthplace	After employment, verification of legal right to work (all new hires).	Whether applicant, parents, or spouse are naturalized or native-born U.S citizens. Birthplace of applicant, parents, or spouse. Requirement that applicant produce naturalization papers.
Dependents		Inquiries regarding: the number and ages of children; what child care arrangements have been made; family planning.
Disability	Whether applicant is able to perform the essential functions of the job with or without reasonable accommodation. That applicant demonstrates how she/he would perform the job and with what accommodation(s). After a job offer, but before hire, require medical examination for all similarly situated entering employees.	Requirement that applicant take medical examination or provide information about workers'compensation claim(s) before a job offer. Generalinquiries into the applicant's state of health or thenature and severity of a disability.
Driver's License	Inquiry if driving is necessary to the job.	Inquiring if all applicants have a valid driver's license regardless of job.
Marital Status		Whether applicant is: single, married, divorced, widowed, etc.; Mr., Mrs., Miss, regarding the Ms. Inquiries names and ages of spouse or children.
Military Service	Job-related inquiries into military experience in the U.S. Armed Forces or state militia (e.g. branch, occupational specialty).	Inquiries regarding foreign military experience. Whether honorably discharged.
Name	Whether the applicant has used another name (for the purpose of verifying past work record).	Inquiries or comments about the name that would reveal applicant's lineage, national origin, marital status, etc. (e.g. maiden name?)Mr., Mrs., Miss, Ms.?

National Origin	What languages applicant reads, speaks, or writes fluently if relevant to the job or if required as a bona fide occupational qualification.	Inquiries regarding: applicant's nationality, ancestry, lineage, or parentage; nationality of applicant's parents or spouse; maiden name of applicant, wife, or mother.
Photograph	May be requested after hire (for identification).	Request before hire.
Polygraph, Lie Detector		Require test to be taken as a condition of employment.
Professional Associations	Inquiries regarding memberships in *job-related* clubs and organizations. Applicants may omit those that reveal the race, religion, age, sex, disability, etc. of applicant.	Requesting the names of *all* organizations, clubs, and associations to which the applicant belongs. Inquiries regarding how the applicant spends his/her spare time.
Race, Color		Inquiries regarding: applicant's race; color of applicant's skin, eyes, hair, or other questions directly or indirectly indicating race or color; applicant's height (unless a bona fide occupational qualification).
References	Inquiring by whom applicant was referred. Requesting names of persons willing to provide professional or character references. Making job-related inquiries of references.	Requiring the submission of religious references. Inquiries of references that would elicit information on applicant's race, color, national origin, age, marital status, disability, or sexual orientation.
Religion	Inquiries regarding the normal hours of work. After hire, inquiries regarding religious accommodations.	Inquiries regarding applicant's religious denomination or affiliation or religious holidays observed. Any inquiry that would indicate or identify religious customs or holidays observed.
Sex	Inquiry only if required as a bona fide occupational qualification.	Inquiries regarding: applicant's sex; Mr., Mrs., Miss, Ms.; if applicant is expecting, planning a family, or uses birth control.
Sexual Orientation		Any inquiry concerning an applicant's heterosexuality, homosexuality, or bisexuality.

Source: Extracted from the State of Maryland Office of Equal Opportunity and Program Equity (OEOPE) Website (January 27, 2006): *www.dllr.state.md.us/oeope/preemp.htm.*

The employment interview has two primary purposes: to evaluate the qualifications and suitability of the applicant to fill the job opening and to give the applicant the information necessary to make an intelligent decision about accepting an offer of employment, should it be given. Be honest about the working conditions, the chances for advancement, and the type of duties you will expect the new employee to perform. Review the job description and the job specification in advance, and have them handy for reference during the interview.

Avoid asking questions that could open you and your employer to accusations of employment discrimination. The information in Exhibit 10.6 also applies to the conduct of interviews. In addition to these, conduct all of your interviews in the same manner, using the same format and questions. The degree of structure can range from complete adherence to the same exact questions and format, as in the pure *structured interview*, to an approach that covers all of the same issues with each applicant, but with some flexibility in how the questions are phrased. The key advantage of adding structure to the interview is that the collection of information from all applicants, on all of the same issues, allows for a more valid comparison among the applicants. With this common framework for comparison, the interview produces more valid and reliable or consistent results because the interviewer is not trying to compare apples with oranges. With greater validity and reliability, the interview becomes a more accurate method for predicting whether the applicant is likely to perform well on the job.[29] (Validity is discussed later in this chapter.) In addition, the use of multiple interviewers, such as a tag-team approach, increases the predictive power of interviews. Questions about how applicants handled issues in their past experience, such as conflicts within teams, also increase the predictive power of interviews.[30] The use of such questions is called *behavior-based interviewing*. This interviewing technique is used by companies such as S.C. Johnson Wax, Merck, Steelcase, and Procter & Gamble.[31]

For many jobs, assessing job applicants on some basic attrributes can prove to be quite valuable for the selection decision. As a result, it is often helpful to obtain information on applicants' (1) ambition or drive, (2) impact or leadership ability, (3) past performance, and (4) problem-solving ability.[32] Lou Adler has posed the following questions in his book, which provides detailed guidance for interpreting responses, while gathering information from applicants on these respective attributes:

Please think of your most significant accomplishment in your career. Now could you tell me all about it?[33]

Give me a quick overview of your current (prior) position and describe the biggest impact (or change) you made.[34]

Please draw an organization chart and tell me about a team project you were involved in, and describe your role. [non-supervisory personnel][35]

If you were to get this job, how would you go about solving this typical problem (describe the problem)?[36]

directive interview
an interview planned and totally controlled by the interviewer

Directive interviews. The **directive interview** is based on a format of specific questions set down in advance (structured) and followed exactly. The questions should ask for information the interviewer considers most essential. Here are some examples: "What did you do between your job with the ABC Company and your employment at XYZ, Incorporated?" "Why did you leave the ABC Company?" Generally, the interviewer will ask the set of questions (questions she has written down in advance) in the order in which they are listed. Certain questions may be more important than others since they may reveal more valuable information. Make sure that the applicant knows the nature of the job for which he is being interviewed and that he also has an opportunity to ask questions.

This type of interview works best when you are dealing with applicants for routine production or clerical positions. It allows you to obtain the maximum amount of job- or performance-related information in the minimum amount of time.

As a supervisor, you need to make job candidates feel at ease. You need to listen carefully. Most important, leave your biases out of the process—pick the most qualified candidate.

Non-directive interviews. The **non-directive interview** also is planned, but it is generally less structured and more flexible. Questions may be written down, but they are designed to be open or loose in order to allow applicants more freedom in their responses and to reveal the attitudes behind their words. Typical questions that might be asked include the following: "Why did you apply for this job?" "Of the jobs you have held, which did you like best (least) and why?" The object of these open-ended questions is to let the applicants talk so that their aspirations, goals, and preferences can come out.

non-directive interview
an interview planned by the interviewer but controlled by the interviewee

The interviewer is not bound to a rigid format with this indirect approach. One question can lead to others, with the applicant's responses determining the direction and flow of the interview. Quite often you will find out a great deal from an applicant's detailed explanations and will uncover much more than you would in a directive interview. People left to talk on their own will say more than they normally would because they are not sure how much you want to know. They will seize the opportunity to speak their minds if they are relaxed and encouraged to speak up. Nonetheless, even with the non-directive interview, you should ask the same general questions of all applicants so that you can make valid comparisons.

Behavioral interviews. In a **behavioral interview,** the interviewer asks the applicant about how she dealt with a critical situation in the past. For example, an applicant might be asked to explain how he dealt with a conflict with a subordinate. Other examples might be to ask the applicant how she coached a work team so that it could meet its goals or how he handled an employee who made a critical mistake. The rationale of behavioral interviews is that past behaviors provide good predictions of how candidates will act in the future. In addition, since interviewees are asked about their past experiences, the information is more reliable than responses to questions posing hypothetical situations. By asking the same questions of all applicants, the interviewer can structure the interview, which helps make it more valid and reliable.[37]

behavioral interview
an interviewing technique in which job applicants are asked to describe how they handled critical incidents in their prior experiences

Work sampling. The job for which you are attempting to hire employees may require skills that can be tested with a work sample or work performance test. For example, you could let the applicants demonstrate their ability to run a machine, meet close tolerances, file correspondence, keyboard, and the like. If your human resources department has not included such tests in the selection procedure, you should work with its selection specialists to develop work sampling or performance tests that can be included as components of the selection process.

Preparing to Interview

Like any other type of interview—whether for counseling, for sharing your evaluations, or for interrogation and fact finding for disciplinary actions—the employment interview should be held in private and in an environment as free from interruptions as you can make it. Since you usually know well in advance when an applicant is due to report, set aside enough time to do the kind of interview you prefer, and do your homework before the meeting. Read the candidate's application thoroughly and review the job description and specification. Prepare a brief checklist of the essentials you wish to cover so that you do not waste time or overlook an important area.

Conducting the Interview

No matter what type of interview you choose, you should observe the following basic procedure:

1. *Put the applicant at ease.* Keep in mind that the applicant will probably be a bit nervous. A comfortable chair, a quiet room, good ventilation, a cup of coffee, and a smile along with your handshake will go a long way toward relieving his tension.

2. *Stick with your schedule.* If you have planned your questions and prepared an outline to follow, stay with them. You must resist the temptation to wander from essential areas and talk about whatever arises. You have certain points to cover, and you do not usually have the luxury of unlimited time.

3. *Listen.* By now you are probably sick of reading about listening, but it is of the greatest importance to the communication process—especially when you are engaged in a discussion. If you do all the talking, you will learn nothing. If you use the time between your questions simply to plan for what you will cover next, you will miss the applicant's answers. If you are not attentive to the applicant, you will cause her to stop talking. Summarize your thoughts about the applicant periodically, in writing, as time and discussion lags permit.

4. *Remain neutral.* Mask your reactions, whether favorable or unfavorable. If the applicant senses your feelings one way or the other, he will begin to tailor responses to your reactions. You will receive what you have indicated you want to hear, not what the applicant wants to say. Try to uncover the applicant's way of looking at things. You will gain a perspective on the individual and her attitudes that otherwise would be denied to you. If an applicant's attitudes or feelings are contrary to yours, simply ask yourself if it really matters. Will those opinions keep the applicant from a successful job performance? If not, forget them.

5. *Avoid asking leading questions.* Questions formulated to lead a person to the answer you want to hear will do just that. An example is "You got along with your boss, didn't you?" If a person answers no, he is pretty stupid. These questions simply waste time. They tell an applicant where your values are, but you will not learn the applicant's values.

6. *Give the applicant a specific time by which she will have your final decision.* Then stick to that time limit as best you can. If you delay your decision too long, you may lose your prospect. You may be surprised to hear the applicant tell you that he is not sure and wishes to examine other opportunities. If you really want that person, set a time by which he should give you a definite answer.

TESTS

Under federal guidelines, tests are any paper-and-pencil or performance measure used as a basis for any employment decision, including selection and hiring. Such measures include interviews, applications, psychological and performance exams, physical requirements for a job, and any other device that is scored or used as a basis for selecting an applicant. The tests you use should attempt to measure only the performance capabilities that can be proven to be essential for success in the job to be filled.

DIVERSITY

Disparate or Adverse Impact

Federal guidelines say that selection devices must have no disparate or adverse impact. **Disparate** or **adverse impact** exists when a significantly different selection rate exists for women or minorities than for other groups. Adverse impact may be determined by several criteria, such as the following guideline:

> A selection rate for any race, sex, or ethnic group which is less than four-fifths (4/5) (or 80 percent) of the rate for the group with the highest rate will generally be regarded by the Federal enforcement agencies as evidence of adverse impact.[38]

For example, if an employer hires 60 percent of white males who apply but less than 80 percent of that figure (less than 48 percent overall) of women and minorities, the selection procedures being used have an adverse impact. As a result, the employer will have to demonstrate that the selection procedures are job-related or valid and reliable. Because of potential challenges to hiring decisions and requirements of the Equal Employment Opportunity Commission (EEOC), accurate records of all those interviewed and hired must be kept. All applicants, whether hired or not, must be classified by sex, race, and ethnic group, including whites.

Some screening criteria or devices that may lead to disparate or adverse impact include tests, educational requirements, height and weight requirements, preferences for relatives of employees, and reference checks. Unless a screening device can be shown to be job related, a business necessity, or a BFOQ, it should not be used. Examples of such business necessity-related qualifications include state-mandated licensing requirements, language abilities, and apprenticeship training for skilled crafts positions.

disparate impact/adverse impact
the existence of a significantly different selection rate between women or minorities and non-protected groups

Validity

Validity is the degree to which a selection criterion or a device measures what it is supposed to measure. With respect to testing for employee selection, the term often refers to evidence that the device is job related—that the device is a valid predictor of future performance on a job. There are several kinds of validity; the ones most relevant to supervisors are *criterion validity* and *content validity.*

Criterion validity involves the demonstration that those who perform well on the test will have high evaluations of actual job performance. Content validity means that the test provides a fair sample of the content of the job. Content validity is established by having experts identify the knowledge required for a job. Test items are then written for various aspects of that knowledge.

An example of a criterion-based or predictive validation follows. To construct a valid physical test, a state agency decided to study the physical demands made on troopers during the execution of their daily duties. A test was developed, made up of a short run with full weight of equipment and a drag-and-carry test simulating the extraction of accident victims. The test was given to recruits but was not used to hire them. After the recruits were selected and had their job performances rated by their superiors, the test results were compared to their ratings. A good relationship was found, and the test was then considered a valid selection device. It simulated with accuracy the physical demands that were made on troopers, and the test included major examples of their daily requirements.

Pre-Employment Drug Testing

Substance abuse has been a widespread problem in the United States for many years. Survey data collected in 2004 indicate that approximately 19 million people, or 7.9 percent of the population over 12 years of age, used illicit drugs in the previous month. Furthermore, 8 percent of the people in the population, who are at least 18 years of age and who work full-time, use illicit drugs. For those working part-time, the proportion using illicit drugs is slightly higher at 10.3 percent.[39] The impact, on an annual basis, of worker substance abuse, in the form of absenteeism, accidents, injuries, and other related costs, has been estimated to range between $75 billion and $200 billion.[40] In view of these statistics, it is unsurprising that drug testing is widespread in the United States. In 2000, approximately 47 percent of U.S. employers administered tests for illicit drug use, compared with 70 percent in 1996. Along with the decline in testing, positive test results declined from 13.6 percent in 1988 to 4.6 percent in 1999. Self-selection may explain some of this decline because drug users are apparently avoiding employment at companies where drug testing is part of the selection process or where there is ongoing drug testing of current employees. Some explanation of this decline may lie with improved methods for cheating on the tests, such as with the use of adulterants.[41]

Nonetheless, drug testing is still widespread and is more important in some industries as the use of illicit drugs varies substantially with industry and occupation. For example, 18 percent of employees working in restaurant and hospitality jobs reported illicit drug use as compared to only 3 percent in protective services.[42] Furthermore, drug and alcohol testing is required for safety reasons in some industries covered by U.S. Department of Transportation regulations, such as truck and bus transportation, aviation, pipelines, railroads, and the maritime industry. The Drug Free Workplace Act also requires large federal contractors to test for drugs.[43] As a supervisor, the extent of your involvement in drug testing will probably be limited to getting the results after the offer of employment has been made and the test(s) given. Offers of employment are usually conditional on successful completion of physical exams and drug tests. Nonetheless, you should have some rudimentary understanding of drug testing procedures.

Drug testing requires careful administration in order to safeguard rights of job applicants, as well as current employees, and to conform with complicated legal requirements. Companies that use drug tests for hiring purposes must require all applicants to undergo such testing and are not allowed to selectively decide who should be tested. They should also inform applicants of their requirement for drug tests by including a notice on the application form. In addition, the testing procedure should provide for challenges of the outcomes and retesting. Furthermore, in order to be in compliance with the Americans with Disabilities Act, there should also be a procedure for applicants, who have been rejected on the basis of a drug test in the past, to apply again at some point in time if they have undergone drug rehabilitation treatment. Finally, employers can also ask their drug testing laboratories to test for adulterants in order to prevent applicants from duping the test.[44]

This chapter's feature on supervisors and performance provides a brief description of one company's experiences with substance abuse and drug testing.

AIDS, HIV, and Hiring

It has been estimated that between 1 to 1.2 million people in the United States had HIV infection or AIDS in 2003.[45] While the initial fears about HIV and AIDs in the workplace, which occurred after the discovery of the disease in the early 1980s, have subsided as a result of greater awareness and understanding, supervisors still need to be aware of the applicable legislation. The Supreme Court has ruled that simple fear of contagion by any virus—without any medical assessment that the fear is well-founded—cannot justify firing an employee with any contagious disease. Through this decision, those who test positive for HIV and AIDS (along with others who suffer from contagious diseases) have been placed under the protection of the 1973 Vocational Rehabilitation Act and the 1990 Americans with Disabilities Act (ADA). Thus, under the provisions of ADA, AIDS or HIV cannot be the basis for refusing to hire an applicant. In addition, under the provisions of the ADA, employers must make "reasonable accommodations" for those with HIV or AIDS and must comply with confidentiality requirements.

Fear of AIDS is a reality in the workplace requiring education for all employees. As a result, many employers have formulated effective and humane policies and training programs to deal with this issue. Many companies have also adopted the guidelines recommended by the American Red Cross and the National Leadership Coalition on AIDS.

Screening by Polygraph

The polygraph, sometimes called the lie detector, was used by 10 percent of U.S. companies to screen job applicants before being banned by federal law in 1988. The Employee Polygraph Protection Act states that private employers may not require, request, or suggest that employees or prospective employees take lie detector tests, except when conducting in-house investigations. Employers may then request employees to take lie detector tests under strict conditions.

SUPERVISORS AND PERFORMANCE

One evening, the plant maintenance engineer contacted the company president at her home and asked if she was aware that employees were using drugs on the job. She replied that she was not and asked how he knew this to be a fact. The engineer replied that he had found drug paraphernalia—syringes, rubber straps, and unidentified pills in various trash containers throughout the work areas. The president immediately contacted the company's attorney and asked for his help.

Together, the president and the attorney worked up a program to deal with possible drug abuse on the company's premises involving company employees. The program involved three distinct phases: education, testing, and rehabilitation opportunities. It was initiated with a two-hour education session on drug abuse, its effects on the workplace, and its costs in both dollars and human terms. The employees were informed that they would be tested for drugs through urine sampling (the most common form of testing) on the following Monday at a nearby testing lab. Employees were assigned a report-in time and given the entire day off with pay. Persons testing positive were required to enroll in a rehabilitation program before being allowed to return to work. Those refusing to be tested or to join the rehab program were fired after explanations and warnings. Each year, all employees would be randomly tested at least once.

This company's policy is typical of a sound approach. It makes no exceptions, it forewarns, it offers treatment, and it is not punitive for those who avail themselves of the opportunity to get straight. Its primary motivations are to prevent injuries and losses and to keep good people on the job.

Screening by Paper-and-Pencil Integrity Tests

Paper-and-pencil integrity or honesty tests, written and graded by vendors, are used to eliminate applicants who are likely to steal from the company. There is substantial evidence that such tests can be valid predictors of tendencies for theft and other undesirable work behaviors. Integrity testing is restricted in only two states: Massachusetts and Rhode Island.[46] The following provides a good summary of the status of paper-and-pencil integrity tests:

> The results of this work [previous research] consistently indicate that these tests are valid in reference to criteria that include theft, detrimental behaviors, and overall job performance. This validity may be demonstrated in spite of attempts by applicants to distort their responses and to appear more honest than they in fact are. Also, integrity tests can add to the prediction of job performance in selection programs that consist of cognitive ability and personality measures. Finally, little data exist that indicate these tests are at variance with any of the laws that govern selection.[47]

THE IMMIGRATION REFORM AND CONTROL ACT

The Immigration Reform and Control Act of 1986 requires most employers to hire only American citizens and aliens who are authorized to work in the United States. When you hire, you must verify the employment eligibility and identity of each employee and complete and retain the one-page federal Form I-9. In general, the person who is hired must complete Section 1 of Form I-9 at the time employment begins. The employer must then examine the employee's identity by looking at various documents and complete Section 2 of Form I-9. The employer must certify, in this section, that he or she has examined the documents that the employee provides as evidence of identity, that the documents appear to be genuine, and that he or she concludes that the person is eligible to be employed in the country. For persons employed for three days or more, the employer must complete Section 2 by the end of the third business day following the beginning of employment. For people hired for employment of fewer than three days, the employer is required to complete Section 2 at the time employment begins. Once Form I-9 is completed by both the employer and the new hire, the documents used to verify identity and employability should be photocopied and kept on file with the Form I-9 for three years after the date of employment, or for one year after the date the employment is terminated, whichever is later.[48] I-9 forms and other immigration information can be obtained at the United States Citizenship and Immigration Services website: *http://uscis.gov.*

Learning Objective Number Five

PITFALLS

In employee selection, as in most of your duties, a number of pitfalls may snare you if you are not aware of them. Since there is a strong similarity between appraisals of subordinates and appraisals of applicants, some of the same pitfalls apply here as well.

1. *The halo effect.* This occurs when you let one outstanding good characteristic in an applicant influence your overall assessment.
2. *The similar to me effect.* This mistake occurs when the hiring supervisor or manager provides a higher evaluation than justified simply because of perceived similarities with applicant. Such mistakes can result in lower team or group performance because they lead to less diverse thinking and less robust problem solving. Too much similarity also restricts the range of experience represented in the team or group and its inventory of knowledge. [49]
3. *The rush job.* If you are inadequately prepared for an interview, how can you find out all you need to know about an applicant?
4. *Failure to follow the principles of sound interviewing.* After you have completed this chapter, you should have a good grasp of what these principles are.
5. *Overreliance on the results of the interview.* Interviews have limited ability to predict job success and should never be the sole basis for hiring decisions. Furthermore, applicants with serious flaws can perform well in interviews even though they may be a disaster on the job.[50]

6. *Use of unvalidated selection procedures and tools.* Despite the prohibitions against using selection procedures that are unrelated to future job performance, a few employers still ask applicants for pictures while on rare occasion others may ask applicants to submit to handwriting analysis. The use of such procedures, which add nothing of value to the selection decision, also run the risk of making a poor impression with job applicants and can lead to future litigation.[51]

7. *Overselling your company or the job.* By overstatements, puffed-up generalizations, and inaccurate or untruthful information, you might be sowing the seeds that eventually frustrate the new person and lead him to quit. The person may accept the job with false hopes as a result of your inaccurate promises.

8. *Omitting pertinent information.* If you leave out vital facts with regard to the applicant's duties or working conditions, she will be forced to make a decision on the basis of incomplete information. Give the facts as clearly as you can, leave out the sugarcoating, and be complete in your description of the job.

9. *Neglecting sound public relations.* If your decision at the close of your interview is a negative one, and you have not left the person with a good impression about your company, you will be promoting unfavorable public opinion about your organization. Such unfavorable opinions could cause a decline in job applicants and even in sales. You want to make an honest but favorable impression so that, no matter what happens, when the visit is over both parties will leave with positive impressions.

10. *Asking discriminatory questions.* Companies can find themselves in major difficulties with federal and state governments if they seek discriminatory information on application forms and during interviews.

11. *Reliance on an absence of negative information.* Because of the fear of litigation, many employers are reluctant to provide information about former employees or share any negative information. Unfortunately, some hiring managers conclude, incorrectly, that because no problems or weaknesses were revealed in a conversation with a former employer that the applicant is satisfactory.[52] Fortunately, many employers have found ways to obtain information about an applicant's performance at previous companies. The following discussion provides practical advice on this process:

    > Information about job candidates is exchanged informally all the time. Friends talk to friends; employees of one company talk to employees of another company; managers talk to other managers in their specialty; and certainly executives talk to other executives. Job seekers often list current members of a company as personal references, which means that they want these people to talk freely with potential employers. The point is simply that job-related information is continually exchanged in the everyday world—regardless of what attorneys may advise.[53]

12. *Hiring friends and relatives who don't qualify.* Pressures from these two groups can be tremendous. Nonetheless, members of these groups must be subjected to the same screening devices and procedures that apply to all other candidates.

WELCOMING AND INDUCTING NEW EMPLOYEES

When you have offered the job and the applicant has accepted, you must now begin your planning to welcome the new arrival. As a result of the interview, you should have a fairly good idea of training needs. If you know that some training will be needed, map out your plans, and get the program organized in a way that allows you to begin as soon as possible. Prepare your department or team for the new person by communicating positive information about him. Plan to make that first day a truly positive experience—one that will tell the applicant that his decision to work for you was a good one.

Learning Objective Number Six

ORIENTATION

Orientation includes the planning and conduct of a program to introduce the new employee to the company, including all policies, practices, rules, and regulations that will immediately affect the employee. Orientation programs are usually conducted by members of the human resources department and typically occur within the first few days after the new person arrives. Typically materials such as handbooks on company policies, descriptions of benefits, rights under various laws, and disciplinary procedures will be distributed and explained.

orientation
the planning and conduct of a program to introduce a new employee to the company and its history, policies, rules, and procedures

Most orientation programs give employees a broad overview of the entire organization, with a special emphasis on how and where the new person fits in with the rest of the organization. The goals usually include the following:

- To instill a favorable first impression with regard to the company, its products, its leadership, and its methods of operation
- To familiarize the new people with the policies, procedures, rules, and benefits that are initially most important
- To outline in detail the specific expectations that the company has for its employees with regard to on-the-job behavior
- To explain the various services that exist for all employees and describe how one can take advantage of them

Learning Objective Number Seven

INDUCTION

Induction includes the planning and conduct of a program to introduce your new person to his job, working environment, supervisor, and coworkers. As the supervisor, induction is your responsibility. You should begin to plan the induction activities of your new subordinate soon after the acceptance of an employment offer. Tailor the induction activities to fit the needs of the subordinate, set specific goals, and work out a timetable to achieve them.

induction
the planning and conduct of a program to introduce a new employee to his or her job, working environment, supervisor, and peers

The Pygmalion effect describes how managers' assumptions about their new people can affect their treatment of them. You must assume the best about your new person and demonstrate trust until your assumptions are proven to be incorrect. You also must have confidence in the person's ability to learn new responsibilities. It is essential to get a new employee started with a positive set of experiences from the first day on the job. Have all materials ready so that she can get right to work. A warm welcome and immediate successful experiences will foster motivation, reassure the new person, and help allay the insecurity or anxiety that comes with a new job. Induction becomes a very important program that can increase the short- and long-term performance of new employees. When done poorly, however, it can sow the seeds for early failure and employee turnover. Accordingly, it is important to shield your people from negative initial experiences by introducing them to successful employees and experiences. Try to keep malcontents away from them until they have firmly established their attitudes and mastery over their tasks.

Induction Goals

Among the typical goals for induction are the following:

- To instill favorable impressions and attitudes about the work section, its operations, and its people
- To remove as many sources of anxiety as possible by helping the new person meet his needs for security, competence, and social acceptance
- To design and provide initial experiences that foster motivation and promote early success
- To begin to build a human relationship that is based on trust and confidence

Exhibit 10.7 contains a checklist that may prove useful to you as you plan your program.

Making Arrangements

You must contact the human resources department and procure the necessary forms, passes, booklets, and so forth so that they are available on the first day. As noted in Exhibit 10.7, the person's work area must be prepared so that the basic inventory of tools, equipment, supplies, and materials is on hand. In addition, access to computer networks should be provided, where appropriate, so that the new employee can receive

---

EXHIBIT 10.7 **Checlist for planning your induction program.**

YES NO

○ ○ 1. Are tools, equipment, supplies, and other things on hand for the newcomer's first day?

○ ○ 2. Have you reserved time with coworkers and others that the newcomer should meet during his induction?

○ ○ 3. Have you planned to give the newcomer a really positive experience the first day?

○ ○ 4. Have you planned a systematic introduction of the new person's duties to her?

○ ○ 5. Have you talked with the newcomer's coworkers, paving the way for a friendly welcome?

○ ○ 6. Have you reserved enough time to spend with the newcomer in the first few days on the job?

communications and obtain information. Everything must be in its place and in working order so that there are no surprises waiting for the new person or for you.

Make arrangements for the new person to join one or another of the formal groups of workers in your department. It is a good idea to get someone to act as the new employee's mentor—a guide and tutor who will be available to answer questions and provide help once you have finished your induction activities. A mentor should be a volunteer who knows the ropes and whose judgment and abilities you respect. This person can provide immediate acceptance and social companionship on and off the job.

Learning Objective Number Eight

THE FIVE BASIC QUESTIONS

As soon as the new employee arrives, the induction or initiation procedure begins. The typical induction answers the following five basic questions for the new worker:

1. Where am I now?
2. What are my duties?
3. What are my rights?
4. What are my limits?
5. Where can I go?

Where Am I Now?

After greeting the new arrival warmly, you should explain in words and graphic form just where he fits into the entire company's operations. By starting with a copy of the company's organization chart, you can move from his slot in your department all the way up the chain of command to the chief executive. Explain the jobs performed in your department and in the departments adjacent to it. Name the personalities involved in each, with particular emphasis on those the new employee is most likely to encounter. Give the newcomer a good idea of how his job and department relate to the ultimate success and profitability of the company.

This initial explanation can be followed by a tour of the department and a look at the work area. Introduce the person to his coworkers and mentor, and give them a chance to chat. Next, familiarize the new person with the facilities within the department and the adjacent areas that he will need to use, and explain the functions of each. Inexperienced new employees often have a challenging transition during the first few days on the job, and they may develop doubts about their ability to survive. The experiences of a recent college graduate reinforce the point as she was the only new person brought into the office when she came on board, and all of the other employees were substantially older than her. She felt like she was at a real disadvantage to the others in terms of experience because she was starting from zero. After an orientation on the first day, she came to work the next day but could not find her desk and needed a map drawn by the receptionist to find her way. Supervisors can help new employees in situations such as this one by helping new employees link up with more experienced employees who have similar interests or backgrounds and by taking the time to provide support and answer what may seem like basic questions.[54]

Introduce the newcomer to people you meet along the way in such a manner as to demonstrate your enthusiasm and pride in having him join your operation. Something like this should do the trick: "Sharon, I'd like you to meet Howard Kramer. Howard, this is Sharon Watkins. Howard has just joined our team, and we are lucky to have him." This gives your new worker a chance to know your true feelings about his decision to come aboard. The newcomer will quickly begin to sense that he is respected and well thought of, as well as needed. Howard will not remember the names of all those to whom he has been introduced, but he will remember your enthusiastic welcome.

During your walk through the company, you should have an excellent opportunity to review the company's history and to reinforce its orientation program. By sharing knowledge of the company, you will give the new person the sense of being an important part of a successful organization. There is tremendous value in this since we all like to feel we belong to groups that are bigger and more powerful than ourselves. Review the company's line of products or services, and point out the major events in the company's history that have contributed the most to its present position. Pass on positive information so that the new employee develops an attractive but honest image of the company, its people, and its future.

What Are My Duties?

Give a copy of the job description to the new person, and go over each duty. Explain the details implied by the general listing, and check his understanding of each. Wherever you can, demonstrate each duty—either by performing it or by giving specific examples. By answering questions for your new worker, you will be helping to accomplish all the goals of your induction program.

What Are My Rights?

Explain the pay periods and how pay is calculated. Also, explain fringe benefits, such as group life and health insurance plans, the company's profit sharing plan, paid holidays, incentive awards, the suggestion plan, and the like. In particular, communicate the eligibility requirements (where they exist) for each benefit. Review the overtime procedures you follow, and explain how workers become eligible for overtime. Go over the appraisal process, and specify what will be rated in it. If there is a union, explain the grievance process and how to file a grievance. Cover all the areas you know from experience that have been sources of misunderstanding in the area of workers' rights. For instance, workers often confuse sick days with personal-leave days.

If there is a union, be certain to introduce the steward and explain the rights employees have in regard to union membership. Where this is voluntary, say so. Do not give your views about unions. Simply advise the newcomer of what he needs to know.

What Are My Limits?

Your first and most important duty regarding discipline is to inform each employee about the limits or boundaries on his conduct and performance. Discipline starts with the induction and orientation of each person. The do's and don'ts that you intend to enforce should be explained, along with the penalties attached to each. Pay particular attention to the areas affecting safety. Each worker should know not only the rules but company policy as well. If safety equipment is needed, be sure that it is issued or purchased, whichever is required. Then be certain to emphasize safety throughout the newcomer's training. Instill respect for safe working habits and conduct right from the start. Enforcement then becomes easier.

Where Can I Go?

This question involves the opportunities for advancement that exist for each new person. Explain the employee's eligibility for training and advanced programs that increase both work skills and the opportunities for promotion. State the criteria you use for making promotion and transfer decisions. People need to know what is required of them in order to advance. Finally, explain the standards they must meet in order to qualify for a raise.

FOLLOWING UP

Plan a follow-up interview to talk with the newcomer about the first day's experiences and answer any questions that may have accumulated. See if you can get a handle on how he really feels.

At the end of the first week, schedule another informal meeting with the new person, and determine if he is making an adequate adjustment to the new job. Your personal daily observations should tell you if he and the group are getting along and if any personal problems are beginning to surface. Watch for warning signals such as fatigue, chronic complaints, lack of interest, or sudden changes from previous behavior patterns. If you spot any of these signals, be prepared to move swiftly to uncover the causes.

You must be prepared for the possibility that the new person may not be cut out for the type of work that has been assigned. If your observations and his responses seem to indicate this, get together with your boss and discuss the matter. You may be able to work something out, such as a transfer to a different job within or outside your section. It may also be possible to redefine duties to compensate for the difficulties. You want to try your best to salvage the new arrival and to avoid costly termination and replacement proceedings.

After the new employee's questions are answered, a **psychological contract** forms between employer and employee that summarizes what both are expected to give and receive from each other. Although unwritten, it should be understood by all concerned. The terms of the contract evolve as time passes and experiences increase. Both parties must feel that the changes are necessary and fair. Each party must believe that the other is living up to his commitments.[55] As you participate in orientation and induction programs and activities, make certain that you know what is likely to happen to the new person once she is on the job. Be honest, and clear up any misconceptions that you sense. Don't promise or let your company promise more than you know it can deliver.

psychological contract
an unwritten recognition of what an employer and an employee expect to give and to receive from each other

Learning Objective Number Nine

THE SOCIALIZATION PROCESS

When people enter a new organization to take a new job, they go through a number of experiences that familiarize them with their new environment—its people, goals,

socialization
the process new employees undergo in the first few weeks of employment through which they learn how to cope and succeed

processes, and systems. **Socialization** is the process through which both the new person and the organization learn about each other. Ultimately, this leads to an understanding by which both parties can live. Through socialization, new employees discover their place in the environment, the restrictions on their freedom, and how to succeed.

All you have to do is treat the new person like a guest in your home whom you wish to impress favorably. Through adequate planning, a warm welcome, a constructive induction program, and conscientious follow-up, you will be doing all that you can do or are expected to do.

INSTANT REPLAY

1. A proper selection procedure usually involves the supervisor in the interviewing process.

2. Selection devices include any interview, form, test, or other instrument that will be used in making the decision to hire.

3. Selection devices and procedures should not adversely affect minorities and women, and they must be valid.

4. The selection process involves both obtaining and giving information. Selection errors can be expensive in terms of both litigation expenses involved with discrimination charges and replacement costs for a person who should not have been hired.

5. Orientation programs are usually conducted by the human resources department and are designed to welcome new employees to the enterprise as a whole.

6. Induction programs are usually conducted by the supervisor of the new employee and are designed to welcome new employees to a specific job, working environment, and peer group.

7. Studies show that the first few days on a new job are extremely important and largely determine the future performance and careers of newcomers.

8. The supervisor of a new person, more than any other factor at work, can mean the difference between success and failure on the job.

QUESTIONS FOR CLASS DISCUSSION

1. Can you define this chapter's key terms?

2. What is the proper role for a supervisor to play in the process of selecting a new subordinate?

3. What will a human resource management department normally do during the selection process?

4. What are the major selection devices used in a typical selection process?

5. How should you prepare to give a selection interview?

6. What are the goals of a good orientation program?

7. What are the goals of a good induction program?

8. What happens to an employee who passes through the socialization process?

9. What are the questions that new employees want answered?

ASSESS THIS SITUATION

Purpose: To test your knowledge of the application of federal human resource laws.

Your Task: Agree or disagree with each of the following statements. Do not consult the key that follows until you have checked each question.

Agree　　**Disagree**

○　　○　1. It is illegal to hire an alien for a job.

○　　○　2. Every employer is required to have an affirmative action plan.

○　　○　3. The Americans with Disabilities Act does not protect job applicants who have HIV or AIDS.

○　　○　4. Employers may use polygraph tests during selection activities.

○　　○　5. Form I-9 must be completed before an applicant is hired.

○　　○　6. Affirmative action programs specify exact numbers of people to be hired.

○　　○　7. Paper-and-pencil integrity tests have low validity for selection purposes.

○　　○　8. People who have been discriminated against cannot sue for punitive damages.

○　　○　9. Unstructured interviews have more validity than structured interviews.

○　　○　10. Drug testing is not a common practice in hiring.
(Key: All are false)

SKILL BUILDING EXERCISE 10.1

Internet technology provides another way for search consultants or headhunters to recruit people who are employed and not currently looking for another job, who are sometimes referred to as passive candidates. Since such people are not in the market, employers have traditionally relied on the personal connections and networks of headhunters to find passive candidates. Interestingly, passive candidates, who are not dissatisfied with their current situation, are often viewed as more attractive in comparison to candidates who are in the market because they are unemployed or are dissatisfied with their present situation. Internet technology now allows recruiters to construct Internet networks of people who are not in the market, but who may respond to an attractive opportunity. The incentive for passive candidates to have their names linked in such networks is that they will have better employment alternatives if something goes wrong at their current job.[56]

It can be safely predicted that networking will be a critical determinant of your ability to obtain the kind of jobs that you prefer in the future. Several companies are involved in establishing such networks or provide the software that enables them to operate.

Your Task: Explore the following websites to learn more about the power of networking and this technology: ZoomInfo *www.zoominfo.com/Search* and LinkedIn Corporation *www.linkedin.com.* Also, investigate the following websites that provide networking services for employers: JobThread *www.jobthread.com* and Jobster *www.jobster.com.*

SKILL BUILDING WRITING EXERCISE 10.2

Your Task: Write a job description for a job in which you have an interest. Be sure to cover all the important duties, to include all significant tasks and activities. Use the *Occupational Outlook Handbook* written by the U.S. Bureau of Labor Statistics (BLS), located on its website at *www.bls.gov/oco,* to help you with the description. After you have written the description, write a job specification that clearly identifies the qualifications that a person must have to perform the job. Refer to the BLS website to obtain information that you need for this task as well. Next, use the BLS website to obtain information about the level of compensation that the employer would be expected to provide and include it in your document. Finally, in the last part of your document, describe the selection procedures that you would recommend for hiring people to perform this job.

DIVERSITY

CASE 10.1	Revolving Door Employment

Winston walked into Lichelle's office, collapsed into the chair and said, "Have you heard the news? Joan just gave two weeks notice. Seems that her husband just got transferred to a job in Milwaukee. With all of these talented women who work here, why is it that they always follow their husbands when these guys get new jobs? Why don't some of the husbands follow their wives when they get new jobs? I just feel like we're totally at the mercy of the husband's job situation and that it has nothing to do with how well we manage around here. Joan really liked it here and was doing a great job!"

LICHELLE: "What do you mean by saying that the women always follow their husbands? I'm here and I haven't left to follow my husband someplace!"

WINSTON: "Well, you know what I mean. Our turnover rate for women is really high and a lot of it has nothing to do with us. We must have had six or seven women who left this year because their husbands or boyfriends got transferred. And the costs of losing these people are really high. We lose their skills and have to suffer through the learning period for their replacements."

LICHELLE: "I know what you mean. We really fell behind when Julie left last month. What do you think we should do?"

WINSTON: "Perhaps we should try to hire more guys since they seem to stay on the job longer."

LICHELLE: "I don't think we can do that legally. Besides, we've got some women here that have been with the company longer than any of the guys. In addition to being illegal, it wouldn't be fair. I don't like that idea at all."

WINSTON: "Yeah, I know. I hate anything related to hiring that sounds like discrimination. But it doesn't seem fair to us either when all of these women leave for reasons that have nothing to do with how well we treated them. This turnover is really going to hurt our profitability this year."

LICHELLE: "I know. This is really bad but I don't know what to do."

WINSTON: "Maybe we should start asking women applicants about the job status of their husbands. You know, how likely it is that they are going to be transferred or take a new job in the next three or four years? It's job-related because if they leave it costs us real money."

LICHELLE: "I don't think you can ask questions like that."

WINSTON: "Okay, why don't we ask the same question of both women and men?"

LICHELLE: "That might be better. But I don't see how asking personal stuff like that could ever be job-related. I don't think you can ask questions like that. I think our hands are tied because of the EEO laws."

WINSTON: "Well, let's check with the HR people on that issue. Here's a related issue. It seems to me that we're also losing lots of women because of pregnancy. Why don't we ask women applicants if they plan to get pregnant in the next two or three years. We won't discriminate against women, we just won't hire the ones that are going to quit because of pregnancy."

Questions

1. If the turnover rate of women is higher, can gender become a job-related selection factor? Explain.

2. Who is right about Winston's proposal to ask both men and women about the likelihood that their spouse will be transferred, Winston or Lichelle? Explain.

3. Would Winston's proposal to ask about pregnancy be legal? Explain.

CASE 10.2 Youth Movement

Scott looked at the new advertising campaign that had just come from the ad agency. He had the task of hiring and supervising five new sales people to promote the new malt liquor product using a new ad campaign. The ads had lots of pictures of young, attractive people in their early 20s to mid-30s. Most of the posters involved sports themes such as rock climbing, beach volleyball, and surfing. A major component of the sales strategy was to have the sales people promote the malt liquor by distributing paraphernalia, such as caps and T-shirts, at sporting events, rock concerts, festivals, and at sports bars. The company had identified people in their 20s and 30s as its primary consumer group, and this segment was expected to account for 80 percent of sales. As Scott finished going through the materials, his boss, Eric, walked into his office.

ERIC: "Well Scott, what do you think of the campaign?"

SCOTT: "I think it's great. This promotional stuff is really going to appeal to these young people who are going to buy our malt liquor."

ERIC: "Yeah, I think so too. The strategy has really worked well for other companies. Do you have a set of applicants to interview for the five sales jobs?"

SCOTT: "Wow, that was a tough job. I had over 125 applications to look through. But I've trimmed the list down to 25."

ERIC: "That's great. But you can't interview 25 people and still get your other work done."

SCOTT: "Yeah, I know. Would you take a look at the applications and help me narrow them down some more?"

ERIC: "Sure. Let's take a look and trim the list down to about 10 or 12." Eric then took a few minutes to look through the stack of applications.

SCOTT: "Well, what do you think?"

ERIC: "These look pretty good. I can see why this was a tough job. But I would eliminate the three guys in here that don't seem to fit."

SCOTT: "Which ones are those?"

ERIC: "Well, they're the older guys. There is one who is 48, another who is 53, and one is 56."

SCOTT: "But they have good solid sales experience and all of them have done sales in the beverage industry."

ERIC: "You're right, but can you see these guys relating to our customers at rock concerts and at beach volleyball tournaments? It's not going to happen."

SCOTT: "Will there be any problems with doing this given that they appear to be the most qualified in terms of sales experience?"

ERIC: "Nah, even if they could do the job they'd just want too much money. So you can just eliminate them on that basis."

Questions

1. Do you agree with Eric's recommendations? Why or why not?

2. Are Eric's recommendations legally acceptable? Explain.

3. How would you attack Eric's argument?

4. What should Scott do if he disagrees with Eric?

REFERENCES

[1] Berry, Leonard L. *Discovering the Soul of Service*, New York: The Free Press (1999): 84.

[2] Greengard, Samuel. "Gimme Attitude," *Workforce Management* (July 2003): 56–60.

[3] Overholt, Alison. "Personality Tests: Back with a Vengeance," *Fast Company*, (November 2004): 115–117.

[4] U.S. Supreme Court, *Griggs versus Duke Power Co., Inc.*, (1971) 401 US 424.

[5] Overholt, "Personality Tests: Back with a Vengence."

[6] Personality Pathways Website (January 27, 2006), *www.personalitypathways.com/type_inventory.html*.

[7] CPP, Inc. Website, (January 27, 2006), *www.cpp.com/products/firo-b/index.asp*.

[8] Kolbe Corporation Website (January 27, 2006), *www.kolbe.com/the_kolbe_concept/what_is_kolbe_a..cfm*

[9] Pfeffer, Jeffrey. *The Human Equation: Building Profits by Putting People First.* Boston: Harvard Business School Press, (1998).

[10] Levering, Robert, and Moskowitz, Milton. "The 100 Best Companies to Work for in America," *Fortune* (January 12, 1998): 84.

[11] Leonard, Arthur S. "Sexual Orientation and the Workplace: A Rapidly Developing Field," *Labor Law Journal* 44(9) (1993): 574–583.

[12] Martin, Justin. "So, You Want to Work for the Best. . . .," *Fortune* (January 12, 1998): 77–78.

[13] Seminerio, Maria, "E-Recruiting Takes Next Step," *eWeek* (April, 23, 2001): 51–54.

[14] Pell, Arthur R. *The Supervisor's Handbook.* New York: McGraw-Hill (1994): 102.

[15] Lee, Barbara A. "Reverse Discrimination," in Lawrence H. Peters, Charles R. Greer, and Stuart A. Youngblood (eds.), *The Blackwell Encyclopedic Dictionary of Human Resource Management.* Oxford, United Kingdom: Blackwell (1997): 294.

[16] Shellenbarger, Sue. "Recent Suits Make Pregnancy Issues Workplace Priorities," *Wall Street Journal* (January 14, 1998): B1.

[17] Ibid.

[18] Ibid.

[19] McKinnon, Jesse. "The Black Population in the United States: March 2002," *Current Population Reports*, U.S. Department of Commerce, Economics and Statistics Administration, U.S. Census Bureau (April 2003). Ramirez, Roberto R., and de la Cruz, G. Patricia, "The Hispanic Population in the United States: March 2002," *Current Population Reports*, U.S. Department of Commerce, Economics and Statistics Administration, U.S. Census Bureau (June 2003).

[20] Gatewood, Robert D., and Feild, Hubert S. *Human Resource Selection*, 4th ed. Fort Worth, TX: Dryden Press, 1998.

[21] McKee, Bradford. "The Disabilities Labyrinth," *Nation's Business* (April 1993): 18–23.

[22] Greer, Charles R. *Strategy and Human Resources: A General Managerial Approach*, 2nd ed. Englewood Cliffs, NJ: Prentice Hall, (2001).

[23] Frierson, James G. "An Employer's Dilemma: The ADA's Provisions on Reasonable Accommodation and Confidentiality," *Labor Law Journal* 43(5) (1992): 308–312. Postol, Lawrence P., and Kandue, David D. "An Employer's Guide to the Americans with Disabilities Act," *Labor Law Journal* 42(6) (1991): 323–342.

[24] Schuler, Randall R. *Managing Human Resources*, 5th ed. New York: West (1995): 261–262.

[25] Pollock, Ellen Joan. "Sir: Your Application for a Job Is Rejected; Sincerely, Hal 9000," *Wall Street Journal* (July 30, 1998): A1, A12.

[26] Rosen, Lester S. *The Safe Hiring Manual: The Complete Guide to Keeping Criminals, Imposters and Terrorists Out of The Workplace*, Tempe, AZ: Facts on Demand Press, (2004).

[27] Heneman, Herbert G., III, and Heneman, Robert L. *Staffing Organizations*. Middleton, WI: Mendota House, Inc., (1994).

[28] Gatewood and Feild. *Human Resource Selection*.

[29] Thomas, Peg. *Finding the Best and the Brightest: A Guide to Recruiting, Selecting, and Retaining Effective Leaders*, Westport, CT: Praeger Publishers, (2005).

[30] Lancaster, Hal. "Making a Good Hire Takes a Little Instinct and a Lot of Research," *Wall Street Journal* (March 3, 1998): B1.

[31] Martin. "So, You Want to Work."

[32] Adler, Lou. *Hire With Your Head Using Power Hiring® to Build Great Companies*, 2nd ed. Hoboken, NJ: John Wiley & Sons, Inc., (2002).

[33] Ibid., 91.

[34] Ibid., 96.

[35] Ibid., 99.

[36] Ibid., 95.

[37] Kleiman, Carol. "True to Life: Behavioral Interviews Focus on Experience," *Fort Worth Star-Telegram* (February 20, 2000): Careers Section.

[38] Equal Employment Opportunity Commission. *1978 Uniform Guidelines on Employee Selection Procedures,* (1978).

[39] U.S. Substance Abuse and Mental Health Services Administration. (2005). *Results from the 2004 National Survey on Drug Use and Health: National Findings* (Office of Applied Studies, NSDUH Series H-28, DHHS Publication No. SMA 05-4062). Rockville, MD. (January 28, 2006): Website: *www.samhsa.gov.*

[40] Rosen, *The Safe Hiring Manual: The Complete Guide to Keeping Criminals, Imposters and Terrorists Out of The Workplace.*

[41] Bennett, Joel B., Reynolds, Shawn, and Lehman, Wayne E. K. "Understanding Employee Alcohol and Other Drug Use: Toward a Multilevel Approach," in Joel B. Bennett and Wayne E. K. Lehman, eds. *Preventing Substance Abuse: Beyond Drug Testing to Wellness,* Washington, DC: American Psychological Association, (2003): 29–56.

[42] Bennett, Reynolds, and Lehman. "Understanding Employee Alcohol and Other Drug Use: Toward a Multilevel Approach."

[43] Rosen, *The Safe Hiring Manual: The Complete Guide to Keeping Criminals, Imposters and Terrorists Out of The Workplace.*

[44] Falcone, Paul. *The Hiring and Firing Question and Answer Book,* New York: American Management Association, AMACOM, (2002).

[45] Center for Disease Control, National Center for HIV, STD, and TB Prevention, "A Glance at the HIV/AIDS Epidemic," *Fact Sheet* (January 28, 2006): Website, *www.cdc.gov/hiv/PUBS/Facts/At-A-Glance.htm.*

[46] Gatewood and Feild. *Human Resource Selection.* Bernardin, H. John, and Cooke, Donna K. "Validity of an Honesty Test in Predicting Theft Among Convenience Store Employees," *Academy of Management Journal 36*(5) (1993): 1097–1108.

[47] Gatewood and Feild. *Human Resource Selection,* 637.

[48] Department of Homeland Security, U.S. Citizenship and Immigration Services, Form I-9, revised May 31, 2005.

[49] Hymowitz, Carol. "Managers Err If They Limit Their Hiring to People Like Them." *Wall Street Journal* (October 12, 2004): B1.

[50] Lousig-Nont, Gregory M. "Seven Deadly Hiring Mistakes," *Supervision* (April 2003): 18–19.

[51] White, Erin. "Focus on Recruitment, Pay and Getting Ahead," *Wall Street Journal,* (June 28, 2005): B6.

[52] Lousig-Nont. "Seven Deadly Hiring Mistakes."

[53] Andler, Edward C. with Herbst, Dara. *The Complete Reference Checking Handbook*, 2nd ed., New York: AMACOM, American Management Association (2003): 58–59.

[54] White, Erin. "Focus on Recruitment, Pay and Getting Ahead," *Wall Street Journal*, (May 31, 2005): B6.

[55] Schein, Edgar H. *Career Dynamics: Matching Individual and Organizational Needs.* Reading, MA: Addison-Wesley (1978): 94–97.

[56] Mintz, Jessica. "Online Tools Aid Job Recruiters in Search of 'Passive' Prospects," *Wall Street Journal* (July 12, 2005): B6.

CHAPTER 1

Live as if you were to die tomorrow.
Learn as if you were to live forever."

Mahatma Gandhi[1]

Objectives

After reading and discussing this chapter, you should be able to do the following:

1. Explain the advantages that a supervisor gains from training an employee.
2. Explain the advantages that a trainee gains from training.
3. List the basic requirements that a trainer must satisfy in order to train.
4. List the basic requirements a trainee must satisfy in order to learn.
5. List and briefly describe the principles that govern training.
6. Briefly describe the training cycle.

Dealing with Shortages of Skilled Workers

Extensive training is one of the few universal best management practices, such as employment security, sharing financial or performance data with employees, and selective hiring, which apply in virtually all situations.[2] It is almost axiomatic in many companies that during economic downturns, expenditures on training are scaled back or eliminated in order to cut costs. In such situations training is not viewed as a necessity. Unfortunately such short-sighted views of training can be very expensive in the long-term. Training differentiates high performing companies from those that are only average.

After many years of outsourcing manufacturing to low-wage countries and plant closures or downsizing in the United States, some industries are experiencing a shortage of skilled machinists, skilled craft workers, and other production workers. For example the National Association of Manufacturers found that in the early 2000s there were shortages of such workers even though the economy was undergoing a recession. Because of impending retirements of Baby Boomers, the association is predicting a demand by 2020 for up to 10 million new skilled workers.[3] It should be noted that even during recessions, not all industries are similarly affected, and that there may be strong demand for skilled workers in some industries even during major restructuring. This was the

Training

case during the mid 2000s in the U.S. even though the auto industry was going through downsizing when Ford and General Motors moved into another phase of plant closures and layoffs.[4]

The lead-time needed to train skilled workers is substantial. For example, Southern Manufacturing Technologies, which is located in Tampa, Florida, has been hiring apprentices who are being trained as machinists to operate machining equipment that requires strong computer skills. The company has been increasing its hiring each year for the past two years but is finding that it needs more skilled machinists in order to meet the demand for its products. Oberg Industries, which is based in Freeport, Pennsylvania, has also been hiring apprentices for tool-and-die making as well as other skills. However, the company acknowledges that such skills require years of training. As a result of the time needed to develop such skills, there is no quick remedy for the shortage of workers.[5]

The National Association of Manufacturers is attempting to address these skill shortages by disseminating information and promoting training through its Center for Workforce Success. One of the policy changes recommended by the center has been for strengthened relationships between community colleges and economic developers for programs dealing with technology.[6] Recent training initiatives, such as the apprenticeships being offered by the United Steelworkers of America and U.S. Steel, have been designed for increased flexibility, less downtime, and more productivity through a **cross-training** approach. Apprentices learn one skill, such as pipe-fitting, while also being trained in a secondary skill.[7] While cross-training is a well-known approach concept, which savvy companies have used for many years, this is a new approach for apprenticeship training.

Companies that understand the importance of training make a commitment to invest in training even during downturns. They understand that adopting innovative approaches to training will make them far more prepared for the future. Supervisors who have the skills to train their employees and who take the time to conduct training will be very valuable to their employers.

cross-training
training employees to do more than one job so that they may fill in for other workers or may be redeployed to other work with changes in demand

Questions for Thought

1. What are some of the issues that supervisors should consider when designing training programs that will add value in the future?
2. How can supervisors balance the demand to focus on current production issues with their needs to devote sufficient time to help their employees become better trained?

Introduction

training
the activity concerned with improving employees' performance in their present jobs by imparting skills, knowledge, and attitudes

This chapter is concerned with how you can help your employees acquire new skills, improve their existing ones, and improve their abilities to handle their jobs. **Training** becomes necessary by the very fact that you have employees. Whether they are old-timers, newcomers, or a mix of the two, you must continually see to it that they are functioning effectively. If they are not, training is in order. Whether you train or rely on others to help you with training, you are responsible for seeing to it that your people are properly trained.

American corporations spend in excess of $55 billion on training each year.[8] The ability to attract, develop (train), and retain employees is one of the criteria *Fortune* uses to select its annual list of the world's most admired companies. An examination of *Fortune's* list reveals that top-ranked companies historically place a great deal of emphasis on training. For example, GE, which has ranked first on numerous occasions, takes pride in being a meritocracy in which developmental opportunities enable employees to reach the top regardless of the schooling they had prior to joining the company. Wal-Mart, which also ranks high on the *Fortune* list, has shifted its emphasis to training and development of its existing workforce rather than simply emphasizing hiring.[9] Such investments in training provide attractive rates of return for the companies' investments. "Motorola [also a leader in training] calculates that every $1 it spends on training delivers $30 in productivity gains within three years."[10]

Arrow Electronics provides an example of a creative approach to training. The company, which is a large distributor of computer and electronic components, has developed a successful approach to training by drawing on a combination of methods. In some respects, the company's approach is relatively traditional as it relies heavily on classroom instruction. Nonetheless, the company is also somewhat opportunistic in is approach. For example, at its yearly sales conference, instead of focusing mainly on recognition and ceremony, the company's sales personnel participate in **simulations** and practice sessions on new products. They actually reach proficiency on the new products prior to the end of the conference.[11]

simulations
training in which participants learn through realistic role-playing exercises or computer software experiences

The choice of high-quality instruction materials that are currently available makes training a much more potent activity than in the past. For example, the quality and range of computer simulations is expanding as vendors are responding to the demand for them to teach a broad range of skills and knowledge. Some simulations teach complex behaviors by having participants play the roles of sales representatives, managers, or even executives. Simulations vary in their sophistication as some include videos of customers or employees while others simply expose learners to scenarios and ask questions about how they would respond. Some training professionals have concluded that simulations provide the best means for developing soft skills, such as how to deal with customers or how to conduct a sales call.[12]

Users of simulations have been impressed by the ability of simulations to develop knowledge that is retained over much longer periods than many others types of training. The consulting firm Accenture has discovered remarkable results for the retentive power of knowledge developed through simulations.[13] Its study found "that those who learn by doing are able to retain 75% of the information taught compared with a 5% retention rate from hearing a lecture and 10% from reading the material.[14]

THE SUBJECTS OF TRAINING

Training imparts attitudes, knowledge, and skills. It is an ongoing process governed by basic principles and provided by people with the aid of machines and methods specially suited to the **subjects** to be covered and the persons to be taught. Training, like daily living, increases our knowledge and understanding of the people and things that surround us.

subjects
the principle of training that requires trainers to know the subject being taught and to know the trainees' needs

ATTITUDES

We have already said much about attitudes, and all of it is related to the training process. You must remember that when you train, you are attempting to instill positive attitudes—either as replacements for improper ones or as useful additions—in the minds of your trainees. Attitudes are taught primarily through your own example and secondarily through your words. Workers learn an attitude by observing what you do. If you talk about safety but act in an unsafe manner or lightly skip over safety during the training period, your workers will adopt the same casual attitudes.

KNOWLEDGE

Knowledge is the body of facts, ideas, concepts, and procedures that enable people to see or visualize what must be done and why. If trainees can understand the whole job and its relationship to the work of others, they have a better chance to master their own jobs. They must understand the theory (fundamental principles and abstract knowledge) that governs their work before they can adequately perform their own tasks. Then, with your help, they must translate theory into practice through training. Knowledge is important but applying knowledge is even more critical.

SKILLS

The best way to teach a skill is to involve the trainees as quickly as possible in performing the skill. Practice and more practice are keys to the successful acquisition of motor skills. Trainees first develop an in-depth understanding of the tools, equipment, or machinery and then move to an actual working knowledge of the trade or craft. In this manner they gain controlled exposure to both the technical side and the manipulative side of their jobs.

Early successes are essential in the early phases of training. Accordingly, you must build in opportunities for small positive accomplishments. It is also important to prevent trainees from developing improper work habits. Often, you may have to ask the trainees to unlearn certain procedures or habits acquired from earlier experiences before you can substitute the proper methods. This is a difficult and time-consuming task that requires a great deal of patience from both you and your trainees.

A major barrier to workforce productivity and training is that about 20 percent of current and new employees lack the basic literacy skills they need to succeed in their jobs.[15] According to the American Management Association, 24 percent of major U.S.

In an effort to improve their workforces, many large companies offer various education programs. Classes, such as the one shown at Aetna Insurance Company, teach workers the skills they need to succeed on the job.

employers are conducting basic remedial training programs to enable their employees to cope with their present and future job demands.[16] R.J. Reynolds invested about $2 billion in automating its factory in Winston-Salem, North Carolina, before discovering that its workforce lacked the reading skills necessary to operate and maintain the new equipment. Of its 6,000 workers, 1,300 had to be put through a basic literacy program. Finally, IBM offered a free college-level course in algebra to its employees but discovered that only 30 out of 280 workers who signed up were able to read and calculate at the twelfth-grade level—a prerequisite for taking the course.[17]

Learning Objective Number One

ADVANTAGES OF TRAINING

ADVANTAGES FOR THE SUPERVISOR

How do supervisors benefit from training an employee? The following are a few of the many benefits you receive when you train your people properly:

1. *You get to know your employees.* When you are dealing with new employees, you hasten the process of learning about their needs, wants, and potential. With your other employees, you get a chance to update your knowledge of each person. This knowledge facilitates decision-making about personnel decisions such as recommendations for promotions, raises, and transfers.

2. *You further your own career.* As each individual increases his efficiency and effectiveness, the whole group benefits. As your employees perform and feel better, they enhance your reputation as a supervisor and leader. As we have stated before, your reputation is largely a product of their performance.

3. *You gain more time.* As a result of training, your people become more self-sufficient and confident. Their improvements in performance reduce the time you must spend on corrections and deficiencies. You then gain more time for planning, organizing, controlling, and coordinating. You may be able to shift from an autocratic style of supervision (so necessary during the training) to a less time-consuming style. A striking example of effective delegation and time management is provided by General George Marshall's leadership during World War II. "Gen. George Marshall ran World War II and still took a daily nap after lunch and went home by 4:30."[18]

4. *You promote good human relations.* One of your primary roles in developing good human relations with your people is that of educator. They gain self-confidence, pride, and security through their training, which promotes cooperation and respect for you. Many will see you as the cause of their improvement and will rely on you more for advice and direction in the future.

5. *You reduce safety hazards.* By engaging in safe behaviors, emphasizing safety rules, and conveying safety-oriented attitudes, you reduce the likelihood of violations and the resulting accidents and injuries. How tragic it would be to have to live with the knowledge that an employee's injury might have been prevented if you had done all that you should have in the area of safety.

This chapter's feature on supervisors and ethics deals with ethics training.

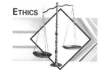

ETHICS

Learning Objective Number Two

ADVANTAGES FOR EMPLOYEES

Training gives your workers many advantages, including the following:

1. *They increase their chances for success.* Through training, workers gain new knowledge and experiences that help reduce the risks of personal obsolescence and increase their value to themselves and to the company. By exposure and practice, workers learn new techniques that enhance their abilities and their enjoyment of work. By successfully completing training, workers confront change, meet challenges, overcome their fears, and gain self-confidence.

2. *They increase their motivation to work.* Through successful training experiences and proper guidance, individuals experience a greater sense of achievement. They find ways to reduce fatigue, increase contributions, and expend less effort to accomplish their tasks. These accomplishments tend to fortify a desire to work harder. We all need a sense of competence.

3. *They promote their own advancement.* As workers become more proficient, they earn the right to receive additional duties, either through delegation or through a job change. By proving themselves through the learning process, they justify the investment of additional company time and money in their development. They become more mobile members of the organization.

SUPERVISORS AND ETHICS

Ethics training has been a priority for some companies for many years, such as defense contractors that must adhere to very rigid standards of conduct in order to do business with the federal government. On the other hand, ethics training was not a priority for many companies until after the scandals at Enron, WorldCom, Tyco, and other organizations. As a result of the subsequent passage of the Sarbanes-Oxley Act of 2002, which requires companies to implement internal controls for financial affairs and to provide more accurate reporting on financial statements, companies are placing more emphasis on such training.

The comprehensive approach of Sun Microsystems to ethics training is explained in the following account:

> There are several telltale signs that an employee is embezzling money from the company, said Ms. Davis, the human resources director for corporate resources at Sun Microsystems in Santa Clara, Calif.
>
> Here's one possibility: If someone on the staff works all year without taking a single vacation day, there is a chance that he is a thief rather than a workaholic. "Employees who are forging documents or stealing from the company need to be in the office all of the time to make sure that everything's in place," she said.
>
> Ms. Davis . . . is one of nearly 1,000 managers at her company who recently went through its Fiduciary Boot Camp, an intense two-day training program that covered ethical issues . . . Dov Seidman, [is] the chief executive of LRN, a Los Angeles company that offers Web-based training on ethical issues to companies like Boeing, United Technologies and Johnson & Johnson . . . LRN has just signed a five-year contract with Pfizer to create 150 online courses for managers covering topics from ethical decision-making to the proper use of e-mail.
>
> Most corporations have had long codes of conduct and have publicized them in employee handbooks and elsewhere. But now, Mr. Seidman said, they are "looking to create ethical athletes out of their managers" who are capable of navigating the gray areas.
>
> Sun is one of the first companies to plunge into the exercise in a big way, by requiring all managers across the globe—not just those who head financial and legal departments—to undergo intense training . . .
>
> After the boot camps were completed, managers were given binders that included information on how to share the information they learned with their employees. In addition, all Sun employees are now undergoing a condensed online ethics course.

4. *Their morale improves.* Mastery of new responsibilities inevitably leads to new prestige and importance. This newfound pride can be translated into higher earnings, a greater commitment to the company, and a renewed self-image. Workers see themselves as necessary and more valuable parts of the whole and as greater contributors to the group's success.

5. *Their productivity increases.* Employees perform their jobs with less wasted effort and lower scrap rates, which results in higher-quality production and a greater return to themselves and the company.

Some or all of these benefits will accrue to everyone who takes part in training. Training tells your people of both your company's interest and your personal interest in their welfare and development. Just be sure to let trainees put their training to use as soon as possible after its completion.

REQUIREMENTS OF TRAINING

REQUIREMENTS FOR TRAINERS

Ideally, you as the supervisor should plan and execute the essential function of training. However, there are times when you cannot train employees. You may lack either the time or the firsthand knowledge of the job to be taught. In such cases, you may have to delegate the training duties to an employee or rely on the various staff specialists your company can provide. Either way, you are accountable for their actions and the results. Therefore, it would be wise for you to assist in the planning of the training and to check up on its execution periodically.

Learning Objective Number Three

Regardless of who does the training, that person must be proficient in the subject matter or skills to be taught and possess a working knowledge of the ways in which people learn. More specifically, she should understand the principles that govern training and the different training methods, along with their respective advantages and disadvantages. Every trainer must recognize that her actions will teach as much as, if not more than, the words spoken during training. Here are a few basic suggestions for trainers that are applicable to almost any training situation:[19]

- *Be enthusiastic.* If you are enthusiastic about training, it is easier for your employees to become enthusiastic about or at least receptive to the training experience.
- *Simplify.* Focus on fewer points that can be learned well rather than try to cover too much material that will not be learned.
- *Be sensitive to body language.* The body language of your employees can indicate whether you need to speed up or slow down in covering the material or make it more interesting.
- *Provide feedback.* Show your employees what they have learned and where they need to acquire more knowledge.
- *Provide reinforcement.* Provide positive reinforcement to your employees as they make progress in mastering the skills or knowledge to be acquired.
- *Expect occasional failures.* Very few training approaches work every time for every employee as people tend to respond differently to different training approaches.

This chapter's feature on supervisors and performance provides an example of how training, when combined with worker empowerment and decision-making, can eliminate the need for policies and restrictions on employees' discretion to perform their jobs.

Learning Objective Number Four

SUPERVISORS AND PERFORMANCE

Robert Slater has described some of Jack Welch's approaches to identifying issues at GE that created a drag on productivity and morale. One of the most notable of these was the "work-out" process that was designed to fix problems and to move decision-making to the level of workers. The process requires a manager to stand in front of an assembly of employees and respond to their proposals for doing things differently. During this process the manager's boss stands behind the manager, but the manager cannot look to his boss for guidance. Managers are allowed three answers for each proposal: yes, no, or more information is needed. During the day-long sessions, a manager might handle more than 100 proposals. Here is an example of a worker's proposal and the manager's response:

> "I've worked for GE for over twenty years, I have a perfect attendance record. I've won management awards. I love this company. It's put my kids through college. It's given me a good standard of living. But there's something stupid that I'd like to bring up."

> The man operated a valuable piece of equipment that required him to wear gloves.

> The gloves wore out several times a month. To acquire another pair he had to call in a relief operator or, if none was available, shut his machine down. He then had to walk a fair distance to another building, go to the supply room,

and fill out a form. He then had to walk around the plant to track down a supervisor of sufficient authority to countersign his request. Only after he had returned the signed form to the supply room was he given a new pair of gloves! Frequently he lost as much as an hour of work.

> "I think it's stupid."

> "I think it's stupid too," said the general manager in front of the room. "Why do we do that?" At that point everyone in the room was dying to hear the answer. Finally, from way back in the room came the answer: "In 1973, we lost a box of gloves."

> "Put the box of gloves on the floor, close to the people," the manager ordered.

As this example indicates, over the passage of time, operational and managerial changes make many operational policies obsolete and counterproductive. It is important that managers and supervisors listen to their employees so that they can respond to suggestions for doing things better or more quickly. Unfortunately, experienced workers are often subjected to mindless and demoralizing policies that dampen productivity. Properly trained employees can make many decisions that enable them to perform their work better and more efficiently. Delegation of decision-making authority also enriches workers' jobs.

Source: Robert Slater, *Jack Welch and the GE Way: Management Insights and Leadership Secrets of the Legendary CEO.* New York: McGraw-Hill, 1999, pp. 159–160. Reproduced with permission of The McGraw-Hill Companies.

REQUIREMENTS FOR TRAINEES

In general, people who are about to go through training should meet the following requirements:

1. They should be informed about what will be taught and why.
2. They should recognize the need to learn the material.
3. They should be willing to learn what is to be taught.
4. They should have the capability to learn what is to be taught.

Given capable trainers and trainees who meet these preconditions, genuine learning and meaningful improvements in performance are possible. Learning theory tells us that without **motivation** or the incentive to learn, no real learning will take place. When learning does take place, motivated trainees and trainers are the central reason for it. The principles that follow will enable you to design and execute a successful training program.

motivation for training
the training principle that requires both trainer and trainee to be favorably predisposed and ready to undergo training

Learning Objective Number Five

THE PRINCIPLES OF TRAINING

You should keep in mind several principles while planning and conducting a training program. Use these principles as a checklist to make certain that you have not overlooked anything important. To remember them, think of the mnemonic MIRRORS:

- Motivation
- Individualism
- Realism
- Response
- Objective
- Reinforcement
- Subjects

These principles are interdependent and interrelated.

MOTIVATION

The trainee's motivation is often a problem. While new employees are usually anxious to get through training successfully so as to gain some level of independence and security, more experienced employees may be less enthusiastic. Experienced employees often do not see the need to learn skills or they have fears about their ability to learn.

Remember that training imparts a sense of competence. If people know what is expected of them, believe that they are capable of mastering those expectations, see the rewards that lie ahead, and desire those rewards, then they should be motivated. Exhibit 11.1 presents several principles of learning theory that apply to adults in a work environment, including issues related to motivation.

INDIVIDUALISM

The principle of **individualism** states that the training you prepare and present must be tailored to meet the needs and situations of individuals. To do this, you must know what

individualism
the training principle that requires a trainer to conduct training at a pace suitable for the trainee

EXHIBIT 11.1	**Adult learning principles.**

- People learn more when their "need to know" is high and their WIFM (what's in it for me) is crystal clear.
- People learn by hearing, seeing, and doing. Try to appeal to visual, audio, and tactile learners. Make training active, not passive.
- People learn by observing and interacting with others. Learning is a social activity.
- People need to use their own life or work-related experience as a basis for learning.
- People learn more when there is a "problem-centered" focus . . . relevant to their world.
- People need opportunities to practice. These practice sessions should occur frequently during training and after training, too.
- People need and will improve with immediate feedback.
- People are motivated to learn by extrinsic and intrinsic motivators.

Source: Extracted from Lisa A. Burke, "Training Transfer: Ensuring Training Gets Used on the Job," Lisa A. Burke, ed., *High-Impact Training Solutions: Top Issues Troubling Trainers*, Westport, CT: Quorum Books, (2001), p. 97. Burke's discussion cites Malcom S. Knowles, *The Adult Learner*, 4th ed., Houston: Gulf Publishing (1990).

When you train your workers, both your technical expertise and attitude are important. Training is a perfect time to instill motivation in an employee.

skills and knowledge people already possess so that you can start from there in designing your program. By building on what they already know, you can use their experiences as a frame of reference. For instance, if people already know how to operate a particular piece of machinery that is similar to but not the same as the one they must now operate, begin by pointing out the similarities and then show the differences or exceptions.

Finally, this principle states that you must vary your presentation of material to fit the people's ability to assimilate it. Let the trainees advance at a comfortable rate, and do not present too much material in large chunks. If you overload them with information, you will only frustrate and confuse them.

You probably already have some experience working with older employees. When older employees go through training, you can individualize your approach by relying on thoroughness rather than speed. Use older employees' backgrounds and experiences as connecting links to the new information or methods. By providing constant feedback to keep them abreast of their progress, you help overcome some of the fear of failure that older workers may have when facing the new and different.

REALISM

Make the learning process as close to the real thing as you can. In most training situations, you should teach people on the job, using their actual equipment, tools, or machinery. In the case of office or clerical employees, use the actual computer software, procedures, and practices. Such **realism** is not always possible. For example, equipment may be unavailable for training because it is being fully utilized in current production. When you cannot train on the job, or deem it wiser not to do so, set up conditions that are as close to actual working situations as possible. Use examples and situations that accurately reflect actual problems the worker is likely to encounter. Then move from the simulated conditions to the actual environment as soon as possible.

A medium-size manufacturer in the Midwest provides a good example. The company was reluctant to purchase the latest manufacturing equipment because it lacked skilled workers who could operate and maintain it. The solution was to find a community college that had the computer-integrated equipment and then send a select group to learn the equipment. After the group was trained, the workers returned to train others in the plant on the equipment that was then being installed.

realism
the training principle that requires training to simulate or duplicate the actual working environment and behavior or performance required

RESPONSE

The principle of **response** reminds you to check regularly on the trainees' receptiveness and their retention of material. Involve the trainees in a two-way conversation. Ask questions and encourage them to do the same. Response also includes the concept of evaluation. Besides oral questions and answers, you can evaluate or measure the trainees' progress by conducting performance tests or written quizzes. Involve the trainees in feedback throughout the training process and share the results of regular evaluations with them. One member of a corporate training program put it this way: "I like the daily quizzes my instructor gives. They let you know right away how well you have caught on to the material covered. It keeps you on your toes and forces you to review each night. I need this course. It means another 25 dollars per week."

response
the principle of training that requires feedback from trainees to trainers and vice versa

OBJECTIVE

objective
the training principle that requires trainers and trainees to know what is to be mastered through training

The principle of the **objective** states that trainees and trainers should always know where they are headed at any given point in the training process. As a trainer, you have to set goals for the training program and for each of the individual training sessions you conduct. These goals must be communicated to the trainees so that they know where they are headed.

The goals of trainees should be realistic, specific, and within the trainees' ability to achieve. They tell employees that their training is planned and professional. We will discuss objectives further in this chapter.

REINFORCEMENT

reinforcement
the training principle that requires trainees to review and restate knowledge learned; also refers to rewards for correct responses

According to the principle of **reinforcement,** if learning is to be retained, it should involve as many senses as possible and be accompanied by rewards such as verbal compliments. When you first explain an idea, you may involve both sight and hearing, using a demonstration coupled with an explanation. Then, you can let the trainees try out their understanding by repeating the demonstration and explanation in their own words. They will then be using sight, touch, and hearing. They will also be reviewing the concepts as well. By using frequent summaries and by reviewing key points, you will be practicing reinforcement. Reinforcement also includes rewarding correct responses. By repetition, practice, and rewards for correct responses you lend emphasis and greatly increase retention.

This chapter's feature on supervising teams describes an exercise for developing teamwork.

Try to put the knowledge and skills that must be learned to work in a real situation as soon as possible. Studies reveal that we retain about 50 percent of what we hear immediately after we hear it and about 75 percent of what we experience immediately after the event. As time passes without further reference to our knowledge or to the application of our skills, our retention of them diminishes still further. More than one training supervisor knows the truth behind the adage "Tell them what you are going to tell them; tell them; and tell them what you told them."

TEAMS

SUBJECTS

The principle of subjects is two-sided: You must know as much about the trainees as possible, and you must have a mastery of the subject to be taught. If you are preparing to teach an entire job, you will want to consult the job description and its corresponding job specification. Next, you will need to know the jobholder's relevant skills and knowledge. To determine the subjects to teach to your current employees, consult their most recent performance evaluations, your current observations, and the workers themselves. Disciplinary actions and records also may point out the need for training. So may the results of exit interviews conducted with employees who quit. Common complaints may signal problems that can be eliminated through training.

A company that switched computer software provides a relevant training example. After a week, the quality of work began to decline. It became obvious to the

SUPERVISING TEAMS

Supervisors who oversee the work of teams sometimes need to improve the quality of teamwork. A number of different exercises have been designed to enable team members to work better as a team rather than as a collection of individuals. Some of the better-known exercises are ropes courses in which participants must work as teams in order to accomplish challenging physical tasks. Recently, some exercises, such as the one described as follows, which rely more on thinking and problem solving, have been used to develop teamwork skills.

It was the waiter's missing shirt button, and the tattoo of a snake and a lizard on his bicep, that clinched it.

Fifteen employees, from managers to plant workers, of the Gates Corporation, a Denver maker of automotive and industrial rubber belts and hoses, had already lifted fingerprints near the chalk outlines of two bodies in an alley and a parking garage and found clues like hair, blood, the steak-knife murder weapon and notes about the killings.

Then over dinner in a restaurant, one of them remarked that the waiter's appearance matched evidence that they had gathered during the day. So the group asked Tim K. Keck, a consultant and retired police chief who was leading the exercise during a quarterly team-building conference in Poplar Bluff, Mo., the location of a company plant, to "arrest" him . . .

Some employees have become believers. "It really helped with thinking and brainstorming, and being observant," said Clover Stout, a health, safety and environmental protection specialist at Gates, of the mock detective work that began at the Gates plant and fanned out into the town. "At the beginning, nobody wanted to share information—there really was a competition on who could find the clue first. Then we had to work with the other team, and everyone huddled up to share information, and the competition aspect started to go away."

William E. Oden, Mr. Keck's partner . . . says the exercise, which they . . . call "C.S.I.: You," is by far their most popular. "Nice-looking people from middle management are crawling through Dumpsters," he said. "We had no idea how much people like that. Some men call afterward and ask if their wives can come."

Source: Sharon McDonnell, "Itineraries; Team Building With a Twist," *New York Times* (August 23, 2005): Copyright (c) (2007) by the New York Times Co. Reprinted with permission.

division manager that many departments were having trouble with the new software. On investigation, the division chief discovered that several supervisors were unable to teach the new software because they themselves had not learned it. Several other supervisors knew the software but seemed unable to teach it to their team members. The division chief worked with the director of training and developed two courses. One course trained supervisors how to train, and the other trained them on the new software.

Learning Objective Number Six

THE TRAINING CYCLE

Exhibit 11.2 shows the four parts of a successful training effort. Training, like planning, demands that you know your destination before you plan your trip. The first step is to identify where training is needed. Once areas are identified, the next step is to write objectives specifying what is to be taught, under what conditions, and how the learning can be verified. Unless all persons undergoing the training have no knowledge of what is to be taught, a pre-test may be needed to determine their levels of knowledge. You can then construct a training plan to answer the questions *who, when, where, how,* and *how much.* Then the program is conducted and the results are evaluated. A post-test may be used for comparison to determine the success of the program and areas that need more improvement or repetition.

PART 1. IDENTIFYING TRAINING NEEDS

You know that your people need training when things are not as they should be. Your efforts at control and supervision should tell you when performances are not meeting expectations or standards. Training is always needed to some degree with new employees, new equipment, and new procedures.

Let's assume that you are a restaurant manager faced with the arrival of a new employee who must be trained to be a waiter. How would you start to determine what should be taught? It would make sense to turn to your copies of the waiter's job description and job specification. You have these, they are up to date, and you have already used them to conduct your recruiting and interviewing prior to your decision to hire. They contain a list of duties and tasks, as well as a list of the personal qualities

---

EXHIBIT 11.2	The four basic components of the training cycle.

1. Identifying Training Needs

Compare performances to standards. Training is needed where significant differences exist. List tasks to be taught.

2. Preparing Training Objectives

Develop descriptions of skills to be learned and performance criteria for tasks.

3. Preparing the Training Process

Deal with the *who, when, where, how,* and *how much.* Reserve facilities and equipment, block out time.

4. Conducting and Evaluating the Training

Demonstrate, let trainees apply what is taught, evaluate the trainees' mastery of tasks, and evaluate the training effectiveness.

demanded of a waiter. The task of greeting customers cordially after the host seats them requires language and interpersonal skills. The task of serving customers their orders requires manual dexterity and coordination—mental as well as physical. Once you know what types of performance are expected of the waiter, you have the raw material necessary to assess training needs. If the new person is experienced, you will probably have to teach your particular restaurant's methods.

The day has arrived. Ben, your new waiter, has two years of experience with the job. Your earlier and present contacts with Ben will tell you the areas in which he needs training. After induction, you show Ben the job description and talk through each of the duties with him, making sure to point out any differences that may arise between what Ben has been doing elsewhere and what he will be expected to do for you. Now that Ben is familiar with his tasks, you are ready to try him out on each and to monitor his performance. But before monitoring, you must have a clear understanding of each task, of the conditions that surround its performance, and of the criteria by which you will judge the quality of performance. These three items constitute what is called a **training objective.**

> **training objective**
> a written statement of what the trainee should be able to do, the conditions under which the trainee is expected to perform, and the criteria used to judge the adequacy of the performance

PART 2. PREPARING TRAINING OBJECTIVES

Before you can train or a person can learn, both parties must have common objectives. These should be in writing to avoid confusion and to ensure mastery. All objectives should state three things as clearly as possible: (1) what the trainee should be able to do (the performance expected); (2) the conditions under which the learner is expected to do it; and (3) how well the task must be done—the performance or criteria.[20] Let's look at each of these in more detail.

Performance

The specific things you want a trainee to do are usually outlined or summarized under the major headings of tasks listed in a job description. But each task may have a series of minor related tasks. For example, Ben's job description states, "Takes orders from patrons." What subtasks or other duties are connected to this one? One might be that the waiter be able to write the orders on a form in a prescribed manner so that the kitchen people can properly interpret it. Before an order can be taken, patrons need to know what is available. Consequently, menus must be distributed and specials for the day announced. All these subtasks must be understood and stated if they are to be taught. Finally, certain skills are connected with these tasks. They, too, must be identified, described, and (in some cases) taught.

Your immediate concern with Ben will be to decide which tasks he can perform, and you cannot do that until you have listed all the detailed tasks. Before you can train Ben or evaluate how much he already knows, you have to possess a complete list of required tasks, skills, and attitudes.

Objectives usually state the performance needed by using active verbs such as *construct, list, identify,* and *compare.* These specified behaviors can be observed or evaluated fairly easily. The more specific the duty, the easier it will be to find out if the trainee has mastered it. Stay away from verbs such as *know, understand, appreciate,* and *believe;* these actions are far too vague to be taught or evaluated with precision.

Conditions

Objectives should list the items needed by the trainee to execute the performance and any limits or constraints that will be placed on performance. In our example of Ben, you already know that he will need the restaurant's prescribed order forms, a writing instrument, and a knowledge of the kitchen staff's shorthand for taking orders from patrons. But there is a time restraint as well at your restaurant. Ben must take the order within a fixed period after patrons are seated or, if they are undecided at his first visit, he must return to the table within five minutes of his first contact (at which he announces the specials of the day).

When preparing to write the conditions for a task, you need to address the equipment, materials, and time restraints.[21] Conditions usually begin with the word *given*. For example, "Given the restaurant's order form, a ballpoint pen, and a working knowledge of the restaurant's order shorthand, the waiter should be able to . . . " Each learning objective at the beginning of each chapter in this text begins with a specification of the conditions that are considered necessary for a student to demonstrate each performance listed. The two conditions are to read and to discuss each chapter. Only then can a student be expected to perform each objective. In a business setting, some objectives may begin with a statement about what will be denied to a trainee. For example, "Given no direct supervision . . . " or "Without the aid of tools, the trainee should be able to . . . ." Such a condition is understood to exist when you as a student take most of your tests. You understand that you are to answer the questions without the aid of notes or the text.

Each major task listed on Ben's job description can be broken down into subtasks. A performance and condition for each can then be written. For example, the subtasks related to "taking a customer's order" may break down as follows:

1. Visit the table.
2. Greet the customer cordially.
3. Introduce yourself and the specials of the day.
4. Offer to take the customer's order.
5. If the customer is undecided, leave and return to take the order.
6. Write the customer's order.
7. Deliver the order to the kitchen.

Each of these subtasks is involved in the major task of taking a customer's order. Each has an attached condition or two. Including your restaurant's policies and procedures in the first performance subtask will give you a complete statement:

1. Visit the table within one minute after the customer is seated by the hostess, armed with the restaurant's order forms, a ballpoint pen, a knowledge of the kitchen shorthand and daily specials, a clean uniform, and a smile on your face.

The performance expected is to visit the customer's table. The conditions surrounding that performance include a one-minute time limit, possession of equipment and knowledge, and a warm and friendly demeanor. Each of the other six subtasks may be given conditions as well. If they are all to be taught together, the conditions in number one will be understood to exist in numbers two, three, four, and six. A new time limit may be required for number five.

The key to writing descriptions of conditions is to be detailed enough to ensure that the desired performance will be executed in the way you want. Add as much description as you feel you must to communicate your intent to the trainee. When in doubt, describe. With detailed lists of tasks and their conditions, both you and the trainee can progress in an orderly manner, leaving little to chance.

Criteria

Criteria state the standards that a trainee must meet in order to give a satisfactory performance. When speed, accuracy, and a quality of performance can be stated, they should be made a part of the training objective. Criteria need not always appear in a training objective. Sometimes they are part of the conditions. Ben's first performance required him to visit a table within one minute after the customer is seated. In this case, time is both a limit and a criterion for evaluating Ben's performance.

Some criteria are best demonstrated or shown. You as a trainer can do this, pointing out the quality of performance you desire through personal demonstrations or by using behavior modeling techniques employing videotape. Nothing needs to be written into the training objective in this case.

As long as you and the trainee know what makes a performance acceptable, you have met the requirement for including criteria in your training objectives. If you cannot find some words or ways to determine acceptability of performance, perhaps you should reconsider its importance to you and to your trainee.[22] It may be of such minor importance that it should not be treated formally in training.

Finally, it is helpful to be aware that there are four different levels of objectives that apply to training in a business or management context. (The first of these three these levels were noted in the earlier discussion as subjects of training.) Not all learning needs to be focused on the level as these vary according to the desired outcomes. These levels of desired outcomes pertain to attitudes, knowledge, skills, and behaviors.[23] The following are examples of good training objectives, which are directed at the four different levels:

> **Attitude (or Awareness)** . . . Upon completing the training, the participants will understand the role of our organization in the transportation industry . . .
> **Knowledge** . . . Upon completing the training, the participants will be able to list by name and position all individuals in their chain of command . . .
> **Skill objectives** . . . Upon completing the training, the participants will be able to calculate overtime pay, based on the current employee contract.
> **Job behavior objectives** . . . Upon completing the training, the participants will follow all rules specified in Section II of the employee handbook.[24]

In addition to considering the level of outcomes, it is also sometimes helpful to think of training outcomes in terms of domains. There are three domains into which training objective outcomes can be categorized: (1) affective or emotional, which is relevant when there is an absence of motivation to learn something new as well as aspects of acceptance or rejection; (2) cognitive, which is relevant when employees have a lack of knowledge about something; and (3) psychomotor, which is relevant when employees are unable to perform a manual skill task.[25] The first three examples of objectives just presented fit best in the cognitive domain while the last one fits best in the attitude domain. Often, supervisors find that their training objectives need to deal with the affective or emotional domain, such as when employees see no need to undergo training or see no reason to change the way they have been doing things.

Finally, the manner in which the accomplishment of each of these objectives could be measured varies according to domain. The first objective could be measured by using a reaction approach, such as a multiple interval response scale item similar to what students complete on teacher evaluations. The second objective could be measured with paper and pencil testing or verbal testing. The third objective could be measured in a similar manner or with use of a computer and the software in a performance test. Lastly, the fourth objective could be measured with observations of the employee's performance.[26]

PART 3. PREPARING THE TRAINING PROCESS

You have determined the needs for training. You have identified the tasks to be taught and have written solid training objectives. These answer the questions "Why should there be training?" and "What will be taught?" The rest of your training program will answer questions relating to *who, when, where, how,* and *how much.* These questions are addressed in Exhibit 11.3. The questions of how and how much are more complicated.

DETERMINING HOW

In what order will the objectives be taught and by what methods? Priorities and a training schedule must be constructed to guarantee that all items are included in an order of presentation that makes sense to the trainee. Many techniques can be used to deliver your training. Exhibit 11.4 lists the major techniques.

Bob Eichinger, consultant and former PepsiCo executive, explains that more companies are using a unique training technique that appears especially well suited for developing employees for future positions as supervisors. In this technique, promising employees are asked to perform assignments at which they are the worst. Eichinger calls these developmental assignments "going against the grain" (GAG) assignments. By having employees work through tasks that they do not perform well, they overcome critical weaknesses that would otherwise limit their upward potential.[27]

EXHIBIT 11.3	Checklist to help you plan your training program.

The Who:	Who will do the training? Who will receive it?
The When:	What times will be set aside for training?
The Where:	What specific physical areas and equipment will be needed to conduct the training?
The How:	In what chronological order will the tasks be taught? What methods of instruction are best for each task?
The How Much:	How much money will be needed to ensure a successful training effort? How much time and equipment will be needed to teach all the objectives?

Apprenticeships	Apprenticeships are formal on-the-job training programs conducted over relatively long periods of time in order to develop high levels of skill. Typically they involve a minimum of several months and sometimes may require several years, as in the case of union apprenticeship programs. Apprentices typically pay for much of their training by working for lower wages during training.
Coaching	Coaching involves informal feedback and suggestions that supervisors provide on a day-to-day basis. Supervisors help employees learn how to perform tasks better and facilitate the acquisition of skills and knowledge.
Computer-Based Training	Computers are used to generate learning material, often in the form of questions or problems, to which students respond. The computer provides positive reinforcement for correct responses and diagnostic information for incorrect responses.
Computer-Aided Instruction	This term is more general than computer-based training. It refers to the use of computers to augment traditional training.
Internships	Internships are similar to apprenticeships. In most business settings, internships are less formal and of shorter duration than apprenticeship training.
DVDs	Employees can observe the performance of actual job tasks in technical work. For non-technical training, such as how to make a sales call, employees can watch experts perform the task.
Job Rotation	With this form of job rotation employees learn and perform various jobs for a relatively short amount of time. Where teams are employed, team members train each other in the various jobs and rotate jobs on a regular basis.
Lecture	Lectures provide a means for quickly disseminating information on new techniques and procedures. A disadvantage is that employees do not gain actual experience. Accordingly, it cannot be assumed that they will be able to apply knowledge acquired from lectures without other forms of training.
Mentoring	In mentoring, supervisors provide career guidance, reassurance, protection, and opportunities for visibility that are useful for career advancement. Mentors often help employers learn the subtleties of how things are done within the organization.
Role Playing and Simulations	Role playing allow trainees to develop skills while dealing with hypothetical situations. For example, an employee may play a role in which she must deal with a difficult customer. Role plays and simulations allow employees to practice skills in realistic but risk-free environments.
Vestibule Training	New employees practice production work using the same equipment as in the real production environment. However, the work product is not used for actual production. As a result, there is less fear of making a mistake, and learning is facilitated.
Virtual Reality Training	This advanced form of computerized training provides a 3D simulation in which trainees can respond to various realistic stimuli such as in the operation of production equipment. It has great applicability to the skilled trades, such as in helping them learn to troubleshoot equipment failures.

Sources: Irwin L. Goldstein and J. Kevin Ford. *Training in Organizations*, 4th ed. Belmont, CA: Wadsworth, (2002). Charles R. Greer. *Strategy and Human Resources: A General Managerial Approach*, 2nd ed. Englewood Cliffs, NJ: Prentice Hall, (2001). Sulaiman Al-Malik in Lloyd L. Byars and Leslie W. Rue. *Human Resource Management*, 3rd ed. Homewood, IL: Richard D. Irwin, (1991). Kenneth N. Wexley and Gary P. Latham. *Developing and Training Human Resources in Organizations*, 2nd ed. New York: HarperCollins, (1991). Irwin L. Goldstein. *Training in Organizations: Needs Assessment, Development, and Evaluation*, 2nd ed. Monterey, CA: Brooks/Cole, (1986).

Buddy Systems

The buddy system is a person-to-person or one-on-one method of training. It may also be known as the teacher–pupil method or the master–apprentice method. Whatever it is called, this method utilizes one trainer and one trainee; a person who knows the job teaches someone who needs to know it. Instruction usually takes place on the job, using the actual workplace, tools, and equipment during regular working hours. When the person doing the training is properly prepared, the buddy system has the following major advantages:

1. *It is flexible.* Learning can take place in a classroom, in a laboratory, or on the job. Changes can be introduced quickly. The system can be tailored in pace and content to meet the individual needs of the trainee.
2. *It allows immediate feedback.* The teacher/trainer works directly with the trainee and can quickly evaluate progress or lack of progress, offering corrections and reviews to improve retention and mastery.
3. *It is personal.* It humanizes the training process and allows for questions and answers, reviews, and additional drills or practices at any time. Personalized corrections may be made, and personalized instructions may be given throughout the duration of training. The system frequently helps the trainees satisfy some of their social needs.

The primary disadvantages of the buddy system are the following:

1. *It is costly.* The trainer's salary goes to pay for the training of just one trainee during any training sessions. Expensive equipment and machines are tied up and used by only one trainee at any given moment.
2. *Extensive preparation is required.* If the real advantages of the buddy system are to be realized, the instructor must adequately assess the needs of the trainee, tailor the instruction to meet those needs, and avoid passing along poor mind-sets, prejudices, and improper shortcuts.

Machine-Based Systems

Computer-based or programmed instruction methods are referred to as *machine-based systems of training* because they rely heavily on a machine to relay information and evaluate trainee responses. Computers and machines that use DVD's can enhance the learning environment and enrich the training that takes place.

All machine-based instruction requires people to (1) prepare the materials; (2) monitor the training process by keeping track of time, maintain equipment, and handle questions; and (3) evaluate the progress of each trainee. This method is more often used to supplement other types of training than to substitute for them. It works well when used to complement other methods.

The advantages of machine-based or computer-based training include the following:

1. *It is uniform.* It ensures that the same material is presented in exactly the same way to each trainee.
2. *It is flexible.* It can be adjusted, or can adjust itself, to fit the needs and pace of the trainees. It involves the learners in the learning process. It frees

trainers for other duties and allows them to handle more than one trainee per session.

3. *It is inexpensive.* The costs of computers and instructional software can be spread over dozens or hundreds of trainees. In addition, software vendors often provide machine-based training, trainers, and free or low-cost instructional materials.

Disadvantages of machine-based training include the following:

1. *It is impersonal.* Computers cannot fully replace the need for human interaction. They cannot provide the warmth of a smile and a compliment from an instructor for a job mastered in training. They cannot sense an employee's fear or frustration or the lack of comprehension of a video or verbal message.

2. *It requires expertise.* Learning materials demand a great deal of money, know-how, and time to prepare. To be economical, instructional materials must not require frequent changing or become obsolete in a short time.

3. *It can be boring.* For trainees with short attention spans, for those who learn quickly, and for those who already know a significant portion of the material, the training can become frustrating and boring.

4. *It needs to serve many trainees in order to be economical.* Computer programs and DVDs cost too much to prepare if only a few trainees are to use them.

5. *It may not teach some behaviors.* General Motors found that it had to supplement computer-based training with classroom instruction when it attempted to get GM dealers to use its computer system. While this example occurred several years ago, it provides a sense of the magnitude of the challenges that are sometimes faced in training. In this particular case, many of the sales people and secretaries who worked for the dealers had little familiarity with computers. As a result GM had to both develop computer skills and change people's mind-sets.[28] An indication of the magnitude of the task is provided by the following: "One person held the mouse up to the screen and tried to use it like a remote control. . . . Another put it on the floor and tried to use it like a sewing machine pedal."[29] The CEO of Learning Tree reinforces the importance of supplementing computer-based training with classroom instruction: "I'm not convinced that a computer-based course can come anywhere near a classroom in changing people's behavior and mind-set."[30]

Group Sessions

DIVERSITY

Lectures, conferences, and role-playing sessions can be quite effective methods of training more than one person at each session. Lectures present basic principles and individual points of view, and they can be used to introduce or summarize. Conferences and discussions can inform, solve problems, clarify situations, and help participants critically evaluate their opinions, attitudes, and methods. Role-playing allows people to act out a situation to what they see as its logical conclusion. Participants see one another in a different light and have a chance to evaluate others' solutions while trying out their own solutions on the group.

Most training requires you to interact with employees. However, technical training, such as learning new computer software, can be done on computers. When you assign computer-based training, be sure to follow up on a personal basis.

Group training can be useful also for developing cooperation and teamwork among your employees. These types of training often involve the completion of a group task requiring participants to work together. Examples include exercises such as the murder mystery noted earlier in this chapter's supervising teams feature, or such activities as working as a team to prepare a meal in a cooking school.[31] The major advantages of the group-sessions method are the following:

1. *It is uniform.* Two or more people are exposed to the same material in the same way at the same time.
2. *It is inexpensive.* Compared to other training methods, group sessions offer savings in hours and salaries for training purposes.

The major disadvantages of the group-sessions method are the following:

1. *It is impersonal.* It does not allow for individual differences or close involvement in the training.
2. *It magnifies errors.* The impact of each mistake or bit of misinformation is magnified by the number of trainees.
3. *It does not overcome a lack of trust.* Group training is not a silver bullet solution for dysfunctional teams or for building trust with individuals who have serious character flaws.[32] Craig Cantoni, the president of Capstone Consulting, has noted the ineffectiveness of group training, such as physically demanding adventure or outdoors training, for dysfunctional teams. More specifically, he notes the following when employees are involved in a potentially dangerous exercise, such as scaling a cliff:

> Distrustful employees may work well with their boss in a rock-climbing exercise, because if they don't, someone will get injured. "But back in the office, he's still a snake . . ."[33]

It is important to recognize the differences among adults regarding how they learn and, therefore, the necessity of adapting to their individual learning styles. For

| **Characteristics of effective trainers.** | **EXHIBIT 11.5** |

- An appreciation that trainees have varied and different learning styles and preferences

- An ability to adapt materials and exercises to a targeted population

- Techniques for gauging whether information has been understood and can be easily applied in the workplace

- Communication skills that denote respect for a training audience, including listening skills, summarizing, paraphrasing, and effective questioning

- A commitment to continued improvement demonstrated by encouraging specific feedback and researching best practices

- A respect for the diversity of today's labor market and diversity within a training audience

Source: Cy Charney and Kathy Conway. *The Trainer's Tool Kit.* 2nd ed., New York: American Management Association (AMACOM), (2005), p. 5.

example, some of your employees may be tactile or bodily–kinesthetic learners who master material better when they can handle the materials or use a hands-on approach. Others may be logical–mathematical style learners who acquire knowledge better through problem solving. Other employees may require demonstrations and some form of interaction before they learn the material. Supervisors should be prepared to train their employees using approaches that fit these varying learning styles. In addition, evolving technology is making lifelong learning a necessity; thus, it is important to use approaches that match the learning styles of employees who may have completed their formal education many years ago.[34] Recognizing that people learn differently is a characteristic of effective trainers. Exhibit 11.5 presents several qualities of effective trainers.

In designing your training program, try to utilize more than one method of training. For most types of training, a single method will not do. A blend or mix will probably suit your purposes better. When you know what has to be taught and what human and material resources are available, think about which methods should work best for you and your trainees.

DETERMINING HOW MUCH

This question needs two answers. You must determine how much time you will need for training and how much money you will have to spend. Break the training into learnable units—units small enough to be effectively taught and absorbed in one session. If the units are too big, the trainee will be unable to digest them. It is far better to have less material—leaving ample time for review and practice—than to have too much. A good rule of thumb is to attempt to teach no more than three major concepts in every 60-minute session.

PART 4. CONDUCTING AND EVALUATING THE TRAINING

Training should begin with the following introductory steps:

1. Put trainees at ease.
2. State the objectives to be achieved during the session.
3. Point out the advantages they will receive from the training.
4. Explain the sequence of the events they are about to follow.

You should stress the fact that when you and the company take the time and make the effort to train workers, it is positive proof of concern for the workers and an expression of confidence in their abilities. If eligibility for training was competitive, let each trainee know of your pride in his selection. Let your trainees know that there is no harm in making mistakes. In fact, we learn more by analyzing our mistakes when we discover their causes and can prevent their recurrence.

Demonstration

During the demonstration phase of your training presentation, you have the opportunity to show and tell. You can perform as your objective specifies or let experienced employees demonstrate the tasks. In Ben's case, you may want to call on your skilled wait staff to demonstrate. Or you may videotape performances and let the trainee view the video, commenting on what is being shown and asking and answering questions. If your trainee has no questions, ask some of your own. Check on Ben's understanding of each critical task. Remember that training involves communication, and communication requires feedback.

Application

The application phase of training asks the trainee to get his feet wet. In this case, Ben will be asked to duplicate the performance that he has just witnessed. You may want to show Ben more than one performance before asking him to repeat it. However, don't try to include too many behaviors before you let the trainee try them. By mixing the demonstration with applications, you provide the trainee with immediate feedback and highlight both what he has mastered and what he has not. You will be applying the principle of reinforcement, as well as providing the early and measured successes that are so important to the mastery of performances and the motivation of the trainee. You may wish to videotape the performance and use the tape for review or to examine progress.

Evaluation

In the evaluation phase, you determine if the trainee has mastered the task performance and if the training effort was successful. The basic question here is whether the trainee can perform, under the prescribed conditions, all the essential tasks at the required level of quality. Evaluation may take place at any point in a demonstration or during a trainee's application of lessons. Performance tests, written or oral quizzes, and the trainer's own observations are the most frequently used devices for evaluating performance.

The effectiveness of training can be measured by five levels of criteria:

1. Reactions—employee satisfaction
2. Learning—employees' comprehension of the material
3. Application—employees' use of the material
4. Business impact—resultant changes in the performance of the business
5. Return on investment—ratio of returns from training relative to its cost [35]

After evaluation, provide trainees with frequent and immediate feedback. Let them know when they are correct and ask them to spot their own mistakes. Let them examine the product of their efforts and try to find any defects. Once they discover an error, explain, or get them to explain, just how it can be prevented from happening again. Point out how one error—the one just made, for example,—can lead to others. Use each mistake as a point for review and then conduct a critique to summarize the entire lesson.

Through evaluation, you can quickly ascertain the need for repeating a training segment. You also will realize how fast you can place people on their own, free from your strict supervision and control. Usually one should gradually reduce the level of supervision and control rather than cause trainees to feel that they will face an abrupt sink-or-swim situation. Be available to them, but simply make your visits and observations less frequent as each person demonstrates an ability to perform to standards. Your follow-up should tell you whether lasting effects have been achieved or whether an individual needs additional training.

DIVERSITY

TRAINING FOR VALUING DIVERSITY

Training that promotes the value of diversity takes many forms. Workshops and seminars—conducted in-house or at training centers by insiders or outsiders—can provide unique approaches and lessons learned by others that enlighten participants and stimulate dialogue. Many companies have created advisory teams or committees to implement diversity training programs. Mentoring programs assign people to sponsor those who differ significantly from themselves. For example, an African American female may be assigned to mentor a Korean American male, while a white male is assigned to mentor a Mexican American female. These efforts, once begun, usually remain part of annual training efforts and may evolve to take on new challenges.

Within these general approaches is a variety of methods and tools that aid diversity training. Some training efforts let participants listen to presentations from individuals representing diverse groups; others show video episodes portraying diverse people in various situations. These then become discussion starters, engaging participants in a give-and-take on the issues presented. A variation on this technique is the interactive video, which stops the action periodically and lets the participants enter the presentation with their own thoughts and suggested outcomes for the situations portrayed. Each episode is a case study or simulation of a real event. Burlington Northern Santa Fe uses this approach followed by group discussions. Shell Oil Company uses an "interactive video . . . in which a learner, using a computer terminal interfaced with a videodisc player and a touch screen, works alone through a self-paced lesson."[36] Folger Coffee Company, a division of Procter & Gamble, uses role-playing exercises to get trainees to empathize with each other. Events are scripted, and participants play roles that are unfamiliar to them.

The purposes of all these efforts are to learn how we form our attitudes and perceptions of others, in what ways people differ from one another, how those differences can give individuals and organizations specific advantages, and how to improve the way we interact with people who differ. As King-Ming Young, head of Hewlett-Packard's Professional Development Group, puts it, "Managers today must demonstrate a larger repertoire of behaviors to get the most out of each employee."[37]

Some of the major conclusions of recent research on diversity training may be summarized as follows: "A focused effort should emphasize that all employees need to understand and are involved in the diversity initiative, that its objectives are tied to the business' success, and that behavior outside desired norms will not be tolerated."[38] In addition to placing value on diversity and diversity training, it is also important to facilitate the movement of minorities and females into higher-skill jobs and managerial jobs. Unless minorities and females are fully represented in these jobs, the full value of diversity will not be attained. Many companies are assigning promising minorities and females to line management jobs very early in their careers in order to build up their level of experience.[39]

PITFALLS

Besides violations of any of the aforementioned principles of training, the following are the major pitfalls:

1. *Leaving it to others.* When you delegate training or use the assistance of staff specialists, you must remain sufficiently involved to ensure that proper training will take place. Remember that you must participate enough in both planning and actual training in order to know whether goals are being achieved.
2. *Making assumptions.* A trainer sometimes makes the mistake of assuming that because trainees are told to read about a concept, they will understand it on their own—or that because the trainer presented the material, all of it has been assimilated. Rely on facts and observations for a proper evaluation of the program and its effectiveness, not on assumptions.
3. *Fearing an employee's progress.* Some people fear the successes and increasing abilities of others because they view them as threats to their own security. Managers sometimes refuse to train employees out of fear that they may be able to replace them. Keep in mind that unless you have a trained successor, you are locking yourself into your present position. Training is the job of every manager who has employees. By failing to train employees you neglect an important duty.
4. *Getting too fancy.* Trainers may get too caught up in methods and training aids and lose sight of what it is they must teach. There may be too much flash and too little substance. Have you ever listened to a speaker or lecturer who talked for hours and said nothing?
5. *Substituting training for proper selection processes.* Training is not a substitute for proper selection procedures. Selection involves trying to hire the best available person to fill a vacancy. It requires skills in such areas as interviewing, testing, and recruiting. Some employers treat selection as an unimportant activity and rely on the training of new employees to impart the skills required to perform a job properly.

INSTANT REPLAY

1. Training is the supervisor's responsibility. It may be delegated, but the supervisor is accountable for it.

2. Training imparts skills, knowledge, and attitudes needed by trainees now or in the near future.

3. Training benefits you, your trainees, and your employer. Be certain that trainees know what they are to learn and why.

4. You are judged on your performance and on the performance of your employees.

5. The training cycle asks you to identify your training needs, to prepare performance objectives, to create a training program, and to conduct the training.

6. The central purpose of training is to improve performance and productivity.

QUESTIONS FOR CLASS DISCUSSION

1. What are the advantages that a supervisor receives when she trains an employee?

2. What are the advantages that a trainee receives from training?

3. What are the basic requirements that a trainer must satisfy?

4. What are the basic requirements that a trainee must satisfy in order to get the most out of training?

5. What are the principles of training, and what does each mean to a trainer?

6. What are the major steps in the training cycle?

7. What are the major pitfalls of which a trainer should be aware?

ASSESS THIS SITUATION

Purpose: To create and conduct a brief training program, following the four basic parts of training as shown in Exhibit 11.2.

Your Task: Create a training program through which you teach another person your way of performing any skill you possess, such as building a model or kneading dough. After you have created your learning objective(s), chosen a method, reserved a location, and gotten a volunteer, write down each step, noting the standards you wish to teach and use them to evaluate the learner's performance. Set a time limit, and conduct your training session in class using the principles learned in this chapter. When you have taught the lesson, evaluate your efforts through the learner's and the class's comments. Don't be surprised if the learner or the class comes up with a better way to do things.

SKILL BUILDING EXERCISE 11.1

The quality of service in large electronics, home improvement, and discount stores is not always at a level expected by customers. It is evident that many retailers could benefit from better-trained store employees. Making a commitment to provide training may also help reduce turnover because employees are likely to feel like they are more highly valued, and therefore more inclined to stay, if the employer invests their training. Furthermore, treating employees well by providing training may have an impact on customer satisfaction because employees tend to treat customers in the same manner in which they are treated.

Your Task: Work in small groups to (1) identify training needs for sales floor clerks in three or four retail stores with which your groups are familiar, (2) develop an estimate of the number of hours it will take to provide such training, (3) develop an estimate of the cost to train a group of 10 clerks, and (4) provide an explanation of why the stores are not currently providing more training.

SKILL BUILDING WRITING EXERCISE 11.2

Assume that you work for a convenience store chain and that you have been assigned the job of designing a training program for new store clerks. There are serious concerns about slower service at the stores because the average time required for a customer to make her purchases at the store has increased by 25 percent over the past six months. Senior management is concerned that with such delays customers will no longer see the stores as a convenience and business will decline. It has been determined that the major reason for longer stop times is that a substantial number of the store's clerks are inexperienced, and as a result, most of them are struggling and need training. You have conducted an analysis of the training needs for the clerks and know what needs to be included in the training. You now want to develop training objectives and tasks for the program that will include the performance expected, the conditions under which the learner will perform the work, and the performance criteria.

Your Task: (1) Prepare a list of five or more major tasks that the clerks will need to perform as a regular part of their jobs. For example, one task would be to handle the check out and payment transaction for alcoholic beverages. Another might be to redeem a winning lottery ticket, while another might be to sell a money order, and so on. (2) After preparing these major tasks, compile a list of the subtasks involved with each major task and then write out two or three conditions for each subtask including equipment, materials, and time constraints. (3) Write out the criteria that will be used to determine whether the task has been performed satisfactorily.

CASE 11.1   North Star Airlines

Abbie Kirkwood is the supervisor of the reservations center at North Star Airlines. As Abbie walked through the rows of cubicles where reservations agents were busy handling calls, Cory Summers, one of the lead persons for the first shift, waved to her and motioned for her to come over to her cubicle. Cory, and the other lead persons, Roberto Garza, Jill Gaither, and Sue Kincaid, were looking at one of the computer screens.

CORY: We're having some problems with this new upgrade to the system. Several times during the past two weeks we've made errors by booking people in the same seats."

JILL: We've also had lots of confusion on fare choices since the special fares were introduced over the weekend. In addition, the ticketless system is really driving us crazy. Since no ticket is issued when we make a mistake on the confirmation number, the passengers have no way of proving that they have a reservation."

ROBERTO: Most of our agents don't know how to enter the new codes for special fares and now we're starting to get complaints from our ticket agents in several airports. I thought that things would calm down after a couple of days but that's not happening. We're getting a continuous stream of problems and complaints."

ABBIE: I've received a few calls too. Maybe we should start tracking the number of errors each agent makes. We could start score boarding and post each agent's performance on the wall here by the coffee machine for everyone to see. We could start offering things like free movie tickets and dinners for people who have the fewest errors. For those that make lots of errors, we could write them up and lower their performance evaluations."

JILL: I'm not sure that our agents can learn these new features on their own. Some of the new features of the upgrade are really complex. The help screens make it a little easier, but it looks to me like we're going to have to do some training."

ABBIE: I'm not sure that training is the answer. If people are really motivated they can learn anything on their own. Some software vendors charge a lot for training and our people aren't doing anything productive while they're in training."

SUE: I agree with Jill. Our agents need some training. We really need to do something and fast. Otherwise we're really going to have a problem when reservations for the holiday start to come in."

ABBIE: Okay, why don't we each just pick out the people we think are having trouble with this software and send them through the training? Each of you can pick out five of your agents who are making the most errors and we'll make them stay late and go through training."

ROBERTO: Why don't we have everybody go through the training during the regular work week?"

ABBIE: We'd have to double staff during the training because someone will have to handle the incoming calls. That would be too expensive. Besides, the smarter agents will learn this upgrade without training. Here's what we'll do. We'll ask the vendor to send a software developer out here to train the agents who are making most of the errors. We'll also include some of our best agents from the first shift and have them go through the training as well. They can learn how to do the training. It will be sort of a 'train the trainer' approach. Then we'll have these agents from the first shift train the weaker agents from the other two shifts. They'll have to come in early or stay late in order to overlap with the second and third shifts to do the training. While they do the training they'll get a little overtime."

ABBIE: Cory, why don't you call the vendor and ask for one of their software developers to conduct the training? They've got some sharp people who ought to be able to explain the upgrades to our agents."

CORY: What shall I tell the vendor to include in the training?"

ABBIE: Oh, they'll know what we need. After all, they designed the upgrade, and they're the experts. Just tell them to put on the standard dog and pony show for our first shift people after work on Monday, Tuesday, and Wednesday."

ABBIE: Roberto, you notify everyone where the training will be conducted."

ROBERTO: What room do you want to use? Will we need to provide a projector for the instructor's laptop computer?"

ABBIE: We'll just have them do the training in the cafeteria. It's always available late in the afternoon or evening. I don't think we'll need a projector. The vendor's expert can just talk us through the changes. Sue, make sure that we have a separate group of tables and chairs for the training. All of you need to send e-mail to notify those you pick for training. Tell them that they'll need to stay late for a couple of hours of training on each of the three nights next week starting with Monday. Any questions?"

Questions

1. What problems do you see in Abbie's approach toward training?

2. What do you think of Abbie's suggestion for scoreboarding? Selection of trainees?

3. How do you think the agents will react? How would you feel?

4. What is the likelihood that the training will be successful?

5. If you were the supervisor, how would you deal with the problems described in the case?

CASE 11.2   BK Custom Products

Jim Brookshire, the training supervisor for BK Custom Products, had received funding to conduct management training for the production supervisors. The training will start today, and he is excited about the opportunity to get the production supervisors up to speed on management techniques. Several months ago, he told Bernice Hernandez, the plant manager, that some basic management training would be necessary with the company's recent expansion and promotion of several employees to supervisory positions. Last month, Bernice acknowledged that several new supervisors, as well as some of the more experienced ones, were struggling with their duties and told Jim to go ahead with the training. They both agreed that, because there had been no supervisory training in the past, all supervisors—both new and experienced—will receive the training.

Jim then proceeded with the development of the training program. He developed a set of supervisory subjects to be taught and found a management trainer, Mark Harper, a management professor at the local university, who agreed to conduct the training. Jim was impressed with Mark's informal manner and down-to-earth approach and was pleased that he would be doing the training.

Because of the volume of production, Bernice had told Jim that the supervisors could not be away from the plant for the whole day. Accordingly, Jim arranged for the training to be conducted on the job site during working hours. The sessions were scheduled for three hours in the afternoon on Tuesdays and Thursdays for six weeks.

It was the first Tuesday of training and the participants were all seated around a U-shaped table arrangement in the break room. Jim introduced Mark Harper and told the participants that he was a professor from the local university. Mark then started into the first training module. About 20 minutes into the session, one of the participant's cell phones rang. It was Harold Miller's. Harold looked down at the number on the phone and said, "I'm sorry, but I've got to take this call," and left the room. About 20 minutes later, a production worker came into the room and motioned for Mary Ferguson, another of the participants, to come to the door. Mary got up and walked around the table to confer with the worker. She then said, "Something's come up in the plant, and I've got to leave for a few minutes."

During the first two hours of the training, 6 of the 20 participants had been in and out of the room for similar interruptions, and 2 did not return at all. During the last hour of the session, Mark had assigned the participants to one-on-one role plays of employee coaching situations. Since many of the participants were in and out of the room, the role players had to be moved around and there was a great deal of confusion.

On Thursday, only 12 of the supervisors showed up for training, and the same interruptions continued as on Tuesday. Mark, who was obviously concerned about the interruptions and lack of attendance, said, "Jim, what's going on here? I thought we were going to have 20 people to work with, and my exercises will have to be changed. People are being pulled out of the training, and it looks like something's come up today because eight of the participants aren't here. This is going to be a disaster if you don't get this situation straightened out!"

As Jim was walking back to his office, he met Bernice Hernandez in the hallway. Bernice said, "How's the training going?" Jim said, "Not well. The supervisors are continually interrupted and today one-third of them didn't even show up! I know we're really busy and there's a real need for the supervisors on the shop floor, but we've got to keep them in the classroom." Bernice said, "Yeah, I know it's a busy time and it's always hard to work in training. By the way, what are you covering in there? One of the department managers said the training was a bunch of 'touchy feely' stuff. Who's this guy Mark Harper? Does this guy know anything about the real world? Do the best you can. I'm counting on you to make this work."

Questions

1. What mistakes do you think Jim has made in his approach to the training?

2. What does Jim's conversation with Bernice Hernandez tell you?

3. What should Jim do in order to turn around the situation?

4. What should he tell Mark Harper?

REFERENCES

[1] Gandhi, Mahandas. (October 17, 2005): *www.brainyquote.com/quotes/authors/m/mohandas_gandhi.html*.

[2] Pfeffer, Jeffrey. *The Human Equation: Building Profits by Putting People First*, Boston: Harvard Business School Press (1999).

[3] Maher, Kris. "Skills Shortage Gives Training Programs New Life," *Wall Street Journal* (May 3, 2005): A2.

[4] Peters, Jeremy W. "Analysts Ask if Ford Overhaul Plan Will Be Spartan Enough," *New York Times* (January 21, 2006). Peters, Jeremy W. "Board Is Told of Fort's Overhaul Plan," *New York Times* (December 8, 2005).

[5] Maher, "Skills Shortage Gives Training Programs New Life."

[6] National Association of Manufacturers, (January 29, 2006): Website *www.nam.org/s_nam/sec.asp?CID=9&DID=7*.

[7] Maher, "Skills Shortage Gives Training Programs New Life."

[8] Bassi, L., and Van Buren, M. E. "Training Investment Can Mean Financial Performance," *Training and Development* (May 1998): 40–42.

[9] Kahn, Jeremy. "The World's Most Admired Companies," *Fortune* (October 11, 1999): 267–275. Stein, Nicholas. "The World's Most Admired Companies." *Fortune* (October 2, 2000): 182–184.

[10] Henkoff, R. "Companies That Train Best," *Fortune* (March 22, 1993): 62–65.

[11] Fred, Charles L. *Breakaway: Using Speed and Expertise to Deliver Value to Customers—Fast.* Boulder, Colorado: Grand River Publishing, LLC (2001).

[12] Totty, Michael. "Learning by Pretending," *Wall Street Journal*, (May 23, 2005): R10.

[13] Ibid.

[14] Ibid.

[15] Grossman, Ron. "The Three R's Go to Work," *Chicago Tribune* (October 29, 1989): sect. 4, 1.

[16] Godin, Seth, ed. *1995 Information Please Business Almanac and Sourcebook.* New York: Houghton Mifflin (1994): 289.

[17] Grossman. "The Three R's Go to Work."

[18] Ricks, Thomas E. "Army's 'Baby Generals' Take a Crash Course in Sensitivity Training," *Wall Street Journal* (January 19, 1998): A1.

[19] Morgan, Rebecca L. "Getting Into Corporate Training—What Does It Take?" *American Salesman* (October 2000): 25–29. Caudron, Shari, Redmon,

Marsha, Suleiman, Anver S., Kaplan-Leiserson, Eva, McDermont, Lynda, and Wagner, Stacey. "Executive Summaries," *Training and Development* (October 2001): 82–83. "20 Teaching Tips to Make Your Training Lessons Stick," *HR Focus* (October 2000): 13. Cone, John W., and Robinson, Dana G. "The Power of E-Performance," *Training and Development* (August 2001): 32–40.

[20] Mager, Robert F. *Preparing Instructional Objectives,* 2nd ed. Belmont, CA: Pitman Learning (1984): 21, 51, 86–87.

[21] Ibid.

[22] Ibid.

[23] Vaughn, Robert H. *The Professional Trainer: A Comprehensive Guide to Training, Delivering, and Evaluating Training Programs,* San Francisco: Berrett-Koehler Publishers, Inc, (2005).

[24] Ibid., 69–70.

[25] Ibid.

[26] Ibid.

[27] Eichinger, Bob. Presentation to the Metroplex Human Resource Planning Society Plano, Texas (April 1994).

[28] Carlton, Jim, and Clark, Don. "Teaching Tech Pays Off for Training Firms," *Wall Street Journal* (February 26, 1998): B8.

[29] Ibid., B8.

[30] Ibid., B8.

[31] Associated Press. "Workers Get Insight from Guided Play," *Dallas Morning News* (September 13, 1997): 2F.

[32] Ibid.

[33] Ibid.

[34] Rajsky, Gregory. "Adult Learning," *Products Finishing* (February 2002): 90–91.

[35] Patterson, Susan C. *The Training Manager's Quick-Tip Sourcebook: Surefire Tools, Tactics, and Strategies to Solve Common Training Challenges,* San Francisco: Jossey-Bass/Pfeiffer (2003).

[36] Jamieson, David, and O'Mara, Julie. *Managing Workforce 2000.* San Francisco: Jossey-Bass (1991): 83–91.

[37] Ibid.

[38] Kilian, Claire McCarty, Hukai, Dawn, and McCarty, E. Elizabeth. "Building Diversity in the Pipeline to Corporate Leadership," *Journal of Management Development 24*(2) (2005): 162.

[39] Eichinger. "Presentation."

CHAPTER 12

"We will remember not the words of our enemies, but the silence of our friends."

Martin Luther King, Jr.[1]

Objectives

After reading and discussing this chapter, you should be able to do the following:

1. Provide a comprehensive overview of the management of diversity.
2. Describe the trends in workforce diversity and the implications for organizations.
3. Describe how supervisors can help capture the potential value provided by workforce diversity.
4. Explain how supervisors can facilitate the inclusion of people of color.
5. Explain how supervisors can help women overcome challenges in the workplace.
6. Explain how supervisors can better utilize older employees.
7. Explain how superviors can improve the inclusion of international employees.
8. Explain how supervisors can facilitate the inclusion of employees with different sexual orientations.
9. Explain how supervisors can facilitate the inclusion and utilization of employees with disabilities.

Managing Diversity at Eastman Kodak

The management of diversity is a topic of growing interest to both employers and employees. Some indication of its importance is provided by Fortune magazine's annual publication of a list of the 50 best companies for minorities. Many of the best-known companies in the United States are on the list, and Eastman Kodak has been on the list for three years in a row. Even though the company has downsized and faces difficult challenges in the market, the company still has good minority representation as minorities account for one-third of the board of directors and one-fifth of senior management. Nonetheless, questions

Managing Diversity

have been raised about the company's management of diversity; it is instructive to consider the diversity challenges the company faces and whether real progress has been made.[2]

Interviews of minority employees at Kodak reveal remarkably different perceptions of the company's progress in managing diversity. For example, "Craig A. Young, an African American human resources manager, says that in 22 years at Eastman Kodak he has never faced discrimination."[3] On the other hand,

> Gladys Alston . . . who worked for Kodak from 1991 to 2002, insists that, if she had been white, she would have progressed well beyond human resource associate, her last job. She filed a formal complaint; Kodak, she said, first offered her $4,992, then raised the offer to $8,268 when she retained a lawyer. She said she spurned that, too."[4]

A number of African American employees and former employees have brought suit charging the company with systematic discrimination. Nonetheless, It is likely that the company's performance in managing diversity is somewhere between these two extremes.[5] "Not all of Kodak's African American employees are unhappy. A few, in fact, suggest that their litigious colleagues may be ascribing racist overtones to ordinary workplace disputes."[6]

Mr. Young and other employees report that the company has taken decisive action when there have been instances of real racism. For example, "Mr. Young noted that Kodak recently fired a shop-floor supervisor who was hurling racial slurs . . . Charles C. Barrentine, an African American vice president, who has worked 32 years at Kodak, [said] 'I've seen hostile environments . . . and this is not one of them.'"[7] While the company has had problems in the past, there is ample evidence that it has taken strong corrective action. More specifically, the company has assessed its supervisors and managers' capabilities to manage diversity. Up to 200 who lacked such abilities were removed. Moreover, the company's actions have not stopped with assessments and the removal of such individuals, as it now has required diversity courses for its supervisors and managers. It also has an external diversity council and has alternative dispute resolution procedures, including panels of employee peers, for employees who want to pursue complaints regarding diversity. Furthermore, the company has agreed to be bound by the dispute resolution procedures, while the employee is not.[8]

Questions for Thought

1. What are the challenges that supervisors are likely to face in managing diversity?
2. How can supervisors obtain performance improvements through the management of diversity?

Learning Objective Number One

TEAMS

management of diversity
managing and leading a heterogeneous workforce in order to accomplish an organization's goals in an effective manner

Introduction

A comprehensive definition of the management of diversity is needed in order to provide a foundation for our discussion of the various aspects of diversity, which are presented in this chapter. The **management of diversity** refers to the process of managing and leading a heterogeneous workforce in order to accomplish an organization's goals. When performed well, it provides a potential competitive advantage by harnessing the distinctive perspectives and talents that are associated with differences. The management of diversity is imbedded with complexity, often requiring the supervisor to be skilled in resolving conflict, communications, and human relations. The concept of managing diversity goes beyond the notion of equal employment opportunity or affirmative action's goal of remedying the under-representation of women and minorities through emphasis on hiring and promotion procedures. Indeed, the management of diversity has the far more ambitious goal of capturing the full value of diversity for business reasons. As with the diversity among employees, organizations are not uniform in their approaches to diversity. There are different views of the concept, three of which will be presented in this chapter in the form of assimilation, differentiation, and integration or inclusion paradigms.

Before proceeding with the management of diversity, it is worth noting that managing diversity does not always carry the same meaning, and there has been confusion about the subject. One source of confusion has been the extension of the term to all conceivable sources of differences. This approach has been criticized because it minimizes the importance of focusing on the differences that have been the source of harmful discrimination.[9]

> What we need . . . theories and practices that help organizations reduce discrimination and enable employees who are increasingly diverse by race, gender, sexual orientation and ability to work together effectively. Managers . . . need to learn how to apply those skills competently and comfortably when the employees in their charge are not like them . . . Since the vast majority of managers in top positions in the United States are still able-bodied, heterosexual white men, the singly largest task is to help those white-male managers understand how to work with people of color, white women, gays and lesbians, people with disabilities, and others. Further, we all need to understand that there is enormous diversity *within* each group, far greater than the difference between and across the individual groups.[10]

While there are benefits from the management of diversity, supervisors also should be aware that there are potential hazards. Supervisors may unintentionally amplify differences between people such that relationships are damaged and employees become too sensitized to differences. In addition, it should be remembered that mistakes will be made in some of the sensitive areas of diversity, and that the organization needs to be supportive of efforts that are intended to improve the diversity climate, even when errors occur.[11] These caveats should be remembered in the discussions that follow.

ENDURING EVIDENCE OF DISCRIMINATION

Unfortunately, while some organizations are well on their way toward full inclusion of diverse employees and have obtained a clear advantage over their competitors because of their skill in managing diversity, there are organizations in which various forms of discrimination are still present to varying degrees.

RACIAL DISCRIMINATION

A recent study examined the response of employers to applicants having names more commonly associated with Caucasians versus African Americans. The researchers, from the University of Chicago and MIT, sent 5,000 résumés in response to 1,250 help wanted ads for administrative, clerical, management, and sales positions. Their study, which was conducted in Chicago and Boston in 2001 to 2002, used calls from employers in response to the applications as potential indicators of discrimination. The researchers varied the names, gender, and quality of credentials; such as experience and honors; in the résumés that were distributed. The black-sounding first names that were used included names such as Tamika, Aisha, Latonya, and Ebony, while some of the white-sounding first names included Kristen, Emily, Anne, and Jill. The corresponding black-sounding family names included such names as Jackson, Washington, Jones, and Williams, while white-sounding family names included names such as O'Brien, Sullivan, Walsh, and Baker.[12] Unfortunately, the results of the study are not encouraging:

> Applicants with white-sounding names were 50 percent more likely to be called for interviews than were those with black-sounding names. Interviews were requested for 10.1 percent of applicants with white-sounding names and only 6.7 percent of those with black-sounding names.[13]

In addition to this study of differences in the responses of employers, other survey data indicate that there are differences in the extent to which Caucasians and African Americans perceive discrimination in employment. A Gallup poll recently found that 55 percent of whites agreed with a statement that the employment opportunities of racial minorities are equal to those of whites, while only 17 percent of blacks agreed.[14]

Aside from research studies, there are also examples of discrimination involving companies that deserve mention. One such example of racial discrimination involved a Hollywood hotel owner who paid a $1.08 million settlement for terminating eight nonwhite bellhops and valets that he determined were "too ethnic."[15] Exhibit 12.1 provides several examples of the costs that companies have incurred for race and gender discrimination.

GENDER DISCRIMINATION

Gender discrimination also continues to be a problem, such as in the financial services industry. For example, gender diversity has been an issue at Merrill Lynch for many

EXHIBIT 12.1	Diversity and the bottom line.	

	COST (IN MILLIONS)	TYPE OF DISCRIMINATION
Coca-Cola	$192.5	Race
State Farm	$250	Gender
Home Depot	$110	Gender
Lucky Stores	$107	Gender
Publix	$82	Gender
Texaco	$176	Race
Shoney's	$132	Race
Denny's	$54	Race

Source: Reprinted from *The Diversity Scorecard: Evaluating the Impact of Diversity on Organizational Performance*, Edward E. Hubbard, page 20, Copyright 2004, with permission from Elsevier.

years. The company, which continues to be criticized over the issue, has now paid over $100 million to women in order to settle sex discrimination and harassment claims.[16]

The former president of Harvard University, Lawrence H. Summers, who is also a labor economist, has hypothesized that the major reason for the under representation of women at the highest-level jobs in science and engineering, is related to time commitment. His argument is summarized as follows:

"Women are, for whatever reasons, less likely to enter jobs that demand enormous time commitments . . . the primary barrier to women in science, as in other high-powered jobs, is that employers demand single-minded dedication to work. 'They expect a large number of hours in the office, they expect a flexibility of schedules to respond to contingency, they expect a continuity of effort through the life cycle' [direct quote of Summers] . . . Married women . . . especially those with children, are far less likely than married men to put up with such demands."[17]

Other researchers have reached similar conclusions about the underrepresentation of women at higher levels in organizations and it is not clear that there is any substitute for long hours and an extremely driven approach to work:

"The higher up you go, jobs get greed-ier [sic] and greedier," says one researcher. "The idea that if only employers would reshape jobs they would be perfectly easy for women to do is just nonsense."[18]

While these conclusions are supported by empirical research, they have created controversies among various groups.[19] Such reactions provide insights into the level of sensitivity that is needed when dealing with these issues. It is important to understand that these comments refer to the very top-level positions in organizations, which are outliers in many respects. Furthermore, it is also worth noting that the differential in hours worked by men and women is simply an average, and there are large numbers of individuals who depart from the average in all occupations and industries.[20] As a result, supervisors need to always remember to treat their associates as individuals and not as members of a class.

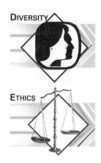

AGE DISCRIMINATION

Age discrimination also continues to be a problem. Between 1999 and 2004 there was a 25 percent increase in the number of age-discrimination cases filed with the Equal Employment Opportunity Commission, with 17,837 filed in 2004.[21] There are numerous examples of this form of discrimination, such as the following:

> Some employers assume that people north of 50 are marking time, or lacking in energy and up-to-date skills. In a survey of 428 HR managers by the Society of Human Resource Management, 53% said older workers "didn't keep up with technology," and 28% characterized them as "less flexible." That certainly rings true for Sam Horgan, 57, a veteran CFO who's spent a lot of time between jobs. A 30-ish job interviewer asked him, "Would you have trouble working with young bright people?" One job interviewer pointedly said to 58-year-old Russ Rakestraw, "You've got a lot of maturity."[22]

> Recently a 63-year old woman was awarded $965,000 by a jury in Texas for age discrimination by the operator of 49 Dairy Queen stores. An incriminating e-mail revealed that the employee had been referred to as "a lazy cowhand 'in the saddle too long'."[23]

DISCRIMINATION AGAINST DISABLED PEOPLE

There are also examples of discrimination against employees who have disabilities. Wal-Mart has been ordered to pay a disabled employee $7.5 million because of disability-related discrimination. The employee, a twenty-one-year-old man with cerebral palsy, had been hired to work in one of the stores' pharmacies but was later reassigned to rounding up shopping carts and garbage collection duties.[24]

In addition to actual discrimination, employees who have disabilities are often apprehensive that they will be subject to discrimination if people at work become aware of their condition. As a result, employees with debilitating diseases often attempt to hide their disabilities because of fears that their careers will be adversely affected. The recent example of a 48-year old man who was employed as head of communications at a non-profit organization is illustrative of such concerns. In this case, the employee, who has multiple sclerosis, a disease, which sometimes progresses with intermittent and variable effects, did not feel that he would be at risk of losing his job. However, he wanted to avoid questions about his health and pity from his coworkers. As a result, the employee took such measures as scheduling his medical appointments with physicians at lunch when he would not be missed and told nobody at work about his condition. He kept the disease a secret for 14 years until the effects became too difficult to conceal before telling his boss and coworkers.[25]

Pregnant women must be treated in the same manner as other employees and cannot be discriminated against because of their pregnancy.

LEGAL PROHIBITIONS AGAINST DISCRIMINATION

Employment discrimination on the basis of race, color, religion, sex, or national origin is prohibited by the Civil Rights Act of 1964, as amended by the Equal Employment Opportunity Act of 1972, and the Civil Rights Act of 1991. These federal laws cover employers having 15 or more employees. Discrimination on the basis of age (40 and over) is also prohibited in companies having 20 or more employees by federal laws. More specifically, these laws are the Age Discrimination in Employment Act of 1967, as amended in 1978 and in 1986, as well as the Older Workers Benefit Protection Act of 1990. There are exceptions to the prohibitions against age discrimination that pertain to executives, firefighters, police, and some governmental officials. Furthermore, another federal law, the Pregnancy Discrimination Act of 1978, which amended the Civil Rights Act, prohibits employers, having 20 more employees, from discriminating against pregnant women. Finally, employers are prohibited by the Americans with Disabilities Act of 1990 from discriminating against disabled individuals. This federal law, which applies to those employers having at least 15 employees, also requires reasonable accommodation of such individuals. In essence, the law requires employers to make reasonable changes in the workplace environment, such as installing more lighting or installing devices allowing easier operation of equipment so that a person with a disability can perform the work.[26] In addition to these federal prohibitions, state laws also prohibit similar forms of discrimination and often include

SUPERVISORS AND ETHICS

There are several reasons for the underrepresentation of women in the executive ranks of corporations in the United States. While one legitimate reason includes withdrawal of women from the labor force for child-rearing activities, others raise serious questions about the extent to which women have been treated ethically and with respect.

Top businesswomen in America give three main explanations for why so few of them reach "C-level"—that group of executives who prefaced their titles with the word "chief." First comes the exclusion from informal networks. In many firms jock-talk and late-night boozing still oil the wheels of progress. In America and elsewhere it has become almost traditional for sales teams to take potential clients to strip clubs and the like. These activities specifically exclude most women . . . The second hurdle is . . . pervasive stereotyping of women's capacity for leadership. Everyone is unconsciously biased and there is strong evidence that men are biased against promoting women inside companies . . . some companies have begun to take special steps to guard against bias . . . The third hurdle is the lack of role models. There are too few women in top jobs to show how it is done.

Source: "The Conundrum of the Glass Ceiling," *The Economist* (July 21, 2005): 63–65.

small employers that may be excluded from coverage by federal laws. Furthermore, most employers have policies prohibiting such discrimination, and most collective bargaining agreements also contain similar prohibitions.

Federal law does not preclude discrimination on the basis of sexual orientation. Nonetheless, 12 states and the District of Columbia prohibit such actions. Such prohibitions are more prevalent at the local level as hundreds of cities and counties have similar prohibitions.[27] Employers also prohibit discrimination on the basis of sexual orientation, and by 2003 2,326 employers had adopted such policies.[28]

In addition to the legal prohibitions, discrimination is also inconsistent with supervisory values. This chapter's feature on supervisors and ethics deals with the unethical treatment of women.

GUIDANCE FOR SUPERVISORS

Better performance is likely when diverse employees feel that they can be themselves in the workplace. A survey by the Society for Human Resource Management and *Fortune* found that 91 percent of respondents felt that their companies obtained a competitive advantage from their diversity initiatives while 79 percent perceived that such initiatives improved morale. In addition, 79 percent believed that diversity efforts improved their company cultures and 77 percent perceived that such efforts facilitated recruitment.[29]

The laws, various court rulings over their application, and the rules of governmental enforcement agencies make up a huge amount of information, and there are frequent regulatory and court decisions, which affect their application. Because of the complexity involved, supervisors should consult their employers' human resource experts to obtain guidance on specific questions about actions that are subject to such laws and regulations. Nonetheless, there is an underlying rationale of these laws and regulations, which supervisors should keep in mind. This rationale is that employers cannot use any of these classifications, such as race, sex, and age, to make employment decisions related to hiring, compensating, promoting, assigning, terminating employees, and so on. Instead, employers must make employment decisions on the basis of individual behaviors and characteristics as opposed to an employee's membership in any class.

The examples of continuing discrimination should serve as strong reminders to supervisors that they should consider all employees as individuals who should be viewed on the basis of how well they can perform the duties of their jobs. It is dangerous to consider employees as members of a class of people, such as African Americans or women, and to use such classifications to make inferences about their abilities to perform jobs. The use of such information to make employment decisions is not only unethical but is also illegal, and the costs to organizations for violations, as noted earlier in Exhibit 12.1, are enormous. Such attributions are also poor management decisions because of the invalidity of the class-based assumptions that are made. It has been observed that instances of outright racial discrimination, where the intention is to deny employment or fail to promote employees because of their race or color, are less frequent today than in the past. Instead, remaining instances of racial discrimination typically result more from faulty assumptions employers make about the qualifications or the abilities of classes of people, such as African Americans or Native Americans, to perform the job. Again, supervisors must guard against the tendency to ascribe characteristics to individuals because of their membership in a class.[30]

Learning Objective Number Two

INCREASING WORKFORCE DIVERSITY

In the United States, the workforce is becoming increasingly diverse and the management of such a workforce is also becoming more complicated. Furthermore, the management of diversity in the future will encompass a wider range of diversity. The breadth of the concept is demonstrated in the following comments of Maia Veal, the president of the Minnesota chapter of Black Engineers:

> "Generally, when someone hears diversity, they think black and white, but it's much more than that," Veal said. "If they think diversity means only African-American then they are in trouble because they will be missing key groups."[31]

The significance of the extent to which diversity is increasing is evident in the following observation about new entrants into the 2008 U.S. workforce, its change from the earlier times, and the economic impact for U.S. businesses:

> "Females, minorities, and foreign-born personnel are projected to produce 85 percent of the net new growth in the U.S. workforce . . . In 1960, nine out of ten consumers were white. Currently, it is estimated that only six out of ten are white . . . Organizations are looking at ways to align their organizations to the new realities of their customer base."[32]

RACIAL DIVERSITY

The United States, which had a total population of almost 291 million people in 2003, is a very racially diverse country, as shown in Exhibit 12.2. Of the total population, approximately 68 to 69 percent of the people are White non-Hispanic, approximately 13 to 14 percent are Hispanic, approximately 13 percent are Black or African American, slightly over 4 percent are Asian, almost 1 percent are American Indian or Alaskan native, and .17 percent are Native Hawaiian and Pacific Islanders. Over 4 million people, or approximately 1.5 percent of the population, belong to two or more races, which adds even greater diversity to the U.S population.[33]

Exhibit 12.3 provides a breakdown on the education of the three largest racial categories in the United States as revealed by supplemental studies to the Bureau of the

Racial diversity in the United States.   EXHIBIT 12.2

	2002 POPULATION (IN MILLIONS)	2002 PERCENT OF U.S. POPULATION	2003 POPULATION*** (IN MILLIONS)	2003 PERCENT OF U.S. POPULATION
White alone, non-Hispanic	194.8	69.0	197.3	67.85
Hispanic or Latino origin*	37.4	13.3	39.9	13.72
Black or African American alone**	36.0	13.0	37.1	12.76
American Indian, Alaska Native alone	n/a	n/a	2.8	.96
Asian alone	n/a	n/a	11.9	4.10
Native Hawaiian, Other Pacific Islander alone	n/a	n/a	.5	.17
Two or More Races	n/a	n/a	4.3	1.48

*The origin of Hispanics is racially heterogeneous.

**Data for 2002 overstate the number of blacks because 3.7 percent are Hispanic Blacks.

***Because of the heterogeneity of the Hispanic category, there is some overlap in the data and the percentages total to slightly more than 100 percent; the population in each category adds to slightly more than the U.S. population total.

Sources: Jesse McKinnon. "The Black Population in the United States: March 2002," *Current Population Reports*, U.S. Department of Commerce, Economics and Statistics Administration, U.S. Census Bureau (April 2003). Roberto R. Ramirez and G. Patricia de la Cruz. "The Hispanic Population in the United States: March 2002," *Current Population Reports*, U.S. Department of Commerce, Economics and Statistics Administration, U.S. Census Bureau (June 2003). U.S. Census Bureau. *USA Statistics in Brief—Race and Hispanic Origin*, (January 18, 2005), *www.census.gov/statab/www/racehiisp.html.*

EXHIBIT 12.3	Educational attainment by race in the United States.		

	NON-HISPANIC WHITES	BLACK	HISPANIC
Percentage of Population, Age 25 and Older, with at Least a High School Diploma	88.7%	79.0%	57.0%
Percentage of Population, Age 25 and Older, with at Least a Bachelor's Degree	29.4%	17.0%	11.1%
Percentage of Population, Under Age 18	22.8%	33.0%	34.4%

Sources: Jesse McKinnon. "The Black Population in the United States: March 2002," *Current Population Reports*, U.S. Department of Commerce, Economics and Statistics Administration, U.S. Census Bureau (April 2003). Roberto R. Ramirez and G. Patricia de la Cruz. "The Hispanic Population in the United States: March 2002," *Current Population Reports*, U.S. Department of Commerce, Economics and Statistics Administration, U.S. Census Bureau (June 2003).

Census, *2002 Current Population Survey*. As can be seen, Hispanic and African American populations have a faster growth rate than Caucasians, as evidenced by the percentage of the population under age 18, and there will be increased diversity in the future. Exhibit 12.3 also reflects another important trend, which is the difference in average levels of educational attainment. As employers look to the future, they will need to develop educational programs that offset the educational lag in the Hispanic population. As indicated in the exhibit, only 57 percent of the Hispanic population has at least a high school diploma, while 88.7 percent of the Caucasian and 79 percent of the Black or African American populations have at least high school diplomas. Although Hispanics account for an increasing proportion of the workforce, they are dramatically underrepresented in the managerial ranks as they account for only 5 percent of managerial positions. African Americans are also underrepresented as they account for only 6.5 percent of managerial positions.[34]

It should be noted that the term "Hispanic" is often misunderstood because it represents several races.[35] Indeed, there is substantial diversity within the category of Hispanics. The category of Hispanics in the United States consists of the following origins: Mexican (66.9 percent), Central and South American (14.3 percent), Puerto Rican (8.6 percent), Cuban (3.7 percent), and other Hispanic (6.5 percent).[36] In addition, within the Hispanic or Latino category, there are major differences in educational attainment, which have implications for workforce issues. More specifically, only 7.6 percent of Hispanics with Mexican origins, ages 25 and older, had at least a bachelor's degree compared with 18.6 percent for Hispanics with Cuban origins and 17.3 percent for Hispanics with Central and South American origins. Another source of diversity within the Hispanic population is that 40.2 percent were foreign born.[37]

DIVERSITY

High performing organizations understand the importance of having the talent that comes from diversity, such as this team of professional women.

Supervisors will need to work effectively with women, as they comprise an increasing proportion of the labor force. As indicated in Exhibit 12.4, the labor force participation rates for women have exhibited a steady increase for many years. For example, their participation rate in 1980 was 59.7 percent, in 1990 it was 68.5 percent, and by 2001, their participation rate had increased to 70.7 percent. The United States is not the only country in which this trend is occurring, as many developed countries have experienced the same shift. Exhibit 12.4 also provides a comparison of the proportion of women who are in the labor force, and women in the United States, have some of the highest participation rates of any country. It is interesting to note that the percentage of the labor force accounted for by women has also grown in Mexico and Canada, two of the closest trading partners of the United States. While the participation rates for women in Mexico are much lower, they have grown substantially over this period. One exception to the increasing representation of women is represented by Turkey's declining proportion of women in the labor force. Supervisors who may take on international assignments will need to be aware of cultural differences that relate to women's involvement in the work environment.

In addition to increasing labor force participation rates, in the United States, women now make up a larger proportion of each year's class of college graduates at the bachelor's degree level. In 2003, women received 57 percent of bachelor's degrees, which was up from 53 percent in 1989. The differential between women and men is expected to increase, and by 2014 women are expected to account for 60 percent of bachelor's degrees. While men still account for more doctoral degree graduates each year, by 2014 women are expected to account for 51 percent of such graduates.[38]

Exhibit 12.4	Comparison of labor force participation rates for women.

	FEMALE LABOR FORCE DIVIDED BY FEMALE POPULATION 15–64 YEARS OLD			
	1980	**1990**	**1995**	**2001**
Denmark	n/a	78.5	73.6	76.0
Sweden	74.1	80.4	76.1	75.5
United States	59.7	68.5	70.7	70.7
Canada	57.8	67.6	67.6	70.5
United Kingdom	58.3	66.5	66.6	67.5
Australia	52.7	62.1	64.8	66.2
Germany	52.8	56.7	61.7	64.5
Japan	54.8	60.3	62.2	64.4
France	54.4	57.8	59.4	63.8
Spain	32.2	41.2	45.1	50.9
Mexico	33.7	n/a	40.1	41.6
Turkey	n/a	36.7	34.2	26.5

Source: Extracted from U.S. Census Bureau, *Statistical Abstract of the United States: 2004–2005*, Last Revised August 1, 2005 [on-line version, accessed September 18, 2005].

While progress could always be better, consider the proportion of management positions held by women in two of *Fortune*'s top 100 companies: Merck—31 percent, and Patagonia—more than 50 percent.[39] Women have earned top positions in other companies as well. For example, Anne Mulcahy is the chairman and CEO at Xerox, where she has successfully returned the company from the verge of bankruptcy to profitability.[40] Myrtle Potter, an African American woman, is president of commercial operations at Genentech, Inc.[41] In addition, Mary Minnick, is president of marketing, strategy, and innovation at Coca Cola.[42] Outside the United States, women are making slow progress into the top positions. For example, although there are very few women in top executive positions in China, Xie Qihua, is the chairwoman of Shanghai Baosteel Group Corp., the largest steel and iron company in China.[43] In Japan, Jumiko Hayashi is the CEO of Daiei, a supermarket chain, while Tomoyo Nonaka is the CEO of Sanyo Electric.[44]

DIVERSITY

AGE DIVERSITY

In addition to a growing representation of minorities in the workforce, there are also changes in the age composition of the workforce. The workforce has a higher

Comparisons of age cohorts.

EXHIBIT 12.5

	CIVILIAN LABOR FORCE PERCENT DISTRIBUTION						
	16–19	20–24	25–34	35–44	45–54	55–64	65 AND OVER
1980	8.8	14.9	27.3	19.1	15.8	11.2	2.9
1990	6.2	11.7	28.6	25.5	16.1	9.2	2.7
1995	5.9	10.3	25.8	27.0	19.1	9.0	2.9
2000	5.8	10.0	23.0	26.3	21.8	10.1	3.0
2003	4.9	10.2	22.1	25.0	22.7	11.8	3.3

Source: Extracted from U.S. Census Bureau. *Statistical Abstract of the United States: 2004–2005*, Last Revised August 1, 2005 [on-line version, accessed September 18, 2005].

representation of older workers, many of which are expected to work longer. In addition, as indicated in Exhibit 12.5, the age distribution of the workforce has cohorts of dramatically different sizes. The exhibit indicates that there have been steady declines in the proportion of the labor force accounted for in the age 20 to 24 and age 25 to 34 cohorts. While some of the declines in the 20 to 24 age cohort may be accounted for by the number of people who are not in the labor force because they are pursuing college degrees, these are meaningful changes in the labor force, which will have a ripple effect in the future. On the other hand, older workers in the 45 to 54, 55 to 64, and 65 and over age cohorts are now at their highest proportions of the labor force going back to 1980. It is important to note that some of the changes in age cohorts involve relatively small percentages. Nonetheless, because the U.S. civilian labor force includes approximately 150 million people, small percentages can represent millions of workers.[45] With changes in age distributions, there will be corresponding differences in the values of the different age cohorts that supervisors will need to consider in managing a diverse workforce.

One interesting development is that more than 25 percent of the present workforce is expected to reach retirement age by 2010. A survey, conducted by the Accenture consulting firm, has reported that approximately 45 percent of companies are not taking actions to capture the knowledge of such employees who are expected to retire in the relatively near future. Unless the knowledge of these workers is captured, such as their business networks, and succession plans are developed, organizations will be at a disadvantage in the future.[46]

Although the racial and gender aspects of diversity probably receive the greatest amount of attention in most organizations, older workers are also an important dimension in the management of diversity. In the United States by 1972, people over 65 years of age accounted for 10 percent of the population, and this proportion is increasing.[47] Over the past 10 years, there has been a substantial increase in the United States in the number of older people who are still working. More specifically, 33 percent of men and

23 percent of women, ages 65 to 69, are working today, as opposed to 27 percent and 18 percent, respectively, in 1994.[48] Furthermore, it is apparent that a large proportion of older workers want to continue working as a recent survey by HSBC Holdings found that only 19 percent of respondents in the United States intend to stop working for compensation when they reach retirement age. Of those who plan to continue working, 11 percent intend to continue working on a full-time basis. Those who desire to keep working want greater flexibility with options for part-time work and the ability to alternate between leisure and work periods.[49]

GLOBAL

INTERNATIONAL DIVERSITY

As indicated in Exhibit 12.6, there is increasing international diversity in developed countries. In some industries, this source of diversity is very pronounced, such as those that are technical in nature. Indeed, immigration laws in the United States provide preferential treatment for individuals who have critical skills.[50] U.S. immigration data from 2002 indicate that the following countries provided the largest number of immigrants: China, El Salvador, India, Mexico, Philippines, and Vietnam. In addition, large numbers of unauthorized or illegal immigrants come from Mexico with smaller numbers from El Salvador, Guatemala, Columbia, Honduras, China, and other countries.[51] Such immigrants may work in a broad range of industries, but unauthorized immigrants are frequently concentrated in manual labor, construction or lower wage jobs, and jobs requiring lower education and skill.

Learning Objective Number Three

EXHIBIT 12.6

Foreign-born labor force representation in developed countries.

COUNTRY	% OF TOTAL LABOR FORCE
Australia	24.9
Canada	19.9
Switzerland	18.1
United States	13.9
Austria	11.0
Germany	9.1
France	6.2
Sweden	5.1
United Kingdom	4.4
Japan	0.2

Source: Extracted from U.S. Census Bureau. *Statistical Abstract of the United States: 2004–2005*, Last Revised August 1, 2005 [on-line version, accessed September 18, 2005].

VIEWS ON MANAGING DIVERSITY

ASSIMILATION APPROACH

Companies have taken three approaches to the management of diversity. The first approach emphasizes a blending in process in which people of color and women are expected to adapt to the culture of the majority. With this approach, the value and uniqueness of their backgrounds, perspectives, and cultures are ignored for the objective of assimilation. The **assimilation paradigm** is more advanced than the older affirmative action view, which tended to place emphasis on compliance with equal employment opportunity legislation, recruitment practices, and fairness issues. Nonetheless, this paradigm still retains the affirmative action focus on quantitative goals, such as hiring and retention goals, and does not attempt to capture the value that diverse perspectives can add. Organizations guided by this view, which are typically somewhat bureaucratic, take actions to insure that employees receive equal treatment and provide protections for due process. Such organizations have increased the level of demographic diversity in their workforces and frequently obtain success in providing fair treatment. However, their blending-in or assimilation approaches, which in essence maintain that gender and race should be ignored, may not enable them to capture some of the benefits of diverse cultural backgrounds, such as a Latin female's insights on an ethnic market segment.[52]

DIFFERENTIATION APPROACH

In contrast to the color and gender blind assimilation approach, the differentiation approach attempts to capture the value of the unique knowledge and the legitimacy associated with a diverse workforce. As noted, people of color or women may have cultural insights, which provide advantages in marketing to or gaining access to a demographic market segment or cultural group. For example, African Americans may be assigned to marketing efforts concerned with urban communities. Organizations following this approach, such as those in consumer products industries, often assign women and people of color to work on ethnic or demographic market segments in order to gain insights of such markets or access. As a result of the **differentiation paradigm,** people of color and women are segregated by their jobs and may sometimes feel that they are being exploited. In addition, organizations following this approach sometimes overlook the other abilities of women and people of color, which keeps them out of the mainstream activities of the organization. They also frequently fail to understand any culturally related practices or skills that enable these employees to achieve success in their market segment assignments.[53]

INTEGRATION APPROACH

In addition to the assimilation and differentiation paradigms, a newer approach is being adopted because of its ability to capture more of the value of diversity. Interestingly, organizations guided by the **integration paradigm,** or inclusion approach, have discovered that the cultural and demographic backgrounds of their employees are

Learning Objective Number Three

assimilation paradigm an approach to diversity in which minorities are expected to adapt to the majority culture and which captures few of the benefits of diversity

differentiation paradigm an approach to diversity in which people of color and women enable the organization to gain access to ethnic and demographic markets and which often results in job segregation

integration paradigm an inclusion approach to the management of diversity in which women and people of color are fully integrated into all aspects of the organization and which captures the full benefit of diversity

often reflected in some of their work decisions and choices. One of the other advantages of this view is that women and people of color perceive greater respect for the value they add to the organization and that they are not viewed as window dressing. Several preconditions of the integrated approach to diversity are relevant to supervisors. One precondition is that there should be an emphasis on openness and tolerance for constructive conflict and debate. In addition, all employees should feel that their culturally or demographic-related perspectives are valued. For example, one firm, which assumed that its model of rewarding fast-paced cold calls was an optimal approach, learned from the success of two top-performing women that more deliberate and relationship-oriented calls, produced excellent results. Other preconditions are that all employees should feel valued and encouraged to apply their unique experiences in their work, should be provided with developmental opportunities related to their jobs, and should be evaluated by the same high performance standards. In addition, egalitarianism should prevail in which all employees are encouraged to contribute ideas and are challenged to do things differently with the merit of the idea being the key determinant of implementation rather than rank.[54] While this approach toward diversity has much to offer, there is evidence that greater progress is still needed. In a recent survey, less than one-third of the employee respondents indicated that their companies' diversity programs were effective.[55]

There are a number of companies that provide good models for managing diversity. PepsiCo has been a leader in this area and has been cited as one of the top five companies for diversity. By 2004, women accounted for 29 percent of the senior management positions above midlevel at PepsiCo. The company has an explicit goal of inclusion, which it is pursuing with multiple initiatives, such as by increasing the level of innovation in products and marketing and by capitalizing on the perspectives of diverse employees. PepsiCo's CEO, Steve Reinemund, has stated that those companies that are the quickest at mastering the challenges of diversity will obtain a clear advantage over their competitors. The company is also pursuing more traditional diversity approaches by working on the retention of its diverse workforce.[56] The views of PepsiCo's president and chief financial officer, Indra Nooyi, on the company's approach to inclusiveness have been summarized as follows:

> "The full potential of diversity is not realized without an inclusive culture."
> She wants employees to become "comfortable being uncomfortable" so
> they're willing to broach difficult issues in the workplace.[57]

PepsiCo's approach to inclusiveness has been described as gutsy as the CEO has assigned explicit responsibilities to his top management team. Reinemund directed his top executives to serve as sponsors for several diverse groups of people within the company, which are defined by race, gender, sexual orientation, and disability. Each executive also has an assignment of mentoring three or more employees in his groups. Furthermore, in the majority of the assignments the executives do not share the same diversity of their groups. For example, the Latino group is sponsored by a white woman, the African American group is matched with a white man, and white men are mentored by an African American, who is also the company's general counsel.[58]

The implications from PepsiCo's example for managing diversity are that supervisors need to be willing to address the difficult issues that sometimes occur with diversity. Those supervisors who approach the issues with sensitivity and think of their employees as unique individuals, rather than uniform members of a class, will be better managers of diversity and will be more likely to be given some slack by their employees when they make a mistake.

PERFORMANCE

GENERAL PRACTICES FOR MANAGING DIVERSITY

RECRUITING

While organizational recruiting policies are normally determined by the human resource function, supervisors need to become actively involved in ensuring that their units or teams have diverse workforces. One of the ways that they can do this is by becoming involved with internship programs. In most organizations, it is relatively easy to obtain support for internships and is often simply a matter of expressing a desire to utilize interns during summers or even during regular academic semesters on a part-time basis. Internships are being increasingly utilized as a recruiting tool as well as a selection process that provides a good assessment opportunity for decisions whether to extend an offer for a permanent job. Internships have become very important for diversity, and there is anecdotal evidence that many companies are very interested in bringing in women and minorities for such opportunities:[59] The director of university relations at General Mills says, "Ultimately we want a workforce that reflects the community we are in."[60]

Increased success is likely when supervisors become involved with organizations for minorities and women at local colleges and universities. An example of the benefits of such involvement is provided by student internships, which can provide a pipeline of diverse candidates for the organization as indicated in the following quote from the president of the Black Engineers chapter in Minnesota: "When you start at the internship level . . . that's the best way to incorporate diversity as a whole into the company."[61]

PERFORMANCE MANAGEMENT

One of the ways in which supervisors can be better managers of diversity is to modify their approach to performance management. Potential improvements are likely when supervisors are sensitive to diversity issues in the performance appraisal process. More specifically, supervisors should be careful to guard against the **like me bias** when evaluating diverse associates. The like me, or **similar to me bias,** can result from unintentional tendencies to evaluate people who are similar to us more highly. Over time, if the pattern persists, there will be a replication of the same majority in higher-level positions because of their more favorable evaluations. One suggestion for reducing the incidence of this bias is that supervisors should focus on results when appraising performance. Such a focus on results should help prevent evaluation on such irrelevant and biased factors, such as appearance.[62]

Supervisors should also take care to develop an awareness of the biases of others as they collect information on which to base their performance evaluations. Other supervisors, associates, customers, and managers provide information that influences evaluations of performance, and supervisors need to consider potential biases from

like me bias or **similar to me bias** the tendency for supervisors and managers to provide higher performance evaluations and selection interview ratings to people similar to them

Diversity enables organizations to expand their knowledge base because of the differences in perspectives that diverse employees bring to the job.

such sources as they conduct their evaluations. In addition, supervisors need to be aware that in some instances, these sources may not provide completely candid views of diverse associates because of concerns that they may be perceived as racist or sexist.[63]

Another practice, which supervisors should adopt, is to provide candid performance feedback and coaching to their diverse associates. Unfortunately, because of concerns that they will be viewed as being prejudiced, some supervisors provide feedback that is too general and unspecific to be of value to their diverse associates. Supervisors obviously need to provide such feedback and can increase the specificity by focusing on the key tasks of the associate's job. By reviewing the key tasks before the appraisal or evaluation, they can develop the detail needed to make the feedback and coaching more valuable. In addition, supervisors should also develop a sense of the frequency with which diverse associates have access to informal information, such as from peers and other supervisors, which is needed for improved performance. Because diverse employees may not have equal access to valuable informal sources of information, their development may be slowed. Accordingly, supervisors need to ensure that this information is made available.[64]

Exhibit 12.7 provides a list of companies that have been successful in managing diversity as it lists the top 10 companies for African Americans, Latinos, and women.

SPECIFIC SKILLS FOR MANAGING DIVERSITY

Supervisors can prevent problems from arising in diverse groups and teams by following some basic practices. While these practices have general applicability to all groups and teams, if these basics are not addressed in the context of diversity, misunderstandings, conflicts, and disappointments may be more likely to occur.

Top ten companies for diversity.		**EXHIBIT 12.7**
TOP 10 COMPANIES FOR AFRICAN AMERICANS	**TOP 10 COMPANIES FOR LATINOS**	**TOP 10 COMPANIES FOR EXECUTIVE WOMEN**
1. PepsiCo	1. PepsiCo	1. Abbott Laboratories
2. Altria Group	2. Citigroup	2. Staples
3. Colgate-Palmolive	3. Unilever Foods, N.A.	3. Altria Group
4. Xerox	4. Health Care Service Corp.	4. Turner Broadcasting System
5. Citigroup	5. Colgate-Palmolive	5. The New York Times Co.
6. Allstate Insurance	6. SBC Communications	6. Sears, Roebuck & Co.
7. Health Care Service Corp.	7. Abbott Laboratories	7. Marriott International
8. Ford Motor Co.	8. The Coca-Cola Co.	8. Knight Ridder
9. Kaiser Permanente	9. JPMorgan Chase	9. Pepsi Bottling Group
10. Turner Broadcasting System	10. Tribune Co.	10. MasterCard

Sources: Sonja Sherwood and Jonny Mendelsson, "Marriott Goes Far Beyond the Numbers," *DiversityInc* (October 2005): 30 and 32. Reproduced with permission. Sonja Sherwood and Jonny Mendelsson, "Pepsico's Reinemund Takes His Faith in Diversity to a New Level," *DiversityInc* (October 2005): 36. Reproduced with permission.

QUICK RESPONSE TO DISAGREEMENTS

When there are disagreements or misunderstandings, the likelihood that serious conflict will occur can be reduced by a quick response on the part of the supervisor. Because supervisors sometimes suppress or ignore divergent views, attempt to avoid the unpleasantness of disagreements, or hope that disagreements will fade away, they do not address the issues and their silence becomes misconstrued. As a result of their failure to respond, they lose the opportunity to obtain clarification and promote resolution of the misunderstanding, and simple misunderstandings may escalate. Those whose inputs were ignored or suppressed may conclude that they are not valued, perhaps because of their diversity. Furthermore, such suppression or disregard of different views is likely to reduce performance. Because good decisions in work settings require **creative tension** and the full considerations of associates' suggestions and perspectives, a failure to work through these inputs is likely to result in sub-optimal decision-making. With greater diversity in groups and organizations, there are typically more varied views and perspectives, which typically produce more disagreements and conflict.[65]

creative tension the interaction of differences in problem solving and creative activities in which diversity-related differences in perspectives leads to superior results

ACTIVE LISTENING

Many communication problems can be avoided with active listening. The essence of active listening is to ensure that the real message is understood and to reassure the speaker that the listener does indeed value and understand his or her perspective. Such listening, which involves such techniques as restating the speaker's message, seeking clarification, asking questions, and not arguing, takes time and involves hard work. Nonetheless, supervisors can probably make some of their most meaningful contributions by listening to associates. In contrast, when associates feel that the supervisor is not listening, they may feel unappreciated, disconnected, and isolated. With diverse groups or teams, where there is increased risk of isolation or marginal inclusion, supervisors' failures to listen seem likely to create a sense of disconnection.[66] In addition to listening actively, improved communication can be promoted with empathetic listening.

EMPATHETIC LISTENING

Empathetic listening is particularly helpful when diversity is involved. One of the communication problems in the context of diversity results from incorrect assumptions that we have about each other. The techniques involved in empathetic listening enable supervisors to avoid such barriers. Aside from the first step of developing a commitment to understand the other person, the next step in such listening is to suspend our assumptions or preconceptions about the person, based on what we expect to hear as a result of cultural conditioning. The third step is to act as a host of the associate who has a message to convey. By acting as if we were the host of the messenger, we acknowledge the feelings of the guest and make him or her feel safe and comfortable. Facts are then pursued but only after feelings are addressed and a safe environment for the guest has been created. The final step is to employ the active listening technique of checking for the accuracy of the message we have heard.[67]

DIRECT AND HONEST COMMUNICATION

mentoring relationships
formal or informal relationships between senior or experienced managers, supervisors, or employees to provide career-enhancing advice, feedback, and information to less experienced employees

As noted earlier, supervisors are sometimes reluctant to provide direct and honest feedback to minority associates because of fear that they will be viewed as biased. As a result, supervisors hold back their real views, and associates are deprived of valuable information that would have enabled them to improve their performance.[68] In addition, because of the importance of more subtle and informal feedback, there is a considerable upside benefit with **mentoring relationships,** in which such honest feedback is shared, especially for women and minorities. While supervisors are not expected to take on the responsibilities for mentoring programs within their organizations, they can arrange for informal mentoring relationships within their own units or by recruiting mentors from other units. In setting up mentoring relationships, it is important to make mentoring available to all employees who wish to be involved because, when they are restricted only to women and minorities, jealousy among excluded associates is a predictable result.[69]

When diverse groups or teams draw on the contributions of everyone, organizations are able to make better decisions.

INPUT FROM EVERYONE

When making group decisions or obtaining input from associates for decisions to be made by the supervisor, it is important to ensure that the views of all employees are obtained. Supervisors must be persistent in encouraging the expression of views or in obtaining the views of all employees.[70] While such input may not be initially forthcoming from women and minorities, at least initially, sincere attempts to get everyone involved should persuade everyone that their views are desired and should produce future involvement.

AVOIDANCE OF EXCLUSION

Unfortunately, women and minorities often find that they are unintentionally excluded from informal activities, such as being left out of an invitation to go to lunch. When a woman is the only one in a group, there may be an inclination to assume that she would not want to participate in an all-male outing. On the other hand, there may be concerns that a woman might be offended by an informal off-site gathering in which salty language and off-color humor may occur. Clearly, supervisors must guard against situations in which women or men feel that they are placed in a hostile environment in terms of sexual harassment. Nonetheless, supervisors should ensure that associates are not insensitive to women and that there is no pattern of exclusion in which women and minorities are simply not invited to participate in common workplace social interactions, such as having opportunities to go to lunch with coworkers. Such exclusion exacts a heavy toll on women and minorities and contributes to a sense of isolation.[71]

REWARD SYSTEMS

While most supervisors are not involved in the design of the organization's compensation system, they should be aware of how such systems can affect efforts that lead to better management of diversity. For example, performance on a diversity dimension now affects the compensation of top executives at Bell South. At United Technologies an executive is designated as the company's director for diversity, with responsibilities for wide-ranging activities and programs.[72] Another example is provided by ALA-GASCO, an Alabama-based utility company, that pays employees $500 for ideas on how to deal with diversity problems in their units.[73]

PRACTICES FOR SPECIFIC GROUPS

Learning Objective Number Four

DIVERSITY

two-way mentoring
mentoring relationships involving people of different races or genders

affinity groups
groups of people, such as women, African Americans, Latinos, and so on, who have minority status in an organization and who are not well represented in senior positions

PEOPLE OF COLOR AND RACIAL DIVERSITY

Mentoring

As noted earlier, mentoring is critical to the successful management of diversity. **Two-way mentoring,** which involves people of different races, is recommended for broader cultural exposure.[74] This is advantageous because there is typically an under-representation of people of color at higher levels in the managerial hierarchy who can serve as mentors.

Affinity Groups

Affinity groups may be particularly helpful for people of color to develop informal sources of information and informal networks within organizations. Supervisors can support affinity groups by attending sessions and making associates aware of such groups. Many leading companies have established these groups, such as Nike, which has established affinity groups for African Americans, other minorities, lesbians, and gays.[75]

Identifying with and Contributing to the Unit

Supervisors can use several approaches to help ensure positive working relationships with racially diverse work groups. Research on intergroup relations suggests that when units are placed in competition with each other, biases between the groups are expected to increase. On the other hand, cooperation between groups tends to reduce such biases. Supervisors can apply these results at the individual level to reduce biases. Strengthening a work team or department's identification with the unit itself has the potential to reduce tensions and biases among members of the unit.[76] Thus, it is important for supervisors to establish a unique positive identity for their unit, clarify a compelling and motivating goal for the unit, stress by actions and words that all employees are members of the unit, and persuade employees that the goal can best be accomplished by cooperation and positive relationships among all employees.

It is critically important that supervisors make racially diverse employees feel that they are critical to the unit's success and that their contributions are valued. This is illustrated in the following account:

In one education session, an African American woman explained that she was willing to stay late to deal with last-minute needs when she was in an organization in which she felt valued and acknowledged. In situations where she felt that going the extra mile was not valued or her effort seen, however, she was unwilling to work beyond what was required.[77]

Critical Mass

While supervisors typically must abide by staffing limits determined at higher levels within the organization, they should be mindful of the benefits of having a critical mass of minorities or people of color in the groups and teams that they supervise. One of the clear findings of empirical research on diversity is that **tokenism** and stereotyping can occur in situations in which there are only individuals or very small numbers of people of color or women. In addition, having larger numbers of diverse employees in the work group tends to build more cooperative interpersonal relations and reduces the likelihood of stereotyping of token numbers of diverse employees. Accordingly, it is desirable to have sufficient integration to move beyond the situation in which only one individual or a very small number of African Americans or Latinos serve as tokens.[78] The problem of very low representation is captured as follows:

> Social scientific studies and the firsthand accounts of outsiders confirm that it is token or near-token outsiders who suffer the most from stereotyping, and from the felt need to "act white," as well as from hostility and harassment. More thoroughly integrated workplaces can foster more symmetrical and more genuine cooperative relations.[79]

Compelling Objective

When racially diverse employees are forced to work together in order to get the job done and buy into a compelling objective, there is greater likelihood that positive interpersonal relationships will develop. The U.S. Army's ability to manage diversity is a shining example of the success that is possible with the application of authority to build effective racially diverse working relationships.[80]

> Hierarchical authority, where it is brought to bear on the project of racial integration, can achieve impressive advances in racial relations. The success of integration in the military, and particularly in the Army, stands as a testament to the potentially democratic uses of hierarchy . . . Even if we could, it would be absurd to argue that the military model could or should be transported into ordinary workplaces. But the military model reminds us of the troubling but familiar tension between freedom and equality. It also reminds us that people can be compelled to get along with each other.[81]

This chapter's feature on supervising teams describes how one company has captured value from using diverse teams.

WOMEN

Flexible Work Policies

It should be no surprise that the number of hours people work in the United States is higher than in other developed countries. For example, each year U.S. workers

tokenism
having only one or very few women or minorities in a unit or job classification solely to provide window dressing for equal employment opportunity purposes

TEAMS

SUPERVISING TEAMS

Diverse interdisciplinary teams are being used to make breakthroughs in marketing in a number of leading companies. One such company is L'Oréal, which makes cosmetics, skincare, haircare, and other personal grooming products. The company has several leading product lines and its Maybelline brand has become the top cosmetics brand in the world, a feat which L'Oréal credits to its commitment to diversity. The French-based company takes pride in its reputation for innovation and touts its emphasis on international diversity, such as in the models and actresses who serve as spokespersons for the company's products. In addition to emphasizing diversity in its advertising and public image, the company embraces diversity throughout the entire organization. L'Oréal attributes its innovation and ability to conquer business challenges to its diverse workforce. Diversity makes a great deal of sense to L'Oréal as the company and its subsidiaries have a presence in 150 countries.

The company's use of diverse teams has led to much of the innovation that made the Maybelline brand, which was not part of L'Oréal until the 1990s, so successful. L'Oréal initiated the process by putting together teams with professionals having widely varying backgrounds and relocated the teams and the headquarters of Maybelline from Memphis to New York City. The diverse teams then developed marketing efforts for its targeted markets. Japan provides an example of one of L'Oréal's successes as the team was able to produce mascara that was appropriate for the eyelashes of Japanese women. L'Oréal's CEO says that diversity, which results from both differences in cultural and national origin backgrounds, is critical to the performance of the company. He also says that, because innovation and creativity are so important to the company's ability to compete in its markets, it is essential for the company to have diverse teams.

Source: L'Oréal website: *www.lorealparisusa.com* (January 20, 2006). Peggy A. Salz. "A Vital Building Block in Attaining That Competitive Edge Calls for the Creation of a Unique Corporate Anatomy," *Wall Street Journal* (May 2, 2005): A8.

***Learning
Objective
Number Five***

PERFORMANCE

put in 500 hours more than their German counterparts and 250 more than those in Britain. Furthermore, men also spend more time on the job in the United States than their women counterparts. In the financial industry, men put in a weekly average of 43.8 hours while women put in an average of 38.7 hours. Men in managerial jobs spend an average of 47.2 hours at work while the average for women is 39.4 hours. The pattern is evident in health services as well as men work 43.1 hours on average while women work 36.4 hours, and there is a similar differential for primary care physicians, with men working an average of 50 hours each week compared with 45 hours for women. The same gender differential also exists for lawyers with men working an average of 47.5 hours per week and women working an average of 43.0 hours. It has been observed that a result of these differences, in hours worked by men and women is that women, are underrepresented in the top positions in their firms.[82]

Supervisors need to remember that women often have greater childcare responsibilities than men and that some of these responsibilities may be reflected in the differential. Accordingly, providing flexibility in work scheduling can be enormously helpful for employees, both women and men, who have such responsibilities. Furthermore, survey data indicate that over 50 percent of women, at lower levels in the organization, have aspirations for senior leadership positions.[83] Nonetheless, work-life conflicts are issues to be considered:

> Those top jobs have become all-consuming . . . You have to give it your life. Since women tend to experience work-life conflicts more viscerally than their male peers, they're less likely to be willing to do that.[84]

Childcare Facilities

Many companies have achieved greater diversity in their workplaces by hiring more women, particularly in non-traditional jobs. In order to attract talented women to their companies and address their needs (and those of men as well), many companies have added on-site child-care facilities. All of the following companies, which have been in *Fortune*'s top 100 companies, have on-site child-care facilities: Fel-Pro, MBNA, S.C. Johnson Wax, ACXIOM, CMP Media, Lucas Digital, Mattel, St. Paul Companies, Quad/Graphics, Amgen, Motorola, Baptist Health Systems, William Beaumont Hospital, and Glaxo Smith Kline.[85]

Critical Mass

As with minorities or people of color, supervisors should attempt to obtain a critical mass of women in groups or teams in order to avoid situations in which there is only one woman. With increasing numbers of women in non-traditional jobs, there should be less difficulty staffing areas in which women have been poorly represented.

This chapter's feature on supervisors and performance discusses ways in which the work environment can be more welcoming for women.

PERFORMANCE

OLDER WORKERS

Learning Objective Number Six

Supervisors will have increased numbers of older workers in their workforces in the future as older people are working longer and account for larger proportions of the populations of many developed countries. This phenomenon is especially pronounced in Japan and Germany where there has been a dearth of younger workers, which has resulted from declining birth rates. In 2006, people aged 65 or older accounted for 20 percent of the Japanese population while Germany will reach the same level in 2009. Because of a shortage of workers, some Japanese employers are recruiting older workers. One such employer advertised for workers over 60 years of age and was overwhelmed with applications. The president of Sanwa Electric Company, which is based in Tokyo, has found that the capacity for workers over 60 years of age does not decrease, and his company has modified equipment to reduce the strain on older employees. For example, one such production modification involves a simple device, which eliminates awkward movements of the wrist.[88]

Leading employers of age-diverse workforces include companies such as Home Depot, Pitney Bowes, Wal-Mart, MetLife, Walgreen, and Principal Financial. Aside

GLOBAL

SUPERVISORS AND PERFORMANCE

One of the ways that supervisors can make the work environment more receptive to women is to adopt policies that allow more flexibility for child-care responsibilities. Such policies also pertain to men who are parents as well as to employees who have responsibilities to care for elderly parents. In addition to the cultural aspects of managing a diverse workforce, improved results can be obtained by providing support and flexibility for women and men with such responsibilities that enable them to be committed to the job without neglecting their family responsibilities.

Some employers have adopted enlightened approaches for helping women balance the demands of work and family responsibilities. More women, whose jobs occasionally involve travel, are taking their young children with them on business trips. Furthermore, an increasing number of hotels, such as Lowes Hotels, now provide camps for children, while others provide babysitting services or referrals. Nonetheless, some women have reported that experiences with very young children have been difficult, particularly when changes in schedules occur.

Marta Kagan, chief executive of Lifeline coaching, a New York firm that counsels people on leading balanced lives, urges clients to take children on business trips only if they expect to have a lot of free time to spend with them. "If you're never going to be available, what's the point?" she asked. "You've got a frazzled child who's off his routine, and you're going to feel like you're split in two."[86]

On the other hand, other women report good experiences with older children when significant personal time to be spent with children is built into the business trip. Supervisors can help make such options realistic possibilities for women by providing advance notice about potential travel requirements. Eva Wisnik, who is the president of a training firm for lawyers, has reported the following:

Still, traveling with them [her children] "is always the highlight of my year," she said. On occasion, it can also make doing business easier. Last year, when her oldest son, David, came along on a drive from Los Angeles to San Diego, he monitored her Black-Berry. "Whenever it buzzed, he would read the messages out to me," she said. "It was like I had my own personal assistant."[87]

Source: Melinda Ligos, "Business Travel: The Pacifier Isn't for the Client," *New York Times* (May 3, 2005). Copyright © (2007) by the New York Times Co. Reprinted with permission.

Learning Objective Number Seven

from the social responsibility aspects of such employment practices, there are sound financial reasons for such enlightened responses such as lower turnover and lower costs for recruitment and training. Borders Bookstores has found turnover to be much lower with older employees, ages 50 and over, as their turnover rate is one-tenth the rate of employees who are less than 30. These savings tend to offset increased costs, such as those associated with medical problems, making overall costs for different age cohorts at Borders about the same.[89]

INTERNATIONALS AND NATIONALITIES

Another source of diversity is related to the culture of people who have emigrated to the United States from other countries. Exhibit 12.8 presents several cultural issues that supervisors may encounter with people in technical occupations.

Some of these issues are related to different views of **power distance,** which pertains to the acceptance of wide or narrow differentials in power in various aspects of a society, such as in employee-employer relationships. Such acceptance of various levels of power distance becomes ingrained while people grow up in a culture. In a high power distance culture, such as Mexico or many Latin American countries, employers or managers are viewed to be on a much higher level, and employees are very deferential. In low power distance cultures, such as in the United States or Western European countries, managers and employees view each other as being on a more equal level, and employees feel more free to differ with them or question their decisions.[90]

As indicated in Exhibit 12.8, different approaches for issues such as giving feedback, are sometimes needed for associates from different cultures because of differences in the ranges of feedback that are considered unacceptable, negative, neutral, positive, and excellent. In Mexican culture, the range of neutral feedback is much narrower than in the United States. As a result, a relatively neutral or slightly negative comment to an employee from Mexico may be perceived as a strong rebuke. On the other hand,

power distance
degree to which differentials in power between people at higher levels in the organization and people lower in the hierarchy are accepted as a normal state of affairs

Practices for managing culturally diverse associates.　　**EXHIBIT 12.8**

ISSUES WITH ASSOCIATES	SUGGESTED SOLUTIONS
Lack of initiative	Providing more information to subordinates. Encouraging them to make decisions on their own.
Excessive deference toward managers and higher-ups	Discussing forms of greetings with them.
"Loose cannon"	Giving them more leeway. Discussing with them who should make what decisions. Explaining their involvement to a greater extent.
Overreaction to negative feedback.	"Soft pedalling" feedback (both negative and positive). Discussing with subordinates the best way to achieve the desired response.
Subordinates do not react to negative feedback.	Discussing with subordinates the best way to achieve the desired result. "Cranking up the volume."

Source: Reprinted from Managing Cultural Diversity in Technical Professions, Lionel Laroche, pp. 54–55, Copyright 2003, with permission from Elsevier.

the neutral range for an associate from France is relatively broad, and slightly negative feedback may not be viewed as something that needs attention. With associates from Germany, supervisors may have to provide relatively blunt feedback, according to U.S. standards, because negative feedback buffered by positive comments up front and in closing will only cause confusion. German associates will understand the feedback better without any positive buffering.[91]

The challenge of supervising diverse employees is especially pronounced in some industries, such as fast food. It has been reported that there are 2.5 million Hispanic employees working in fast food restaurants who do not speak English. There are some initiatives by employers to help their employees learn English, such as the Coca-Cola Company's work with the Sed de Saber program, the National Restaurant Association Educational Foundation's English immersion program, and other companies' offerings of English-as-a-second language classes. Other efforts are directed at helping supervisors, who do not speak Spanish, learn enough to communicate with their employees. Because of the high turnover rates in the industry, employers see the advantages of training supervisors to learn Spanish instead of teaching all employees English. Some employers have provided their managers with phrase books, such as *Gringo Lingo*, which provides English-Spanish language that is specific to the industry.[92]

Some practical advice for supervisors facing such challenges is provided by a restaurant manager, Tom Norr, who has learned some Spanish in a short language essentials course:

Learning Objective Number Eight

> "Every day I talk a little bit in Spanish," Norr said . . . "The biggest thing for me is, I think it's a sign of respect to try to speak their language."[93]

GAYS, LESBIANS, AND BISEXUALS

Increasing numbers of organizations are dealing with differences in sexual orientation in a similar manner to other forms of diversity. For example, 5,815 companies had implemented domestic partner benefits by 2003.[94] Furthermore, some companies in the consumer product and service industries view different sexual orientations as market segments with different marketing opportunities. On the other hand, other organizations are still dealing with sexual orientation as a moral issue.[95] Unfortunately, lesbian and gay employee have not been treated well in the workplace in the past, and many have taken elaborate procedures to hide their sexual orientations.

> Gay men and lesbian women generally kept their sexual orientation a closely guarded secret on the job. Many of them fabricated social lives that included dates with persons of the opposite sex, and they rarely shared their vacation photographs with their coworkers. If there was a social event with coworkers, many would bring opposite sex dates that had been secured to help cover their secret. Some even chose careers on the basis of their safety in the event they decided to come out . . . Others carefully guarded their sexual orientation for fear that the promotions would be denied them if they were more "out."[96]

Regardless of the supervisor's views of the moral issues on sexual orientation, it is difficult to argue with the following as a fundamental requirement:

> The first priority must be creating a safe place for lesbians and gays to come out in the organization. It must be made clear that this is a business imperative. Far too many people who are lesbian or gay experience hostile work environments in which jokes and biased remarks are allowed to prevail, and divulging one's sexual orientation would negatively affect her or his career opportunities.[97]

*Learning
Objective
Number Nine*

As with many issues, supervisors do not determine organizational policies about domestic partner benefits, and so on. However, they have the power to determine whether all employees will be treated with respect and dignity and whether they work together effectively and creatively. Furthermore, they can help create a culture of inclusiveness in which lesbians and gays feel comfortable in communicating with coworkers about issues such as breakups or the illness of a partner, and their partners can attend the organization's social functions.[98]

EMPLOYEES WITH DISABILITIES

The concept of workforce diversity also includes employees with disabilities. A recent survey of people who have disabilities revealed that of those who are of working age, only 35 percent had jobs. As a result of the somewhat limited number of people with disabilities in the work environment, there is typically some uncertainty about the manner in which one should interact with such employees. People with disabilities have different sensitivities to treatment, just like other people. As a result, supervisors and coworkers need to act with sensitivity toward employees who have disabilities. For example, an employee in a wheelchair may feel as if the wheelchair is an extension of his body. As a result, an action such as leaning on it or pushing the employee without asking whether assistance is desired, may be offensive. It is clear that communication is a key to enlightened interactions with employees who have disabilities.[99] The following advice from Roy Grizzard, Jr., an official in the federal government's Office of Disability Employment Policy, describes such communication:

> "What you want in a work situation is for people to feel comfortable. It's my opinion that the person with the disability needs to be open and upfront about it . . . especially it it's a condition that is physical and observable . . . Get it out there and let your colleagues know if you have any special needs at work to put them at ease. Make them comfortable."[100]

More specific insights about working with people with disabilities may be found at the websites of the Office of Disability Employment Policy, U.S. Department of Labor, *www.dol.gov/odep/welcome.html.* Specific suggestions for accommodating disabilities may be found at the Job Accommodation Network, *www.jan.wvu.edu,* and the Searchable Online Accommodation Resource (SOAR), *www.jan.wvu.edu/soar/wheelchair.html.*

Exhibit 12.9 provides several suggestions about etiquette for improved interactions with employees who have disabilities.

EXHIBIT 12.9	Accommodating employees with disabilities.

Pointers for Managers

Do not exempt employees with disabilities from high expectations. Equal rights for people with disabilities [means] . . . to be allowed to succeed or fail like everyone else.

There should be no concessions, lowering of standards, or waiving of requirements.

Working with People with Visual Disabilities

When escorting someone who is blind, ask, "Would you like to be guided?" Most are comfortable gently holding an arm at just about the elbow when guided. Describe any obstacles in your path (for example, stairs, narrow aisles, low ceiling, and so on).

Don't avoid phrases like "Do you see what I mean?" and "Looking around here." People who are blind use these phrases themselves and won't be offended.

Working with People with Hearing Disabilities

Look directly at the hearing-impaired person to whom you are speaking; . . . avoid . . . activities that obscure lipreading.

Speak slowly and clearly, but do not overemphasize or exaggerate words or speak loudly.

Make sure that you have the person's attention before you begin speaking. Tap the individual's shoulder or wave. Make eye contact before beginning.

Maintain eye contact with the person who is deaf, even if an interpreter is present. The hearing-impaired person will look for cues from both of you and the interpreter and prefers to be responded to directly.

Find out how the employee prefers to communicate. Do not assume what the person will need without asking.

Encourage other employees who express interest to learn sign language.

Working with People with Learning Disabilities

Consider restructuring minor parts of the job that present a major challenge to the worker.

Choose either to accommodate workers with learning disabilities or find alternate ways of getting the task done. A worker with a learning disability may never do some tasks as quickly as you'd like. You can accommodate the worker by finding alternative ways of getting the job done.

Ask questions. If a worker with a learning disability is having difficulty on the job, sit down together and try to identify the problem.

Think about the employee's work environment. For example, employees with auditory perceptual impairments need a quiet place to work.

Source: Deborah Dagit, "A Guide to Accommodating People With Disabilities," *DiversityInc* (October 2005): 88. Reproduced with permission.

INSTANT REPLAY

1. Despite progress in providing equal opportunity employment and the management of diversity, there are still remnants of enduring racial and gender discrimination, as well as discrimination against people with disabilities.

2. Discrimination on the basis of age appears to be occurring with increased frequency.

3. Supervisors must not treat employees as members of a class based on an attribute, such as their gender or race, but instead should treat them as individuals with unique abilities and skills.

4. Supervisors sometimes slow the career progress of minority employees by failing to provide them with candid feedback about their performance.

5. Responding quickly to disagreements, listening actively, and listening empathetically are skills that are particularly helpful for managing diversity.

6. Several industries are characterized by extensive international diversity. Supervisors must be sensitive to cultural differences in order to avoid misunderstandings with such diversity.

QUESTIONS FOR CLASS DISCUSSION

1. How is the management of diversity different than affirmative action?

2. What are the three approaches to the management of diversity and how do they differ?

3. Describe some of the major trends in the diversity of the U.S. workforce. Provide comparisons with the trends in other countries.

4. Explain how having a critical mass of minorities or women and a compelling objective are important for improving the management of diversity.

5. Describe an approach to the treatment of lesbians and gays that would meet the standard of effective management of diversity.

ASSESS THIS SITUATION

Purpose: To assess the need for diversity training in your organization.

Your Task: Take the following quiz by agreeing or disagreeing with each statement, based on your own experiences in your organization:

Agree	Disagree	
○	○	1. There is high turnover among diverse groups.
○	○	2. There is a lack of diversity at all levels of the company's hierarchy.
○	○	3. Some associates feel isolated from their peers because of their diversity.
○	○	4. One or more diverse groups are the subject of inappropriate behavior and ridicule.
○	○	5. Diversity is not reflected in those with powerful positions.
○	○	6. The company seems to be demanding that diverse individuals conform to the dominant culture.
○	○	7. No programs currently exist that encourage people to share and celebrate their differences.
○	○	8. There have been/are charges of discrimination.

SKILL BUILDING EXERCISE 12.1

Purpose: To encourage you to value the diversity in your teams and employees.

Your Task: Perform the exercise described here (after the list) with your team members and employees.

- Race—the result of inheritance
- Ethnicity—the result of upbringing
- Languages mastered
- Gender
- Sexual orientation—straight, bisexual, gay, or lesbian
- Place of birth—native born or immigrant
- Age—young, middle-aged, older, or elderly
- Physical characteristics—height and weight, able-bodied or physically challenged
- Education
- Religious affiliation and beliefs
- Mental characteristics—able or mentally challenged

Workshops in industry that focus on valuing diversity often begin by asking participants to introduce themselves to each other, using the preceding list. In one workshop, Juan starts the introductions by saying, "I am Puerto Rican by birth and of Spanish heritage; both my parents were born in Puerto Rico. I consider myself young at age 28 and speak Spanish and English fluently. I am a straight male with a high school diploma and two years of college credit toward my bachelor's degree. I am hearing-impaired and a practicing Roman Catholic."

Imagine yourself in this workshop, and write out your own introduction to its participants. Then, list the differences and similarities that exist between you and Juan. Which will draw you together? Which seem to form a barrier between you two? Ask yourself what additional information you would like to have from Juan in order to get to know him as an individual. Everyone in a workplace must do what you have just done if the goal of valuing diversity is to be realized. Next time you and your team or teams meet, consider performing this exercise, and make sure everyone participates. You will be surprised to discover that these are characteristics that bring people together more than drive people apart.

SKILL BUILDING WRITING EXERCISE 12.2

Consider a situation in which a female employee who has worked for a long time where you work or have worked. She has recently been confined to a wheelchair as a result of a traffic accident, which left her a paraplegic. Assume that you are this employee's supervisor and that you need to develop a plan for any changes in the physical work environment that will be required to accommodate her return to work.

Your tasks are as follows: (1) Develop a list of changes that may be needed and budget for each of the changes. (2) Develop a plan for ensuring that she will be treated in a sensitive manner, consistent with the principles of this chapter, by coworkers as well as yourself. (3) Prepare a guide that you can use when talking to her to obtain her input on all aspects of both of these plans. (4) Describe any problems that she is likely to encounter when she returns to work, and how you will attempt to avoid them or deal with them if they occur.

Use the following websites to obtain information needed for your plans: the Job Accommodation Network, *www.jan.wvu.edu* and the Searchable Online Accommodation Resource (SOAR), *www.jan.wvu.edu/soar/wheelchair.html.*

CASE 12.1   Tyrone's Opportunity

Tyrone has been working for eight months at the St. Louis distribution facility of a large parcel delivery service. The facility employs approximately 475 people who transfer packages from large incoming trucks and express railroad cars to delivery trucks. Tyrone's job involves sorting and loading packages on the trucks for delivery to customers. The work is hard, and it is often very hot when he is working in the back of the trucks. However, the loaders and drivers are union and wages are good for a low-skill job. During the evenings, he has been attending a local university and has completed 90 credit hours. While he has been able to attend classes only at night, he has been able to get involved with an organization for African American students.

Last week, Greg Johnson, the manager of the distribution facility, called Tyrone into his office to tell him about a special program. Greg said that he would like for Tyrone to consider participating in a new developmental program for minorities that will streamline their entry into managerial positions. The company's progress in hiring African Americans and Latinos has been slow and their turnover rates have been high, approximately 16 percent compared to 9 percent for non-minority employees. Only 5 percent of the employees at the facility are African Americans and 6 percent are Latinos. Furthermore, although there is one African American crew leader and there are two Latino crew leaders, there are no minorities in the supervisory and managerial ranks. Approximately half of the minority employees work in delivery truck loading operations where working conditions are the least favorable. Women make up 10 percent of the employees, and most of them work in the operations office in clerical positions.

Greg explained that the program, which would be open only to African Americans and Latinos, would provide a fast track preparation for entry into the managerial ranks. After rotating assignments through the five units in the facility as a crew leader for one year, followed by a one-year assignment as a supervisor, those who perform well will be promoted to assistant terminal managers. Greg explained that the union had gone along with the program. However, he acknowledged that the union agreed only because the company would be in danger of losing important federal contracts if it did not make more rapid progress in diversity. He also stated that Tyrone's performance ratings had been good and that his immediate supervisor recommended him for participation in the program. Greg also told Tyrone that he would begin as a crew leader responsible for five or six other workers in the loading area and that he would have a salary about 25 percent higher than his present earnings. He then asked Tyrone to think about whether he wanted to participate and asked him to decide before next week. When Tyrone asked whether he would have time to still attend night classes in order to finish his degree, Greg said that the job would probably be a little too demanding for any evening classes and that the shift assignments were too uncertain for him to make plans very far into the future. He also said that the company's high standards of performance placed high value on the ability of people to survive in "sink or swim" situations.

A couple days later, Tyrone talked to Devon Washington, the only African American crew leader at the facility, about his conversation with Greg Johnson. Devon had worked at the facility for 12 years and was widely respected by all employees at the facility. While Devon was very knowledgeable about the facility's operations and was self-educated in scheduling and warehousing systems and the software used in the facility, he had only a high school diploma and still led a crew in the truck loading area. When Tyrone told Devon about the program, Devon was surprised that he had not heard about it but said that he was pleased that the company had finally decided to do something about diversity. Tyrone then asked Devon whether he should participate in the program. He was surprised when Devon told him that the company had tried a similar program about three years ago and the program at that time had been restricted to women. Of the eight women in the program only two were still with the company. One was a supervisor in the claims area where the employees were all women, and the other worked in the accounts receivable program in the company's Milwaukee office. When Tyrone asked Devon why the women left the company, Devon said that there was a great deal of resentment that they had been placed in crew leader and supervisor jobs ahead of men who had much more seniority. He also said that there had been a great deal of criticism of their supervisory skills and their purported lack of in-depth knowledge of operations, particularly by the men who reported to them, and that the situation had not been a good one. Devon also said there were other issues as well but that he didn't want to say much about them. When Tyrone pressed, Devon told him that he had heard that two of the women had been rumored to have had affairs with the facility manager.

Tyrone thought about Devon's comments and whether he should participate in the program. His present job involved nothing more than a strong back and willingness to work hard under bad conditions. He could surely use the extra money as he and his fiancé were getting married next summer. Furthermore, he hadn't been able to apply any of the things he was studying in his classes, and the crew leader job and the supervisor job would be more interesting. He knew what crew leaders did, but he didn't know what was entailed in the job of an assistant manager. Nonetheless, he was concerned about the experience of the women who had been in the previous program.

Questions

1. How would you categorize the company's view of diversity?

2. What advice would you give Tyrone? What problems is he likely to face as a crew leader and supervisor?

3. What questions should he ask Greg before he accepts his offer to participate in the program?

4. What conditions are needed to ensure success for Tyrone? For the success of the program?

5. Do you think Tyrone should accept his employer's offer? Why or why not?

CASE 12.2   Responding to a Complaint

It was 10:00 A.M. on Tuesday. Victoria Sanchez had finished a store manager's teleconference with the regional manager when her assistant, Cary Wright, came into her office and told her that a customer, Mr. Felipe Fernandez, appeared to be very angry and wanted her to call him right away. While the customer relations staff ordinarily dealt with customer complaints, Felipe Fernandez was a member of the city council. Victoria had seen him on the local news a couple of times and knew that he was well-known in the city. In addition, as a matter of policy, Victoria tried to return all calls to irate customers because she hated to expose the staff to such calls.

Victoria took a deep breath, picked up the phone, and called Mr. Fernandez. She had hardly gotten him on the line when he began to rant about the racist people who worked in her store. He also told her that he was only calling her out of courtesy because he was probably going to follow up with a formal complaint to company headquarters about the incident that he had observed. Victoria told him that she was sorry that he had experienced any bad treatment and asked him to explain what had happened.

After a little more venting, Fernandez then explained that he had come to the store about a half hour before closing time last night in order to buy a high-definition digital television. As he approached the television display area, he overheard a conversation between two young clerks. One had asked the other to help him with the cable and accessories displays. The other one laughed and said that he could not help him because their section manager had asked him to "watch a bunch of Mexicans in the store to make sure that they weren't stealing anything." The other clerk laughed and replied, "yeah, he's asked me to do that a couple of times as well. Last week he had me watching them too—I don't trust them either."

Fernandez went on to say that such comments were a clear indication of racism. He also said that Victoria should be ashamed of herself since she allowed racists to work in the store and that if she didn't fire the section manager, Phil Carter, and the clerks, he would follow through with a formal complaint to corporate headquarters. He finished by telling her that he wanted a return call by Friday telling him that she had done what he asked.

After Victoria got off the phone, she thought for a few minutes. Phil Carter was one of her best supervisors, and the two clerks, although high school seniors, were good workers about whom there had never been any previous complaints. The store had the usual number of customer complaints as well as average to moderate personnel issues, which had involved allegations of discrimination a couple of times when employees had been terminated. Neither of these past allegations had been proven to be valid.

Questions

1. What are the key factors that Victoria should consider in deciding what to do?

2. What information should Victoria obtain from Phil Carter? From the two clerks?

3. Do you have enough information to assess the diversity climate in the store?

4. What course of action would you outline for Victoria? For Phil Carter?

5. What should she tell Felipe Fernandez?

REFERENCES

[1] King, Martin L., Jr. (October 17, 2005): *www.brainyquote.com/quotes/authors/m/martin_luther_king_jr.html.*

[2] Deutsch, Cladia H. "Race Remains a Difficult Issue for Many Workers at Kodak," *New York Times* (August 24, 2004) Copyright © (2007) by the New York Times Co. Reprinted with permission.

[3] Deutsch, Cladia H. "Race Remains a Difficult Issue for Many Workers at Kodak," *New York Times* (August 24, 2004) Copyright © (2007) by the New York Times Co. Reprinted with permission.

[4] Deutsch, Cladia H. "Race Remains a Difficult Issue for Many Workers at Kodak," *New York Times* (August 24, 2004) Copyright © (2007) by the New York Times Co. Reprinted with permission.

[5] Ibid.

[6] Deutsch, Cladia H. "Race Remains a Difficult Issue for Many Workers at Kodak," *New York Times* (August 24, 2004) Copyright © (2007) by the New York Times Co. Reprinted with permission.

[7] Deutsch, Cladia H. "Race Remains a Difficult Issue for Many Workers at Kodak," *New York Times* (August 24, 2004) Copyright © (2007) by the New York Times Co. Reprinted with permission.

[8] Ibid.

[9] Cross, Elsie Y. *Managing Diversity—The Courage to Lead,* Westport, CT: Quorum Books (2000).

[10] Ibid., 138.

[11] Thomas, R. Roosevelt, Jr. "From Affirmative Action to Affirming Diversity," *Harvard Business Review* (March–April, 1990): 107–117.

[12] Kruger, Alan B. "Sticks and Stones Can Break Bones, but the Wrong Name Can Make a Job Hard to Find," *New York Times* (December 12, 2004): C2. "What's in a Name?" *MIT News* (January 24, 2003): *http:web.mit.edu/ newsoffice/nr/2003/resumes.html* [accessed on-line October 16, 2003].

[13] Kruger. "Sticks and Stones Can Break Bones, but the Wrong Name Can Make a Job Hard to Find."

[14] Wessel, David. "Racial Discrimination: Still at Work in the U.S." *Wall Street Journal* (September 4, 2003).

[15] Greenhouse, Steven. "Going for the Look, but Risking Discrimination," *New York Times* (July 13, 2003).

[16] McGeehan, Patrick. "What Merrill's Women Want," *New York Times* (August 22, 2004).

[17] Postrel, Virginia. "Some Economists Say the President of Harvard Talks Just Like One of Them," *New York Times* (February 24, 2005): C2. Copyright © (2007) by the New York Times Co. Reprinted with permission.

[18] Tischler, Linda. "Where Are the Women?" *Fast Company* (February 2004): 52–60.

[19] Postrel. "Some Economists Say the President of Harvard Talks Just Like One of Them."

[20] Tischler. "Where Are the Women?"

[21] Helyar, John, and Cherry, Brenda M. "50 and Fired," *Fortune* (May 16, 2005), 78–90.

[22] Ibid.

[23] Shlachter, Barry. "Texas Woman Wins Discrimination Suit," *Fort Worth Star Telegram* (April 12, 2005): C2.

[24] Hays, Constance L. "Wal-Mart Is Found Liable in Bias Against Disabled Man," *New York Times* (February 24, 2005): C3.

[25] Marcus, Amy Dockser. "After Diagnosis, A New Dilemma: What to Tell Boss?" *Wall Street Journal* (March 31, 2005): A1–A8.

[26] Greer, Charles R. *Strategic Human Resource Management: A General Managerial Approach*, 2nd ed., Upper Saddle River, NJ: Prentice Hall (2001).

[27] Barrier, Michael. "Mixed Signals," *HR Magazine* (December 2001): 64–68. Greer, *Strategic Human Resource Management*.

[28] Pope, Mark, Barret, Bob, Szymanski, Dawn M., Chung, Barry Y., Singaravelu, Helma, McLean, Ron, and Sanabria, Samuel. "Culturally Appropriate Career Counseling with Gay and Lesbian Clients," *Career Development Quarterly*, (December 2004): 158–177.

[29] Diversity Programs Support Recruitment, Retention, and More," *HR Focus* (January 2002): 3.

[30] Thomas. "From Affirmative Action to Affirming Diversity."

[31] George, Libby, and Pritchard, Andrew. "Minorities Enjoy Firms' Attention," *Minnesota Daily* (February 3, 2003): *www.mndaily.com/articles/2003/02/03/4743*.

[32] Hubbard, Edward E. *The Diversity Scorecard: Evaluating the Impact of Diversity on Organizational Performance*, Boston: Elsevier Butterworth-Heinemann (2004): 9.

[33] McKinnon, Jesse. "The Black Population in the United States: March 2002," *Current Population Reports*, U.S. Department of Commerce, Economics and Statistics Administration, U.S. Census Bureau (April 2003). Ramirez, Roberto R., and de la Cruz, G. Patricia, "The Hispanic Population in the United States: March 2002," *Current Population Reports*, U.S. Department of Commerce, Economics and Statistics Administration, U.S. Census Bureau (June 2003). U.S. Census Bureau, *USA Statistics in Brief—Race and Hispanic Origin*, (January 18, 2005), *www.census.gov/statab/www/racehiisp.html*.

[34] Hymowitz, Carol. "The New Diversity," *Wall Street Journal*," (November 14, 2005): R1–R3.

[35] McKinnon. "The Black Population in the United States: March 2002."

[36] Ramirez and de la Cruz, "The Hispanic Population in the United States: March 2002."

[37] Ibid.

[38] "Big (Lack of) Men on Campus," *USA Today* (September 23, 2005): 13A.

[39] Ibid.

[40] Schoenberger, Chana R. "Technicolor Dreams," *Forbes* (July 4, 2005): 90–92.

[41] Brown, Paul B. "What I Know Now," *Fast Company* (December 2004): 104.

[42] Terhune, Chad. "Coca-Cola CEO Shuffles Managers," *Wall Street Journal* (March 24, 2005): B3. Coca-Cola Website: *www2.coca-cola.com/ourcompany/bios/bio_08.html.*

[43] Wonacott, Peter, and Areddy, James T. "China's Woman of Steel," *Wall Street Journal* (June 1, 2005): B1–B4.

[44] The Conundrum of the Glass Ceiling," *The Economist* (July 21, 2005): 63–65.

[45] U.S. Census Bureau, *Statistical Abstract of the United States: 2004–2005,* Last Revised August 1, 2005 [on-line version, accessed September 18, 2005].

[46] Heffes, Ellen M. "Dramatic Workforce Trends Require Planning Now," *Financial Executive* (July/August 2005): 18–21.

[47] Moffett, Sebastian. "Fast-Aging Japan Keeps Its Elders on the Job Longer," *Wall Street Journal* (June 145, 2005): A1–A8.

[48] Freudenheim, Milt. "Help Wanted: Older Workers Please Apply," *New York Times* (March 23, 2005): A1, C3.

[49] Maher, Kris. "U.S. Retirement Security Improves," *Wall Street Journal* (June 22, 2005): D2.

[50] Laroche, Lionel. *Managing Cultural Diversity in Technical Professions,* New York: Butterworth-Heineman (2003).

[51] Extracted from U.S. Census Bureau, *Statistical Abstract of the United States: 2004–2005,* Last Revised August 1, 2005 [on-line version, accessed September 24, 2005].

[52] Thomas, David A., and Ely, Robin J. "Making Differences Matter: A New Paradigm for Managing Diversity," *Harvard Business Review* (September–October, 1996): 79–90.

[53] Ibid.

[54] Ibid.

[55] Holstein, William J. "Office Space: Armchair M.B.A.; Diversity as Policy, Not as Window Dressing," *New York Times* (September 12, 2004).

[56] Terhune, Chad. "Pepsi, Vowing Diversity Isn't Just Image Polish, Seeks Inclusive Culture," *Wall Street Journal* (April 19, 2005): B1.

[57] Ibid.

[58] Ibid.

[59] George and Pritchard. "Minorities Enjoy Firms' Attention."

[60] Ibid.

[61] Ibid.

[62] Cross. *Managing Diversity—The Courage to Lead.*

[63] Ibid.

[64] Ibid.

[65] Miller, Frederick A., and Katz, Judith H. *The Inclusion Breakthrough: Unleashing the Real Power of Diversity,* San Francisco: Berrett-Koehler Publishers, Inc. (2002).

[66] Miller and Katz. *The Inclusion Breakthrough: Unleashing the Real Power of Diversity.*

[67] O'Neil, Patrick. "The Sangoma's Gift: Building Inclusion Through Honor, Respect, and Generosity of Spirit," in Angeles Arrien, ed., *Working Together: Producing Synergy by Honoring Diversity,* Pleasanton, CA: Berrett-Koehler Publishers (1998), pp. 133–145.

[68] Miller and Katz. *The Inclusion Breakthrough: Unleashing the Real Power of Diversity.* Cross. *Managing Diversity—The Courage to Lead.*

[69] McKinnon, Tom. "Building a Diverse Succession Plan You Can Really Use," Presentation at the American Society for Training and Development, ASTD 2003 International Conference and Exposition, San Diego, CA (May 19, 2003).

[70] Miller and Katz. *The Inclusion Breakthrough: Unleashing the Real Power of Diversity.*

[71] Cross. *Managing Diversity—The Courage to Lead.*

[72] Raphael, Todd. "Diversity Lives at Bell South," *Workforce* (January 2002): 18. Gale, Sarah Fister. "Companies Find EAPs Can Foster Diversity," *Workforce* (February 2002): 66–69.

[73] Levering and Moskowitz. "The 100 Best": 84–95.

[74] Miller and Katz. *The Inclusion Breakthrough: Unleashing the Real Power of Diversity.*

[75] Jung, Helen. "Few Women, Minorities in Top Positions at Nike," *The Oregonian* (April 21, 2005): B01.

[76] Estlund, Cynthia, *Working Together: How Workplace Bonds Strengthen a Diverse Democracy,* New York: Oxford University Press, Inc. (2003).

[77] Miller and Katz, *The Inclusion Breakthrough: Unleashing the Real Power of Diversity,* 60.

[78] Estlund. *Working Together*. Miller and Katz. *The Inclusion Breakthrough: Unleashing the Real Power of Diversity*.

[79] Estlund. *Working Together*, 82.

[80] Ibid.

[81] Ibid., 133.

[82] Tischler. "Where Are the Women?"

[83] Ibid.

[84] Ibid.

[85] Levering and Moskowitz. "The 100 Best": 84–95.

[86] Ligos, Melinda. "Business Travel: The Pacifier Isn't for the Client," *New York Times* (May 3, 2005).

[87] Ligos. "Business Travel: The Pacifier Isn't for the Client."

[88] Moffett. "Fast-Aging Japan Keeps Its Elders on the Job Longer."

[89] Freudenheim, Milt. "Help Wanted: Older Workers Please Apply."

[90] Laroche. *Managing Cultural Diversity in Technical Professions*. Graham, John L., Mintu, Alma T., and Rodgers, Waymond. "Explorations of Negotiation Behaviors in Ten Foreign Cultures Using a Model Developed in the United States," *Management Science 40*(1) (1994): 72–95.

[91] Laroche. *Managing Cultural Diversity in Technical Professions*.

[92] Berta, Dina. "English-Speaking Managers Learn to Use Spanish in Workplace," *Nation's Restaurant News* (June 27, 2005): 6–22.

[93] Berta, "English-Speaking Managers Learn to Use Spanish in Workplace," 22.

[94] Pope, Barret, Szymanski, Chung, Singaravelu, McLean, and Sanabria. "Culturally Appropriate Career . . . "

[95] Miller and Katz. *The Inclusion Breakthrough: Unleashing the Real Power of Diversity*.

[96] Pope, Barret, Szymanski, Chung, Singaravelu, McLean, and Sanabria. "Culturally Appropriate Career . . . ," 159.

[97] Miller and Katz. *The Inclusion Breakthrough: Unleashing the Real Power of Diversity*, 84.

[98] Ibid.

[99] Hinton, Eric L. "How to Communicate with Coworkers with Disabilities," *DiversityInc* (October 2005): 83–92.

[100] Ibid., 84.

"Feedback is an anomaly. People have a general sense that feedback is good to give and receive. But many people avoid it like the plague."

Manuel London[1]

Objectives

After reading and discussing this chapter, you should be able to do the following:

1. Understand the process of performance management.
2. Understand the value of evaluating outcomes and processes.
3. Explain why clear objectives and standards are needed in order to prepare proper appraisals.
4. List and give examples of appraisal methods.
5. List and give examples of pitfalls in the appraisal process.

Problems with Performance Appraisals at Leading Companies

Performance appraisals or evaluations have been subject to criticism since their inception. Nonetheless, as will be discussed in this chapter, they are a critical component of performance management and an important process for supervisors to understand and master. Before delving into the details, it will be helpful to review some negative experiences with performance evaluations of two people. These experiences should help provide perspective for the lessons in this chapter.

Executive at General Electric

The 43-year-old chief executive of Aviation Materials at General Electric sued the company over his treatment, alleging that the company discriminated on the basis of race.[2] Key information about the executive, who is black, may be summarized as follows:

> *The chief executive of GE Aviation Materials has been promoted three times since he joined the General Electric Company in 2001. His base salary of $205,000 ranks him 18th among 314 United States-based executives at GE Transportation, his unit's parent company. Until this year he has received stellar evaluations and hefty bonuses. But this year, despite a big*

Performance Management

increase in his unit's sales and profits, he received a low rating and a negligible compensation increase . . . already the suit offers an example of how people can look at the same numbers and draw opposing conclusions . . . "G.E. has a well-run diversity program without any glaring holes," said Carl Brooks, president of the Executive Leadership Council . . . G.E. acknowledges that sales and earnings at this unit, Aviation Materials, have risen since . . . [he] took over early last year, but says his bad evaluation reflected the low ratings he got from subordinates—black and white—on aspects of his leadership style like listening skills, ability to train, or to build and lead teams. Management experts say that G.E. puts heavy weight on such employee feedback. "When they fault someone who makes his numbers for being an impersonal turkey, you can bet they have the data to support it," said Noel M. Tichy, a professor at the University of Michigan's Business School who once worked for G.E.[3]

Associate at Financial Services Company

Being blindsided by a negative review is more common than it should be as there should be communication between the manager and his or her employees throughout the year, and the evaluation should come as no surprise. The experiences of employees in such situations serve as a warning of how supervisors or managers should not conduct performance appraisals:

An associate at a large New York financial services company was well into her third year with a new manager before she received a performance review, and it turned out to be the worst of her career . . . The associate thought she had been handling challenges on her own. But her boss said the associate wasn't alerting her early enough when there were problems with projects and she felt blindsided when she heard about project difficulties further down the road . . . What the associate figured out was that her style of working independently with minimal communication—a very successful strategy in her previous job with the same company— wasn't working for this boss. "I was hurt and angry, but I had a bigger goal. I have kids and a mortgage and I need this job," the associate said . . . In this case, the associate pressed her boss for details on what would be acceptable . . . She spent the next few months shadowing her boss, telling her about the tiniest developments on projects. She worked longer hours, and when on vacation she checked her e-mail and called in. The result? Within six months, her boss was pleased enough to discuss a potential promotion with her.[4]

Questions for Thought

1. Why do problems such as these occur with performance appraisals?
2. How can supervisors and managers use the process to increase performance while being helpful and beneficial for employees?

Introduction

Performance Management

**performance
management**
a systematic
approach for
improving
performance that
includes
performance
appraisal, follow-up
such as rewards or
action plans,
improved
communication,
and eliminating
barriers to
performance

Performance management is a systematic approach that involves the determination of employee performance through performance appraisal or performance evaluation, conducting the performance appraisal session, and rewarding success or positive results. It implies a systematic approach to sustaining or improving performance. As such, it involves removing barriers to performance in the work environment, increasing the quality of communication between the supervisor and employee, such that there is more of a regular coaching relationship and a supportive environment. Performance management also involves following up on negative results by developing action plans for improving performance, such as through additional training or taking actions to reassign under-performing employees to work in which they are better suited. It also involves termination in cases where performance does not improve.[5] It should be noted that performance management is a term that is also used in a broader sense to describe organization-wide efforts to measure and improve organizational performance. This broader concept monitors critical measures, such as financial performance, employee productivity, and so on. It uses such measures to guide decision-making in various management processes, such as budgeting, cost control, marketing, and strategic planning.[6]

One of the contributions of the broader or organization-wide view of performance management, is that individual employee performance can be improved by the regular communication of key performance indicators to employees. Sharing such results tells employees that they are trusted members of the team, and as such, their contributions are critical to the organization's accomplishment of its goals. Some organizations combine such key indicators or results into summaries of performance indicators called **performance scorecards,** which are developed down to the level of individual employees and linked to the scorecards for managers and various units.[7] For example:

**performance
scorecard**
combined and
weighted measures
of performance
designed for each
employee,
manager, and
organizational unit

Every individual has an individual scorecard. Every branch and department has a scorecard. And the company has a scorecard. Performance measurements built into performance scorecards must be SMART—specific, measurable, achievable (stretch), realistic and time-bound. Goals must be linked.[8]

Individual rewards are then distributed on the basis of performance indicated on the employee's scorecard, and the scorecards for the branch and the organization. A **balanced scorecard** for a branch manager might include measures of the following: (1) financial health, to include sales, gross margins, same store sales growth, and so on; (2) customer focus, such as an index of customer satisfaction; (3) service excellence, such as percentages of on-time delivery and order-accuracy; and (4) employee learning and growth, to include training and employee satisfaction.[9]

A key activity in performance management involves appraising or evaluating employees' performance. A primary duty for both supervisors and self-managing teams is to periodically conduct performance appraisals of their employees. In the **appraisal process,** supervisors evaluate each employee or team member's job performance. Skill levels and potential also may be appraised as a part of the process. The appraisal process is usually referred to as performance appraisal, performance evaluation, or performance review. In most organizations, performance appraisal is formalized—put in writing and made a matter of record—once or twice each year. Because of the value of frequent feedback, it is unsurprising to see that companies are conducting performance appraisals more frequently. A survey by Development Dimensions International in 2003 found that 41 percent of responding companies conducted appraisals at least two times per year. This result compares with a decline, from 78 percent in 1997 to 58 percent in 2003, of companies that conduct appraisals only on an annual basis.[10]

Performance appraisals provide needed feedback to all employees, letting them know what their superiors, or sometimes even their peers, think of their performance. The day-to-day coaching in which supervisors critique an employee's performance, make suggestions for improvement, or provide praise for good work provides the groundwork for the formal appraisal.

balanced scorecard
a combined indicator of performance that includes multiple and weighted measures of performance, such as financial health, customer focus, service excellence, and employee learning and growth

appraisal process
periodic evaluations of each employee's on-the-job performance as well as skill levels, attitudes, and potential

GOALS OF APPRAISALS

Here are the major goals of employee appraisals:

- To measure employee performance
- To measure employee potential
- To analyze employee strengths and weaknesses—providing recognition for the former and ways to eliminate the latter
- To set goals for the improvement of performance
- To substantiate decisions about pay increases and eligibility for promotion, transfer, or training programs
- To eliminate hopelessly inadequate performers

If the appraisal process is to accomplish these goals, it must be objective and accurate. It must also comply with company policies and the constraints of moral, ethical, and legal conduct. Throughout the remainder of this chapter, we deal with the appraisal process from the supervisor's perspective. When team leaders or team members perform appraisals, the process generally remains the same.

Learning Objective Number Two

As a team leader, you may visit clients periodically to gather feedback on service and quality. As with any appraisal, you must be as objective and accurate as possible

WHAT TO APPRAISE

Appraisals can focus on (1) outcomes, such as the results of effort, or (2) work processes or work-related behaviors, such as the actions of employees. The first approach focuses on the end product, with quantity and quality measures. The second focuses on how the work is performed, as it appraises the behaviors involved in the work. Appraisal or work behaviors often include measures of intangibles, such as cooperation, initiative, team spirit, and the relative difficulty of tasks being performed. Most appraisal programs try to measure both outcomes and behaviors.

As a supervisor or team leader, you will be appraised on the work results of your employees as well as on the quality of the processes or behaviors by which you manage—decision-making, planning, communicating, and problem solving. As a team facilitator, you will be appraised by the teams you serve on and how well you aid their efforts.

Your company's appraisal procedures and appraisal forms will dictate what you appraise. Look at the forms and determine their emphasis on outcomes and behaviors. The best producers from among your employees should be the ones to receive the greatest financial rewards you have to distribute. Those who demonstrate weaknesses should be counseled and scheduled for training to improve their weaknesses.

This chapter's supervising teams feature discusses performance reviews for teams and their clients.

TEAMS

Learning
Objective
Number Three

STANDARDS

Whether you are appraising outcomes or behaviors, you must do so with well-defined, specific, realistic, measurable, and mutually understood criteria or **standards.** Training objectives require such criteria so that both the trainer and trainee can tell when a

SUPERVISING TEAMS

Changes in performance appraisal methods may occur with the introduction of teams into the workplace. Business journals identify three generic approaches currently in use. One or a combination of them may be just right for your teams.

Peer Reviews

Because the nature of teams makes each member dependent upon the performance of others, teammates are asked to evaluate each other's contributions. Peer reviews work best when each member cares about the other members, knows how to perform other members' jobs as a result of cross-training, and has been taught to make honest, valid, and candid appraisals using precise performance standards. In self-managing teams, members hire, discipline, reward, and terminate team members. They usually have the authority to act on their appraisals by identifying those in need of help, and they work with members to improve their performance. If needed improvements do not occur, team members may recommend the termination of poor performers.

Client Reviews

A team's clients are any individuals or groups receiving its output. Clients are found inside and outside the team's department and organization. The team needs to know about dissatisfied clients. Various methods for gathering client input are available. Team leaders may visit clients regularly and interview them, in person or by use of surveys, to gather feedback on performance. Typical questions are: "What are we doing well?" "What are we doing poorly?" "What can we do for clients that we are not now doing?" The answers provide goals for the future.

Self-Assessments

Each team member conducts an evaluation of his own performance as both an individual worker and a team member. This evaluation can then be compared to peer reviews. Any variances may require a meeting with the affected parties to gain understanding of differing perspectives. When disputes and disagreements occur, the team leader or a supervisor may be called on to adjudicate and negotiate solutions.

behavior is being demonstrated with sufficient mastery. Appraising people in different job categories may require the use of different work factors and criteria. Regardless of the forms you use for appraisals, be certain that the descriptive words on them have clear and precise meanings to you and to those being rated. Ambiguity in these measures can provide the basis for legal challenges of the use of performance appraisals.[11]

Be certain to inform your employees or team members of the standards by which their work performance will be appraised. Keep in mind that standards will vary in proportion to the employee's time on a job and to the training received. You should not expect the same output from a new person that you expect from a seasoned veteran. Consider the following guidelines when selecting performance standards or criteria:

1. *Relevance.* Standards must relate directly to successful performance on a specific job.
2. *Freedom from contamination.* When comparing the performance of production workers, for example, the appraiser must allow for differences in the equipment they are using. Similarly, a comparison of the performances

standard
a quantity or quality designation that can be used as a basis for judging outcomes and behaviors

of field sales representatives will be contaminated if territories differ in sales potential. Since diverse employees have diverse styles, the appraisal should focus on the results they achieve. You must exercise care to avoid making judgments on the basis of stereotypes, biases, or an employee's deviation from an approach typical of your company's dominant culture.

3. *Validity.* To avoid charges of discrimination, employees in each job category must be evaluated by the same standards and methods.

4. *Acceptance.* Regardless of the criteria and methods used, the appraisal system will succeed only if those subjected to it accept it as being valid, fair, and understandable. If you are stuck with an appraisal system in which you and your people do not believe, get together with your peers who feel as you do and work with higher authorities to change things. If an appraisal system has no support from either the appraisers or the appraisees, it will be worthless and will create negative results for all concerned.

DIVERSITY

APPRAISALS AND DIVERSITY

When evaluating diverse employees, supervisors have to consider the fairness and applicability of various standards of performance. Companies on the cutting edge of the management of diversity have discovered that efforts must be made "to distinguish style from substance—so that many styles and approaches can be accommodated without sacrificing effectiveness within the organization." They do not hold employees to a "homogeneous ideal." Such inflexibility has a discriminatory impact and may exclude diverse groups from positions of leadership, particularly minorities and women. "By shifting the focus away from style to performance results, . . . organizations are enlarging the range of acceptable behavior for diverse employees while remaining focused on quality performance."[12]

Some companies have improved their management of diversity by adopting new philosophies, policies, programs, and operating procedures for hiring, promoting, and appraising employees. Such actions often change the company's culture to one that accepts (not simply tolerates) the existence of subcultures and taps into their unique strengths and contributions. These companies recognize that diverse people have diverse needs and expectations. Training can then focus on meeting these expectations so that these types of employees can survive and prosper in the organization. Support for diverse employees may include support networks, mentors, skills training, and encouragement for self-development. At the same time, all employees should be encouraged to be themselves and to act in ways comfortable for them that accomplish the company's goals.[13]

In some companies, performance standards are developed with input from diverse groups of employees "who understand the organization's needs and also recognize the untapped talent that those outside the mainstream can offer."[14] After all, empowering people means delegating authority and granting autonomy. Once people are trained to perform their duties, they must be given the latitude to do so effectively. Rewards for outstanding performance should be varied as well. Just as people work for differing motives, it takes different incentives to entice and satisfy diverse individuals. One size will not fit all.

Some practical guidance seems in order on the issue of diversity and performance appraisal. For example, what should be done when the performance appraisals of the only three women or minorities are the lowest in the unit? While low performance obviously justifies such appraisal results, it would be prudent to examine the potential reasons for such results and seek advice from human resource staff members.[15] For example, other than the possibility of bias on your part, there could be historical differences in opportunities for training that need to be eliminated or differences in informal mentoring that need to be addressed. Consulting with your boss and staff experts in human resources allows you to work through the potential reasons for these ratings and conclude whether the ratings are warranted.

THE SUPERVISOR AS AN APPRAISER

Effective appraisals require supervisors to have the following attributes, information, and skills:[16]

1. Willingness to communicate performance standards and to obtain employee input and agreement on appropriate personal goals for the period
2. Knowledge of the key job-related behaviors, objective outcomes, and goals on which the evaluation is based
3. Sufficient objectivity to focus on the behaviors and outcomes while recognizing that some subjective dimensions of appraisal, such as employee cooperation, are critical
4. Willingness to provide informal performance feedback and coaching at regular intervals throughout the year
5. Communication skills to provide respectful and timely feedback that employees internalize
6. Familiarity with the appraisal instrument and knowledge of the meaning of the ratings
7. Courage to provide honest appraisals to employees and to seek such feedback from superiors

If you feel uncomfortable when it comes to appraising employees, try to determine the source of your discomfort. When it is inadequate firsthand knowledge about their performance, it may mean that you do not spend enough time with them, you fail to record observations of their performance, or you do not oversee their work as much as you should. If you need training as an appraiser, you should ask for it. Appraisals are far too important to be done improperly.

Unless you oversee the work of self-managing teams, you will usually not share appraisal duties with employees. With or without self-managing teams, the appraiser has the responsibility to keep results confidential and share them only with those who are approved to receive appraisal results.

AVOIDING THE BLAME GAME

Blame placing is not the purpose of performance appraisal. Although organizations may want to assign blame for mistakes, you will most probably have to continue to work with the blamed person. At the same time, that person will have to continue to work with you and his or her coworkers. The purpose of appraisal is to reinforce the positive, identify areas in which improvement is needed, and map out actions for commitment to improved performance in the future. An appraisal goes well if it rewards good performance and helps the individuals involved to learn from errors.

On the other hand, while placing blame for mistakes and poor performance is counterproductive, it is important that supervisors use the appraisal to address poor performance. When supervisors fail to address poor performance, they tend to reward mediocrity and demoralize high performers. Some of the best-managed companies, such as Intel, Microsoft, and GE, are adamant about the need to confront poor performance and to deliver bad news to poor performers. Top performers appreciate a work environment that emphasizes excellence and eliminates noncontributors.[17]

CHALLENGES OF PERFORMANCE APPRAISALS

The following federal laws have some applicability to the appraisal process: Equal Pay Act of 1963, Age Discrimination in Employment Act of 1967 (as amended), and Title VII of the 1964 Civil Rights Act (as amended in 1972 and 1991). While there are many ways in which an ill-conceived and poorly executed appraisal process or even very sound process can encounter legal challenge, the following should help make the process less vulnerable:

1. Base the performance appraisal on an analysis of the job.
2. Define your performance dimensions in behavioral terms and support assessments with observable, objective evidence.
3. Keep things simple.
4. Monitor and audit for discrimination.
5. Train raters to assess performance accurately and to conduct effective performance appraisal discussions.
6. Provide upper-management review before the appraisal is reviewed with the individual.
7. Provide some appeal mechanism.[18]

Performance appraisals also need to convey an overall description of the employee's performance so that decision-makers have confidence in their value. One of the common problems of performance appraisals is that supervisors do not express what they really think about their employees' performance. In other instances, the performance appraisal process simply fails to capture critical aspects of job performance that differentiate between excellent, average, and poor performance.

One of the authors is familiar with a situation in which the performance appraisal system really did not serve its intended purposes. In this situation, a unionized company was downsizing its workforce and the contract allowed the company to use performance as one of the layoff criteria. When the company's managers attempted to determine which employees to layoff, they realized that the performance appraisals the company had been using for many years did not provide useful performance information. Because the managers wanted to lay off the worst performers, they essentially ignored the appraisals in the employees' files and conducted new appraisals. It was almost as if the managers were saying, "We really didn't mean what we said in your previous performance appraisals, but this time we're serious." After performing the new appraisals, the managers used them for the layoff decisions. Unsurprisingly, the union filed a large number of grievances over the layoffs that were based on the new appraisal process and won many of its cases in arbitration. Needless to say, a company is putting itself at risk when it sets aside several years of performance appraisals, which presumably tell employees that their performance is satisfactory, and then ignores those appraisals when it is time to actually use appraisals for important decisions.

Learning Objective Number Four

APPRAISAL METHODS

Organizations often make use of several performance appraisal methods. Each has advantages and disadvantages, and none is adequate for all employees or groups. Company policy will typically dictate the appraisal method or combinations of methods that will be used. The methods must be valid and standardized, have no disparate impact on minorities and women, be based on current and objective job-related standards, and be conducted in conformance with the preceding legal guidelines.

360-DEGREE REVIEW PROCESS

The 360-degree review process involves multiple performance appraisers. The individual is appraised by employees, peers, and superiors, and also performs a self-appraisal. In some companies, customers are asked to provide appraisals.[19] The rationale for the 360-degree performance review or 360-degree feedback is that a supervisor's performance should be appraised from all directions. Traditional top-down appraisals offer no direct way of determining the quality of supervision from the employee's perspective. Furthermore, when peers contribute to the evaluation, the supervisor has more incentive for cooperating with them on a regular basis.

The 360-degree feedback process offers a number of potential benefits. For these reasons, many companies, such as Levi Strauss, AT&T, and General Motors, are using 360-degree feedback and multi-rater assessment.[20] Other companies using the process include Exxon Mobil, General Electric, Tenneco, Caterpillar, TRW, Bank of America, and Mass Mutual Insurance. Furthermore, for the past 20 years, IBM has had employees evaluate their superiors.[21]

This performance feedback or review system gives supervisors an unusually objective and diverse look at how others perceive them. Managers learn of their annoying traits as well as supportive ones. "Many companies are using feedback for cultural change, to accelerate the shift to teamwork and employee empowerment. Bosses who charged up the corporate ladder by controlling everything and barking like a drill sergeant often get an earful from eagerly critical underlings."[22] When the system was used at Du Pont for providing feedback to some 80 research scientists and support personnel, it strengthened their abilities to work in teams. In other companies, the 360-degree evaluation process has been expanded to include suppliers as evaluators of employees.[23] The key factor for successful application of the feedback system is to "pick a small number of shortcomings to fix and decide on a few concrete remedies."[24]

While 360-degree feedback provides a number of advantages, some companies view such systems as being incompatible with their organizational cultures and have not

SUPERVISORS AND PERFORMANCE

Genentech, a San Francisco-based company, was selected as *Fortune's* best company to work for in 2006. The company, which was the first company in the biotech industry, has grown from a start-up in 1976 to an organization with market capitalization value of over $100 billion and over 9,500 employees. Genentech has a low-key culture with many practices of other benchmark high-performance companies, such as highly selective hiring, de-emphasized status differentials including no reserved parking places, little importance attached to the job titles of executives, and austere offices for executives. In addition, there is a general emphasis on informality, and there are regular Friday night beer busts.

While the culture is informal, Genentech is very serious about its mission to create lifesaving drugs. The company encourages collaboration and its CEO has pushed research units to cross boundaries and work together. Genentech has a system of annual or semi-annual reviews of the research of its scientists and researchers by a committee of 13 Ph.D.'s who determine future funding of their projects. These reviews, which have the objective of guiding funds to projects that have the best chances of producing viable drugs, are rigorous and are conducted to eliminate favoritism and politics from the process by which research funds are allocated. While similar processes may be used to determine research budgets in other biotech or pharmaceutical companies, Genentech's process is not punitive. Genentech's CEO says that the review process is not designed to terrify researchers, but it is also not taken as an unimportant formality. Genentech's performance review process is guided by the purpose of the organization, and the people who understand the research actually perform the reviews. There are consequences in that when projects are terminated, scientists and researchers do not lose their jobs but are reassigned to projects that have a higher likelihood of succeeding.

As can be seen, while performance appraisals for many employees will be far different from the research project reviews at Genentech, there is some value in using the company as an example for improving appraisal processes. More specifically, supervisors and managers can improve their performance appraisals by working to align the process with the mission of the organization, ensuring that they are knowledgeable about the work of employees whose performance they are evaluating, taking actions to minimize the influence of politics or favoritism, and following up the appraisal with consequences.

Source: Betsy Morris. "Genentech: The Best Place to Work Now," *Fortune*, (January 9, 2006). Genentech website, (February 5, 2006), *www.gene.com/gene/index.jsp.*

implemented them. Recent survey data reveal that the 360-degree systems, or systems that include feedback from peers or customers, are actually used by only 19 percent of companies.[25] Nonetheless, because of the advantages of such systems, it seems reasonable to speculate that we will see more companies adopt them in the future.

This chapter's supervisors and performance feature discusses how Genentech evaluates the performance of its researchers.

Robert D. Rockey, Jr., president of North American operations for Levi Strauss, is evaluated through his company's 360-degree review process. Based on the feedback he received from his superior, peers, and employees, Rockey decided to "loosen up somewhat, to command less, to listen more."[26] Unsurprisingly, appraisees appear to obtain more value from the written comments than the ratings on the scales. Raters also favor the use of their evaluations for developmental feedback rather than for personnel decisions such as raises. In addition, it appears that appraisals should be anonymous because when raters have to sign their evaluations, they rate their managers higher.[27]

GRAPHIC RATING SCALE METHODS

One of the most common appraisal methods is the graphic rating scale. Supervisors rate their employees on several graphic rating scale items, such as the one shown in Exhibit 13.1. Typically, the performance of employees is appraised on several factors or dimensions of the job. Examples of common factors include effort, knowledge, cooperation with others, and quantity of output. The person's performance on each factor is then measured on a scale. With graphic rating scale items, each interval on the scale often has a descriptive phrase for the specific level of performance. In Exhibit 13.1, the factor is quantity of output. The rater must decide and mark where the person's performance is on this scale, such as very good, average, fair, and so on. After all items are completed, the numerical values are then totaled for an overall performance score.

RANKING AND FORCED DISTRIBUTION METHODS

Because leniency bias and rater inflation are common errors in performance appraisals, your company may require you to complete a *ranking* of your employees. With this method, you will be required to rank your people from the most productive to least productive or from the most valuable to least valuable. You may be required to make a simple list of your employees, ranking one over another on their abilities and contributions.

The *forced distribution* or forced ranking method provides another remedy for leniency errors or rater inflation. With this approach, no more than a certain percentage of your people may be ranked in each of the performance categories. Performance categories often approximate the percentages of a normal distribution or bell curve. In order

Graphic rating scale item.					EXHIBIT 13.1

FACTOR	SUPERIOR	VERY GOOD	AVERAGE	FAIR	POOR
QUANTITY OF OUTPUT	Extraordinary Volume and Speed of Output	Above-Average Output	Expected Output- Normal Output	Below-Average Output	Unsatisfactory Level of Output
	✓	◯	◯	◯	◯

EXHIBIT 13.2	**Forced distribution method of worker appraisal.**

Instructions to Rater: List your employees by their overall rating in one or another of the categories below. Use their complete initials and do not exceed the percentages listed.

Percentage	Category	Employee(s)
5%	Superior	GBH
12.5%	Above Average	SAB, RFL
65%	Average	PTC, BCT, LH, NPB, SDO
		LMR
12.5%	Below Average	GSW, TFM
5%	Unacceptable	PBC

to promote more emphasis on performance, a number of leading companies have adopted these approaches. GE uses a system in which 20 percent of employees are rated as top-performing, 70 percent are rated in a high-performing middle group, and 10 percent are rated in a bottom-performing group. Other well-known companies that use forced ranking systems, with set percentages of employees being ranked in a small number of performance categories include Cisco Systems, EDS, Microsoft, and PepsiCo. However, these companies also evaluate their employees with other appraisal formats, such as objectives, and do not rely solely on the forced distribution since these formats do not provide much information for developmental purposes or guidance.[28]

Exhibit 13.2 illustrates a forced distribution approach. When all of your employees perform identical tasks, the ranking and forced distribution methods are appropriate. However, when your employees perform different jobs, the rankings are less valid because the system requires you to compare apples and oranges.[29] Unfortunately, this same criticism applies to many performance appraisal methods. In addition, supervisors usually complain about ranking or forced distribution methods because they often feel that they have a disproportionate number of above-average (or below-average) performers. They argue that the arbitrariness of the forced distribution method makes them give invalid ratings to some of their employees.

A limitation of the ranking and forced distribution methods is that, by themselves, they provide very little information of value for providing feedback in a performance appraisal session.[30] For example, a supervisor would find it difficult to conduct a meaningful performance appraisal session if all she could tell the employee is that his rank is 8 out of 12. However, because such methods are typically used in conjunction with other appraisal methods, they can make a valuable contribution. Ranking and forced distribution methods force you to make a choice and to evaluate your people in a new way. It is conceivable that performance appraisals may become the criterion for making layoff decisions at some point in the future. If supervisors have failed to distinguish between the performance levels of their employees, the appraisals will not be useful. Unlike the citizens of Garrison Keillor's fictitious Lake Wobegone, where all the children are above average, all of your employees cannot be ranked above average with forced distributions.

PAIRED COMPARISON METHOD

The *paired comparison* method requires supervisors to compare employees in a pair-wise manner. The supervisor counts the number of times an employee is picked as the better of the pairs and a numerical total is obtained. This technique has the advantage of providing a realistic framework of comparison. It is easier for most evaluators to decide whether one employee is better than another than it is to decide whether she fits in the average, above average, good, and other categories of a graphic rating scale. However, paired comparison methods become unwieldy with large numbers of employees because of the very large number of comparisons that must be made. They also provide only limited information for the performance appraisal session.[31]

Exhibit 13.3 provides an example of the paired comparison method.

Paired comparison method.	**EXHIBIT 13.3**

Compare the overall performance of each of your employees on a pair-wise basis with every one of your other employees. Assign a value of 1 if the first employee is better than the second for each pair of subordinates:

PAIRED COMPARISONS:

Roberto vs. Jay	1	Jay vs. Alice	1	Josie vs. Jay	1
Roberto vs. Alice	1	Jay vs. Felicia	1	Josie vs. Alice	1
Roberto vs. Felicia	1	Jay vs. Roberto	0	Josie vs. Felicia	1
Roberto vs. Josie	1	Jay vs. Josie	0	Josie vs. Roberto	0'
Roberto's Score =	4	Jay's Score =	2	Josie's Score =	3

Alice vs. Jay	0	Felicia vs. Jay	0
Alice vs. Felicia	1	Felicia vs. Alice	0
Alice vs. Roberto	0	Felicia vs. Roberto	0
Alice vs. Josie	0	Felicia vs. Josie	0
Alice's Score =	1	Felicia's Score =	0

OVERALL RANKING (4 = BEST, 0 = WORST):

Roberto	4
Jay	3
Josie	2
Alice	1
Felicia	0

ESSAY, NARRATIVE, AND CRITICAL-INCIDENT METHODS

The most flexible method, but clearly the most demanding method of appraisal, is the *essay* or *narrative* method. In this method, the supervisor describes the employee's performance in written comments that address all of the relevant performance dimensions of the job. This method offers the maximum degree of expression for precise and informative evaluations and is valuable for conducting an appraisal session. This method applies well to highly educated professionals and to managers who are rated by other managers. However, narratives and essays are time-consuming to prepare.

With the *critical-incident* method, the rater records personal observations about both positive and negative occurrences in order to dramatize the particular point under examination. In this method, the supervisor refers to specific situations—critical incidents—that highlight or illustrate a worker's performance. These incidents are of great value in discussing an employee's performance in appraisal sessions because they deal with specific observable behaviors. The disadvantage is that critical incidents can only come from frequent observations and recording. Supervisors may not have sufficient opportunities for observation and collection of critical incidents when employees work at remote locations. Sales people, construction workers, research people, and staff specialists are a few examples of workers who are often based at different locations. In their cases, comments from the people they serve may provide examples of critical incidents. Exhibit 13.4 provides examples of critical incidents.

BEHAVIORALLY ANCHORED RATING SCALES

The *behaviorally anchored rating scale* (BARS) method of appraisal uses a series of statements that describe performance behaviors ranging from effective through ineffective. The statements are often constructed from critical incidents written by people who have intensive knowledge of the job, such as supervisors or job incumbents.[32] These statements describe behaviors that pertain to a specific dimension of job performance. The statements are then placed on a scale in order of their desirability, and a point

EXHIBIT 13.4	**Critical-incident appraisal.**

Initiative: Constance requests additional work when she runs out and lends a hand to her less experienced coworkers.

Cooperation: Routinely, she coordinates with coworkers, recognizing that her work is the basis for theirs.

Conscientiousness: She always calls to make sure that special orders are delivered to customers when expected and sends a follow-up shipment via FedEx when they do not.

Judgment: When there are equipment failures on the third shift, she checks inventory levels and backlogs before calling outside maintenance people at premium rates.

value is assigned to each statement. The rater must choose the statement that best describes the ratee's performance for each dimension and then total the points. The following three statements illustrate the use of BARS for rating a trainer's punctuality while conducting training sessions:

- The trainer always arrives 30 minutes early for each training session and makes sure that all equipment is functioning (5 pts.)
- The trainer usually arrives for each training session just before the session is scheduled to begin (3 pts.)
- The trainer is often late for sessions and frequently leaves early (0 pts.)

Notice that these statements describe specific observable behaviors that were drawn from critical incidents, and that the method requires the appraiser to select one of the descriptive statements. Statements like the ones shown can be constructed for each behavior or dimension considered crucial to successful performance on a job. Input from those who will be rated should be sought during construction of the statements to ensure that a complete list of essential behaviors is included and to help enlist the support of those who will be rated under the BARS method.

A disadvantage of BARS is that the statements are specific to only one job, and they are expensive to develop because of the time and statistical expertise required.[33]

CONCLUDING REMARKS ABOUT APPRAISAL FORMATS

The most common approach to appraisal is to combine various formats. For example, a company's standard appraisal form may include several graphic rating scales. It also may require the supervisor to conduct a forced distribution rating of the employee's overall performance (e.g., top 10 percent, next 20 percent, etc.). The form also may require the supervisor to include three or four objectives developed from an MBO approach. In addition, it may require a short narrative about the employee's performance. Use of multiple appraisal approaches enables the company to offset the weaknesses of each and provides a better overall appraisal.

It should be remembered that all appraisal approaches are affected by the personal interests, preferences, and prejudices of the appraiser. No appraisal method will completely eliminate bias. It is up to you, the rater, to be as objective as you can by making every effort to leave bias and personality clashes out of each rating. Your emphasis should be foremost on the employee's performance on the job. Try to act like a camera. State as clearly as you can what each person did and how well it was done.

MANAGEMENT BY OBJECTIVES

In this chapter, we discuss MBO as a useful method for appraising the performance of teams, team members, and traditional employees. Superiors and employees agree on the goals employees will work to achieve and strategies required for achieving them. The goals may be related to outcomes or behaviors. The primary advantage of MBO as an appraisal method is that people are more committed to achieving goals when they have had a role in setting them.

As part of the appraisal process, you may need to watch workers perform their jobs. The objective notes you take can be used in your written evaluation.

As noted in the earlier quote about performance scorecards, good objectives are identifiable by the acronym, SMART, and should include the following characteristics: specificity, measurability, attainability, realism, and time-bound. Objectives should also be subjected to the test of their priority relative to alternate goals. Another suggestion is that one should not place too much emphasis on measurability by focusing on goals that lend themselves to objective measures. When this happens, there may be too much emphasis on unimportant objectives while important objectives, which are more difficult to measure, are set aside or ignored.[34]

Stretch goals are "big, athletic leaps of progress on measures like inventory turns, product development time, and manufacturing cycles."[35] Another way of defining a stretch goal or stretch objective, in operational terms, is that "there is only a fifty-fifty chance of achieving it."[36] Setting and reaching such goals are rapidly becoming ordinary behaviors for individuals and teams. To leap ahead of the competition, incremental changes and gradual improvement are not enough. Reengineering demands discarding the old, rethinking everything a company does, and coming up with a whole new effort. Chrysler chose this route with its cab-forward design. "Getting an organization to embrace wrenchingly difficult new goals—particularly in the absence of a crisis—can traumatize employees. Managers who can't stand the relentless new pace quit or get fired."[37] To motivate employees to reach stretch goals, management must explain the urgency and consequences of not reaching the goal. Next, it must convince everyone that the goal is possible and point out, through benchmarking, how others have achieved the goal. Then, it must empower people to find their own means and get out of their way.

Stanford professors James C. Collins and Jerry I. Porras have found that long-lasting visionary companies have several common traits. Among them is the continuous setting and achieving of what they call big, hairy, audacious goals (BHAGs). When President John F. Kennedy set a national goal in 1961 to place Americans on the moon and return them safely to earth by the end of that decade, he was setting a BHAG. In like fashion, when Sam Walton, founder of Wal-Mart, set the goal to become "a $1 billion company in four years (more than doubling of the company's size)" he was setting a BHAG.[38]

Both stretch goals and BHAGs need little explanation, are "clear and compelling and [serve] as a unifying focal point of effort—often creating immense team spirit. [Each] has a clear finish line . . . is tangible, energizing, highly focused."[39] When working with your teams and employees, encourage them to articulate and strive for such goals. The rewards for doing so are incredible for both the individuals involved and their organizations.

Supervisors should also note that there are criticisms of MBO and the process by which objectives are set and implemented. One concern is that the time period for their accomplishment is often too short for meaningful and sustainable results to be evident. Another concern is that teamwork may not receive the emphasis it deserves, and there may not be sufficient recognition of the effect of interdependencies. In addition, with the shift toward a service economy, the requirements for spontaneity and decentralized decision-making do not always match up well with pre-established goals. Finally, the pressure for quantitative measures tends to diminish the attention paid to non-quantitative influences, which are critical to the quality of performance.[40] Thus, MBO has limitations, as do many supervisory tools, but there are ways to offset some of the weaknesses as will be explained in the next section.

Today's supervisors and managers should not forget the importance of goals or objectives, whether they are the normal or stretch variety, as well as some of the criticisms of their use. This is especially important for performance management, and the appraisal process in particular, because an important part of the appraisal session should be developmental and future oriented. It is important for supervisors to remember the following:

> Successful managers help others achieve their goals and dreams. Ultimately, managing others is a career that involves helping others. If you want to get the help you need from your employees in order for you to be successful, you must help employees get what they want.[41]

APPRAISING WITH MBO

Approaches to appraising by MBO differ widely, although most efforts begin with implementation at top management levels. Gradually, as the upper echelons gain expertise with MBO, it is used at progressively more levels. If you do not have the permission of your superior to use MBO, you should not use it. Exhibit 13.5 outlines a

EXHIBIT 13.5	Basic steps in appraising through MBO.

Step 1. *Setting goals.* Goals must be mutually determined through discussions between supervisors and employees. Areas for improvement can be determined from past appraisals, current situations, job descriptions, and the employee"s ambitions to improve and gain higher responsibilities.

Step 2. *Identifying resources and actions needed.* The amount of time, money, and materials required to reach an objective must be determined. To attain any goal, the efforts of the goal setter and others may be required. Accurate predictions must be made.

Step 3. *Arranging goals in order of priority.* Both the rater and the ratee need to agree as to the importance of each goal and the order in which they should be pursued.

Step 4. *Setting timetables.* Precise times need to be set for the completion of actions and the attainment of goals. These times will allow evaluations of progress and will facilitate appropriate adjustments in either methods or goals.

Step 5. *Appraising the results.* The summary judgment of success or failure that occurs at this step sets the stage for a return to step one. Thus the cycle repeats.

series of distinct steps that can make MBO work for you. It represents only one of many approaches, but it is a comprehensive method that can prevent some of the major problems others have encountered in their early MBO efforts.

STEP 1: SETTING GOALS

As stated earlier, goals are ends or end states that have to do with a person's or a unit's growth and development. If they are to be meaningful, they should meet the criteria set forth earlier. They must be set through a dialogue or discussion between superiors and employees, and both parties must recognize their importance and be committed to them.

STEP 2: IDENTIFYING RESOURCES AND ACTIONS NEEDED

Before superiors and employees can agree on goals, they should examine whether the organization and the employee have the resources and abilities to achieve them. Resources include human energy, effort, time, money, and materials. Some actions may require the commitment and cooperation of several persons and units.

STEP 3: ARRANGING GOALS IN ORDER OF PRIORITY

Which goal should be worked on first, second, and so on? What end state is considered by both parties to be the most essential? One guideline for answering these questions is the level of inefficiency that needs to be eliminated. An attack on the most expensive areas of waste or problems could be placed first on the list of objectives. Lesser areas of waste could be attacked simultaneously or sequentially.

Some additional criteria to consider when appraising with MBO.	EXHIBIT 13.6

In addition to the achievement or non-achievement of a goal, consider the following when evaluating performance:

1. How has the employee grown as a result of pursuing the goal?

2. Was the employee effective? Did she do the right things in a proper sequence?

3. Was the employee efficient? Did he use only the necessary amounts of resources?

4. Did the individual help or hinder fellow workers?

5. Were due dates met? Were goals achieved earlier than planned?

6. Were obstacles overcome or circumvented?

7. Were the goals easy or difficult to achieve?

8. Is the employee getting better at choosing goals, setting priorities, and establishing timetables?

STEP 4: SETTING TIMETABLES

Besides agreeing on priorities, the boss and employee must agree on the times by which each goal is to be achieved. Time estimates must be made, and calendars must be prepared for future reference. Dates for completion become guideposts and serve as checkpoints to determine progress and problems. As these dates arrive, boss and employee coordinate to determine if adjustments are necessary. New times, new approaches, or refinements may be required.

STEP 5: APPRAISING THE RESULTS

At the intervals dictated by your company, you and your employees meet to discuss the progress and events that have taken place since the last evaluation. Your appraisal of your employees' efforts is not based solely on goal achievement. Your appraisals should consider both processes and behaviors. Additional criteria for use with MBO appraisals are presented in Exhibit 13.6.

APPRAISING BY COMPUTER

Some companies are using software to develop more refined measures of the time their employees spend in productive work. For example, British Airways uses software to measure how much time a service representative spends in break time or making personal calls. Such software can also measure performance in resolving customer complaints.[42] Employers may legally monitor the amount of time employees spend surfing the Internet as the Electronic Communications Privacy Act enables employers to monitor employees' e-mail and Internet activity on company computers. A recent survey examined the rationales for

Using computers to monitor employees is an increasingly popular, but controversial, trend. The computerized checkouts at markets can objectively monitor the productivity of workers.

companies that monitor their employees. The responding executives cited the following reasons for such monitoring: 31 percent—client interaction quality, 27 percent—productivity, and 20 percent—to detect illegal or criminal activities.[43]

Computer monitoring
using computers to measure how employees achieve their outputs by monitoring work as it takes place

Computer monitoring measures how employees achieve their outputs—monitoring work as it takes place—in addition to keeping track of their total output. It counts such things as the number of keystrokes per minute, the use of individual machines per hour, and the number and kinds of items processed by a sales clerk per hour. Computer monitoring allows employers to rate employee productivity and rank employees according to how completely and effectively they use each minute of each working hour. Computer monitoring can provide the specific quantifiable measures of performance needed for meaningful pay-for-performance compensation systems.

Critics of computer monitoring argue that it creates additional worker stress, fatigue, and turnover. Workers fear unauthorized access to and disclosure of highly "personal and private information."[44] From management's point of view, computer monitoring helps control costs, improve security, increase productivity, and obtain more precise information needed for objective appraisals. [Life insurance] "industry representatives also contend that some workers like the monitoring because they view it as a way to prove they are doing a good job and see it as protection in the case of disputes with customers."[45]

Software packages also are used for performance appraisal. While only 20 percent of companies use performance management software or systems accessed on-line, substantially greater usage is expected in the future.[46] There is an extensive array of products available, such as noted in Skill Building Exercise 13.1, and some of them utilize multiple appraisal or evaluation formats, which were discussed earlier in the chapter, such as BARS, critical incidents, and goal setting.[47]

This chapter's supervisors and ethics feature deals with the role that Enron's performance evaluation system played in maintaining the company's flawed organizational culture and in promoting unethical behavior.

Each of the appraisal packages has various legal and consistency checkpoints built in. You should investigate them for their possible application to your situation.

Learning
Objective
Number Five

PITFALLS

Be aware of the common types of errors that can be made by raters, and try to eliminate them from your appraisals of employees. Committing any one of them will render your rating inaccurate. Some of the pitfalls discussed here also apply to the selection of new employees.

THE HALO AND HORN EFFECTS

One common rating error is known as the **halo effect.** The rater allows one outstanding positive trait or incident about a person to color the overall rating and image of that employee. Because one of your people dresses well and has good manners and bearing, you may tend to let this blind you to other traits or the whole performance record. Conversely, if the most vivid incident you can recall about a person is his commission of a major mistake, you might allow this to obscure other fine qualities and be influenced by the **horn effect.** You must guard against letting isolated events or appearances dominate your total impression and objectivity toward a worker.

halo effect
one positive
characteristic,
behavior, or
incident favorably
biases the appraisal

horn effect
one negative
characteristic,
behavior, or
incident adversely
biases the appraisal

RATING THE PERSON—NOT THE PERFORMANCE

There is a strong tendency to give higher ratings if the supervisor and the employee get along well and low ratings if they do not. Human nature is such that we have more favorable perceptions of people we like most. On the other hand, a rater's personality and attitudes may clash with those of an employee. As a result, the employee may receive an unsatisfactory appraisal even though her performance and potential are above average. Your job in appraisals is to rate each person according to his performance in a particular job. Unless an individual's personality traits are interfering with his performance, there is no reason for you to consider them in the appraisal. You may not like an individual, but if a fair appraisal requires that you rank her as superior, you must do so. Leave your biases and prejudices out of the appraisal and avoid personal attacks.

SUPERVISORS AND ETHICS

On July 8, 2005, Lea Fastow, a former assistant treasurer at Enron, left a halfway house, after completing a one-year term in a federal prison. Fastow's prison sentence resulted from a misdemeanor tax violation of filing a tax return, which did not report income that her husband, Andrew Fastow, Enron's former chief financial officer, received from kickbacks related to illegal financial schemes at the company. She was one of the first executives of the company to complete her sentence for involvement in the company's unethical and illegal activities.

The collapse of Enron exemplifies the terrible consequences that occur when business leaders and others fail to adhere to fundamental ethical standards. In less than 12 months, shareholders saw the value of their stock drop from over $80 per share to less than $1 when the firm declared bankruptcy. Thousands of employees lost their jobs as well as their retirement savings as the value of the Enron stock in their 401(k) accounts plummeted. Companies that dealt with Enron were left with tens of millions of dollars in losses. The credibility of financial analysts reached rock bottom as their ratings advised investors to buy Enron's stock until just days before Enron's bankruptcy. In addition, politicians of both parties were tainted by their acceptance of large campaign contributions and the effects these contributions may have had on their failure to enact regulatory reforms that could have prevented some of Enron's practices.

The scandal revealed ethical lapses at the highest levels of Enron's leadership as executives enriched themselves to the tune of tens of millions of dollars at the expense of shareholders through lucrative options and financial arrangements that posed severe conflicts of interest. As investigators closed in, documents were shredded. Executives called before Congressional investigative committees exercised their Fifth Amendment rights against self-incrimination and refused to testify. Even the organizational culture of Enron and its performance management systems appear to have contributed to unethical conduct. The company's "rank and yank" performance evaluation system, which quickly forced out employees who fell in the bottom 20 percentile, placed tremendous pressure o.n employees to achieve results regardless of the means by which results were obtained.

Sources: "Lea Fastow's Prison Term Is Over, *Wall Street Journal* (July 11, 2005): C6. Hanney, Brian. "Called to Account," *Accountancy Magazine* (June 2004): 160. Andy Serwer. "Dirty Rotten Numbers," *Fortune* (February 18, 2002): 74–81. "The Lessons from Enron," *Economist* (February 9, 2002): 9–10. Wendy Zellner. "A Hero—and a Smoking Gun Letter," *Business Week* (January 28, 2002): 34–35. Allan Sloan, Keith Naughton, Kevin Peraino, Temma Ehrenfeld, and Donna Foote. "Who Killed Enron?" *Newsweek* (January 21, 2002): 18–24. Anne Belli Gesalman, Kevin Peraino, Martha Brant, and Tamara Lipper. "The Gambler Who Blew It All," *Newsweek* (February 4, 2002): 18–24.

To keep your actual or potential biases in check, you should avoid the following specific behaviors in appraising employees:

1. *Stereotyping*—ignoring a person's uniqueness and individuality by assuming that any member of a group must have characteristics that conform to a preformed image of the group. For example, Bill is a sales person, and therefore Bill is . . ., or Jane is Hispanic, and therefore she is. . . . Our perceptions of a member of any specific group may or may not be rooted in fact.

2. *Projecting*—accusing others of the very faults you possess. Examine the anger you feel toward another person, and beneath it you may find that you contributed to the situation.

3. *Screening*—noticing only the negative aspects of a person or his performance, interpreting events in the most negative way possible, recording only events that support a preformed judgment about a person, and ignoring positive contributions.

As noted earlier in the discussion of the manner in which to conduct the appraisal session, a focus on behavior should help avoid the pitfall of appraising the person instead of performance. For example, the supervisor should use the following approach:

Rather than simply commenting that an employee, "needs to improve the way he works with others," a better approach is to state that, "on several occasions Joe went outside the chain of command to press home his opinion about project changes not accepted by his team leader."[48]

RATING EVERYONE AS AVERAGE

This error, which often is referred to as the *error of central tendency,* occurs when you rate everyone as average. You may be tempted to do so because you lack sufficient data. Supervisors also commit errors of central tendency because they seek safe, uncontroversial methods of handling appraisals. They may fear that if they rate a person below average, they will face a confrontation at the appraisal session. You will avoid having to justify a below average rating with this approach, but you will also discourage your high performers. Conversely, rating someone high does not make it so. If you falsify employees' ratings, they will know it and so will your boss.

SAVING UP FOR THE APPRAISAL

Some supervisors spot a deficiency, record it, and save their discussion of it for the formal appraisal. When this happens, employees reasonably feel that they have been treated unfairly. Employees should not be surprised by a criticism they receive during an appraisal session. The supervisor should have discussed problems with them at the time when they occurred. The formal appraisal interview should provide a review of past events that exhibits a concern for preventing the recurrence of past infractions, and it should offer a focus for future improvement.

Observe your people on an appropriately frequent basis and make on-the-spot corrections and comments about their work. Let them know where they stand with you on a regular basis. Be open and available—if you are, there will be no shocks or surprises at the appraisal interview. Your informal appraisals will have prepared them for what you will say at the formal appraisal. You also will have the facts to support your appraisal.

THE RUSH JOB

Last-minute, hurry-up rating is related to most other appraisal errors. Whether you have two employees or 20, you have to give yourself enough lead-time for thinking things through and searching your memory and files for tangible data on which to prepare your appraisals. How would you like it if your boss spent only 15 minutes to appraise your past six months of performance?

Your formal appraisals are important. Your people know that they represent your written opinion of them and their performances. They know that what you say will directly affect their futures and their earnings. They also know that you go on record with your superiors in these appraisals. Give deserved praise and help employees to develop programs for improvement. This should be a task that you tackle with great concern and eagerness. You are laying foundations that will have to support future plans and programs. Make those foundations firm and strong.

NOT SHARING THE RESULTS

We have assumed that your formal appraisal of an employee will be discussed with him or her. To do otherwise defeats the purpose behind appraising people—to improve their performance individually and collectively. Yet, some organizations have actually prohibited or discouraged the communication of results to the rated individuals. Such policies may be adopted to counter the tendency for the ratings to be more lenient when managers are required to discuss them with their employees. Nonetheless, failure to share the results of the evaluation reduces the impact of the appraisal process. If appraisals are not shared in your company, you must realize how this failure affects your employees. A sense of fear and distrust is created by this secrecy, and employees will be frustrated because they do not know what their boss has said about their performance. If your company has such a policy, work to change it.

LACK OF PROPER TRAINING

All too often, companies sow the seeds for management failures by neglecting to train supervisors in the conduct of performance appraisals. A supervisor who has not been taught how to appraise, how to prepare for an appraisal interview, and how to conduct such an interview will make preventable mistakes. Self-study, conferences with your boss, college courses in human resource management, and management seminars are all good ways to establish or improve your skills in this area.

LACK OF PROPER DOCUMENTATION

When you attempt to criticize an employee's performance, you must be prepared to give specific information. You must have concrete evidence to back up your observations and criticisms. For example, be specific by giving dates and the amount of time missed when noting an employee's tardiness.

Appraisals are used as a basis for decisions about promotions, demotions, raises, and termination. You should appraise specific performances that are essential for good overall performance and document your ratings. Documentation that justifies your ratings is necessary because you may someday find yourself a party to a lawsuit claiming that your appraisal of an employee was discriminatory. A few years ago Ford Motor Company announced its intention to trim the ranks of salaried employees who were either poor performers or average performers who were not expected to be promoted. Although the program was classified as voluntary, Ford managers planned to tell employees that they recommended acceptance of a separation package. In order to limit litigation costs, challenges over its appraisal system, and the adequacy of its documentation, observers expected Ford to reduce its exposure to litigation by providing buyouts accompanied by legal releases from employees.[49]

Problems with documentation are common as supervisors typically feel that there are more pressing issues that demand their attention on a daily basis. However, documentation is becoming increasingly important for challenges of appraisals and personnel actions. More fundamentally, such regular documentation of performance throughout the year provides the basis for a more accurate and comprehensive appraisal than reliance on one's memory for the previous time period.[50] Getting into the routine of reporting such documentation should also serve as a stimulus to provide more frequent feedback and coaching.

THE ERROR OF RECENT EVENTS

Supervisors often find that recent events inordinately influence their judgment about employees, especially if the events are strongly negative or positive, and there is a lack of notes or documentation. You must guard against letting the most recent events overshadow those of the previous months. The best defense is to keep accurate records of individuals' performances, recording significant events as they occur. Your appraisal should give equal consideration to all that has occurred over the appraisal period.

FOCUSING ONLY ON NEGATIVES OR POSITIVES

Employees are demoralized when supervisors focus solely on the negative aspects of their performance. Unless the employee is at the stage where he or she would be terminated, there should be positive aspects that deserve commendation. Conversely, unless the employee is truly exceptional, there should be tactful and clear discussion about the areas in which the employee needs to improve. One helpful approach for such discussions involves self-evaluation with the supervisor asking the employee to provide insights about the probable causes of substandard performance.[51]

FAILURE TO PROVIDE DIRECTION FOR THE FUTURE

Some supervisors also make the mistake of failing to tell employees the behaviors and actions that they would like to see them pursue in the future. When discussing these actions, supervisors need to tailor their approach to the level at which the employee is performing, the employee's level of experience and knowledge, and receptivity to guidance. As discussed later in this chapter, different appraisal styles are appropriate for different employees and situations.[52]

FAILURE TO ASSIGN RESPONSIBILITIES

The appraisal session should not be the end of the process. There should be an agreement on what needs to be done in the future, the responsibilities that belong to the employee and those that need action on the part of the supervisor, such as checking into opportunities for specialized training for the employee.[53]

THE APPRAISAL SESSION

Your daily contacts should provide you with the facts you need to prepare and support your formal evaluations. The big event for both you and your employee is the appraisal session, where you both can discuss the judgments you have made. This meeting should occur in private and without interruption.

Sharing the results of your appraisal efforts takes place in three stages: preparing for the session, conducting the session, and following up on its results.

PREPARING FOR THE SESSION

The session should not just happen. It must be planned with the same thoroughness you would apply to the planning of any important event. Then, you can anticipate and prevent problems and misunderstandings that might permanently damage your relationship. One suggestion is to ask your employees to provide input for the appraisal session. Typically, they will appreciate knowing that you want to be sure not to overlook anything about their performance, and it will help them prepare for the appraisal session as well. Another technique is to request employees to provide a list of their most important accomplishments over the past year or shorter period depending on the time period used for reviews.[54]

Be certain that you review each appraisal in detail before you attempt to meet with your employee. Even though you wrote it, you probably wrote several others at the same time, and it is amazing how easily you can confuse them in your own mind. Anticipate the areas or individual remarks that might give rise to controversy. Be clear in your own mind about why you rated a person below average on a given point and what led you to that conclusion. If you have recorded a failure that the person has overcome and is not likely to repeat, be sure that you state this on the rating. You do not want to put much emphasis on such a situation because most of our learning takes place through trial and error, and we learn best by analyzing our mistakes.

Having analyzed your employee's weaknesses as probable points for discussion and questions, construct a list of his strong points. Label what he does extremely well. These points represent excellent introductory material to begin the session. Some managers use what is referred to as the *sandwich approach*. This technique gives the worker a strength, then a weakness, then a strength, and so on. It tends to soften the blows to a person's ego and to promote confidence in the person being rated. Use whatever approach you feel is best for both you and your worker. Watch for a reaction and be ready to adjust your approach as necessary.

Finally, set down a list of goals or objectives that you would like to see the person achieve. The list should relate most specifically to improving performance and growth. Then determine the possible ways in which she might go about achieving each one. For example, suppose that your employee has recurring difficulty in making logical and practical decisions. Be ready to get her views on how to improve. Have a suggested plan on hand, and recommend that the employee follow it if she does not have a plan. For every weakness, there should be a suggestion for improvement. Let us hope that your employee will concur.

CONDUCTING THE SESSION

Make arrangements for adequate time and facilities, and ensure that you will be free of unnecessary interruptions. This is time for just you two, and there should be no distractions. It also is important to remember that you may need to obtain additional information, such as on training programs, that will help an employee improve in an area of weakness. You may need to schedule additional sessions to work through developmental plans.

A useful suggestion for supervisors is to focus on behaviors instead of unchangeable employee characteristics or attitudes that you can only presume to exist. As noted earlier, performance appraisal experts often suggest that the appraiser should act like a camera and report what she sees. Supervisors will conduct better appraisal sessions by adhering to the following advice:

> Instead of using characteristics to describe employee problem areas (e.g., lazy, slow, bad attitude, not a team player), use descriptive behaviors. Replace "lazy" with "doesn't perform duties in a timely fashion, misses deadlines, does not respond quickly to changing priorities." Or let the employee who doesn't act in the best interests of the team know that he or she "doesn't pitch in to help others when time is available and help is needed." Go from "bad attitude" to "shows unwillingness to support management decisions that he or she may not agree with." Just this simple method of letting the employee know the specific behavior that is creating the problem . . . can let the employee know that you are not being critical or judgmental.[55]

It is important for supervisors to recognize that different employees require different approaches in performance appraisal sessions. In performance appraisal, one approach does not fit all situations. Norman Maier's classic work on performance appraisal sessions identifies three basic approaches. These are the (1) tell and sell, (2) tell and listen, and (3) problem-solving approaches. The *tell and sell* approach is essentially a directive style in which the supervisor describes the evaluation and then outlines the actions needed for improvement in the future. The supervisor then "sells" the evaluation and attempts to obtain the employee's commitment to the actions outlined for improvement. This approach works best for younger and inexperienced employees, those who are insecure, and those who are easygoing and unimaginative.

In the *tell and listen* approach, the supervisor describes the appraisal to the employee and then allows him to talk through any disagreements with the appraisal. The supervisor practices active listening, notes any inaccuracies, and works through any misunderstandings. This approach tends to reduce defensiveness on the part of the employee, which may facilitate acceptance of the appraisal. Unfortunately, with the tell and listen approach, the employee may not obtain a clear message about the actions needed for improvement.

For experienced, competent employees, the *problem-solving* approach is appropriate. The supervisor helps the employee talk through any performance problems and helps draw out the employee's ideas for how to solve the problems. The supervisor helps to channel the employee's solutions toward approaches that are consistent with the company's goals or practices.[56]

After making preliminary decisions about the most appropriate style, begin the session by emphasizing that its purpose is to promote improvement in the individual and the department. Then move into the specifics. Be brief and to the point. One good approach is to begin with some rather general questions such as, "Well, Tom, how would you rate yourself on your progress since our last interview?" or, "If you had to appraise yourself for the past six months, what would you say about your performance?" This method gets your employee talking and gives you insight into his perception of things. Moreover, it makes the point that this interview is to be a dialogue and an exchange of points of view. Avoid lecturing and get your employee's feelings and observations into the open. Work for mutual agreement and accord.

It usually is better to give your employees their written appraisals at least a day before the appraisal session. It also is useful to have employees submit a self-appraisal prior to the session, which can be used in the appraisal process. Both help the employee to prepare for the session. For each weakness noted, provide evidence of the validity of the rating. Then discuss how the weakness can be overcome. If your employee sees no immediate way to improve on the weakness, introduce your thoughts on the matter.

Finally, set some specific short-range goals with your employee to remedy the list of shortcomings. These should tackle the questions of what should be done, by what time it should be completed, and how each goal should be reached. You will be instilling hope in each person you work with, and, more concretely, you will be showing a way out of the present difficulties. Here again is a chance to convince your employee of your honest concern for his welfare and progress.

FOLLOWING UP ON THE RESULTS

After the session, and as a part of your normal duties, check on each person's progress toward the goals set in the appraisal session. If Ann said she would brush up on her basic skills, visit with her to see if she has. If Wally said he was going to try a new method, find out how well he is doing. Your people will soon realize, as you do, that appraisals are daily routines that are only periodically summarized through the formal appraisal report and review session. This realization should cause them to give their best regularly and not just at appraisal time.

REWARDS FOR THOSE WHO EXCEL

The extent to which you can provide tangible rewards for employees who excel is determined by many factors. These include the degree of your authority, your control over the purse strings through budget requests, and your boss's willingness to delegate to you. Often, all you can do from a dollar-and-cents point of view is to recommend a fixed amount as a raise. A worker who is near or at the top of the salary range may be eligible for only a token increase. Until a worker gets a promotion to a higher pay grade, she will have peaked. The incentive to hasten the promotion may be sufficient to impel that person to work at an above-average pace. Or, if she is trapped by being the least-senior person, it could mean frustration.

You have many intangible awards you can give each person. These include a pat on the back for a job well done and the frequent appreciation you show each person in public and in private. Your demonstration of your dependence on each team player goes a long way toward satisfying his need for esteem and status. You can make your people aware that you understand the value of their individual contributions in a number of ways. For example, you can send a letter of commendation to higher management levels for any exceptional contributions by your people, or you can sometimes grant time off from work. Try to make each reward appropriate for the behavior or outcome. Such rewards have greater impact when they follow quickly on the heels of the event. The appraisal process should make you keenly aware of which employees are carrying the load in your department and the extent of your dependence upon them.

Company celebrations of employee contributions vary widely. Most companies stage regular events to honor and celebrate jobs well done. Bonuses, certificates of achievement, induction ceremonies, and peer recognition are but a few of the ways in which companies recognize outstanding performances and behaviors. At 3M,

> The company recognizes success not so much by giving shares or bonuses but by holding events where peers cheer peers. Honorees get a certificate and backpat from [the CEO] and waves of applause. The top awards come once a year, 3M's Oscar night. With considerable fanfare, three or four eminent innovators are inducted into the Carlton Society, a hall of fame for company immortals. Call it corny but it works.[57]

The Hotel Inter-Continental in Miami started a monthly rewards program it calls "It Pays To Do It Right."

> The hotel's 650 full- and part-time hourly employees are recognized for exceptional service. Nominated by guests and managers in two categories, the employee with the most votes in each wins a plaque and $500.[58]

Such celebrations create a climate that encourages excellence by providing positive reinforcement for the behaviors the organization values. All of us need regular feedback and positive recognition when we do well. Rewards and ceremonies help satisfy employee needs for recognition and security.

NEGATIVE RESULTS

Just as good appraisals should lead to rewards and tangible improvements, poor appraisals should lead to negative consequences. When performance has been judged to be below standard, requirements for additional training and denials of positive benefits may be in order. It may be appropriate to eliminate raises and bonuses, or to deny promotions. Demotion also may be appropriate depending on management policy or a union agreement. In extreme cases where people can but will not perform, termination may be the only alternative. Inform your people that good and bad consequences are associated with performance appraisals. Be certain that the link between performance and rewards or punishments is clear to each of your employees. As with rewards, punishments should be appropriate and timely.

As a summary of the appraisal process review the checklist in Exhibit 13.7. Keep in mind that appraisals can either help or hinder the development of good human relations between you and individuals or groups you supervise. Make appraisals

| **EXHIBIT 13.7** | **Checklist to help you prepare for the appraisal process.** |

1. Do I observe my subordinates regularly? If not, I must have a means of obtaining information about their performance and potential.

2. Do I often let them know how they stand with me? Am I honest when I do so?

3. Do I really know each of my people as individuals? If not, how will I develop such knowledge?

4. Can I detail in writing each of their specific duties? Would my list agree with theirs?

5. Do my appraisals emphasize an individual's performance on the job? Am I using established and approved standards for comparison?

6. Can I back up my opinions with facts? With specific incidents?

7. Have I commented on my employees' potential?

8. Have I planned to share the results with each person?

9. Have I thought about ways that each person can improve his or her rating?

10. Is this rating something I will be proud to sign?

---

positive experiences in order to cement team spirit and individual morale. Lock away any biases you may have, and stick to the facts. Use observable, measurable job-related standards to rate people on their performances and outcomes. Use your appraisal interview to coach and counsel as well as to praise and to criticize.

INSTANT REPLAY

1. Efforts to evaluate employees take place daily. Formal appraisals usually take place once or twice each year.

2. The appraisal process is too important for a supervisor to delegate.

3. Appraisals look at the rate of personal development and changes in performance capabilities.

4. Appraisals must be based on known standards and linked to definite rewards and punishments.

5. The many approaches and methods of appraising employees all have advantages and disadvantages. All are affected to some extent by bias and subjective judgments.

6. If you are aware of the pitfalls of performance appraisal, you can act to prevent them.

7. The real value of appraisals lies in sharing them with the rated individual. Specific problems and achievements can be noted, and plans can be made for improvement.

QUESTIONS FOR CLASS DISCUSSION

1. Can you define this chapter's key terms?
2. Why do supervisors appraise their employees? What in the process will benefit supervisors? What will benefit their employees?
3. Why are clear objectives and standards needed in the appraisal process?
4. Which of the appraisal methods described in this chapter would you as a supervisor prefer to use? Why?
5. What are the major pitfalls of the appraisal process?
6. How often are you appraised at work? How often in your management course? Would you like to be appraised more often? Why?

ASSESS THIS SITUATION

Purpose: To experience the difficulties connected with the use of vague, general, usually unobservable traits as rating criteria.

Your Task: Listed here are traits sometimes used by companies when rating their employees. After each, write a definition of the trait. When you have finished, compare your definitions with those of your fellow students. Then list reasons why rating on the basis of traits is not a valid substitute for rating on the basis of clear, observable, job-related behaviors and standards of work performance.

1. Initiative:
2. Drive:
3. Persistence:
4. Human relations:
5. Promotability:

SKILL BUILDING EXERCISE 13.1

Critical incidents can be very helpful for performance appraisal or performance evaluation, as well as for training and selection purposes. As noted in the discussion of the various methods of appraisal, critical incidents are behaviors that provide the basis for some rating systems, and examples are provided in the discussion of BARS and in Exhibit 13.4. For sophisticated rating systems, such as BARS, large numbers of critical incidents are winnowed down through a statistical process in order to obtain ones that truly differentiate between different levels performance. For example, a behavioral incident on which bad employees are rated similarly to good employees would not be a critical incident.

Your Task: Working in groups of three of four students, do the following tasks: (1) Recall work behaviors qualifying as critical incidents, which you have observed or performed yourself, that represented excellent or poor performance. (2) Describe your examples to other members of the group. (3) After the discussion of each incident, report the consequences of each of these incidents for the individual, coworkers, customers, or the organization.

SKILL BUILDING WRITING EXERCISE 13.2

As discussed in this chapter, several software products are available for streamlining the performance appraisal or evaluation process. The availability of these products has been expanding at such a rapid pace that decision-makers should spend some time investigating the various products in order to find the ones that best fit their needs. Some examples of software packages include: Halogen Software's Appraisal, SilkRoad Technology's WingSpan, Promantek's TrakStar, Dick Grote's GroteApproach and the HRN Management Group's Performance Pro.

Your Task: Go on-line to investigate the various software products that are available to help with the performance appraisal or employee performance management processes. Select five of these software packages and provide a written description of the following: (1) the specific functions that each package can perform, (2) the extent to which they are targeted for use by supervisors or managers, and (3) the extent to which they are designed to be integrated with other software systems that a company may be using.

CASE 13.1   Virginia's Performance Appraisal

Steve Knapp sat down to fill out the appraisal form for his secretary, Virginia Penna. It was a few minutes before he needed to leave for home, but he had forgotten about doing Virginia's appraisal. He had just received a reminder from human resources telling him that he needed to complete Virginia's appraisal and turn in the form by tomorrow morning. It had been a hectic day, and Steve had not enjoyed a minute of peace since arriving for work. As he looked at the form, he tried to think about Virginia's performance on each of the rating scale items. There were 10 items on which he had to evaluate her performance: (1) knowledge of duties, (2) accuracy of work, (3) taking initiative, (4) attention to detail, (5) promptness, (6) willingness to take on responsibilities, (7) cooperation with others, (8) effort, (9) developing new skills, and (10) dependability. There also was an item that requested a global evaluation of her overall performance.

As Steve thought about Virginia's performance with respect to each of the items, he knew that he had a problem. In reality, Virginia's performance over the year had been below average on each of the items except for cooperation. Nonetheless, she had performed better over the past 30 days and was always pleasant and friendly to everyone. Steve knew that if he rated Virginia below average on any of the items, she would be upset. Unfortunately, Virginia was not good at her job, but she had been with the company a long time and was well liked by others as well as himself. He had learned to make up for some of Virginia's weaknesses by doing more secretarial work himself on his personal computer. Nonetheless, he knew that he would be better off with another secretary and that he shouldn't be spending time doing clerical tasks. He wished that Virginia would take a job somewhere else.

Steve looked at the form again. All it required was the completion of the 10 graphic rating scale items. The scales had the following rating categories for each item: needs improvement, below average, average, above average, and superior. Steve knew that he didn't want to have a session with Virginia like he had last year. He had given her two ratings of "needs improvement," and she had started crying immediately after reading the form. As he worked through the form, he told himself that better ratings would help make Virginia feel more confident about herself and that perhaps she would perform better if she received higher ratings this time. Upon completion of the form, he quickly reviewed the ratings. All of the ratings he had assigned were average to above average. Furthermore, he had given Virginia a rating of superior on the item for cooperation with others, and the overall rating was above average.

Steve knew these ratings were higher than Virginia's performance warranted, but he told himself that the appraisal process should be forward-looking. Why dwell on the past since he was powerless to change it? Instead, he told himself that the higher ratings were justified because he expected Virginia to do better next year. He reassured himself that Virginia would be pleased with the ratings. He thought that she also might work harder because of a Pygmalion effect or out of gratitude. Why go through a painful process like he did last year? He had given Virginia low ratings last year, but the appraisal had no effect on her performance. Besides, as a result of an economic downturn, there weren't going to be raises for anyone this year. It wasn't like Virginia's ratings would affect anyone else. As Steve completed the last item on the form, he reached for the phone to ask Virginia to come in for her appraisal.

Questions

1. How do you think Virginia's performance will be affected by Steve's ratings of her?

2. Will his approach to Virginia's ratings affect those he assigns when he rates his other employees?

3. What mistakes has Steve made in rating Virginia's performance? How do you think Steve should have approached the appraisal process?

4. What are the likely consequences of Steve's appraisal of Virginia?

CASE 13.2   Rating Monroe's Performance

Liz Jarrell was trying to complete Monroe Moore's performance appraisal. Monroe was one of 12 financial analysts who worked for her. She had been on the job for about two months since being transferred back to the United States from the company's operations in Brazil. Liz had been working on the evaluation for over an hour and was making little progress. The problem was that she simply did not know how to rate Monroe's performance. Monroe did not stack up well with the other people in the unit in terms of completed financial analyses. On the other hand, it appeared that he was highly respected within the department as well as by people in other departments. He seemed to spend a lot of time helping other analysts and was very good at some of the more sophisticated analyses that were becoming more important. It looked like several of the analysts called Monroe when they needed help on difficult issues. In addition, she knew that he had spent a couple of days teaching a workshop for new employees in another department. The other department had requested his assistance, and her predecessor, Peg Flynn, who had retired from the company, had authorized it before her arrival.

As she looked at the ratings on the form, she didn't know whether Monroe's performance should be rated as needs improvement, below average, average, above average, or superior. Liz knew that Monroe had completed 40 percent fewer analyses than any other member of the department and that he was often late with the ones he completed. The records for the rest of the year before she arrived at the department showed a similar pattern of performance. In addition, since her arrival in the department, Liz had emphasized the importance of productivity and timely work.

Questions

1. What rating should Liz assign to Monroe's performance?
2. Explain your justification for the rating.

Source: The underlying concepts for this case are based on a case developed by Development Systems International, located in Studio City, California.

REFERENCES

[1] London, Manual. *Job Feedback: Giving, Seeking, and Using Feedback for Performance Improvement,* 2nd ed., Mahwah, N.J.: Lawrence Erlbaum Associates, Publishers (2003): xiii.

[2] Deutsch, Claudia H. Black, White or Gray; Statistics and Emotions Clash in Corporate Bias Cases, *New York Times,* (June 7, 2005).

[3] Ibid.

[4] Dahle, Cheryl. "Office Space: Career Couch; Blindsided by the Boss in Your Annual Review," *New York Times,* (May 2, 2004), Copyright © (2007) by the New York Times Co. Reprinted with permission.

[5] Cardy, Robert L., and Dobbing, Gregory H. "Performance Management," in Lawrence H. Peter, Charles R. Greer, and Stuart A. Youngblood, eds., *The Blackwell Encyclopedic Dictionary of Human Resource Management*, Oxford, United Kingdom: Blackwell Publishers, Ltd., (1997): 255–256.

[6] AMIFs Research Committee. "Basic Tenets of Performance Management in Financial Institutions," *Journal of Performance Management* (November 2005): 17–21.

[7] O'Connor, Thomas J. "Driving High Performance," *Electrical Wholesaling,* (October 2005): 34–39.

[8] Ibid., 36.

[9] Ibid.

[10] Bernthal, Paul, Rogers, Robert W., and Smith, Audrey. *Executive Summary—Managing Performance: Building Accountability for Organizational Success,* Development Dimensions International (2003).

[11] Schuler, Randall S., and Jackson, Susan S. *Human Resource Management: Positioning for the 21st Century.* Minneapolis: West (1996).

[12] Loden, Marilyn, and Rosener, Judy B. *Workforce America!* Homewood, IL: Business One Irwin (1991): 161–178.

[13] Ibid.

[14] Ibid.

[15] Flynn, Gillian. "Getting Performance Reviews Right," *Workforce* (May 2001): 76–77.

[16] Neal Jr., James E. "Doing Performance Appraisals Right," *Credit Union Executive Newsletter* (September 10, 2001): 4. Flynn, "Getting Performance Reviews Right." "How Our Readers Make Performance Management Work," *HR Focus* (October 2001): S1–S3. Fandray, Dayton. "The New Thinking in Performance Appraisals," *Workforce* (May 2001): 36–39. Clarke-Epstein, Chris. "Truth in Feedback," *Training and Development* (November 2001): 78–80.

[17] Grote, Dick. "The Secrets of Performance Appraisal," *Across the Board* (May 2000): 14–20.

[18] Grote, Dick. *The Performance Appraisal Question and Answer Book,* New York: American Management Association (AMACOM), (2002): 13–14.

[19] O'Reilly, Brian. "360 Feedback Can Change Your Life," *Fortune* (October 17, 1994): 93–94, 96, 100.

[20] Ibid.

[21] Antonioni, David. "Designing an Effective 360-Degree Appraisal Feedback Process," *Organizational Dynamics* 25(2) (1996): 24–38.

[22] Ibid.

[23] Taylor III, Alex. "The Auto Industry Meets the New Economy," *Fortune* (September 5, 1994): 58.

[24] O'Reilly. "360 Feedback Can Change Your Life."

[25] "Parallels Between Performance Management Quality and Organizational Performance," *Supervision*, (August 2005): 19–20.

[26] Mitchell, Russell. "Managing by Values," *Business Week* (August 1, 1994): 48–49.

[27] Antonioni. "Designing an Effective 360-Degree Appraisal Feedback Process."

[28] Grote. *The Performance Appraisal Question and Answer Book.*

[29] Cascio, Wayne F. *Applied Psychology in Personnel Management,* 4th ed. Englewood Cliffs, NJ: Prentice Hall (1991).

[30] Schuler and Jackson. *Human Resource Management.*

[31] Cascio. *Applied Psychology in Personnel Management.*

[32] Ibid.

[33] Ibid.

[34] Grote. *The Performance Appraisal Question and Answer Book.*

[35] Tully, Shawn. "Why to Go for Stretch Targets," *Fortune* (November 14, 1994): 145–146.

[36] Grote. *The Performance Appraisal Question and Answer Book,* p. 43.

[37] Ibid.

[38] Collins, James C., and Porras, Jerry I. *Built to Last: Successful Habits of Visionary Companies.* New York: HarperBusiness (1994): 91–99.

[39] Ibid.

[40] Levinson, Harry. "Management by Whose Objectives?" *Harvard Business Review on Appraising Employee Performance,* Boston: Harvard Business School Press (2005): 1–28.

[41] Hill, Joe B. "Strategies of Successful Managers," *Supervision* (February 2005): 10.

[42] Conlin, Michelle. "The Software Says You're Just Average: Technology Alters How Performance Is Gauged—and Rewarded," *Business Week* (February 25, 2002): 126.

[43] "E-mail: What You Don't Know Can Get You Fired," *The Columbus Dispatch* (May 7, 2001): 01E. "Watching Employees," *USA Today* (February 25, 2002): B.01.

[44] Ibid.

[45] Ibid.

[46] Bernthal, Rogers, and Smith. *Executive Summary—Managing Performance: Building Accountability for Organizational Success.*

[47] Totty, Patrick. "How Do Your Employees Stack Up?" *Credit Union Magazine,* (November 2002): 33–34.

[48] Painter, Charles N. "Ten Steps for Improved Appraisals," *Supervision*, (October 2003): 12–14.

[49] Schellhardt, Timothy D., and Goo, Sara. "At Ford, Buyout Plan Has a Twist," *Wall Street Journal* (July 22, 1998): B1.

[50] Painter. "Ten Steps for Improved Appraisals."

[51] London. *Job Feedback: Giving, Seeking, and Using Feedback for Performance Improvement.*

[52] Ibid.

[53] Ibid.

[54] Painter. "Ten Steps for Improved Appraisals."

[55] Frankel, Lois P., and Otazo, Karen L. "Employee Coaching: The Way to Gain Commitment, Not Just Compliance," *Employment Relations Today* 19(3) (1992): 311–320.

[56] Maier, Norman R.F. *The Appraisal Interview: Three Basic Approaches.* La Jolla, CA: University Associates (1976).

[57] Loeb, Marshall. "Ten Commandments for Managing Creative People," *Fortune* (January 16, 1995): 136.

[58] Barciela, Susana. "Attaboys Pay Dividends in Work Place," *Chicago Tribune* (January 4, 1995): sect. 6, 5.

14

"He who lives without discipline dies without honor."

Icelandic Proverb[1]

Objectives

After reading and discussing this chapter, you should be able to do the following:

1. List and briefly explain the principles of discipline.
2. Explain what it means to discipline your subordinates fairly.
3. Explain the role of penalties in the exercise of discipline.
4. Differentiate between positive discipline and negative discipline.
5. Describe why supervisors should know themselves and their employees well before they attempt to discipline their employees.
6. List and briefly explain common pitfalls that can affect a supervisor's efforts at discipline.

Maintaining Discipline at Citigroup

In 2004, the government of Japan told Citigroup, the largest banking and financial services company in the world with operations in over 100 countries and approximately 300,000 employees, that it could no longer conduct private banking in the country. The Japanese government's concerns focused on rule violations within the Citigroup's private banking unit, such as inadequate safeguards that would prevent money laundering. As a result of this fiasco, Citigroup's CEO, Charles Prince, ordered an independent review of the unit's problems and concluded the following:[2]

> *"The people on the ground in Japan, based on what I've read, I think they were pretty conscious over a long period of time about doing things that were simply violative of the rules . . . We've been kicked out of the private banking business in Japan because the regulator has said that we're not fit to run that kind of business in Japan. It's embarrassing. That's a big deal; that's a really big deal."[3]*

After considering the evaluation of the bank's conduct, Mr. Prince then terminated three top executives and several employees who were responsible for the violations. He then traveled to Japan and formally apologized for the

Discipline

Introduction

By **discipline,** we mean two distinct and related concepts: education and training to foster compliance with reasonable rules and standards (called *positive discipline*), and the dispensing of appropriate sanctions for wrongdoing (called *negative discipline*). Both approaches are necessary to promote reasonable and safe conduct at work and to sustain acceptable performance. As a supervisor, you are the person closest to your employees and are the member of management best suited to deal with them when they violate rules. If you hire new people, you should be thinking about how well they will fit in with the work environment. Your training and appraisals can either prevent problems or be the cause of them. Both can either foster self-discipline or sow the seeds for future performance problems.

discipline
the management duty that involves educating employees to foster obedience and self-control and dispensing appropriate punishment for wrongdoing

THE SUPERVISOR AND DISCIPLINE

Employees and team members depend on their supervisors, team leaders, and team facilitators to satisfy many of their needs at work. They expect and deserve to be treated ethically and to have their employment rights respected. Employees at all levels need to know the standards that will be applied to their behaviors. They also must be given the training to meet these standards. Finally, all of us need regular feedback to know how we are doing and to help in our efforts to improve. When superiors fail to help employees, others stand ready to do so. Unions, cliques, and lawyers are three such groups. If employees, teams, and team members like their jobs and respect their supervisors, leaders, and facilitators, they have the best reasons for avoiding punitive action. Such workers are bent not on disruption but on construction. When people know that their leaders have their best interests at heart, they will not intentionally let them down.

Effective discipline depends on many things, not the least of which is the individual employee's willingness to accept responsibility for his behaviors. Too many organizations rely on controls imposed on the individual to enforce compliance with standards. There is no real substitute in organizations for employee self-control and willingness to comply with standards. When individuals accept responsibility for their own efforts, punitive efforts are seldom needed. This point is echoed in the following conclusion by Nigel Nicholson:

> It is easy to energize employees who want to be motivated. But how do you crack the tough cases, the people who never seem to do what you want—yet take up all of your time? . . . I have concluded that these are precisely the wrong questions to ask. That's because, as it turns out, you can't motivate these problem people: Only they themselves can. Your job is to create the circumstances in which their inherent motivation—the natural commitment and drive that most people have—is freed and channeled toward achievable goals.[7]

Nicholson's comment provides wonderful advice for supervisors. Nonetheless, while supervisors should try to discover the keys to unlocking the motivational potential even with problem people, it is not always possible. While disciplinary systems may be needed for only a small number of employees, they are absolutely essential.

A FAIR AND EQUITABLE DISCIPLINARY SYSTEM

Learning Objective Number One

As is the case with appraisal systems, unless your employees view the disciplinary system as both fair and equitable, it will cause more problems. Disciplinary efforts must consider a person's dignity, her legal rights, and the union agreement if one exists. A fair and equitable disciplinary system has the following characteristics:

1. It has reasonable policies, rules, and procedures that govern conduct at work. These exist to prevent problems and do not violate any federal, state, or local laws.
2. It communicates the rules and provides prior warning of the consequences that one can expect when guilty of a deliberate violation.

Understanding diversity comes into play in discipline. When disciplining Hispanic and Korean workers, don't expect them to look you in the eye. In these and other cultures, it is a sign of respect to lower one's eyes to the ground.

3. It enforces rules, policies, and procedures consistently, and consistently applies sanctions for infractions.
4. It has progressively more severe penalties for repeated infractions by the same party.
5. It places the burden of proving guilt on management.
6. It considers the circumstances surrounding an infraction and allows for appropriate mitigation of punishment.
7. It has appeals and review procedures.
8. It has a short memory—it purges memories of wrongdoing after a reasonable time and avoids holding a grudge.
9. It is delivered in a pleasant manner.

Evaluate the disciplinary system you live with by these standards. If you suspect or know that there are problems, get together with your fellow supervisors and go to those who can change things. You cannot expect to enjoy the respect of your employees if you have to violate the preceding standards when performing your role as judge.

AN APPROPRIATE NUMBER OF RULES

A contributing cause of rules violations is that organizations have too many rules. When there are too many rules, employees often find that some of the rules are unreasonable or outdated. They also learn that many rules are simply not enforced. In general, rules are reasonable when they are needed for safety or to promote operational efficiency. Employees tend to obey reasonable rules while they tend not to obey unreasonable rules. When asked whether their organizations have too many rules, supervisors often deny that this is the case. However, when asked if their organizations have any rules that are not enforced, they almost universally agree. They then often change their position and agree that their companies have too many rules. When there are too many rules, employees see that some are not enforced and perceive the inconsistency. As a result, they may not understand which behaviors are tolerated and which are prohibited.

THE RED-HOT STOVE CONCEPT

Professor Douglas McGregor (who gave us Theories X and Y) offered a useful analogy to keep in mind when approaching disciplinary tasks and handing out penalties. Called the *red-hot stove concept,* it compares the organization's disciplinary system to a red-hot stove and the employee who has earned punishment to someone who has been burned. Edwin Leonard and Raymond Hilgert put it this way:

> Everyone knows what happens if they touch a red-hot stove (advance warning). Someone who touches a hot stove gets burned right away, with no questions of cause and effect (immediacy). Every time a person touches a hot stove, that person gets burned (consistency). Whoever touches a hot stove is burned, because the stove treats all people the same (impersonality).[8]

Anyone who touches the hot stove will experience the same result. Initially, the victim will feel anger and hostility toward the stove, but normally this reaction is a result of the realization that he has acted incorrectly. The anger fades in time, and the victim learns respect for the stove. The victim's behavior will change in the future. So it should be with your disciplinary actions. The term "immediate" from the red-hot stove rule is a bit overstated, however, for a good point. Disciplinary action should be taken as soon as possible or practical when rule violations occur. However, violations require investigations before disciplinary action is taken, but these should be quick enough so that employees see the cause and effect relationships. People should not be in doubt that burns will occur when rules, procedures, standards, and policies are violated. Make sure that they know the stove is hot and that it will burn anyone who fails to respect its heat.

Learning Objective Number Two

PROGRESSIVE DISCIPLINE

progressive discipline
a system using warnings about what is and is not acceptable conduct; specific job-related rules; punishments that fit the offense; punishments that grow in severity as misconduct persists; and prompt, consistent enforcement

Progressive discipline uses warnings about what is and is not acceptable conduct; specific, job-related rules; penalties that fit the offense; sanctions that grow in their severity as misconduct persists; and prompt, consistent enforcement. Exhibit 14.1 highlights the characteristics of an effective and equitable discipline system in more detail. Many of the requirements for **"just cause"** for discipline are also incorporated in the characteristics presented in Exhibit 14.1. Union contracts universally require just cause or simply cause before employers can discipline employees. Employees protected by civil service rules also have protections similar to the concept of just cause. The specific components of just cause include the following: adequate warning, reasonable rules, fair investigation of the incident, substantial evidence, fair or consistent application of rules, and an appropriate penalty (proportional to the severity of the offense).[9]

Managers lose the respect of employees (and lawsuits in court) when they attempt to enforce vague rules, penalize in an inconsistent manner, fail to follow their own disciplinary procedures, fail to warn employees of rule changes, and fail to warn them of unacceptable conduct. The progressive discipline system is formal; it is familiar to all who are governed by it. It places limits on managers' actions and their flexibility to

Characteristics of an effective and equitable discipline system.

EXHIBIT 14.1

- Specific rules
- Reasonable rules (necessary for safety and efficiency)
- Relevance to job
- Clearly defined punishments
- Punishments that fit the severity of the offense
- Punishments that increase with repeated infractions
- Careful investigation
- Prompt enforcement
- When enforcement has become lax, new warnings are provided before any discipline
- Consistent enforcement
- Documentation of offenses committed and punishments given
- Effective communication of standards and what happens when they are violated
- Effective communication during disciplinary meetings
- Disciplinary actions administered in private
- An appeals process
- Follow-up to prevent recurrence and to cement relations

---

deal with problem employees. But it must do so in order to be perceived as just and fair. It offers the best defense against accusations of bias and discrimination.[10]

This chapter's feature on supervising teams describes the role of discipline in a high-performing small business.

Exhibit 14.2 presents several vignettes of common disciplinary incidents. As you read through these, think about whether discipline was warranted and the severity of discipline that you think is appropriate. Although these vignettes describe disciplinary actions against employees in union environments that were eventually appealed to arbitration, a progressive approach to discipline should be used with both unionized and non-union employees. With progressive discipline, the intent is not to punish but to correct the employee's problem behavior and to rehabilitate his performance. Accordingly, successively more severe punishments are meted out only if the unacceptable behavior continues. Typically, the first instance of a rule violation or unacceptable behavior results in an oral warning. A written warning is given for the second violation. Further violations of a similar type generally result in suspensions of one to seven days. A very serious violation might result in a 30-day suspension if there have been previous

just cause
discipline of appropriate severity for violation of reasonable rules; it follows a warning with consistent rule enforcement and substantial proof

TEAMS

SUPERVISING TEAMS

Small businesses are often viewed as being somewhat behind large corporations in the sophistication of their approach to management. Nonetheless, a closer examination of some leading small businesses reveals that they have mastered a broad set of managerial skills and are very effective in developing and maintaining highly effective teams. One example of a high-performing small business is C&M Auto Service, which has 15 technicians and service facilities in both Vernon Hills and Glenview, Illinois. One of the first indicators of the performance of this firm is that there is very low turnover among the firm's technicians. In fact, the firm has a flow of people who want to work there. Automobile technicians are often in high demand and those having five years of experience can earn as much as $60,000 per year while some can earn over $80,000 per year.

Some of the keys to the success of C&M Auto Service are that the technicians are empowered and well-trained. Technicians are mentored during a two-year apprenticeship program, which provides financial incentives for the mentors to provide good training.

The firm also provides financial incentives as technicians acquire higher certifications through a national skill development program. It is clear that the firm invests heavily in training as its annual training program includes 40 hours of training for technicians and it relies on outside professionals for instruction.

In addition, the firm provides all technicians with a computer, e-mail, and a phone so that they can communicate with family members and others during the day just like people who work in offices. The co-owner of the business says that he has changed his managerial approach from an initial authoritarian approach to one that emphasizes participation. The technicians all understand their responsibilities and the importance of meeting time standards. In addition, he has developed a very effective incentive-based compensation system that has a substantial impact on productivity. Finally, he uses discipline effectively as he does not terminate employees until after he has tried to improve their performance with additional training or has attempted to find a position better suited to their skills.

Sources: Maren Goldberg. "Team Building," *Motor Age*, (December 2004): 44–48. Diane Smith. "A Calling for Cars," *Fort Worth Star Telegram*, (February 6, 2005).

suspensions. Most employers do not suspend employees for more than 30 days, and demotions are relatively rare because they seldom produce desired results. After multiple suspensions, a further violation typically results in termination. Another aspect of progressive discipline warrants explanation because it is sometimes misunderstood. While progressive discipline applies to successive violations of the same rule, it also applies to violations of different rules. The progressive requirement is met when an employee has been disciplined a number of times for different rule violations and then is terminated for a subsequent violation.[11]

PERFORMANCE

Arbitrators who have been asked to rule on the fairness of a disciplinary action of unionized employees look for progressiveness in the disciplinary actions as well as adherence to a regular procedure for assessing discipline and consistent treatment of employees who receive discipline. (Judges apply some of the same criteria when nonunion employees find a way to litigate their terminations.) It should be noted that a

Examples of disciplinary action.	**EXHIBIT 14.2**

Evaluate the appropriateness of the discipline applied in each of the following situations and formulate the reasons for your decisions: (*Note:* The arbitrator's decisions appear at the end of this section.)

Repeated Tardiness. A water pipeline mechanic, who had an excellent work record over 19 years at a utilities department, had begun to accumulate tardiness violations. The department's rules, which defined tardiness as being one minute late, imposed discipline for an accumulation of three tardiness violations in 30 days or six violations in a six-month period. The department also had a Constructive Action Plan that would clear violations from the employee's record if there were no more in a six-month period. Because of the employee's seven violations in a 12-month period and three disciplinary actions, he chose to participate in the Constructive Action Plan. (Most of his instances of tardiness occurred for violations of one, two, or three minutes.) During his fifth month in the plan he had another tardiness violation. The last violation occurred when he was 10 minutes late to work on a night call-out for emergency repairs while working on the rotating night shift. During the four-day period leading up to the incident the employee had worked over 19 hours of mandatory overtime with two 16-hour days and little opportunity for sleep. On the night of the incident, he was called back less than two hours after working a full eight-hour shift. As a result of this violation, his record of tardiness violations, and the conditions of the Constructive Action Plan, the employee was given a five-day suspension and placed on last chance warning status with one more violation being termination.

Sleeping on the Job. An electrician employed for 11 years at a beverage production facility was assigned the job of repairing a flow meter during the night shift. After diagnosing the problem, he went to a computer terminal to order the part. His supervisor, who found him seated in front of the terminal with his eyes closed and his chin on his chest, concluded that he was sleeping. When confronted by his supervisor the employee denied being asleep. In the two-year period leading up to the suspension, the employee had been disciplined six times with two written reprimands, two 1-day suspensions, one 3-day suspension, and a 1-week suspension. As a result of this incident, he was suspended for one week for sleeping on the job.

Insubordination. A mechanic who had been employed for nine years at a manufacturing plant frequently used his vacation time to take time off Fridays in order to be off work for three-day weekends. Because this practice caused his coworkers to work more weekends than they desired, the employee, who had a good disciplinary record, began to incur the displeasure of his boss and coworkers. Typically, he also would not stay when needed to complete work after his regular shift because he had a second job. In addition, he was sometimes argumentative, disrespectful of management, and uncooperative. Company policy required employees to provide 24-hour advance notice for vacation requests and one-hour notices for sick leave requests. On a day leading up to the incident, the employee called in approximately four hours before he was supposed to report to work and requested vacation time for that day. Although his supervisor denied his request, the employee failed to show up for work and was given a written warning the next week. After receiving the warning, the employee told a coworker that they needed to "get together and get rid of that big-nosed ____ ____ [the supervisor]." Five days after this incident, the company terminated the employee for gross insubordination and attempting to discredit a supervisor.

Arbitrator Decisions. Tardiness case: reduced the five-day suspension to a one-day suspension and removed the "last chance" status because discipline was too severe for the circumstances. Sleeping case: denied the grievance because employer's determination of sleeping was credible. Insubordination case: reduced termination to a four week suspension because of lack of progressive discipline.

few acts of misconduct are so serious that employees may be terminated with the first incident without the application of progressive discipline. These very serious types of misconduct are discussed later in this chapter.

POSITIVE DISCIPLINE

Learning Objective Number Four

positive discipline the part of discipline that promotes understanding and self-control by letting employees know what is expected of them

ETHICS

Positive discipline promotes understanding and self-control. The primary aim of discipline by any manager in the organization should be to prevent undesirable behavior or to change it into desirable behavior. You must communicate what is expected of each individual with regard to her behavior on the job. This process begins with the arrival and induction of each new employee and continues throughout her employment.

The subject of your communication should be the limits placed on individuals by company policies, departmental rules, job descriptions, and the union contract (if one exists). By communicating rules and expectations of acceptable behavior before any infraction occurs, you forewarn your employee about the type of conduct you want on the job. If employees stay within these boundaries, they risk nothing, but if they step outside them, they can expect management to react in certain predictable ways. Once established, these boundaries need to be maintained by regular review of their usefulness and by the judicious application of fair punishments.

Employees gain security when they know their jobs and the standards they must meet. They are aware of the degree of freedom allowed and have definite limits that they know they must not overstep. If they cross one or another of these limits, they know that a punishment will follow the violation.

Positive discipline can be illustrated by a police officer traveling in the flow of traffic in a well-marked, easily identifiable police car. She is visible to other motorists, serves as a reminder to obey traffic regulations, and represents a warning that violators will be apprehended and given a penalty. There is nothing sneaky about her behavior, and the officer's main purpose is to prevent violations from occurring. Contrast this with an unmarked squad car parked out of the view of passing motorists. In this case, prevention is de-emphasized, and detection and punishment are emphasized.

An example of positive discipline comes from a Florida company, Tampa Electric. The company has a procedure it calls a "discipline-making leave day." When an employee below the rank of top management commits an offense or series of offenses that would ordinarily lead to a suspension, the company gives the employee a one-day suspension with pay. The employee is given that day to think seriously about whether or not he wants to continue to work for Tampa Electric. Since the procedure has been used, attendance problems have been cut in half. Supervisors who had been reluctant to give an earned suspension, now see it as a positive step toward improving conditions.[12] Another advantage is that since pay is not withheld for the day off, there is less justification for a disciplinary appeal.

Do not leave your people guessing about the limits imposed on them or about their chances of getting caught in wrongdoing and being penalized. Be visible and obvious, and let them have no doubts about your intentions and your punitive powers. You are not trying to trap anyone. Rather, you are serving to inform them by your actions and words that you wish to promote reasonable behavior and to prevent any unacceptable conduct.

People resent rules that they consider unnecessary or unfair. It often is insufficient to issue prohibitions. People need to know why they cannot do certain things. For example, if employees cannot smoke in department A, the supervisor should explain why they cannot. If your employees are not to use company tools at home on a loan basis, tell them why not. Resentment follows from a lack of understanding the need for rules or regulations. Be sure your people have adequate explanations so that their obedience will be based on logic. This should provide an incentive to cooperate.

LEGAL CONCERNS

Equal employment opportunity laws affect disciplinary and dismissal decisions. It is unlawful to discipline, deny employment rights, or terminate someone because of race, color, religion, sex, national origin, age, or handicap status. Worker compensation laws from the 50 states prohibit discipline and termination of employees who make compensation claims. Similarly, the Occupational Safety and Health Act protects employees from terminations and other disciplinary actions when they exercise their rights under the act. Labor laws prohibit the disciplining of workers for involvement in efforts to unionize and for engaging in lawful union activities. In addition, some cities have enacted laws that prevent discrimination on the basis of one's sexual preference or orientation.

A number of federal and state laws protect **whistleblowers**—employees who notify authorities of violations of laws by their employers that are contrary to public policy (the good of society). In addition, it generally is unlawful to penalize individual employees in any way for refusing to engage in unlawful activities. Clearly, every organization needs a specialist in the area of the law and discipline. Check with your human resource specialists before you decide to take any disciplinary actions.

whistleblower
an employee who notifies authorities of violations of laws committed by his or her employer that are contrary to public policy

RESOLVING COMPLAINTS

Complaints should be a warning to you that something is not right for your people. Complaints can be symptoms of deep-seated or long-standing problems with work or its environment. If they are not dealt with in a fair and equitable way, they can lead to employee misconduct. For example, a person's job may be so boring and unfulfilling that she seeks conversations with others at work, disrupting their work and taking her away from her own.

When your employee or team member comes to you with a complaint, give it a fair hearing. Show sincere interest, and give the person enough time to say what he thinks. Listen without passing judgment. Get the person's perspective. If you can do something to help, do it. If you cannot, find someone who can. If necessary, send the complaint or the complainer to another person for assistance. Let people know that you and the company don't want their employees to be dissatisfied.

Some companies have open-door policies that encourage employees to go beyond their immediate supervisor, all the way to the top if necessary. Others have individuals or committees to allow for a fair hearing and adjudication of disputes. For example, the Red Lobster restaurant chain uses a peer review panel of employees and managers to review disciplinary action. If the panel finds that the discipline is too severe, it can reverse the action. In one case, the panel reversed the termination of a waitress who had worked for the company for 19 years. The panel addressed the issue only three weeks after her termination. More companies, such as Marriott, TRW, and Rockwell International, are using these procedures as a means of improving employee relations and reducing litigation.[13]

EMPLOYEE ASSISTANCE PROGRAMS

Programs created to help employees with personal and job-related problems at work are collectively called employee assistance programs (EAPs). A person with a family, health, financial, stress-related, or substance abuse problem may need immediate help. Exercise, diet, and access to medical professionals offer employees a way to handle a variety of problems, which, if left unattended, can lead them into disciplinary troubles. Drug intervention programs offer substance abusers a way to overcome addictions and to remain employed. People who are unable to cope with their problems will become problems for themselves and others at work. Some of the symptoms of troubled workers are absenteeism, tardiness, implausible excuses, lateness in completing assignments, difficulties in working with others, and turnover.

This chapter's feature on supervisors and ethics deals with procedures that can help firms identify employees who have the greatest likelihood to be involved with fraud.

The hospitality industry suffers from high rates of absenteeism and employee turnover. Some hotels experience as much as 100 percent turnover in a year. The Chicago Hilton and Towers has reduced its turnover rate to about 38 percent thanks in large part to its EAPs focus on wellness: smoking cessation, diet, exercise, training in interpersonal relations, and regular meetings with new hires and staff.[14]

When an employee or team member begins to exhibit signs of trouble, supervisors may gain insights by initially taking a somewhat counter-intuitive approach by examining their own behavior and treatment of the employee. Perhaps they have not

Employee assistance programs, such as company-sponsored health clubs, help reduce employee stress. EAPs help employees deal with personal problems that could otherwise hurt productivity.

SUPERVISORS AND ETHICS

Employee theft is a widespread problem in some businesses, such as the retailing and hospitality industries. Restaurants and bars are particularly susceptible to such unscrupulous behaviors. Almost all types of businesses are at risk to fraud and embezzlement. Because of the magnitude of the losses to firms each year, many companies are interested in finding ways to prevent dishonest behaviors.

An auditing firm, Deloitte & Touche, which also provides consulting services, has been investigating profiling techniques that will enable employers to identify employees who have a high likelihood of engaging in such behaviors. The firm has reported that psychological profilers will probably be needed to develop the technology for eventual commercial use. The firm currently provides "DTect Services" that enable firms to avoid embezzlement in their financial and accounting operations. The characteristics of employees, who are likely to engage in fraudulent behaviors, have been identified through surveys conducted by the Association of Certified Fraud Examiners. Unsurprisingly, personal circumstances, such as substance abuse and dissatisfaction with the employer, are often the key to an employee's decision to engage in fraudulent behaviors.

Although there is a demonstrated need to prevent embezzlement or fraud, there will be problems to overcome before employers will be able to use such technology in the future. One of the major concerns is related to the need to protect the privacy of employees. Furthermore, the collection of highly personal data from employees in order to develop profiles entails the risk that the information will somehow get into the wrong hands and inflict harm. Privacy laws are becoming more prevalent and any use of such technology in the future will need to conform to the requirements of such laws.

Source: Karen Richardson. "Find the Bad Employees: A Tool Can Do It, Privacy Issues Aside," *Wall Street Journal* (February 1, 2006): C3.

shown interest or have somehow alienated the employee. After looking at their own approach as a potential explanation, supervisors should attempt to develop a comprehensive understanding of the employee, to include potential sources of motivation and how these motivational levers may be frozen at work. As a part of this process, the supervisor should attempt to identify developments in the employee's personal life, which may be affecting performance, such as serious illnesses of family members. The supervisor then needs to follow up with a problem-solving session with the employee in which various approaches for dealing with the problem behavior are discussed.[15]

DIVERSITY AND DISCIPLINE

The following guidelines promote positive discipline in any organization by all people regardless of gender, religion, race, age, ethnic background, and physical challenges. They have been culled from the writings of several experts in the area of managing diversity.

- Make certain that individuals know the standards that will be applied to outcomes and behaviors and why those standards are necessary.
- Make sure that people have the necessary resources to succeed.
- Tailor rewards and punishments to fit the circumstances.
- Remove any rewards for poor or negative performances. For example, don't give a poor performer less to do and overburden your star performers as a consequence.
- Remove any punishments for positive performances. For example, do not punish people for exercising their authority and initiative when it results in honest failures. Empowering means the freedom to experiment and fail.
- Encourage all employees to respect and value the individuality and uniqueness of each organizational member and the subcultures to which each belongs.
- Give each person prompt, objective feedback on performance. In particular, make sure that when you have negative feedback for a minority person that you tell him or her in a timely manner. Unfortunately, some white supervisors are hesitant to take disciplinary action against minority employees or provide critical feedback because of concerns about the potential that their actions will be considered as discriminatory. It is unfair to deprive your minority employees of negative feedback that would help them avoid discipline or assist their development.[16]

NEGATIVE DISCIPLINE

negative discipline
the part of discipline that emphasizes the detection and punishment of wrongdoing

Negative discipline emphasizes the detection of wrongdoing and punishment. Such discipline can become bureaucratic and impersonal, relying heavily on records, rules, and procedures, but it need not be this way. It is sometimes characterized by a lack of trust in employees, by demands for blind obedience, and by employees' willful disobedience of rules and regulations. Many employees play a game with their supervisors when they work in such an environment. They become covert and sneaky in their behavior. They deliberately plot to break rules to see if they can beat the system and get away with it or simply to keep management off balance and irritated. They do so because they resent the approach to discipline taken by their employer and supervisors, and they delight in frustrating their efforts. They have not developed the attitudes that support a willing compliance with their organization's rules.

A climate in which negative discipline thrives—one in which the need for penalties is frequent—should be examined and restructured to promote willing compliance and positive discipline. Individual counseling is absolutely essential in order to turn the situation around. Human relationships need development, nourishment, and maintenance. The disciplinary system must be worthy of respect and have the confidence of employees.

PENALTIES

Learning Objective Number Three

Penalizing wrongdoers is an important aspect of discipline. Sometimes preventive actions fail; then the need for prompt and fair action takes over. Your power to take

Common disciplinary problems.		Exhibit 14.3
Absenteeism and tardiness	Insubordination	
Discourtesy	Off-duty misconduct	
Dishonesty	Possession of drugs on the premises	
Drinking on the job and intoxication	Safety violations	
Failure to follow procedures	Sexual harassment	
Failure to pass a drug test	Sleeping on the job	
Falsifying records	Substance abuse	

Source: BNA Editorial Staff, *Grievance Guide,* 10th ed. Washington, D.C.: Bureau of National Affairs, Inc., (2000).

action in dealing with infractions is probably limited. Typically, most supervisors can issue oral and written warnings on their own. Suspensions generally require approval by the manager of employee relations. Your formal disciplinary power depends on your company's policies, and, if your company has a union, the union contract will spell out many of these responsibilities.

COMMON PROBLEMS

As a supervisor, you will likely face one or more of the problems identified in Exhibit 14.3 during any given year. Rule violations usually carry the penalty of a verbal reprimand for the first offense, a written reprimand for the second, and a suspension without pay for a third violation. The person's intentions and work history, as well as the circumstances surrounding the offense, must be considered before any punishment can reasonably be given. Illegal activities may require immediate suspension or dismissal as well as criminal prosecution. However, not all illegal or criminal activities that occur off the job provide legitimate justification for discipline. If such activities do not pose a threat to coworkers, repel customers, or interfere with the performance of the job, the employer may lack justification for imposing discipline.

Absenteeism and sexual harassment will account for many of the problems you are likely to encounter. Most companies say that absenteeism is their biggest problem, and sexual harassment is a growing concern for many companies. Dealing with these problems effectively requires that you be aware of the causes and your options for responding to them.

PERFORMANCE

ABSENTEEISM

People miss work for a variety of reasons. If the employee has a legitimate excuse, the first time it happens you may just let her know that you are concerned. If there is a possibility that the reason will recur, discuss it with the employee, and try to prevent it from occurring. Suppose that Jill, a single parent, has not been late or absent in the past. Yesterday, she called in with a request to take the day off because her babysitter was not available. Is this a legitimate reason? Maybe. But it can recur, and Jill should be working on an alternative to her regular sitter.

Sometimes your company may be to blame for absent employees. Suppose your company offers five sick days each year that cannot be banked and if not used are lost. Suppose employees with legitimate gripes are experiencing job-related stress about which the company has done nothing. At some point, the stress becomes too much to deal with, and the employee feels a real need to escape the source of the stress, at least for a time. Finally, suppose your employee has come to you with a plea to enrich his job. If you fail to deal with your worker's boredom and loss of motivation, you may have an absent worker in the not-too-distant future.

Treat all absentees seriously. Talk to each when he returns. Keep an eye open for patterns in absenteeism—for example, Jack is always out the third Friday of every month. Be sure that you are setting a good example through your own attendance before you decide to discipline others for poor records. Remember also that under the Family and Medical Leave Act employees can request up to 12 weeks of unpaid leave per year for serious illnesses; to take care of newly born children or newly adopted children; or to take care of seriously ill parents, spouses, and children.

Stay in touch with all of your people regularly. Greet them warmly when they come in each day. Listen to their concerns, and deal with their problems promptly. Give those who can handle it a larger say in what they do and how they do it. Through thoughtful delegation, you empower people to become more responsible and to take more pride in themselves and their work.

Sexual harassment destroys the morale and productivity of victims. Employees should be trained to know what conduct is inappropriate and you must take every complaint seriously.

SEXUAL HARASSMENT

Guidelines issued by the Equal Employment Opportunity Commission have interpreted Title VII of the Civil Rights Act to prohibit **sexual harassment.** More specifically, the guidelines define sexual harassment by the following conditions:

> Unwelcomed sexual advances, requests for sexual favors, and other verbal or physical conduct of a sexual nature when:
>
> 1. submission to such conduct is made either explicitly or implicitly a term or condition of employment;
> 2. submission to or rejection of such conduct by an individual is used as a basis for employment decisions affecting such individual; or
> 3. such conduct has the purpose or effect of unreasonably interfering with an individual's work performance or creating an intimidating, hostile, or offensive working environment.[17]

sexual harassment unwelcomed sexual advances, requests for sexual favors, and other physical and verbal conduct of a sexual nature

ETHICS

Although sexual harassment has been illegal for many years a great deal of such harassment still occurs in the workplace.[18] The following account of sexual harassment at a Mitsubishi plant in Illinois indicates how severe the problems can become and the financial consequences to the employer:

> Male coworkers routinely groped women. Some women claimed they were forced to agree to sex to win jobs. Sketches of genitals, breasts, and various sexual acts were drawn on car fenders labeled with female workers' names and sent down the assembly line. Off-site sex parties were held and photographs were distributed around the breakroom . . . Mitsubishi entered into a consent decree to pay $34 million to the victims.[19]

An increasing number of sexual harassment cases in Europe indicate that sexual harassment is not a problem unique to the United States.[20] Because of the increasing numbers of men and women working together, opportunity for possible harassment also increases.[21] Furthermore, employers can incur very high costs when they have to defend themselves against suits for harassment. With harassment cases, the cost for defending the employer may be as much as $250,000, especially when there is a trial.[22] In addition, the 1991 Civil Rights Act allows victims to sue their employers for both actual and punitive damages. Supervisors sometimes worry about their personal liability but the courts have generally considered that they are not liable under federal laws because they are not employers.[23] Nonetheless, the federal courts are not in agreement on this and there have been conflicting rulings.[24] Furthermore, supervisors may incur liability under state laws, such as in Illinois under the Illinois Human Rights Act and in New York under that state's Human Rights Law. Supervisors may also incur liability under common law. The career of a supervisor can be badly damaged by a failure to take action when he or she becomes aware of sexual harassment or should have known that it was occurring.[25] Exhibit 14.4 provides several examples of sexual harassment.

ETHICS

Types of Sexual Harassment

Sexual harassment can occur with a blatant quid pro quo approach in which a supervisor requests sexual favors from an employee in return for favorable treatment.

| EXHIBIT 14.4 | Examples of sexual harassment and responses. |

EXAMPLES

- Unwelcome touching, patting, or pinching
- Sexually offensive language, pictures, or objects
- Derogatory, sexually based humor
- Pressure to engage in sexual activity
- Disparaging remarks to a person about his or her gender
- References to an assumed or desired sexual relationship
- Suggestive references about a person's body or appearance
- Unsolicited, unwanted notes, e-mail messages, graphics, calls, or requests for dates
- Obscene gestures

RESPONSES

- Say no. Sexual harassment is a pattern of behavior that continues after you say no.
- Don't blame yourself. It's not your fault.
- Don't ignore it. The behavior is likely to continue.
- Tell someone.

SUPERVISORY RESPONSES

- Do not ignore the behavior.
- Confront the alleged perpetrator and determine the facts.
- Report findings to superiors.
- Follow up on superiors' decisions.

This type of sexual harassment is less frequent than the hostile environment form, which involves behavior in which a reasonable person would be offended. For example, a hostile environment may be created by vulgar language, conversations about sexual exploits, statements about a person's physical attributes, unwelcome touching, and similar activities. The frequency of such incidents, their severity, the degree of an employee's humiliation, and effect on job performance are factors that courts apply in assessing whether there was a hostile environment.[26]

The number of sexual harassment complaints is increasing despite the efforts of companies to deal with the issue and the publicity associated with the problem.

The news media was filled with reports of former President Clinton's problems related to the lawsuit of Paula Jones over sexual harassment. Clearly, the repercussions from this incident undermined his effectiveness as the Chief Executive of the United States. More recently, Bill O'Reilly, the host of *The O'Reilly Factor*, and the show's associated companies were sued for $60 million by one of the show's producers, who claimed that O'Reilly had sexually harassed her.[27] Problems continue at the corporate level. Two former employees of an investment company claimed that they were sexually harassed while management ignored their problems. One of the former employees claimed that her supervisor "on several occasions . . . exposed himself to her." The other claimed that her manager "offered to pay her rent if she would become his mistress, asked repeatedly to see her breasts, put his tongue in her ear and bragged to her about his sexual prowess."[28]

When sexual harassment is not as obvious or blatant as in the examples cited earlier, there is room for confusion about what actions constitute sexual harassment. One of the points of confusion is that companies sometimes set higher standards than the law requires in order to protect themselves against litigation. An example is the so-called Seinfeld case in which a jury, which included 10 women, ordered Miller Brewing Co. to pay an employee $26 million and return him to his job after the company terminated him for pointing out material in a dictionary."[29] Another source of confusion is that no uniform standard exists for sexual harassment, because juries appear to take the environment of the industry or work community into consideration. A final source of confusion is the mixed signals of recent court decisions on the issue.[30]

Consensual Relationships in the Workplace

Another problem is related to romance in the workplace, a common occurrence in most organizations. Employees are free to become romantically involved, although most companies prohibit one participant from supervising the other. Furthermore, even sexual affairs between supervisors and their direct subordinates do not meet the conditions required for sexual harassment in the absence of unwelcome conduct. However, aside from the negative managerial consequences of these types of relationships, such as the creation of perceptions of favoritism and associated declines in the morale of coworkers, these relationships create potential liability because sexual harassment claims and liability can occur when the relationship sours. At this point, the employee may then claim retaliation on the part of the supervisor and that he or she received adverse or unfavorable treatment in subsequent personnel actions.[31] One of the authors knew a senior executive who provided the following advice to all managers: "Remember that today's willing participant in an office romance is tomorrow's litigant."[32]

Policies and Procedures

A strong, clear stand against sexual harassment must be taken because the company is usually liable for violations it finds out about. It may even be liable for those it should have known about, and it is usually liable for those committed by supervisors that it did not know about. However, the company can take actions to reduce its liability.[33] In addition to prevention efforts, supervisors must deal with any accusations as soon

EXHIBIT 14.5	Examples of issues to be addressed in sexual harassment policies

- A precise definition of sexual harassment
- Tasteful examples of unacceptable harassing behaviors
- Communication of a hard stance against such behaviors
- Clarification of the meaning of *unwelcome*
- Steps to get the harasser to stop
  - Inform the harasser to stop the harassment behavior
  - Report to a designated person when the supervisor is the harasser
- Invitation to employees to file complaints if they have been harassed
- At least three persons (with contact information) to whom complaints can be reported
- Procedures for reporting harassment
- Assurance that complaints do not have to go through the supervisor
- Procedures that will be used to investigate complaints
- Assurances that complaints will be investigated
- Assurances of confidentiality in handling complaints
- Assurances of timely disciplinary action to be imposed on harassers
- Promises of no retaliation for filing complaints

Source: Gary R. Kessler. "Adequate Sexual Harassment Policies for the Productive Workforce," *Employee Rights Quarterly*, (Autumn 2001): 32–39. Darlene Orlov and Michael T. Roumell. *What Every Manager Needs to Know About Sexual Harassment*, New York: American Management Association (AMACOM), (1999).

as they become aware of them. A written company policy spelling out what sexual harassment is and the consequences of harassment must be communicated to all employees. Exhibit 14.5 provides examples of the issues that should be addressed or included in such policies.

A specific procedure for filing a sexual harassment complaint must also be established. The complaint procedure should enable employees to appeal to higher-level managers or an internal authority without going through their supervisors. This cut-out around the immediate supervisor is necessary because in the vast majority of cases the supervisor is the harasser.[34] The importance of having effective anti-harassment policies was emphasized in two 1998 U.S. Supreme Court decisions. The Court ruled that employers have some protection against suits claiming harassment when they have such policies, have complaint procedures, and the employee has not sought relief through the procedure.[35]

Training

It is important for supervisors to be trained on how to recognize and respond to sexual harassment. It is also critical for companies and supervisors to provide such training for all employees. More specifically, employees need to be able to recognize sexual harassment, the procedures for dealing with it, the consequences for engaging in such conduct, and to understand that the organization will not tolerate it. Aside from the responsibility of protecting employees from harassment by supervisors and managers, supervisors must ensure that employees are not harassed by other employees as well as customers. In addition to its managerial value, such training helps employers gain more favorable treatment when they are faced with sexual harassment charges or litigation. Furthermore, companies operating in California that have at least 50 employees are now required to train their supervisors on procedures for preventing sexual harassment.[36]

Many companies are providing training and other support in response to the need to prevent sexual harassment and to minimize their legal exposure. For example, Du Pont "maintains a 24-hour hot line that provides advice to employees on dealing with sexual harassment."[37] Ford Motor Company also has a toll-free number for reporting complaints.[38] One woman who provides sexual harassment training for companies uses the following question to make her point about the unacceptability of sexually harassing behavior:

ETHICS

"Even the most thick headed people will suddenly 'get it' if you ask them, Would you like someone to treat your daughter this way?"[39]

Investigations

When investigating charges of sexual harassment, the supervisor must be careful not to violate the rights of the accused. Claims of sexual harassment are sometimes false and should be investigated with diligence and discretion.[40] Anyone who feels the need to complain should be allowed to do so in privacy and with dignity. No implied or expressed penalty or fear of retribution should be connected with filing a complaint.

BEFORE TAKING ACTION

The actions you take when your employees violate rules and regulations should be governed by the following principles:

Learning Objective Number Five

1. Know each employee, his record, and the nature and causes of the offense.
2. Know your powers as laid down in your job description. When in doubt, check with your boss and your peers.
3. Check on the precedents, if any, that have governed similar situations in the past.
4. Be consistent. If you have given an oral warning on the first minor offense as a general rule, do so in every similar case.
5. Consider the circumstances surrounding the misconduct. Was it willful or accidental? Was the person aware of the limits placed on her conduct? Is this her first offense? Get the facts. Remember that in employee relations, unlike the law, ignorance of the rule *is* an excuse.

6. If an employee has made the same mistake more than once, make the sanctions progressively more severe. Generally, you progress from an oral warning to a written reprimand and eventually to suspension.
7. Coordinate with the other supervisors on enforcement. Every manager should enforce every policy, rule, standard, and procedure with equal weight and effort. It is better not to have a rule that is unenforced or unenforceable.
8. Be reasonable and fair.

The most important aspects of fairness involve basing your decisions on the circumstances. What may be an appropriate penalty for one party to an infraction of the rules may not be so for another. For example, suppose that you find two of your people in a shoving match; before you can break it up, one of them hits the other. Both people are guilty of fighting, but can you think of reasons for which justice might dictate coming down harder on one than on the other? Consider the circumstances and the motives underlying the action you observed. Someone started the fight. Shouldn't that person be dealt with more severely than the person who was provoked? What if one of them had done this before, whereas the other had a clean record? Wouldn't these facts influence your decision?

This chapter's feature on supervisors and performance deals with e-mail and the problems supervisors may encounter.

Being fair does not mean treating everyone the same. You are not a machine that operates automatically or in the same manner with everyone. When we talk about precedents, we mean treating similar offenses in a similar manner. But the key word is "similar." Be certain that what you are dealing with and the people you are dealing with are sufficiently similar to warrant concern for precedents.

When you punish, you must look at the person and the circumstances. This does not mean that you do so in order to exercise prejudice or to get even. If you are vindictive or carry a grudge, you are bound to attack people personally. They will know it, even if you do not admit it. You will be basing your actions on a personal dislike for them and not on their actions. As in conducting appraisals, you must be as objective as you can in order to prevent criticism of your motives or intent. Your job and your reputation are too valuable to risk on immature behavior.

Do not be the cause of your employees' mistakes. Set the example, and let them know you mean what you say. Give them the security that comes with knowing what they must do and why.

A man who audited stores for a large retail chain for more than 30 years once told one of the authors that where he uncovered dishonest employees, there was usually a dishonest manager. For example, a dishonest manager would, on the way out of the store each day, help himself to a handful of peanuts or candy. At other times, such a manager might be too lenient in enforcing rules or regulations or deal weakly with dishonest employees. Honest employees began to resent the extras enjoyed by their peers and decided to get into the action, too. It may start with a pen or pencil, but it may not end until there are substantial losses.

Keep in mind that you are not the final voice in matters of discipline. Your company and the union may have procedures providing for review of your decision, since matters of discipline are often considered too important to entrust to any one manager. If you are wrong, you will be overruled. If not, you should be able to count on your boss for backing. Your employees will hear about your disciplinary decisions.

SUPERVISORS AND
PERFORMANCE

Companies are increasingly concerned about the content of e-mail messages that their employees send and receive beyond the confines of the organization, as well as the messages that they send to each other. Because of such concerns, companies are increasing their surveillance of the content of employees' e-mail through the use of scanning software. Survey data indicate that between 2001 and 2005 the proportion of companies scanning employees' e-mail increased from 47 percent to 60 percent. The software used for such scanning can be customized for the particular issues of concern to employers. For example, investment firms may want to scan for words, such as high yield or guarantee, which might indicate that their sales representatives are over-promising customers on the returns that can be expected from their investment products.

Although the current emphasis of such scanning is on e-mail exchanges outside of the organization, scanning e-mail within organizations is increasing. The proportion of companies doing such scanning in 2005 was 27 percent, which is an increase from the 19 percent reporting such use in 2003. One of the obvious purposes of internal scanning is to identify sexually harassing behaviors or evidence of a hostile environment so that disciplinary action can be taken to eliminate such activities. The example of Harry Stonecipher, the former CEO of Boeing, whose e-mails to a female employee with whom he was having an affair, led to his discharge, should put all employees on notice that their use of company e-mail for inappropriate purposes will place them in danger of serious discipline or termination.

In addition to concerns about sexual harassment, employee fraud, and leakages of competitive information, computer monitoring can also be used to determine how employees are spending their time at work. For example, computer software can track the Internet websites they visit. In addition, software can be used to determine the activity level of employees as an indication of their productivity.

Supervisors should be very clear with their employees about the inappropriateness of behaviors that can constitute sexual harassment or the creation of a hostile work environment. They should also emphasize that such behaviors are not limited to in-person conversations or action, because sexual harassment can occur through e-mail messages. Furthermore, supervisors need to warn their employees that the organization may be monitoring their e-mail without their knowledge and that e-mails provide very strong evidence of misconduct. Connecticut and Delaware require organizations to inform their employees of such monitoring, but other states have no such regulations. Finally, supervisors need to emphasize that employees should assume, when they send an e-mail, that anyone may see it.

Source: Piu-Wing Tam, Erin White, Nick Wingfield, and Kris Maher. "Snooping E-Mail by Software Is Now a Workplace Norm," *Wall Street Journal*," (March 9, 2005): B1–B3.

Do not jeopardize your relations with them by hasty or irrational actions. Be sure that you have the facts and that you have put them together properly. Consult with superiors before you act.

Consider the case of a supervisor named John and his employee, Harry. John has given a verbal order to Harry. Harry has failed to respond. Orders are intended to provoke an immediate positive response and usually do if they are not over-utilized, so John immediately assumes that Harry is being insubordinate. Without any further investigation, John suspends Harry for one week while he and the company decide whether or not to fire Harry. But wait a moment. Aren't there legitimate reasons Harry could have had for not following the supervisor's order? Here are but a few:

1. Harry did not hear the order.
2. Harry was told to do something illegal.
3. Harry was told to perform a task outside his job description or beyond his capabilities or training.
4. John was unclear in his order, and Harry did not understand it.

All these and more could get Harry off the hook. If John relies solely on his observations, without any further investigation, he is likely to make an improper decision and be reversed. In that case, Harry will be back at work, with pay for his time off. Meanwhile, John will have damaged his reputation and alienated Harry, among others. It pays to get the employee's point of view.

GIVING THE REPRIMAND

You have studied the case of wrongdoing, gathered your facts, touched base with experts, and reached the conclusion that disciplinary action is necessary. You have chosen the penalty to fit the offense and scheduled a meeting with the offender. Now begins one of the least pleasant tasks of being a supervisor. Here are some tips to make the disciplinary session as productive as possible:

- Choose a time and place that ensures privacy and freedom from interruptions.
- Have your facts in writing and your mind clear about the who, what, when, where, and how.
- Be businesslike and serious. The meeting is not the time or place for discussion about anything other than the offense and the consequences of it.
- Adopt a pleasant approach in administering the discipline. The manner in which discipline is administered is important. Empirical evidence shows that when discipline is delivered in a pleasant manner and the supervisor makes an accurate diagnosis of the situation, there is less damage to the relationship and greater likelihood that the discipline will be viewed as appropriate. Emotional reactions to discipline also are less likely when supervisors administer discipline in a pleasant manner.[41]
- Take charge of the meeting. Lay out your case with specifics. Get agreement on essentials, and listen for any new information.
- Be clear about the fact that the behavior is at issue, not the person.
- Try to get a commitment from the offender for improvement and for no repetitions of the offense.

THE DECISION TO TERMINATE

The decision to terminate a person usually rests with the person or persons who have the authority to hire. In most disciplinary cases, this is the last resort, and it should take place only when all else has failed. Some situations, however, usually demand that the guilty party be dismissed immediately. These include the following cases:

1. Gross insubordination, such as refusal to comply with a direct, lawful order accompanied by a statement of an intention to refuse the order
2. Drunkenness on the job
3. Willful destruction of company property
4. Serious cases of dishonesty or theft
5. Bringing a firearm on company premises

Certainly there will be exceptions, even in these extreme situations, and whatever circumstances surround each of these exceptional cases must be considered. It is nevertheless true that a large majority of companies require that the penalty for these infractions be automatic dismissal.

EMPLOYMENT AT WILL

Employment at will means that both the employer and the employee have the right to terminate the employee's employment at any time, with or without just cause. Along with employment discrimination laws and the other federal laws already discussed in this chapter, nearly all the states have some laws that restrict an employer's right to fire anyone for any reason. The courts have added to these restrictions. While the employment-at-will rule from the common law still generally prevails, there are some important exceptions. Important areas of exception are of the following: (1) public policy exceptions,[42] (2) implied covenant of good faith and fair dealing,[43] and (3) an implied employment contract.[44]

The public policies exceptions prevent employers from terminating employees because of such actions as refusal to perjure themselves in order to protect the employer's interests, reporting infractions of regulations or laws when they are obligated to do so, and refusing to engage in activities that are legally prohibited.[45] For example a public policy exception would arise when an employee is terminated for missing work because he or she has been serving on a jury.[46] As for implied covenants, good faith and fair dealing, an example of such an exception would extend protection to an employee who has been discharged to keep the employee from becoming vested in the company's pension plan.[47] Finally, exceptions to employment-at-will under the implied contract view are based on the rationale that the language in an employee handbook conveys tenure or restricts the employer's basis for terminations.[48] As a result, employers who wish to retain the power to terminate employees at will must refrain from making any promises, guarantees, or covenants that may lead the employee to believe that she has a right to long-term employment. Accordingly, their employee handbooks are careful not to imply any such rights. In addition, in order to obtain more specific protection against implied employment contract interpretations, employers typically have noncontractual disclaimers that new employees must sign. Employees acknowledge in these disclaimers their understanding that the employment arrangement is at-will.[49]

One state, Montana, has actually adopted a wrongful discharge law that severely constrains the at-will employment approach.[50] In Montana, the state's Wrongful

employment at will
the common law doctrine that holds that employment will last until either employer or employee decides to terminate it, with or without cause

EXHIBIT 14.6	Definition of "just cause" in Puerto Rico's Discharge Indemnity Act.

Sec. 185b. Discharge without just cause

Good cause for the discharge of an employee of an establishment shall be understood to be:

(a) That the worker indulges in a pattern of improper or disorderly conduct.

(b) The attitude of the employee of not performing his work in an efficient manner or of doing it belatedly and negligently or in violation of the standards of quality of the product produced or handled by the establishment.

(c) Repeated violations by the employee of the reasonable rules and regulations established for the operation of the establishment, provided a written copy thereof has been timely furnished to the employee.

(d) Full, temporary, or partial closing of the operations of the establishment.

(e) Technological or reorganization changes as well as changes of style, design, or nature of the product made or handled by the establishment and in the services rendered to the public.

(f) Reductions in employment made necessary by a reduction in the volume of production, sales, or profits, anticipated or prevalent at the time of the discharge.

A discharge made by mere whim or fancy of the employer or without cause related to the proper and normal operation of the establishment shall not be considered as a discharge for good cause.

Source: P.R. Laws Ann. Tit. 29, Sect. 185a–185i.

Discharge Act protects employees from being terminated under the following circumstances:

    a. it was in retaliation for the employee's refusal to violate public policy or for reporting a violation of public policy;

    b. the discharge was not for good cause and the employee had completed the employer's probationary period of employment; or

    c. the employer violated the express provisions of its own written personnel policy.[51]

In addition, Puerto Rico has enacted the Discharge Indemnity Act, which details just causes for terminating an employee (see Exhibit 14.6).

To summarize, while there are exceptions, employment at will is still broadly applicable, and supervisors must understand that their companies can terminate employees when it is appropriate to do so. Accordingly, the safest or most conservative approach for employers is to terminate employees only when there is just cause or good reason. As such, there should have been the elements of discipline discussed previously in this chapter, such as reasonable rules, prior warning, due process, progressive discipline, a thorough investigation, and documentation.[52]

PITFALLS

The major problems you encounter when you attempt to carry out your disciplinary duties can be minimized by an awareness of their causes.

Learning Objective Number Six

Starting Off Soft

Supervisors, especially those who are new at the job, are apt to associate being lenient with being liked. They sometimes feel that if they look the other way on occasion or mete out less than a deserved penalty for an infraction, they will endear themselves to their employees. This is inaccurate. In actuality, their leniency will be the cause of more trouble. If Mary arrives late and you say nothing, she will be encouraged to do it again. So will the others who witness the event and your failure to take constructive action.

It is always easier to start out tough, with an emphasis on the letter of the law. As you gain self-confidence and additional knowledge about your duties and your people, you can shift the emphasis to the spirit of the law as well, tempering your judgment within the framework of your understanding of your people, their personalities, and the group pressures at work on them. This is what justice means. Each person and most events are unique and should be dealt with as such. If you are soft, those who toe the line will resent you for it. They will see no tangible reward for proper behavior, while they witness some for improper conduct. Your softness will be interpreted as weakness, and you can expect your employees to test you further to find the limits.

Acting in Anger

How many times have you wished you could take back remarks made to another in anger? If you are like most people, the answer is: too often. With emotions influencing your observations and judgment, you will seldom make a sound decision. Too often you will have to back down and apologize for a demonstration of your lack of self-control. Never attempt to discipline while you or the other persons involved are angry. It helps to move physically away from the situation and the environment of a wrongdoing in order to regain your composure. Tell the persons involved to report to you in your office in a few minutes. This will give you time to recapture your composure and reason.

Disciplining in Public

If you have some critical remarks for an individual, make them in person and in private. Each person has a reputation to uphold, both with you and with his peers. He has pride and self-esteem, which need protection. He does not wish to be subjected to ridicule or embarrassment. It may not be penalties that your people fear, but your way of dispensing them. Your methods may make the difference between a constructive and a destructive kind of discipline. Human resource experts say that when an employee is disciplined in public, those who observe the discipline also are punished because most people do not like to observe such actions.

Incomplete Research and Analysis

Let us assume that you see a man stretched out on a packing crate 30 feet away, and, because he has his eyes shut, you jump to the conclusion that he is sleeping on the job or, at the very least, goofing off. You should know by now—from your experience and from this book—that appearances do not always reveal the whole truth. Where discipline is involved, it takes more than one observation to make a sound case. Unless you go to the man (preferably with a witness you can count on) and ask him some questions, you cannot really be sure that your observations are correct.

If you intend to penalize someone, be certain that you have a firm case that will stand up to review by a higher authority. Have the details clearly in mind, and make some notes of your observations for later reference. Memory loses certainty and eliminates details with the passage of time between a disciplinary action and the appeal of that action. Answer questions such as who was there and what was said by each person. If all you have is your word against the employee's, you will lose the case, especially when a union is involved.

Exceeding Your Authority

Keep in mind that, like your people, you have limits on your power and conduct. Check with your boss and your peers when you are in doubt about what action to take. There is no legitimate excuse for falling into the trap of exceeding your authority.

Being Vindictive

Be sure that your actions and words are not based on personality clashes or personal prejudice. Put your biases aside, or they will shine through with a neon brilliance for all to see. If you single out one person for disciplinary action, and your reasons rest in your personal biases, you certainly will lose your case and face the wrath of those who must review your actions.

Like your employees, you have personal preferences. It would not be reasonable to expect you to like all your people. But you are being paid to serve all of them, regardless of their personal feelings toward you or yours toward them. Unless an employee's personality is defective and interferes with performance, you cannot in conscience hold it against that individual.

Leaving It to Others

Like appraising your people, disciplining them is your exclusive right and duty. You cannot be asked to part with it if you are expected to control and direct your workers properly. Some companies allow the human resource department or some other authority to mete out discipline. This reduces the supervisor's role to that of an arresting officer. Your employees will soon realize that you cannot punish but can only report violations. As a result, your status will be reduced greatly. This represents a tremendous handicap to a supervisor. Although some managers prefer this arrangement because it releases them from a difficult responsibility, they fail to see that giving up this power makes them impotent and subjects them to additional and needless harassment from above and below.

Even worse than losing disciplinary powers to a higher authority is giving them away to a top worker or "straw boss"—someone acting with your authority on your behalf. Remember, these people are extensions of yourself and, as such, represent you and your other employees. Do not give them the power to cause you and themselves trouble. You are responsible for your people and are accountable for their actions. If your top worker or straw boss made the wrong decisions, you would have to correct them, thus injuring their already difficult position, possibly beyond repair. Most straw bosses do not want such authority. If they do try to assume it, make it clear to them that they cannot have it.

Failing to Keep Adequate Records

To gain and keep a perspective on each of your people, you should keep records of their performance appraisals, reprimands, and needs. These files will prove quite helpful when you face tough personnel decisions. They also come in handy when you want to justify your opinions or take specific disciplinary actions.

INSTANT REPLAY

1. Both positive discipline and negative discipline are needed if reasonable and safe conduct at work is to be promoted.

2. When an organization or a supervisor tolerates a poor performer, the organization or the supervisor cannot, in conscience, discipline anyone whose performance exceeds the poor performer's.

3. The best kind of disciplinary system is one based on the individual employee's sense of responsibility for her own work and on each employee's self-control.

4. People need to know what is expected of them and how well or poorly they are doing; they have a right to expect consistent enforcement of rules, policies, and standards.

5. People need to know that good work will be rewarded and that poor performance will earn swift and predictable responses from management.

6. People do not resent punishment that they know they deserve. They do resent being punished for something they did not know was wrong— for not being forewarned.

7. The majority of your employees will not need negative discipline if the positive side of discipline has been developed.

QUESTIONS FOR CLASS DISCUSSION

1. Can you define this chapter's key terms?

2. What is the difference between negative and positive discipline? In what ways are they similar?

3. What is the purpose of punishment in a disciplinary system?

4. What are the basic principles of discipline?

5. What are the major pitfalls a supervisor can fall victim to when carrying out disciplinary functions?

6. What does it mean to be fair when disciplining employees?

7. Why should you know yourself and your employees well before attempting to discipline or punish them?

ASSESS THIS SITUATION

Purpose: To test your knowledge and ability to identify sexual harassment in a work setting.

Your task: After each of the following statements, indicate if you agree or disagree with it. The answers are shown at the end of the exercise. Don't look at them until after you have completed the quiz.

Agree	*Disagree*	
O	O	1. If I don't think I am sexually harassing another person, that means I am not doing so.
O	O	2. If no complaints of sexual harassment come to a manager's attention, none is occurring.
O	O	3. Same-sex harassment is not covered by the law.
O	O	4. Fear can keep people who are harassed from complaining.
O	O	5. When a man enters what has been an all-female environment, some behaviors of the women will have to change.
O	O	6. Sexually suggestive visual material, when placed in one's private office, cannot be grounds for sexual harassment.

(Answers: 1, 2, 3, and 6 should be marked "Disagree")

SKILL BUILDING EXERCISE 14.1

Supervisors sometimes encounter reports of sexual harassment or may even themselves observe questionable behaviors. Although they may need to obtain assistance from specialists in human resources or the legal department, they should have some sense of problematic behavior and know how to respond.

Your Task: Work in small groups and answer these questions about the three situations that follow: (1) Does the behavior constitute sexual harassment? (2) What additional information, if any, would you need in order to reach a definitive conclusion? (3) What actions would you take if an investigation of the incident confirmed the information presented here?

Situation A: A manager frequently told dumb-blonde jokes to one of his employees who happened to be a blonde woman. She was offended by his jokes.

Situation B: A customer at a café comes in almost every day, places his laptop computer on the table, and logs on to a porn site. The waitresses who serve him can see the computer screen when they come to his table to take his orders.

Situation C: A senior citizen in a retirement home hugs and kisses women who help him get into bed and who help him get into the shower. Occasionally he grabs some of the younger ones.

Sources: Diane Molvig. "Squelch Sexual Harassment," *Credit Union Executive Newsletter,* (September 6, 2004): 2. Gillian Flynn, "Third-Party Sexual Harassment: Commonplace and Laden with Liability," *Workforce* (November 2000): 88–92.

SKILL BUILDING WRITING EXERCISE 14.2

Progressive discipline systems have been subject to criticism because they do not always produce desired changes in employee behaviors. It is true that progressive disciplinary systems take time to administer correctly because they require attention to detail and documentation of actions taken. Attention to detail and consistency are required for fair administration of such systems and for them to be able to withstand challenges in arbitration or legal proceedings. Unfortunately, some of the criticisms of such systems are probably unfair because disappointing results were caused by sloppy administration, inconsistent handling of incidents, or weak supervision rather than flaws with the systems. Nonetheless, progressive discipline systems are better suited to some types of problem employee behaviors than others. Consider the following behaviors:

- Absenteeism
- Abuse of sick leave
- Insubordination
- Lack of initiative
- Low productivity
- Poor quality
- Tardiness
- Safety violations
- Substance abuse
- Verbal abuse of coworkers

Your Task: Prepare brief written responses for each of these problem behaviors, which answer the following questions: (1) Is progressive discipline appropriate? Provide justification for your answer. (2) For those behaviors for which progressive discipline is inappropriate, describe another approach that is likely to be more effective.

CASE 14.1   Disciplinary Situations

Assume that you are the supervisor who must decide what to do with employees in each of the following situations. Your options include the following: ask your boss to handle the situation, refer the worker to human resources or an employee assistance program, obtain more information, provide training, administer a verbal warning, write up a written reprimand, recommend a suspension of three days, recommend a suspension of 30 days, or recommend termination. You may also choose combinations of these actions. Be prepared to justify your choices.

Situation 1. An employee just sent a sexual joke by e-mail to all members of your department. Within 30 minutes after the joke was sent, two females and a male employee come to your office to complain about the joke. Company policy forbids employees from using e-mail for personal use and explicitly forbids the distribution of material of a sexual nature.

Situation 2. You read in the paper before coming to work this morning that one of your employees was arrested by the police for a domestic disturbance and suspected spousal abuse. It is the third time that he has been arrested. In the first two incidents, his wife had facial bruises and scrapes on her arms but she refused to file charges. Later on this morning, you learn that his wife had similar injuries again but refused to file charges, and the police have released him.

Situation 3. Your company sells and installs home security systems. All repair and installation technicians carry cell phones so that they can be contacted about emergency work or changes in jobs. In addition, your scheduler maintains a list of service calls each technician is to make during the day. Technicians are required to call in when they arrive at a job, leave the job, and take breaks for more than 20 minutes. One of your best technicians, Richard Titus, could not be located for three hours yesterday afternoon. He did not respond to calls on his cell phone and failed to show up at a job. The dispatcher finally got in touch with Richard by calling the apartment of a friend whom she thought was dating Richard. Richard is married and does not live at this apartment.

Situation 4. You manage a team of heating and air conditioning specialists who install custom systems in large buildings. Every morning you have a conference with all of the team members to go over developments that will need special attention. It is essential that the team members exchange information so that they can coordinate their efforts. Cooperation, good relations, and respectful treatment among your team members are vital for economical and efficient installations. At this morning's conference, you were going over a foul-up by one of the team members on the previous day that would require a substantial amount of rework. You and he explained the situation so that the others would know how to conduct the rework. After he finished, one of the other team members said, "What kind of an idiot would make a mistake like this?"

Situation 5. This morning you were making a presentation to other supervisors, support staff members, and the plant manager about new classroom facilities and equipment that will be used for training. The classroom equipment includes a computer with Internet access and a projector that displays the computer images on a large screen. Prior to the meeting, you had set up the computer to display a website about technical manufacturing standards and then left to coordinate other issues. Later, as you were addressing the group, you switched on the projector and there in living color was a pornographic scene from a website. Afterward, you found out that one of your employees had set you up by switching the Internet address.

Situation 6. Two customers at the expensive restaurant you manage have come to you with a complaint about one of the waiters. The husband and wife, who were part of a dinner party of eight, are outraged at the waiter's treatment of the wife. According to the husband, the waiter had given their party menus and was taking their orders. When it came time for his wife to order she asked the waiter about a particular item on the menu. The waiter replied that he would not recommend it to her. When she asked why, the waiter said that the item was over her calorie limit. The wife, who was obese, was humiliated by the comment, and the husband was outraged. Furthermore, they stated that the same waiter had made a similar insinuating remark about his wife's obesity on a previous occasion. The waiter has 20 years' service with the restaurant and also is the maitre d'.

Source: Situation 6 is based on an arbitration case by Samuel Kaynard, "Union Club of New York and Hotel Employees International Union, Local 6," *Labor Award Reporter: Summary of Labor Arbitration Awards, Report No. 460* (July 1997): 6–7.

Questions

1. Review the options listed at the beginning of these situations. What will you do in each of these situations? Explain your reasoning.

2. Might these incidents be related to the quality of supervision these employees have received? Explain.

CASE 14.2   Sticky Business

You are a supervisor in a sugar refinery that processes sugar cane into sugar. Recently the shut-off valve to one of the molasses vats failed to work properly, and approximately 300 gallons of molasses spilled onto the plant floor. You directed several people to work overtime to help clean up the mess. One of the production workers you ordered to help was a long-time employee of 24 years. He refused to stay, saying the following: "I've got things to do. . . . I've got a life outside this refinery. . . . I've got business of my own to take care of." At the regular quitting time, he clocked out and left the refinery.

The next day you confronted the employee about his refusal to obey your directive to stay and help clean up the molasses. He said that he had left work the previous day instead of helping because he had a personal emergency. Your employee stated that he had to help find his teenage daughter who was missing. You told him that you would check out his story and meet with him later.

You talked to several people about the missing daughter excuse and determined that your employee was lying. In addition, you reviewed his disciplinary record and found that he had been disciplined twice in the past for similar behaviors, although these incidents occurred over five years ago.

Source: Based on an arbitration case by Diane Massey, "Domino Sugar Corp. and United Food and Commercial Workers International Union, Local 1101," *Labor Award Reporter: Summary of Labor Arbitration Awards, Report No. 468* (March 1998): 6–7.

Questions

1. What disciplinary action will you take in this situation?

2. What factors influenced your decision? Explain the basis for your decision.

REFERENCES

[1] World of Quotes.Com Website, (February 11, 2006), *www.worldofquotes.com/topic/Discipline/1.*

[2] O'Brien, Timothy L., and Thomas, Landon, Jr. "It's Cleanup Time at Citi," *New York Times,* (November 7, 2004).

[3] Ibid.

[4] Ibid.

[5] Ibid.

[6] Ibid.

[7] Nicholson, Nigel. "How to Motivate Your Problem People," *Harvard Business Review,* (January 2003): 57–58.

[8] Leonard, Edwin C., Jr, and Hilgert, Raymond L. *Supervision: Concepts and Practices of Management,* 9th ed. Mason, Ohio: Thomson South-Western, (2004): 180.

[9] BNA Editorial Staff. *Grievance Guide,* 10th ed. Washington, DC: Bureau of National Affairs, (2000).

[10] Ledvinka, James, and Scarpello, Vida G. *Federal Regulation of Personnel and Human Resource Management,* 2nd ed. Boston: PWS-Kent (1991): 315–325.

[11] BNA Editorial Staff. *Grievance Guide.*

[12] "Disciplining Employees with Dollars," *Success!* (April 1987): 25.

[13] Jacobs, Margaret. "Red Lobster Tale: Peers Decide Fired Waitress's Fate," *Wall Street Journal* (January 20, 1998): B1.

[14] Kleiman, Carol. "Employee Turnover a Bottom-Line Issue," *Chicago Tribune* (October 21, 1990): sect. 8, 1.

[15] Nicholson. "How to Motivate Your Problem People."

[16] Thomas, David A., and Wetlaufer, Suzy. "A Question of Color: A Debate on Race in the U.S. Workplace," *Harvard Business Review* (September–October 1997): 124.

[17] Equal Employment Opportunity Commission. *Guidelines on Discrimination Because of Sex.* Section 1604.11, November 10, 1980.

[18] "Anita Hill and Sexual Harassment," *Workforce* (January 2002): 32.

[19] Shepard, Glenn. *How to Manage Problem Employees.* New Jersey: John Wiley & Sons, Inc., (2005): 88–89.

[20] "Women in Suits," *Economist* (March 2, 2002): 60–61.

[21] Zachary, Mary-Kathryn. "Labor Law for Supervisors," *Supervision* (July 2001): 23–26.

[22] Dobrich, Wanda, Dranoff, Steven, and Maatman, Gerald, Jr. *The Manager's Guide to Preventing a Hostile Work Environment,* New York: McGraw-Hill, (2002).

[23] Orlov, Darlene, and Roumell, Michael T. *What Every Manager Needs to Know About Sexual Harassment,* New York: American Management Association (AMACOM) (1999).

[24] Dobrich, Dranoff, and Maatman. *The Manager's Guide to Preventing a Hostile Work Environment.*

[25] Orlov and Roumell. *What Every Manager Needs to Know About Sexual Harassment.*

[26] Dobrich, Dranoff, and Maatman. *The Manager's Guide to Preventing a Hostile Work Environment.*

[27] Shepard. *How to Manage Problem Employees.*

[28] Pusey, Allen. "Ex-Mayor Folsom, Companies Sued," *Dallas Morning News* (September 25, 1997): 34A.

[29] Fisher, Anne. "After All This Time, Why Don't People Know What Sexual Harassment Means?" *Fortune* (January 12, 1998): 156.

[30] Ibid.

[31] Dobrich, Dranoff, and Maatman. *The Manager's Guide to Preventing a Hostile Work Environment.*

[32] Greer, Charles R. *Strategy and Human Resources: A General Managerial Approach,* 2nd ed. Englewood Cliffs, NJ: Prentice Hall (2001): 78.

[33] Jacobs, Roger B., and Koch, Cora S. *Legal Compliance Guide to Personnel Management.* Englewood Cliffs, NJ: Prentice Hall, (1993).

[34] Greer. *Strategy and Human Resources: A General Managerial Approach* 78.

[35] Greenhouse, Linda. "High Court Clarifies Sex Harassment Law," *Fort Worth Star Telegram* (June 27, 1998): A1, A15.

[36] "Lawsuits Could Follow Failure to Train," *HR Focus.* (September 2005): 2.

[37] Campbell, Linda P. "Examining Workplace Behavior," *Chicago Tribune* (October 20, 1993): sect. 1, 3.

[38] Felsenthal, Edward. "Rulings Open Way for Sex-Harass Cases," *Wall Street Journal* (June 29, 1998): A3, A10.

[39] Fisher, "After All This Time, Why Don't People Know What Sexual Harassment Means?" 56.

[40] Greer. *Strategy and Human Resources: A General Managerial Approach* 78.

[41] Greer, Charles R., and Labig, Chalmer E., Jr. "Employee Reactions to Disciplinary Action," *Human Relations 40*(8) (1987): 507–524.

[42] Coleman, Francis T. *Ending the Employment Relationship Without Ending Up in Court*, Washington, D.C.: Society for Human Resource Management, (2001).

[43] Ibid.

[44] Ruben, Alan, and Miles, Ed. *Elkouri & Elkouri: How Arbitration Works*, 6th ed. Washington, D.C.: Bureau of National Affairs, Inc., 2003.

[45] Coleman. *Ending the Employment Relationship Without Ending Up in Court.*

[46] Ruben. *Elkouri & Elkouri: How Arbitration Works.*

[47] Coleman. *Ending the Employment Relationship Without Ending Up in Court.*

[48] Ruben. *Elkouri & Elkouri: How Arbitration Works.*

[49] Coleman. *Ending the Employment Relationship Without Ending Up in Court.*

[50] Ruben, *Elkouri & Elkouri: How Arbitration Works.*

[51] Ibid., 930.

[52] Falcone, Paul. *The Hiring and Firing Question and Answer Book.* New York: American Management Association (AMACOM) (2002).

CHAPTER 5

"It is one of the characteristics of a free and democratic nation . . . [that it has] free and independent labor unions."

President Franklin Delano Roosevelt[1]

Objectives

After reading and discussing this chapter, you should be able to do the following:

1. List the steps for handling complaints, and comment about what happens in each.
2. List prohibitions of the Wagner Act.
3. List prohibitions of the Taft–Hartley Act.
4. Compare the roles of supervisors and stewards in labor relations.
5. Outline typical grievance procedures for a large organization and a small organization.

Union Cooperation at Harley Davidson

Harley Davidson motorcycles are considered an American icon, and the company's customers have incredible loyalty to the company's products. Nonetheless, in the 1980s the company was in serous trouble as a result of quality problems, issues related to a merger, and difficulties with the company's unions. In 1983, the company began its turnaround with the help of tariffs against imported motorcycles, which protected its market for four years, and a number of management changes including improved relationships with the unions that represented the company's workers.[2] With these changes in labor relations, the relationship with the unions moved from a more traditional adversarial relationship to more of a problem-solving approach. For example, the unions were given a larger role in major decisions that affected the workers, such as the following:

> *Harley's managers made an unusual deal with their unions, the International Association of Machinists and the Paper, Allied-Industrial, Chemical and Energy Workers. A partnership arrangement was written into the union contracts, requiring labor and management to agree on decisions affecting workers.[3]*

Complaints, Grievances, and Unions

The unions, for example, had a say in the selection of a new assembly plant site in the mid-1990s. Two of the three members of the site selection committee were from the unions, and Kansas City, Mo., got the nod, rather than a lower-wage state with a right-to-work law (which wouldn't require workers to join or support a union). Assembly is done at the Kansas City plant and at an older facility in York, Pa., while engineers and transmissions are made in Milwaukee, the headquarters city. The pay for all this is $17 to $33 an hour and rising at 2.5 percent a year. Still, with the partnership as a framework, labor costs are continuously whittled down as a condition for keeping production in America.[4]

Management recently proposed going to Germany to buy the gears for a new transmission, rather than making them at the main plant here. The union wanted the work in-house and got it, but only after agreeing, as an offset, that future retirees would pay health insurance premiums beyond a certain cap. The company now pays the premiums without a cap. "The Unions have been forced to negotiate things we would have preferred not to negotiate," said Richard Krause, president of the Paper, Allied-Industrial, Chemical and Energy Workers local here, who was laid off himself for nearly five years in the early 1980s. We've changed work rules, and we've reduced job classifications considerably [which allows more flexible work assignments]. But we are involved in running the business, and that means accepting changes that keep the company competitive."[5]

Management, on the other hand, cannot transfer "core production" overseas without union consent. Nor can it lay off workers unilaterally. Adhering to this restriction, the company retrained and reassigned more than 60 workers who were displaced when Harley went to robotic welding of motorcycle frames at the Kansas City plant.[6]

Harley's example of labor and management cooperation provides an indication of the benefits that can be obtained when managers work closely with unions to help control costs and increase productivity while providing for job security. Supervisors should work to improve the relationship with the unions representing their employees so that the dual needs of company productivity and competitiveness can be reached in a way that enables companies to preserve job security.

Questions for Thought

1. In what ways can supervisors establish a good working relationship with union stewards and union workers while maintaining a focus on efficiency, cost control, and productivity?
2. How can supervisors build a relationship with union stewards and unionized employees where trust between the parties has been damaged?

Introduction

This chapter discusses the proper ways of dealing with the complaints of employees. First, we consider how to handle complaints in a company where there is no union. Next, we discuss what unions are and why workers join them. Finally, we learn how complaints are handled in a company where there is a union contract.

COMPLAINTS

complaint
any expression of unhappiness with working conditions or on-the-job relationships that comes to a manager's attention

For our purposes, a **complaint** is any expression of unhappiness with working conditions or on-the-job relationships that comes to a manager's attention. A complaint may be based on a worker's assumption that she has been treated unfairly or inequitably. Complaints often begin with a worker's perception that she has been or is being treated differently from others in similar circumstances.

A complaint may be a symptom of a very different problem from the one it seems to state. The worker may be complaining about his level of pay or job classification, but the real issue may be dissatisfaction with the job—even though the worker may feel that more pay or a higher job classification would make the job more bearable. If this is the case, even after a careful explanation of why a certain level of pay goes with the labor grade, the worker will likely remain dissatisfied because the real problem has not been resolved.

HANDLING COMPLAINTS: A COMPANY-WIDE SYSTEMS APPROACH

Most companies have a recommended or required set of procedures to follow when a supervisor, team leader, or team facilitator is confronted with employee complaints. Typically, the first step is to identify the nature of the complaint and the problem or challenge it poses for an individual or group. This involves getting the facts and perspectives from all those affected by a complaint. Once a complaint is accurately stated, the causes for it—a rule, policy, people problems, or a change of some kind—need to be discovered. If corrective action is warranted, the complaining employee is asked what he views as an adequate remedy. Alternative courses of action are then considered and evaluated for consistency with company policies and applicable precedents. Prompt action usually is called for, and the results must be evaluated to determine if the complaint has been satisfactorily resolved.

Be ready to handle worker complaints. Understand that their complaints are very important to them. Be ready to help.

QUALITIES OF AN EFFECTIVE COMPLAINT SYSTEM

One of the most important characteristics of effective formal complaint systems or procedures is that they promote *two-way communication*. While supervisors, managers, and executives may think that they have a great sense of what is going on in their own organizations, they are often surprised. On the other hand, supervisors are much closer to the action and typically have a better sense of organizational reality than higher-level managers. Nonetheless, they can be badly mistaken when they conclude that they have a complete understanding of the work environment from the employee's perspective. Effective complaint systems are designed to ensure an airing of the facts because someone designated by the procedure must conduct a fair *investigation* of the complaint in order to determine whether it has merit. Supervisors and managers who conduct the investigation have to talk to employees about the complaint in order to determine the facts. Essentially, the complaint procedure forces this communication. It is important that the manager conduct an absolutely *fair investigation* by examining the complaint from all perspectives and by talking to everyone who can provide information about the issue before deciding on merits of the complaint.[7] Another characteristic of effective complaint systems is that there is a *resolution* of the complaint. With non-union complaint systems, a higher-level manager or executive will generally make the final decision on what is to be done about the compliant, after lower-level appeals are exhausted. While employees will understand that the complaint may not be resolved in their favor, they will appreciate the process if they believe that the final decision-maker was *fair*. In union settings with formal grievance systems, after lower-level appeals are exhausted, the final appeal is made to an impartial arbitrator, who has been selected by both the company and the union, which ensures a fair resolution of the complaint.

The importance of dealing with complaints in an effective manner is emphasized by an example in which the complaint system was completely ineffective. In this example, a U.S. District Court awarded $171.6 million to Henry Boisvert, a former supervisor at the FMC Corporation. In previous litigation, a jury directed FMC to pay Mr. Boisvert $200,000 for wrongful termination. Boisvert, who worked in testing, blew the whistle on the company about problems with the Bradley Fighting Vehicle. He had initially written a report critical of the vehicle that he wanted to give to the Army, but an FMC manager quashed the report. In 1986, FMC terminated Boisvert because he would not sign a report about the Bradley Fighting Vehicle, which he claimed was falsified.[8] According to Boisvert, the amphibious vehicle had the following problem:

> In many circumstances, he charged, the Bradley swam like a rock . . . he had one driven into a test pond and watched it quickly fill with water . . . former FMC welders who worked on Bradleys claimed they weren't given enough time to do their work properly and so would simply fill gaps with putty.[9]

Employees who believe that a complaint will not get a fair hearing, or who fear consequences of complaints, can become negative influences at work. Some turn hostile to management. Others waste time, infect others with negative attitudes, and actively work to harm their companies. Do what you can to eliminate the fears of employees and encourage your people to air their complaints. Accept the complaints of employees as a fact of working life, and use the information they provide to mold better employees and working environments.

While some complaint systems are formal, such as where unions represent employees and in larger organizations, informal alternatives can also be helpful as we will discuss later in this chapter.[10]

THE FUNCTIONS OF AN EFFECTIVE COMPLAINT SYSTEM

Exhibit 15.1 presents the requirements for an effective formal complaint procedure, which provides an alternative to the informal open-door policy of dealing with complaints. When a company implements a complaint procedure, it is important to communicate to employees that the procedure does not take the place of an open-door policy of passing on complaints to managers. Instead, it provides a formal alternative that is helpful when previous attempts to use the open-door policy have failed to satisfy the employee.[11] In unionized environments, the grievance procedure would be used for many of the functions of a complaint procedure.

HANDLING COMPLAINTS: DEVELOPING YOUR OWN APPROACH

If you are not fortunate enough to work in an environment that has instituted a system for handling complaints, you still must deal with them more or less on your own. The following discussion can help you formulate your approach. Keep in mind that you should include as many of the aforementioned qualities and functions as you can.

Key features of an internal complaint procedure.

EXHIBIT 15.1

1. Standardized complaint form that collects the following:

   - Background information—complainant's name, work location, and date

   - Issue of the complaint

   - Previous discussions with management representatives on the issue

   - Remedy sought by the complainant

   - In cases of sexual harassment—any previous communication with management

   - In cases of problems with coworkers—any previous attempts to resolve the issue with peers

   - Signature of the complainant

2. Centralized processing with unique complaint tracking numbers

3. Acknowledgment of complaint that provides the following information to the complainant:

   - Complaint tracking number

   - Name of investigator

4. Utilization of competent complaint investigators

5. Discussion of potential remedies

   - Investigator first discusses findings with manager who will make decisions on remedies

   - Investigator may make recommendations about a remedy

   - Result of the investigation and decision on remedy is communicated to complainant

6. Complainant receives written report detailing the conclusions to include:

   - Background information

   - Tracking number

   - Investigator's name

   - Summary of the issues

   - Summary of key facts

   - Summary of investigation outcome (may or may not include details of action taken)

7. Documentation stored at central location to include:

   - Complaint form

   - Acknowledgment letter to complainant

   - Notes and statements of witnesses

   - Investigator's recommendations

   - Detailed account of action taken as remedy

8. Appeal procedure

   - Complainant is informed of procedure for appealing to senior management

   - Appeals should be in writing

9. Sound implementation

   - Managers encouraged to continue with informal open-door approaches to complaints

   - Managers and employees informed about the internal complaint procedure

   - Distribution of literature about the program to managers and employees

   - Program described in employee handbook

   - Complaint forms made available

Source: Adapted from Erin S. Hendricks, "Do More than Open Doors," *HR Magazine* (June 2000): pp. 171–176. Reprinted with the permission of *HR Magazine* published by the Society for Human Resource Management, Alexandria, VA.

To begin with, your attitude toward the complaints of your employees or team members should be to treat them seriously. Your employees think that their complaints have merit; they would not bring them to your attention if they believed otherwise. Complaints may also come to your attention indirectly through overheard conversations or through uninvolved third parties. In such cases, an investigation is warranted to determine if the complaints have substance. Watch for any sudden changes in established patterns of behavior; these often indicate the existence of an unexpressed complaint. If complaints are not dealt with as soon as they are discovered, situations worsen, and the damage can spread quickly to other persons or teams.

One suggestion is that the supervisor should invite employees to bring their complaints to him or her. While there may be some cynicism, some employees will start to bring in their complaints, and the supervisor will learn a great deal about what is going on in the organization. There are several advantages to this approach, with some of the more important being that the employee will have an opportunity to identify a problem and express some frustration. When employees bring complaints to their supervisors, they should reasonably expect a resolution of their legitimate complaints or at least clarification if the complaint is unfounded. Supervisors should remember that the issue is of importance to the employee and that it has probably been bothering the employee for some time. As a result, the supervisor must be careful not to respond in a manner that minimizes the importance of the employee's concern, even though from the supervisor's broader perspective, it may sometimes appear unimportant. Other advantages to the approach are that the supervisor will have an opportunity to be of assistance to the employee, which can do a great deal for the employee's respect and appreciation for the supervisor. Often after implementing such an approach to complaints, there will be an increase in employee morale.[12]

An open-door policy, which generally means letting employees know that you are available and eager to discuss their problems, can prevent problems from getting out of hand. If your people feel that you care about them, will act swiftly, and will use sound judgment, you will find them willing to air their irritations and observations. However, this can come about only after you have established solid human relations with them on an individual or group basis. If you hear complaints only through the grapevine, your people are probably fearful and at least reluctant to bring their complaints to you directly. This means that they may distrust either your judgment or your willingness to deal with their complaints. Find out what is preventing open, honest communication and then go to work on the problems. If employees do not bring their complaints to you, take the initiative and conduct confidential meetings on a regular basis in which you ask employees if anything is bothering them.[13]

Learning Objective Number One

A RECOMMENDED APPROACH

The steps that follow will help you deal effectively with your employees' complaints. You should find them useful even if your company does not have prescribed complaint procedures.

1. Listen to the Complaint

Determine its causes and the complainer's feelings and motives. Be prepared to give the complaining employee your undivided attention. If the complainer's timing is not right, set up an appointment as soon as possible.

Remain calm. If the complainer is agitated and emotional, you should be the opposite. You cannot counsel effectively unless you are in control of yourself and the situation. Try to uncover what the complainer is feeling by allowing him to verbalize his feelings and motives. Avoid passing judgment, because you seek information about the other person's perceptions, not your own. Take notes, and reserve your own opinions and facts for later in the meeting. By listening attentively and drawing people out, you may find that the initial complaint gradually slips away as the real, underlying issue comes to the surface. It may be the first time that the employee has been able to express what was really on his mind. Gradually, all the facts will emerge in your employee's words, and the problem will come into focus. Then, and only then, can it be intelligently resolved.

Remember that people frequently just want to talk with someone about their problems. By talking, they are expressing confidence in you and showing respect for your opinion. Often, employees know that the solutions to their difficulty are beyond either their control or yours. In discussing such a situation, we often find a clarity and perspective that is almost impossible to discover alone. Employees may come to realize that the problem is not as serious as they originally thought, or they may actually discover a solution as they attempt to explain their views.

2. Push for Solutions

Once your employee has talked about the real issues, ask her for her solutions. What would she do if she were in your shoes? What does she think would be a fair disposition of her complaint? You want to know what she thinks will make her happy. If it is within your power to grant such a solution, and if you believe it to be a wise one, then do so. If you need more information or wish to check out her side of the story, defer your answer, and give a specific time for a response. Seek a win-win situation where no meaningless compromises are necessary and where no one is viewed as a loser.

3. Make a Decision and Explain It

Before you can make a decision, you need to consider who is best qualified to make it. If it is yours to make and you have all the facts you need, give your employee your decision and the reasons for it. If higher authorities are involved, identify them. If rules, policy, or procedures are involved, explain their meanings and their applicability to the situation. Your employees may not receive the answers that they were looking for, but they will know that you have done your homework.

4. Explain How to Appeal

If your workers are dissatisfied with your decision and want to pursue the matter further, tell them how to do so. Let them know whom they should see and how they can make an appointment. If your workers decide to appeal your decision, you should not hold that action against them, and you should let them know that you do not.

The proportion of the labor force accounted for by traditionally unionized workers has steadily declined as the workforce has grown.

5. Follow Up

Regardless of the outcome, it is sound management practice to get back to the people who have made a complaint within a reasonable time after its resolution. Assess their present attitudes and make it clear that you want your people to come to you with their complaints. Be sure you keep a record of any proceedings for future reference.

By being sincere, listening attentively, asking exploratory questions, and acting on each complaint promptly, you will minimize conflicts and reduce barriers to productivity and cooperation.

LABOR UNIONS

So far in this chapter, we have discussed handling complaints in companies where there is no union. We now shift to companies that are unionized. Before considering complaint resolution in unionized companies, however, we need to take a brief look at unions in the United States.

labor union
a group of workers employed by a company or in an industry who have banded together to bargain collectively with their employer

A **labor union** consists of a group of workers (a) who are employed by a company or who work in the same industry or (b) who are practicing the same skilled craft and have banded together to bargain collectively with employers for improvements in their wages, hours, benefits, and working conditions. *Craft* or *trade unions* are composed of workers in the same skilled occupation. For example, the International Brotherhood of Electrical Workers (IBEW) is a union organized to represent skilled craftspersons. *Industrial unions* include workers in the same company or industry, regardless of their specific occupations. The United Auto Workers (UAW) and the United Food and Commercial Workers are two examples of industrial unions.

According to the U.S. Bureau of Labor Statistics, 12.5 percent of the workers employed in private and public (government) sectors of the U.S. economy belonged to unions in 2005. The total of 15.7 million union members accounted for 7.8 percent of private sector workers and approximately 36.5 percent of public sector workers in 2005. An additional 1.5 million were covered by union contracts but did not have union membership. Union membership as a proportion of the employed labor force declined 7.6 percentage points from the comparable figure in 1983 of 20.1 percent.[14] Here are the major reasons behind this decline:

- The proportion of the labor force accounted for by traditionally unionized workers (blue-collar or manufacturing jobs) has steadily declined as the workforce has grown.
- The primary growth areas in the economy are made up of jobs that are traditionally non-union.
- Manufacturing jobs have moved offshore and to the South and Southwest, traditionally non-union areas.
- Workers have shown a trend to decertify their unions, moving from unionized to non-unionized status.
- Many of the foreign-owned companies that have come to the United States to establish production facilities have created non-union workforces.
- Enlightened, people-focused enterprises have created work environments built on trust, mutual respect, and genuine concern for the welfare of their employees, removing major causes for the formation of unions.

There have been concerns that unions have negotiated health care benefits, particularly in the auto industry, which have contributed to cost disadvantages for U.S. manufacturers.[15] In some countries, health care costs are paid by governmental programs, while in the United States such costs are mostly paid for by employers. In the long run, such cost differentials are expected to contribute to reductions in employment in heavily unionized industries. Recently, after thousands of job losses, the United Automobile Workers Union (UAW) agreed to pay a higher share of workers' health care costs, in contrast to the past in which the companies picked up almost the entire cost.[16] Interestingly, Japanese auto companies manufactured 31 percent of the automobiles and trucks produced in North America in 2005 while providing health care benefits in their U.S. plants, that were approximately the same as in the U.S. auto manufacturers' plants. Nonetheless, pension benefits and starting wages have been lower in the Japanese companies compared to the U.S. companies. Japanese companies typically do not have union representation in their plants that are located in the South.[17]

Exhibit 15.2 lists the proportion of workers in several major industries who are union members.

UNIONS AND PRODUCTIVITY

Unions are still a political and economic force in our economy. They have achieved some success in replacing their lost blue-collar members with white-collar, service, and professional employees. Increasingly, unions have become partners with management,

EXHIBIT 15.2	Union membership statistics according to industry.

INDUSTRY	PERCENT OF EMPLOYED WORKERS IN 2005
Utilities	28.2
Transportation and Warehousing	24.2
Telecommunications	22.4
Construction	14.7
Manufacturing	12.9
Mining	11.4
Broadcasting	9.3

Source: Extracted from U.S. Department of Labor, Bureau of Labor Statistics, *Union Members Summary*, Released on January 20, 2006, *www.bls.gov/news.release/union2.nr0.htm.*

Workers join unions in an effort to gain bargaining power against management. Union membership is declining because of better management in some companies, a decline in manufacturing jobs, and more legislation designed to protect workers' rights.

working to remove barriers to productivity and to quality. They have done so out of necessity to preserve employment opportunities for their members. They have shown a willingness to trade restrictive work rules and past economic gains for job security.

For example, Detroit Diesel had productivity problems, and relations between the union and management needed improvement. When Roger Penske took over the company, he quickly started building trust with employees and the UAW union. As a result of improved relations and changes in work design, a huge turnaround in labor relations and an increase in productivity took place. The UAW even split the cost of building a new training center for the company's employees.[18]

Because restrictive work practices often have been associated with unionization in the past, it may come as a surprise that a model employer and icon of good management would be heavily unionized. Nonetheless, this is exactly the case with Southwest Airlines as between 84 and 89 percent of the company's employees are represented by unions. Southwest has excellent relationships with its unions. The Southwest Airlines Pilots Association (SWAPA) has operated under an unprecedented 10-year contract with the company. Obviously, both parties must have had a great deal of trust in each other to enter into an agreement of this length. Early in their relationship, Herb Kelleher, the former CEO of Southwest Airlines, and the lead lawyer for the pilots' union came to an understanding. Kelleher said that if the union's lawyer would not "nit pick" him, he would not "nit pick" the union.[19]

Another unusual feature of labor relations at Southwest Airlines is that the pilots' union tells its members that the name of the game is productivity. This is reflected in the fact that Southwest's pilots fly more hours than pilots do at other major airlines. One of the reasons the pilots' union emphasizes productivity is that the pilots have an incentive to be productive—they receive lucrative stock options. For example, pilots with 10 years of service each receive stock options worth approximately $100,000. The pilot's union tells its members "if you didn't come here to work, you're not going to make it." At a session for approximately 20 newly hired pilots, the vice president of the pilots' union said, this is "Golden Goose Airlines. If you think we're going to let you screw it up you're crazy."[20]

The example of the quick turnaround of Southwest's airplanes provides a good example of high performance that can be possible with unionized workers. The ground crew, who are all union members, work like a highly coordinated race track pit crew. On a flight on Southwest Airlines, one of the authors observed a Southwest pilot doing his part with a quick turnaround of the plane. He was helping to clean up trash in the passenger cabin while the ground crew did its work.

PUBLIC SECTOR UNIONS

Governmental workers have increasingly turned to unions for representation. In 2005, among governmental employees, those who work at the local level were the most highly unionized with 41.9 percent of those employed. Firefighters, police, and teachers were the most heavily unionized public sector employees at the local level. State government employees were the next highest with union members representing 30.7 percent of workers. In the federal government 29.9 percent of workers were represented by unions.[21] While we have included the term "employee association," the distinction between unions and employee associations has become blurred and is now largely a matter of semantics. Still, members of employee associations often have a strong preference for the term *employee association.*

In 1962, federal employees were aided in their attempts to unionize when President Kennedy signed Executive Order 10988. This executive order required federal agencies to recognize and bargain with the associations that represented a majority of their employees, as determined by secret-ballot elections. Executive Order 11491, issued by President Nixon, further encouraged and improved collective bargaining rights for federal employees. Although some public sector unions have occasionally struck in major cities such as New York, Chicago, and San Francisco, they typically do not have the legal right to do so and frequently have been ordered back to work through court orders.

PROFESSIONAL EMPLOYEES

Salaried and professional employees traditionally have resisted attempts to unionize them, but this reluctance has diminished in recent years. In addition to the trend toward unionization noted for governmental workers, other professionals that have gravitated toward unionization include nurses, teachers (most of whom are also government employees), and engineers. Some of the most interesting developments have occurred with engineers. For example, the Seattle Professional Engineering Employees Association (SPEEA) represents 24,500 of Boeing's engineering and technical employees. In 2000, SPEEA conducted a lengthy strike against Boeing. The strike, which has been termed the first cyber strike, demonstrated the union's technical expertise, as the union utilized the Internet to keep its members unified and informed about the daily progress of negotiations. Airline pilots provide another example of professional employees who have chosen to unionize. The Allied Pilots Association, which represents 11,500 American Airlines employees, also provides an example of a highly sophisticated union of professional employees.[22]

WHY EMPLOYEES BAND TOGETHER

Workers join employee associations and unions for many reasons. They want equity, job security, more pay, and better benefits. By banding together, they improve their bargaining position with employers and are better able to avoid unfair and discriminatory treatment.

Better Bargaining Position

Compared with their employers, individuals have little bargaining power. A company can simply make an offer on a take-it-or-leave-it basis or make no offer at all. The employee is free to say yes or no. The individual's bargaining power rests on his ability to refuse to accept an employment offer or to quit when dissatisfied. But where all the employees at a company or in a craft or department bargain as one with the employer, the business would have to shut down or operate under severe handicaps if the whole group of workers were to strike.

Fair and Uniform Treatment

Pay raises, transfers, promotions, layoffs, and eligibility requirements for company training programs can be quite arbitrary without union checks on management's prerogatives. Favoritism and discrimination can influence these decisions, resulting in inequities with little hope for appeal. As a result, unions have pushed for greater reliance on seniority and objective standards. The best man or woman may not always benefit, but the decision will be objective. Unions place great emphasis on job security and constantly try to obtain greater security for themselves and their members'

SUPERVISORS AND PERFORMANCE

Firestone's recall of 6.5 million tires in 2000, mostly from Ford Explorers, and suspicions that defective tires may have contributed to the deaths of 62 people have raised questions about the importance of good labor relations and the implications for quality. Although Firestone, which is Japanese owned, denied that its tires were to blame, a two-year strike by the United Rubber Workers (URW) at the Decatur, Illinois, plant where most of the tires were manufactured is being scrutinized for its role in the production of defective tires. The union claims that Firestone sought to get rid of the union. " 'Firestone's sole purpose was to bust the union,' says the union vice president, Randy Gordon. 'But we made life miserable for the company.' "

All three parties involved denied that they were to blame. Firestone asserted that the tires were not defective, while Ford maintained that the Explorer is a safe vehicle. On the other hand, the union has speculated that the Explorer has a flaw in its design, and that Ford's instructions to its customers incorrectly tell them to under-inflate the tires. Some plaintiffs' lawyers have pointed to the union as the cause of the problem. Plaintiffs' lawyers have asserted that employees allowed flawed tires to be shipped from the plant and alleged that replacement workers who worked in the plant during the strike were to blame. Conversely, it has been argued that the strike was not the cause of flaws in the tires, because the plant had quality problems even prior to the strike.

Supervisors need to keep in mind that they are a key to maintaining good relations with the union. They obviously do not have control over larger company policies that affect the quality of labor relations, but they have much influence on the factors at work that can lead to dissatisfaction. Good labor relations and good quality require a continued commitment from both companies and employers over long periods of time. Attempts to take shortcuts around good labor relations typically fail.

Source: "Workers to Ford: Don't Tread on Us," *Newsweek* (August 28, 2000): 44. Quoted material from this source is indicated in the first paragraph.

financial futures. Safer working conditions also are a focus of unions, and their efforts have been instrumental in the passage of state and federal safety legislation.

UNION SECURITY PROVISIONS

Unions have fought for years to win recognition from employers. They want to increase their strength by requiring all employees to belong to a union once it is recognized as their legitimate bargaining agent. In an election for certification, a union may win by only a slim majority. Those workers who voted against it may not be willing to join the union voluntarily. To counter this resistance, unions have tried to enforce various types of *shop agreements.*

This chapter's supervisors and performance feature describes problems that companies may encounter when skilled production workers are replaced during labor disputes.

With a *union shop* agreement, all current employees must join the union as soon as it is certified as their legitimate bargaining agent. Newcomers have to join after a specified probationary period—normally 30 days. The majority of union contracts with employers call for a union shop. The union shop is illegal in the 22 states that have enacted *right-to-work laws*—so named for granting people the right to work with or without membership in a union.[23]

In a *modified union shop,* employees may elect not to join the union that is representing them. Part-time employees, students in work-study programs, and people employed before a specified date may refuse to join.

Employees do not have to belong to the union under an *agency shop,* but they must pay a fee to the union. The reason for this is that union negotiations benefit all employees—members and nonmembers alike. Since all employees benefit, each should pay a share of the costs of winning those benefits.

In an *open shop,* membership in the elected union is voluntary for all existing and new employees. Individuals who decide not to join the union do not have to pay any dues to the union.

A *closed shop* requires an employer to hire only union members. This kind of shop is forbidden by the Taft–Hartley Act (described later in this chapter). However, a close relative of the closed shop still exists in the form of *hiring halls.* Hiring halls exist in construction, longshoring, trucking, and skilled-craft areas. For example, if a construction company needs skilled craftspeople, it will generally contact a union's hiring hall to fill its employment needs. Hiring halls are legal as long as they refer nonmembers for jobs in a nondiscriminatory manner.[24]

LABOR LEGISLATION

*Learning
Objective
Number Two*

NATIONAL LABOR RELATIONS ACT (1935)

As the Great Depression dragged on, Congress began to analyze its causes and soon realized that the low wages of so many workers had been a significant factor. To achieve a balance of power between labor and management, the National Labor Relations Act (often called the Wagner Act) was passed as one of the measures of the New Deal. It has often been referred to as organized labor's Magna Carta (great charter or birth certificate) because it guaranteed the right of unions to exist. It gave the individual worker the right to join a union without fear of persecution by the employer. In the words of Section 7 of the Act:

> [E]mployees shall have the right to self-organization, to form, join, or assist labor organizations, to bargain collectively through representatives of their own choosing, and to engage in concerted activities for the purpose of collective bargaining or other mutual aid or protection.

The Wagner Act also listed as unfair practices the following management activities by employers:

- Restraining employees from joining a union
- Contributing financially to or interfering in any way with union operations

- Discriminating in any way against a worker because of union affiliation
- Punishing union members who report management violations of the Act
- Refusing to bargain with a duly elected union of employees

The second and third prohibitions are most significant to supervisors. These provisions have been interpreted as forbidding management from making threats or promises of financial gain to employees who are considering union affiliation or who are about to engage in an election to determine a bargaining agent.

The Wagner Act also established the National Labor Relations Board (NLRB), consisting of five members appointed by the President of the United States. The NLRB is empowered to investigate alleged violations of the Act and to oversee elections to determine a bargaining unit. Its decisions have the power of law and bind both unions and employers. However, as a result of the Wagner Act, another law had to be passed to curb some of the labor excesses it helped create.

This chapter's feature on supervisors and ethics deals with the measures that employers sometimes take to avoid unionization.

ETHICS

LABOR–MANAGEMENT RELATIONS ACT (1947)

Learning Objective Number Three

During the years between the passage of the Wagner Act and the end of World War II, this country witnessed phenomenal growth in union membership and also in abuses of union power. Organized labor grew from about 4 million members in 1935 to about 15 million (35 percent of the workforce) by 1947. Unions were becoming a powerful force and were exercising financial and economic power that was almost totally unchecked. Postwar strikes threatened the economy.

Congress again felt compelled to balance the two forces. Despite the protests of labor and a veto of the bill by President Truman, it passed the Labor–Management Relations Act, usually called the Taft-Hartley Act. The Act was intended to curb many of the abuses that organized labor had been guilty of in the 1930s. It amended the Wagner Act to include a list of provisions against specific practices by unions:

- Workers could not be coerced to join or not to join a union.
- The closed shop was prohibited.
- Unions (and employers) were required to bargain in good faith.
- Complex restrictions were placed on certain kinds of strikes and boycotts. The Act prohibited the *secondary boycott,* by which the union forces a company, uninvolved in a labor dispute, to stop dealing with or purchasing from another company involved in a labor dispute. Also prohibited were *jurisdictional strikes,* which were designed to force an employer to give work to one union rather than to another.
- Unions could not charge their members excessively high initiation fees.
- Employers were not required to pay for services not performed (featherbedding).

Other provisions allow states to enact right-to-work laws "which make union security agreements, such as union shops and agency shops, illegal."[25] In addition, an emergency

SUPERVISORS AND ETHICS

As noted in the discussion of unfair labor practices, managers are prohibited from interfering with workers' efforts to unionize. Employers are not allowed to intimidate workers who attempt to unionize coworkers nor are they allowed to retaliate when workers are successful in winning a union representation election and negotiate a contract with the company. When employers and their supervisors or managers interfere with or retaliate against workers for union activities in the private sector, they commit an unfair labor practice, which is a violation of the National Labor Relations Act. Nonetheless, some employers have played fast and loose with workers' efforts to unionize and have taken advantage of the law's absence of penalties for violations, except for the most egregious actions.

As the world's largest retailer, with over a million employees, Wal-Mart has become a lightning rod for criticism by many interest groups and labor unions. With few exceptions, the company has managed to remain non-union although there have been attempts by unions to organize Wal-Mart employees. Recently, the United Food and Commercial Workers Union sought information about the activities of a former Wal-Mart executive, who it was alleged, had paid for information about Wal-Mart employees who were sympathetic toward unions. Wal-Mart explained that the allegations were false and that the executive in question misappropriated company funds for personal use instead of for prohibited anti-union activities.

At about the same time, Wal-Mart also came under criticism when it closed a store in Canada. Approximately six months earlier, the store had become the only Wal-Mart in the United States or Canada in which employees were represented by a union. Wal-Mart announced that the company was closing the store because of low revenues and union demands. While Canadian labor law applied to this store in Jonquiere, Quebec, there are many similarities between Canadian and U.S. labor law in the protections of workers' rights to unionize. Union leaders charged that Wal-Mart closed the store to discourage unionization efforts at other Wal-Mart stores in Canada. The labor relations board in Quebec has also directed Wal-Mart Canada to cease intimidation and harassment of employees involved in a union-organizing effort in one of the company's stores in another Quebec city. Unionization is widespread in the Quebec workforce with approximately 40 percent of employees being represented by unions.

Supervisors should remember that their behaviors will be observed by their employees and that any departures from high ethical standards will send a strong signal that they do not take workers' rights or the welfare of their companies seriously. Supervisors must respect their employees' rights to engage in protected union activities at the same time that they represent the interests of their employers.

Source: James Bandler and Ann Zimmerman. "Union Seeks Wal-Mart Documents," *Wall Street Journal* (April 11, 2005): A6. Clifford Krauss. "For Labor a Wal-Mart Closing in Canada Is a Call to Arms," *New York Times*, (March 10, 2005): C5.

provision in the Taft-Hartley Act allows the President of the United States, through the attorney general's office, to seek a court order to stop a strike or lockout that threatens the nation's general health or welfare. The court's order can last for up to 80 days. During this cooling-off period, the federal government attempts to mediate the disputes that are separating the parties. The NLRB can hold a secret-ballot vote among the striking or locked-out union members after the injunction is 60 days old to see if the company's latest offer is acceptable.

REPRESENTATION ELECTIONS

The NLRB has established procedures that must be followed by both management and workers when the latter express their desire to be represented by a union. The certification process (the process of getting the NLRB to certify a particular union as the legitimate bargaining agent for employees) begins when at least 30 percent of the workers sign authorization cards calling for a union to represent them. Then the workers can ask the NLRB to schedule a representation (certification) election.

An election will then be scheduled and conducted by NLRB representatives. Once the election is held, the results tabulated, and the disputes settled, the NLRB certifies a bargaining agent. The employer is then obligated to enter into negotiations with the certified union toward a collective bargaining agreement. On average, about 3,000 certification elections are sponsored each year by the NLRB, and about 46 percent are won by unions.[26]

The effort by employees to get rid of their bargaining agent (union) works in the same way as the process of obtaining such an agent. Decertification, as it is called, first requires 30 percent of the bargaining agent's members to call for a decertification election. On average, about 420 decertification elections result in the decertification of unions each year.[27]

ETHICS

THE SUPERVISOR'S ROLE DURING REPRESENTATION ELECTIONS

Your job is the same as any other manager's during employee certification or decertification elections. You should remain neutral and preserve an atmosphere in which workers can express their uninhibited choices. In general, do nothing that is not expressly authorized by higher management. Do not express your opinions—pro or con—toward unions or union membership by your employees. Make no threats, and make no promises. Do not give or announce any increases in pay or benefits just before or during representation elections, unless the increases are totally unrelated to the election campaigns.

You may point out to workers the economic costs that are connected to union membership. Such costs include the dues paid to support union officers and activities, the costs of processing employee complaints through the union contract's complaint procedures, and the costs connected with strikes that take people off the payroll. You may also point out that both the union contract and its constitution place restrictions on workers. Rules and punishments are prescribed in both.

TEAMS

This chapter's feature on supervising teams deals with the limits that labor legislation places on the implementation of teams in unionized companies.

SUPERVISING TEAMS

As indicated in this chapter, the Wagner Act, which became law in 1935, established a number of unfair labor practices, specified prohibited employer actions, and preserved the rights of employees to form unions and to engage in collective bargaining. The unfair labor practice specified in Section 8(a)(2) states that it is an unfair labor practice for employers "to dominate or interfere with the formation or administration of any labor organization or contribute financial or other support to it . . ." As indicated earlier, this provision prohibits company unions, which are unions dominated, financed, and supported by companies. This provision was necessary when the Wagner Act became law because some employers had thwarted the efforts of their employees to be represented by independent unions. In the absence of such a provision, employers could still use company unions to sidestep real union representation.

The adoption of work team approaches, which provide a number of advantages, such as increasing employee involvement in the workplace, sharing decision-making responsibilities, and expanding the skill sets of employees, has been prevalent in many high-performing companies since the 1980s. Because of their potential for enhancement of productivity, the utilization of work teams has been a key means for companies that need to compete on a global basis. Since work teams have such advantages and are often critical for company success, it is somewhat ironic that the adoption of work teams can constitute a violation of the Wagner Act.

In general, supervisors and managers need to understand that work teams should not be used to perform any of the functions of a union. For example, teams should not be used to deal with issues such as wages, hours, complaints, grievances, working conditions, or in any manner in which the team represents other employees. The NLRB has provided some clarification of the permissible applications of work teams. More specifically, they may be used for brainstorming or the suggestion of ideas, providing information to management without making proposals, or in situations in which the team has the power to make the decision without getting approval from management.

Additional guidance has also been provided in various NLRB decisions. This guidance indicates that the use of teams to address quality issues does not pose problems. However, problems are likely when the company forms a worker committee, provides a place for the committee to meet, and asks the committee to make decisions on various union functions, such as grievances, pay issues, and working conditions. Finally, employers need to be cautious about the timing of their formation of work teams. If a company implements work teams during the period when a union is attempting to organize the company's employees, there will probably be an inference that the employer is motivated by a desire to prevent unionization. As a result, union organizers will probably file charges with the NLRB arguing that there has been an unfair labor practice. Because of the complexity of this issue, supervisors and managers should seek the advice from the company's labor lawyers before forming teams. Finally, it should be noted that if there is a mistake in the utilization of teams and a violation of the Wagner Act, the action taken by the NLRB is typically not severe. Often the company will simply be directed to stop its use of teams in a manner inconsistent with the law or to disband the teams.

Source: Steven L. Thomas and Judy Best. "Work Teams and Unions: Keeping Employee Involvement Legal," *Business Forum 26* (2001): 4–13.

LABOR RELATIONS

The area of **labor relations** includes all the activities within a company that involve dealings with a union and its members. Specifically, two main areas are the most important and time consuming: **collective bargaining** (arriving at a contract that covers workers' wages, hours, and working conditions) and **grievance processing** (dealing with complaints that allege violations of the collective bargaining agreement).

COLLECTIVE BARGAINING

Bargaining collectively—the union representatives on one side of the table, management's representatives on the other—is the traditional way in which labor disputes are settled and labor-management agreements are formed. Some time before the expiration date of a labor contract, the two groups begin a series of meetings that ultimately leads to the signing of a new agreement. Bargaining may take place on the local level, where only one local union and employer are involved, or on an industry-wide basis, where the agreement sets the standard for the industry—as in the automotive and trucking industries.

The usual process involves a specialist in labor relations from the company's labor relations department (usually at the vice-presidential level) and the union's negotiating committee. Both sides employ labor lawyers who are well versed in the most recent developments in labor law to help them hammer out specific contract provisions and wording.

Both sides bring a list of demands to the bargaining sessions and, in their own minds, assign to each a priority that will become apparent as negotiations develop. Some demands are made merely to serve as trading material. Negotiations involve give and take so each side must be prepared to bargain away some of its demands in order to obtain others.

Each side attempts to resolve the many minor issues as quickly as it can, reserving the major issues for the final meetings immediately preceding expiration of the contract. It is then that the pressure for a settlement is greatest. Ultimately, through compromises and trading, a new contract emerges. The agreement is then offered to the union membership, which votes to accept or reject it. A simple majority vote is usually required.

The union contract with management spells out in rather precise terms the rights of workers with regard to wages, hours, and working conditions. It is a formal written document that both managers and union members must thoroughly understand. It can and does limit management's authority.

ENFORCING THE LABOR CONTRACT

Enforcement of the terms of the agreement depends on communication of the contract provisions and of the demands they make on labor and management. Managers must be made aware of their rights and duties. Copies of the agreement are made available to each manager, along with an explanation that is easy to understand. Any questions that may arise in a manager's mind can quickly be answered through consultation with the human resources department or labor relations officials. The union must also make its

labor relations
management activities necessitated by the fact that the organization has a union that represents its employees

collective bargaining
the process of negotiating a union agreement that covers wages, hours, and working conditions

grievance procedure
the process by which grievances are filed and either settled or elevated to higher union and company representatives with unresolved grievances being submitted to arbitration

*Learning
Objective
Number Four*

members aware of their rights and duties. Copies of the contract are distributed to each member, and meetings are held to explain the contract's terms.

THE SUPERVISOR AND THE STEWARD

steward
the union's elected or appointed first-line representative in the areas in which employees work

The **steward** is first of all an employee and a worker. He has the additional responsibilities of a union officer because the union members have elected or appointed him. Stewards receive some release time from work to carry out their duties. Exhibit 15.3 lists the responsibilities of supervisors and stewards. More points draw them together than keep them apart.

Just as a supervisor is management's spokesperson, a steward is labor's spokesperson. She has the duty to represent workers in the early stages of the grievance process. The steward must be able to interpret the contract both to the supervisor and to fellow workers. A worker's complaint usually cannot win the union's backing without the steward's consent.

Stewards, like managers, have a difficult and demanding position. They are workers and must conform to company standards or risk disciplinary action. On the other hand, they have the status of elected union officers who, if they wish to retain their posts, must be effective representatives of their constituents. They may, therefore, feel a

EXHIBIT 15.3

The responsibilities of supervisors and stewards in labor relations.

SUPERVISORS	STEWARDS
Know the contract	Know the contract
Enforce the contract	Enforce the contract
Look out for the welfare of employees	Look out for welfare of constituents
Serve as spokesperson for both management and employees	Serve as spokesperson for the union and constituents
Settle grievances fairly (in line with management's interpretation of the contract)	Settle grievances fairly (in line with union interpretation of the contract)
Keep abreast of grievance solutions and changes in contract interpretation	Keep abreast of grievance solutions and changes in contract interpretation
Maintain good working relationships with stewards	Maintain good working relationships with supervisors
Keep stewards informed about management's decisions and sources of trouble	Keep supervisors informed about union positions and sources of trouble
Protect management rights	Protect labor rights

good deal of pressure to push complaints to grievance status, even when their own best judgment says they should not. In circumstances where there are few complaints or grievances, some stewards may feel the need to escalate issues or manufacture discontent in order to justify their position and to prove that they are serving a useful purpose.

HANDLING GRIEVANCES

When a worker is dissatisfied with a supervisor's disposition of a work-related complaint, she may appeal that decision by filing a formal charge called a **grievance.** A grievance alleges that a violation has occurred of one or another of the provisions of the labor agreement. A complaint that is improperly handled can and usually does become a grievance. Managers should consider every gripe about wages, hours, and working conditions a potential grievance.

grievance
an alleged violation of the labor-management agreement

If the details of the grievance are not clear to you after you hear the complaining employee's case, ask questions. Conduct your own investigation to determine whether or not the facts presented to you are complete and true. If they are not or if you are uncertain about any of them, gather the evidence needed to clarify the situation. If you are unsure about the proper interpretation or application of the specific language of the labor contract, seek counsel from the labor relations specialists. Exhibit 15.4 provides recommendations to follow while handling grievances.

If you determine that the grievance is without merit, give the worker and the steward your facts, your (management's) interpretation and application of the labor contract provisions, and your specific reasons for denying the grievance. If your verbal answer is accepted by the complaining employee and the union steward, prepare a written record of the complaint and your disposition of it. Be certain that any remedy you grant is within your power to give and has your boss's approval.

On the other hand, your verbal answer to the complaining employee may not be acceptable to him or to the steward. If it is not, your involvement will continue. You will probably be given a written copy of the complaint and will probably have to provide a written response. You will probably be questioned by various labor relations people and union officials during later phases of the grievance procedure.

Normally, grievances are not put into writing until they progress from the first step to the second. This is especially true in large corporations, where the number of grievances is quite large and where the majority are usually solved at the level of the steward and supervisor. From this step on, the number of people involved increases, as does the need for precise language.

Learning Objective Number Five

THE GRIEVANCE PROCEDURE

Where a collective bargaining agreement exists between the company and a union, a formal procedure for handling grievances will be included 99 percent of the time.[28] The following **grievance procedure** is typical, although one or two intermediate steps may be left out in some agreements:

grievance processing
settling an alleged violation of the labor-management agreement in accordance with the method outlined in that agreement

1. The employee makes a verbal complaint to the supervisor. If the employee (grievant) is unsatisfied with the supervisor's response, the procedure moves to the next step.

| EXHIBIT 15.4 | **Dos and don'ts for the supervisor when handling a grievance.** |

DO

- Begin by assuming that every complaint has merit.
- Give the employee (grievant) your time and listen carefully to each word.
- Identify the specific contractual wording that the grievance alleges was violated.
- Visually check out the location where the grievance supposedly took place.
- Interview every person who may have knowledge of the grievance, the parties to it, the event, the location, and the circumstances.
- After gathering all your facts, check out all past grievances that have a bearing on this one.
- Hold all your interviews and discussions with concerned parties in private.
- Before giving any answer to the grievance, touch base with your boss.
- Give your answer as completely as you can within any time limit prescribed by the union contract.
- Keep written records of all your findings, your interviews, and your answers.

DON'T

- Settle any grievance outside the terms of the written contract.
- Engage in trading one grievance settlement for the withdrawal of another.
- Engage in bargaining over issues that are not part of the written contract.
- Agree to any changes in the precise wording of the contract.
- Fail to deliver any remedy endorsed by the parties as a settlement for the grievance.

2. If the steward feels the grievance is meritorious, the grievance is prepared in written form and signed by the employee. The steward then meets with the supervisor and tries to work out a solution. (Supervisors should research the issue carefully and consult with the labor relations specialists in preparation for this meeting.) If, after hearing the steward's arguments, the supervisor believes nothing new has been added to change the situation, she will stick to the original decision.

3. Union officials meet with the supervisor's immediate superior or a representative from the labor relations department. They examine issues to determine if any precedents from earlier grievance processing apply. If no solution can be agreed on, the grievance advances to the next step.

4. Higher-level union officials meet with the labor relations director or plant manager. Costs and time devoted to the problem are increasing, and both sides will want to solve the issues as quickly and as equitably as they can. If no agreement is reached, the grievance advances to the next step.
5. Arbitration is invoked.[29]

MEDIATION

Mediation is the attempt to resolve a dispute by using the conflict resolution skills of a neutral outsider who is allied with neither labor nor management. Mediators are asked to bring the two sides together and to facilitate their agreement on a settlement. Mediators have no formal authority and cannot impose a settlement on the parties. Nonetheless, mediators help the parties to reach agreement through a variety of means. They can provide more objective assessments of the costs of disagreement, reestablish communication, clarify the intentions of the parties toward each other, suggest potential solutions (which might be unacceptable if the solution came from the other side), clarify misunderstandings, and help the parties save face.[30] For high-level disputes, such as between large companies and national unions, the mediator may be a distinguished public official, such as a judge, who has a fine reputation and whose insights, wisdom, and power are respected by both sides.

mediation
the use of a neutral third party in a labor-management dispute to facilitate resolution of the dispute by the parties

ARBITRATION

In **arbitration,** a neutral third party is called in to decide the case. He or she is a professional arbitrator, selected by the two parties from panels of experts meeting the standards of the American Arbitration Association (AAA) or the Federal Mediation and Conciliation Service (FMCS). In fiscal year 2005, FMCS received 16,787 requests for panels of arbitrators to rule on grievances that companies and unions were unable to resolve. After requesting arbitration services, however, the parties often settle the cases on their own. In fiscal year 2005, FMCS arbitrators issued 2,629 arbitration awards (decisions). Approximately 50 percent of the grievances that make it to arbitration in the private sector involve discipline or termination of employees.[31]

arbitration
the use of a neutral third party to resolve differences between management and labor unions over contract interpretation issues

The arbitrator holds a hearing on the grievance. During the hearing, advocates for the union and the company present their arguments and evidence. In most cases, lawyers represent one or both sides. At the hearing, the advocates make opening statements on the merits of the case, call witnesses, and conduct direct and cross-examinations of witnesses. The arbitrator is in charge of the hearing and conducts the proceedings in much the same manner as a judge, although with less formality. The hearing may be quite informal depending on the arbitrator's style. Formal rules of evidence are not required, although most arbitrators understand such rules and rely on them to some extent. The arbitrator then writes an award in which the grievance is either sustained or denied. This award or ruling becomes binding on both union and management and can be enforced in federal courts if needed. In addition to resolving grievances, interest arbitration sometimes is used in the public sector to overcome an impasse in collective bargaining because the parties are usually not permitted to strike.

INSTANT REPLAY

1. Complaints are serious matters to be dealt with in a serious way. In a unionized organization, complaints can and often do turn into grievances.

2. Handling complaints requires honesty, sincerity, and an open discussion of all the relevant facts and emotions involved.

3. The grievance procedure begins when you and an employee or the union steward meet to discuss a formal complaint alleging a violation of a union contract.

4. When you manage in a union environment, you must know your labor agreement's provisions and how a ruling on a grievance can affect the future interpretation of the agreement.

5. You need to know federal and state laws that regulate your treatment of employees in all matters—not just in labor relations areas.

6. You should develop a cooperative relationship with your steward. Both of you are paid to look out for special interests and to reach accommodations when it is in your mutual interests to do so.

7. Unions exist to serve their members. In many companies, they are a fact of life.

QUESTIONS FOR CLASS DISCUSSION

1. Can you define this chapter's key terms?

2. How should a supervisor handle complaints?

3. What does the Wagner Act prohibit?

4. What does the Taft-Hartley Act prohibit?

5. In what ways are the supervisor and the steward similar? In what ways are these labor relations roles different?

6. Can you outline a typical grievance procedure for a large organization? What might be left out in a small company?

ASSESS THIS SITUATION

Purpose: To get a union member's view about a union—its benefits and drawbacks.

Your Task: Interview a union member (family member, classmate, friend, or the like) using the following questions and any others you may wish to add. Compare your results with those of your classmates.

1. Why did you join your union?

2. What are the costs—psychological and financial—connected with your union membership?

3. What direct benefits does your union provide you in the following areas:
   a. Wages and benefits?
   b. Working conditions?
   c. Employee assistance during a strike?

4. Have you ever been involved in a strike?

5. What were the issues that led to the strike?

6. Does your union contract prescribe a grievance process?

7. What is the process?

8. In general, how would you describe the working relationship between management and the union?

9. What do you think your working life would be like if your union did not exist?

SKILL BUILDING EXERCISE 15.1

The Internet provides an efficient and low-cost way for unions to provide information to their members and a means for improving the various services that unions make available to their members. The Internet also plays an important role in making information available to potential members who do not yet have union representation. An examination of union websites will reveal that unions provide a substantial amount of information about issues on which they are seeking improvements, either through negotiations with employers or political action. In addition to issues that are specific to individual companies and workplaces, union websites also provide information on issues that affect a broad cross-section of their members.

Your Task:

1. Search the websites of the following international or national unions that represent workers in the private sector and identify five issues that appear to be very important to each of these unions: (a) International Brotherhood of Teamsters, *www.teamster.org*; (b) International Brotherhood of Electrical Workers (IBEW), *www.ibew.org*; (c) International Association of Machinists and Aerospace Workers, *www.iamaw.org*; (d) United Mine Workers of America (UMWA), *www.umwa.org*; and (e) Communication Workers of America (CWA), *www.cwa-union.org*.

2. After completing your examination of these websites, work in small groups and discuss the issues of concern to the different unions and the means the unions are using to address these concerns. Discuss how any of these issues may be related to the supervisor's interaction with unionized workers.

3. Speculate on the types of information that is presented in the "members only" portions of the websites.

SKILL BUILDING WRITING EXERCISE 15.2

In addition to representing workers in such traditional areas, such as in manufacturing industries, unions also represent professional workers and governmental workers. Some of these professional unions and public sector unions are listed as affiliates of the American Federation of Labor–Congress of Industrial Organizations (AFL-CIO) on the AFL-CIO website at *www.aflcio.org*, while others are independent unions.

Your Task:

1. Explore the websites of three of the following unions of professional employees and provide a brief written description of the major issues on which each of the unions is trying to make progress: (a) Airline Pilots Association (ALPA), *www.alpa.org*; (b) United American Nurses (UAN), *www.uannurse.org*; (c) Society of Professional Engineering Employees in Aerospace, *www.speea.org*; and (d) American Federation of Teachers, *www.aft.org*.

2. Explore the websites of three of the following public sector unions and provide a brief written description of the major issues on which each of the unions is trying to make progress: (a) American Federation of Government Employees (AFGE), *www.afge.org*; (b) American Federation of State, County, and Municipal Employees (AFSCME), *www.afscme.org*; (c) International Association of Fire Fighters, *www.iaff.org*; and (d) American Postal Workers Union (APWU): *www.apwu.org*.

3. Provide a brief written discussion of any differences in the issues of concern to the unions of professional employees and those that represent public sector employees. Note that there is some overlap in these classifications as professional unions may also represent public sector employees, such as teachers and nurses. Explain how such issues of concerns to the unions could affect the supervisors of such professionals or public sector employees.

CASE 15.1   Beer Mints?

Marty Cole, an outside sales representative, was walking through the parking lot to go to his temporary office in the tire manufacturing plant when he noticed a pickup truck with a man sitting in it. The man was drinking a bottle of beer. Marty concluded that there must be a shift change, and he was drinking a beer before driving home. However, when Marty arrived at the plant entrance, he noticed that people were returning from break and that it was not time for a shift change. He then realized that he had seen an employee on break drinking a beer in his pickup. Marty also realized that the pickup had been parked with the back facing the plant entrance. The man had appeared to have been looking in the rearview mirror, and it was now obvious that he had adjusted the rearview mirror toward the plant so that he could see anyone come out and approach in his direction. Marty had approached from the opposite direction and, therefore, had not been seen.

Marty walked back to the security hut and told the supervisor of security what he had seen. He and the security supervisor went out to the parking lot and walked up to the pickup. There was no one in the pickup, but there was a partially opened case of beer on the seat. In addition, there were lots of empty beer bottles in the cargo area of the truck. The supervisor of security returned to the security hut and looked up the license plate of the truck. The owner of the pickup was Buford Collins, one of the tire builders who had worked at the plant for five years. The security supervisor then called Gina Pitts, the director of human resources. Gina came to the security hut, where Marty and the supervisor of security told her what they had seen.

Gina and the two men went to find Buford. The company had a strict policy against drinking on the job specifying that such a violation was grounds for termination. When they found Buford, he was working on the line where the raw tire casings were placed in the hot tire molds. His eyes were runny and his face was flushed and puffy. Gina was convinced that Buford had been drinking and concluded that he looked like someone who drank a lot on a regular basis. Buford, however, denied that he had been drinking and said his face was flushed because of the heat. He explained that he had gone to his truck to get some candy mints but that he had not had a beer. He also explained that he kept mints in his truck and that he liked to go to his truck during his breaks to listen to music and eat mints. Buford's explanation for the empty beer bottles was that he and a friend had been hunting last weekend, and they had put all of their empties in the truck.

Gina told Buford to go home and that he would be on suspension until she and the plant manager decided what to do. Buford then volunteered that he would be willing take a blood alcohol test. Gina told him that it wasn't necessary but that he could do so if he wished. She sent him to the office where a secretary made arrangements for a blood alcohol test. The test was conducted approximately $1\frac{1}{2}$ hours later at a nearby hospital. The test results that came back two days later simply stated, "Negative results. No alcohol detected at the .04 percent level or above." Two days later Gina and the plant manager met with Buford. They told him that he would be terminated for drinking on the job unless he agreed to go through a substance abuse program paid for by the company's employee assistance program. Buford refused. He said that he had not been drinking and would not go through such a program. The plant manager terminated Buford, and the union appealed the case to arbitration. The applicable provision of the union contract says that employees may be terminated only for just cause.

Questions

1. Do you think the discipline of Buford was fair? On what factors do you base your reasoning?

2. What is your opinion of the company's investigation and disciplinary procedure?

3. How strong is the company's case against Buford? Does it have just cause for termination?

4. How do you think an arbitrator will rule in this case?

CASE 15.2 Downsizing Dilemma

The order from the CEO was unambiguous. Costs at the plant would have to be reduced by 20 percent. Since labor constituted a high proportion of total costs, it was clear that layoffs would be necessary. The plant manager, director of human resources, production manager, and production supervisors all agreed that the best way to conduct the layoffs would be to first identify the nonessential work activities in each job classification. They would then eliminate a corresponding number of employee full-time equivalents (FTEs) by cutting out these activities in each classification. Although the employees were represented by a union, the contract with the union did not require the company to conduct layoffs according to inverse seniority. The contract only required seniority to be applied when employees had equal ability to perform the job.

The company then conducted an activity value analysis (AVA) of all jobs in order to identify the nonessential activities. Employees wrote out all of the activities they performed each year and the amount of time they devoted to each. Committees of managers then reviewed the activities and decided, on the basis of their essentiality, the number of FTEs to eliminate in each job classification. Because the management team had no confidence in the validity of past performance appraisals, they had teams of three supervisors reevaluate each employee for purposes of the layoff decisions. Employees in each job classification were placed in three categories for purposes of the layoffs: (1) above average, (2) average, and (3) marginal. A point system was used to place employees in each category based on an overall evaluation of ability, skill, and qualifications. The cut-off levels for each category were as follows: 20 or more equaled above average, 10 to 19 equaled average, and 0 to 9 equaled marginal. Employees in the marginal category would be laid off first, followed by the lowest-ranked employee in the average category, next lowest ranked, and so on.

When the plant manager and director of human resources reviewed the list of employees who would be laid off by this approach, they realized that the two union stewards, Judy Cooper and Kelvin Hastings, would be laid off. The stewards received point totals of 9 and 6, respectively. Because they felt that the union would find it unacceptable if no union stewards remained on the job, the plant manager and director of human resources decided to add three points to Judy Cooper's evaluation, making her total points 12. They reasoned that Judy had demonstrated leadership on the job by guiding the union to an agreement in the last contract negotiations with the company. Thus, Judy Cooper's point total of 12 placed her in the "average" category and one point above Henry Gilbert's total of 11. As it turned out, the company needed to lay off more employees than the number in the marginal category. As a result, it was necessary to go to the lowest-ranking employee in the average category. Thus, Henry Gilbert was laid off, and Judy Cooper was retained.

The union then filed a grievance on behalf of Henry, contending that he had been unfairly laid off. The union argued that the layoffs were not conducted in accordance with fair procedures equally applied to all employees. It challenged management's use of the special evaluations conducted for the layoffs instead of the regular appraisals Henry and other employees had received on an annual basis for many years. The union requested that Henry be reinstated to his position and paid back pay for the time he was off the job. Approximately eight months later, Henry's case came before an arbitration hearing.

Questions

1. Evaluate the company's layoff procedures. Do they appear to be fair?

2. What is your opinion of the special evaluation procedure used for the layoffs?

3. How do you think the arbitrator should rule in this case? Why?

4. What would you have done if you were making these decisions for the company?

REFERENCES

[1] Wisdom Quotes website (February 12, 2006): *www.wisdomquotes.com/ cat_ labor.html.*

[2] Source: Uchitelle, Louis. "If You Can Make It Here," *New York Times,* (September 4, 2005).

[3] Ibid.

[4] Ibid.

[5] Ibid.

[6] Ibid.

[7] Pollock, Ted. "Dealing with Employee Complaints," *Products Finishing,* (April 2004): 8, 102–103.

[8] Gomes, Lee. "A Whistle-Blower Finds Jackpot at the End of His Quest," *Wall Street Journal* (April 27, 1998): B1, B12.

[9] Ibid.

[10] Pollock. "Dealing with Employee Complaints."

[11] Adapted from Erin S. Hendricks, "Do More than Open Doors," *HR Magazine* (June 2000): pp. 171–176. Reprinted with the permission of *HR Magazine* published by the Society for Human Resource Management, Alexandria, VA.

[12] Pollock. "Dealing with Employee Complaints."

[13] Ibid.

[14] U.S. Department of Labor, Bureau of Labor Statistics, *Union Members Summary*, Released on January 20, 2006, *www.bls.gov/news.release/union2.nr0.htm.*

[15] White, Joseph B., Hawkins, Lee Jr., and Lundegaard, Karen. "UAW Is Facing Biggest Battles in Two Decades," *Wall Street Journal*, (June 10, 2005): B1–B2.

[16] Durbin, Ann. "Ford Workers Approve Health Care Cuts; Judge Backs Similar GM Benefits Deal," *Buffalo News*, (December 23, 2005): D7.

[17] Welch, David, Foust, Dean, and Coleman, Cowan. "The Good News About America's Auto Industry," *Business Week*, (February 13, 2006).

[18] Noe, Raymond A., Hollenbeck, John R., Gerhart, Barry, and Wright, Patrick M. Video tape segment, "Detroit Diesel," accompanying *Human Resource Management*. Burr Ridge, IL: Austin Press/Richard D. Irwin, 1994.

[19] Menaker, Marvin, Kearns, Gary, Parker, James, and Landau, Ruth. Presentation on Labor Relations at Southwest Airlines, Southwest Academy of Arbitrators, Dallas, Texas (March 1996).

[20] Ibid.

[21] U.S. Department of Labor, Bureau of Labor Statistics, *Union Members Summary*, Released on January 20, 2006, *www.bls.gov/news.release/union2.nr0.htm.*

[22] Greer, Charles R. "E-Voice: How Information Technology Is Shaping Life Within Unions," *Journal of Labor Research 23*(2) (Spring 2002): 41–61.

[23] Delaney, John T. "Right to Work," in Lawrence H. Peters, Charles R. Greer, and Stuart A. Youngblood (eds.), *The Blackwell Encyclopedic Dictionary of Human Resource Management*. Oxford, UK: Blackwell (1997): 295.

[24] Cibon, Partick J., and Castagnera, James O. *Labor and Employment Law*, 2nd ed. Boston: PWS-Kent Publishing Company (1993).

[25] Joel, Lewin G. III. *Every Employee's Guide to the Law*. New York: Pantheon Books (1993): 326.

[26] Farber, Henry S. "Union Success in Representation Elections: Why Does Unit Size Matter?" *Industrial and Labor Relations Review* (January 2001): 329–348. Hatfield, Donald E., and Murrman, Kent F. "Diversification and Win Rate in NLRB Certification Elections," *Journal of Labor Research* (Fall 1999): 539–555.

[27] Ibid.

[28] Holley, William H., Jr. "Grievance Procedure," in Lawrence H. Peters, Charles R. Greer, and Stuart A. Youngblood, Editors, *Blackwell Encyclopedic Dictionary of Human Resource Management*, Oxford, U.K.: Blackwell Publishers, Ltd., (1997): 134–135.

[29] Miner, John B., and Miner, Mary Green. *Personnel and Industrial Relations,* 3rd ed. New York: Macmillan Publishing Company (1977). Middlemist, R. Dennis, Hitt, Michael A., and Greer, Charles R. *Personnel Management: Jobs, People, and Logic,* Englewood Cliffs, NJ: Prentice Hall (1983).

[30] Kolb, Deborah M. *The Mediators.* Cambridge, MA: MIT Press (1983).

[31] Federal Mediation and Conciliation Service, *Arbitration Statistics, Fiscal Year 2005,* (February 16, 2006), website: *www.fmcs.gov/assets/files/Arbitration.*

16

"It's a very sobering feeling to be up in space and realize that one's safety factor was determined by the lowest bidder on a government contract."[1]

Alan B. Shepard
Former Astronaut

Objectives

After reading and discussing this chapter, you should be able to do the following:

1. Describe the issues of concern to supervisors with respect to physical security.
2. Outline security measures that supervisors can take to prevent theft by employees.
3. Describe a supervisor's duties in the event of a fire and with regard to fire prevention.
4. Describe OSHA enforcement procedures and an employer's rights with regard to OSHA inspectors.
5. Describe the supervisor's role in preventing and dealing with employee substance abuse.

Continuing Safety Issues in Mining

As a result of increasing oil and gas costs, there has been a resurgence in the coal mining industry. This industry was in decline for many years, and for communities in which coal mining was the dominant industry, there were years of economic decline. With the increase in the price of coal that has resulted from shortages of oil and gas, coal mining companies have been attempting to supply coal to meet the demand. Coal mining, particularly underground mining, has always been a dangerous industry, and the dangers continue today even with advances in safety and communications equipment. A series of coal mining accidents have called attention to the safety issues in coal mining. In January 2006, 12 miners in West Virginia were killed from carbon monoxide poisoning in the Sago Mine.[2] A few days later, two more miners died in the Alma Mine 1, also in West Virginia, as a result of a conveyer belt fire.[3]

Security, Safety, and Health

While there are numerous conditions that make underground mining a dangerous business, there are also some management issues that appear to contribute to safety issues. For example:

> *"Many miners look at inspectors as their enemies," said Tony Oppegard, a former top federal mine official in the Clinton administration and the former prosecutor of mine safety violations in Kentucky. . . . For some mining operations, paying fines is less expensive than adhering to the rules, miners say. And a few mines do not bother to pay at all . . . . Indeed, miners say that they are sometimes forced to accept unsafe working conditions in return for employment . . . . another reason that coal mining continues to be dangerous: workers who complain about unsafe conditions are sometime fired or penalized. . . . Some miners say that they are expected to put up with such problems to keep their jobs, Mr. Oppegard said.[4]*

While keeping coal mines safe for workers is complex, it can be done as experts report that there are mines that have not had accidents in 20 to 30 years of operations. Management attention to safety rules and training play a critical role in keeping coal mines safe. Without a constant focus on safety, rules and procedures get ignored and accidents occur. The approach to mining and safety technology, such as sensors, is also important.[5] In the Sago Mine disaster, the miners ran out of oxygen and were killed by carbon monoxide while waiting to be rescued. Interestingly, laws in Canada require mines to have stock reserve supplies in the mines of oxygen, food, and water so that miners can survive while awaiting rescue. Such supplies have been credited for saving the lives of 72 miners who waited 20 hours for rescue in a Canadian mine.[6]

In the Alma Mine conveyer belt fire that killed two workers, one worker who talked to a newspaper reporter on an anonymous basis, said the following:

> *"I work at the belt that caught fire and had to put out a fire at the same exact spot just a couple weeks ago when the sprinkler system didn't work," the miner said, referring to a fire that occurred on Dec. 23. "I reported the fire to my supervisor, and he ignored it."[7]*

Questions for Thought

1. How can supervisors ensure that their employees have a safe working environment, and why do they and their employers sometimes fail to provide safe conditions?
2. How can supervisors ensure that their employees receive the safety training that they need and that employees obey safety rules?

Introduction

In this chapter, we are concerned with the supervisor's duties in the following areas:

security
efforts at protecting physical facilities and other resources from loss or damage

- **Security**—protecting physical facilities and other resources from loss or damage
- **Safety**—protecting employees and customers from accidents and injuries
- **Health**—preventing employee illness, both physical and emotional, and treating injuries when they occur

safety
efforts at protecting human resources from accidents and injuries

Our focus will be on prevention—the ways in which supervisors and others can head off trouble and minimize damage to the company's human, financial, informational, and material resources. We will explore supervisors' responsibilities to protect these resources. Your security and safety duties begin with the screening of new applicants and continue every day as you carry out your managerial functions. Fortunately, staff specialists or outside consultants frequently are available to provide assistance in these areas, particularly in larger organizations.

health
the general condition of a person physically, mentally, and emotionally, or, efforts at preventing illness and treating injuries when they occur

As you provide direction for your employees through training and discipline, you can help to prevent accidents and theft. As a part of organizational efforts, you can build a structure for preventing accidents and enforcing safety rules. Furthermore, as you plan for the future, you can design programs, procedures, and practices that will help workers comply with management policies and state and federal safety standards. You can also develop effective preventive, diagnostic, and therapeutic controls to deal with safety and security problems. Through effective communications, committee action, and peer-group cooperation, you can ensure the coordination of safety and security efforts throughout the company.

PHYSICAL SECURITY

Learning Objective Number One

The terrorist attacks on the World Trade Center in New York and the Pentagon in Washington, D.C., on September 11, 2001, killed over 3,000 people while they were at work in their offices. In addition, shortly after these attacks, anthrax sent through the mail posed hazards for postal facilities.[8] These attacks highlight the vulnerability of workplaces to extraordinary dangers. However, violence has reached a point where homicide is the "leading cause of occupational death for women."[9] Furthermore, it has been estimated that each year 13,000 instances of violence occur in the workplace against women in which the attackers are the targets' husbands or boyfriends.[10] These levels of violence pose serious threats for organizations. In addition to the devastating effects of violence on the

| Some risk factors associated with potential violence. | Exhibit 16.1 |

- Personality conflicts (between coworkers or between worker and supervisor)
- Mishandled termination or other disciplinary action
- Bringing weapons onto a work site
- Drug or alcohol use on the job
- Grudge over a real or imagined grievance
- Breakup of a marriage or romantic relationship
- Other family conflicts
- Financial or legal problems
- Emotional disturbance
- Increasing belligerence
- Ominous, specific threats
- Hypersensitivity to criticism
- Recent acquisition/fascination with weapons
- Apparent obsession with a supervisor or coworker or employee grievance
- Preoccupation with violent themes
- Interest in recently publicized violent events
- Outbursts of anger
- Extreme disorganization
- Noticeable changes in behavior
- Homicidal/suicidal comments or threats

Source: Critical Incident Response Group, National Center for the Analysis of Violent Crime, Federal Bureau of Investigation, U.S. Department of Justice, *Violence in the Workplace: Issues in Response*, March 1, 2004, pp. 21–22.

workforce, the employer may incur financial liabilities from failing to prevent a disgruntled or terminated employee from attacking others in the workplace.[11]

In order to prevent violence in the workplace, supervisors need to be in close contact with their subordinates and must recognize the indicators that an employee is troubled. Employees also must be trained to alert their superiors to potential problems. Several risk factors or problematic behaviors for which supervisors should be alert are presented in Exhibit 16.1. Some of the factors are obvious, but in the interest of providing a comprehensive treatment, we have retained them in the exhibit. Supervisors should be alert to these indicators but also need to understand that the presence of such factors or even a

ETHICS

combination of them cannot conclusively predict whether any particular individual will engage in violence. However, supervisors should keep in close contact with employees exhibiting such behaviors or undergoing such circumstances and help them obtain assistance. They should also confer with their manager and the director of security. Such concerns should be expressed in confidence and with concern for employees' privacy.

Employee assistance programs (EAPs) can be helpful in preventing employees from reaching a breaking point, and these programs have much greater utilization when counselors are located on site. In addition, it is important for employees to be assured that they can seek assistance from their EAP on a confidential basis. It is important that the EAP provide other services than substance abuse and depression counseling so that employees who seek EAP assistance will not be associated with such problems simply because their coworkers find out that they are going to the EAP. Better selection procedures can also help firms avoid hiring people who have greater potential for violence. For example, the inclusion of a few carefully crafted behavioral questions in selection interviews can help screen out applicants with angry personalities. In addition, the company should make clear policy statements that it will not tolerate threats, harassment, or violence and that it will investigate all reports of such behaviors.[12]

PERFORMANCE

Exhibit 16.2 presents important points about the role that supervisors play in reducing the terrible consequences of substance abuse to people and businesses.

EMPLOYEE THEFT

ETHICS

Learning Objective Number Two

Each year businesses lose billions of dollars to thefts by customers, employees, and outside criminals. "The International Association of Professional Security Consultants says losses of cash and inventory alone range from $10 billion to $40 billion annually."[13] Thefts of employee property cause suspicion, low morale, dollar losses, and employee turnover. The largest loss to most U.S. businesses results from employee theft. It has been estimated that "sixty to 80 percent of all inventory 'shrinkage' . . . can be blamed on workers. . . . The norm for shrinkage is 2 to 2.5 percent of inventory, although it might run as high as 7 percent in some businesses."[14] "In employee surveys conducted by academics and other specialists, as many as 30 percent of workers interviewed admitted stealing from their employers."[15] According to a Chicago testing company, Reid Psychological Systems, "about 17 percent of applicants admit to stealing from a previous employer."[16]

Employees steal time, money, company assets, and secrets. For money and other motives, employees steal vital information about product designs, marketing plans, customers, finances, and research projects. This information in the competition's hands can do great harm. According to the consulting firm Ernst & Young, "more than half the country's businesses are likely to have suffered financially because of information losses stemming from inadequate computer security measures. And at least some of the financial losses have exceeded $1 million per occurrence."[17] In spite of the size of these losses, only 58 percent of senior managers consider computer security to be very important. "Those who do consider computer security to be very important tend to be in the banking and insurance industries" according to an Ernst & Young survey.[18] Losses of vital information also occur when managers talk too much or to the wrong people, through improper disposal of waste paper, and from uncontrolled access to information by visitors and suppliers.

The supervisor's role in making employee assistance programs (EAPs) effective.	EXHIBIT 16.2

- Supervisors refer employees having problems to the EAP instead of attempting to deal with the issue on their own. Where there are effective EAPs supervisors recognize that they lack the professional training and objectivity needed to help an employee with substance problems.

- Supervisors are careful not to treat the employee in a manner that enables a substance abuse problem. Because of friendships between supervisors and employees, the supervisor sometimes attempts to overlook or even cover up employee behaviors that are being caused by substance abuse.

- Supervisors understand how to conduct a constructive confrontation with the employee about substance abuse. For example, they include the three messages of (a) the supervisor and organization value the employee, (b) specifics with documentation of how work performance has been affected, and (c) help is available through the EAP.

- Supervisors recognize that employee problems that seem trivial can become large problems without assistance. Accordingly, they have effective communications with EAP personnel, while maintaining strict confidentiality of individual employee cases, and know when to refer employees for assistance.

- Supervisors understand that it is important to focus on work performance and are aware that declining productivity, absenteeism, or tardiness can indicate substance abuse. When supervisors focus on work performance, they also have an objective basis for talking to employees about the issue. With a focus on work performance, it is less likely that the employee will perceive the supervisor's intervention as an unwarranted personal intrusion.

- Supervisors are careful to maintain confidentiality in their referrals to the EAP and understand the procedures.

- Supervisors have good listening skills and a supportive attitude, which helps encourage employees to come to them when they have problems.

Sources: Fred Dickman. "Ingredients of an Effective Employee Assistance Program," in William G. Emenger, William S. Hutchison, Jr., and Michael A. Richard, eds., *Employee Assistance Programs: Wellness/Enhancement Programming,* 3rd ed. Springfield, IL; Charles C. Thomas, Publishers, LTD, (2003), pp. 47–56. Lawrence P. Mannion. *Employee Assistance Programs: What Works and What Doesn't,* Westport Connecticut: Praeger Publishers, (2004).

Electronic thieves working from within companies steal billions of dollars each year through a variety of schemes. Computer criminals can siphon money from business accounts into their personal accounts. They can create phony charges from nonexistent vendors and then authorize payment of those charges. Computer theft may be committed by programmers, computer operators, clerks, bank tellers, executives, and disgruntled or fired employees. Losses to computer thieves tend to be much larger than losses to conventional thieves.

Among the electronic security problems that threaten businesses are: bugged facsimile machines, intercepted cellular phone calls, and intercepted Internet or e-mail messages. Facsimile (fax) machines use telephone lines or cellular networks to transmit printed copy. It is possible to tap into a fax machine by making a secret connection with its telephone line. Thieves can also intercept messages by monitoring cellular calls. Eavesdropping equipment is readily available through most electronics stores.[19]

Computer fraud provides another risk factor, which requires preventive action and vigilance by supervisors. Most of the computer crimes against companies, approximately 75 percent, are committed by employees.[20] While information systems executives and their staffs typically take the lead in securing information systems and preventing threats to the organization's assets through theft by computer, supervisors also have responsibilities. Simple lapses in security, which can be prevented by supervisory vigilance, such as employees giving their passwords to other employees, can create the means for computer theft.[21] Even very small businesses are subject to computer fraud, often times because one employee has all of the responsibilities for accounting duties, such as reconciling bank accounts, handling cash, writing checks, and tracking and recording receivables. In some cases, the use of computers to perform these functions has eliminated audit trails and, as a consequence, has made embezzlement more attractive. Supervisors should ensure that such responsibilities are separated and to be performed by more than one person.[22]

The array of people who want to steal from the company or harm it through its information systems is expanding and now includes, the following: (a) hackers, who generally break into computer systems for the challenge involved; (b) spies from other companies seeking competitive information; (c) intelligence agents from foreign countries who are attempting to find ways to disable communications and supply chain systems; (d) phishers, who rely on phony e-mail messages, such as a bogus requests from eBay or banks, in order to obtain confidential information for credit card fraud or other scams; (e) **spyware,** which infiltrates computer systems to gather critical information and send it to external clients; and (f) terrorists, who seek to or inflict casualties among the populace by damaging business systems and organizations.[23]

Computer viruses have become a huge problem, and an entire virus protection software industry has evolved in response. Viruses have changed the way we use our computers, such as by not opening attachments in e-mail from senders we do not know.[24] Supervisors should see to it that anti-virus software is installed on their employees' computers and that it is appropriately maintained and updated. Similarly, they need to ensure that **anti-spyware software** is installed and maintained so that thieves cannot obtain such information as credit card data.[25] The danger posed by outside hackers, thieves, or people trying to obtain competitive intelligence about the organization is revealed by the following account:

> Studies show that small companies are subject to several attacks every day and that giant corporations are under attack virtually every minute of the day. The vast majority of these are virus attacks, most of which are repelled.[26]

Finally, some other simple actions often prove to be very helpful in preventing outsiders from doing damage to the organization's computer systems or from obtaining critical information. One such action involves educating employees on the importance of maintaining the security of their organization's computer and information systems and making sure that they report any suspected intrusions or threats to the system.[27] Another is to ensure that employees keep the automatic

spyware
software that infiltrates computer systems for the purpose of obtaining information that can be used for fraudulent purposes

computer virus
a rogue computer program that can reproduce itself endlessly or cause other havoc, such as the destruction of stored data

anti-spyware software
software packages that remove probing software that has been imbedded in an organization's computers in order to obtain critical information

update features of their software turned on so that the latest security patches or fixes will be installed.[28]

Some companies use various types of tags and coded strips to track assets and to detect the theft of merchandise or unauthorized use of facilities. Software loss-prevention systems enable companies to detect theft by their own employees. Such software, when combined with television surveillance systems, provides a powerful means for controlling theft. One of the advantages of such software is that it streamlines searches of video records because they are matched up with cash register transactions. Supervisors, loss prevention personnel, and risk managers, can quickly review key video segments that capture transactions, such as refunds, no-sale rings, and so on.[29]

Your job also may entail enforcing procedures designed to control access to and use of data. Security software, passwords, access codes, encryption, and virus scanners are but a few of the readily available and inexpensive solutions to computer security. Access to databases can be limited in various ways to keep unauthorized personnel from viewing or working with them. Devices that defend against the bugging of fax machines are available. E-mail and Internet communications software, such as Microsoft Internet Explorer, and newer fax machines have encryption features.

ETHICS

SELECTION AND PREVENTION

Preventing crimes committed by employees begins with the selection of each new employee. During the screening process, both supervisors and members of the human resources department should be alert for telltale signs of a potentially dishonest employee (see Exhibit 16.3). In addition to this list of clues, you should check the

---

Some warning signs of a potentially dishonest applicant.	**EXHIBIT 16.3**

1. Gaps in employment	Obtain information about these gaps during the employment interview.
2. Criminal record	A criminal record check must be job-related. The failure to check for a potentially violent criminal background can create employer liability.
3. Lies on the application	Significant falsehoods on an employment application signal future falsehoods.
4. Frequent job changes	Changes that indicate the person does not know what she wants to do (absence of focus or linkage between past jobs) may be predictive of short tenure with your organization.
5. Financial problems	A strong focus on money issues by the applicant may mean over-extension and temptations to profit at others' expense.
6. Overqualification	Someone seeking a job for which he is overqualified may view the job as only a temporary way to make ends meet.

applicant's lifestyle for any hints that the person is living above his or her level of income. When conducting orientation activities, inform all new employees of your company's policy on dishonesty and the penalties. Further, many security experts recommend insuring an organization against employee theft through the purchase of fidelity bonds for all those employees who will have access to large amounts of money or valuable goods.

Ask for and verify a recommendation from the applicant's most recent employer. This precaution will not always uncover a person with a history of theft or willful destruction of company property because many employers simply ask an employee caught stealing to resign. They often do not fire such an employee or prosecute him because they want to avoid embarrassment or do not want to admit to themselves that they have hired a thief. Few employers provide negative information about former employees because they fear lawsuits for defamation of character. In addition, courts have been notoriously lenient toward white-collar criminals, who often receive only small fines or jail terms of less than a year following convictions for theft amounting to thousands of dollars in cash or goods.

To prevent losses from employee dishonesty, supervisors and managers should look for the following behaviors:

- Pocketing checks from presumably uncollectible accounts . . .
- Issuing checks in payment of invoices from fictitious suppliers and cashing them through the dummy corporation . . .
- Final purchasing decisions are made by one person, with no technical staff to assess each purchase . . .
- Pocketing the proceeds of cash sales and not recording the transactions . . .
- A buyer turns down a promotion that would move her or him to another department . . .
- Purchasing staffers come in early and leave late, and never take vacations.[30]

Proper security gives employees a feeling of safety where they work. It also reduces losses due to theft.

OFFICE SECURITY

Most companies have tangible assets to protect, such as computer equipment and highly sensitive information. The main problem in protecting office equipment, machines, and sensitive information is preventing access by unauthorized personnel. It should not be possible for someone to enter an office without being screened at the entrance. To make this screening process easier, many offices have only one entrance; it is usually the only non-fire exit as well. Someone should be on hand at all times to greet visitors from the moment the office is opened until it is closed for the day. People who have no legitimate reason to go farther should not be allowed to do so.

This chapter's feature on supervisors and ethics deals with the physical security issues and the responsibilities employers have and their role in the fight against terrorism.

SHOP SECURITY

Shop or plant security has some parallels to office security. Again, access by unauthorized personnel is the biggest problem standing in the way of safety and security. Similar controls can be exercised over people who attempt to enter the area. Employees may secure their personal belongings in lockers or check them with the company's security personnel on entering the plant or shop. However, plant and office security pose some additional problems. Besides protecting property and information from theft, you must be concerned with the prevention of vandalism and fires.

Vandalism is generally considered to be wanton or willful destruction of or damage to another's property. Disgruntled employees and outsiders sometimes vandalize company property. Whoever does the damage, some simple precautions can help prevent or minimize losses.

To begin with, make control over and security for all equipment, machines, tools, and other expensive pieces of company property the responsibility of specified people. Portable pieces of equipment should be issued only on request and should be returned by the persons to whom they were issued. Physical facilities must be kept clean and under observation at regular and irregular intervals. Storage areas require extra security measures if they contain sensitive or highly valuable materials. Closed-circuit television, guards, proximity devices, and alarm systems are popular but expensive prevention and detection measures. Locks remain the primary means of security used by business firms, but they cannot prevent trouble or vandalism if they are not used properly.

vandalism
wanton or willful destruction of or damage to another's property

SHOPLIFTING

Surveys in the retailing industry indicate that shoplifting is a major problem. For example, survey data reveal that shrinkage in the supermarket industry is 2.26 percent of sales. While shoplifting accounts for 23 percent of shrinkage in supermarkets, 26 percent is accounted for by cashiers.[31] Another survey, focusing on theft, collected data from 30 retail companies having 10,663 stores. This survey provided evidence of widespread shoplifting: 503,860 shoplifters were apprehended in one year.[32] We all lose because stores must raise prices and spend money to prevent thefts by customers. When stores raise their prices, they become less competitive. Dollars lost to theft and spent on security are not available to make businesses more productive and profitable.

ETHICS

SUPERVISORS AND ETHICS

One of the realities of the post-9/11 era is that supervisors must also worry about the dangers that terrorism poses for their employees, workplaces, and the companies for which they work. The potential for terrorism appears greater in some uniquely vulnerable industries, such as airlines, nuclear power generation, defense, and rail transportation. In addition, employees of the federal government who provide security for federal buildings or work in embassies face dangers from terrorism. A lesson from 9/11 is that it is important to anticipate the circumstances in which terrorists could strike and take preventative actions instead of waiting to be attacked. The need for proactive or anticipatory responses has created ethical dilemmas for supervisors and employers.

FedEx is in a unique position to help prevent terrorism by passing on information about suspicious shipments and activities to governmental agencies that have responsibilities for the nation's security. The company's 250,000 employees have many opportunities to note suspicious deliveries, and they have opportunities to observe activities that may indicate terrorist preparations or plots. In addition, the company has a vast amount of information in its computer systems on domestic and international shipments, including the names and addresses of shippers and recipients as well as credit card information. Before 9/11, the company did not want to provide information to governmental agencies because it felt that such reporting interfered with its fast-paced deliveries.

However, almost immediately after 9/11, the company changed its approach with governmental security agencies and began a practice of cooperating closely with governmental agencies that are charged with preventing terrorism. Aside from data on shipments and financial information, the company's thousands of delivery drivers have almost unequalled opportunities to observe dangerous activities in neighborhoods and businesses. While some of the federal government's initial efforts to collect information from meter readers, letter carriers, and couriers in a program called the Terrorism Information and Prevention System (TIPS) ran into political opposition, FedEx has continued to provide assistance to governmental agencies, such as the FBI. This is in contrast to the approach of United Parcel Service (UPS), which refuses to provide data on customer shipments except where compelled to do so by legal regulations. The U.S. Postal Service also does not share information on mail or package shipments unless ordered to do so by the courts.

Supervisors need to determine how their companies want employees to handle sensitive information about customers and whether the company's rules are consistent with the law as well as the supervisor's ethical standards. When weighing such concerns, the supervisor needs to consider the dangers to society that may be prevented by passing on such information to security agencies. Conversely, the supervisor must also consider the threats to the privacy rights of the individuals and businesses that utilize the company's services. However, assistance for such decisions is available within many companies so supervisors and managers are not alone when they make such decisions. FedEx had decided that it has an obligation to be a leader in the fight against terrorism.

Source: Robert Block. "In Terrorism Fight, Government Finds a Surprising Ally: FedEx," *Wall Street Journal*, (May 26, 2005): A1–A5.

Most experts agree that companies can reduce losses by training employees to look out for shoplifters. As a supervisor of retail sales people, you can train your employees never to leave a customer alone or out of sight long enough to pocket merchandise. Employees can be trained to catch credit card thieves and users of invalid credit cards by teaching and enforcing proper clearance procedures. Finally, you can enforce anti-theft procedures, such as keeping display cases locked and displaying one item to one customer at a time.

Your employer may offer other remedies and prevention measures as well, such as rewards for catching shoplifters and for recovering stolen or void credit cards. Store detectives posing as shoppers and closed-circuit TVs provide a means of monitoring shoppers. Shops can protect merchandise with price tags that self-destruct when tampered with or with tags that only store personnel can remove. Checkpoint Systems, Inc., an electronic security firm in New Jersey, manufactures electronic circuits that set off alarms at exits. Such circuits are quite small and can be built into a product's packaging or affixed to a piece of paper and inserted in a product. The cost of installing the system can be recovered in a relatively short time through loss prevention.[33]

Cub Foods in Colorado Springs had a big shoplifting problem until it created and installed two cardboard cops in its aisles. Each is a six-foot stand-up photograph of a real cop in uniform. The figures are placed in aisles where there have been shoplifting losses. Since their installation, shoplifting is down 30 percent.[34] Wal-Mart's famous senior citizen "greeters" became a fixture in its stores when it became obvious that they reduced store losses to shoplifters.

Learning Objective Number Three

FIRE PREVENTION

Each year, fire departments in the United States are called out to almost 2 million fires. Fires cause approximately 4,000 U.S. deaths and 25,000 injuries each year. In addition, annual property damage from fires amounts to approximately $8 billion.[35]

Although you are not expected to be a professional firefighter, you are expected to minimize the risk of a fire starting in any area over which you have control. A concern for fire prevention begins with the initial training of each employee and continues to be reinforced by fire prevention programs throughout the year. Every department should conduct regularly scheduled inspections. All of your people can cause fires if they are not careful about fire prevention, just as they can also provide detection and prevention. All employees should be made to feel that fire prevention and detection is a personal responsibility. Such an attitude is instilled through your actions and words and by your responding in a positive way each time an employee tells you about a potential fire hazard or takes time to remove one. Exhibit 16.4 is a sample fire prevention checklist.

Be certain that all pieces of firefighting equipment, such as extinguishers and hoses, are visible, accessible, and in proper working order, and make sure that you and your people know where they are and how to use them. Different kinds of fires require different kinds of firefighting equipment. The wrong type of extinguishing agent—such as water used on a grease fire—can spread the fire and increase the likelihood of injuries and property damage. Periodic but unpredictable fire drills will prepare your people for the worst and will reinforce proper evacuation procedures and routes.

EXHIBIT 16.4	Sample checklist for fire prevention.

Fire Protection	OK	Needed
1. Is your local fire department familiar with your facility, its location and specific hazards?	○	○
2. If you have a fire alarm system, is it certified as required and tested annually?	○	○
3. If you have interior standpipes and valves, are they inspected regularly?	○	○
4. If you have outside private fire hydrants, are they flushed at least once a year and on a routine preventive maintenance schedule?	○	○
5. Are fire doors and shutters in good operating condition?	○	○
6. Are fire doors and shutters unobstructed and protected against obstructions, including their counterweights?	○	○
7. Are fire door and shutter fusible links in place?	○	○
8. Are automatic sprinkler system water control valves, air and water pressure checked periodically as required?	○	○
9. Is maintenance of automatic sprinkler systems assigned to responsible persons or to a sprinkler contractor?	○	○
10. Are sprinkler heads protected by metal guards if exposed to potential physical damage?	○	○
11. Is proper clearance maintained below sprinkler heads?	○	○
12. Are portable fire extinguishers provided in adequate number and type and mounted in readily accessible locations?	○	○
13. Are fire extinguishers recharged regularly with this noted on the inspection tag?	○	○
14. Are employees periodically instructed in the use of fire extinguishers and fire protection procedures?	○	○

Source: Extracted from Occupational Safety and Health Administration, U.S. Department of Labor, *Small Business Handbook*, OSHA 2209-02R, 2005, pp. 19–20.

PROTECTING PEOPLE

Protecting people from illness, accidents, and injuries is not only smart business, it is required by law as well. By law, a business is responsible for injuries suffered by its employees if the injuries occur during or arise as a result of the employee's employment.

An **accident** is defined as any unforeseen or unplanned incident or event. An accident does not necessarily result in damage to people or property. Although accidents usually are unforeseen, many are not unforeseeable. Planning and safety programs can and do yield significant decreases in accidents. In addition, engineering **ergonomics**—the design of work sites, machinery, equipment, and systems to minimize stress and injury on the job—can produce dramatic improvements in accident rates. We will discuss several approaches for providing safer and healthier workplaces in this chapter.

accident
any unforeseen or unplanned incident or event

ergonomics
concern about the design of work sites, machines, equipment, and systems to minimize stress and job-related injuries

OVERWORK

Downsizing and other lean staffing practices have resulted in overwork for millions of workers in the United States. Overwork has both physical and mental effects. In order to cope with overwork, many workers take unscheduled days off by calling in sick. Human resource managers were asked about this practice in a survey of 305 companies. The respondents reported a substantial increase in the number of unscheduled days that employees are taking off. Some workers viewed such days off as a means of protesting downsizing, work overload, and stress as well as a kind of entitlement attitude that appears to be associated with overwork and stress.[36]

> Now, it appears, employees are simply taking the time off when they need it, whether or not their employers formally sanction it . . . "What we see now is the individual saying, 'There are some things I have to do, too.'" Increasingly, "it's a two-way street."[37]

Supervisors in work environments that utilize teams can also work closely with their teams to ensure that they are working effectively and are not consumed by overwork and stress. In spite of overworking conditions in many organizations, teams can also accomplish great things, such as helping to transform a negative environment into a positive one or in increasing the productivity of a work unit. This chapter's feature on supervising teams provides an example of a very positive experience that can occur when employees work as a team.

PREVENTIVE APPROACHES TO SAFETY AND HEALTH

Although each working environment is unique, each has certain hazards and types of accidents that can be identified and removed or neutralized so that they cause a minimum amount of damage and human suffering. Studies over the years by the Occupational Safety and Health Administration (OSHA) have found the following basic elements in workplaces that have good accident prevention programs and records:

Learning Objective Number Four

1. The top manager assumes the leadership role.
2. Responsibility for safety and health activities is clearly assigned.

SUPERVISING TEAMS

The power of teams can sometimes be revealed in the manner in which they respond to emergency situations, such as when the safety and welfare of people are at stake. In such situations, remarkable things can be accomplished by committed teams that have coordinated their efforts to accomplish a difficult goal with a higher calling. In such situations, team members freely contribute their unique knowledge in order to find solutions to difficult problems. When they work as teams in such situations, they often derive great satisfaction from their collaborative efforts.

During the aftermath of Hurricane Katrina, there were wonderful examples of superb teamwork. One such example occurred at United Parcel Service (UPS) in which 15 employees were able to work as a team in order to deliver a vital power generator part to the New Orleans City Hall. Without the part there was no way to obtain the power needed to run the lights in the building. An emergency call for the part reached a UPS manager in Shreveport, who then contacted several UPS facilities until he found the package that night in Oklahoma. Because air transportation was unavailable at that time of night, UPS had to find a way to deliver it to New Orleans, which was 764 miles away from the part's location. The UPS team devised a five-person pony express chain that enabled the part to be delivered the next day in New Orleans at noon. In this instance, UPS people in multiple locations coordinated their efforts to perform an important mission. One veteran employee on the team told *Wall Street Journal* reporter Carol Hymowitz that the team "felt wonderful when we got the job done."

Source: Carol Hymowitz. "Team Work Fosters Faster Solutions Than Going Solo," *Wall Street Journal,* (September 20, 2006): B6.

3. Possible accident causes are properly identified and either eliminated or controlled.
4. Appropriate safety- and health-related training is instituted.
5. An accident record system is maintained.
6. A medical and first aid system is ready for possible use.
7. Continued activity is designed to foster on-the-job awareness and acceptance of safety and health responsibility by every employee.
8. People are forewarned about and told how to cope with the hazards they must face on the job.

Many symptoms in the workplace can let you know that you have a problem or will have one in the future. Some obvious signs are accident and injury statistics, employee illnesses that are linked to the workplace, and absentee figures related to these. Not-so-obvious signals include labor turnover, excessive waste or scrap, increases in the number of "near misses" that could have caused injuries or property damage, and the pending receipt of new equipment and new employees. These last two signal a need for safety training.

A rising concern for most employers is the presence of indoor pollution in the plant and office. What has become known as *sick-building syndrome* (SBS) may be caused by one contaminant or by several acting in concert. Indoor locations commonly have chemicals, such as asbestos and formaldehyde as well as radon gas. Indoor locations also serve as incubators for various forms of viruses and bacteria with fungal agents, such as molds, that can cause a number of illnesses. Some fungal agents can cause esophageal cancer and deforming arthritis.[38] The EPA has discovered a number of potential cancer-causing substances in offices:

> Many studies conducted by EPA over the last 25 years have shown measurable levels of more than 107 known carcinogens in modern offices. The presence of these volatile organic compounds (VOCs) is due to the change from open windows to energy-efficient living and working environments—modifications made necessary during the energy crisis of the 1970s. Combined with the advent of modern building methodology and products, the result has been energy-efficient offices that contain amounts of known cancer-causing chemicals.[39]

As indoor air pollution becomes a larger problem (since more structures are built or renovated to become more energy efficient), it will be important to address these health hazards. The symptoms of sick-building syndrome include headaches; irritations of the nose, throat, and eyes; skin rashes; dizziness; nausea; frequent respiratory infections; and wheezing and cough. While employees do not always become sufficiently ill to miss work, these health hazards probably detract from their productivity. Ergonomics consultant John Jukes maintains that investments in improving building environments to eliminate such health hazards provide good economic returns in less absenteeism, improved productivity, and better morale.[40]

INSUFFICIENT WORK BREAKS

Insufficient work breaks have become another problem, according to OSHA. In a number of industries, employees simply do not get sufficient opportunities to use the restroom facilities. For example, teachers are often unable to leave students unattended and must find another teacher or staff person to fill in while they go to the restroom. People who work in factories, such as where there is machine pacing, sometimes find that they are not free to use restroom facilities without first obtaining permission.[41]

> [For some employees] meeting this simple need can mean humiliating pleas for permission and even risking the loss of their job. Some try not to drink liquids or go to the toilet all day—habits that court medical problems.[42]

While OSHA regulations mandate that employers have adequate numbers of bathrooms, no requirement for allowing employees to use these facilities existed prior to 1998, when OSHA remedied this situation with a directive for bathroom access. Employers who treat their employees with such disregard are prime candidates for unionization. The food processing industry has been criticized for poor treatment of employees in this area.[43]

AIDS IN THE WORKPLACE

AIDS has claimed the lives of 25 million people throughout the world since the disease was identified some 25 years ago. While there have been breakthroughs in drug therapies that prolong life, the disease remains a terrible threat to life.[44] Unfortunately, employers are sometimes ill prepared to deal with HIV-positive employees or ones with AIDS. Employers must have an AIDS policy and offer an ongoing educational effort to deal with the epidemic.

In their search for guidelines, many companies have taken advantage of a variety of volunteer speakers' programs, such as those offered by the HIV Peer Network in New York, and have adopted as policy the guidelines developed by the Citizens Commission on AIDS of New York and New Jersey. Among these are:

- People with HIV-positive status and AIDS sufferers are entitled to the same rights and opportunities as people with other serious or life-threatening illnesses.
- At the very least, all policies should comply with all relevant laws and regulations, such as the Americans with Disabilities Act (ADA), which protects all persons with AIDS and HIV from discrimination.
- Employers should provide up-to-date information and training on risk reduction for employees.
- Employers should protect the confidentiality of employee medical records.
- Employers should provide education programs for all employees before any problems arise in the workplace.

Learning Objective Number Five

A manager's kit, which includes posters and pamphlets with guidance on dealing with AIDS in the workplace, is available from the Centers for Disease Control and Prevention in Atlanta. Their AIDS Hotline is 1-800-342-AIDS. Your local chapter of the American Red Cross or the Equal Employment Opportunity Commission's ADA Hotline at 1-800-669-EEOC can provide additional information.

DRUGS AND EMPLOYEES

Employees whose performance is affected by dependency on alcohol or other drugs are a danger to themselves and to others. The drug-dependent employee may steal from the employer or from fellow employees to get the money needed to support a habit. Small mistakes can become major problems and can lead to accidents, injuries, and worse. Consider the following statistics about substance abuse:

- Over 7.4 million U.S. workers use illicit drugs.
- Drug and alcohol use is a contributing cause of 38 to 58 percent of on-the-job injuries.
- The likelihood of injuring oneself or others is 3.6 times higher for workers under the influence of illicit drugs.
- The probability of filing worker compensation claims is five times greater for employees on illicit drugs.
- Workers who are heavy alcohol users have 16 more days of annual absenteeism than non-abusers.[45]

To determine if your organization, unit, or team has a substance abuse problem or the potential for developing one, the U.S. Department of Labor suggests the following:

- Look at the statistics on such things as absenteeism, accidents, property losses, security breaches, and workers' compensation claims. Compare them to the past and to national, state, local, and industrial averages for your type of business.

■ Consult with all organizational members to get their observations and sense of the extent of the problem. Employees should be part of the investigation and help formulate policy and corrective measures.

■ Employees can play various roles to achieve and maintain a workplace free of substance abusers.

Because substance abuse tends to be a hidden problem, many organizations have decided to proceed on the assumption that there may be individuals in the workplace who have or are developing a problem with alcohol or other drugs. The U.S. Department of Labor recommends a workplace substance abuse program that includes several components that are described in the following discussion:

1. A written substance abuse policy
2. An employee education and awareness program
3. A supervisory training program
4. Access to an employee assistance program
5. An appropriate drug testing program[46]

Step one communicates a clear commitment to creating and maintaining a workplace free of substance abuse. An effective substance abuse policy should:

■ state why the policy is necessary and what it is meant to encourage and prevent.

■ define what constitutes an infraction, and describe the consequences.

■ recognize that substance abuse is treatable, and identify company or community resources where employees with problems can obtain help.

■ describe the responsibility of an employee with a substance abuse problem to seek and complete required treatment.

■ state the company's position on drug testing and, if testing occurs, the consequences of a positive test result.

■ assure employees that participation in assistance programs is confidential and will not jeopardize employment or advancement.[47] However, you must also inform employees that participation will not protect them from disciplinary action for continued unacceptable job performance or rule violations. It is important to keep the results of drug tests confidential because of the potential for lawsuits over defamation. In such a case, "the truth is not necessarily a defense. Even if the information is true, you can be held liable for telling others 'with malice.' Accordingly, think carefully about whether the people you're passing information to really need to know."

Exhibit 16.5 provides a model for a substance abuse policy.

Step two requires companies to inform employees about drug and alcohol abuse and its effect on the company's safety, security, health care costs, productivity, and quality. Companies must explain their policies and how testing and assistance programs will be utilized. To be truly effective, an education and awareness program must be an ongoing one, not just a one-time effort.[48]

Step three requires supervisors, team leaders, and team facilitators—those most directly responsible for enforcing the policy—to learn how to detect performance

EXHIBIT 16.5	Sample drug abuse policy statement.

Drug Abuse Policy Statement

[Company Name] is committed to providing a safe work environment and to fostering the well-being and health of its employees. That commitment is jeopardized when any [Company Name] employee illegally uses drugs on the job, comes to work under their influence, or possesses, distributes, or sells drugs in the workplace. Therefore, (Company Name) has established the following policy:

1. It is a violation of company policy for any employee to possess, sell, trade, or offer for sale illegal drugs or otherwise engage in the illegal use of drugs on the job.

2. It is a violation of company policy for anyone to report to work under the influence of illegal drugs.

3. It is a violation of company policy for anyone to use prescription drugs illegally. (However, nothing in this policy precludes the appropriate use of legally prescribed medications.)

4. Violations of this policy are subject to disciplinary action up to and including termination.

It is the responsibility of the company's supervisors to counsel employees whenever they see changes in performance or behavior that suggest an employee has a drug problem. Although it is not the supervisor's job to diagnose personal problems, the supervisor should encourage such employees to seek help and advise them about available resources for getting help. Everyone shares responsibility for maintaining a safe work environment, and coworkers should encourage anyone who may have a drug problem to seek help.

The goal of this policy is to balance our respect for individuals with the need to maintain a safe, productive, and drug-free environment. The intent of this policy is to offer a helping hand to those who need it, while sending a clear message that the illegal use of drugs is incompatible with employment at (Company Name).

If your company is subject to the requirements of the Drug-Free Workplace Act of 1988 (by nature of a grant/contract with the federal government) you should add the following statement to your drug policy:

As a condition of employment, employees must abide by the terms of this policy and must notify (Company Name) in writing of any conviction of a violation of a criminal drug statute occurring in the workplace no later than five days after such conviction.

Source: Extracted from the President's Drug Advisory Council, Office of the Assistant Secretary for Policy, U.S. Department of Labor, *Drugs Don't Work in America: A Step-by-step Guide to a Drug-Free Workplace* (February 21, 2006), website: *www.dol.gov/asp.*

problems that may indicate substance abuse. Although supervisors at every level are responsible for observing and documenting unsatisfactory work performance or behavior, they are not responsible for diagnosing substance abuse or treating substance abuse problems. They do need to know the signs that may accompany substance abuse and what to do when they observe them. For example, supervisors may be required to counsel employees and refer them to an assistance program, a company physician, or drug testing program. [49]

Step four specifies ways for dealing with substance abuse. Providing access to a substance abuse EAP communicates a clear commitment by a company (and its unions) that it wishes to save valued employees and help them remain or once again become effective performers. With or without an EAP, all employees should be able to inform coworkers about alcohol and other drugs, confront users with their unacceptable work behaviors, and provide referral information. [50]

These four steps must occur before drug testing can be initiated. Nonetheless, drug testing of new applicants for jobs is rapidly becoming the norm. Although routine drug testing for existing employees was controversial in the past and is affected by union contracts and various laws, there is greater clarity today.

> Private employers may screen employees with pre-employment testing, investigate accidents by testing those involved, and conduct random drug tests. Recent litigation has focused not on whether an employer may test but on how the test is done.[51]

The legal environment is more complex, however, than this general statement would seem to indicate. For example, approximately 10 states have laws that regulate drug testing in employment situations.[52] Fortunately, there are publications, such as the *Guide to State and Federal Drug-Testing Laws,* that are available from the Institute for a Drug-Free Workplace at *www.drugfreeworkplace.org* and other sources.

Organizations doing business with the federal government are covered by the Drug-Free Workplace Act of 1988. These organizations must certify that they provide a drug-free workplace, have a substance abuse policy, conduct ongoing drug awareness programs, and require all employees to notify their companies of any criminal drug statute conviction. They also must notify the federal government of such violations and impose sanctions for an employee convicted of drug abuse violations in the workplace. The U.S. Department of Transportation (DOT) requires drug testing of employees in safety-sensitive positions and drug abuse awareness education for supervisors and employees. In the federal government, routine, random drug testing has been the rule in the armed services for military and some civilian employees since the early 1980s. The DOT began urine tests for drug and alcohol use during annual physicals at about the same time and began random testing of air-traffic controllers, aviation and railway safety inspectors, electronics technicians, and employees with top secret clearances in 1987.

As noted earlier, state and local laws tend to limit drug testing of employees. For example, a Connecticut statute allows random testing only in certain highly restricted circumstances. But when drug testing is used selectively, in sensitive work settings, and testing is performed with proper collection and safeguards, the courts have ruled in its favor. The U.S. Department of Labor suggests asking the following questions before testing employees for drugs:

- *Who will be tested?* Options may include all staff, job applicants and/or employees in safety-sensitive positions.
- *When will tests be conducted?* Possibilities including pre-employment, upon reasonable suspicion or for cause, post-accident, randomly, periodically, and post-rehabilitation.
- *Which drugs will be tested for?* Options including testing applicants and employees for illegal drugs and testing employees for a broader range of substance, including alcohol and certain prescription drugs.
- *How will tests be conducted?* Different testing modes are available, and many states have laws that dictate which may and may not be used. Employers

SUPERVISORS AND PERFORMANCE

According to public health reports, smoking costs the United States over $72 billion each year in health care costs, with losses in productivity accounting for $40 billion of that amount. The public is aware of the consequences of smoking; a Gallup survey found that 94 percent of the survey's U.S. respondents wanted some type of workplace restrictions on smoking. Because of such views of smoking, many state and local governments have implemented regulations that restrict smoking in the workplace, but such regulations vary greatly. Because of the toll of smoking on health, the financial costs associated with smoking, and legal regulations, the number of companies that forbid smoking on the premises has increased dramatically. A survey by the Society of Human Resource Management in 2004 found that the vast majority of companies (72 percent) restricted smoking to designated areas other than employee offices. This result is dramatic when it is considered that during the mid-1980s, only 3 percent of companies prohibited smoking on the premises.

Some companies have been aggressive in their attempts to deal with smoking in the workplace. For example, FedEx prohibits smoking in its buildings and aircraft. CDW Computer Center, Inc, which has 1,500 employees, not only prohibits smoking in its buildings, but also in the parking lots. Controls Unlimited also prohibits smoking on the premises and allows employees to smoke outside only on their own time during lunch. In addition, some companies and organizations do not hire smokers. For example, the American Cancer Society does not hire smokers. While there is no law preventing employers from discriminating against smokers, legal issues remain to be resolved. One practical consideration is that even if the company has the right to exclude smokers from being hiring, rejected applicants can still sue the company, and it will cost the company to defend itself, even if it has the right to reject such applicants.

Another positive employer practice for dealing with smoking is to provide support for employees who wish to quit smoking. FedEx provides as much as $150 to reimburse employees for Nicorette gum, the drug Zyban (which is prescribed to help people quit smoking), and acupuncture treatments for smoking. The company also has a registered nurse who runs a smoking cessation program for the company.

Sources: Lin Grensing-Pophal. "Smoking Is a Burning Issue for HR Policy Makers," *HR Magazine* (May 1999): 58–66. *Managing Benefit Plans,* "Workplace Smoking: How Far Should You Go?" *Managing Benefit Plans,* (June 2005): 2–3.

also must be familiar with any local, state, and Federal laws or any collective bargaining agreements that may impact when, where and how testing is performed. It is strongly recommended that legal counsel be sought before starting any testing program.[53]

This chapter's feature on supervisors and performance deals with the actions that some employers are taking to help employees stop smoking.

Various organizations and hotlines can give you more information and help you create a drug-free workplace and an employee assistance program. Here are several that you will find eager to help:

- The National Clearinghouse for Alcohol and Drug Information: 1-800-729-6686
- The Drug-Free Workplace Helpline: 1-800-967-5752
- 800 Substance Abuse Line: 1-800-662-HELP
- The American Council on Alcoholism Helpline: 1-800-527-5344

FAMILY LEAVE

The Family and Medical Leave Act provides certain protections to employees who have health and other problems. The act affects employers—businesses, nonprofits, and governmental units—with 50 or more employees by granting their employees up to 12 weeks unpaid leave for the birth or adoption of a child; caring for a spouse, child, or parent; or taking care of one's own illness. During the leave, the employer must guarantee that the employee will be able to return to the same or a comparable job. If employees have health care benefits, those benefits must be continued during the term of the leave. Employers may apply employees' accrued sick leave to the leave period. They may choose to exempt employees in the top 10 percent of compensation, those who have not worked at least a year, and those who have not worked at least 25 hours per week or 1,250 hours during the past 12 months. Employees must provide 30 days' notice to their employers for foreseeable leaves.[54]

THE SUPERVISOR'S ROLE

Safety

Nearly all efforts at promoting safety and identifying and getting help to the troubled worker depend on you as the supervisor. Safety programs, regulations, procedures, and committees need your input and enforcement efforts in order to work effectively and efficiently. Many sources of help are available to you for identifying problem areas and taking corrective actions. Exhibit 16.6 lists the most important areas to consider when conducting safety and health inspections. When you have identified the hazards, you are ready to set up and implement controls to prevent, eliminate, or deal with each of them. These controls eliminate hazards or reduce their potential to cause harm. Dangerous machines can be eliminated or fitted with proper safeguards. Operators can be thoroughly trained and drilled in safety procedures. Personal protective gear can be purchased, issued, and checked regularly to see that it works and is being used correctly. Access to hazards can be carefully controlled by restricting it to those who are aware of and equipped to deal with hazardous situations.

Substance Abuse

Your role as a supervisor is crucial in spotting troubled workers who need special assistance and in getting them started on a program designed to meet their needs. Look for warning signs such as changes in an employee's routine and behaviors. Increases in

EXHIBIT 16.6	**Typical scope of a self-inspection program.**

Processing, Receiving, Shipping, and Storage—equipment, job planning, layout, heights, floor loads, projection of materials, materials handling and storage methods, training for material handing.

Building and Grounds Condition—floors, walls, ceilings, exits, stairs, walkways, ramps, platforms, driveways, aisles.

Housekeeping Program—waste disposal, tools, objects, materials, leakage and spillage, cleaning methods, schedules, work areas, remote areas, storage areas.

Electricity—equipment, switches, breakers, fuses, switch boxes, junctions, special fixtures, circuits, insulation, extensions, tools, motors, grounding, code compliance.

Lighting—type, intensity, controls, conditions, diffusion, location, glare and shadow control.

Heating and Ventilation—type, effectiveness, temperature, humidity, controls, natural and artificial ventilation and exhausting.

Machinery—points of operation, flywheels, gears, shafts, pulleys, key ways, belts, couplings, sprockets, chains, frames, controls, lighting for tools and equipment, brakes, exhausting, feeding, oiling, adjusting, maintenance, lockout/tagout, grounding, work space, location, purchasing standards.

Personnel—training, including hazard identification training; experience; methods of checking machines before use; type of clothing; PPE (personal protective equipment); use of guards; tool storage; work practices; method of cleaning, oiling, adjusting machinery.

Hand and Power Tools—purchasing standards, inspection, storage, repair, types, maintenance, grounding, use and handling.

Chemicals—storage, handling, transportation, spills, disposals, amounts used, labeling, toxicity or other harmful effects, warning signs, supervision, training, protective clothing and equipment, hazard communication requirements.

Fire Prevention—extinguishers, alarms, sprinklers, smoking rules, exits, personnel assigned, separation of flammable materials and dangerous operations, explosive-proof fixtures in hazardous locations, waste disposal, and training of personnel.

Maintenance—provide regular and preventive maintenance on all equipment used at the worksite, recording all work performed on the machinery and by training personnel on the proper care and servicing of the equipment.

PPE [personal protective equipment]—type, size, maintenance, repair, storage, assignment of responsibility, purchasing methods, standards observed, training in care and use, rules of use, method of assignment.

Transportation—motor vehicle safety, seat belts, vehicle maintenance, safe driver programs.

First Aid Program/Supplies—medical care facilities locations, posted emergency phone numbers, accessible first aid kits.

Evacuation Plan—establish and practice procedures for an emergency evacuation (e.g., fire, chemical/biological incidents, bomb threat), include escape procedures and routes, critical plant operations, employee accounting following an evacuation, rescue and medical duties and ways to report emergencies.

Source: Extracted from Occupational Safety and Health Administration, U.S. Department of Labor, *Small Business Handbook*, OSHA 2209-02R, 2005, pp. 17–18.

Supervisors of workers in hazardous situations need to make sure their employees understand their jobs and are properly protected. Safety of workers is foremost.

an employee's tardiness, absenteeism, ineffectiveness, or need for disciplinary action may signal that the employee has a personal or drug-related problem. Employees who suddenly isolate themselves from fellow workers and who become argumentative with their peers are asking for help.

When you think you have a troubled employee on your hands, let the person know what you think, and recommend or refer him to those in your company who can help. Your company's medical department will work with the individual or refer him to an appropriate agency for treatment. Failure to comply with the company's directives may leave the employee subject to disciplinary measures and termination. You need to keep your people aware of the help that is available to them, and your company should have an ongoing educational program to alert employees to the dangers of drug abuse.

THE OCCUPATIONAL SAFETY AND HEALTH ACT (1970)

In 1970, Congress passed the Occupational Safety and Health Act, which created the **Occupational Safety and Health Administration (OSHA)** "to assure so far as possible every working man and woman in the nation safe and healthful working conditions to preserve our human resources." The law, which became effective in April 1971, applies to all employers engaged in any business affecting commerce and employing people. Its terms apply to all the states, territories, and possessions of the United States as well as to employees of the federal government. The law does not apply to working conditions protected under other federal occupational safety and health laws such as the Federal Coal Mine Health and Safety Act, the Atomic Energy Act, and the Migrant Health Act.

Occupational Safety and Health Administration
the federal agency that administers the Occupational Safety and Health Act

According to OSHA, each employer has the duty to furnish employees a working environment free from recognized hazards that cause or are likely to cause death or serious physical harm. Administration and enforcement of OSHA are vested in the secretary of labor and in the Occupational Safety and Health Review Commission, a quasi-judicial board of three members appointed by the president. Research and related functions are vested in the secretary of health and human services, whose functions will for the most part be carried out by the National Institute for Occupational Safety and Health. The institute conducts research and experimental programs for developing criteria for new and improved job safety and health standards.

OCCUPATIONAL SAFETY AND HEALTH STANDARDS

Various safety and health standards have been issued by OSHA and are available to you through your company or from one of the many local OSHA offices in major cities around the country. Exhibit 16.7 shows a representative OSHA regulation. All help define protective measures or ways in which to deal with an identifiable hazard. We will discuss the activities of OSHA in more detail at the end of this chapter.

It is not enough to warn and instruct employees about safety hazards. Employers are responsible for unsafe behaviors of their employees, such as the failure to wear safety equipment. Thus, supervisors also must enforce instructions and remove or eliminate hazards. Supervisors who ignore company or OSHA safety rules and standards can cause a doubling of the OSHA-prescribed penalties if accidents are the result of such behavior. All employers and supervisors are obligated to familiarize themselves and their employees with the standards that apply to them.

COMPLIANCE COMPLAINTS

Employees may file complaints about safety and health violations to any local OSHA office. Complaining employees may not be persecuted in any way by their employers. Furthermore, since the *Whirlpool Corporation v. Marshall* case in 1980, workers have had the right to refuse a job assignment or to walk off the job "because of a reasonable apprehension of health [hazards] or serious injury coupled with a reasonable belief that no less drastic alternative is available." This wording and other words in the Supreme Court decision have been interpreted to mean that workers may refuse to perform work that constitutes a clear and present danger, in their minds, to their safety. Employers are not required to pay workers who do not perform such work, but they may not reprimand them in any way.

OSHA INSPECTIONS

OSHA is allowed to select firms for regular inspection visits if they have 10 or more employees, below-average safety records, or employees who have filed complaints. Since the 1979 Supreme Court decision in *Marshall v. Barlow's, Inc.,* employers do not have to admit OSHA inspectors who do not have a search warrant. But all companies (except those with 9 or fewer employees) must keep OSHA records on accidents, illnesses, and employee exposure to potentially toxic materials or other harmful physical agents. Millions of employees have the right to demand information about hazardous chemicals at their work sites. They can demand to know the identities and compositions of chemicals that

Sample component of OSHA standard for eye and face protection.	EXHIBIT 16.7

1910.133(a)

General requirements.

1910.133(a)(1)

The employer shall ensure that each affected employee uses appropriate eye or face protection when exposed to eye or face hazards from flying particles, molten metal, liquid chemicals, acids or caustic liquids, chemical gases or vapors, or potentially injurious light radiation.

1910.133(a)(2)

The employer shall ensure that each affected employee uses eye protection that provides side protection when there is a hazard from flying objects. Detachable side protectors (e.g., clip-on or slide-on side shields) meeting the pertinent requirements of this section are acceptable.

1910.133(a)(3)

The employer shall ensure that each affected employee who wears prescription lenses while engaged in operations that involve eye hazards wears eye protection that incorporates the prescription in its design, or wears eye protection that can be worn over the prescription lenses without disturbing the proper position of the prescription lenses or the protective lenses.

1910.133(a)(4)

Eye and face PPE shall be distinctly marked to facilitate identification of the manufacturer.

1910.133(a)(5)

The employer shall ensure that each affected employee uses equipment with filter lenses that have a shade number appropriate for the work being performed for protection from injurious light radiation . . .

Source: Occupational Safety and Health Administration, U.S. Department of Labor, Occupational Safety and Health Standards, (February 21, 2006): Website *www.osha.gov.*

they are exposed to at work. When OSHA compliance officers (inspectors) call, they may be on a routine inspection, or they may be responding to an employee's complaint. In the latter case, the inspectors need not limit their visits to investigating the complaint.

ON-SITE CONSULTATION

OSHA has developed a free on-site consultation service that is available to any employer on request. An OSHA consultant will visit a business and tour the facilities, pointing out what operations are governed by OSHA standards and how to interpret the applicable standards. The inspector will point out any violations and offer suggestions for how to correct them. No citations are issued, but—as part of the decision to request a consultation— the employer must agree to eliminate, within a reasonable time, all hazards discovered.

STATE PROGRAMS

When the Occupational Safety and Health Act was passed in 1970, many states already had their own state safety laws. Some of these laws were criticized for their weak standards, ineffective administration, and lax enforcement. Others were considered quite acceptable. States have the opportunity to develop and administer their own safety and health programs, provided that they can demonstrate that their programs are "at least as effective" as the federal program. State safety and health programs must be approved by OSHA. About half of the states have developed and are administering their own safety and health programs.

Workers' compensation is another major area of state legislation. Prior to 1910, workers were injured frequently on the job. Their lost wages and medical bills were usually their own problems unless they could prove in a court of law that their employers were the sole cause of their injuries. If a worker contributed in any way to the injury suffered or if a worker knew the work to be dangerous, the employer could usually avoid legal responsibility for damages.

workers' compensation federal and state laws designed to compensate employees for illnesses and injuries that arise out of and in the course of their employment

Workers' compensation insurance programs compensate employees for medical and disability expenses, as well as for income lost because of an illness or injury. They are state mandated and may be either elective or compulsory. Under elective laws, a company may provide the protection the law requires on its own by insuring itself against worker claims. But employees or their families would then be free to sue the employer for damages for injuries, illnesses, or deaths. "Large employers that self-insure pay these claims out of the corporate kitty, while smaller concerns typically purchase insurance."[55] A worker who suffers an illness or injury on the job can file a claim with the state's compensation board. Benefits are paid to individuals according to schedules stating fixed maximums that may be awarded by compensation boards.

Under compulsory workers' compensation laws, each employer within the state's jurisdiction must accept the application of the law and provide the benefits required. When the company provides the protection required by law through workers' compensation insurance, the employee who suffers an injury or illness may not sue.

The cost of workers' compensation insurance varies, depending on a company's history of worker claims. The more claims filed against a company, and the more benefits paid by an insurance company, the greater the premium charged for workers' compensation protection. Most businesses, therefore, try to insure workers' safety through the latest in safety devices and safety rules. They do this not only to protect their workers from injury but also to protect their profits from the drain of insurance premiums and self-insurance funds.

OshKosh B'Gosh, a maker of children's clothing, had a routine inspection from OSHA and received a citation. Plant operations were at the root of a growing number of cumulative trauma disorders (CTDs) such as carpal tunnel syndrome. According to Pat Hirschberg, the plant's safety chief, "the directive to fix the problem 'was the best thing that could have happened to us.'" A committee was created "to inspect every aspect of production and uncover the sources of injury. It found that most of the worker's problems arose from small, awkward motions that required force and were highly repetitious."[56] Operations caused abnormal use of fingers, wrists, and hands, and neither tables nor chairs were adjustable. The committee presented its findings and recommendations to senior management and convinced them to make several changes. As a result, the company hired engineers to design special equipment to facilitate production operations, introduced job rotation to vary employee activities, instituted training to teach proper equipment adjustment and work positions, and encouraged workers to bring their concerns to management so that changes could be made. The results were as follows:

> The number of claims jumped by a third when the program was introduced, as people began to pay attention to symptoms they might previously have ignored. But because these ailments were caught in the early stages, they never became costly or severe. [Workers' compensation] claims eventually retreated as the company's prevention strategy took effect.[57]

INSTANT REPLAY

1. The security of your company's and employees' assets is partly your responsibility.

2. Your people depend on you and the company's policies and programs to protect them from recognized and recognizable hazards.

3. Although safety and security are everyone's legitimate concern, your organization depends on you and its other managers for planning, implementing, and enforcing proper programs.

4. Engineering, education (training), and enforcement are the keys to successful safety and security efforts.

5. Supervisors play a critical role in maintaining a drug-free work environment.

6. Supervisors who really care about safety and security listen to their employees, look for hazards, assign responsibility for safety and security, enforce standards and procedures, and discipline violators of safety and security policies.

QUESTIONS FOR CLASS DISCUSSION

1. Can you define this chapter's key terms?

2. As a supervisor, how would you go about the task of safeguarding your office or shop environment?

3. What are a supervisor's duties with regard to fire prevention? With regard to fighting a fire?

4. How can a supervisor act to prevent losses from vandalism?

5. What are the major purposes of the Occupational Safety and Health Act? When did it become effective in enforcement efforts? How does it enforce its regulations?

6. What are an employer's rights with regard to OSHA inspectors?

ASSESS THIS SITUATION

Purpose: To acquaint you with the help available from public and private sources for creating a drug-free workplace.

Your Task: Using the telephone numbers provided in this chapter, contact three sources and request their free materials. Summarize the materials and present your summary to your class. Together with classmates, create a policy for your school or company.

SKILL BUILDING EXERCISE 16.1

As discussed in this chapter, supervisors play an important role in protecting the resources of their employers from theft by shoplifters as well as shrinkage losses from employee theft of merchandise. In addition, supervisors also need to be on the alert for instances of employee fraud and embezzlement. Fortunately, the Internet provides a means for rapid dissemination of recent information on various fraudulent schemes. The Federal Bureau of Investigation (*www.fbi.gov*) maintains case studies of various types of white-collar crime on its website. While most website contents and navigation formats are subject to change, a search of the site map of the FBI's website should reveal the location of the cases. Recent examination of the FBI website reveals that the pressroom section contains a series of these case files in its "Gotcha Archive" (*www. fbi.gov/gotcha/archive/gotarchive.htm*).

Your Task: Prepare for class by reviewing the cases that are relevant to business and work situations. During the time set aside in class, work in small groups to do the following: (1) Provide a basic description of the various schemes and the financial damage to the businesses. (2) Describe the flaws in the companies' security systems and any management practices that enabled the schemes to work, (3) Identify the key changes that should be adopted by businesses in order to prevent such losses. (4) Outline the actions that supervisors will have to take in order to support such loss prevention measures.

SKILL BUILDING EXERCISE 16.2

OSHA maintains a number of helpful tools on its website at *www.osha.gov/index.html.* The website has a wide range of valuable information that is helpful for supervisors. For example, there is an eTools section, which has a number of critical safety issues, such as eye protection, hearing conservation, machine guarding, silica, and steel erection. There is also an eTools section on ergonomics, which has features on such topics as baggage handling and beverage delivery. There is also an expert adviser section with information on such issues as asbestos, fire safety, and hazard awareness. In addition, there are PowerPoint and multimedia presentations on a wide variety of safety and occupational health issues.

Your Task: Explore the PowerPoint section of the OSHA website and review the PowerPoint safety presentations for various work activities, such as operating an industrial truck or forklift, how to handle asbestos, or how to prevent exposure to tuberculosis. Provide a brief written review of three different PowerPoint presentations, or other multimedia training materials on the OSHA website and describe how a supervisor might ensure that employees master this material and obey the safety and health procedures that are presented.

It's Not My Dope	CASE 16.1

Gerald Haley was the plant manager of the ALU-GULF aluminum smelting plant. As Gerald was reviewing the maintenance schedule for the next week, Del Walsh knocked on his door. Del was a consultant who was advising the company on the installation of new computer controls for the smelter.

DEL: "You're not going to be happy with some news I have for you."

GERALD: "Don't tell me the new controls aren't going to be ready on schedule! We can't take another delay."

DEL: "No, no, that's not it. About 20 minutes ago I went out to take a look at the ducks that are flying in to land on the water out by the pier where the bauxite ships dock. I was walking back from the pier, and when I came by the storage warehouse, I thought I smelled marijuana smoke. I looked through a small space in the big sliding doors and saw a couple of maintenance guys smoking a joint. I didn't get a good look at who they were, but I thought you ought to know."

GERALD: "You're right, I'm not happy about this. Are they still out there?"

DEL: "I don't think so because a truck pulled up to the doors of the warehouse and they probably slipped out the back door to avoid being seen. There was no way to see the back door from where I was, and when the truck pulled in, I couldn't see anyone in the warehouse."

GERALD: "Thanks for telling me, Del. We really can't have that stuff around here. As you know, our guys work around dangerous equipment and high voltage all the time. In addition, a lot of the work they do on the power lines to the smelter takes place about 250 feet in the air. There just isn't any room for error or inattention. Because of the danger, we have a policy that makes use or possession of drugs or alcohol on the premises a basis for termination."

Gerald called the police, and they responded by sending three officers with drug detection dogs. The police took the dogs through the employees' locker room. The dogs detected no drugs in the locker room so they shifted the search to the employees' cars in the parking lot. In about 10 minutes, the dogs detected drugs in one of the cars. The police could see what looked like a joint in the ashtray. The police then called in the license tag of the car and obtained the name of the owner. It turned out to be Harry Snider, one of the plant's maintenance workers. Gerald confronted Harry.

GERALD: "Harry, we received a report that two workers were smoking a joint in the warehouse this afternoon. When we brought in the drug dogs, they searched the company parking lot and found what appears to be a marijuana joint in your car. As you know, we have a strong policy against using drugs or having drugs on the premises. Do you have anything to say?"

HARRY: "I don't smoke marijuana. If it really is marijuana then somebody else must have left it in there. It's not my dope."

GERALD: "Well, we're going to need a drug test. Are you willing to give us a specimen for a drug test?"

HARRY: "I told you I don't use drugs and that whatever the cops found isn't mine. I'm not going to go through any drug test. I've got some rights to privacy. The answer's no."

GERALD: "I will take your refusal to mean that you have declined the opportunity to establish your innocence. We're going to suspend you until we complete the analysis of the joint and the rest of our investigation."

Three days later, after receiving positive test results on the alleged joint, the company terminated Harry. Harry filed a grievance with the union and the union pursued the case on to arbitration. The union argued that no employee should be fired for mere possession of marijuana, and that Harry should be given a second chance.

Source: This case is based on a management brief written by Brian Meiners. Reprinted with permission.

Questions

1. Do you agree with Gerald's actions in this situation? Explain.

2. Do you think Harry has a legitimate argument about privacy rights? Explain.

3. How do you think an arbitrator will rule in this case? What are the critical issues that will determine the ruling on Harry's case?

4. What do you think Gerald should do to prevent another drug incident like this? Why do you think an outsider discovered the marijuana use?

CASE 16.2 | **No Chance for a Smoke Break**

Sonny Nygaard had not had a minute's rest all morning. Two shipments had gone out under rush conditions. As he and his coworker, Dixy Paxon, started the production run for the third shipment, the pulverizer had broken down. Sonny and Dixy had been lucky and could see the burned-out relay as soon as they removed the inspection cover. Unfortunately, it was in a difficult position to replace. While Sonny crawled under the pulverizer to remove the old relay, Dixy left to obtain a replacement. Dixy's departure left Sonny alone in the pulverizer room while other equipment was running. As a result, he had not been able to take his 10:00 A.M. break. Sonny finished removing the relay and crawled out from under the pulverizer. As he stood up, he brushed the dust off his clothes and reached into his pocket for a cigarette. He had just lit the cigarette and taken two puffs when his supervisor, Web Daniel, walked into the pulverizer room. Web saw his lit cigarette and said, "Put that damn thing out before you blow us all to Hell along with the rest of the whole plant! Are you crazy!"

Sonny said, "It just happened sort of automatically. I just didn't think about it. I haven't had a smoke break since we've been so busy this morning, and I couldn't leave the area because Dixy left to get a new relay."

Web said, "I don't care what your excuse is. One spark and this place blows sky high. We've given you safety training, plastered this place with no-smoking signs, and enforced the rules. What does it take to get your attention? Go down to the plant manager's office. I'll be down in a few minutes."

Later, at the meeting with Web, the plant manager, and the union steward, Sonny explained that he had not intended to break the rule. He also said that he smoked three packs of cigarettes a day and couldn't go very long without having a smoke. The plant manager reminded him of the extreme danger of smoking in his work area and that violation of the no-smoking rule was grounds for termination on the first offense. He suspended Sonny pending completion of an investigation of the incident and a review of his work record.

Web and the plant manager reviewed Sonny's work and disciplinary records. Sonny had good performance evaluations. Web explained that Sonny was a good, dependable worker, had very low absenteeism, and had worked at the plant for seven years. Nonetheless, the disciplinary record indicated that Sonny had been disciplined on a previous occasion for smoking in an unauthorized area. This incident had taken place two years ago, before Sonny had been transferred into Web's section. Sonny had been suspended for two weeks for the rule violation, but it had taken place in a much less dangerous area than in the pulverizer room. The two managers also interviewed Sonny's coworkers and found that they considered him to be a solid worker. However, one of them came by the plant manager's office after their interviews and said that he had seen Sonny smoking in the pulverizer room on two previous occasions.

The plant manager and Web decided that the appropriate action would be to terminate Sonny. The union's business agent was informed of the pending termination. The business agent said that instead of firing Sonny, the company should first get treatment for his smoking addiction through the employee assistance program. If he smoked in a restricted area after treatment, then termination would be warranted, but not before.

The next day the plant manager called Sonny in and terminated him for violating the no-smoking policy.

Source: Case based on an arbitration case written by Bruce Fraser, "Stone Container Corp. and International Brotherhood of Teamsters, Chauffeurs, Warehousemen and Helpers of America, Local 25," Labor Award Reporter: Summary of Labor Arbitration Awards, *Report No. 469 (April 1998): 4–5.*

Questions

1. Do you agree with the plant manager's termination of Sonny Nygaard? Why or why not?

2. What is the significance of the fact that a coworker had seen Sonny smoking in the pulverizer room before? What is the significance of the fact that he did not report the incident at the time?

3. What is your view of the union business agent's argument that Sonny should first be given an opportunity to get treatment for his smoking addiction?

4. If the case is appealed to arbitration, how do you think the arbitrator will weigh the plant's safety concerns with Sonny's smoking problem, work history, and past smoking violations? Explain.

REFERENCES

[1] Brainy Quote Website (February 20, 2006): *www.brainyquote.com/quotes/authors/a/alan_shepard.html.*

[2] Harris, Gardner. "Endemic Problems of Safety in Coal Mining," *New York Times*, (January 10, 2006): A14.

[3] Urbina, Ian. "2 Missing Workers Are Found Dead in West Virginia Mine," *New York Times*, (January 22, 2006): Section 1, p. 14.

[4] Harris, Gardner. "Endemic Problem of Safety in Coal Mining," *New York Times* (January 10, 2006): Section A., P. 14, Copyright © (2007) by the New York Times Co. Reprinted with permission.

[5] Fountain, Henry. "For a Safer Mine, Try More Training," *New York Times*, (January 8, 2006): sect. 4, 2.

[6] Editorial. "Tolerating Death in the Mines," *New York Times*, (February 5, 2006): sect. 4, 11.

[7] Urbina, Ian. "2 Missing Workers Are Found Dead in West Virginia Mine," *New York Times*, (January 22, 2006): Section 1, p. 14, Copyright © (2007) by the New York Times Co. Reprinted with permission.

[8] Gatehouse, Jonathon. "Terror by Mail," *Maclean's* (November 15, 2001): 22–24.

[9] McFarland, Jennifer. "Violence in the Workplace," *Harvard Management Update* (April 2001): 8.

[10] Ibid.

[11] Mayer, Merry. "Breaking Point," *HR Magazine* (October 2001): 111–114.

[12] Ibid.

[13] Randle, Wilma. "When Employees Lie, Cheat, or Steal," *Working Woman* (January 1995): 55–56, 76.

[14] Employees Top Shoplifters," *Chicago Tribune* (December 19, 1994): sect. 4, 3.

[15] Emshwiller, John R. "Businesses Lose Billions of Dollars to Employee Theft," *Wall Street Journal* (October 5, 1992): B2.

[16] Ibid.

[17] Ziemba, Stanley. "Study Finds Lax Computer Security Is Costing Business," *Chicago Tribune* (November 20, 1994): sect. 7, 5.

[18] Ibid.

[19] Cullison, A. E. "Fax Machines an Open Book to Hackers," *Chicago Tribune* (September 9, 1990): sect. 7, 11B.

[20] Hanna, Greg. "Preventing Computer Fraud," *Strategic Finance*, (March 2005): 31–35.

[21] Ibid.

[22] Bologna, Jack, and Shaw, Jack. *Corporate Crime Investigation*, Boston: Butterworth-Heinemann (1997).

[23] Bank, David, and Richmond, Riva. "Where the Dangers Are," *Wall Street Journal*, (July 18, 2005): R1–R3.

[24] Hayes, Frank. "Secure Your Users," *Computerworld* (September 24, 2001): 70.

[25] Hanna. "Preventing Computer Fraud."

[26] Ibid., 32.

[27] Ibid., 31–35.

[28] Sullivan, Andrew. "Programs in Peril," *PCWorld.Com*, (March 2006): 16–18.

[29] Weir, Tom. "Caught on Camera," *Supermarket Business Magazine* (November 15, 2001): 11.

[30] Bologna and Shaw. *Corporate Crime Investigation*, 19–21.

[31] Turcsik, Richard, and Summerour, Jenny. "Monitoring Shrink," *Progressive Grocer* (October 2001): 7. Weir. "Caught on Camera."

[32] Clark, Ken. "On Guard," *Chain Store Age* (October 2001): 45–48.

[33] Reitman, Valerie. "Alarm Sounded on Shoplifting," *Chicago Tribune* (January 28, 1990): sect. 7, 12.

[34] Hagedorn, Ann. "It's Why Employees Don't Want the Boss's Portrait on the Wall," *Wall Street Journal* (November 29, 1990): B1.

[35] Fire Prevention Week, 2000 by the President of the United States of America: A Proclamation," *FDCH Regulatory Intelligence Database* (October 7, 2000).

[36] Wah, Louisa. "The Emotional Tightrope," *Management Review*, (January 2000): 38–43.

[37] Shellenbarger, Sue. "Overloaded Staffers Are Starting to Take More Time off Work," *Wall Street Journal* (September 23, 1998): B1.

[38] Sandler, Howard M. "Microbiologics in the Workplace," *Occupational Hazards* (May 2000): 95–96.

[39] Kim, Arnold L. "Sick Building Syndrome Solutions," *Professional Safety* (June 2001): 43.

[40] Turner, Toni. "The Phantom Menace," *Director* (September 2001): 90–94.

[41] Jackson, Maggie. "Toilet Training for Businesses: OSHA Will Issue New Mandate," *Fort Worth Star Telegram* (March 13, 1998): F1, F4.

[42] Ibid.

[43] Ibid.

[44] Statements by HHS Secretary Tommy G. Thompson Regarding World AIDS Day," *FDCH Regulatory Intelligence Database* (November 30, 2001).

[45] Fletcher, Lee. "Drug Testing Promoted as Loss Prevention Measure," *Business Insurance* (May 8, 2000): 16.

[46] U.S. Department of Labor (February 24, 2006), website: *http://www.dol.gov/asp/programs/drugs/workingpartners/dfworkplace/dfwp.asp.*

[47] Ibid.

[48] Ibid.

[49] Ibid

[50] Ibid.

[51] Bahls, Jane Easter. "Dealing with Drugs: Keep It Legal," *HR Magazine* (March 1998): 105–116.

[52] U.S. Department of Labor, website (February 24, 2006): *http://www.dol.gov/asp/programs/drugs/workingpartners/dfworkplace/dfwp.asp.*

[53] U.S. Department of Labor, Office of the Assistant Secretary for Policy, "Drug-Free Workplace," (February 24, 2006), website: *www.dol.gov/asp/programs/drugs/workingpartners/dfworkplace/dt.asp.*

[54] O'Brien, Timothy L., Gupta, Udayan, and Marsh, Barbara. "Most Small Businesses Appear Prepared to Cope with New Family-Leave Rules," *Wall Street Journal* (February 8, 1993): B1.

[55] Fefer, Mark D. "Taking Control of Your Workers' Comp Costs," *Fortune* (October 3, 1994): 131–132, 134, 136.

[56] Ibid.

[57] Ibid.

GLOSSARY

Abilene paradox group decision-making error related to group dynamics in which group members do not press for their real needs

accident any unforeseen or unplanned incident or event

accommodating style allowing the other party to satisfy his or her needs

accountability having to answer to someone for your performance or failure to perform to standards

active listening listening that clarifies, restates, and summarizes in order to obtain a deep understanding of the speaker

adjourning the fifth stage of team development where the team dissolves

affiliative manager a manager with affiliation needs greater than power needs

affinity groups groups of people, such as women, African Americans, Latinos, and so on, who have minority status in an organization and who are not well represented in senior positions

anchoring trap a decision-making trap that places inordinate emphasis on the first information of which the decision-maker becomes aware

anti-spyware software software packages that remove probing software that has been imbedded in an organization's computers in order to obtain critical information

appraisal process periodic evaluations of each employee's on-the-job performance as well as skill levels, attitudes, and potential

arbitration the use of a neutral third party to resolve differences between management and labor unions over contract interpretation issues

assimilation paradigm an approach to diversity in which minorities are expected to adapt to the majority culture and which captures few of the benefits of diversity

attitude a person's manner of thinking, feeling, or acting toward specific stimuli

authority a person's right to give orders and instructions to others and to use organizational resources

autocratic style a management and leadership style characterized by the retention by the leader of all authority for decision-making

avoiding style not addressing the conflict by ignoring it

balanced scorecard a combined indicator of performance that includes multiple and weighted measures of performance, such as financial health, customer focus, service excellence, and employee learning and growth

behavioral interview interview in which interviewees are asked to describe how they have coped with a past situation, or how they would act in a hypothetical situation

behavioral perspective a view that in complex organizations conflict is inevitable and as a result, conflict is not necessarily symptomatic of bad management

belief a perception based on a conviction that certain things are true or probable in one's own mind

benchmarking identifying better practices and processes by making comparisons with top performing companies

benchmarks performance levels or best practices of the most exceptional companies in an industry

brainstorming group idea generation processes in which creativity is encouraged while evaluation is limited to a separate phase

bureaucratic style a management style characterized by the manager's reliance on rules, regulations, policies, and procedures to direct employees

change agent a champion or proponent who provides the driving force to implement and maintain a change

charismatic leaders leaders who excel at communicating a vision for the future and in persuading others to become committed to achieving the vision

clique an informal group of two or more people who come together primarily on the basis of social rationales

collaborative style pursuing mutual need satisfaction in the resolution of a conflict

collective bargaining the process of negotiating a union agreement that covers wages, hours, and working conditions

command-and-control leadership leadership that emphasizes power based on authority and obedience to a supervisor's directives

communication the transmission of information and common understanding from one person or group to another through the use of common symbols

competing style pursuing your own needs at the expense of the other party

complaint any expression of unhappiness with working conditions or on-the-job relationships that comes to a manager's attention

compressed work week a work week made up of four 10-hour days

compromising style an approach for resolving conflict in which each party gives up some need satisfaction

computer monitoring using computers to measure how employees achieve their outputs by monitoring work as it takes place

computer virus a rogue computer program that can reproduce itself endlessly or cause

other havoc, such as the destruction of stored data

confirming-evidence trap seeking information about a decision that is expected to align with one's initial inclinations

constructive conflict conflict that results in problem solving because it clarifies issues and alternatives

controlling the management function that sets standards for performance and attempts to prevent, identify, and correct deviations from standards

counselor the human relations role in which a supervisor is an adviser and director to subordinates

creative tension the exchange of differences in problem solving and creative activities in which diversity-related differences in perspectives leads to superior results

cross-training training employees to do more than one job so that they may fill in for other workers or may be redeployed to other work with changes in demand

cultural diversity the co-existence of two or more cultural groups within an organization

deconstructive conflict conflict that is emotion laden, may involve attacks of a personal nature, often includes insults, and may lead to retaliation

delegation the act of passing formal authority by a manager to another

democratic style a management and leadership style characterized by a sharing of decision-making authority with employees

differentiation paradigm an approach to diversity in which

people of color and women enable the organization to gain access to ethnic and demographic markets and which often results in job segregation

directing the supervision or overseeing of people and processes

direction in communication, the flow or path a message takes in order to reach a receiver

directive interview an interview planned and totally controlled by the interviewer

discipline the management duty that involves educating employees to foster obedience and self-control and dispensing appropriate punishment for wrongdoing

disparate impact/adverse impact the existence of a significantly different selection rate between women or minorities and non-protected groups

diversity differences among people and groups that serve to both unite and separate them from others

downsizing to reduce in number or size

EGR theory motivation theory based on existence, growth, and relatedness needs

electronic data interchange a paperless business-to-business approach, which relies on electronic communications technology for the transmission of orders, invoices, and other business transactions

emotional intelligence a multidimensional theory of leadership behavior based on personal skills and knowledge associated with maturity

emotionally unintelligent managers managers who lack empathy and are oblivious to the effect of their emotions on others

empathetic listening active listening with a purpose of understanding the speaker's real needs

employment at will the common law doctrine that holds that employment will last until either employer or employee decides to terminate it, with or without cause

empower to equip people to function on their own, without direct supervision

ergonomics concern about the design of work sites, machines, equipment, and systems to minimize stress and job-related injuries

estimating and forecasting traps assuming greater accuracy in one's estimates and forecasts than warranted

expectancy belief that effort will result in performance

feedback any effort made by parties to a communication to ensure that they have a common understanding of each other's meaning and intent

feeling a personality component that emphasizes one's values in evaluating information

flexibility the ability of members of a workforce to perform different tasks

flexible manufacturing a computer-based manufacturing approach that quickly shifts production from one product to another

flextime a work schedule with flexible starting and ending times

follow-up checking with others to ensure that a message was received and that action is being taken

force-field analysis a method for visualizing the driving and restraining forces at work within an individual so as to assess what

is needed to make a change in a person's behavior

foreman a supervisor of workers in manufacturing

formal group two or more people who come together by management decision to achieve specific goals

formal organization an enterprise that has clearly stated goals, a division of labor among specialists, a rational design, and a hierarchy of authority and accountability

forming the first stage of team development in which team members determine the parameters of interpersonal relations and task behaviors

framing placing a decision option in a background context that increases the likelihood that the option will be selected or accepted

framing traps being overly influenced by the context of the decision, which may have been crafted by an advocate to guide the decision-maker toward a preferred alternative

functional authority the right that a manager of a staff department has to make decisions and to give orders that affect the way things are done in specific functions in another department

goal the objective, target, or end result expected from the execution of programs, tasks, and activities

golden rule principle an ethics principle that specifies that people should treat others in a manner in which they would like to be treated

grapevine gossip or informal communication in an organization that often occurs when there is inadequate information from the managerial hierarchy

grievance an alleged violation of the labor-management agreement

grievance procedure the process by which grievances are filed and either settled or elevated to higher union and company representatives with unresolved grievances being submitted to arbitration

grievance processing settling an alleged violation of the labor-management agreement in accordance with the method outlined in that agreement

group developmental sequence phases of group development that typically include forming, storming, norming, performing, and adjourning

group two or more people who consider themselves a functioning unit and share a common goal

groupthink a decision-making error caused by group dynamics

groupware software enabling group members to work together without close proximity

halo effect one positive characteristic, behavior, or incident favorably biases the appraisal

health the general condition of a person physically, mentally, and emotionally, or, efforts at preventing illness and treating injuries when they occur

hierarchy the management levels and people who staff an organization's positions of formal authority

horn effect one negative characteristic, behavior, or incident adversely biases the appraisal

human needs physiological and psychological requirements that all humans share and that act as motives for behavior

human relations the development and maintenance of sound on-the-job relationships with subordinates, peers, and superiors

individualism the training principle that requires a trainer to conduct training at a pace suitable for the trainee

induction the planning and conduct of a program to introduce a new employee to his or her job, working environment, supervisor, and peers

informal group two or more people who come together by choice to satisfy mutual needs or to share common interests

information any facts, figures, or data that are in a form or format that makes them usable to a person who possesses them

institutional manager a manager who has a high need for power, high inhibitions, and low need for affiliation

instrumentality belief that performance will result in desired outcomes

integration paradigm an inclusion approach to the management of diversity in which women and people of color are fully integrated into all aspects of the organization and which captures the full benefit of diversity

interactionist view that some conflict is necessary and that managers should attempt to manage conflict at an optimal level

interview a two-way conversation under the control of one of the parties

intuition a personality component that emphasizes gut feelings or hunches as a means of obtaining information

job description a formal listing of the duties that make up a position in the organization

job enlargement increasing the number of tasks or the quantity of output required in a job

job enrichment providing variety, deeper personal interest and involvement, greater autonomy and challenge, or increased responsibility on the job

job rotation movement of people to different jobs, usually for a temporary period, in order to inform, train, or stimulate cooperation and understanding among them

job sharing splitting the hours of a job between two or more employees

job specification the personal characteristics and skill levels that are required of an individual to execute a job

just cause discipline of appropriate severity for violation of reasonable rules; it follows a warning with consistent rule enforcement and substantial proof

just-in-time delivery systems information systems that indicate times when components will be needed with components being delivered "just-in-time"

justice-based principle an ethics perspective that emphasizes the criterion of fairness

Keirsey-Bates Temperaments an instrument that measures personality types

labor relations management activities necessitated by the fact that the organization has a union that represents its employees

labor union a group of workers employed by a company or in an industry who have banded together to bargain collectively with their employer

leadership the ability to get work done with and through others while winning their respect, confidence, loyalty, and willing cooperation

leadership by example modeling the way for others to act, such as a supervisor who sets high standards for her own performance

lean manufacturing an integrated approach, which combines several manufacturing approaches, such as just-in-time methods, to reduce costs

Level 5 leaders fiercely competitive leaders who combine humility and personal sacrifice with high performance expectations and a commitment to the organization

like me bias or similar to me bias the tendency for supervisors and managers to provide higher performance evaluations and selection interview ratings to people similar to them

line authority a manager's right to give direct orders to subordinates and appraise, reward, and discipline those who receive those orders

maintenance factor a factor that can be provided in order to prevent job dissatisfaction

management the process of planning, organizing, directing, and controlling human, material, and informational resources for the purposes of setting and achieving stated goals; also, a team of people making up an organization's hierarchy

management by exception (MBE) a management principle asserting that managers should spend their time on those matters that require their particular expertise

management by objectives (MBO) a management principle

that uses performance objectives to guide, evaluate, and reward employee behavior

management by wandering around (MBWA) a leadership principle that encourages supervisors to get out of their offices regularly so that they can touch base with their employees and customers

management of diversity managing and leading a heterogeneous workforce in order to accomplish an organization's goals in an effective manner

management skills categories of capabilities needed by all managers at every level in an organization

manager a member of an organization's hierarchy who is paid to make decisions; one who gets things done with and through others, through the execution of the basic management functions

matrix organization an organizational structure in which there are dual reporting relationships, which commonly involve functional and project reporting relationships

mediation the use of a neutral third party in a labor-management dispute to facilitate resolution of the dispute by the parties

medium a channel or means used to carry a message in the communication process

mentoring relationships formal or informal relationships between senior or experienced managers, supervisors, or employees to provide career-enhancing advice, feedback, and information to less experienced employees

message the ideas, intent, and feelings that you wish to communicate to a receiver

micro-management close supervision, which leaves little room for employee discretion

middle management the members of the hierarchy below the rank of top management but above the rank of supervisor

middle manager a manager of other managers or supervisors who reports to executives

minority according to the EEOC, a member of one of the following groups: Hispanics, Native Americans, African Americans, Asians or Pacific Islanders, Alaskan natives

mission the expression in words—backed up with both plans and actions—of the organization's central and common purpose, its reason for existing

motivation the drive within a person to achieve a goal

motivation for training the training principle that requires both trainer and trainee to be favorably predisposed and ready to undergo training

motivation factor a factor that has the potential to stimulate internal motivation to provide better-than-average performance and commitment from those to whom it appeals

Myers Briggs Type Inventory (MBTI) an assessment instrument that provides measures of personality components

negative discipline the part of discipline that emphasizes the detection and punishment of wrongdoing

nominal group group idea generation process in which members develop their ideas individually, and then the leader elicits all ideas for group consideration

non-directive interview an interview planned by the interviewer but controlled by the interviewee

norming third stage of team development where cohesiveness within the team is found

objective the training principle that requires trainers and trainees to know what is to be mastered through training

Occupational Safety and Health Administration the federal agency that administers the Occupational Safety and Health Act

offshoring outsourcing work to vendors in other countries or shifting work to a company-owned facility in another country

open book management sharing all financial information with employees so that they can make informed decisions and earn a share of increased profits

operating management the level of the hierarchy that oversees the work of non-management employees (workers)

organizational development a planned, managed, systematic process used to change the culture, systems, and behavior of an organization to improve its effectiveness in solving problems and achieving goals

orientation the planning and conduct of a program to introduce a new employee to the company and its history, policies, rules, and procedures

outsourcing contracting with outside vendors to perform work that was previously performed in-house

overconfidence trap failure to anticipate a sufficiently broad range for the outcomes of a forecasted event

peer a person with the same level of authority and status as another

performance management a systematic approach for improving performance that includes performance appraisal, follow-up such as rewards or action plans, improved communication, and eliminating barriers to performance

performance scorecard combined and weighted measures of performance designed for each employee, manager, and organizational unit

performing the fourth stage of team development where roles are well-understood, and the interpersonal relationships provide a supporting mechanism for the performance of work tasks

permanent part-time workers employees who wish to work less than 40 hours per week

personal power manager a manager with strong power and affiliation needs and low inhibition

planning the management function through which managers decide how they will proceed toward future goal accomplishment

pluralistic leaders leaders who capture the benefits of diverse workforces by seeking input from all employees

policy a broad guideline constructed by top management to influence managers' approaches to solving problems and dealing with recurring situations

positive discipline the part of discipline that promotes understanding and self-control by letting employees know what is expected of them

power the ability to influence others so that they respond favorably to orders and instructions

power distance degree to which differentials in power between people at higher levels in the organization and people lower in the hierarchy are accepted as a normal state of affairs

procedure general routine or method for executing day-to-day operations

productivity the amount of input needed to generate a given amount of output

program plan listing goals and containing the answers to the who, what, when, where, how, and how much of the plan

progressive discipline a system using warnings about what is and is not acceptable conduct; specific job-related rules; punishments that fit the offense; punishments that grow in severity as misconduct persists; and prompt, consistent enforcement

psychological contract an unwritten recognition of what an employer and an employee expect to give and to receive from each other

Pygmalion effect a self-fulfilling prophecy in which a supervisor's high expectations for an associate result in high performance because of the manner in which the supervisor treats the employee and the resultant response

quality the totality of features and characteristics of a product or service (or process or project) that bear on its ability to satisfy stated or implied goals (requirements of producers and customers)

quality of working life (QWL) a general label given to various programs and projects designed to help employees satisfy their needs and meet their expectations from work

realism the training principle that requires training to simulate or duplicate the actual working environment and behavior or performance required

receiver the person or group intended by a transmitter to receive the message

reinforcement the training principle that requires trainees to review and restate knowledge learned; also refers to rewards for correct responses

reliability the trait of being dependable or reliable

response the principle of training that requires feedback from trainees to trainers and vice versa

responsibility the obligation each person with authority has to execute his duties to the best of his ability

rights-based principle an ethics perspective that maintains that people have basic rights, which must be respected

role ambiguity uncertainty about the role that one is expected to play

role conflict a situation that occurs when contradictory or opposing demands are made on a manager

role prescription the collection of expectations and demands from superiors, employees, and others that shapes a manager's job description and perception of his or her job

rule a regulation on human conduct at work

rule-based principle an ethics perspective that evaluates the desirability of a behavior in accordance to whether it could withstand scrutiny as a universal standard

safety efforts at protecting human resources from accidents and injuries

scoreboarding providing feedback on individual and team efforts to reach goals

security efforts at protecting physical facilities and other resources from loss or damage

selection the human resource management function that determines who is hired

sensing a personality component that emphasizes gathering information through the senses

sexual harassment unwelcomed sexual advances, requests for sexual favors, and other physical and verbal conduct of a sexual nature

simulations training in which participants learn through realistic role-playing exercises or computer software experiences

six sigma a statistics-based approach for reducing variance in manufacturing or service outcomes with the goal of improving quality and reducing waste

socialization the process new employees undergo in the first few weeks of employment through which they learn how to cope and succeed

span of control the number of employees over which a manager has direct supervisory control

spectator style a management style characterized by treating employees as independent decision-makers

spokesperson the human relations role through which a supervisor represents management's views to workers and workers' views to management

spyware software that infiltrates computer systems for the purpose of obtaining information that can be used for fraudulent purposes

staff authority the right of staff managers to give advice and counsel to all other managers in an organization in the areas of their expertise

standard a definition of acceptable performance levels for people, machines, or processes

standard operating procedure (SOP) set of procedures providing guidance for decision making given different routine circumstances

status-quo trap a decision error that presumes that past conditions will remain in the future and places too much weight on maintaining the status quo

steward the union's elected or appointed first-line representative in the areas in which employees work

storming the second stage of team development where individuals begin thought and often have conflict

subjects the principle of training that requires trainers to know the subject being taught and to know the trainees' needs

sunk-cost trap failure to stop a course of action because of a reluctance to write off costs and acknowledge a previous mistake in making a decision

supervisor a manager responsible for the welfare, behaviors, and performances of non-management employees (workers)

synergy cooperative action or force of two or more elements pulling together that yields a result greater than the sum of the results that could be achieved separately by the elements

team a work group in which members feel a compelling need for teamwork, assume joint responsibility for accomplishment of the team's goals, and hold each other accountable for results

team facilitator a supervisor in charge of teams but who is working outside them

team leader a supervisor working in a team who is responsible for its members

telecommuting working at home through telecommunications

temporary workers workers employed by a temporary work agency to provide labor for other employers

Theory X a set of attitudes traditionally held by managers that includes assuming the worst with regard to the average worker's initiative and creativity

Theory Y a set of attitudes held by today's generation of managers that includes assuming the best about the average worker's initiative and creativity

thinking a personality component that emphasizes rational thought in evaluating information

tokenism having only one or very few women or minorities in a unit or job classification solely to provide window dressing for equal employment opportunity purposes

top management the uppermost part of the management hierarchy, containing the positions of the chief executive and immediate subordinates

toxic managers manipulative managers who lack emotional intelligence and tend to be over-controlling

traditional view a view that all conflict is dysfunctional or symptomatic of bad management and that conflict resolution should be emphasized

training the activity concerned with improving employees' performance in their present jobs by imparting skills, knowledge, and attitudes

training objective a written statement of what the trainee should be able to do, the conditions under which the trainee is expected to perform, and the criteria used to judge the adequacy of the performance

transmitter the person or group that sends a message to a receiver

two-way mentoring mentoring relationships involving people of different races or genders

understanding all parties to a communication are of one mind regarding its meaning and intent

utilitarian principle an ethics perspective relying on cost-benefit analysis

valence the value or attractiveness of an outcome

validity the degree to which a selection device measures what it is supposed to measure or is predictive of a person's performance on a job

value judgment about what is right or wrong and important or unimportant

vandalism wanton or willful destruction of or damage to another's property

virtual teams geographically disbursed teams, which rely on electronic communications technology to coordinate their work

vision a statement of what kind of company the organization wants to be in the future and the direction in which it will go

whistleblower an employee who notifies authorities of violations of laws committed by his or her employer that are contrary to public policy

work ethic a person's attitude about the importance of working, the kind of work he chooses, and the quality of his efforts while performing work

worker any employee who is not a member of the management hierarchy

workers' compensation federal and state laws designed to compensate employees for illnesses and injuries that arise out of and in the course of their employment

working to the rule following work procedures down to very minute details, thereby bringing production to a standstill

INDEX